# Communications
# in Computer and Information Science 1515

More information about this series at https://link.springer.com/bookseries/7899

Fuchun Sun · Dewen Hu · Stefan Wermter ·
Lei Yang · Huaping Liu · Bin Fang (Eds.)

# Cognitive Systems and Information Processing

6th International Conference, ICCSIP 2021
Suzhou, China, November 20–21, 2021
Revised Selected Papers

 Springer

*Editors*
Fuchun Sun
Tsinghua University
Beijing, China

Stefan Wermter 🆔
Universität Hamburg
Hamburg, Germany

Huaping Liu
Tsinghua University
Beijing, China

Dewen Hu 🆔
National University of Defense Technology
Changsha, China

Lei Yang
Tsingzhan Artificial Intelligence Research
Institute
Nanjing, China

Bin Fang
Tsinghua University
Beijing, China

ISSN 1865-0929               ISSN 1865-0937 (electronic)
Communications in Computer and Information Science
ISBN 978-981-16-9246-8        ISBN 978-981-16-9247-5 (eBook)
https://doi.org/10.1007/978-981-16-9247-5

This Springer imprint is published by the registered company Springer Nature Singapore Pte Ltd.
The registered company address is: 152 Beach Road, #21-01/04 Gateway East, Singapore 189721, Singapore

# Preface

This volume contains the papers from the Sixth International Conference on Cognitive Systems and Information Processing (ICCSIP 2021), which was held in Suzhou, China, during November 20–21, 2021. ICCSIP is a prestigious biennial conference with past events held in Beijing (2012, 2014, 2016, 2018) and Zhuhai (2020). Over the past few years, ICCSIP has matured into a well-established series of international conferences on cognitive information processing and related fields. Similar to the previous event, ICCSIP 2021 provided an academic forum for the participants to share their new research findings and discuss emerging areas of research. It also established a stimulating environment for the participants to exchange ideas on the future trends and opportunities of cognitive information processing research.

Currently, cognitive systems and information processing are applied in an increasing number of research domains such as cognitive sciences and technology, visual cognition and computation, big data and intelligent information processing, bioinformatics, and applications. We believe that cognitive systems and information processing will certainly exhibit greater-than-ever advances in the near future. With the aim of promoting research and technical innovation in relevant fields, domestically and internationally, the fundamental objective of ICCSIP is defined as providing a premier forum for researchers and practitioners from academia, industry, and government to share their ideas, research results, and experiences.

ICCSIP 2021 received 105 submissions, all of which were written in English. After a thorough reviewing process, 41 papers were selected for presentation as full papers, resulting in an approximate acceptance rate of 39%. The accepted papers not only address challenging issues in various aspects of cognitive systems and information processing but also showcase contributions from related disciplines that illuminate the state of the art. In addition to the contributed papers, the ICCSIP 2021 technical program included four plenary speeches by Bo Zhang, Shiqing Chen, Yaonan Wang, and Lining Sun and six invited speeches by well-known scholars and entrepreneurs. We would also like to thank the members of the Advisory Committee for their guidance, the members of the International Program Committee and additional reviewers for reviewing the papers, and members of the Publications Committee for checking the accepted papers in a short period of time.

Last but not the least, we would like to thank all the speakers, authors, and reviewers as well as the participants for their great contributions that made ICCSIP 2021 successful and all the hard work worthwhile. We also thank Springer for their trust and for publishing the proceedings of ICCSIP 2021.

November 2021

Fuchun Sun
Dewen Hu
Lei Yang
Stefan Wermter
Huaping Liu
Bin Fang

# Organization

ICCSIP 2021 was hosted by the Chinese Association for Artificial Intelligence, the Chinese Association of Automation, and the IEEE Computational Intelligence Society. It was organized by the Cognitive Systems and Information Processing Society of Chinese Association for Artificial Intelligence, the Cognitive Computing and Systems Society of Chinese Association of Automation, Tsinghua University, and the Gusu Laboratory of Material Science with the help of the following co-organizers: the Nanjing Tsingzhan Institute of Artificial Intelligence, the China Center for Information Industry Development, and the Artificial Intelligence and Sensing Technology Institute (SIP) Co., Ltd.

## Conference Committee

### Honorary Chairs

| | |
|---|---|
| Bo Zhang | Tsinghua University, China |
| Nanning Zheng | Xi'an Jiaotong University, China |
| Deyi Li | Chinese Association for Artificial Intelligence, China |

### Advisory Committee Chairs

| | |
|---|---|
| Qionghai Dai | Tsinghua University, China |
| Fuji Ren | University of Tokyo, Japan |
| Shiming Hu | Tsinghua University, China |
| Hui Yang | Gusu Laboratory of Material Science, China |

### General Chairs

| | |
|---|---|
| Fuchun Sun | Tsinghua University, China |
| Angelo Cangosi | University of Manchester, UK |
| Jianwei Zhang | University of Hamburg, Germany |

### Program Committee Chairs

| | |
|---|---|
| Dewen Hu | National University of Defense Technology, China |
| Lei Yang | Tsingzhan Artificial Intelligence Research Institute, China |
| Stefan Wermter | University of Hamburg, Germany |
| Huaping Liu | Tsinghua University, China |

### Publication Chair

| | |
|---|---|
| Bin Fang | Tsinghua University, China |

## Program Committee

| | |
|---|---|
| Chenguang Yang | University of the West of England, UK |
| Guang-Bin Huang | Nanyang Technological University, Singapore |
| Katharina Rohlfing | University of Paderborn, Germany |
| Antonio Chella | Università degli Studi di Palermo, Italy |
| Yufei Hao | EPFL, Switzerland |
| Zhen Deng | Fuzhou University, China |
| Jun Ren | Hubei University of Technology, China |
| Chunfang Liu | Beijing University of Technology, China |
| Changsheng Li | Beijing Institute of Technology, China |
| Mingjie Dong | Beijing University of Technology, China |
| Peng Su | Beijing Information Science and Technology University, China |
| Rui Huang | University of Electronic Science and Technology of China, China |
| Tian Liu | Beijing Information Science and Technology University, China |
| Haiyuan Li | Beijing University of Posts and Telecommunications, China |
| Yong Cao | Northwestern Polytechnical University, China |
| Taogang Hou | Beijing Jiaotong University, China |

## Technical Sponsor

NVIDIA-IM

# Contents

## Algorithm

# Algorithm

# WeaveNet: End-to-End Audiovisual Sentiment Analysis

Yinfeng Yu[1]([✉]), Zhenhong Jia[1], Fei Shi[1], Meiling Zhu[2], Wenjun Wang[3],
and Xiuhong Li[1]

[1] College of Information Science and Engineering, Xinjiang University, Urumqi, China
yuyinfeng@xju.edu.cn
[2] No. 59 Middle School of Urumqi, Urumqi, China
[3] Shanxi Datong University, Datong, China

**Abstract.** The way of analyzing sentiment by the proposed model in this paper is strikingly similar to the mechanism by which one person perceives another's sentiment. In this paper, We proposed a novel neural architecture named WeaveNet to "listen" and "watch" a person's sentiment. The main strength of our model comes from capturing both intra-interactions of one modal and inter-interactions of different modals stage by stage. Intra-interactions were modeled by convolution operations in the first few stages for each modality respectively and by bidirectional LSTM in the final stage for both audio clips and video clips. Inter-interactions were recognized at each stage applying various fusion effectively. At the same time, our model concentrated on the delicate design of the neural network rather than handcrafted features. The inputs of the network in our model were raw audios and natural images. In addition, audio clips and frames of a video were aligned by keyframe rather than by time in time order. We performed extensive comparisons on three publicly available datasets for both sentiment analysis and emotion recognition. WeaveNet outperformed state-of-the-art results in three publicly available datasets.

**Keywords:** Audiovisual · End-to-end · Sentiment analysis

## 1 Introduction

Sentiment analysis is one of the most active research areas in natural language processing and video processing. It is the computational study of individuals' emotions, sentiments, and so on [33]. With the rapid development of social networks, individuals can widely express their opinions. These opinions provide precious resources for sentiment analysis, which assists the development of automatic sentiment analysis [23]. The early methods were based on just only one modal extracting features by external tools [2,12,27]. Then the models transforming one modal to another were developed. For example, text-based sentiment analysis continued advanced by utilizing automatic speech recognition technology to convert speech into texts. With the development of automatic speech recognition, bimodal-based methods were introduced to sentiment analysis tasks [5,21,28].

Supported by Xinjiang Natural Science Foundation under Grant 2020D01C026 and Grant 2015211C288.

Recently, with the rapid development of communication technology, large amounts of data were uploaded by web users in the form of audios or videos, rather than just only texts. A large number of videos were readily available, which considerably promoted the research in the field of multimodal sentiment analysis and emotion recognition. Multimodal sentiment analysis has achieved advancement in performance and become an emerging research field of artificial intelligence [3, 8, 11, 14, 15, 18, 19, 29, 31].

At the same time, there are still some challenges that need to be overcome.

The first challenge is how to capture the inter-interactions of different modals effectively. Sometimes, there exists a contradiction among three modals in multimodal sentiment analysis. For example, "Cry with joy". In the above scene, the sentiment analysis result of textual is neutral, which was contradicted with that of both visual(negative) and acoustic(positive). Some researchers have observed that bimodal sub-tensors are more informative when used without other sub-tensors during their second set of ablation experiments in Tensor Fusion Network [30]. Whether it is the best choice to join audio, visual and textual together or not in multimodal emotion recognition and sentiment analysis is still a question.

The second challenge is how to capture the intra-interactions of one modal effectively. The intra-interactions of one modal vary from person to person. The way of expressiveness of affection varies widely from person to person. The amount of sentiment information in a specific modal varies widely from scene to scene. For example, some people express their affections more vocally, some more visually and others rely heavily on logic express little emotion [20].

Much of research work in multimodal sentiment analysis was based on handcrafted features extracted from raw videos, raw audios, and texts. The affection representation of these models was learned from the handcrafted features. Whether it is reasonable or not is still a question. To overcome the above challenges, lots of research has been done. These research achievements are mainly divided into the following three categories. The first category of models has relied densely on handcrafted features. The input of the neural network in these models [4, 9, 13, 17, 22] is handcrafted features extracted by external tools. The second category of models has relied lightly on handcrafted features, which is called end-to-end. The input of the neural network in these models is raw data. Meanwhile, there is a layer for extricating handcrafted features at the following layer of the neural network in these models [24, 26, 34]. The third category of models named end-to-end audiovisual model has never relied on any handcrafted features. They rely heavily on the design of models with very deep neural networks, using raw data as their input. They are different from the first category models since they accept raw audios and videos as the input of the model. They are also different from the second category models since it never uses any handcrafted features from the input layer to the output layer through the whole network. The representation completely got through neural networks without any handcrafted features. The proposed model in this paper was endeavored to overcome some of the above challenges via well designing a third category model. The model was performed to capture intra-interactions by a highlight in several multistage fusion. The model aimed to capture inter-interactions by fusing and summarizing in several multistage fusion. The inputs of the proposed model were raw audios and videos. The model never used any handcrafted features from the input layer to the output layer through the whole network.

The main contributions of this paper are as follows:

- We proposed a novel model named WeaveNet for audiovisual sentiment analysis. Our model was designed to capture both intra-interactions and inter-interactions stage by stage through the whole audio clips and video clips. Intra-interactions were modeled by convolution operations in the first few steps and by bidirectional LSTM in the final stage. Inter-interactions were identified at each stage using multistage fusion.
- Our model was concentrated on the delicate design of the neural network rather than handcrafted features. The inputs of the network in our model were raw audios and natural images. Furthermore, audio clips and frames of a video were aligned by keyframe rather than by time in time order.
- WeaveNet achieved state-of-the-art results for audiovisual sentiment analysis in three publicly available datasets.

The rest of the paper is organized as follows. In the following section, we will review related work. In Sect. 3, we will exhibit more details of our methodology. In Sect. 4, experiments and results are presented, and the conclusion follows in Sect. 5.

## 2   Related Work

### 2.1   Multistage Fusion

Multistage fusion is a divide-and-conquer approach which distributes the fusion burden at several stages, letting any stage to perform in a more specialized and effective way [10].

### 2.2   Fusion Strategies

With the development of multimodal sentiment analysis, the fusion strategies have increased in quantity. There are concatenation fusion, add fusion, dot multiply fusion, and so on. Here $z^a$ denotes the representation tensor of audios. $z^v$ denotes the representation tensor of images. $z^f$ denotes the fusion tensor.

**Concatenation Fusion.** The paper [7] provided a fusion formula for the representation of an utterance generated by concatenating all three multimodal features. The formula used in our model is as follows: $z^f = \tanh((W^f[z^a; z^v]) + b^f)$.

**Add Fusion.** Add fusion should make sure the dimension is identical between $z^a$ and $z^v$, $z^f = \tanh((W^f(z^a + z^v)) + b^f)$.

**Dot Multiply Fusion.** Dot Multiply fusion should make sure the dimension is the same between $z^a$ and $z^v$, $z^f = \tanh((W^f(z^a \odot z^v)) + b^f)$, Where $\odot$ indicates dot multiple by element-wise. $W^f$ denotes the weight parameters. $b^f$ denotes the parameters of bias.

# 3    Proposed Approach

In this section, we first describe the overall architecture of our proposed model in Sect. 3.1. Section 3.2 provides formulation and alignment. Then we give the detailed formulas of every module in Sect. 3.3.

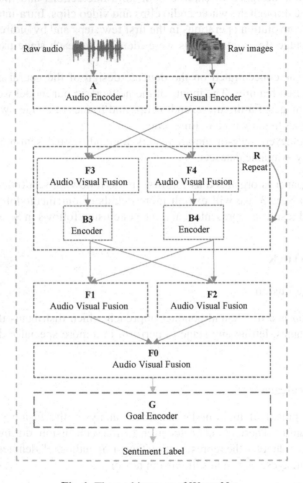

**Fig. 1.** The architecture of WeaveNet.

## 3.1    Overview of Network Architecture

The overall architecture is detailed in Fig. 1. **A** in bold is short for **A**udio module; **V** in bold is short for **V**isual module; **R** in bold is short for **R**epeatable module; **F0, F1, F2, F3, F4** in bold is short for submodule of **F**usion between audio and visual; **B3, B4** in bold is short for submodule of **B**roadcast of fusion information between audio and visual; **G** in bold is short for module of **G**oal output. It is an end-to-end network with the inputs of raw audios and raw images. The raw audios processed by the module **A** and the raw images handled by the module **V** were woven with each other. Both module **A** and **V** were designed to highlight intra-interactions in audios and images respectively. The module **R** included four sub modules named **F3, F4, B3, B4**. Audios handled by module **A** and images processed by module **V** performed an fusion (e.g., add) by sub module **F3** and did a fusion(e.g., dot multiply) by sub module **F4**. Both sub module **F3** and sub module **F4** aimed to capture inter-interactions between audios and images. Then the output of sub module **F3** was processed by the sub module **B3**, and the output of sub module **F4** was processed by sub module **B4**. Both sub module **B3** and sub module **B4** were also designed to highlight intra-interactions in audios and images respectively. The procedure in module **R** was called weave. The process of weaving could iterate n times according to a specific situation. The module **R** performed to capture both intra-interactions and inter-interactions between audios and images. In our experiments, we only repeated one time. When finished the process of weaving, the results processed by sub module **B3** and the results processed by sub module **B4** would make a weave fusion again. Both module **F1** and module **F2** also aimed to capture inter-interactions between audios and images. The output of module **F1** and the product of module **F2** would make a fusion (e.g., concatenate). The module **F0** performed to make a summarize between audios and images. The results of concatenating fusion would process by module **G**. The output of module **G** was a sentiment score, which was transformed to sentiment label.

## 3.2 Formulation and Alignment

**Problem Formulation.** Given a dataset with data, $X = (X^a, X^v)$, where $X^a, X^v$ stand for auditory and visual modality inputs, respectively. Usually, a data set is indexed by videos, which means that if we have N videos, then $X = (X_0, X_1, ..., X_{N-1})$, where $X_i = (X_i^a, X_i^v), 0 \leq i < N$. The corresponding labels for these N videos are $Y = (Y_0, Y_1, ..., Y_{N-1}), Y_i \in \mathbb{R}$ [17]. C denotes the number of all the classes (e.g. sentiment or emotion type) in a data set. In this work, we were tackling to learn a prediction function h, such that $h : X \longrightarrow Y$.

$y_{i,c}$ denotes an binary indicator, if the class label $Y$ is the correct classification for observation $X_i$ it is "1", else it is "0". Where $0 \leq c < C$.

$p_{i,c}$ denotes the predicted probability that observation $X_i$ is of class c by prediction function h. The $p_{i,c}$ is as follows:

$$p_{i,c} = \frac{exp^{h(X_i^a, X_i^v; y_{i,c})}}{\sum_{k=0}^{C-1} exp^{h(X_k^a, X_k^v; y_{k,c})}} \tag{1}$$

The cross-entropy was our optimization goal.

**Alignment of Audio Clips and Frames.** How to align audio clips and frames of a video? $f^v$ denotes the frame rate per second of a video clip. $f^a$ denotes the sampling frequency of an audio clip. $t^a$ denotes the length of an audio clip in the time domain. $N_s^a$ denotes the number of slices for an audio clip. $s_t^a$ denotes the stride of a slice in an audio clip in the continuous domain. $w_t^a$ denotes the length of a slice in an audio clip in a continuous domain. $s^a$ denotes the stride of a slice in an audio clip in the discrete domain. $w^a$ denotes the length of a slice in an audio clip in the discrete domain.

$$N_s^a = \lceil \frac{t^a - w_t^a}{s_t^a} \rceil + 1 \tag{2}$$

When $w_t^a$ and $s_t^a$ have the following relation:

$$w_t^a = 2 \times s_t^a \tag{3}$$

Then the $N_s^a$ is calculated by the following:

$$N_s^a = \lceil \frac{t^a}{s_t^a} \rceil - 1 \tag{4}$$

When $t^a = 1$ and $f^v = 30.0$, it satisfy the following equation:

$$\lceil \frac{1}{s_t^a} \rceil - 1 = f^v \tag{5}$$

By solving Eq. (5), $s_t^a = \frac{1}{31}$ in second can be derived. $w^a$ and $s^a$ are calculated by the following:

$$w^a = \lceil f^a \times w_t^a \rceil \tag{6}$$

$$s^a = \lceil f^a \times s_t^a \rceil \tag{7}$$

The above is a solution for aligning audio clips and frames of a video in time.

### 3.3 Modules in Details

**Module A.** $X_i^a(t)$ denotes the i-th raw audio, where $0 \leq i < N, t \in \mathbb{R}$. $X_i^a(n)$ denotes the i-th sampled audio. $N_{i1}^a$ denotes the length of $X_i^a(n)$.

$$X_i^a(n) = X_i^a(t) \times \delta(t - \frac{n}{f^a}) \tag{8}$$

where $\delta(t)$ is unit impulse function, $0 \leq n < N_{i1}^a, n \in \mathbb{N}$. Discrete audio $X_i^a(n)$ was obtained. $X_i^a(:, w^a)$ denotes the reshaped one of $X_i^a$. $N_{i2}^a$ denotes the first dimension size of $X_i^a(:, w^a)$.

$$N_{i2}^a = \lceil \frac{N_{i1}^a - w^a}{s^a} \rceil + 1 \tag{9}$$

$$X_i^a(m, w^a) = X_i^a[m \times s^a : m \times s^a + w^a] \tag{10}$$

where $0 \leq m < N_{i2}^a, m \in \mathbb{N}$. We segmented the discrete audio by the width of $w^a$ and the stride $s^a$ to make sure each segment have overlapped with its neighbors. Then we flattened all the segments in order and reshaped them to the length of $f^a$. So, every audio has several segments at the length of $f^a$. Then we padded $X_i^a(:, w^a)$ with zeros to make sure it's length is integer times of $f^a$. $N^b$ denotes the number of segments of sampled audio in a second.

$$N_i^{ap} = N_{i2}^a - N^b \times \lfloor \frac{N_{i2}^a}{N^b} \rfloor \tag{11}$$

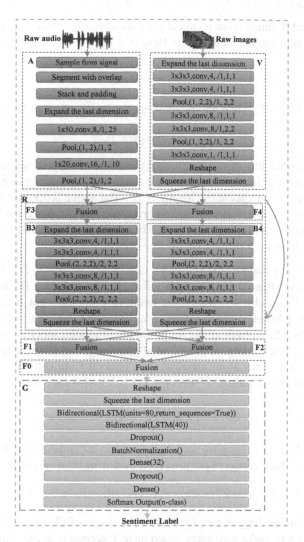

**Fig. 2.** The details of WeaveNet.

Where $N_i^{ap}$ denotes the padding length of $X_i^a$.

$$X_i^{ap} = zeros((N_i^{ap}, w^a))  \qquad (12)$$

Where $X_i^{ap}$ denotes the padding part of $X_i^a$.

$$X_i^a = stack[X_i^a; X_i^{ap}]  \qquad (13)$$

Then we reshaped $X_i^a$ to the shape $(N_{i3}^a, f^a)$. Where $N_{i3}^a$ is compute as follows:

$$N_{i3}^a = \lfloor \frac{N_{i2}^a + N_i^{ap}}{N^b} \rfloor  \qquad (14)$$

Then we sampled T times at an identical time interval from 0 to $N_{i3}^a$. $k^a$ denotes the index of audio segments in an audio clip. Here $0 \le k^a < N_{i3}^a$, $k^a \in \mathbb{N}$.

$$k^a = \lfloor \frac{N_{i3}^a}{T} \times j \rfloor \tag{15}$$

where $0 \le j < T$, $j \in \mathbb{N}$. Then we sorted all the $k^a$ in ascendant order and put them in a list named $\mathbf{K}^a$.

$$Z_i^a(j,:) = X_i^a(\mathbf{K}^a[j],:) \tag{16}$$

$Z_i^a$ denotes the embedding of raw audio with the shape of (T, $f^a$), which can conserve the time information of intra-interactions. We made re-sample techniques to make sure every audio have T segments at the length of $f^a$. The above procedure for raw audios named "slice" in this paper. After the slicing procedure, we expanded the last dimension to make every audio has the shape(T, $f^a$, 1). Then 1-d convolution and 1-d max-pooling were used twice to make a summarize for raw audios.

**Module V.** $X_i^v(:,:,:)$ denotes the i-th video clip, where $0 \le i < N$. $N_i^v$ denotes the number of frames extracted from the i-th video clip. $h^v$ indicates the height of every face got from a video clip. $w^v$ means the width of every face got from a video clip. To make a balance between computation complexity and the intra-interactions of one modal, we obtained faces from all the frames in the i-th video applying python package face recognition[1]. Succeeding, We re-sized all the images with the shape of $(h^v, w^v)$. Then we sampled T times at an identical time interval from 0 to $N_i^v$ with the same solution as a process of audios. $k^v$ denotes the index of frames in a video clip. Here $0 \le k^v < N_i^v$, $k^v \in \mathbb{N}$.

$$k^v = \lfloor \frac{N_i^v}{T} \times j \rfloor \tag{17}$$

where $0 \le j < T$, $j \in \mathbb{N}$. Then we sorted all the $k^v$ in ascendant order and put them in a list named $\mathbf{K}^v$, which conserve the time information of intra-interactions.

$$Z_i^v(j,:,:) = X_i^v(\mathbf{K}^v[j],:,:) \tag{18}$$

$Z_i^v$ denotes the embedding of raw faces with the shape of (T, $h^v$, $w^v$). We made re-sample techniques to make sure every video have T segments at the shape of $(h^v, w^v)$ maintaining the time information of intra-interactions. Following the slicing process, We expanded the last dimension to make every video with the shape(T, $h^v$, $w^v$, 1). Later 2-d convolution, 2-d convolution, and 2-d max-pooling were used twice to make a summarize for the raw images. Following made a reshape and squeezing transformation to the output of 2-d convolution.

**Module R.** The module **R** included four sub modules named **F3, F4, B3, B4**. The sub module **F3** and sub module **F4** were designed to capture inter-interactions between audios and images. However, there was a subtle difference between them. The sub module **F3** focused on audio representation with the complementary of images. The sub module **F4** centered on visual representation with the attention of audio. The fusion strategy in sub module **F3** and sub module **F4** were choosable. The fusion strategy

---

[1] https://pypi.org/project/face_recognition/.

could be tensor fusion, add fusion, dot multiply fusion and so on. The sub module **B3** and sub module **B4** aimed to capture intra-interactions. The architecture of them could be identical or distinctive. In our model, weighing the convenience of the repeated of module **R**, the architecture of sub module **B3** and sub module **B4** were sketched to the same. In the sub module **B3** or sub module **B4**, we first expanded the last dimension of the input. Then repeated twice of the procedure of 3-d max-pooling after two 3-d convolutions. Then the output of the last 3-d max-pooling was reshaped. When completed the repeated of module R, the output of both sub module **B3** and sub module **B4** were squeezed the last dimension respectively after reshaped.

**Module F1 and F2.** The module **F1** and module **F2** were designed to capture inter-interactions between audios and images. There was a subtle difference between them. The module **F1** concentrated on audio representation with the complementary of images. The module **F2** focused on visual representation with the attention of audio. The fusion strategy in module **F1** and module **F2** were choosable. The fusion strategy could be tensor fusion, add fusion, dot multiply fusion and so on. In our model, the fusion strategy in module **F1,F2,F3,F4** are as follows:

$$z^f = \lambda_k \times \tanh((W^f(z^a + z^v)) + b^f) + (1 - \lambda_k) \times \tanh((W^f(z^a \odot z^v)) + b^f) \quad (19)$$

where $1 \leq k \leq 4$, $\lambda_k \in [0, 1]$ is a parameter corresponding with module **Fk** respectively.

**Module F0.** The module **F0** was designed to capture inter-interactions between audios and images. The fusion strategy in this model could be tensor fusion, add fusion, dot multiply fusion, concatenate fusion and so on.

**Module G.** The module **G** aimed to capture the temporal information from the summary of audio and images. To make an alignment the representation of both audios and images, we reshaped the input of this module. Then the last dimension of the output of reshaping transformation was squeezed. After that, two layers of bidirectional Long short time memory Layer were designed to capture the temporal information. The result of the procedure by the two bidirectional LSTM was transferred to a Batch Normalization and two dense layers. The last layer was a dense layer with a "softmax" activation function, which acted to transform a sentiment score of more than two class to sentiment label.

## 4   Experiments

### 4.1   Experimental Setup

**Datasets.** To examine the effectiveness of the proposed model, we designed various experiments to evaluate the performance of WeaveNet. We had chosen two domains: sentiment analysis and emotion recognition. The first two datasets were sentiment analysis. The final one was emotion recognition. All benchmarks involved two modals with raw audios and raw images.

**MOSI.** Multi-modal Opinion level Sentiment Intensity [32]. It is an opinion-level anno-tated corpus of sentiment and subjectivity analysis in online videos, which including 2199 segments. Sentiment intensity is assigned from strongly negative to strongly pos-itive with a linear range from minus 3 to plus 3. For every video clip, the annotators possed seven choices: strongly positive, positive, weakly positive, neutral, weakly neg-ative, negative, strongly negative. We transformed them into 3, 5, 7 labels with identical distribution, and conducted 3-class, 5-class, and 7-class sentiment classification using MOSI video clips.

**MOUD.** Multimodal Opinion Utterances Dataset [16]. The MOUD dataset contains 498 video clips. Every video clip was labeled to be either positive, negative or neutral. However, there are 20 video clips in MOUD, which has an extraordinary name. We failed to extract frames from these video clips. We dropped these video clips in our experiments. In MOUD experiment, we conducted binary sentiment classification using 478 video clips.

**IEMOCAP.** Interactive Emotional dyadic Motion Capture database [1]. It was collected by the Speech Analysis and Interpretation Laboratory at the University of Southern California. The database recorded from ten actors in dyadic sessions with markers on the face, head, and hands. The actors performed selected emotional scripts and also improvised hypothetical scenarios designed to elicit specific types of emotions. The dataset had 7532 video clips. Every video clip was annotated for the presence of 10 emotions (anger, disgust, excited, fear, frustration, happiness, neutral state, sadness, surprise, and others). We dropped the clips annotated as "others". We conducted binary (anger, happiness, neutral state) sentiment classification using IEMOCAP video clips. We got frames from video clips of MOUD and IEMOCAP and then extracted faces from frames using face recognition python package.

**Evaluation Criteria.** Different datasets in our experiments have different labels. For binary classification and multiclass classification, we reported accuracy $A^C$, where C is the number of all the classes in a dataset. Higher values denote better performance.

**Implementation Details.** $T$ denotes video time-steps. The time-steps $T$ in our exper-iments was set to 32. Every raw audio was sampled at the sample rate of 16K Hz. $f^a = 16000$. $s^a = \frac{1}{31}$. $N^b = 5$. Every face was re-sized with $h^v$(height) = 128, $w^v$(width) = 128. We randomly select 8:1:1 for training, validation, and test set for all three datasets. One NVIDIA Tesla K80 GPU was used for training and testing. Our model was trained using Adam with an initial learning rate at 1e-3 and with an orig-inal epoch at 44. We combined drop out with early stopping to get our model rid of overfitting. The parameters of module **F1,F2,F3,F4** are $\lambda_1 = 0.9$, $\lambda_2 = 0.1$, $\lambda_3 = 0.9$, $\lambda_4 = 0.1$ respectively. The fusion tactics of module **F0** in our experiments was concate-nation fusion. The details were in Fig. 2.

### 4.2   Performance Comparison with State-of-the-art

**Baseline Models.** We compared the performance of WeaveNet with current state-of-the-art models for audiovisual sentiment analysis. Due to space constraints, each base-line name denoted by a symbol(in parenthesis) which used in Table 1 to refer to specific baseline results.

**EndToEnd1($\triangleright$).** This was an end-to-end model that applied a convolutional neural network to get an affectionate representation of the acoustic modality, which employed a deep residual network to get an emotional description of the visual modality. This model did a regression for both arousal and valence of emotion using the RECOLA database of the AVEC 2016 research challenge on emotion recognition [25].

**EndToEnd2($\triangleleft$).** This was an end-to-end audiovisual deep residual network for multimodal apparent personality trait recognition. This model was evaluated on the dataset that was released as part of the ChaLearn First Impressions Challenge. The network was trained end-to-end for predicting the five personality traits of people from their videos. It made five continuous prediction values corresponding to each trait for the video clip [6]. The type of the model used in above two papers($\triangleleft$, $\triangleright$) was a regression rather than classification. We modified the activation function of the output layer of the model in those papers to "softmax" and remained all the same as the original models. To make a comparison with the proposed model, we built the model of those papers and tested them on MOSI, MOUD, and IEMOCAP.

**Quantitative Evaluation.** We performed comparisons of the proposed model and two state-of-the-art methods in audiovisual sentiment analysis on three datasets. The comparison results in Table 1 illustrated that our model consistently outperformed others, which demonstrate the effectiveness of our proposed model.

**Table 1.** Results were for sentiment analysis on both MOSI and MOUD, emotion recognition on IEMOCAP. SOTA1 refer to the previous best state of the art. Best results were highlighted in bold. $\triangle_{SOTA}$ showed the change in performance over SOTA1. Improvements were highlighted in green. Those to be improved were highlighted in red. The WeaveNet slightly outperformed some of SOTA.

| Model | MOSI | | | MOUD | IEMOCAP | | |
|---|---|---|---|---|---|---|---|
| | Accuracy(%) | | | Accuracy(%) | Accuracy(%) | | |
| | $A^7$ | $A^5$ | $A^3$ | $A^2$ | $A^2$ | | |
| | | | | | ang.[a] | hap.[b] | neu.[c] |
| [25] | 17.73 | 30.91 | 55.91 | 59.09 | 85.53 | 92.77 | 77.87 |
| [25] | 22.73 | 34.55 | 51.36 | 63.64 | 84.82 | 90.21 | 76.60 |
| WeaveNet | **25.00** | **36.36** | **55.92** | **68.18** | **87.66** | **92.78** | **77.88** |
| $\triangle_{SOTA}$ | ↑ 2.27 | ↑ 1.81 | ↑ 0.01 | ↑ 4.54 | ↑ 2.13 | ↑ 0.01 | ↑ 0.01 |

[a]Denotes anger. [b]Denotes happiness. [c]Denotes neutral state.

### 4.3 Analysis of the Proposed Approach

The most significant factor of the proposed model outperformance than baseline models is that the proposed model fusion between audios and images stage by stage. Apprehend all the detailed characterization of the sentiment in a video is an unrealistic idea since the computation cost is so high that the result is unachievable. Coarser much detailed information gravely makes the fine classification impossible. We dropped some information subtly after the fusion step by step, which makes the ability to capture the sentiment improved very much. The second critical factors are the time alignment between audios and images. We aligned the keyframe of both audio and images from the entire video clip rather than by time, which has a summarize function. The high accuracy of keyframe alignment between audio clips and video clips performs a sparse representation with a low computational cost, which made the proposed model possess a high ability to capture the inter-interactions. The convolution layer located before the bidirectional LSTM at the head of the whole network in our model is a powerful way to reduce computation cost. Convolution operation holds a very high-level share of parameters. It does well at taking the characteristic of sentiment in both audios and images. At the same time, the parameters of convolution are relatively less than other networks such as RNN with the same ability in representation. However, both the audios and images are a sequence. So in our model, we captured the intra-interactions stage by stage with convolution operation. After summarizing, the data volume of the representation for sentiment decreased. We sent the representation to the bidirectional LSTM to capture the intra-interactions. The order of the convolution layer and bidirectional LSTM is reasonable.

## 5 Conclusion

In this paper, we proposed an effective model named WeaveNet for audiovisual sentiment analysis. Our model was designed to capture both intra-interactions and inter-interactions stage by stage through the whole audio clips and video clips. Intra-interactions modeled by convolution operations in the first few steps and by bidirectional LSTM in the final stage. Inter-interactions were identified at each stage using multistage fusion. Our model concentrated on the delicate design of the neural network rather than handcrafted features. The inputs of the network in our model were raw audios and natural images. Besides, audio clips and frames of a video were aligned by keyframe rather than by time in time order. We performed extensive comparisons on three publicly available datasets for both sentiment analysis and emotion recognition. WeaveNet achieved state-of-the-art results in three publicly available datasets.

## References

1. Busso, C., et al.: Iemocap: interactive emotional dyadic motion capture database. Lang. Resour. Eval. **42**, 335–359 (2008)
2. Cambria, E.: Affective computing and sentiment analysis. IEEE Intell. Syst. **31**, 102–107 (2016)
3. Chen, M., Wang, S., Liang, P.P., Baltrusaitis, T., Zadeh, A., Morency, L.P.: Multimodal sentiment analysis with word-level fusion and reinforcement learning. In: ICMI (2017)
4. Etienne, C., Fidanza, G., Petrovskii, A., Devillers, L., Schmauch, B.: Speech emotion recognition with data augmentation and layer-wise learning rate adjustment. CoRR abs/1802.05630 (2018)

5. Gievska, S., Koroveshovski, K., Tagasovska, N.: Bimodal feature-based fusion for real-time emotion recognition in a mobile context. In: 2015 International Conference on Affective Computing and Intelligent Interaction (ACII), pp. 401–407 (2015)
6. Güçlütürk, Y., Güçlü, U., van Gerven, M., van Lier, R.: Deep impression: audiovisual deep residual networks for multimodal apparent personality trait recognition. In: ECCV Workshops (2016)
7. Hazarika, D., Poria, S., Mihalcea, R., Cambria, E., Zimmermann, R.: Icon: Interactive conversational memory network for multimodal emotion detection. In: EMNLP (2018)
8. Kim, D.H., Lee, M.K., Choi, D.Y., Song, B.C.: Multi-modal emotion recognition using semi-supervised learning and multiple neural networks in the wild. In: ICMI (2017)
9. Kim, J., Englebienne, G., Truong, K.P., Evers, V.: Deep temporal models using identity skip-connections for speech emotion recognition. In: ACM Multimedia (2017)
10. Liang, P.P., Liu, Z., Zadeh, A., Morency, L.P.: Multimodal language analysis with recurrent multistage fusion. CoRR abs/1808.03920 (2018)
11. Liu, Z., Shen, Y., Lakshminarasimhan, V.B., Liang, P.P., Zadeh, A., Morency, L.P.: Efficient low-rank multimodal fusion with modality-specific factors. In: ACL (2018)
12. Ma, X., Yang, H., Chen, Q., Huang, D., Wang, Y.: Depaudionet: an efficient deep model for audio based depression classification. In: AVEC@ACM Multimedia (2016)
13. Mistry, K., Zhang, L., Neoh, S.C., Lim, C.P., Fielding, B.: A micro-GA embedded PSO feature selection approach to intelligent facial emotion recognition. IEEE Trans. Cybern. 47, 1496–1509 (2017)
14. Nasir, M., Jati, A., Shivakumar, P.G., Chakravarthula, S.N., Georgiou, P.G.: Multimodal and multiresolution depression detection from speech and facial landmark features. In: AVEC@ACM Multimedia (2016)
15. Nguyen, D.L., Nguyen, K., Sridharan, S., Ghasemi, A., Dean, D., Fookes, C.: Deep spatio-temporal features for multimodal emotion recognition. In: 2017 IEEE Winter Conference on Applications of Computer Vision (WACV), pp. 1215–1223 (2017)
16. Pérez-Rosas, V., Mihalcea, R., Morency, L.P.: Utterance-level multimodal sentiment analysis. In: ACL (2013)
17. Pham, H., Manzini, T., Liang, P.P., Póczos, B.: Seq2seq2sentiment: Multimodal sequence to sequence models for sentiment analysis. CoRR abs/1807.03915 (2018)
18. Poria, S., Cambria, E., Hazarika, D., Mazumder, N., Zadeh, A., Morency, L.P.: Multi-level multiple attentions for contextual multimodal sentiment analysis. In: 2017 IEEE International Conference on Data Mining (ICDM), pp. 1033–1038 (November 2017). https://doi.org/10.1109/ICDM.2017.134
19. Poria, S., Cambria, E., Bajpai, R., Hussain, A.: A review of affective computing: from unimodal analysis to multimodal fusion. Inf. Fusion 37, 98–125 (2017)
20. Poria, S., Chaturvedi, I., Cambria, E., Hussain, A.: Convolutional MKL based multimodal emotion recognition and sentiment analysis. In: 2016 IEEE 16th International Conference on Data Mining (ICDM), pp. 439–448 (2016)
21. Seng, K.P., Ang, L.M., Ooi, C.S.: A combined rule-based & machine learning audio-visual emotion recognition approach. IEEE Trans. Affect. Comput. 9, 3–13 (2018)
22. Sivaprasad, S., Joshi, T., Agrawal, R., Pedanekar, N.: Multimodal continuous prediction of emotions in movies using long short-term memory networks. In: ICMR (2018)
23. Soleymani, M., García, D., Jou, B., Schuller, B.W., Chang, S.F., Pantic, M.: A survey of multimodal sentiment analysis. Image Vis. Comput. 65, 3–14 (2017)
24. Trigeorgis, G., et al.: Adieu features? end-to-end speech emotion recognition using a deep convolutional recurrent network. In: 2016 IEEE International Conference on Acoustics, Speech and Signal Processing (ICASSP), pp. 5200–5204 (2016)

25. Tzirakis, P., Trigeorgis, G., Nicolaou, M.A., Schuller, B.W., Zafeiriou, S.: End-to-end multi-modal emotion recognition using deep neural networks. IEEE J. Sel. Top. Sign. Proces. **11**, 1301–1309 (2017)
26. Tzirakis, P., Zhang, J., Schuller, B.W.: End-to-end speech emotion recognition using deep neural networks. In: 2018 IEEE International Conference on Acoustics, Speech and Signal Processing (ICASSP), pp. 5089–5093 (2018)
27. Wu, A., Huang, Y., Zhang, G.: Feature fusion methods for robust speech emotion recognition based on deep belief networks. In: ICNCC 2016 (2016)
28. Yan, J., Zheng, W., Xu, Q., Lu, G., Li, H., Wang, B.: Sparse kernel reduced-rank regression for bimodal emotion recognition from facial expression and speech. IEEE Trans. Multimedia **18**, 1319–1329 (2016)
29. Yang, L., Jiang, D., Xia, X., Pei, E., Oveneke, M.C., Sahli, H.: Multimodal measurement of depression using deep learning models. In: AVEC@ACM Multimedia (2017)
30. Zadeh, A., Chen, M., Poria, S., Cambria, E., Morency, L.P.: Tensor fusion network for multi-modal sentiment analysis. In: Empirical Methods in Natural Language Processing, EMNLP (2017)
31. Zadeh, A., Liang, P.P., Poria, S., Vij, P., Cambria, E., Morency, L.P.: Multi-attention recurrent network for human communication comprehension. CoRR abs/1802.00923 (2018)
32. Zadeh, A., Zellers, R., Pincus, E., Morency, L.P.: Mosi: Multimodal corpus of sentiment intensity and subjectivity analysis in online opinion videos. CoRR abs/1606.06259 (2016)
33. Zhang, L., Wang, S., Liu, B.: Deep learning for sentiment analysis : a survey. Wiley Interdisc. Rew. Data Min. Knowl. Discov. **8**, e1253 (2018)
34. Zhu, B., Zhou, W., Wang, Y., Wang, H., Cai, J.J.: End-to-end speech emotion recognition based on neural network. In: 2017 IEEE 17th International Conference on Communication Technology (ICCT), pp. 1634–1638 (2017)

# Unsupervised Semantic Segmentation with Contrastive Translation Coding

Runfa Chen[1(✉)], Hanbing Sun[1], and Ling Wang[2]

[1] Institute for Artificial Intelligence, Tsinghua University (THUAI), Beijing National Research Center for Information Science and Technology (BNRist), State Key Lab on Intelligent Technology and Systems, Department of Computer Science and Technology, Tsinghua University, Beijing, People's Republic of China
{crf21,sunhb19}@mails.tsinghua.edu.cn
[2] Department of Air Defense Early Warning Command System, Air Force Early Warning Academy, Wuhang, People's Republic of China

**Abstract.** The proposed new method constructs a contrastive learning task through unsupervised image-to-image translation and indirectly extracts domain-invariant features by maximizing mutual information. Specifically, by reusing the semantic segmentation network for image-to-image translation, the probability space of the segmentation output is projected into the RGB space, thereby constructing positive and negative samples to maximize the mutual information between the input image and the semantic segmentation RGB projection map. Meanwhile, the output space of the target domain is transferred to the source domain, and then the robust domain-invariant semantic features are extracted. We develop two adversarial transfer methods and a three-stage training paradigm of pre-training, cross-domain transfer, and self-supervised training. Experiments on benchmarks demonstrate that this method is reasonable and feasible. Comprehensive ablation studies and analyses are also carried out to reveal the advantages and disadvantages of the two designed transfer schemes and the effect and significance of color-invariant semantic information for unsupervised semantic segmentation tasks. The contrastive learning task, which is constructed through unsupervised cross-domain image-to-image translation, provides a new insight for cross-domain transfer learning to overcome the problem of domain shift.

**Keywords:** Domain shift · Unsupervised semantic segmentation · Unsupervised image-to-image translation · Contrastive learning

## 1 Introduction

Semantic segmentation is one of the most challenging tasks in visual understanding. Compared with simpler problems such as image classification and object detection, semantic segmentation is a deeper understanding of visual content.

F. Sun et al. (Eds.): ICCSIP 2021, CCIS 1515, pp. 17–36, 2022.
https://doi.org/10.1007/978-981-16-9247-5_2

Semantic segmentation needs to assign labels pixel by pixel, and its labels correspond to its semantic content. Therefore, it is also called a dense label classification task. Semantic segmentation is a pervasive research field, and the academic community has proposed many methods to solve these issues.

In addition, with the development of computer graphics, it has become a feasible solution to generate large amounts of automatically labeled simulation data for many vision-related tasks. Using computer graphics technology to simulate the virtual environment and automatically generate images and segmentation annotations is an economical choice. For example, GTA5 [37] and SYN-THIA [38] are two popular urban street simulation data sets. It is similar to the real-world data set and has shared classes (for example, CityScapes [5]). Although the appearance of the simulation image is similar to the real image, there are still differences in texture, layout, color, and lighting conditions [13], which leads to the problem of domain shift with different data distributions. Therefore, a certain model trained on the simulation data set will fail when applied to a real scene. This requires us to solve the problem of domain shift between simulation data and real-world data to fully use the labeled samples in the source domain simulation data and a large number of unlabeled samples in the target domain real data. To solve this challenge, we need to study unsupervised cross-domain transfer learning. Unlike cross-domain transfer learning for image classification, cross-domain transfer learning for unsupervised semantic segmentation has received less attention due to its difficulties.

One method learns transferable knowledge by solving the visual domain shift between virtual simulation data and real-world data. The cross-domain transfer learning based on the generative adversarial network focuses attention on the pixel-level transfer of the input space, *i.e.*, image translation. This transfer method is not limited to specific downstream tasks and has become a powerful weapon for cross-domain transfer learning. In the traditional unsupervised image-to-image translation methods, the cycle-consistency loss has emerged as the de facto gold standard [21,47,49]. With the recent rise of contrastive learning, a powerful tool has been brought to the field of self-supervised representation learning [3,12,34,46]. In the work of CUT [35], the effectiveness of contrastive learning in unsupervised image-to-image translation is demonstrated. They use a multilayer, patch-based approach rather than operate on entire images to calculate the contrastive loss. And they only sample positive and negative samples in a single image. To replace the cycle-consistency loss, they learn the cross-domain similarity function between input and output image patches to maximize the mutual information, which is used to avoid mode collapse. Thus, they not only improve the effect of image-to-image translation, but also achieve high-efficiency single-directional cross-domain translation.

In this paper, the contrastive loss of CUT [35] is used to replace the two-directional cycle-consistency loss. At the same time, we reuse the feature extractor of the semantic segmentation network as the encoder of the image-to-image translation network. In addition, in order to fine-grained transfer, we reuse the classifier of the semantic segmentation network as a generator of the image-to-image translation network and project the probability space of the segmentation output to the RGB space. By maximizing the mutual information between the input image and the semantic projection map, we can extract the features that are invariant with color and style. We resort to a discriminator at the output of the semantic projection map to guide the output of the target domain to transfer to the source domain. The feature extractor can extract domain-invariant features in the process of unsupervised image-to-image translation. Specifically, we hope that the semantic projection map, which is generated by the target domain after the feature extractor and classifier, can obtain some of the attributes of the source domain, while retaining the content and structural attributes of the target domain input image (*i.e.* the position and shape of the object).

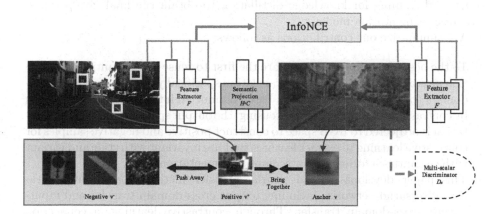

**Fig. 1.** Based on mutual information maximization cross-domain transfer

Figure 1 shows an illustration of our cross-domain transfer network for unsupervised semantic segmentation. In the figure, the image patch marked by the red box represents a car, so it can be considered that its semantic features are different from the signs, roads, and leaves marked by the yellow boxes. Based on this assumption, we can construct positive and negative samples and use the recently prevalent contrastive loss InfoNCE [34] to bring together the positive samples and push away the negative samples in the feature space to learn the universal representations. Maximizing the mutual information between the input and the output (*e.g.* the representation similarity between the car of the input image and the car of the semantic projection map), the representations can retain position and class information while ignoring attributes such as color and texture to distinguish between positive and negative samples. At the same time, through the introduction of a generative adversarial network, the semantic projection map can be transferred across domains to help further the feature extractor learn the domain-invariant representations.

Finally, a remaining issue of our approach is how to perform adversarial training. One solution is output cross-domain transfer (*i.e.*, the discriminator is used to distinguish the semantic projection map of the source domain and that of the target domain) and further extracts the common semantic features of the input and output space by contrastive learning; Another solution is input-output cross-domain transfer (*i.e.*, the discriminator is used to distinguish the input RGB image of the source domain and the semantic projection map of the target domain), so that the semantic segmentation projection space of the target domain can be transferred to the RGB color space of the source domain. This input-output cross-domain transfer method can provide a reconstruction regularization term for the projection of the source domain. Still, it may damage the capacity to extract the semantic features by contrastive learning forcibly. We will give a comparison of these two adversarial transfer methods in the experimental part. After cross-domain adversarial training, we will conduct self-supervised training for knowledge distillation to obtain the final unsupervised semantic segmentation model.

We summarize our contributions as follows:

- To the best of our knowledge, we are the first to reuse the semantic segmentation network for image-to-image translation specifically for unsupervised cross-domain transfer learning, which is based on mutual information maximization by contrastive learning. By such a reusing, the output space of semantic segmentation is projected to RGB space to construct positive and negative samples for contrastive learning to extract features that are invariant with style and variant with semantics information for semantic segmentation tasks.
- This paper develops two adversarial transfer methods based on generative adversarial networks, including output cross-domain transfer and input-output cross-domain transfer. Through contrastive learning, a connection between the input and output spaces can be established to extract domain-invariant representations in the feature space further.
- This paper designs a simple and effective three-stage training paradigm, including pre-training, cross-domain transfer, and self-supervised training. Extensive experimental evaluations on main benchmarks reveal that the proposed method outperforms various famous counterparts. The comprehensive ablation studies and visual analysis are also conducted to dig further and explain the principles.

## 2    Related Work

**Unsupervised Semantic Segmentation.** The first work to introduce adversarial learning for semantic segmentation is FCNs in the wild [17], which aligns the global and local features of the two domains in the feature space. Curriculum domain adaption[48] estimates the worldwide distribution and labels of superpixels and then learns a more refined semantic segmentation model. Adapt-SegNet [41] uses multiple discriminators to perform a multi-level cross-domain transfer of features at different levels. Another method is to migrate the foreground, and background classes separately [45].

Another method learns transferable knowledge by solving the visual domain shift between virtual simulation data and real-world data. Using the cross-domain transformed image as input, CyCADA [16] further aligns the feature distribution between the two domains in the feature space. BDL introduced a two-way learning framework [25], in which image-to-image translation and semantic segmentation models can both promote each other in a closed loop. In addition, there is also much work devoted to aligning different attributes between the two domains, such as entropy [43] and information [30].

**Unsupervised Image-to-Image Translation.** In terms of unsupervised image-to-image translation with unpaired training data, CycleGAN [49], Disco-GAN [21], DualGAN [47] preserve key attributes between the input and the translated image by using a cycle-consistency loss. Various studies have been proposed towards the extension of CycleGAN. The first kind of development is to enable multi-modal generations: MUNIT [18] and DRIT [24] decompose the latent space of images into a domain-invariant content space and a domain-specific style space to get diverse outputs. Another enhancement of CycleGAN is to perform translation across multiple (more than two) domains simultaneously, such as StarGAN [4]. A more functional line of research focuses on the transformation between domains with a larger difference. For example, CoupledGAN [28] and UNIT [27] using domain-sharing latent space, and U-GAT-IT [20] resort to attention modules for feature selection.

**Contrastive Representation Learning.** Recently, a family of methods based on contrastive learning has emerged to learn universal representations [3,12,15, 34,46]. Contrastive losses measure the distance, or similarity, between representations in the latent space, one of the critical differences between contrastive learning methods and other representation learning approaches [23]. CPC [34] first proves that minimizing this loss based on NCE is equivalent to maximizing a lower bound on the mutual information. SimCLR [3] further elaborate on it advantages over other losses. These methods make use of noise contrastive estimation [11], learning an embedding where associated samples are brought together, in *contrast* to other samples in the dataset. Associated samples can be an image with itself [12,46], neighboring patches within an image [34], or multiple views of the input image [40], and an image with a set of transformed versions of itself [3,33]. Inspired by CUT [35], we are the first to use InfoNCE loss for the unsupervised semantic segmentation tasks.

## 3   Methods

This section presents the detailed formulation of our method. We first introduce the general idea and then follow it up by providing the details of each component. The three-stage training mechanism is specified as well.

## 3.1   General Formulation

**Source and Target Domains Definition.** We perform data augmentation of color jitters on the simulation image, and call this augmented image domain as the source domain $\mathcal{X}$. And we call the real-world image domain without data augmentation as the target domain $\mathcal{Y}$. The semantic projection map of the source domain is denoted as $x^l = f_{y\to x}(x) \in \mathcal{X}^l$, and the semantic projection map of the target domain is denoted as $y^l = f_{y\to x}(y) \in \mathcal{Y}^l$.

**Unsupervised Image-to-Image Translation Definition.** Unsupervised image-to-image translation is ill-posed, which learns $f_{y\to x}$ with only the marginals $p(\mathcal{X})$ and $p(\mathcal{Y})$ provided, since there are infinitely many conditional probabilities corresponded to the same marginal distributions. We use the same method as CUT [35] to solve the problem, maximizing mutual information of input and output. We only need to learn the translation map in one direction, avoiding the use of reverse generators and discriminators, so that a more compact and more effective architecture is derived. Considering that the source domain image has annotated information, data augmentation can be performed during the supervised semantic segmentation training process to enhance the generalization of the semantic segmentation model. In this paper, we resort to unsupervised image-to-image translation from the target domain $\mathcal{Y}$ to the source domain $\mathcal{X}$ and extract features that are invariant with style.

The image-to-image translation module $f_{y\to x}$ is composed of an encoder $E_y$ and a generator $G_{y\to x}$. By combining the encoder and generator, we get $y^l = f_{y\to x}(y) = G_{y\to x}(E_y(y))$. The adversarial training [10] is usually used to align the translated output to the source domain. Specifically, the multi-scale discriminator $D_x$ is used to classify and discriminate between the source domain semantic projection map $x^l$ (or the source domain input image $x$) and the target domain semantic projection map $y^l$ to measure the distance between the generated distribution and the source domain distribution.

**Unsupervised Semantic Segmentation Definition.** Semantic segmentation aims to predict the unique label [36] pixel by pixel for the input image, and minimize the cross-entropy $H(l, p) = \frac{1}{hw} \sum_{i=1}^{h} \sum_{j=1}^{w} \sum_{k=0}^{K-1} -l_k^{(i,j)} \log\left(p_k^{(i,j)}\right)$ between the real label $l_k^{(i,j)} \in \mathcal{L}$ and the network output $p_k^{(i,j)}$, where $h$ and $w$ represent the length and width of the image, $i$ and $j$ represent the pixel position, $K$ represents the total number of classes, and $k$ represents the class.

In the unsupervised semantic segmentation setting, you can sample the label-image pairs $(x, l) \in \mathcal{X} \times \mathcal{L}$ from training set $S$ of the source domain $\mathcal{X}$, and image data $y \in \mathcal{Y}$ from training set $T$ of target domain $\mathcal{Y}$, where source domain $\mathcal{X}$ and target domain $\mathcal{Y}$ share $K$ semantic classes $k \in \{0, \cdots, K-1\}$. For non-shared classes, we ignore the relevant areas and ignore them during training and testing. The training goal is to learn a semantic segmentation model to achieve the lowest prediction risk in the target domain. Generally, the semantic segmentation network can be divided into feature extractor $F$ and classifier $C$. Traditional cross-domain transfer generally uses the binary domain discriminator $D_x$ to perform the overall transfer, but this coarse-grained transfer method can easily lead to negative transfer. In this paper, by maximizing the mutual information between input and output, semantic information is indirectly considered for fine-grained transfer.

**Other Definition.** As mentioned in the introduction, the model reuses the feature extractor $F$ for encoding, reuses the classifier $C$ for decoding, and uses a small two-layers $1 \times 1$ convolution as the projection network $H$ to map the probability space to the RGB space. Formally, the feature extractor $F$ will replace the original encoder $E_y$ in $f_{y \to x}$, and the classifier $C$ and the projection network $H$ will replace $f_{y \to x}$ in the original generator $G_{y \to x}$, resulting in a new translation $f_{y \to x}(y) = (H \circ C)(F(y))$. The cross-domain transfer process is divided into two steps to alternate training to optimize $f_{y \to x}$ and multi-scale discriminator $D_x$.

## 3.2 Architecture

**Feature Extractor $F$.** We use two backbone networks widely used in this field as the feature extractor $F$ to prove the universality of the new method. Two mainstream feature extractors in this field are $F$ backbone networks: ResNet-101 [14] and VGG-16 [39], with feature output dimensions of 2048 and 1024 respectively. And load the pre-trained model on ImageNet [7].

**Classifier $C$.** We adopt Deeplab-V2 [1]'s classifier $C$, which integrates multi-scale information (Atrous Spatial Pyramid Pooling, ASPP). The feature extractor $F$ and classifier $C$ of the semantic segmentation network used in the self-supervised training stage are the same as the pre-training and cross-domain transfer stage network structure, but the network weights are different.

**Table 1.** Projection network architecture

| Component | Input → Output shape | Layer information |
|---|---|---|
| Projection | $(\frac{h}{8}, \frac{w}{8}, K) \to (\frac{h}{8}, \frac{w}{8}, 256)$ | CONV-(N256, K1, S1, P0), LIN, ReLU |
| | $(\frac{h}{8}, \frac{w}{8}, 256) \to (\frac{h}{8}, \frac{w}{8}, 3)$ | CONV-(N128, K1, S1, P0), Tanh |

**Projection Network $H$.** The composition and parameters are shown in the Table 1, where $h$ represents the length, $w$ represents the width, CONV represents the convolutional layer, N represents the number of output channels, K represents the size of the convolution kernel, S is the convolution step size, P is the convolution padding size, and $K$ represents The number of semantic classes, LIN stands for layer-instance normalization.

**Multi-scale Discriminator $D_x$.** Our multi-scale discriminator is inspired by the previous work [6,8,19,44]. In these works, discriminators of different scales are applied to images of different sizes (small-size images obtained from the original images by downsampling). In this paper, we consider a more effective method, which treats the feature maps in different layers of a single input as images of different scales, and then input each feature map into a classifier of corresponding size, similar to the feature pyramid in objection detection (e.g., SSD [29] and FPN [26]).

As mentioned above, the discriminator $D_x$ contains two parts: the encoder $E_x$ and the classifier $C_x$. In order to achieve multi-scale processing, the classifier $C_x$ is further divided into three sub-classifiers: $C_x^0$ is used for local-scale ($10 \times 10$ receptive field), and $C_x^1$ is used for medium Scale ($70 \times 70$ receptive field), and $C_x^2$ for the global scale ($286 \times 286$ receptive field). $C_x^0$ is directly connected to the output of $E_x$. Then, a down-sampling-convolution layer is conducted on $E_x$ to provide the feature maps of smaller scale, which are concatenated to two branches: one is linked to $C_x^1$, and the other one is further down-sampled through convolution layers followed by $C_x^2$. For a single input image, $C_x^0$, $C_x^1$, and $C_x^2$ are all trained to predict whether the image is true or false. In addition to the multi-scale design, we also design a residual attention mechanism to promote further the propagation of feature gradients in the discriminator [2].

**Table 2.** Discriminator network architecture

| Component | Input → Output Shape | Layer Information |
|---|---|---|
| Encoder Down-sampling0 | $(h, w, 3) \to (\frac{h}{2}, \frac{w}{2}, 64)$ | CONV-(N64, K4, S2, P1), SN, Leaky-ReLU |
| | $(\frac{h}{2}, \frac{w}{2}, 64) \to (\frac{h}{4}, \frac{w}{4}, 128)$ | CONV-(N128, K4, S2, P1), SN, Leaky-ReLU |
| RA of Encoder& Classifier0 | $(\frac{h}{4}, \frac{w}{4}, 128) \to (\frac{h}{4}, \frac{w}{4}, 256)$ | Global Average & Max Pooling, MLP-(N1), Multiply the weights of MLP |
| | $(\frac{h}{4}, \frac{w}{4}, 256) \to (\frac{h}{4}, \frac{w}{4}, 128)$ | CONV-(N128, K1, S1), RA, Leaky-ReLU |
| Down-sampling1 | $(\frac{h}{4}, \frac{w}{4}, 128) \to (\frac{h}{8}, \frac{w}{8}, 256)$ | CONV-(N256, K4, S2, P1), SN, Leaky-ReLU |
| Classifier1 | $(\frac{h}{8}, \frac{w}{8}, 256) \to (\frac{h}{8} - 1, \frac{w}{8} - 1, 512)$ | CONV-(N512, K4, S1, P1), SN, Leaky-ReLU |
| | $(\frac{h}{8} - 1, \frac{w}{8} - 1, 512) \to (\frac{h}{8} - 2, \frac{w}{8} - 2, 1)$ | CONV-(N1, K4, S1, P1), SN |
| Down-sampling2 | $(\frac{h}{8}, \frac{w}{8}, 256) \to (\frac{h}{16}, \frac{w}{16}, 512)$ | CONV-(N512, K4, S2, P1), SN, Leaky-ReLU |
| | $(\frac{h}{16}, \frac{w}{16}, 512) \to (\frac{h}{32}, \frac{w}{32}, 1024)$ | CONV-(N1024, K4, S2, P1), SN, Leaky-ReLU |
| Classifier2 | $(\frac{h}{32}, \frac{w}{32}, 1024) \to (\frac{h}{32} - 1, \frac{w}{32} - 1, 2048)$ | CONV-(N2048, K4, S1, P1), SN, Leaky-ReLU |
| | $(\frac{h}{32} - 1, \frac{w}{32} - 1, 2048) \to (\frac{h}{32} - 2, \frac{w}{32} - 2, 1)$ | CONV-(N1, K4, S1, P1), SN |

Leaky-ReLU with a negative slope of 0.2 is used for the discriminator network, and the spectral normalized is used for all convolutional layers. The Table 2 introduces the composition of the discriminator in detail, where: $h$ represents the length, $w$ represents the width, CONV represents the convolutional layer, MLP represents the fully connected layer, and N represents the number of output channels. K represents the size of the convolution kernel, S is the convolution step size, P is the convolution padding size, and SN represents the normalization of the spectrum. In addition, in the residual attention module, the feature maps of global average pooling and maximum pooling are spliced, so the number of input channels of MLP-(N1) is 256.

## 3.3   Three-Stage Training Paradigm

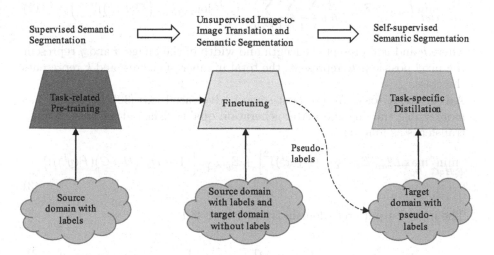

**Fig. 2.** Three-stage training paradigm

Figure 2 shows the three-stage training paradigm of pre-training, cross-domain transfer and self-supervised training.

**Pre-training stage:**

– **Cross-entropy loss:** Load the ImageNet [7] pre-trained model, and use the source domain labeled data for model fine-tuning training. Calculate the cross-entropy loss for $(x, l)$, minimize the difference between the predicted value and the real label, and pre-train a semantic segmentation network $C \circ F$:

$$\min_{C \circ F} L_{seg} = \mathbb{E}_{x \sim \mathcal{X}} \frac{1}{hw} \sum_{i=1}^{h} \sum_{j=1}^{w} \sum_{k=0}^{K-1} -l_k^{(i,j)} \log_{\text{softmax}} \left( C(F(x))_k^{(i,j)} \right), \quad (1)$$

where $h$ and $w$ represent the length and width of the image, $i$ and $j$ represent the pixel position, $K$ represents the total number of classes, and $k$ represents the class.

## Cross-domain transfer stage:

- **Cross-entropy loss:** In the source domain, the cross-entropy loss is calculated by using the image label pair $(x, l)$ to further fine-tune the feature extractor $F$ and classifier $C$:

$$\min_{C \circ F} L_{seg} = \mathbb{E}_{x \sim \mathcal{X}} \frac{1}{hw} \sum_{i=1}^{h} \sum_{j=1}^{w} \sum_{k=0}^{K-1} -l_k^{(i,j)} \log_{\text{softmax}} \left( C(F(x))_k^{(i,j)} \right), \qquad (2)$$

where $h$ and $w$ represent the length and width of the image, $i$ and $j$ represent the pixel position, $K$ represents the total number of classes, and $k$ represents the class.

- **Adversarial loss:** We use least-square adversarial loss [32], because it has more stable training and better generation quality. The output cross-domain transfer is as follows:

$$\min_{F, H \circ C} \max_{D_x} L_{gan}^{y \to x} \mathbb{E}_{x^l \sim \mathcal{X}^l} \left[ \left( D_x(x^l) \right)^2 \right] + \mathbb{E}_{y^l \sim \mathcal{Y}^l} \left[ \left( 1 - D_x((H \circ C)(F(y^l))) \right)^2 \right];$$
$$(3)$$

The input-output cross-domain transfer is as follows:

$$\min_{F, H \circ C} \max_{D_x} L_{gan}^{y \to x} = \mathbb{E}_{x \sim \mathcal{X}} \left[ \left( D_x(x) \right)^2 \right] + \mathbb{E}_{y^l \sim \mathcal{Y}^l} \left[ \left( 1 - D_x((H \circ C)(F(y^l))) \right)^2 \right]$$
$$(4)$$

- **Mutual information maximization loss:** We use the prevalent loss function InfoNCE of the current noise contrastive estimation framework to maximize the mutual information between input and output. The contrastive learning based on noise contrastive estimation brings together the anchor sample and the positive samples in the feature space and pushes it further away from the negative samples. We use the normalized version of InfoNCE, and uses the temperature factor $\tau = 0.07$ to adjust the output of softmax. This version is called NT-Xent in SimCLR [3], with adaptive adjustment weight of negative examples. We sample one anchor sample, one positive sample and $N$ negative samples, which are mapped into hidden vectors by the network of different levels of the feature extractor $v$, $v^+$ And $v^-$, where $v_n^-$ represents the n-th negative sample. NT-Xent loss is as follows:

$$\min L_{\text{NT-Xent}}^{y \to x}(v, v^+, v^-) = -\log \left[ \frac{\exp(v \cdot v^+ / \tau)}{\exp(v \cdot v^+ / \tau) + \sum_{n=1}^{N} \exp(v \cdot v_n^- / \tau)} \right]$$
$$(5)$$

- **Multilayer-patchwise contrastive loss:** We use a multilayer-patchwise contrastive learning strategy like CUT [35]. Due to the large image size, we take a larger number of negative samples $N = 1024$ and take the features of the $L = 6$ layer to calculate the multilayer-patchwise contrastive loss. The features of each layer and each spatial position in the neural network represent a region of the input image, and the spatial position corresponding to the deeper network layer corresponds to the larger region. We select $L$ interest layers of network features, and perform feature mapping through the small two-layer fully-connected network $\hat{H}$ used in SimCLR [3] to generate the feature set of target domain image $y$ $\{z_l\}_L = \{\hat{H}_l(F^l(y))\}_L$, where $F^l(y)$ represents the $l \in \{1, 2, ..., L\}$ output of selected layers. The sampling spatial position of the $l$th selected layer is denoted as $s \in \{1, ..., S_l\}$, where $S_l$ represents the number of space positions of each layer. Denote the corresponding hidden layer vector as $z_l^s \in \mathbb{R}^{C_l}$, and other hidden layer vectors as $z_l^{S \backslash s} \in \mathbb{R}^{(S_l-1) \times C_l}$, where $C_l$ represents the corresponding feature dimension. Similarly, the image $y^l$ after the projection of the target domain image is encoded to obtain the feature set $\{\hat{z}_l\}_L = \{\hat{H}_l(F^l((H \circ C)(F(y))))\}_L$. Our purpose is to calculate contrastive loss between the corresponding image patches of the input and output images. The image patch corresponding to the spatial position can be used as the positive sample, and the other image patches in the image can be used as the negative sample. Further, define the PatchNCE loss function:

$$\min_{F, H \circ C, \hat{H}} L_{\text{PatchNCE}}^{y \to x} = \mathbb{E}_{y \sim y} \sum_{l=1}^{L} \sum_{s=1}^{S_l} L_{\text{NT-Xent}}^{y \to x}(\hat{z}_l^s, z_l^s, z_l^{S \backslash s}), \qquad (6)$$

where, only the optimized gradient is calculated for $\hat{z}_l$ to update the model parameters.

– **Full objective:** The translated image $y^l$ should be as close as possible to the input space or output space of the source domain $\mathcal{X}$. At the same time, the corresponding image patches before and after the translation should retain mutual information as much as possible, as shown in Fig. 1. In addition, we also use the PatchNCE loss function to perform regularization constraints on the source domain $\mathcal{X}$, guiding the feature extractor $F$ and generator $(H \circ C)$ to not cause unnecessary changes, which is consistent with the idea of reconstruction loss in the field of unsupervised cross-domain image-to-image translation. The whole objective of the discriminator $D_x$ is as follows:

$$\max_{D_x} \lambda_1 L_{gan}^{y \to x}; \qquad (7)$$

The full objective of the feature extractor $F$, classifier $C$, projection $H$, and two-layer fully-connected network $\hat{H}$ is as follows:

$$\min_{F, C, H, \hat{H}} L_{seg} + \lambda_4 \left( \lambda_1 L_{gan}^{y \to x} + \lambda_2 L_{\text{PatchNCE}}^{y \to x} + \lambda_3 L_{\text{PatchNCE}}^{x \to x} \right), \qquad (8)$$

where, $\lambda_1$, $\lambda_2$, $\lambda_3$ and $\lambda_4$ are the trade-off weights.

**Self-supervised training stage:**

- **Cross-entropy loss:** Load the ImageNet pre-trained model, and use the image-pseudo-label pair $(y, \hat{l})$ to calculate the cross-entropy loss on the target domain, minimize the difference between the predicted value and the pseudo-label, and help re-distill a new semantics segmentation network $C \circ F$:

$$\min_{C \circ F} L_{seg} = \mathbb{E}_{y \sim \mathcal{Y}} \frac{1}{hw} \sum_{i=1}^{h} \sum_{j=1}^{w} \sum_{k=0}^{K-1} -\hat{l}_k^{(i,j)} \log_{\text{softmax}} \left( C(F(y))_k^{(i,j)} \right), \qquad (9)$$

where $h$ and $w$ represent the length and width of the image, $i$ and $j$ represent the pixel position, $K$ represents the total number of classes, and $k$ represents the class.

## 4   Experiments

### 4.1   Dataset

**GTA5:** contains 24966 simulation images, and the original image size is $1914 \times 1052$ pixels resolution. During training, the image size is scaled to $1280 \times 720$ pixels without random cropping, and color jitters are used for data augmentation in the cross-domain transfer stage. Use the 19 semantic classes shared with the real-world city street CityScapes dataset, denote other classes as the "ignore" class and ignore the "ignore" class area during the training process.

**Synthia-Rand-CityScapes:** contains 9400 simulation images, the original image size is $1280 \times 760$ pixels resolution. During training, the image size is scaled to $1024 \times 512$ pixels, without random cropping, and color jitters are used for data augmentation in the cross-domain transfer stage. Similarly, only 16 semantic classes shared with the real-world city street CityScapes dataset are used for training. Other classes are set to "ignore" class, and the "ignore" class area is ignored during training. However, this dataset generally selects the following two evaluation settings: performed on 16 classes or a subset of 13 classes.

**CityScapes:** contains 2975 real images, and the original image size is $2048 \times 1024$ pixels resolution. The image size is scaled to $1024 \times 512$ pixels in the cross-domain transfer stage, without random cropping and color jitters. In the self-supervised training stage, the image size is scaled to $1024 \times 512 - 3072 \times 1536$ pixels, and $1024 \times 512$ pixels are randomly cropped, using color jitters and random flipping data augmentation methods. The two cross-domain transfer tasks are GTA5CityScapes and SYNTHIACityScapes. Only use the semantic classes shared with the simulation data set for testing, set other categories as the "ignore" class, and ignore the "ignore" class area during the test. Following the standard protocol [16,17,42], we use 2975 images in the training set as the unlabeled target domain training set and evaluate the proposed cross-domain transfer model on 500 images in the validation set.

## 4.2  Setup

For the feature extractor $F$ and classifier $C$, use the SGD optimizer (momentum 0.9, weight decay $10^{-4}$). The initial learning rate is $2.5 \times 10^{-4}$ (classifier $C$ learning rate $\times 10$), and the learning rate is decayed according to the "poly" learning rate decay strategy with an exponent of 0.9.

The output of the classifier $C$ is softened by the temperature adjustment factor $\tau = 1.8$. $\lambda_4$ is set to $10^{-3}$. Use ReLU as the activation function in the projection $H$ and the double-layer fully-connected network $\hat{H}$, and use Leaky-ReLU with a slope of 0.2 in the discriminator $D_x$. Use Adam [22] optimizer to train with a learning rate of $10^{-4}$ and $(\beta 1, \beta 2) = (0.5, 0.999)$. $\lambda_1$, $\lambda_2$, and $\lambda_3$ are all set to 1.

When using the contrastive learning InfoNCE to calculate the mutual information maximization loss, select the $L = 6$ features layers of the feature extractor, sample $S_l = 1024$ random regions, and use the two-layer fully-connected layer to extract the output features of the corresponding layer 256-dimensional similarity feature, temperature adjustment factor $\tau = 0.07$. Specifically, when the feature extractor $F$ is ResNet-101, the input layer, the first relu layer, layer1, layer2, layer3, and layer4 are respectively selected to calculate the PatchNCE loss; when the feature extractor $F$ is VGG-16, the input layer and the 4th, 9th, 16th, 28th, and 32nd layers are selected respectively to calculate the PatchNCE loss.

Considering that data augmentation methods such as flipping and scale change are used in the self-supervised training stage, a multi-scale testing scheme is used to integrate the prediction results of different augmentation methods in the final model test.

## 4.3  Evaluation Metrics

The metrics used to evaluate the algorithm are consistent with ordinary semantic segmentation tasks. Specifically, we calculate the PSACAL VOC intersection ratio of the predicted output and the real label (IoU) [9]: $\text{IoU} = \frac{\text{TP}}{\text{TP}+\text{FP}+\text{FN}}$, where TP, FP and FN are the true positive examples, false positive examples and false negative examples. In addition to IoU for each semantic class, we also report the mean value of all semantic classes mIoU.

## 4.4  Comparisons with State of the Arts

Table 3 and Table 4 show the semantic segmentation performance of GTA5 $\rightarrow$ CityScapes and SYNTHIACityScapes tasks, and our model achieves better results compared with the classic prevalent methods. At the same time, the effects of the two training schemes of output transfer and input-output transfer are compared. Although the input-output transfer performs well on the GTA5CityScapes task, it does not perform well on the SYNTHIACityScapes task. This result may be because the difference between the source domain dataset SYNTHIA and the target domain dataset CityScapes is huge. Not only

**Table 3.** GTA5 → CityScapes

| Backbone | Method | Road | Sidewalk | Building | Wall | Fence | Pole | Light | Sign | Vegetation | Terrain | Sky | Person | Rider | Car | Truck | Bus | Train | Motorbike | Bike | mIoU |
|---|---|---|---|---|---|---|---|---|---|---|---|---|---|---|---|---|---|---|---|---|---|
| VGG-16 | FCNs in the wild [17] | 70.4 | 32.4 | 62.1 | 14.9 | 5.4 | 10.9 | 14.2 | 2.7 | 79.2 | 21.3 | 64.6 | 44.1 | 4.2 | 70.4 | 8.0 | 7.3 | 0.0 | 3.5 | 0.0 | 27.1 |
| | CDA [48] | 74.9 | 22.0 | 71.7 | 6.0 | 11.9 | 8.4 | 16.3 | 11.1 | 75.7 | 13.3 | 66.5 | 38.0 | 9.3 | 55.2 | 18.8 | 18.9 | 0.0 | 16.8 | 14.6 | 28.9 |
| | CBST [50] | 90.4 | 50.8 | 72.0 | 18.3 | 9.5 | 27.2 | 28.6 | 14.1 | 82.4 | 25.1 | 70.8 | 42.6 | 14.5 | 76.9 | 5.9 | 12.5 | 1.2 | 14.0 | 28.6 | 36.1 |
| | CyCADA [16] | 85.2 | 37.2 | 76.5 | 21.8 | 15.0 | 23.8 | 22.9 | 21.5 | 80.5 | 31.3 | 60.7 | 50.5 | 9.0 | 76.9 | 17.1 | 28.2 | 4.5 | 9.8 | 0.0 | 35.4 |
| | AdaptSegNet [41] | 87.3 | 29.8 | 78.6 | 21.1 | 18.2 | 22.5 | 21.5 | 11.0 | 79.7 | 29.6 | 71.3 | 46.8 | 6.5 | 80.1 | 23.0 | 26.9 | 0.0 | 10.6 | 0.3 | 35.0 |
| | SIBAN [30] | 83.4 | 13.0 | 77.8 | 20.4 | 17.5 | 24.6 | 22.8 | 9.6 | 81.3 | 29.6 | 77.3 | 42.7 | 10.9 | 76.0 | 22.8 | 17.9 | 5.7 | 14.2 | 2.0 | 34.2 |
| | CLAN [31] | 88.0 | 30.6 | 79.2 | 23.4 | 20.5 | 26.1 | 23.0 | 14.8 | 81.6 | **34.5** | 72.0 | 45.8 | 7.9 | 80.5 | **26.6** | **29.9** | 0.0 | 10.7 | 0.0 | 36.6 |
| | AdaptPatch [42] | 87.3 | 35.7 | 79.5 | **32.0** | 14.5 | 21.5 | 24.8 | 13.7 | 80.4 | 32.0 | 70.5 | 50.5 | 16.9 | 81.0 | 20.8 | 28.1 | 4.1 | 15.5 | 4.1 | 37.5 |
| | AdvEnt [43] | 86.9 | 28.7 | 78.7 | 28.5 | **25.2** | 17.1 | 20.3 | 10.9 | 80.0 | 26.4 | 70.2 | 47.1 | 8.4 | 81.5 | 26.0 | 17.2 | **18.9** | 11.7 | 1.6 | 36.1 |
| | Output transfer | **91.5** | **47.9** | **82.0** | **32.0** | 19.6 | **30.3** | 25.8 | 13.2 | 78.9 | 26.0 | 81.4 | 54.5 | 22.0 | **84.5** | 18.9 | 12.1 | 0.1 | 14.3 | 10.0 | 39.2 |
| | Input-output transfer | 87.3 | 44.0 | 80.7 | 28.8 | 20.4 | 30.0 | **28.8** | 11.8 | 79.3 | 31.7 | **81.9** | **57.3** | **26.2** | 84.4 | 20.5 | 11.4 | 0.0 | **18.6** | 11.7 | **39.7** |
| ResNet-101 | CyCADA [16] | 86.7 | 35.6 | 80.1 | 19.8 | 17.5 | 38 | **39.9** | **41.5** | 82.7 | 27.9 | 73.6 | **64.9** | 19 | 65 | 12 | 28.6 | 4.5 | 31.1 | **42** | 42.7 |
| | AdaptSegNet [41] | 86.5 | 36.0 | 79.9 | 23.4 | 23.3 | 23.9 | 35.2 | 14.8 | 83.4 | 33.3 | 75.6 | 58.5 | 27.6 | 73.7 | 32.5 | 35.4 | 3.9 | 30.1 | 28.1 | 42.4 |
| | SIBAN [30] | 88.5 | 35.4 | 79.5 | 26.3 | 24.3 | 28.5 | 32.5 | 18.3 | 81.2 | 40.0 | 76.5 | 58.1 | 25.8 | 82.6 | 30.3 | 34.4 | 3.4 | 21.6 | 21.5 | 42.6 |
| | CLAN [31] | 87.0 | 27.1 | 79.6 | 27.3 | 23.3 | 28.3 | 35.5 | 24.2 | 83.6 | 27.4 | 74.2 | 58.6 | 28.0 | 76.2 | 33.1 | 36.7 | **6.7** | 31.4 | 31.4 | 43.2 |
| | AdaptPatch [42] | **92.3** | **51.9** | 82.1 | 29.2 | 25.1 | 24.5 | 33.8 | 33.0 | 82.4 | 32.8 | 82.2 | 58.6 | 27.2 | 84.3 | 33.4 | 46.3 | 2.2 | 29.5 | 32.3 | 46.5 |
| | AdvEnt [43] | 89.4 | 33.1 | 81.0 | 26.6 | 26.8 | 27.2 | 33.5 | 24.7 | 83.9 | 36.7 | 78.8 | 58.7 | 30.5 | 84.8 | **38.5** | 44.5 | 1.7 | 31.6 | 32.4 | 45.5 |
| | Output transfer | 89.5 | 43.5 | **85.5** | 42.5 | **30.5** | 32.9 | 30.6 | 17.6 | **85.9** | 33.6 | **84.7** | 64.2 | 36.2 | **87.0** | 36.6 | 46.6 | 0.0 | 34.5 | 33.8 | 48.2 |
| | Input-output transfer | 87.5 | 40.7 | 83.3 | **42.9** | 22.4 | 30.9 | 38.2 | 15.4 | 85.7 | **40.6** | 83.5 | 63.4 | **36.6** | 85.9 | 37.3 | **47.7** | 0.0 | **36.5** | 39.5 | **48.3** |

the texture style is significantly different, but the perspective is also very different, which makes the transfer across the input and output too difficult to learn effective transferred knowledge, and even causes serious negative transfer. These phenomena will damage the capacity of the extraction of input and output common semantic features (for example, using VGG-16 as a feature extractor, the road class's IoU is only 11.2%, using ResNet-101 as a feature extractor, and the road class's IoU is only 29.7%). Since the output transfer scheme only considers the alignment of the semantic output space, it can ignore more information such as texture and perspective, so the semantic segmentation performance is more stable and robust. In summary, it is possible to consider using the input-output transfer scheme for slight domain shift, and use the output transfer scheme for significant domain shift.

**Table 4.** SYNTHIA → CityScapes

| Backbone | Method | Road | Sidewalk | Building | Wall | Fence | Pole | Light | Sign | Vegetation | Sky | Person | Rider | Car | Bus | Motorbike | Bike | mIoU$_{16}$ | mIoU$_{13}$ |
|---|---|---|---|---|---|---|---|---|---|---|---|---|---|---|---|---|---|---|---|
| VGG-16 | FCNs in the wild [17] | 11.5 | 19.6 | 30.8 | 4.4 | 0.0 | 20.3 | 0.1 | 11.7 | 42.3 | 68.7 | 51.2 | 3.8 | 54.0 | 3.2 | 0.2 | 0.6 | 20.2 | 22.9 |
| | CDA [48] | 65.2 | 26.1 | 74.9 | 0.1 | **0.5** | 10.7 | 3.5 | 3.0 | 76.1 | 70.6 | 47.1 | 8.2 | 43.2 | 20.7 | 0.7 | 13.1 | 29.0 | 34.8 |
| | ST [50] | 0.2 | 14.5 | 53.8 | 1.6 | 0.0 | 18.9 | 0.9 | 7.8 | 72.2 | 80.3 | 48.1 | 6.3 | 67.7 | 4.7 | 0.2 | 4.5 | 23.9 | 27.8 |
| | CBST [50] | 69.6 | 28.7 | 69.5 | **12.1** | 0.1 | 25.4 | 11.9 | 13.6 | **82.0** | 81.9 | 49.1 | **14.5** | 66.0 | 6.6 | 3.7 | 32.4 | **35.4** | – |
| | AdaptSegNet [41] | 78.9 | 29.2 | 75.5 | – | – | – | 0.1 | 4.8 | 72.6 | 76.7 | 43.4 | 8.8 | 71.1 | 16.0 | 3.6 | 8.4 | – | 37.6 |
| | SIBAN [30] | 70.1 | 25.7 | 80.9 | – | – | – | 3.8 | 7.2 | 72.3 | 80.5 | 43.3 | 5.0 | 73.3 | 16.0 | 1.7 | 3.6 | – | 37.2 |
| | CLAN [31] | **80.4** | **30.7** | 74.7 | – | – | – | 1.4 | 8.0 | 77.1 | 79.0 | 46.5 | 8.9 | **73.8** | 18.2 | 2.2 | 9.9 | – | 39.3 |
| | AdaptPatch [42] | 72.6 | 29.5 | 77.2 | 3.5 | 0.4 | 21.0 | 1.4 | 7.9 | 73.3 | 79.0 | 45.7 | **14.5** | 69.4 | 19.6 | 7.4 | 16.5 | 33.7 | **39.6** |
| | AdvEnt [43] | 67.9 | 29.4 | 71.9 | 6.3 | 0.3 | 19.9 | 0.6 | 2.6 | 74.9 | 74.9 | 35.4 | 9.6 | 67.8 | 21.4 | 4.1 | 15.5 | 31.4 | 36.6 |
| | Output transfer | 65.3 | 27.6 | 73.0 | 1.4 | 0.0 | 24.6 | 0.0 | 6.5 | 71.2 | 79.2 | 50.5 | 7.4 | 64.9 | 30.2 | 10.1 | 13.2 | 32.8 | 38.4 |
| | Input-output transfer | 11.2 | 13.6 | 72.0 | 1.8 | 0.0 | **25.9** | 0.0 | 6.3 | 74.0 | 80.5 | **52.5** | 9.7 | 66.1 | **33.9** | **13.0** | **16.8** | 29.8 | 34.6 |
| ResNet-101 | SIBAN [30] | 82.5 | 24.0 | 79.4 | – | – | – | 16.5 | 12.7 | 79.2 | 82.8 | **58.3** | 18.0 | 79.3 | 25.3 | 17.6 | 25.9 | – | 46.3 |
| | AdaptSegNet [41] | 84.3 | **42.7** | 77.5 | – | – | – | 4.7 | 7.0 | 77.9 | 82.5 | 54.3 | 21.0 | 72.3 | 32.2 | 18.9 | 32.3 | – | 46.7 |
| | CLAN [31] | 81.3 | 37.0 | 80.1 | – | – | – | 16.1 | 13.7 | 78.2 | 81.5 | 53.4 | 21.2 | 73.0 | 32.9 | 22.6 | 30.7 | – | 47.8 |
| | AdaptPatch [42] | 82.4 | 38.0 | 78.6 | 8.7 | **0.6** | 26.0 | 3.9 | 11.1 | 75.5 | **84.6** | 53.5 | 21.6 | 71.4 | 32.6 | 19.3 | 31.7 | 40.0 | 46.5 |
| | AdvEnt[43] | **85.6** | 42.2 | 79.7 | 8.7 | 0.4 | 25.9 | 5.4 | 8.1 | 80.4 | 84.1 | 57.9 | **23.8** | 73.3 | 36.4 | 14.2 | 33.0 | 41.2 | 48.0 |
| | Output transfer | 72.1 | 30.2 | **81.7** | 10.2 | 0.0 | **31.5** | 16.3 | **17.9** | 83.3 | 81.4 | 55.2 | 17.0 | **84.3** | **50.1** | **23.8** | **39.3** | **43.4** | **50.2** |
| | Input-output transfer | 29.7 | 15.9 | 81.3 | **11.8** | 0.0 | 29.8 | 13.7 | 16.3 | **83.9** | 81.7 | 56.7 | 19.0 | 84.1 | 47.9 | 21.5 | 31.3 | 39.0 | 44.8 |

Table 5 shows the experimental results of using the ResNet-101 feature extractor on the GTA5CityScapes task of the three-stage training paradigm. Taking the input-output transfer scheme as an example, the mIoU of the proposed model on the semantic segmentation task of the target domain has been increased from 38.4 in the pre-training stage to 45.3 in the cross-domain transfer stage, which verifies the proposed method can realize effective knowledge transfer under the framework of reusing semantic segmentation network for unsupervised image-to-image translation. After self-supervised training of the proposed model, mIoU is further increased to 48.3, indicating that the pseudo-labels retain sufficient semantic information, and the semantic segmentation performance can be further improved by distilling pseudo-labels.

**Table 5.** Training results of each stage

GTA5 → CityScapes, ResNet-101

| Transfer methods | Training stage | Road | Sidewalk | Building | Wall | Fence | Pole | Light | Sign | Vegetation | Terrain | Sky | Person | Rider | Car | Truck | Bus | Train | Motorbike | Bike | mIoU |
|---|---|---|---|---|---|---|---|---|---|---|---|---|---|---|---|---|---|---|---|---|---|
| Output transfer | Pre-training stage | 66.5 | 18.4 | 72.2 | 24.2 | 17.4 | 25.7 | 32.2 | 16.9 | 82.7 | 29.2 | 79.6 | 57.0 | 33.5 | 62.8 | 23.5 | 28.0 | 12.6 | 28.0 | 19.7 | 38.4 |
| | Cross-domain transfer stage | 86.3 | 32.6 | 83.4 | 38.3 | 26.6 | 29.4 | 35.5 | 18.3 | 82.5 | 27.5 | 83.4 | 58.9 | 33.0 | 83.9 | 34.6 | 36.6 | 16.3 | 23.0 | 28.0 | 45.2 |
| | Self-supervised training stage | 89.5 | 43.5 | 85.5 | 42.5 | 30.5 | 32.9 | 30.6 | 17.6 | 85.9 | 33.6 | 84.7 | 64.2 | 36.2 | 87.0 | 36.6 | 46.6 | 0.0 | 34.5 | 33.8 | 48.2 |
| Input-output transfer | Pre-training stage | 66.5 | 18.4 | 72.2 | 24.2 | 17.4 | 25.7 | 32.2 | 16.9 | 82.7 | 29.2 | 79.6 | 57.0 | 33.5 | 62.8 | 23.5 | 28.0 | 12.6 | 28.0 | 19.7 | 38.4 |
| | Cross-domain transfer stage | 84.3 | 30.7 | 82.3 | 36.3 | 22.0 | 28.9 | 34.7 | 19.0 | 82.8 | 35.3 | 84.1 | 58.6 | 33.3 | 83.5 | 34.7 | 39.2 | 11.7 | 26.9 | 32.6 | 45.3 |
| | Self-supervised training stage | 87.5 | 40.7 | 83.3 | 42.9 | 22.4 | 30.9 | 38.2 | 15.4 | 85.7 | 40.6 | 83.5 | 63.4 | 36.6 | 85.9 | 37.3 | 47.7 | 0.0 | 36.5 | 39.5 | 48.3 |

## 4.5 Ablation Study

**Table 6.** The ablation study of GTA5 → CityScapes

| Output transfer | Input-output transfer | Color jitters | mIoU |
|---|---|---|---|
| | | | 38.4 |
| ✓ | | | 42.5 |
| | ✓ | | 40.4 |
| | | ✓ | 44.3 |
| ✓ | | ✓ | 45.2 |
| | ✓ | ✓ | **45.3** |

This section uses the ResNet-101 feature extractor on the GTA5CityScapes task data set to conduct an ablation study in the cross-domain transfer stage, mainly for two cross-domain transfer schemes and color jitters augmentation for ablation analysis. As shown in the Table 6, under the condition of not performing color jitters augmentation on the source domain data, only the output transfer scheme is used, and the mIoU is increased from 38.4 to 42.5, but using input-output transfer scheme can only be increased to 40.4. One possible reason is that the transfer across the input and output is affected by the RGB color space of the input. With color jitters, it is more helpful to extract semantic information that is irrelevant to color. While the output transfer scheme is to transfer in the output space, and the reconstruction of the source domain is not constrained by the input color space, so more semantic information invariant with color can be extracted through contrastive learning.

Furthermore, only the color jitters augmentation is performed on the source domain without any explicit transfer scheme. mIoU is increased from 38.4 to 44.3, which further proves that the color jitters augmentation is helpful to extract the color-invariant representations and the color-invariant semantic information is essential for unsupervised semantic segmentation tasks. By combining color jitters augmentation and the cross-domain transfer scheme based on contrastive learning, the ability to extract color-invariant semantic information can be better improved, and mIoU is further increased to 45.2 and 45.3.

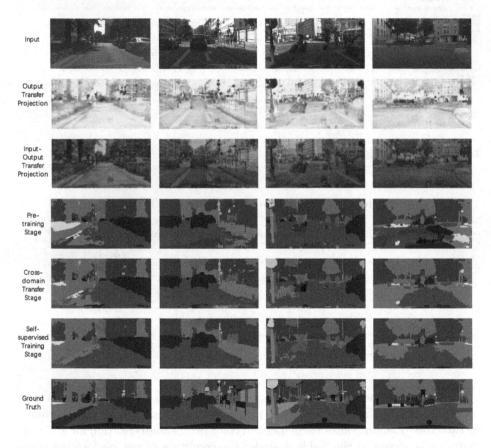

**Fig. 3.** Visualization of results on GTA5 → CityScapes. From top to bottom, the input images of the target domain CityScapes, the projection maps with the output transfer scheme, the projection maps with the input-output transfer scheme, the semantic segmentation maps after pre-training, the input-output transfer training, and after self-supervised training.

## 4.6    Visualization of Results

Figure 3 shows the visualization results of the proposed model using the ResNet-101 feature extractor on the GTA5CityScapes task. Observing the semantic segmentation projection maps with the output transfer scheme, we can find that the projection maps are more abstract, so it may be possible to retain more abstract high-level semantic information while ignoring unimportant style details, and further reduce the burden of transfer learning, which may avoid the occurrence of negative transfer when the source domain and target domain are quite different.

Observing the semantic segmentation projection map with the input-output transfer scheme, we can find that the projection maps seem to overlay different color semantic layers on different objects in the foreground and background. Such translated images look like a semantic attention mechanism added to the original input images. This phenomenon indirectly shows that reusing the semantic segmentation network as an unsupervised image-to-image translation network can integrate the semantic segmentation information into the image-to-image translation process. Therefore, the input-output transfer scheme can be used when the difference between the source domain and the target domain is small, so as to effectively use the segmentation label information to realize the positive feedback loop of image-to-image translation and semantic segmentation.

Further observation of the semantic segmentation output results of the three training stages shows that the semantic segmentation images of each stage are more refined and accurate than the previous stage, which qualitatively verifies the steady improvement of the semantic segmentation performance through the three-stage training paradigm.

## 5    Conclusion

We attempt to combine contrastive learning with generative adversarial networks to achieve the fusion of semantic priors and unknown "dark energy", and proposes a transfer method for unsupervised semantic segmentation tasks. Specifically, it uses an unsupervised image-to-image translation framework to maximize mutual information by a generative adversarial network and contrastive learning while bringing together the input and output distribution and indirectly extracting domain-invariant features. First, the feature extractor and classifier of semantic segmentation are reused for the encoder and generator in the image-to-image translation framework. Specifically, the features of the exact spatial location at the corresponding level of the images before and after the translation are brought closer to each other. The features of different spatial locations at the same level are pushed away from each other so that the feature extractor can learn features that are domain-invariant and sensitive to spatial locations and semantic classes. We conduct an experimental evaluation on the benchmark datasets, compare other prevalent methods and two transfer schemes, and prove that the proposed method is reasonable and practical. The input-output transfer scheme performs well in tasks with slight domain shift but is not up to tasks with large domain shift, while the output transfer scheme has better robustness. At the same time, the importance of color-invariant semantic information for unsupervised semantic segmentation tasks is explained through an ablation study.

# References

1. Chen, L.C., Papandreou, G., Schroff, F., Adam, H.: Rethinking atrous convolution for semantic image segmentation. arXiv preprint arXiv:1706.05587 (2017)
2. Chen, R., Huang, W., Huang, B., Sun, F., Fang, B.: Reusing discriminators for encoding: towards unsupervised image-to-image translation. In: Proceedings of the IEEE/CVF Conference on Computer Vision and Pattern Recognition, pp. 8168–8177 (2020)
3. Chen, T., Kornblith, S., Norouzi, M., Hinton, G.: A simple framework for contrastive learning of visual representations. In: International Conference on Machine Learning, pp. 1597–1607. PMLR (2020)
4. Choi, Y., Uh, Y., Yoo, J., Ha, J.W.: StarGAN v2: diverse image synthesis for multiple domains. In: Proceedings of the IEEE/CVF Conference on Computer Vision and Pattern Recognition, pp. 8188–8197 (2020)
5. Cordts, M., et al.: The cityscapes dataset for semantic urban scene understanding. In: Proceedings of the IEEE Conference on Computer Vision and Pattern Recognition, pp. 3213–3223 (2016)
6. Demir, U., Unal, G.: Patch-based image inpainting with generative adversarial networks. arXiv preprint arXiv:1803.07422 (2018)
7. Deng, J., Dong, W., Socher, R., Li, L.J., Li, K., Fei-Fei, L.: ImageNet: a large-scale hierarchical image database. In: 2009 IEEE Conference on Computer Vision and Pattern Recognition, pp. 248–255. IEEE (2009)
8. Durugkar, I., Gemp, I., Mahadevan, S.: Generative multi-adversarial networks. arXiv preprint arXiv:1611.01673 (2016)
9. Everingham, M., Eslami, S.A., Van Gool, L., Williams, C.K., Winn, J., Zisserman, A.: The pascal visual object classes challenge: a retrospective. Int. J. Comput. Vis. 111(1), 98–136 (2015). https://doi.org/10.1007/s11263-014-0733-5
10. Goodfellow, I.J., et al.: Generative adversarial nets. In: NIPS (2014)
11. Gutmann, M., Hyvärinen, A.: Noise-contrastive estimation: A new estimation principle for unnormalized statistical models (2010)
12. He, K., Fan, H., Wu, Y., Xie, S., Girshick, R.: Momentum contrast for unsupervised visual representation learning. In: Proceedings of the IEEE/CVF Conference on Computer Vision and Pattern Recognition, pp. 9729–9738 (2020)
13. He, K., Gkioxari, G., Dollár, P., Girshick, R.: Mask R-CNN. In: Proceedings of the IEEE International Conference on Computer Vision, pp. 2961–2969 (2017)
14. He, K., Zhang, X., Ren, S., Sun, J.: Deep residual learning for image recognition. In: Proceedings of the IEEE Conference on Computer Vision and Pattern Recognition, pp. 770–778 (2016)
15. Hjelm, R.D., et al.: Learning deep representations by mutual information estimation and maximization. In: International Conference on Learning Representations (2018)
16. Hoffman, J., et al.: CyCADA: cycle-consistent adversarial domain adaptation. In: International Conference on Machine Learning, pp. 1989–1998. PMLR (2018)
17. Hoffman, J., Wang, D., Yu, F., Darrell, T.: FCNs in the wild: Pixel-level adversarial and constraint-based adaptation. arXiv preprint arXiv:1612.02649 (2016)

18. Huang, X., Liu, M.Y., Belongie, S., Kautz, J.: Multimodal unsupervised image-to-image translation. In: Proceedings of the European Conference on Computer Vision (ECCV), pp. 172–189 (2018)
19. Iizuka, S., Simo-Serra, E., Ishikawa, H.: Globally and locally consistent image completion. ACM Trans. Graph. (ToG) **36**(4), 1–14 (2017)
20. Kim, J., Kim, M., Kang, H., Lee, K.H.: U-GAT-IT: unsupervised generative attentional networks with adaptive layer-instance normalization for image-to-image translation. In: International Conference on Learning Representations (2019)
21. Kim, T., Cha, M., Kim, H., Lee, J.K., Kim, J.: Learning to discover cross-domain relations with generative adversarial networks. In: International Conference on Machine Learning, pp. 1857–1865. PMLR (2017)
22. Kingma, D.P., Ba, J.: Adam: A method for stochastic optimization. arXiv preprint arXiv:1412.6980 (2014)
23. Le-Khac, P.H., Healy, G., Smeaton, A.F.: Contrastive representation learning: a framework and review. IEEE Access **8**, 193907–193934 (2020)
24. Lee, H.-Y., Tseng, H.-Y., Huang, J.-B., Singh, M., Yang, M.-H.: Diverse image-to-image translation via disentangled representations. In: Ferrari, V., Hebert, M., Sminchisescu, C., Weiss, Y. (eds.) ECCV 2018, Part I. LNCS, vol. 11205, pp. 36–52. Springer, Cham (2018). https://doi.org/10.1007/978-3-030-01246-5_3
25. Li, Y., Yuan, L., Vasconcelos, N.: Bidirectional learning for domain adaptation of semantic segmentation. In: Proceedings of the IEEE/CVF Conference on Computer Vision and Pattern Recognition, pp. 6936–6945 (2019)
26. Lin, T.Y., Dollár, P., Girshick, R., He, K., Hariharan, B., Belongie, S.: Feature pyramid networks for object detection. In: Proceedings of the IEEE Conference on Computer Vision and Pattern Recognition, pp. 2117–2125 (2017)
27. Liu, M.Y., Breuel, T., Kautz, J.: Unsupervised image-to-image translation networks. In: Proceedings of the 31st International Conference on Neural Information Processing Systems, pp. 700–708 (2017)
28. Liu, M.Y., Tuzel, O.: Coupled generative adversarial networks. arXiv preprint arXiv:1606.07536 (2016)
29. Liu, W., et al.: SSD: single shot multibox detector. In: Leibe, B., Matas, J., Sebe, N., Welling, M. (eds.) ECCV 2016, Part I. LNCS, vol. 9905, pp. 21–37. Springer, Cham (2016). https://doi.org/10.1007/978-3-319-46448-0_2
30. Luo, Y., Liu, P., Guan, T., Yu, J., Yang, Y.: Significance-aware information bottleneck for domain adaptive semantic segmentation. In: Proceedings of the IEEE/CVF International Conference on Computer Vision, pp. 6778–6787 (2019)
31. Luo, Y., Zheng, L., Guan, T., Yu, J., Yang, Y.: Taking a closer look at domain shift: category-level adversaries for semantics consistent domain adaptation. In: Proceedings of the IEEE/CVF Conference on Computer Vision and Pattern Recognition, pp. 2507–2516 (2019)
32. Mao, X., Li, Q., Xie, H., Lau, R.Y., Wang, Z., Paul Smolley, S.: Least squares generative adversarial networks. In: Proceedings of the IEEE International Conference on Computer Vision, pp. 2794–2802 (2017)
33. Misra, I., van der Maaten, L.: Self-supervised learning of pretext-invariant representations. arXiv preprint arXiv:1912.01991 (2019)
34. Oord, A.v.d., Li, Y., Vinyals, O.: Representation learning with contrastive predictive coding. arXiv preprint arXiv:1807.03748 (2018)
35. Park, T., Efros, A.A., Zhang, R., Zhu, J.-Y.: Contrastive learning for unpaired image-to-image translation. In: Vedaldi, A., Bischof, H., Brox, T., Frahm, J.-M. (eds.) ECCV 2020, Part IX. LNCS, vol. 12354, pp. 319–345. Springer, Cham (2020). https://doi.org/10.1007/978-3-030-58545-7_19

36. Pathak, D., Shelhamer, E., Long, J., Darrell, T.: Fully convolutional multi-class multiple instance learning. arXiv preprint arXiv:1412.7144 (2014)
37. Richter, S.R., Vineet, V., Roth, S., Koltun, V.: Playing for data: ground truth from computer games. In: Leibe, B., Matas, J., Sebe, N., Welling, M. (eds.) ECCV 2016, Part II. LNCS, vol. 9906, pp. 102–118. Springer, Cham (2016). https://doi.org/10.1007/978-3-319-46475-6_7
38. Ros, G., Sellart, L., Materzynska, J., Vazquez, D., Lopez, A.M.: The SYNTHIA dataset: a large collection of synthetic images for semantic segmentation of urban scenes. In: Proceedings of the IEEE Conference on Computer Vision and Pattern Recognition, pp. 3234–3243 (2016)
39. Simonyan, K., Zisserman, A.: Very deep convolutional networks for large-scale image recognition. arXiv preprint arXiv:1409.1556 (2014)
40. Tian, Y., Krishnan, D., Isola, P.: Contrastive multiview coding. arXiv preprint arXiv:1906.05849 (2019)
41. Tsai, Y.H., Hung, W.C., Schulter, S., Sohn, K., Yang, M.H., Chandraker, M.: Learning to adapt structured output space for semantic segmentation. In: Proceedings of the IEEE Conference on Computer Vision and Pattern Recognition, pp. 7472–7481 (2018)
42. Tsai, Y.H., Sohn, K., Schulter, S., Chandraker, M.: Domain adaptation for structured output via discriminative patch representations. In: Proceedings of the IEEE/CVF International Conference on Computer Vision, pp. 1456–1465 (2019)
43. Vu, T.H., Jain, H., Bucher, M., Cord, M., Pérez, P.: ADVENT: adversarial entropy minimization for domain adaptation in semantic segmentation. In: Proceedings of the IEEE/CVF Conference on Computer Vision and Pattern Recognition, pp. 2517–2526 (2019)
44. Wang, T.C., Liu, M.Y., Zhu, J.Y., Tao, A., Kautz, J., Catanzaro, B.: High-resolution image synthesis and semantic manipulation with conditional GANs. In: Proceedings of the IEEE Conference on Computer Vision and Pattern Recognition, pp. 8798–8807 (2018)
45. Wang, Z., et al.: Differential treatment for stuff and things: a simple unsupervised domain adaptation method for semantic segmentation. In: Proceedings of the IEEE/CVF Conference on Computer Vision and Pattern Recognition, pp. 12635–12644 (2020)
46. Wu, Z., Xiong, Y., Yu, S.X., Lin, D.: Unsupervised feature learning via non-parametric instance discrimination. In: Proceedings of the IEEE Conference on Computer Vision and Pattern Recognition, pp. 3733–3742 (2018)
47. Yi, Z., Zhang, H., Tan, P., Gong, M.: DualGAN: unsupervised dual learning for image-to-image translation. In: Proceedings of the IEEE International Conference on Computer Vision, pp. 2849–2857 (2017)
48. Zhang, Y., David, P., Gong, B.: Curriculum domain adaptation for semantic segmentation of urban scenes. In: Proceedings of the IEEE International Conference on Computer Vision, pp. 2020–2030 (2017)
49. Zhu, J.Y., Park, T., Isola, P., Efros, A.A.: Unpaired image-to-image translation using cycle-consistent adversarial networks. In: Proceedings of the IEEE International Conference on Computer Vision, pp. 2223–2232 (2017)
50. Zou, Y., Yu, Z., Vijaya Kumar, B.V.K., Wang, J.: Unsupervised domain adaptation for semantic segmentation via class-balanced self-training. In: Ferrari, V., Hebert, M., Sminchisescu, C., Weiss, Y. (eds.) ECCV 2018, Part III. LNCS, vol. 11207, pp. 297–313. Springer, Cham (2018). https://doi.org/10.1007/978-3-030-01219-9_18

# Multi-class Feature Selection Based on Softmax with $L_{2,0}$-Norm Regularization

Shumei Zeng[1], Yuanlong Yu[1(✉)], and Zhenzhen Sun[2(✉)]

[1] College of Mathematics and Computer Science,
Fuzhou University, Fuzhou, Fujian 350116, China
yu.yuanlong@fzu.edu.cn
[2] College of Computer Science and Technology,
Huaqiao University, Xiamen, Fujian 361021, China

**Abstract.** In recent years, feature selection (FS) methods based on sparsity have been extensively investigated due to their high performance. These methods solve the FS problem mainly by introducing some kinds of sparsity regularization terms. However, recent existing feature selection algorithms combine sparsity regularization with simple linear loss function, which may lead to deficient in performance. To this end, we propose a fresh and robust feature selection method that combines the structured sparsity regularization, *i.e.*, $\ell_{2,0}$-norm regularization, with the Softmax model to find a stable row-sparse solution, where we can select the features in group according to the solution of the projected matrix, and the classification performance can be improved by Softmax. Extensive experiments on six different datasets indicate that our method can obtain better or comparable classification performance by using fewer features compared with other advanced sparsity-based FS methods.

**Keywords:** $L_{2,0}$-norm regularization · Feature selection · Structured sparsity · Softmax

## 1 Introduction

Recently, with the development of high-dimensional datasets, feature selection (FS) has been investigated extensively in many fields due to it can decrease the number of features without deteriorating model's performance, and has been playing an important role in many real-world applications, *i.e.*, data compression, biometric identification, and pattern recognition.

Generally, FS algorithms can be roughly divided into three families in terms of how they combine the model learning algorithms with features search: filter methods, wrapper methods, and embedded methods. The learning algorithm and feature search are independent in the filter methods, which select the most

This work is supported by National Natural Science Foundation of China (NSFC) under grant #61873067.

F. Sun et al. (Eds.): ICCSIP 2021, CCIS 1515, pp. 37–48, 2022.
https://doi.org/10.1007/978-981-16-9247-5_3

important features based on the statistics and intrinsic properties of the data. Typical filter method includes F-statistic [1], Relief-F [2,3] and mRMR [4]. The wrapper methods generate a subset of features under a classifier and use an objective function to evaluate the subset of features, as in the recursive feature elimination-based support vector machine(SVM-RFE) [5]. Embedded methods outperform filter and wrapper methods in terms of computational efficiency and classification performance because they integrate feature selection and model learning into a single optimization problem. Therefore, the embedded methods receive more and more attention in the last few years. In this paper, we focus on embedded methods.

Sparsity regularization is currently being studied extensively in embedded feature selection methods. For binary classification problems, $\ell_1$-norm and $\ell_0$-norm are used to perform feature selection, which is called LASSO [6,7]. Since the LASSO is designed only for univariate-output problems which are not suitable for multi-class feature selection tasks, researchers are increasingly concentrating on structured sparsity for multi-class feature selection tasks. In the work of [8], the authors proposed a robust feature selection (RFS) method by combining a $\ell_{2,1}$-norm based loss function with a $\ell_{2,1}$-norm regularization. From then on, $\ell_{2,1}$-norm regularization gets more and more attention in multi-class feature selection tasks [9–11]. Although $\ell_{2,1}$-norm can achieve satisfactory results, there exist some disadvantages. First, $\ell_{2,1}$-norm will over-penalize the features with large weights, which may hurt the performance of data approximation. Second, exact row-sparse solutions are difficult to obtain with the $\ell_{2,1}$-norm, even a large regularization factor (e.g., $10^5$) cannot produce strong row-sparsity. Therefore, in the work of [12], authors develop a novel feature selection method called RPMFS which imposes a $\ell_{2,0}$-norm equality constraint to perform feature selection. Comparing with $\ell_{2,1}$-norm based methods, RPMFS can balance data approximation and joint sparsity of feature weights. Also, in the work of [13], authors proposed an efficient sparse feature selection (ESFS) approach based on $\ell_{2,0}$-norm equality constraint, which introduces a new label coding method and transforms the model into the same structure as linear discriminate analysis (LDA). Unfortunately, the aforementioned methods share the same limitation in regularizing the structured sparsity with a linear loss function for feature selection, which has limited performance in classification.

In order to achieve this, this paper proposes a novel robust feature selection approach that combines the Softmax model with the $\ell_{2,0}$-norm regularization, in which the features can be selected in group, and the classification performance can be improved. Unlike the linear loss function which computes uncalibrated and not easy to interpret scores for all classes, the softmax computes probabilities for all labels. In general, the correct class always has a higher probability and the incorrect class has a lower probability. Thus, the softmax can give a better interpretation in each class. Then, the proposed objective function is optimized using an Accelerated Matrix Homotopy Iterative Hard Thresholding (AMHIHT) algorithm. Extensive experiments on six biological datasets are conducted to evaluate the effectiveness of the proposed method, and the experimental results have shown that the proposed approach can achieve better or comparable classification performance by using selected features than other advanced sparsity based FS approaches.

The following is a summary of the rest of the paper. The notations and definitions used in this paper are introduced in Sect. 2, as well as some related works on sparsity based feature selection. In Sect. 3, We give a thorough explanation of our method. In Sect. 4, the experimental results are reported and analyzed. Finally, in Sect. 5, the conclusion is presented.

## 2   Related Work

### 2.1   Notations and Definitions

The notations and definitions used in this paper are summarized in this section. Matrices and vectors are written in boldface uppercase letters and boldface lowercase letters, respectively. For a matrix $\mathbf{W} = \{w_{ij}\} \in R^{n \times m}$, its $i$-th row is denoted as $\mathbf{w}^i$ and its $j$-th column is denoted as $\mathbf{w}_j$. For a vector $\mathbf{w} \in R^n$, its $i$-th element is denoted by $w_i$.

The $\ell_p$-norm of the vector $\mathbf{w}$ is defined as

$$\|\mathbf{w}\|_p = \left( \sum_{i=1}^n |w_i|^p \right)^{\frac{1}{p}},$$

where $p \neq 0$.

The $\ell_0$-norm of the vector $\mathbf{w}$ is defined as

$$\|\mathbf{w}\|_0 = \sum_{i=1}^n \sigma(w_i) \text{ where } \sigma(w_i) = \begin{cases} 1, & if \ w_i \neq 0 \\ 0, & if \ w_i = 0 \end{cases},$$

which is a pseudo-norm and used to calculate the amount of non-zero elements of $\mathbf{w}$.

The matrix $\mathbf{W}$'s Frobenius norm is defined as

$$\|\mathbf{W}\|_F = \sqrt{\sum_{i=1}^n \sum_{j=1}^m w_{ij}^2},$$

The matrix $\mathbf{W}$'s $\ell_{2,0}$-norm is defined as

$$\|\mathbf{W}\|_{2,0} = \sum_{i=1}^n \mathbb{1}_{\|\mathbf{w}^i\|_2 \neq 0},$$

where $\mathbb{1}_A$ stands for the indicator function. For a scalar $w$, if $w \neq 0$, $\mathbb{1}_w = 1$, otherwise $\mathbb{1}_w = 0$. Also, the $l_{2,0}$-norm is a pseudo-norm that is used in $\mathbf{W}$ to calculate the number of non-zero rows.

## 2.2   Structured Sparsity Based Feature Selection

Given a training dataset $\mathbf{X} = \{\mathbf{x}_1, \mathbf{x}_2, ..., \mathbf{x}_N\} \in R^{d \times N}$, where $\mathbf{x}_i \in R^{d \times 1}$ is the $i$-th sample, and its associated class label $\mathbf{Y} = \{\mathbf{y}_1, \mathbf{y}_2, ..., \mathbf{y}_N\} \in R^{C \times N}$ is one-hot form, i.e. $y_{ij} = 1$ if $\mathbf{x}_i$ belongs to class $j$, $y_{ij} = 0$; otherwise. $N$ denotes the number of samples, and $C$ is the total number of classes. Generally, the least square regression is one of the simplest models used to obtain the projection matrix $\mathbf{W} \in R^{d \times C}$ and bias $\mathbf{b} \in R^{C \times 1}$ for classification, which has the form of

$$\min_{\mathbf{W}} \ \left\| \mathbf{W}^T \mathbf{X} + \mathbf{b}\mathbf{1}^T - \mathbf{Y} \right\|_F^2, \tag{1}$$

where $\mathbf{1} \in R^{N \times 1}$ is a column vector with all its entries being 1.

Cai et al. [12] proposed the RPMFS, a novel robust and pragmatic feature selection approach that extends the model (1) for feature selection. For the loss function, RPMFS replaces the Frobenius norm with the $\ell 2, 1$-norm, and imposes a $\ell_{2,0}$-norm equality constraint with respect to $\mathbf{W}$ for feature selection. The optimization problem is formulated as:

$$\min_{\mathbf{W},\mathbf{b}} \ \left\| \mathbf{W}^T \mathbf{X} + \mathbf{b}\mathbf{1}^T - \mathbf{Y} \right\|_{2,1}$$
$$s.t. \ \|\mathbf{W}\|_{2,0} = k. \tag{2}$$

In the work of [13], authors proposed an efficient sparse feature selection (ESFS) by combining $\ell_{2,0}$-norm equality constraint with the least square regression model. The optimization problem is

$$\min_{\mathbf{W},\mathbf{b}} \ \left\| \mathbf{W}^T \mathbf{X} + \mathbf{b}\mathbf{1}^T - \mathbf{Q}\mathbf{Y} \right\|_F^2$$
$$s.t. \ \|\mathbf{W}\|_{2,0} = k, \tag{3}$$

where $\mathbf{Q} \in R^{C \times C}$ is a reversible matrix used to code labels.

The aforementioned $\ell_{2,0}$-norm feature selection methods share the same limitation in regularizing the structured sparsity with a linear loss function for feature selection, which has limited performance in classification. Next, we will introduce a new approach that combines the $\ell_{2,0}$-norm with cross entropy loss function.

## 3   Ours Method

In this paper, we propose to combine the cross entropy loss function (Softmax model) with the $\ell_{2,0}$-norm regularization. Given a training sample set $\mathbf{X} = \{\mathbf{x}_1, \mathbf{x}_2, ..., \mathbf{x}_N\} \in R^{d \times N}$ and its corresponding class labels $\mathbf{Y} = \{\mathbf{y}_1, \mathbf{y}_2, ..., \mathbf{y}_N\} \in R^{C \times N}$, the Softmax function has the following form:

$$z_i^j = \frac{\exp\left(\mathbf{w}_j^T \mathbf{x}_i\right)}{\sum_{c=1}^C \exp\left(\mathbf{w}_c^T \mathbf{x}_i\right)}, \tag{4}$$

where $\mathbf{Z} = \{z_i^j\} \in R^{C \times N}$ denotes the model's outputs. Then, the objective function of Softmax is

$$J(\mathbf{W}) = -\sum_{i=1}^{N} \sum_{j=1}^{C} y_i^j \log z_i^j. \tag{5}$$

Thus, the optimization objective function of our method is

$$\varphi_\lambda(\mathbf{W}) = \min_{\mathbf{W}} J(\mathbf{W}) + \lambda ||\mathbf{W}||_{2,0}. \tag{6}$$

## 3.1 Optimization Algorithm

Since $J(\mathbf{W})$ is a differentiable convex function, according to Taylor Formula, it can be approximated as

$$J(\mathbf{W}) \approx J(\mathbf{W}_0) + tr\left(\nabla J(\mathbf{W}_0)^T (\mathbf{W} - \mathbf{W}_0)\right)$$
$$+ \frac{1}{2}||\mathbf{H}^{-\frac{1}{2}}(\mathbf{W} - \mathbf{W}_0)||_F^2, \tag{7}$$

where $\nabla J(\mathbf{W})$ and $\mathbf{H}$ is the gradient and Hessian matrix of $J(\mathbf{W})$, respectively. Then, the projected gradient method can be used to approximately iterative update $J(\mathbf{W})$

$$\mathbf{W}^{t+1} = \mathbf{W}^t - \eta \mathbf{H}^{-1} \nabla J(\mathbf{W}^t), \tag{8}$$

where $\eta$ is the learning rate. Replacing $\eta \mathbf{H}^{-1}$ by $\frac{1}{L}\mathbf{I}$, (8) can be rewritten as

$$\mathbf{W}^{t+1} = \mathbf{W}^t - \frac{1}{L}\nabla \mathbf{J}(\mathbf{W}^t). \tag{9}$$

Adding $\lambda ||\mathbf{W}||_{2,0}$, (6) can be solved by iterative optimizing the subproblem

$$\mathbf{W}^{t+1} = arg \min_{\mathbf{W}} ||\mathbf{W} - (\mathbf{W}^t - \frac{1}{L}\nabla \mathbf{J}(\mathbf{W}^t))||_F^2$$
$$+ \frac{2\lambda}{L}||\mathbf{W}||_{2,0}. \tag{10}$$

Each row of $\mathbf{W}$ can be updated individually due to the Frobenius norm and the $\ell_{2,0}$-norm are all separable function. The update form is shown below:

$$(\mathbf{w}^i)^{t+1} = arg \min_{\mathbf{W}^i} ||\mathbf{w}^i - ((\mathbf{w}^i)^t - \frac{1}{L}\nabla \mathbf{J}((\mathbf{w}^i)^t))||_2^2$$
$$+ \frac{2\lambda}{L} \mathbb{1}_{||\mathbf{w}^i||_2 \neq 0}, \tag{11}$$

We have proposed an accelerated matrix homotopy iterative hard thresholding (AMHIHT) to solve this problem in [14], which can be used to update $\mathbf{W}$ in this paper directly, where $\mathbf{W}$ has a closed-form solution at each iteration as

$$\left(\mathbf{w}^i\right)^{t+1} = \begin{cases} s_L(\mathbf{w}^i)^t, if \ ||s_L(\mathbf{w}^i)^t||_2^2 > \frac{2\lambda}{L} \\ \mathbf{0}, \text{otherwise} \end{cases} \tag{12}$$

where $s_L(\mathbf{w}^i)^t = (\mathbf{w}^i)^t - \frac{1}{L}\nabla J\left(\mathbf{w}^i\right)^t$.

The procedure of the AMHIHT method is described in Algorithm 1, and the convergence analysis of Algorithm 1 can be found in [14].

---

**Algorithm 1.** Acceleration Matrix Homotopy Iterative Hard Thresholding Algorithm for solving problem (6)

---

**(Input:)** Training data $\mathbf{X} \in R^{d \times N}$, class labels $\mathbf{Y} \in R^{C \times N}$,
      $\mathbf{W}^0$; parameters $\lambda, L_0, \lambda_0, L_{min}, L_{max}$;
**(Output:)** $\mathbf{W}^*$;
1: initialize $\rho \in (0,1), \gamma > 1, \eta > 0$, set $t \leftarrow 0$;
2: **repeat**
    *An L-tuning iteration*
3:   update $\mathbf{W}^{t+1}$ by Eq. (12);
4:   **while** $\varphi_{\lambda_t}(\mathbf{W}^t) - \varphi_{\lambda_t}(\mathbf{W}^{t+1}) < \frac{\eta}{2}||\mathbf{W}^t - \mathbf{W}^{t+1}||_F^2$
5:     $L_t \leftarrow min\{\gamma L_t, L_{max}\}$;
6:     update $\mathbf{W}^{t+1}$ by Eq. (12);
7:   **end while**
8:   $L_{t+1} \leftarrow L_t$;
9:   $\lambda_{t+1} \leftarrow \rho\lambda_t$;
10:  $t \leftarrow t + 1$;
11: **until** $\lambda_{t+1} \leq \lambda$
12: $\mathbf{W}^* \leftarrow \mathbf{W}^t$.

---

## 4   Experiments

We conducted a series of experiments to evaluate the efficiency and effectiveness of the proposed method and compared the results with several state-of-the-art sparsity based feature selection methods.

### 4.1   Datasets Descriptions

The six biological benchmark datasets used in the experiment are: Brain [15], Leukemia [16], Lymphoma [17], NCI [18], Prostate [19], and Srbct [20]. Table 1 shows the details of these datasets.

### 4.2   Experiment Setup

In the experiments, we verify the effectiveness of the proposed method through classification accuracy (Acc) induced by the selected features, where two popular classifiers, *i.e.*, Softmax and KNN, are used. Each dataset is randomly divided into a training set and a testing set, and the ratio of training samples and testing samples is 2 : 1. We compare our approach with Baseline (no feature selection) and six advanced feature selection methods: (1) Relief [2] and mRMR [4]

**Table 1.** Datasets description

| Datasets | Samples | Features | Classes |
|----------|---------|----------|---------|
| Brain | 42 | 5597 | 5 |
| Leukemia | 38 | 3051 | 2 |
| Lymphoma | 62 | 4026 | 3 |
| NCI | 61 | 5244 | 8 |
| Prostate | 102 | 6033 | 2 |
| Srbct | 63 | 2308 | 4 |

which are basic filter method; (2) RFS [8] and RLSR [21] which have $\ell_{2,1}$-norm regularization; (3) RPMFS [12] and EFSF [13] which have $\ell_{2,0}$-norm equality constrained. On each dataset, we conducted 10 repeated experiments and compared the average results. For each method, the number of select feature is tuned from $\{20, 40, ..., 400\}$. For the proposed method, we tuned the parameter $\lambda$ from $\{10^{-5}, 10^{-4}, ..., 10^{-1}\}$.

### 4.3 Experiment Result

Table 2 shows the classification accuracy result of each feature selection method and the corresponding number of selected features, where the mark with the red color represents the best result, and the mark with the blue color represents the second best result. Figure 1 and Fig. 2 shows the classification accuracy with respect to a different number of the selected feature. As the results show, when compared to other approaches, our method achieves the highest classification accuracy on most datasets. When the number of selected features is small (e.g., 20), our method can gain a much better result than other methods, which demonstrates that our method can select more discriminative features than other methods.

We show the average computational time of each sparsity regularization method on the six data sets in Fig. 3. As it can be seen, the proposed method has a relatively short running time which is suitable for practical application.

### 4.4 Parameter Sensitivity

The sensitivity of $\lambda$ is evaluated in this part, and the classification accuracy with respect to different values of $\lambda$ is shown in Fig. 4. Due to the space limitation, we only show results on two datasets (i.e., Lymphoma, Prostate). It can be seen that the classification accuracy does not fluctuate much with the change of $\lambda$, which indicates that our method is robust to the regularization parameter $\lambda$, thus there is no need to spend much time to tune the value of $\lambda$.

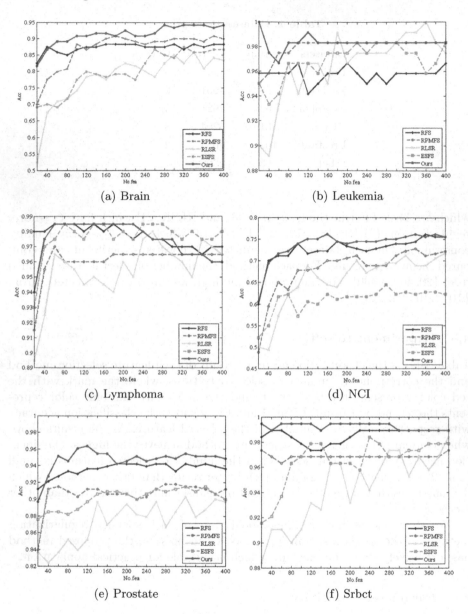

**Fig. 1.** The classification accuracy with respect to different number of selected features where the results obtained by using Softmax

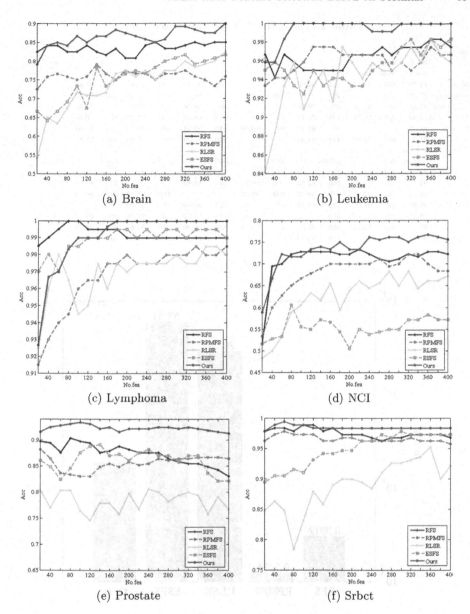

**Fig. 2.** The classification accuracy with respect to different number of selected features where the results obtained by using KNN.

**Table 2.** The optimal classification accuracy

| Dataset | KNN | | | | | | | | | | | | | | |
|---|---|---|---|---|---|---|---|---|---|---|---|---|---|---|---|
| | Baseline | Relief | | mRMR | | RFS | | RPMFS | | RLSR | | ESFS | | Ours | |
| | Acc | No.fea | Acc | No.fea | Acc | No.fea | Acc | No.fea | Acc | No.fea | Acc | No.fea | Acc | No.fea | Acc |
| Brain | 77.78 | 400 | 84.17 | 360 | 80.00 | 260 | 85.00 | 400 | 82.50 | 140 | 79.17 | 320 | 81.67 | 400 | 90.00 |
| Leukemia | 97.22 | 200 | 100.00 | 20 | 98.33 | 360 | 98.33 | 360 | 98.33 | 120 | 97.50 | 320 | 98.33 | 80 | 100.00 |
| Lymphoma | 98.67 | 300 | 99.00 | 200 | 100.00 | 80 | 100.00 | 360 | 98.50 | 340 | 98.50 | 180 | 99.50 | 180 | 100.00 |
| NCI | 72.22 | 320 | 70.00 | 140 | 71.11 | 220 | 73.33 | 280 | 68.33 | 320 | 72.22 | 80 | 60.56 | 360 | 76.67 |
| Prostate | 81.01 | 20 | 92.42 | 40 | 92.12 | 80 | 90.30 | 240 | 80.61 | 20 | 88.18 | 140 | 89.09 | 100 | 93.33 |
| Srbct | 91.93 | 340 | 98.95 | 120 | 98.95 | 100 | 98.95 | 360 | 95.26 | 60 | 97.89 | 300 | 97.89 | 60 | 99.47 |
| Dataset | Softmax | | | | | | | | | | | | | | |
| | Baseline | Relief | | mRMR | | RFS | | RPMFS | | RLSR | | ESFS | | Ours | |
| | Acc | No.fea | Acc | No.fea | Acc | No.fea | Acc | No.fea | Acc | No.fea | Acc | No.fea | Acc | No.fea | Acc |
| Brain | 84.44 | 260 | 82.50 | 360 | 87.50 | 160 | 88.33 | 340 | 85.83 | 180 | 90.83 | 320 | 87.50 | 280 | 94.17 |
| Leukemia | 99.44 | 160 | 99.17 | 140 | 99.17 | 100 | 96.67 | 360 | 100.00 | 100 | 98.33 | 220 | 98.33 | 20 | 100.00 |
| Lymphoma | 96.00 | 360 | 93.00 | 220 | 94.50 | 60 | 98.50 | 260 | 98.00 | 60 | 97.00 | 80 | 98.50 | 60 | 98.50 |
| NCI | 75.93 | 320 | 71.67 | 360 | 71.67 | 360 | 76.11 | 400 | 71.67 | 340 | 72.78 | 280 | 64.44 | 160 | 76.11 |
| Prostate | 91.72 | 400 | 92.12 | 280 | 93.64 | 180 | 94.24 | 320 | 90.30 | 280 | 91.82 | 320 | 91.52 | 120 | 96.36 |
| Srbct | 97.54 | 40 | 98.95 | 100 | 98.42 | 40 | 98.95 | 400 | 98.42 | 20 | 97.37 | 240 | 98.42 | 20 | 99.47 |

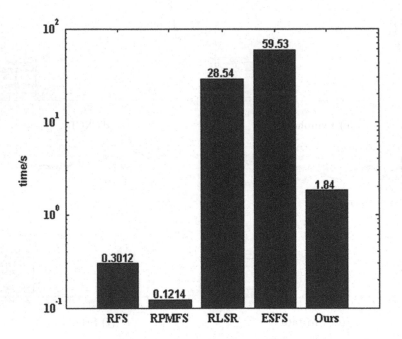

**Fig. 3.** Average running time

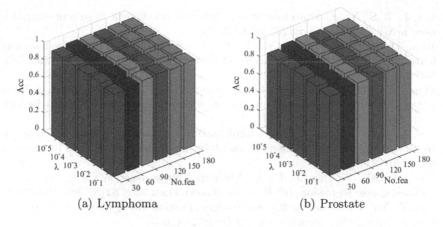

(a) Lymphoma                    (b) Prostate

**Fig. 4.** The sensitivity of the parameter $\lambda$

# 5 Conclusion

In this paper, we propose a novel and robust feature selection method that combines the $\ell_{2,0}$-norm regularization with the cross-entropy loss function, where the features can be selected in group according to the solution of the projected matrix, and the Softmax model can improve classification efficiency. We verify the validity of the proposed method through extensive experiments, the results show that the proposed method has better classification accuracy with fewer selected features compared with several state-of-the-art sparsity based feature selection methods.

# References

1. Ding, C., Peng, H.: Minimum redundancy feature selection from microarray gene expression data. J. Bioinf. Comput. Biol. **3**(02), 185–205 (2005)
2. Kira, K., Rendell, L.A.: A practical approach to feature selection. In: Proceedings of the 9th International Workshop on Machine Learning, pp. 249–256 (1992)
3. Kononenko, I.: Estimating attributes: analysis and extensions of relief. In: Proceedings of the 7th European Conference on Machine Learning, pp. 171–182 (1994)
4. Peng, H., Long, F., Ding, C.: Feature selection based on mutual information criteria of max-dependency, max-relevance, and min-redundancy. IEEE Trans. Pattern Anal. Mach. Intell. **27**(8), 1226–1238 (2005)
5. Guyon, I., Weston, J., Barnhill, S., Vapnik, V.: Gene selection for cancer classification using support vector machines. Mach. Learn. **46**(1), 389–422 (2002)
6. Tibshirani, R.: Regression shrinkage and selection via the lasso. J. Roy. Stat. Soc. Ser. B (Methodological) **58**(1), 267–288 (1996)
7. Liu, J., Chen, J., Ye, J.: Large-scale sparse logistic regression. In: Proceedings of the 15th ACM SIGKDD International Conference on Knowledge Discovery and Data Mining, pp. 547–556 (2009)
8. Nie, F., Huang, H., Cai, X., Ding, C.: Efficient and robust feature selection via joint $\ell_{2,1}$-norms minimization. Adv. Neural Inf. Process. Syst. **23**, 1813–1821 (2010)

9. Liu, J., Ji, S., Ye, J.: Multi-task feature learning via efficient $\ell_{2,1}$-norm minimization. arXiv preprint arXiv:1205.2631 (2012)
10. Wen, J., Lai, Z., Zhan, Y., Cui, J.: The $\ell_{2,1}$-norm-based unsupervised optimal feature selection with applications to action recognition. Pattern Recogn. **60**, 515–530 (2016)
11. Peng, Y., Sehdev, P., Liu, S., Li, J., Wang, X.: $\ell_{2,1}$-norm minimization based negative label relaxation linear regression for feature selection. Pattern Recogn. Lett. **116**, 170–178 (2018)
12. Cai, X., Nie, F., Huang, H.: Exact top-k feature selection via l2, 0-norm constraint. In: Proceedings of the 23rd International Joint Conference on Artificial Intelligence, pp. 1240–1246 (2013)
13. Pang, T., Nie, F., Han, J., Li, X.: Efficient feature selection via $\ell_{2,0}$-norm constrained sparse regression. IEEE Trans. Knowl. Data Eng. **31**(5), 880–893 (2018)
14. Sun, Z., Yu, Y.: Robust multi-class feature selection via $\ell_{2,0}$-norm regularization minimization. arXiv preprint arXiv:2010.03728 (2020)
15. Pomeroy, S.L., et al.: Prediction of central nervous system embryonal tumour outcome based on gene expression. Nature **415**(6870), 436–442 (2002)
16. Nutt, C.L., et al.: Gene expression-based classification of malignant gliomas correlates better with survival than histological classification. Cancer Res. **63**(7), 1602–1607 (2003)
17. Alizadeh, A.A., et al.: Distinct types of diffuse large b-cell lymphoma identified by gene expression profiling. Nature **403**(6769), 503–511 (2000)
18. Ross, D.T., et al.: Systematic variation in gene expression patterns in human cancer cell lines. Nat. Genet. **24**(3), 227–235 (2000)
19. Singh, D., et al.: Gene expression correlates of clinical prostate cancer behavior. Cancer Cell **1**(2), 203–209 (2002)
20. Khan, J., et al.: Classification and diagnostic prediction of cancers using gene expression profiling and artificial neural networks. Nat. Med. **7**(6), 673–679 (2001)
21. Chen, X., Yuan, G., Nie, F., Huang, J.Z.: Semi-supervised feature selection via rescaled linear regression. In: Proceedings of the 26th International Joint Conference on Artificial Intelligence, pp. 1525–1531 (2017)

# Dynamic Network Pruning Based on Local Channel-Wise Relevance

Luxin Lin, Wenxi Liu[✉], and Yuanlong Yu

College of Computer and Data Science, Fuzhou University, Fuzhou, China
{wenxiliu,yu.yuanlong}@fzu.edu.cn

**Abstract.** In recent years, deep convolutional neural networks (CNNs) significantly boost the various applications, but the high computational complexity of these models hinder the further deployment on device with limited computation resources. Hence, dynamic channel pruning has been recently proposed and widely used for compressing CNN-based models. In this paper, we propose a novel plug-and-play dynamic network pruning module. With very slight extra computation burden, it can achieve the comparable performance as the original model. Specifically, our proposed module measures the importance of each convolutional channel to prune the CNNs with small decrease in accuracy. The module reduces the computation cost by global pooling and channel-wise 1-dimensional convolution that considers the channels' locality. Comprehensive experimental results demonstrate the effectiveness of our module, which makes a better trade-off between the performance and the acquired computational resources, comparing to its competing methods. In concrete, our dynamic pruning module can reduce 51.1% FLOPs of VGG16 with only 0.18% top-1 accuracy degradation on CIFAR10.

**Keywords:** Model compression · Dynamic pruning · Local channel information

## 1 Introduction

Convolutional neural networks (CNNs) have been widely used in many domains, such as image classification [15], object detection [14] and so on. With development of deep neural networks, their computational complexity and the amount of their parameters have been increasing rapidly, which thus hinder these models from being deployed on mobile devices with limited computational resources.

To solve this problem, researchers propose shallow neural networks that contain fewer learnable parameters to replace deep networks [10,24]. However, the shallow models with low capacity can hardly extract high-level semantic features from raw samples, resulting in poor performance comparing to deep models. Therefore, research efforts have been spent on how to design efficient network compression approaches. Prior studies [1,7] demonstrate that deep CNNs are over-parameterized, which motivates network pruning techniques that compress

F. Sun et al. (Eds.): ICCSIP 2021, CCIS 1515, pp. 49–60, 2022.
https://doi.org/10.1007/978-981-16-9247-5_4

the models by removing redundant parameters [3]. Conventional pruning methods [6,8,13,16,20] focus on finding the universal characteristics of weights or output in the model, and they prune redundant weights based on the metrics that measure the importance of the weights in a heuristic manner. Nevertheless, these methods ignore the relationship between weights and input samples, as well as the difference between network layers, which thus cannot well compress deep models. Furthermore, dynamic pruning methods [2,3,5,26] have been proposed to improve model compression. Generally, these methods rely on the global channel attention to attentively choose some channels to pass through while skipping the remaining ones during forward propagation. Yet, the global attention, though powerful, suffers from quadratic increase of the inference time and model size, giving rise to huge computational costs for pruning large models.

To strengthen the prior dynamic pruning approaches, we propose a novel lightweight dynamic network pruning module that can be easily integrated into the standard Conv-BN-ReLU blocks of CNNs. In particular, our proposed module follows the two-stage procedures: 1) predicting channel attention that prediction the redundancy of the convoluted feature channels, and 2) pruning dynamiclly the channels according to the channel attention. On the first stage of our module, We firstly employ different downsampling methods for the expansion/reduction of convolutional channels: for the expansion of convolutional channels, we downsample input feature maps by average pooling method, and form a single vector that contains compact semantic information; For the reduction case, the inputs are downsampled into two vectors by channel-wise global average pooling and global max pooling operations, respectively, and they are then aggregated into a new vector by an interleaving manner. Then, the new descriptors can be utilized to generate channel attention. The attention of each channel not only concerns with its own semantic representation but also correlates with other feature channels. On the other hand, to bridge the feature channels, fully connected layers are often deployed to leverage their non-local dependency [3]. Over utilization of fully connected layers may not bring about sufficient performance gains than the computation overhead it sacrifices, especially for those deep large network models. Therefore, to reduce the computation cost, we can simply project the local channel information into the scores via a 1-dimensional convolution instead of fully connected layers. On the second stage, to accelerate the model computation, we rank the channels according to the value of attention. In specific, we keep the channels with the top-$k$ scores and rescale their scores to attentively strengthen the features, while suppress the less important channels by skipping their convolution operations to reduce the computation burden.

To evaluate our approach, we employ the proposed efficient channel dynamic pruning module to prune different deep CNN models, e.g., VGGNet and ResNet, on the CIFAR10 dataset. The experimental results demonstrate that our proposed module can reduce the number of FLOPs while maintaining the comparable performance comparing to the original models and the state-of-the-art dynamic pruning approaches.

# 2    Related Work

Channel pruning [3,5,8,16,20] remove the unimportant filters of the convolution kernel according to certain metrics. In such pruning methods, the weights for the removed filters are set to zeros in a row-by-row manner, making structured weight matrices. Compared with the traditional pruning methods with non-structured sparse matrices, these methods are hardware-friendly and accelerate models' inference without extra storage. It can be broken down into the two groups: static pruning and dynamic pruning.

**Static Pruning.** Static pruning methods evaluate channel importance by all the samples, and it will remove the redundant channels permanently. Early works focus on the channel scores generated from the pre-trained weights and samples without considering the effects of the following fine-tuning of the models. For example, Li et al. [13] calculate the norm of model weight, and remove channels with small value. Similarly, Lin et al. [16] conduct research on feature maps. They argue that the feature maps with the higher average rank over samples contain more information, and therefore remove the low-rank maps. However, with only the empirical evidence as shown by them, the exact link between the maps' ranks and the information is unclear. Subsequently, researchers move towards finding the minimum set of convolutional kernels that make the model achieve a reasonable accuracy. Liu et al. [19] formulate the task of channel pruning as a nonconvex optimization problem, and use the ADMM algorithm to solve it efficiently. In [17], Lin et al. adopted generative adversarial network (GAN) to produce the indices of the channels retained in the compressed models.

**Dynamic Pruning.** For a given model, the complexity of its forward propagation varies across instances, e.g., an image with less noise is easier to be accurately recognized. To this end, there is another set of methods proposed to prune channels conditioned on instances fed into the model by just skipping the redundant channels in terms of the instances. To achieve this goal, some methods focus on the potential relationship between samples. For instance, Tang et al. [26] excavate models' redundancy maximally by a proposed paradigm in which some filters, considered redundant by the manifold information from the samples, are dynamically removed. In [18], Liu et al. introduces structural feature regularization to make the intermediate feature maps of each input become sparse. Recent works use extra end-to-end trainable blocks generating channel scores in the process of dynamic pruning. Dong et al. [2] propose an auxiliary block with slight extra computation, which predicts the indices of channels to be removed after the activations and helps skip the unnecessary convolution of these channels in advance. Li et al. [12] propose multi-ratio branches that will be selected to optimize the performance of the model conditioned on the inputs. Gao et al. [3] introduce channel attention block to evaluate each channel and use the attention to boost and suppress channel.

# 3    Efficient Channel Dynamic Pruning

## 3.1    Preliminaries

To formulate our proposed module, we consider the CNN model $\mathcal{F}$ with $N$ convolution layers as $\{L_1, L_2, \ldots, L_N\}$. For the $i$-th layer $L_i$, we denote its weights as $\mathbf{W}^i \in \mathcal{R}^{C^{i-1} \times C^i \times k^i \times k^i}$, which have $C^{i-1}$ input channels and $C^i$ output channels, with $k^i \times k^i$ kernel size.

Let $\mathbf{X}^i = \{\mathbf{x}_1^i, \mathbf{x}_2^i, \cdots, \mathbf{x}_n^i\} \in \mathcal{R}^{n \times C^{i-1} \times H^{i-1} \times W^{i-1}}$ and $\mathbf{Y}^i = \{\mathbf{y}_1^i, \mathbf{y}_2^i, \cdots, \mathbf{y}_n^i\} \in \mathcal{R}^{n \times C^i \times H^i \times W^i}$ denote its input and output, where $n$ denotes the batch size of samples, and $\mathbf{y}_j^i$ represents the $j$-th output with the height $H^i$, width $W^i$ and channel number $C^i$. Therefore, the $i$-th convolution operation can be written as:

$$\mathbf{Y}^i = \mathbf{W}^i \star \mathbf{X}^i, \tag{1}$$

where $\star$ represents the convolution operation.

## 3.2    Proposed Module

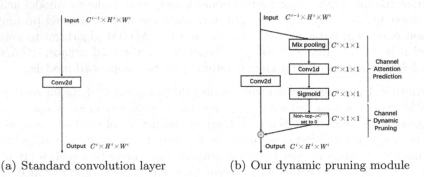

(a) Standard convolution layer        (b) Our dynamic pruning module

**Fig. 1.** Illustration of our dynamic pruning module, comparing to the standard convolution layer.

As shown in Fig. 1, the proposed dynamic pruning module is composed of two stages: channel importance score prediction and channel pruning. We will elaborate the details in the following.

## 3.3    Channel Attention Prediction

Recent works [2,3,5,26] show that dynamic pruning with the global attention paradigm that considers all channels per layer performs well. The computational and space complexities are both $O(C^i C^{i-1})$, leading to a quadratic increase in the computational cost. Thus, pruning large models requires extra computational

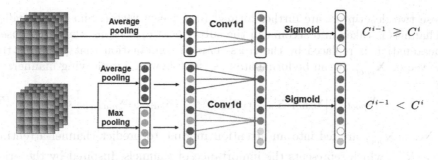

**Fig. 2.** Illustration of the first stage of our proposed module. We firstly employ different downsampling methods for the expansion/reduction of convolutional channels to produce a new descriptor, and the detail will be introduced in the Sect. 3.3. Next, this descriptor is fed into the following 1-dimensional convolution layer to extract the features across the channels. Finally, it are mapped into the range of $[0, 1]$ by sigmoid functions.

resources to reduce the general complexity of the models' inference. To address this problem, we introduce the local attention paradigm that incorporates the locality of channels to prediction each channel attention. Figure 2 shows the structure of our proposed module.

For the first step of predicting the channel attention, the feature maps are commonly downsampled by a global average-pooling operation to produce a compact representation, which will further reduce the complexity of the succeeding operations. In our work, we use it as our downsampling method. Note that some convolutional layers project low-dimensional features into high-dimensional space. It is hard to makes exact predictions by using small sample size. For these layers, we adopt interleaving feature manner. We will describe the details below.

For the expansion of convolutional channels ($C^{i-1} \geq C^i$), we adopt global average-pooling $F_{avg}$ only to extract spatial information of input tensor $\mathbf{X}^i$. Thus, the new features $\mathbf{X}^i_{pool}$ which obtained after downsampling is formulated as follow:

$$\mathbf{X}^i_{pool} = F_{adv}(\mathbf{x}^i) = \frac{1}{C^i} \sum_{m=1}^{H^i} \sum_{n=1}^{W^i} \mathbf{x}^i(m,n) \tag{2}$$

For the reduction of convolutional channels ($C^{i-1} < C^i$), we adopt both average-pooling $F_{avg}$ and max-pooling $F_{max}$ to extract spatial information of input tensor $\mathbf{X}^i$. Thus, two spatial context descriptors $\mathbf{X}^i_{adv} \in \mathcal{R}^{C^i}, \mathbf{X}^i_{max} \in \mathcal{R}^{C^i}$ can be produced below:

$$\mathbf{x}^i_{adv,j} = F_{adv}(\mathbf{x}^i_j) = \frac{1}{C^i} \sum_{m=1}^{H^i} \sum_{n=1}^{W^i} \mathbf{x}^i_j(m,n), \tag{3}$$

$$\mathbf{x}^i_{max,j} = F_{max}(\mathbf{x}^i_j) = max(\mathbf{x}^i_j). \tag{4}$$

These two descriptors are further formed into a new vector. Since the locality of channels is taken into account in the subsequent operations, the widely used concatenation is replaced by the cross-channel combination that produces the new vector $\mathbf{X}_{pool}^i$. It can be formulated as the following interleaving manner:

$$\mathbf{X}_{pool}^i = \left[\mathbf{x}_{adv,1}^i, \mathbf{x}_{max,1}^i, \mathbf{x}_{adv,2}^i, \cdots, \mathbf{x}_{adv,C^i}^i, \mathbf{x}_{max,C^i}^i\right]. \tag{5}$$

Next, $\mathbf{X}_{pool}^i$ are fed into an attention module to predict channel attention $\mathbf{M}^i \in \mathcal{R}^{C^i}$, which represents the importance of channels. Inspired by the prior module [23], the proposed module that incorporates the cross-channel information satisfies the following criteria: 1) it is computationally friendly; 2) the multiple channels can be boosted simultaneously by the attention (rather than getting a single channel boosted by a one-hot like attention); 3) only a small subset of the channels are activated by the sparse results with each element in $[0, 1]$. In particular, we leverage the 1-dimension convolution with a sigmoid activation maps $\mathbf{M}^i$ into the range of $[0, 1]$. Thus, this module is formulated as follows.

$$\begin{aligned}\mathbf{M}^i &= Sigmoid(\sum_{j=1}^k \mathbf{W}_{att,j}^i \mathbf{x}_{pool,j}^i), \quad \mathbf{x}_{pool,j}^i \in \Omega^{k'} \\ &= Sigmoid(\mathbf{W}_{att}^i \star \mathbf{X}_{pool}^i),\end{aligned} \tag{6}$$

where $k'$ represent the kernel size of the 1-dimension convolution (Fig. 3).

### 3.4   Channel Dynamic Pruning

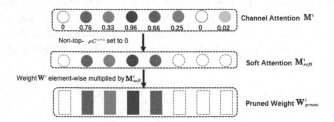

**Fig. 3.** Illustration of the second stage of our proposed module. We first suppress the channel attention $\mathbf{M}^i$ of the non-top-$\rho C^{i-1}$ elements to 0, so as to generate soft attention $\mathbf{M}_{soft}^i$. Then, it accomplishes dynamic pruning by multiplying soft channel attention $\mathbf{M}_{soft}^i$ with the weight $\mathbf{W}^i$.

The predicted channel attention $\mathbf{M}^i$ are utilized to remove the redundancy across the channels on the channel pruning stage. The higher attention value indicate larger importance of the corresponding channels, while the channels with zero value are considered redundant, since each score is within $[0, 1]$.

Although the elements of attention are all non-zero due to the sigmoid function, it is straightforward to set a very threshold to prune the channels with the predicted channel attention below the threshold. However, the predefined threshold as hyperparameter often depends on datasets and models, which thus is hard to tune. Moreover, the threshold-based method might lead to the unstable channel sparsity. Thus, we utilize these attention to perform pruning via a fixed pruning rate. Given the pruning rate, the certain number of channels with less importance will be removed. Instead of removing or reserving channels, we want to utilize the channel attention to strengthen the representation capability of features. Therefore, we preserve the attention values to weigh channels instead of setting them to 1, denoted as soft attention. We will elaborate the algorithm below.

Given the pruning rate $\rho$, $\mathbf{M}^i$ is split into two groups: a set $\mathbf{U}^i \in \mathcal{R}^{\rho C^i}$, with less important channel scores which is consisted of the $\rho C^i$ lowest scores, and another set $\mathbf{I}^i \in \mathcal{R}^{(1-\rho)C^i}$ that is consisted of the $(1-\rho)C^i$ highest importance scores. In specific, we treat these channels differently. For the less important channels, they will be set zero to accelerate the computation. For the important ones, their scores stay the same. Hence, the $j$-th channel of the soft attention $\mathbf{M}^i_{soft}$ can be computed as:

$$\mathbf{M}^i_{soft,j} = \begin{cases} \mathbf{M}^i_j, & if \ \mathbf{M}^i_j \in \mathbf{I}^i \\ 0. & if \ \mathbf{M}^i_j \in \mathbf{U}^i \end{cases} \tag{7}$$

Finally, we combine $\mathbf{M}^i_{soft}$ with the weights of convolution by element-wise multiplication, and the sparse weights $\mathbf{W}_{prune}$ are produced as below.

$$\begin{aligned} \mathbf{Y}^i &= (\mathbf{W}^i \odot \mathbf{M}^i_{soft}) \star \mathbf{X}^i, \\ &= \mathbf{W}^i_{prune} \star \mathbf{X}^i, \end{aligned} \tag{8}$$

where $\odot$ represents element-wise multiplication, and $\star$ represents convolution operation.

## 3.5  Computation Complexity

The computational will be significantly reducedby applying the pruning module. As an example, take the $i$-th convolutional layer $L_i$. Before pruning the channels, with an input consisting $C^{i-1}$ feature maps fed into $L_i$,the computation complexity is $O(C^{i-1}C^i H^i W^i (k^i)^2)$. By pruning the channels of $L_i$ and $L_{i-1}$ with the ratio $\rho$, the complexity decreases to $O(\rho^2 C^{i-1} C^i H^i W^i (k^i)^2)$. Moreover, the proposed pruning module with time complexity of $O(2k'C^i)$ brings negligible extra computation due to the low-cost 1-dimensional convolution.

## 4  Experimental Results

**Datasets and Models.** We evaluate the proposed module for the tasks of image classification on the CIFAR10 dataset [11]. This dataset includes 50k train samples and 10k test samples, which are all $32 \times 32$ images belonging to 10 classes. We apply the augmentation method proposed by [5] to train the networks, and follow the recent works on dynamic pruning by using the VGGNet [25] and ResNets [4] as network backbones.

**Evaluation Metrics.** All methods are evaluated in terms of the prediction accuracy, floating point operations (FLOPs) [21] and the number of the parameters for the pruned networks. To reduce the bias caused by network initialization, the accuracy of each model is calculated by the average results of multiple runs. The number of FLOPs is computed in the same way as [5]. A better module will generate a pruned model with better accuracy or less FLOPs/parameters.

**Implementation Detail.** All experiments are implemented in Pytorch [22]. This paper supposes that different layers of the CNN model have the same contributions to the performance of the model. Thus, the pruned ratio of each convolutional layer was set to the same value $\rho$. In the train phrase, we adopt the SGD optimizer with 0.1 initial learning rate, 0.9 momentum and 0.0005 weight decay, and train each model for 200 epochs.

### 4.1 Experimental Results and Analysis

**Theoretical Complexity.** Note that with the same pruning rate in the pruning process, the number of all pruned channels in the models are generally fixed, leading to the same FLOPs of various models without considering the extra computation of the pruning modules. Moreover, these methods of dynamic pruning keep all the weights, from which only a subset is chosen to perform pruning dynamically in the inference, resulting in no decrease in the space for storing the weights. Therefore, we only present a comparison in the computational complexity of the extra pruning modules brought by various modules. The comparative result of our proposed module is reported in Table 1, where it achieves the lowest computational complexity. In details, it reduces the time complexity from $O(N^2)$ to $O(N)$, with the significant reduction of the space complexity, which is only $O(1)$.

**Table 1.** Comparison of the theoretical complexity for adding dynamic pruning modules.

| Module | FLOPs | Parameters |
|---|---|---|
| MIL [2] | $HWC^iC^{i-1}k'^2$ | $C^iC^{i-1}k'^2$ |
| FBS [3] | $2C^iC^{i-1}$ | $C^iC^{i-1}$ |
| Ours | $2k'C^{i-1}$ | $k'^2$ |

**Results on VGG16.** We compare our module with traditional static pruning methods, like L1 [13], SSS [9], GAL [17] and Hrank [16], and mainstream dynamic pruning methods, i.e., SFP [5] and FBS [3]. The results are reported in Table 2, where the proposed module generally outperforms the others. Compared with static pruning methods, our module can obtain better accuracy (93.78% vs. 93.40% by L1, 93.02% by SSS and 90.73% by GAL) with more FLOPs reduction. Although we have more participants than static pruning, ours proposed method can stay outstanding performance (93.1% vs. 91.23% by Hrank) especially in high pruning rate. Compared with SFP, our module introduce tiny FLOPs and the number of parameters (<1% of the original parameters), it can perform more better top-1 accuracy than SFP. Compared with FBS, ours module's performance is inferior to FBS (93.78% vs. 93.85%; 93.10% vs. 93.22%). However, FBS introduces a large number of parameters (10.9% of the original parameters), it creates difficulties to apply in the edge devices. Hence, these experiments demonstrates our module can excellently accelerate the calculation of neural network with a plain structure.

**Table 2.** Comparison results of pruning VGG16 on CIFAR10. "PR." denotes *Pruning Ratio.*

| Model | Method | Dynamic | Acc. (%) | FLOPs (PR.) | Params. (PR.) |
|-------|--------|---------|----------|-------------|---------------|
| VGG16 | L1 [13] | × | 93.96→ 93.40 | 206.00M (34.3%) | 5.40M (−64.0%) |
|  | SSS [9] | × | 93.96→ 93.02 | 183.13M (41.6%) | 3.93M (−73.8%) |
|  | GAL-0.1 [17] | × | 93.96→ 90.73 | 171.89M (45.2%) | 2.67M (−82.2%) |
|  | SFP [5] | ✓ | 93.96→ 92.93 | 153.41M (51.2%) | 14.99M (+0.0%) |
|  | FBS [3] | ✓ | 93.96→ 93.85 | 155.06M (50.5%) | 16.63M (+10.9%) |
|  | Ours | ✓ | 93.96→ 93.78 | 153.45M (51.1%) | 14.99M (+<0.1%) |
|  | Hrank [16] | × | 93.96→ 91.23 | 73.70M (76.5%) | 1.78M (−92.0%) |
|  | SFP [5] | ✓ | 93.96→ 92.04 | 80.04M (74.6%) | 14.99M (+0.0%) |
|  | FBS [3] | ✓ | 93.96→ 93.22 | 81.69M (73.9%) | 16.63M (+10.9%) |
|  | Ours | ✓ | 93.96→ 93.10 | 80.08M (74.5%) | 14.99M (+<0.1%) |

**Results on ResNet56.** We prune ResNet56 on CIFAR10, and Table 3 displays the compress results. Our module can reduce 52.5% FLOPs with the high accuracy 93.72%. It outperforms significantly static pruning methods in terms of higher accuracy (93.80% vs. 93.06% by L1, 93.01% by NISP; 93.72% vs. 90.36% by GAL; 92.68% vs. 90.72% by Hrank) and faster calculation speed (39.6% vs. 27.6% by L1 and 35.5% by NISP; 74.1% vs. 60.2% by GAL 74.1% by Hrank in FLOPs reduction). Furthermore, compared with SFP, our module achieves higher accuracy (93.80% vs. 93.47%; 93.72% vs. 93.10%). than it with almost the same FLOPs Besides, our module makes a better trade-off between the accuracy and the computational resources required.

## 4.2  Ablation Studies

**Effect of Kernel Size.** To evaluate the kernel size ($k$) effect on the convolution layer, we change $k$ from 3 to 9 and employ these changed modules to VGG16 on CIFAR10. Figure 4(Left) reports the corresponding top-1 accuracy for each variant at the different pruning rate. We can see that the module, whose $k$ value is equal to 9, can obtains the best results at the most pruning ratio. The result demonstrates the 1-dimensional convolution with suitable kernel size can model excellently channels potential connections with little extra computation cost. In the subsequent experiments, we set the kernel size as 9.

**Table 3.** Comparison results of pruning ResNet-56 on CIFAR10. "PR." denotes *Pruning Ratio*.

| Model | Method | Dynamic | Acc. (%) | FLOPs (PR.) | Params. (PR.) |
|---|---|---|---|---|---|
| ResNet-56 | L1 [13] | × | 93.26→ 93.06 | 90.90M (27.6%) | 0.73M (−14.1%) |
| | NISP [27] | × | 93.26→ 93.01 | 81.00M (35.5%) | 0.49M (−42.4%) |
| | SFP [5] | ✓ | 93.59→ 93.47 | 89.80M (28.4%) | 0.85M (0%) |
| | Ours | ✓ | 93.59→ 93.80 | 75.71M (39.6%) | 0.85M (+<0.1%) |
| | GAL-0.8 [17] | × | 93.26→ 90.36 | 49.99M (60.2%) | 0.29M (−65.9%) |
| | SFP [5] | ✓ | 93.59→ 93.10 | 59.40M (52.6%) | 0.85M (0%) |
| | Ours | ✓ | 93.59→ 93.72 | 59.55M (52.5%) | 0.85M (+<0.1%) |
| | Hrank [16] | × | 93.26→ 90.72 | 32.52M (74.1%) | 0.27M (−68.1%) |
| | Ours | ✓ | 93.59→ 92.68 | 31.71M (74.7%) | 0.85M (+<0.1%) |

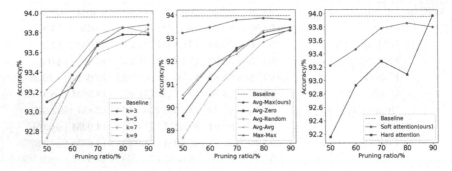

**Fig. 4.** (Left) Comparison results for the different kernel size convolution layers. (Middle) Comparison results for different donwsampled methods. (Right) Comparison results for the model pruned with soft attention and hard attention.

**Effect of Downsampled Method.** To evaluate the downsampled method effect, we proposed several downsampled feature mixing variants, including: 1) *Avg-Zero*: Average-pooling descriptor and zero value; 2) *Avg-Random*: Average-pooling descriptor and random value which satisfy the gaussian distribution; 3) *Avg-Avg*: Average-pooling descriptor and average-pooling-pooling descriptor; 4) *Max-Max*: Max-pooling descriptor and max-pooling descriptor. Figure 4(Middle) reports the corresponding experimental results. Among these variants, our method obtained the best performance. In particular, the avg-pooling feature describes the global information of the sample, and the max-pooling descriptor focus more on the local information. Mixing global and local information can achieve a balance by explicitly predicting the interdependencies from the input features of the convolution layer.

**Effect of Channel Soft/Hard Attention.** To validate our proposed channel soft attention method, we proposed the variant (channel hard attention) which generate hard attention matrix $\mathbf{M}_{hard}$ with 0 and 1 according to channel attention $\mathbf{M}$. Figure 4(Right) shows the corresponding top-1 accuracy based on two method. Our method obviously shows the best performance. The result demonstrates that it can strengthen the representational capability of pruned model by boosting or suppressing the channel according channel attention.

## 5   Conclusion

In this paper, we focus on the design of the low-cost and high-performance CNN-based channel pruning module. To this end, we propose an efficient dynamic channel pruning method based on the local cross-channel interaction strategy via a 1-dimentional convolution. Experimental results demonstrate that our method makes a better trade-off between the accuracy and the computational overhead, and it is easy to deploy on different network architectures. As the future work, we want to further explore the latent relation among network channels by introducing network interpretation techniques that can imply the latent correlation between the input sample and the channels activation, in order to verify the dynamic pruning method validity. Moreover, we aim to improve the pruning method that can automatically balance computational cost and accuracy to maximally mine redundancy in the given model.

## References

1. Denton, E., Zaremba, W., Bruna, J., LeCun, Y., Fergus, R.: Exploiting linear structure within convolutional networks for efficient evaluation. In: International Conference on Neural Information Processing Systems(NIPS), pp. 1269–1277 (2014)
2. Dong, X., Huang, J., Yang, Y., Yan, S.: More is less: A more complicated network with less inference complexity. In: International Conference on Computer Vision and Pattern Recognition (CVPR), pp. 5840–5848 (2017)
3. Gao, X., Zhao, Y., Dudziak, Ł., Mullins, R., Xu, C.Z.: Dynamic channel pruning: feature boosting and suppression. In: International Conference of Learning Representation (ICLR) (2018)
4. He, K., Zhang, X., Ren, S., Sun, J.: Deep residual learning for image recognition. In: International Conference on Computer Vision and Pattern Recognition (CVPR), pp. 770–778 (2016)
5. He, Y., Kang, G., Dong, X., Fu, Y., Yang, Y.: Soft filter pruning for accelerating deep convolutional neural networks. In: International Joint Conference on Artificial Intelligence (IJCAI), pp. 2234–2240 (2018)
6. He, Y., Liu, P., Wang, Z., Hu, Z., Yang, Y.: Filter pruning via geometric median for deep convolutional neural networks acceleration. In: International Conference on Computer Vision and Pattern Recognition (CVPR), pp. 4340–4349 (2019)
7. Hinton, G.E., Srivastava, N., Krizhevsky, A., Sutskever, I., Salakhutdinov, R.R.: Improving neural networks by preventing co-adaptation of feature detectors. arXiv preprint arXiv:1207.0580 (2012)
8. Hu, H., Peng, R., Tai, Y., Tang, C.: Network trimming: A data-driven neuron pruning approach towards efficient deep architectures. CoRR (2016)
9. Huang, Z., Wang, N.: Data-driven sparse structure selection for deep neural networks. In: European Conference on Computer Vision (ECCV), pp. 304–320 (2018)

10. Jafarian, K., Vahdat, V., Salehi, S., Mobin, M.: Automating detection and localization of myocardial infarction using shallow and end-to-end deep neural networks. Appl. Soft Comput. **93**, 106383 (2020)
11. Krizhevsky, A., Hinton, G., et al.: Learning multiple layers of features from tiny images. Technical report (2009)
12. Li, C., Wang, G., Wang, B., Liang, X., Li, Z., Chang, X.: Dynamic slimmable network. In: International Conference on Computer Vision and Pattern Recognition (CVPR) (2021)
13. Li, H., Kadav, A., Durdanovic, I., Samet, H., Graf, H.P.: Pruning filters for efficient convnets. In: International Conference on Learning Representations (ICLR) (2016)
14. Li, K., Wan, G., Cheng, G., Meng, L., Han, J.: Object detection in optical remote sensing images: a survey and a new benchmark. ISPRS J. Photogrammetry Remote Sens. **159**, 296–307 (2020)
15. Li, Y., Zhang, H., Xue, X., Jiang, Y., Shen, Q.: Deep learning for remote sensing image classification: a survey. Wiley Interdisc. Rev. Data Min. Knowl. Discov. **8**(6), e1264 (2018)
16. Lin, M., et al.: Hrank: filter pruning using high-rank feature map. In: International Conference on Computer Vision and Pattern Recognition (CVPR), pp. 1529–1538 (2020)
17. Lin, S., Ji, R., Yan, C., Zhang, B., Cao, L., Ye, Q., Huang, F., Doermann, D.: Towards optimal structured CNN pruning via generative adversarial learning. In: International Conference on Computer Vision and Pattern Recognition (CVPR) (2020)
18. Liu, C., Wang, Y., Han, K., Xu, C., Xu, C.: Learning instance-wise sparsity for accelerating deep models. In: International Joint Conference on Artificial Intelligence (IJCAI) (2019)
19. Liu, N., Ma, X., Xu, Z., Wang, Y., Tang, J., Ye, J.: Autocompress: an automatic DNN structured pruning framework for ultra-high compression rates. In: Proceedings of the AAAI Conference on Artificial Intelligence, vol. 34, pp. 4876–4883 (2020)
20. Luo, J.H., Wu, J.: An entropy-based pruning method for CNN compression. arXiv preprint arXiv:1706.05791 (2017)
21. Molchanov, P., Tyree, S., Karras, T., Aila, T., Kautz, J.: Pruning convolutional neural networks for resource efficient inference. In: International Conference of Learning Representation (ICLR) (2016)
22. Paszke, A., et al.: Pytorch: An imperative style, high-performance deep learning library. In: International Conference on Neural Information Processing Systems (NIPS) (2019)
23. Qilong, W., Banggu, W., Pengfei, Z., Peihua, L., Wangmeng, Z., Qinghua, H.: Eca-net: efficient channel attention for deep convolutional neural networks. In: International Conference on Computer Vision and Pattern Recognition (CVPR) (2020)
24. Saikia, P., Baruah, R.D., Singh, S.K., Chaudhuri, P.K.: Artificial neural networks in the domain of reservoir characterization: a review from shallow to deep models. Comput. Geosci. **135**, 104357 (2020)
25. Simonyan, K., Zisserman, A.: Very deep convolutional networks for large-scale image recognition. arXiv preprint arXiv:1409.1556 (2014)
26. Tang, Y., et al.: Manifold regularized dynamic network pruning. In: International Conference on Computer Vision and Pattern Recognition (CVPR) (2019)
27. Yu, R., et al.: Nisp: pruning networks using neuron importance score propagation. In: International Conference on Computer Vision and Pattern Recognition (CVPR), pp. 9194–9203 (2018)

# High-Confidence Sample Labelling for Unsupervised Person Re-identification

Lei Wang[1], Qingjie Zhao[1]([✉]), Shihao Wang[2], Jialin Lu[1], and Ying Zhao[3]

[1] Beijing Institute of Technology, Beijing 100081, China
zhaoqj@bit.edu.cn
[2] The Australian National University, Canberra ACT, Canberra 2600, Australia
[3] The University of Hong Kong, Hong Kong 999077, China

**Abstract.** Person re-identification (re-ID) is factually a topic of pedestrian retrieval across camera scenes. However, it is challenging due to those factors such as complex equipment modeling, light change and occlusion. Much of the previous research is based on supervised methods that require labeling large amounts of data, which is expensive and time-consuming. The unsupervised re-ID methods without manual annotation usually need to construct pseudo-labels through clustering. However, the pseudo-labels noise may seriously affect the model's performance. To deal with this issue, in this paper, we use Density-Based Spatial Clustering of Applications with Noise (DBSCAN) to assign pseudo-labels to samples and propose a model with the high-confidence samples' labels (HCSL), which is a fully unsupervised learning method and does not use any labeled data. The model constructs high-confidence triplets through cyclic consistency and random image transformation, which reduces noise and makes the model finely distinguish the differences between classes. Experimental results show that the performance of our method on both Market-1501 and DukeMTMC-reID performs better than the latest unsupervised re-ID methods and even surpasses some unsupervised domain adaptation methods.

**Keywords:** Re-identification · Unsupervised learning · Deep clustering · Pseudo-labels

## 1 Introduction

Person re-identification (re-ID) is a crucial task to retrieve the same person's identity across various devices. The challenge is how to alleviate the influence of different cameras, various postures, occlusion, and pedestrians' wear. In recent years, re-ID has been widely used in video surveillance systems and intelligent security, and has become the focus of academic research. Although deep learning approaches [32,42] exhibit superior performance, they typically rely on manually annotated datasets to train the model. Unsupervised re-ID approaches can avoid laborious data annotation with highly generalized models and they are more suitable for video surveillance and other cases. Therefore, it is more concerned by people at present.

© Springer Nature Singapore Pte Ltd. 2022
F. Sun et al. (Eds.): ICCSIP 2021, CCIS 1515, pp. 61–75, 2022.
https://doi.org/10.1007/978-981-16-9247-5_5

Recently, unsupervised re-ID approaches has made good progress. Existing approaches mainly include cross-domain unsupervised re-ID and single-domain unsupervised re-ID. The cross-domain [14, 23] unsupervised approaches usually need a manually annotated source dataset. They use the generative adversarial networks (GAN) to transfer the source domain's image style to fit the target domain's style. However, due to differences in background, equipment, pedestrian wear, and postures between different datasets, the target domain features may not be sufficiently distinguishable from the model pre-trained on the source domain dataset [39] as shown in Fig. 1. Performance of the cross-domain unsupervised models is still lagging behind supervised learning. In addition, it is challenging to select the appropriate source domain data for transfer learning in unsupervised re-ID because of domain differences [22, 35]. The single-domain methods belong to fully unsupervised re-ID and do not require any manual labeled data. Their traditional methods [8, 15, 19] focus on hand-made features. However, the performance of these methods is lower than that of supervised methods. To relieve these problems, we choose to use self-supervised learning.

CUHK01                    Market1501                    GRID

**Fig. 1.** Differences in background, equipment, pedestrian wear, and postures between different datasets

The self-supervised approach [5, 12] can be regarded as a particular unsupervised learning method. Its supervised information is self-mined from the unsupervised dataset, then the network is trained through this information. Deep clustering [2, 25, 41] is a self-supervised learning approach. It combines convolutional neural networks (CNN) [13] and unsupervised clustering to propose an end-to-end model. In re-ID, a fully unsupervised approach, Bottom-up Clustering (BUC) [17], is based on deep clustering. BUC uses bottom-up hierarchical clustering to merge samples, and after each step of merging, it uses the result clusters as pseudo-labels for deep neural network training. It then uses the trained network to get features and update clustering and the pseudo-labels continuously until the model achieves the best performance. However, BUC may not distinguish between complex samples in early model merging, leading to wrong merging and getting many wrong pseudo-labels. Simultaneously, these errors cause superimposition errors in subsequent merging, thereby severely degrade the model's performance.

To address these issues and reduce pseudo-labels noise impact in re-ID tasks that do not use any labeled data, we propose a method that trains the network with the high-confidence samples labels (HCSL). Moreover, HCSL is also a deep clustering method that does not require any manual labels. The iterative process of HCSL includes (1) training the network to extract features, (2) clustering pseudo-labels, (3) training classification tasks and updating the network's weights, (4) reusing the model to extract features. Specifically, HCSL assigns a pseudo-label to each sample and extracts image features through a pre-trained feature extractor. Then the model clusters the samples through Density-Based Spatial Clustering of Applications with Noise (DBSCAN) [6] and updates the pseudo-labels. The last and most significant thing is that model fine-tunes the network using high-confidence triplet loss (HCTL) and saves the best performing model after several iterations.

In summary, the main contributions of this paper are: This paper aims to improve the accuracy of unsupervised re-ID without using any labeled data. To reduce pseudo-labels noise impact in fully unsupervised re-ID, the model uses high-confidence triplet loss to optimize the model. At the same time, the loss can balance noise-free pseudo-label samples and hard negative sample mining. Experimental results show that our performance on Market-1501 and DukeMTMC-reID is better than that of the latest unsupervised re-ID methods.

## 2    Related Work

### 2.1    Supervised Person Re-identification

Early research on re-ID focused on extracting robust and discriminative low-level visual features, such as color features [10,29], shape features [44], and texture features [3]. And traditional machine learning methods are used for metric learning [24] in the process of feature matching. Because re-ID faces severe challenges such as scenes, pedestrian postures, and occlusion, the above-mentioned traditional methods are difficult to achieve good results. Momentarily, deep learning has been introduced in re-ID, and significant progress has been made. Furthermore, in re-ID, deep learning is mainly used to extract more discriminative feature representations. By early 2021, the best performance on the re-ID general dataset Market-1501 reached Rank-1 = 96.2%, mAP = 91.7%, and reached Rank-1 = 91.6% and mAP = 84.5% on DukeMTMC-reID [47]. However, these supervised methods usually rely on labeled datasets to train the model. When the trained model is applied to other datasets, the performance is significantly reduced, and it may not be practical to label each new scene. Therefore, unsupervised re-ID will become a new research hot spot.

### 2.2    Unsupervised Person Re-identification

In recent years, cross-domain person re-ID has achieved encouraging results, and most studies use the style transfer theory. Zhong et al. [46] effectively utilize camera invariance in domain adaptation, and they use starGAN to generate a series of different camera-style images. Liu et al. [20] perform style transfer on ambient light, resolution, and camera field of the view separately and then integrate them. Deng et al. [4] use CycleGAN to convert the source domain's image style to that of the target domain without changing the image labels. And then, it trains the network on the generated images. Also, some cross-domain methods use the thought of clustering. Fu et al. [9] train the model on the source domain and then segment the target domain images, they cluster the patch and whole target domain images respectively to obtain pseudo-labels. However, these methods require the source dataset labels, and the style widely differs between the source domain and the target domain datasets. The generalization ability of unsupervised domain adaptation is insufficient.

The self-supervised re-id methods usually use pseudo-labels generated by clustering for deep learning. Fan et al. [7] use source domain data to train the network, use Kmeans to cluster target domain samples to generate pseudo labels, and use pseudo labels to fine-tune the model. However, it is not a fully unsupervised method. Lin et al. propose BUC [17], using CNN to extract image features. Then BUC stipulates hierarchical clustering to merge a fixed number of classes at each step and uses the pseudo-labels generated in each step as supervision to fine-tune the model. Although this method achieves confident performance, this simple combination cannot solve pseudo-labels noise, and it is difficult for the deep networks to propose more discriminative features.

To solve the noise issue caused by pseudo-labels, Wang et al. [33] propose to use multi-label instead of single-label classification, they consider similarity and consistency of style to construct the feature bank, and then determine the soft multi-label. Lin et al. [18] propose a method that does not require clustering, but it uses a classification network with softened labels to reflect the similarity between images. Because these methods for constructing soft labels do not have hard-labels learning, errors caused by the hard classification are eliminated. Although some improvements have been made in these approaches, most approaches require domain adaptation or other auxiliary information to help estimate the similarity. After removing these aids that require much calculation, their performance is still not satisfying [18]. However, HCSL reduces the noise generated by pseudo-labels using a more efficient loss function and obtains better performance than previous methods.

## 3   Proposed Method

This paper proposes a self-supervised method with high-confidence samples' labels (HCSL). This model combines the deep learning network and unsupervised clustering, and it is optimized in an end-to-end manner.

### 3.1   HCSL Architecture

Figure 2 shows the overall framework of HCSL. This model mainly consists of three steps: pseudo-labels initialization, unsupervised clustering, and fine-tuning.

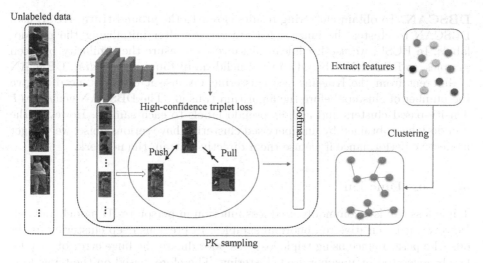

**Fig. 2.** The structure of HCSL. The framework does three steps alternatively: extract features, unsupervised clustering, and fine-tuning with high-confidence triplet loss.

Specifically, in the first stage, the model extracts image features through a pre-trained feature extractor and assigns pseudo-labels to each sample; in the second stage, the model uses unsupervised clustering methods: DBSCAN to cluster samples and assign new pseudo-labels; in the third stage, HCSL uses PK sampling [37] to obtain mini-batch from the dataset and fine-tune the network. Furthermore, we develop a high-confidence triplet loss (HCTL) to minimize the pseudo-labels noise caused by unsupervised clustering. HCTL, through cycle consistency, selects suitable *negative simples* to construct triples to calculate the loss. Compared with other methods, it can further improve the identification ability.

## 3.2   Iterative Pseudo Labeling

Inspired by Tang et al. [31], HCSL uses DBSCAN to cluster the initialized dataset. The advantage of DBSCAN is that there is no need to set the number of clustering. In addition, its clustering speed is fast, and it can effectively deal with noise points and find spatial clusters of arbitrary shapes.

**Pseudo-Labels Initialization.** To use the loss function to optimize the models, models need to generate pseudo-labels as supervision. For a dataset containing $N$ image samples $X = \{x_1, x_2, \cdots, x_N\}$, HCSL treats each sample as a separate cluster to obtain pseudo-labels $Y = \{y_1, y_2, \cdots, y_N\}$. And then, HCSL uses ResNet [11] pre-trained by ImageNet as the extractor's backbone network and replaces the original fully connected (FC) layer with the new FC-1024 layer to output the feature vector. Through this feature extractor, we can get the feature embedding of each image for subsequent clustering.

**DBSCAN.** To obtain clustering results closer to the ground truth, HCSL uses DBSCAN to cluster the images' feature vectors after initializing the pseudo-labels. In HCSL, we use Euclidean distance to measure the similarity between samples, so DBSCAN is based on the Euclidean distance matrix $dist$. DBSCAN is different from the Kmeans [38] clustering because it does not need to give the number of clusters before the algorithm runs [6]. The DBSCAN generates $k$ density-based clusters and assigns pseudo labels to each sample. However, the pseudo-labels obtained by unsupervised clustering have serious noise, we will get ineffective performance if we use them directly to train the network.

### 3.3 Loss Function

Triple loss [30] is a commonly used loss function in person re-ID model training. However, it is sensitive to abnormal samples. In previous deep clustering methods, the performance using triple loss was poor due to the huge error of pseudo-labels generated by unsupervised clustering. Therefore, based on the triple loss, we get inspiration from a common way of constructing supervision signals in self-supervised learning: cyclic consistency. And we propose another loss HCTL that can reduce the influence of pseudo-labels noise. Because the core thought of triple loss is to develop a triple of *anchor*, *positive sample* and *negative sample*, then it shortens the distance between *positive sample* and *anchor*, at the same time pushes *negative sample* away. In unsupervised learning, the choice of *positive* and *negative* samples has a decisive influence. The core thought of HCTL is to construct triples with more high-confidence samples through the random transformation of images and cyclic consistency. Thereby, the influence of abnormal samples is reduced to improve model performance. To meet the need of HCTL loss, we use PK sampling to generate mini-batches for training in each iteration. PK sampling means that we randomly select $K$ instances from $P$ identities to generate mini-batches according to clustering results, so it is easily to combine triples required by HCTL.

**Positive Samples.** Obviously, the image $x_i^*$ generated after a series of random transformations of image $x_i$ must be the *positive sample* of $x_i$. Therefore, when the HCSL performs PK sampling on the dataset $X^*$ to construct a mini-batch, it stores a randomly transformed *positive sample* for each image.

**Negative Samples.** Self-supervised learning usually uses the cyclic consistency principle to construct self-supervised signals. Therefore, HCTL mines *negative sample* in a mini-batch for *anchor* images by cycle consistency. As shown in Fig. 3, the HCTL can search the image bidirectionally according to the cyclic consistency to mine *negative sample* for *anchor*. We set a non-negative threshold $q$ and a pseudo-labelled mini-batch $\{x_i\}_{i=1}^{P \times K}$. This mini-batch selects $P$ identities from all identities and selects $K$ samples from each identity. For each sample $x_i$, HCTL calculates the Mahalanobis distance between $x_i$ and other $(P-1) \times K$ samples of other clusters. Mahalanobis distance is different from Euclidean distance. It can consider the relationship between various attributes

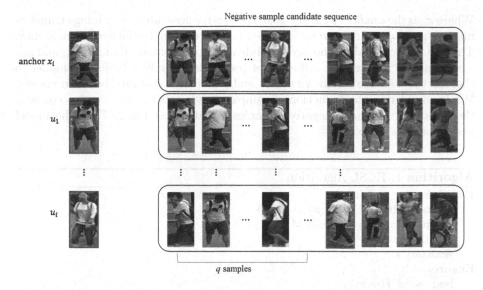

**Fig. 3.** Mining *negative sample*. We calculate the negative sample candidate sequence $U$ of the *anchor*, and then calculate the negative sample candidate sequence of each sample in $U$ starting from $u_1$. When the order of *anchor* in the sequence is greater than $q$, we find the *negative sample* of anchor $x_i$ and stop the algorithm.

and pay more attention to the correlation between samples, while Euclidean distance treats the differences between multiple attributes equally. So Mahalanobis distance learning is a prominent and widely used approach for improving classification results by exploiting the structure of the data [28]. Given $n$ data points $x_i \in R_m$, the goal is to estimate a matrix $M$ such that:

$$d_\mathbf{M}(x_i, x_j) = (x_i - x_j)^T \mathbf{M}(x_i - x_j)$$

Where $R_m$ is a batch of the dataset with pseudo-labels. According to the distance, we sort them to obtain a negative sample candidate sequence $\{u_i\}_{i=1}^{(P-1) \times K}$ from small to large. The further back in the sequence, the more likely it is to be a negative sample, but more likely to be a simple negative sample. To balance noise-free pseudo-labels and hard negative samples mining, HCTL will not simply select the last sample of the sequence as the negative sample. For each sample $u_i$ in the sequence, HCTL also calculates its *negative sample* candidate sequence. If $x_i$ does not appear in the first $q$ positions, then $u_i$ is a *negative sample* of $x_i$. At the same time, we specify that the first $u_i$ found is a hard *negative sample* of $x_i$.

HCTL can be expressed as:

$$L = \left\{ \|x_a - x_p\|_2 - \|x_a - x_n\|_2 + margin, 0 \right\}_+$$

Where $x_a$ is the *anchor*, $x_p$ is the *positive sample* generated after image transformation, and $x_n$ is the *negative sample* mined according to the cycle consistency. The loss is calculated by the high-confidence triples composed of $x_a$, $x_p$, and $x_n$, which further reduces the influence of pseudo-labels noise, helps the model to shorten the distance within the class and pushes the distance between classes. While considering the reduction of sample pseudo-label noise, we also consider the importance of hard negative samples for model training. Thus the model performance is improved.

---

**Algorithm 1.** HCSL Algorithm

---

**Require:**
    unlabeled data $X = \{x_1, x_2, \cdots, x_N\}$
    non-negative sample threshold $q$
    iteration $t$
    similarity $s$
**Ensure:**
    best model $f(w, x_i)$
  1: initialize:
      iteration $iter = 0$
      pseudo-labels: $\{y_i\}_i^N = 1$
  2: train model with $X$ and $Y$, the model without high-confidence triplet loss
  3: **while** $iter < t$ **do**
  4:    initialize pseudo-labels: $\{y_i\}_i^N = 1$
  5:    extract features
  6:    calculate the Euclidean distance matrix $dist$
  7:    calculate the minimum of the $dist$
  8:    clustering with k-means clustering: $c$
  9:    update $Y$ with new pseudo-labels
10:    fine-tune model with $X$ and $Y$, the model with high-confidence triplet loss
11:    evaluate model performance: $P$
12:    **if** $P > P_{best}$ **then**
13:      $P_{best} = P$
14:      best model: $f(w, x_i)$
15:    **end if**
16:    $iter = iter + 1$
17: **end while**

---

### 3.4    Model Updating

As shown in Algorithm 1, at the beginning of each iteration, HCSL assigns $N$ image samples to $N$ different clusters to obtain the initial pseudo-labels. The initialization, clustering, and fine-tuning processes make up an iteration. In every iteration, HCSL generates $k$ high-quality clustering centers through DBSCAN clustering and allocates $N$ image samples to $k$ clusters to update the dataset $X$ with new pseudo-labels. Then HCSL fine-tunes the model with the dataset

$X$ according to HCTL. We iterate over the model and evaluate its performance until it stops improving.

# 4 Experiments

## 4.1 Datasets

**Market-1501.** Market-1501 [43] is collected in the campus of Tsinghua University. It consists of 32,668 images of 1,501 people and is shot by six cameras. The training set includes 12,936 images of 751 people, 17.2 training data per person on average. Moreover, the test set includes 19,732 images of 750 people, 26.3 test data per person on average.

**DukeMTMC-reID.** Dukemtmc-reID [45] is a person re-identification subset of the DukeMTMC dataset, which contains 36,411 images of 1,404 people and is shot by 8 cameras. The training set includes 16,522 images of 702 people, and the test set contains 17,661 images of 702 people.

## 4.2 Training Details

**HCSL Training Setting.** We use the ResNet-50 pre-trained by ImageNet as the backbone network and replace the original FC layer with a new FC-1024 layer to output the feature vectors. An image size of the model input is adjusted to $224 \times 224$. The *batchsize* is 64, and a mini-batch is generated by selecting $P = 16$ identities and $K = 4$ images randomly. In the model initialization phase, we use SGD [1] to optimize the model, and the momentum parameter is 0.9, *weight decay* is 5e−4. We train the model with *learning rate* 0.1 for 20 epochs. In the fine-tuning model stage, we use RAdam [21] to optimize the model, and the *learning rate* is 0.01 for 20 epochs, *weight decay* is 5e−4. Moreover, HCTL *margin* is 1, and the non-negative sample threshold $q$ is 14 on Market-1501. The *positive sample* is obtained after random cropping, random flipping, and random erasure of the input image.

**HCSL Evaluating Setting.** We use the mean average precision (mAP) and the Cumulative Matching Characteristic (CMC) curve to evaluate the model performance. The mAP reflects the model's recall rate, and the CMC curve reflects the model's retrieval accuracy. We use Rank-1, Rank-5, and Rank-10 scores to represent the CMC curve.

## 4.3 Effectiveness of HCSL

Table 1 shows the performance comparison between the HCSL and the most advanced methods on the Market-1501 and DukeMTMC-reID. Our method achieved the best performance with Rank-1 = 73.6% and mAP = 51.3% on the Market-1501. Compared with our unsupervised baseline, BUC method, our model's accuracy on Rank-1 is improved by 7.4% and mAP by 13%. And our

**Table 1.** The performance comparison between the HCSL and several most advanced methods on the Market-1501 dataset and DukeMTMC-reID dataset. "None" means that these methods do not use labeled labels, and "Transfer" means that these methods need to be trained on the source domain and then applied to the target domain. "Weakly" means weakly supervised method.

| Methods | Labels | Reference | Market-1501 | | | | DukeMTMC-reID | | | |
|---------|--------|-----------|------|--------|--------|---------|------|--------|--------|---------|
| | | | mAP | Rank-1 | Rank-5 | Rank-10 | mAP | Rank-1 | Rank-5 | Rank-10 |
| BOW [43] | None | ICCV15 | 14.9 | 35.6 | 52.3 | 60.1 | 8.3 | 17.0 | 28.5 | 34.7 |
| UMDL [26] | Transfer | CVPR16 | 12.3 | 34.5 | 52.4 | 59.7 | 7.2 | 18.7 | 31.5 | 37.4 |
| PUL [7] | Transfer | TOMM18 | 20.3 | 44.9 | 59.4 | 65.7 | 16.3 | 30.1 | 46.2 | 50.7 |
| SPGAN [4] | Transfer | CVPR18 | 26.6 | 57.9 | 75.8 | 81.4 | 26.4 | 46.7 | 62.3 | 68.4 |
| HHL [46] | Transfer | ECCV18 | 31.7 | 62.3 | 78.4 | 84.6 | 27.4 | 46.7 | 61.1 | 66.7 |
| TJ-AIDL [34] | Transfer | CVPR18 | 26.4 | 58.4 | 74.7 | 81.3 | 23.2 | 44.7 | 59.6 | 65.1 |
| BUC [17] | None | AAAI19 | 38.3 | 66.2 | 79.6 | 84.5 | 27.5 | 47.4 | 62.6 | 68.4 |
| ATNet [20] | Transfer | CVPR19 | 25.7 | 55.9 | 73.7 | 79.8 | 25.2 | 45.3 | 59.9 | 64.8 |
| UCDA [27] | Transfer | ICCV19 | 34.5 | 64.3 | – | – | 36.7 | 55.4 | – | – |
| CSCL [36] | Transfer | ICCV19 | 35.6 | 64.7 | 80.2 | 85.6 | 30.5 | 51.5 | 66.7 | 71.1 |
| WFDR [40] | Weakly | CVPR20 | 50.1 | 72.1 | 80.5 | – | 42.4 | 62.0 | **75.1** | – |
| SSL [16] | None | CVPR20 | 37.8 | 71.1 | 83.8 | 87.4 | 28.6 | 52.5 | 63.5 | 68.9 |
| HCSL (Ours) | None | This work | **51.3** | **73.6** | **87.5** | **91.2** | **47.9** | **62.7** | 70.2 | **75.7** |

method also has superior performance with Rank-1 = 62.7%, mAP = 47.9% on DukeMTMC-reID. The improvement of HCSL performance is mainly due to high-confidence triplet loss (HCTL) that can distinguish image details better. Furthermore, it not only surpassing previous fully unsupervised methods but even surpasses some unsupervised domain adaptation (UDA) methods.

**Table 2.** The impacts of using high-confidence triplet loss (HCTL) on model performance.

| Methods | Market-1501 | | DukeMTMC-reID | |
|---------|-------------|-----|---------------|-----|
| | Rank-1 | mAP | Rank-1 | mAP |
| HCSL (with triplet loss) | 34.5 | 19.2 | 21.3 | 17.1 |
| HCSL (with HCTL) | **73.6** | **51.3** | **62.7** | **47.9** |

**Comparison with Triple Loss.** Table 2 shows the model's performance using high-confidence triple loss (HCTL) and using triple loss. Using HCTL has a remarkable performance improvement on both benchmarks. In Market-1501, using the high-confidence triple loss, compared with using the triple loss directly, the Rank-1 improves 39.1%, and the mAP improves 32.1%. Compared with BUC that does not use triple loss, triple loss makes the model performance worse because it is sensitive to abnormal samples. In unsupervised re-ID, the pseudo-labels noise generated by clustering can seriously affect triple loss calculation, but HCTL can achieve better results by reducing the impact. In addition, we also compared the performance of Mahalanobis distance and Euclidean distance when applied to HCTL. From Table 3, the Mahalanobis distance has a better effect. The experimental results prove our analysis in 3.3.

**Table 3.** Compare Euclidean distance and Mahalanobis distance. "*" means that HCSL uses Euclidean distance to obtain a negative sample candidate sequence

| Methods | Market-1501 | | DukeMTMC-reID | |
|---|---|---|---|---|
| | Rank-1 | mAP | Rank-1 | mAP |
| HCSL* | 64.1 | 50.2 | 57.6 | 47.1 |
| HCSL | **73.6** | **51.3** | **62.7** | **47.9** |

**Comparison with Different $q$ in HCTL.** In HCTL, the non-negative sample threshold $q$ controls the selection of hard negative samples, and finally affects the confidence of triplet. To get the best performance, we set $P = 4$, $K = 16$ and evaluate the impact of different $q$ on Market-1501. Our results are reported in Fig. 4(a). When we set $q = 14$, we get the best performance of HCSL. We believe

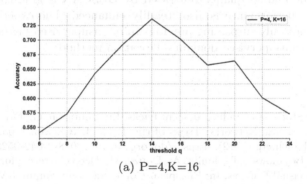

(a) P=4,K=16

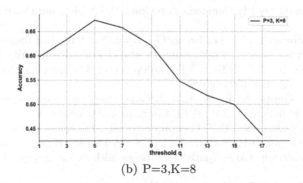

(b) P=3,K=8

**Fig. 4.** Performance curve with different values of the non-negative sample threshold parameter q on Market-1501.

that in HCTL, the threshold $q$ is affected by $K$ in PK sampling. Although the re-ID dataset may not be ideal for calculating the negative sample candidate sequence due to pedestrian clothing and lighting factors, the difference between the classes still exists and can be HCTL obtained. At the same time, because of the limitations of unsupervised learning, HCSL does not work well at $q = 17$. To confirm the above conclusion, we set $P = 3$, $K = 8$ and evaluate the impact of different $q$ on Market-1501. It can be seen in Fig. 4(b) that the performance when $q = 5$ is better than other cases, but the overall performance is worse than batchsize $= 64$.

## 5   Conclusion

In this paper, we propose a fully unsupervised re-ID method, HCSL. Different from previous works, this method does not require any labeled datasets. HCSL optimizes the following issue: in the previous deep clustering methods, the large amount of noise in the clustering pseudo-labels affects the model performance. Specifically, HCSL constructs high-confidence triplets through cyclic consistency and random image transformation, which reduces noise and makes the model finely distinguish differences between classes. With the model iteration, the pseudo-labels quality generated by DBSCAN is gradually improved, and the model performance is also steadily enhanced. The experiments prove that HCSL is not only surpassing previous fully unsupervised methods but even surpasses some unsupervised domain adaptation methods.

## References

1. Bottou, L.: Stochastic gradient descent tricks. In: Montavon, G., Orr, G.B., Müller, K.-R. (eds.) Neural Networks: Tricks of the Trade. LNCS, vol. 7700, pp. 421–436. Springer, Heidelberg (2012). https://doi.org/10.1007/978-3-642-35289-8_25
2. Caron, M., Bojanowski, P., Joulin, A., Douze, M.: Deep clustering for unsupervised learning of visual features. In: European Conference on Computer Vision (2018)
3. Dalal, N., Triggs, B.: Histograms of oriented gradients for human detection. In: IEEE Computer Society Conference on Computer Vision and Pattern Recognition (2005)
4. Deng, W., Zheng, L., Ye, Q., Kang, G., Yang, Y., Jiao, J.: Image-image domain adaptation with preserved self-similarity and domain-dissimilarity for person re-identification. In: 2018 IEEE/CVF Conference on Computer Vision and Pattern Recognition, pp. 994–1003 (2018)
5. Doersch, C., Gupta, A., Efros, A.A.: Unsupervised visual representation learning by context prediction. In: 2015 IEEE International Conference on Computer Vision (ICCV), pp. 1422–1430. IEEE Computer Society, December 2015
6. Ester, M., Kriegel, H.P., Sander, J., Xu, X.: A Density-Based Algorithm for Discovering Clusters in Large Spatial Databases with Noise. AAAI Press, Palo Alto (1996)
7. Fan, H., Zheng, L., Yan, C., Yang, Y.: Unsupervised person re-identification: clustering and fine-tuning. ACM Trans. Multim. Comput. Commun. Appl. 83:1–83:18 (2018)

8. Farenzena, M., Bazzani, L., Perina, A., Murino, V., Cristani, M.: Person re-identification by symmetry-driven accumulation of local features. In: 2010 IEEE Computer Society Conference on Computer Vision and Pattern Recognition, pp. 2360–2367 (2010)
9. Fu, Y., et al.: Self-similarity grouping: a simple unsupervised cross domain adaptation approach for person re-identification. In: 2019 IEEE/CVF International Conference on Computer Vision (ICCV), pp. 6111–6120 (2019)
10. Gou, M., Fei, X., Camps, O., Sznaier, M.: Person re-identification using kernel-based metric learning methods. In: Computer Vision-ECCV 2014 (2014)
11. He, K., Zhang, X., Ren, S., Sun, J.: Deep residual learning for image recognition. In: 2016 IEEE Conference on Computer Vision and Pattern Recognition (CVPR), pp. 770–778 (2016)
12. Komodakis, N., Gidaris, S.: Unsupervised representation learning by predicting image rotations. In: International Conference on Learning Representations (ICLR), Vancouver, Canada, April 2018
13. Krizhevsky, A., Sutskever, I., Hinton, G.E.: ImageNet classification with deep convolutional neural networks. In: Proceedings of the 25th International Conference on Neural Information Processing Systems, vol. 1, pp. 1097–1105. NIPS 2012, Curran Associates Inc., Red Hook, NY, USA (2012)
14. Li, Y.J., Lin, C.S., Lin, Y.B., Wang, Y.: Cross-dataset person re-identification via unsupervised pose disentanglement and adaptation. In: 2019 IEEE/CVF International Conference on Computer Vision (ICCV) (2019)
15. Liao, S., Yang, H., Zhu, X., Li, S.Z.: Person re-identification by local maximal occurrence representation and metric learning. In: 2015 IEEE Conference on Computer Vision and Pattern Recognition (CVPR) (2015)
16. Lin, Y., Xie, L., Wu, Y., Yan, C., Tian, Q.: Unsupervised person re-identification via softened similarity learning. In: 2020 IEEE/CVF Conference on Computer Vision and Pattern Recognition (CVPR) (2020)
17. Lin, Y., Dong, X., Zheng, L., Yan, Y., Yang, Y.: A bottom-up clustering approach to unsupervised person re-identification. In: Proceedings of the AAAI Conference on Artificial Intelligence, vol. 33, pp. 8738–8745 (2019)
18. Lin, Y., Xie, L., Wu, Y., Yan, C., Tian, Q.: Unsupervised person re-identification via softened similarity learning. In: 2020 IEEE/CVF Conference on Computer Vision and Pattern Recognition (CVPR), pp. 3387–3396 (2020)
19. Lisanti, G., Masi, I., Bagdanov, A.D., Bimbo, A.D.: Person re-identification by iterative re-weighted sparse ranking. IEEE Trans. Patt. Anal. Mach. Intell. **37**, 1629–1642 (2015)
20. Liu, J., Zha, Z.J., Chen, D., Hong, R., Wang, M.: Adaptive transfer network for cross-domain person re-identification. In: 2019 IEEE/CVF Conference on Computer Vision and Pattern Recognition (CVPR) (2019)
21. Liu, L., et al.: On the variance of the adaptive learning rate and beyond. In: International Conference on Learning Representations (2020)
22. Long, M., Wang, J.: Learning transferable features with deep adaptation networks. JMLR.org (2015)
23. Lu, Y., et al.: Cross-modality person re-identification with shared-specific feature transfer. 2020 IEEE/CVF Conference on Computer Vision and Pattern Recognition (CVPR) (2020)
24. Martinel, N., Micheloni, C., Foresti, G.L.: Saliency weighted features for person re-identification. In: Agapito, L., Bronstein, M.M., Rother, C. (eds.) ECCV 2014. LNCS, vol. 8927, pp. 191–208. Springer, Cham (2015). https://doi.org/10.1007/978-3-319-16199-0_14

25. Niu, C., Zhang, J., Wang, G., Liang, J.: GATCluster: self-supervised gaussian-attention network for image clustering. In: Vedaldi, A., Bischof, H., Brox, T., Frahm, J.-M. (eds.) ECCV 2020. LNCS, vol. 12370, pp. 735–751. Springer, Cham (2020). https://doi.org/10.1007/978-3-030-58595-2_44

26. Peng, P., et al.: Unsupervised cross-dataset transfer learning for person re-identification. In: 2016 IEEE Conference on Computer Vision and Pattern Recognition (CVPR), pp. 1306–1315 (2016)

27. Qi, L., Wang, L., Huo, J., Zhou, L., Shi, Y., Gao, Y.: A novel unsupervised camera-aware domain adaptation framework for person re-identification. In: 2019 IEEE/CVF International Conference on Computer Vision, ICCV 2019, 27 October–2 November 2019, Seoul, Korea (South), pp. 8079–8088. IEEE (2019)

28. Roth, P.M., Hirzer, M., Kstinger, M., Beleznai, C., Bischof, H.: Mahalanobis distance learning for person re-identification. Person Re-Identification (2014)

29. Rui, Z., Ouyang, W., Wang, X.: Person re-identification by salience matching. In: Proceedings of the 2013 IEEE International Conference on Computer Vision (2013)

30. Schroff, F., Kalenichenko, D., Philbin, J.: FaceNet: a unified embedding for face recognition and clustering. In: 2015 IEEE Conference on Computer Vision and Pattern Recognition (CVPR), pp. 815–823 (2015)

31. Tang, H., Zhao, Y., Lu, H.: Unsupervised person re-identification with iterative self-supervised domain adaptation. In: 2019 IEEE/CVF Conference on Computer Vision and Pattern Recognition Workshops (CVPRW) (2019)

32. Tay, C.P., Roy, S., Yap, K.H.: AANet: attribute attention network for person re-identifications. In: 2019 IEEE/CVF Conference on Computer Vision and Pattern Recognition (CVPR) (2020)

33. Wang, D., Zhang, S.: Unsupervised person re-identification via multi-label classification. In: 2020 IEEE/CVF Conference on Computer Vision and Pattern Recognition (CVPR), pp. 10978–10987 (2020)

34. Wang, J., Zhu, X., Gong, S., Li, W.: Transferable joint attribute-identity deep learning for unsupervised person re-identification. In: 2018 IEEE/CVF Conference on Computer Vision and Pattern Recognition, pp. 2275–2284 (2018)

35. Wei, L., Zhang, S., Wen, G., Qi, T.: Person transfer GAN to bridge domain gap for person re-identification. In: 2018 IEEE/CVF Conference on Computer Vision and Pattern Recognition (2018)

36. Wu, A., Zheng, W.S., Lai, J.H.: Unsupervised person re-identification by camera-aware similarity consistency learning. In: 2019 IEEE/CVF International Conference on Computer Vision (ICCV), pp. 6921–6930 (2019)

37. Wu, C.Y., Manmatha, R., Smola, A.J., Krhenbühl, P.: Sampling matters in deep embedding learning. In: 2017 IEEE International Conference on Computer Vision (ICCV) (2017)

38. Wu, J., Xiong, H., Chen, J.: Adapting the right measures for k-means clustering. In: Proceedings of the 15th ACM SIGKDD International Conference on Knowledge Discovery and Data Mining, pp. 877–886. Association for Computing Machinery (2009)

39. Yan, H., Ding, Y., Li, P., Wang, Q., Xu, Y., Zuo, W.: Mind the class weight bias: weighted maximum mean discrepancy for unsupervised domain adaptation. In: 2017 IEEE Conference on Computer Vision and Pattern Recognition (CVPR) (2017)

40. Yu, H.X., Zheng, W.S.: Weakly supervised discriminative feature learning with state information for person identification. In: 2020 IEEE/CVF Conference on Computer Vision and Pattern Recognition (CVPR) (2020)

41. Zhan, X., Xie, J., Liu, Z., Ong, Y.S., Loy, C.C.: Online deep clustering for unsupervised representation learning. In: 2020 IEEE/CVF Conference on Computer Vision and Pattern Recognition (CVPR) (2020)
42. Zhao, Y., Shen, X., Jin, Z., Lu, H., Hua, X.: Attribute-driven feature disentangling and temporal aggregation for video person re-identification. In: 2019 IEEE/CVF Conference on Computer Vision and Pattern Recognition (CVPR), pp. 4908–4917, June 2019
43. Zheng, L., Shen, L., Tian, L., Wang, S., Wang, J., Tian, Q.: Scalable person re-identification: a benchmark. In: 2015 IEEE International Conference on Computer Vision (ICCV), pp. 1116–1124 (2015)
44. Zheng, W.S., Gong, S., Xiang, T.: Reidentification by relative distance comparison. IEEE Trans. Softw. Eng. **35**, 653–668 (2012)
45. Zheng, Z., Zheng, L., Yang, Y.: Unlabeled samples generated by GAN improve the person re-identification baseline in vitro. In: Proceedings of the IEEE International Conference on Computer Vision (2017)
46. Zhong, Z., Zheng, L., Li, S., Yang, Y.: Generalizing a person retrieval model hetero- and homogeneously. In: Proceedings of the European Conference on Computer Vision (ECCV), September 2018
47. Zhu, Z., Jiang, X., Zheng, F., Guo, X., Zheng, W.: Viewpoint-aware loss with angular regularization for person re-identification. In: Proceedings of the AAAI Conference on Artificial Intelligence, pp. 13114–13121 (2020)

# DAda-NC: A Decoupled Adaptive Online Training Algorithm for Deep Learning Under Non-convex Conditions

Yangfan Zhou[1,2,3] (iD), Cheng Cheng[1,2,3], Jiang Li[1,2,3], Yafei Ji[1,2,3], Haoyuan Wang[1,2,3], Xuguang Wang[1,2,3], and Xin Liu[1,2,3(✉)] (iD)

[1] University of Science and Technology of China, 96 Jinzhai Road, Hefei, Anhui, China
[2] Suzhou Institute of Nano-Tech and Nano-Bionics (SINANO), Chinese Academy of Sciences, 398 Ruoshui Road, Suzhou Industrial Park, Suzhou, Jiangsu, China
{yfzhou2020,ccheng2017,jli2018,yfji2020,hywang2015,xgwang2009, xliu2018}@sinano.ac.cn
[3] Gusu Laboratory of Materials, 388 Ruoshui Road, Suzhou Industrial Park, Suzhou, Jiangsu, China

**Abstract.** Adam is a famous adaptive optimization algorithm for model training of deep learning. However, its weak generalization capability under non-convex conditions is still an open problem. To tackle this problem, we proposed a decoupled weight decay adaptive algorithm, named DAda-NC, for solving non-convex optimization issues and improving generalization capability. In our proposed algorithm, we use the $sign(\cdot)$ function to re-design the second order momentum of adaptive algorithm that makes our proposed algorithm converging in non-convex cases. Moreover, we respectively add a decoupled weight decay factor to the calculation of the gradient and stepsize of the proposed algorithm, which improves the generalization capability for our proposed algorithm. Finally, plenty of experiments conducted on public datasets demonstrate that our proposed algorithm outperforms other executed algorithms.

**Keywords:** Adaptive algorithm · Deep learning · Model training · Non-convex optimization · Online learning

## 1 Introduction

Deep neural networks (DNNs) have become a significant paradigm of artificial intelligence in many fields such as industrial visual [1,2], nature language process [3,4], auxiliary medical [5], auto driving [6], etc. In this paradigm, deep model training of DNN is an arduous and important task because the neural network model is extremely complex. To address this problem, deep model training is generally transformed into an optimization problem that minimizes the value of a loss function. For this reason, optimization algorithms are necessary when training deep models. Moreover, to implement the optimization algorithm easily

© Springer Nature Singapore Pte Ltd. 2022
F. Sun et al. (Eds.): ICCSIP 2021, CCIS 1515, pp. 76–88, 2022.
https://doi.org/10.1007/978-981-16-9247-5_6

and quickly, many algorithms based on stochastic gradient descent method have been widely concerned and applied [7,8].

Stochastic gradient descent (SGD) algorithm is a classical and simple optimization algorithm for deep neural network training. Moreover, SGD is easily applied to various deep training tasks because of its simple algorithm logic. Importantly, SGD superior to other optimization algorithms in terms of generalization ability in many applications. However, the convergence rate of SGD is unsatisfactory, so a large number of label samples are required. To speed up the convergence rate of SGD, many fast optimization algorithms with adaptive stepsize have been proposed, for instance, Adam [9], AMSGrad [10], AdamW [11], etc. In fact, these adaptive algorithms not only design the adaptive stepsize, but also fully consider the help of the historical gradient information to the convergence speed. Therefore, the adaptive algorithms have received extensive attentions in recent years.

Although the above algorithms have been applied in some scenarios, they all restricted to convex conditions. However, in many practical scenarios, the convex condition is not easy to satisfy, which will cause the performance of the above convex optimization algorithms to be greatly reduced, or even fail to converge. Consequently, the research of non-convex optimization algorithms is crucial to the wide application of DNN. To tackle the non-convex problem, many non-convex optimization algorithms have been proposed in last few decades, such as [12–14]. However, these methods are all fixed stepsize with slow convergence rate, and exhibit poor performance in non-convex problems. For this reason, many researchers further studied the non-convex issues for Adam with adaptive stepsize. For example, non-convex optimization for Adam [15], non-convex stochastic optimization for Adam-type algorithms [16], and Yogi [17]. It is however, whether the AdamW optimization algorithm conveges under non-convex conditions is still an open problem.

AdamW is a better optimizer than Adam with its generalization capabilities that decoupling the weight decay from the adaptive stepsize. However, AdamW is a typical convex optimization algorithm that fails converging in the non-convex case. Therefore, it is urgent to propose an optimization method to ensure that AdamW still converges in the non-convex case. In this paper, we propose a non-convex optimization algorithm, named DAda-NC, which uses decoupled method to recover the weight decay regularization of AdamW. Importantly, DAda-NC also conbines the $sign(\cdot)$ function with its stepsize to ensure that it converges even under non-convex conditions. In addition, our mainly contributions are summarized below:

- We propose a decoupled adaptive training algorithm for deep learning under non-convex conditions, named DAda-NC.
- We solve the non convergence problem in the case of non-convex for adaptive algorithms by exploiting the $sign(\cdot)$ function.

- We further improve the generalization ability of adaptive algorithms by exploiting a decoupled weight decay factor.
- We present sufficient experiments for both image classification and language processing tasks on different public datasets.

The rest of this article is structured as follows: Sect. 2 presents the notation and preliminaries of this work. Moreover, the algorithm design of DAda-NC is provided in Sect. 3. Furthermore, the results of experiments are shown in Sect. 4. We put the conclusion of this work in Sect. 5, and provide our future works in Sect. 6. Finally, we state our acknowledgements for this work in Sect. 7.

## 2 Notation and Preliminaries

### 2.1 Notation

In this paper, we use bold letters to denote vectors, such as $\mathbf{x}$ and $\mathbf{y}$. For all $\mathbf{x}, \mathbf{y} \in \mathbb{R}^d$, $\mathbf{x}^2$ denotes the element-wise square, $\sqrt{\mathbf{x}}$ represents the element-wise square root, and $\frac{\mathbf{x}}{\mathbf{y}}$ denotes the element-wise division. Moreover, $\mathbf{x}_t$ represents the value of $\mathbf{x}$ at the $t$-th time. In addition, $x_{t,i}$ denotes the $i$-the coordinate of vector $\mathbf{x}_t$.

### 2.2 Online Non-convex Optimization

In this paper, we consider an online learning problem. In this problem, the decision vectors $\mathbf{x}_t$ and the loss functions $f_t(\cdot)$ are different from time $t$ to time $t+1$. Specifically, the optimizer generates a decision $\mathbf{x}_t$ for $t$-th time. Thus, deep model outputs a result that following the decision. Then, the adversary (i.e., the loss function) returns a regret to the optimizer based on the output result. Finally, the optimizer utilizes its strategy to update the decision $\mathbf{x}_{t+1}$ for the next time. Consequently, the optimization goal of online leaning can be formed as follows:

$$\min_{\mathbf{x}_t \in \mathbb{R}^d} R(T) = \frac{1}{T} \sum_{t=1}^{T} (f_t(\mathbf{x}_t) - f_t(\mathbf{x}^*)), \tag{1}$$

where $T$ is a time horizon, $f_t(\cdot)$ is the loss function at time $t$, $R(T)$ denotes the regret of time $T$, $\mathbf{x}_t$ is the decision vector at time $t$, and $\mathbf{x}^*$ represents the global optima solution.

In our work, we focus on an online learning problem under non-convex conditions. For this reason, we next introduce a non-convex optimization problem. Specifically, we give the following non-convex form to intuitively describe the problems:

$$f_t(\mathbf{x}_t) := \mathbb{E}_{\mathbf{s}_t \sim \mathbb{P}} [\ell_t(\mathbf{x}_t, \mathbf{s}_t)], \tag{2}$$

where time $t \in \{1, \ldots, T\}$, $\mathbf{x}_t \in \mathbb{R}^d$, $\ell$ is a smooth loss function which possibly non-convex, the vector $\mathbf{x}_t$ is model parameters of DNN at time $t$, $\mathbf{s}_t$ is the labeled sample for training at time $t$, and $\mathbb{P}$ is an unknown data distribution.

## 2.3    Adam

In this section, we review the design of Adam. The Adam optimization algorithm is shown in Algorithm 1. According to the original design of Adam, it is to solve the optimization problem under convex conditions. Therefore, the loss functions $f_t$ and the feasible region for Adam are both convex.

---

**Algorithm 1:** Adam

---
**Input:** $\alpha = 0.001, \beta_1 = 0.9, \beta_2 = 0.999, \epsilon = 10^{-8}$
**Output:** $x_{t+1}$
1  **Initialize:** $x_0, m_0, v_0$
2  **for** $t = 1 \ldots T$ **do**
3  $\quad$ $t \leftarrow t + 1$
4  $\quad$ $--\rightarrow$ Calculate the learning rate:
5  $\quad$ $\alpha_t \leftarrow \frac{\alpha}{\sqrt{t}}$
6  $\quad$ $--\rightarrow$ Calculate the gradient $g_t$:
7  $\quad$ $g_t \leftarrow \nabla f_t(x_{t-1})$
8  $\quad$ $--\rightarrow$ Calculate the first order momentum $m_t$:
9  $\quad$ $m_t \leftarrow \beta_1 m_{t-1} + (1 - \beta_1) g_t$
10 $\quad$ $--\rightarrow$ Calculate the second order momentum $v_t$:
11 $\quad$ $v_t \leftarrow v_{t-1} - (1 - \beta_2)(v_{t-1} - g_t^2)$
12 $\quad$ $--\rightarrow$ Return the output with adaptive stepsize:
13 $\quad$ $x_{t+1} \leftarrow x_t - \alpha_t m_t / (\sqrt{v_t} + \epsilon)$

14 **return** $x_{t+1}$

---

As shown in Algorithm 1, the first order moment of Adam is designed as a exponential moving average of gradient, which is formed as follows:

$$m_t = \beta_1 m_{t-1} + (1 - \beta_1) g_t. \tag{3}$$

The first-order momentum in adaptive optimization algorithms is to consider the influence of historical gradient information on the current gradient, which refers to the effect of the inertia of object motion in physics. In fact, an important significance of the first-order momentum is to speed up the iteration speed of the optimization algorithm, which is similar to the second-order momentum. In particular, the second order momentum is an exponential moving average with respect to the square of the gradient, and its form is shown below:

$$v_t = v_{t-1} - (1 - \beta_2)(v_{t-1} - g_t^2). \tag{4}$$

Importantly, the second order momentum realizes the adaptation of the step size of the optimization algorithm, thereby avoiding the invalid oscillation of the algorithm near the optimal point. Finally, Adam updates the decision vector based on the two momentums and the learning rate $(\alpha_t)$, which is shown below:

$$x_{t+1} = x_t - \alpha_t m_t / (\sqrt{v_t} + \epsilon). \tag{5}$$

Although Adam has received a lot of attention and applications, its applicable condition is that the loss function is convex. Therefore, in the case of non-convex, the effect of Adam is very unsatisfactory. For this reason, we propose a novel adaptive momentum optimization algorithm, which is specifically applied to non-convex situations.

## 3   Algorithm Design of DAda-NC

In this section, we first present some definitions and assumptions that guarantee the usability of the proposed algorithm. Secondly, we introduce the design details for our proposed algorithm.

**Definition 1.** *If function $\ell$ is L-smooth, then for $\forall \mathbf{x}, \mathbf{y} \in \mathbb{R}^d$, it satisfies the following condition:*

$$\|\nabla \ell(\mathbf{x}) - \nabla \ell(\mathbf{y})\| \le L \|\mathbf{x} - \mathbf{y}\|. \tag{6}$$

**Definition 2.** *For the function $\ell$, its gradient calculation number with respect to the first parameter of an algorithm is equal to the stochastic first-order (SFO) complexity of the algorithm.*

**Definition 3.** *The SFO complexity of SGD to obtain a $\delta$-accurate solution is $O(1/\delta^2)$.*

The definitions in this paper are common in many previous similar works, such as [17,18].

**Assumption 1.** *This work assumes that the gradient of the function $\ell$ is bounded, i.e., for $\forall \mathbf{x}, \mathbf{y} \in \mathbb{R}^d$, we have $\|\nabla \ell(x_{t,i})\| \le G$.*

**Assumption 2.** *This work assumes that the variance in stochastic gradients is bounded, i.e., for $\forall \mathbf{x} \in \mathbb{R}^d$, we have $\mathbb{E}\|\nabla \ell(x_{t,i}) - \nabla f(x_{t,i})\|^2 \le \sigma^2$.*

The assumptions in our work are typical in many similar works that with respect to the first order momentum based optimization algorithms, such as [19,20].

Next, we turn to particular introduce our proposed algorithm, DAda-NC. For the first step of DAda-NC, it stochastic chooses a batch of samples from training dataset and return the corresponding gradient. In order to eliminate the excessive influence of the second-order weight, we design a decoupled weight decay strategy. Therefore, we add a decoupled operation into the gradient as follows:

$$\mathbf{g}_t = \nabla f_t(\mathbf{x}_{t-1}) + \lambda \mathbf{x}_{t-1}. \tag{7}$$

Moreover, DAda-NC uses a same update strategy as Adam for the first order momentum, which is shown below:

$$\mathbf{m}_t = \beta_1 \mathbf{m}_{t-1} + (1 - \beta_1)\mathbf{g}_t. \tag{8}$$

---

**Algorithm 2:** DAda-NC: Adam with decoupled weight decay for non-convex conditions.

---
**Input:** $\alpha = 0.001, \beta_1 = 0.9, \beta_2 = 0.999, \epsilon = 10^{-8}, \lambda \in \mathbb{R}$

**Output:** $\mathbf{x}_{t+1}$

1 **Initialize:** $\mathbf{x}_0, \mathbf{m}_0, \mathbf{v}_0$

2 **for** $t = 1 \ldots T$ **do**

3     $t \leftarrow t + 1$

4     $\dashrightarrow$ Calculate the learning rate:

5     $\alpha_t \leftarrow \frac{\alpha}{\sqrt{t}}$

6     $\dashrightarrow$ Select batch and return the corresponding gradient:

7     $\nabla f_t(\mathbf{x}_{t-1}) \leftarrow SelectBatch(\mathbf{x}_{t-1})$

8     $\dashrightarrow$ Calculate the decoupled gradient $\mathbf{g}_t$:

9     $\mathbf{g}_t \leftarrow \nabla f_t(\mathbf{x}_{t-1}) + \lambda \mathbf{x}_{t-1}$

10     $\dashrightarrow$ Calculate the first order momentum $\mathbf{m}_t$:

11     $\mathbf{m}_t \leftarrow \beta_1 \mathbf{m}_{t-1} + (1 - \beta_1)\mathbf{g}_t$

12     $\dashrightarrow$ Calculate the second order momentum $\mathbf{v}_t$:

13     $\mathbf{v}_t \leftarrow \mathbf{v}_{t-1} - (1 - \beta_2)sign(\mathbf{v}_{t-1} - \mathbf{g}_t^2)\mathbf{g}_t^2$

14     $\dashrightarrow$ Return the output with decoupled weight decay:

15     $\mathbf{x}_{t+1} \leftarrow \mathbf{x}_t - \alpha_t \left( \mathbf{m}_t / (\sqrt{\mathbf{v}_t} + \epsilon) + \lambda \mathbf{x}_{t-1} \right)$

16 **return** $\mathbf{x}_{t+1}$

---

Importantly, DAda-NC applies the $sign(\cdot)$ function to the second order momentum, thus solving the non convex optimization problem. The form of the second order momentum in DAda-NC is shown as follows:

$$\mathbf{v}_t = \mathbf{v}_{t-1} - (1 - \beta_2)sign(\mathbf{v}_{t-1} - \mathbf{g}_t^2)\mathbf{g}_t^2. \tag{9}$$

Finally, the update rule of the decision vector with decoupled weight decay is shown below:

$$\mathbf{x}_{t+1} = \mathbf{x}_t - \alpha_t \left( \mathbf{m}_t / (\sqrt{\mathbf{v}_t} + \epsilon) + \lambda \mathbf{x}_{t-1} \right). \tag{10}$$

Therefore, the details of the proposed algorithm have been shown in full. In order to demonstrate the performance of our proposed algorithm in practices, we next apply it in various deep learning tasks.

## 4    Experiments

In this section, we evaluate the performance of Dada-NC on different datasets and learning rate settings for non-convex conditions. In our experiments, we conduct two group tasks of deep learning, i.e., image classification and language processing. Moreover, we use one 1080Ti GPU and the Pytorch module of Python 3.6 for all model training tasks.

## 4.1    Datasets and Parameter Settings

In our experiments, we use different public datasets for image classification task and language processing task, respectively. The summary of datasets utilized in our experiments are shown in Table 1. In the image classification tasks, we use a famous public dataset, i.e., CIFAR-10, which is a image dataset including 10 classes and 60000 images with $32 * 32$ size. Furthermore, we conduct three classical architectures, i.e., VGG-11 [21], ResNet-34 [22] and DensetNet-121 [23], for this dataset. For the language processing tasks, we use a famous language dataset, Penn Treebank, with $1, 2, 3$-Layer LSTM architectures, respectively. Moreover, the Penn Treebank is a dataset obtained by tagging the corpus, and its tagging content includes part of speech tagging and parsing. In addition, the corpus of the Penn Treebank data set comes from the Wall Street Journal in 1989, and its word size is $1M$ extracted from 2499 articles.

Table 1. Datasets and architectures used in our experiments.

| Task | Dataset | Architecture |
|------|---------|--------------|
| Image classification | CIFAR-10 | VGG-11 |
| Image classification | CIFAR-10 | ResNet-34 |
| Image classification | CIFAR-10 | DenseNet-121 |
| Language processing | Penn Treebank | 1,2,3-Layer LSTM |

We compare our proposed algorithm with the classical adaptive optimization algorithm Adam and the latest adaptive non-convex optimization algorithm Yogi. We set all the algorithms executed in our experiments as follows:

- **Adam** [9] is with the stepsize: $\alpha = 0,001$, the coefficient of first order momentum: $\beta_1 = 0.9$, the coefficient of second order momentum: $\beta_2 = 0.999$, the regularization item: $\epsilon = 10^{-8}$. Moreover, the initialization momentums are set as $\mathbf{m}_t = 0$ and $\mathbf{v}_t = 0$.
- **Yogi** [17] is with the stepsize: $\alpha = 0,01$, the coefficient of first order momentum: $\beta_1 = 0.9$, the coefficient of second order momentum: $\beta_2 = 0.999$, the regularization item: $\epsilon = 10^{-3}$. Moreover, the initialization momentums are set as $\mathbf{m}_t = 0$ and $\mathbf{v}_t = 0$.
- **DAda-NC** (Ours) is with the stepsize: $\alpha = 0,5$, the decoupled coefficient: $\lambda = 0.125 * 10^{-3}$, the coefficient of first order momentum: $\beta_1 = 0.9$, the coefficient of second order momentum: $\beta_2 = 0.999$, the regularization item: $\epsilon = 10^{-3}$. Moreover, the initialization momentums are set as $\mathbf{m}_t = 0$ and $\mathbf{v}_t = 0$.

## 4.2    Image Classification

In this group of experiments, we conduct the image classification task, which is a standard and focused problem in machine learning, on the public dataset

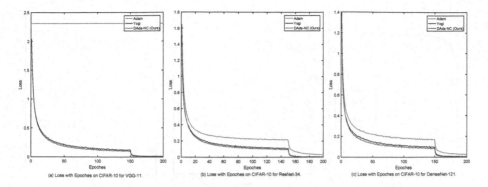

**Fig. 1.** Comparison of each executed algorithm with respect to loss *vs.* epochs on CIFAR-10.

CIFAR-10. Furthermore, three different neural network architectures, VGG-11 (with 11 layers), ResNet-34 (with 34 layers) and DenseNet-121 (with 121 layers), are utilized for the experiments on CIFAR-10, respectively. Next, we present the results and analysis of our experiments.

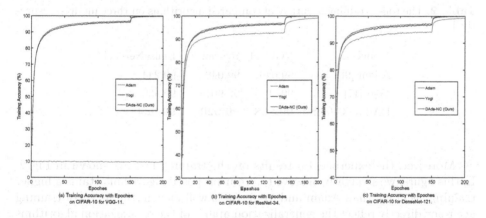

**Fig. 2.** Comparison of each executed algorithm with respect to training accuracy *vs.* epoches on CIFAR-10.

The experimental results about the loss with respect to the epoches are shown in Fig. 1. In this figure, we intuitively see that the loss of our proposed algorithm can reach the lowest of all executed algorithms at the end of the experiment. In fact, the purpose of model training is to minimize the value of the loss, thereby the extent of the loss can potentially reflect the quality of the model training results. In other words, the stable loss value output by the optimization algorithm in the training process potentially reflects the generalization ability of the

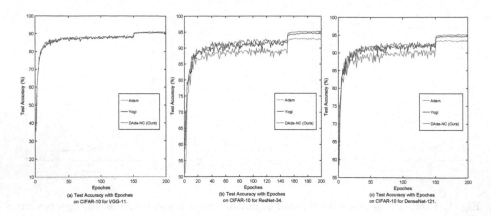

**Fig. 3.** Comparison of each executed algorithm with respect to test accuracy *vs.* epoches on CIFAR-10.

algorithm. Therefore, the Fig. 1 shows that our proposed algorithm outperforms Adam and Yogi in non-convex conditions.

**Table 2.** The top-1 training accuracy of compared algorithms on three models, respectively.

| Model | VGG-11 | ResNet-34 | DenseNet-121 |
|---|---|---|---|
| Adam [9] | 99.046 | 99.046 | 99.244 |
| Yogi [17] | 99.80 | 99.901 | 99.936 |
| DAda-NC (ours) | **99.858** | **99.920** | **99.964** |

Moreover, the experimental results on the training loss are shown in Fig. 2. In this figure, we straightly observe that our proposed algorithm attains a higher training accuracy than Adam and Yogi. As is well-known, the index of training accuracy directly reflect the generalization ability of the optimization algorithms used for the training process. Therefore, the Fig. 2 demonstrates that our proposed algorithm performs better than Adam and Yogi on training accuracy for image classification tasks. Furthermore, we present the summary of top-1 training accuracy of each compared algorithms under non-convex conditions as shown in Table 2. The results in this table further demonstrate that our proposed algorithm performs the best in terms of the training accuracy.

In addition, another important indicator that reflects the performance of the optimization algorithm is the test accuracy after model training. For this reason, we also conduct a set of experiments on test accuracy with respect to image classification tasks. And the experimental results are shown in Fig. 3. Note that the training samples will be used repeatedly, while the test samples are usually extra, so the training accuracy will be slightly higher than the test accuracy.

**Table 3.** The top-1 test accuracy of compared algorithms on three models, respectively.

| Model | VGG-11 | ResNet-34 | DenseNet-121 |
|---|---|---|---|
| Adam [9] | 10.000 | 92.880 | 93.480 |
| Yogi [17] | 90.650 | 94.510 | 94.680 |
| DAda-NC (ours) | **91.070** | **94.730** | **94.750** |

Nonetheless, the Fig. 3 reveals that our proposed algorithm obtain a higher test accuracy than Adam and Yogi after model training. Moreover, we compare the top-1 test accuracy of all the executed algorithms in this group of experiments, and show them in Table 3. The results also verify that our proposed algorithm outperforms Adam and Yogi in terms of the test accuracy.

### 4.3 Language Processing

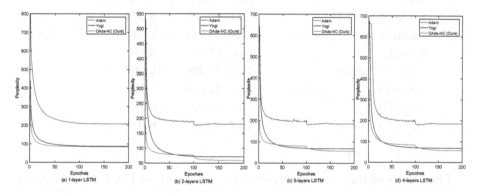

**Fig. 4.** Comparison of each executed algorithm with respect to perplexity *vs.* epoches on Penn Treebank. **The lower perplexity, the better.**

Language processing is one of the important applications in artificial intelligence. Therefore, we also conduct another group of experiments on language processing. In this group of experiments, we utilize the classic 1, 2, and 3-layer LSTM models on the Penn Treebank dataset, respectively. Moreover, the total number of model parameters of 1,2,3-Layer LSTM are 5293200, 13632400 and 24221600, respectively. It is well known that the perplexity is an important evaluation indicator for language models, therefore, we also use the perplexity to evaluate the performance of executed optimization algorithms. Moreover, if it is known that the sentence $(w_1, w_2, \ldots, w_m)$ will appear in the corpus, then the higher the probability of the sentence calculated by the language model, the better the language model predicts the corpus. For this reason, we usually use the perplexity to characterize the predictive ability of language models. Furthermore, the perplexity $P$ of the language model $S$ can be formed as follows:

$$P(S) = p(w_1, w_2, \ldots, w_m)^{-\frac{1}{m}}$$

$$= \left[ \prod_{i=1}^{m} \frac{1}{p(w_i | w_1, w_2, \ldots, w_{i-1})} \right]^{\frac{1}{m}}, \quad (11)$$

where $p$ denotes the probability.

**Table 4.** The results of test process on LSTM.

| Algorithm | Architecture | Loss | Perplexity | Bits-per-character |
|-----------|--------------|------|------------|--------------------|
| Adam [9] | 1-Layer | 5.34 | 207.57 | 7.697 |
| Yogi [17] | | 4.46 | 86.59 | 6.436 |
| DAda-NC (ours) | | **4.43** | **84.28** | **6.397** |
| Adam [9] | 2-Layers | 5.17 | 176.51 | 7.464 |
| Yogi [17] | | 4.27 | 71.33 | 6.156 |
| DAda-NC (ours) | | **4.21** | **67.27** | **6.072** |
| Adam [9] | 3-Layers | 5.19 | 180.15 | 7.493 |
| Yogi [17] | | 4.21 | 67.51 | 6.077 |
| DAda-NC (ours) | | **4.16** | **64.28** | **6.006** |
| Adam [9] | 3-Layers | 5.19 | 179.00 | 7.484 |
| Yogi [17] | | 4.22 | 68.23 | 6.092 |
| DAda-NC (ours) | | **4.17** | **64.87** | **6.019** |

The results of this group of experiments are shown in Fig. 4. Moreover, this figure firsthand show that our proposed algorithm attains the least perplexity in all 1, 2 and 3-layers LSTM models. Note that the lower the perplexity value, the better the model performance. Both Adam and Yogi perform worse than our proposed algorithm. Therefore, our proposed algorithm also has a good performance in the training of language processing models under non-convex conditions. In addition, we further show the results of the test process in Table 4. We directly see that our proposed algorithm attains the least value of loss, perplexity and bits-per-character among all the compared algorithms in the test process.

## 5    Conclusion

In this paper, we focus on the problem of convergence and generalization ability of adaptive optimization algorithms under non-convex conditions. In our propose algorithm, we first use a decoupled weight decay method to further improve the generalization ability. And then we re-design the second order momentum of adaptive algorithms with the $sign(\cdot)$ function that ensures our proposed algorithm converges under non-convex conditions. Finally, we conduct sufficient experiments on both image classification and language processing tasks. All the experimental results demonstrate that our proposed algorithm outperforms Adam and Yogi on standard public datasets under non-convex cases.

## 6  Future Work

Nonetheless, it is not known whether our proposed algorithm still has such good performance except in the case of non-convex, such as convex, strongly convex and so on. Therefore, we will explore these issues in our future works. Furthermore, the theoretically proof of convergence of our proposed algorithm is also left for our future work.

**Acknowledgement.** This work was supported by the Hundred Talents Program of Chinese Academy of Sciences under grant No. Y9BEJ11001. This research was primarily conducted at Suzhou Institute of Nano-Tech and Nano-Bionics (SINANO).

## References

1. Ge, C., Wang, J., Wang, J., Qi, Q., Liao, J.: Towards automatic visual inspection: a weakly supervised learning method for industrial applicable object detection. Comput. Ind. **121**(11), 103232 (2020)
2. Shu, Y., Huang, Yu., Li, B.: Design of deep learning accelerated algorithm for online recognition of industrial products defects. Neural Comput. Appl. **31**(9), 4527–4540 (2018). https://doi.org/10.1007/s00521-018-3511-4
3. Dong, H., Wang, W., Huang, K., Coenen, F.: Automated social text annotation with joint multi-label attention networks. IEEE Trans. Neural Netw. Learn. Syst. **32**(5), 2224–2238 (2020)
4. Chen, Q., Wang, W., Huang, K., Coenen, F.: Zero-shot text classification via knowledge graph embedding for social media data. IEEE Internet Things J. (2021)
5. Zhang, F., Li, Z., Zhang, B., Du, H., Zhang, X.: Multi-modal deep learning model for auxiliary diagnosis of Alzheimer's disease. Neurocomputing **361**, 185–195 (2019)
6. Hu, J., Zhang, X., Maybank, S.: Abnormal driving detection with normalized driving behavior data: a deep learning approach. IEEE Trans. Veh. Technol. (2020)
7. Zhou, Y., Zhang, M., Zhu, J., Zheng, R., Wu, Q.: A randomized block-coordinate Adam online learning optimization algorithm. Neural Comput. Appl. **32**(16), 12671–12684 (2020). https://doi.org/10.1007/s00521-020-04718-9
8. Zhou, Y., Huang, K., Cheng, C., Wang, X., Hussian, A., Liu, X.: FastAdaBelief: improving convergence rate for belief-based adaptive optimizers by exploiting strong convexity. CoRR, abs/2104.13790 (2021)
9. Kingma, D., Ba, J.: Adam: a method for stochastic optimization. Comput. Sci. (2014)
10. Reddi, S.J., Kale, K., Kumar, S.: On the convergence of Adam and Beyond. In: Proceedings of the Sixth International Conference on Learning Representations, pp. 13–23 (2018)

11. Loshchilov, I., Hutter, F.: Decoupled weight decay regularization. In: International Conference on Learning Representations (2019)
12. Reddi, S.J., Hefny, A., Suvrit, S., Póczos, B., Smola, A.J.: Stochastic variance reduction for nonconvex optimization. In: Proceedings of the 33ND International Conference on Machine Learning, ICML 2016, pp. 314–323, New York City, NY, USA (2016)
13. Zhu, Z.A., Hazan, E.: Variance reduction for faster non-convex optimization. CoRR, abs/1603.05643 (2016)
14. Reddi, S.J., Sra, S., Póczos, B., Smola, A.J.: Fast stochastic methods for nonsmooth nonconvex optimization. CoRR, abs/1605.06900 (2016)
15. De, S., Mukherjee A., Ullah, E.: Convergence guarantees for RMSProp and ADAM in non-convex optimization and an empirical comparison to Nesterov acceleration. CoRR, abs/1807.06766 (2018)
16. Chen, X., Liu, S., Sun, R., Hong, M.: On the convergence of a class of adam-type algorithms for non-convex optimization. In: International Conference on Learning Representations, ICLR 2019, New Orleans, Louisiana, United States (2019)
17. Zaheer, M., Reddi, S., Sachan, D., Kale, S., Kumar, S.: Adaptive methods for non-convex optimization. In: Thirty-second Conference on Neural Information Processing Systems, NeurIPS 2018, Palais des Congrès de Montréal, Montréal CANADA (2018)
18. Jin, X., Zhang, X., Huang, K., Geng, G.: Stochastic conjugate gradient algorithm with variance reduction. IEEE Trans. Neural Netw. Learn. Syst. **30**(5), 1360–1369 (2019)
19. Ghadimi, S., Lan, G.: Stochastic first- and zeroth-order methods for nonconvex stochastic programming. SIAM J. Optim. **23**(4), 2341–2368 (2013)
20. Ghadimi, S., Lan, G., Zhang, H.: Mini-batch stochastic approximation methods for nonconvex stochastic composite optimization. Math. Programm. (16), 267–305 (2014). https://doi.org/10.1007/s10107-014-0846-1
21. Simonyan, K., Zisserman, A.: Very deep convolutional networks for large-scale image recognition. Comput. Sci. (2014)
22. He, K., Zhang, X., Ren, S., Sun, J.: Deep residual learning for image recognition. In: IEEE Conference on Computer Vision and Pattern Recognition (CVPR), pp. 770–778 (2016)
23. Huang, G., Liu, Z., Van Der Maaten, L., Weinberger, K.Q.: Densely connected convolutional networks. In: IEEE Conference on Computer Vision and Pattern Recognition (CVPR), pp. 2261–2269 (2017)

# A Scalable 3D Array Architecture for Accelerating Convolutional Neural Networks

Yafei Ji[1,2], Xiang Wang[1,2], Yangfan Zhou[1,2] (iD), Chen Cheng[1,2],
Jiang Li[1,2], Haoyuan Wang[1,2], Xuguang Wang[1,2],
and Xin Liu[1,2(✉)] (iD)

[1] Suzhou Institute of Nano-Tech and Nano-Bionics (SINANO), Chinese
Academy of Sciences, 398 Ruoshui Road, Suzhou Industrial Park, Suzhou,
Jiangsu, China
{yfji2020, xwang2018, yfzhou2020, ccheng2017, jli2018,
hywang2015, xgwang2009, xliu2018}@sinano.ac.cn
[2] Gusu Laboratory of Materials, 388 Ruoshui Road, Suzhou Industrial Park,
Suzhou, Jiangsu, China

**Abstract.** Convolutional neural network (CNN) is widely used in computer vision and image recognition, and the structure of the CNN becomes more and more complex. The complexity of CNN brings challenges of performance and storage capacity for hardware implementation. To address these challenges, in this paper, we propose a novel 3D array architecture for accelerating CNN. This proposed architecture has several benefits: Firstly, the strategy of multilevel caches is employed to improve data reusage, and thus reducing the access frequency to external memory; Secondly, performance and throughout are balanced among 3D array nodes by using novel workload and weight partitioning schemes. Thirdly, computing and transmission are performed simultaneously, resulting in higher parallelism and lower hardware storage requirement; Finally, the efficient data mapping strategy is proposed for better scalability of the entire system. The experimental results show that our proposed 3D array architecture can effectively improve the overall computing performance of the system.

**Keywords:** 3D array · Acceleration · Convolutional neural network

## 1 Introduction

In recent years, with the continuous development of artificial intelligence and deep learning technology, convolutional neural network (CNN) has received great attention and extensive research, because of its excellent performance in wide range applications such as computer vision, image recognition and classification. However, due to higher precision requirements in complicated application scenarios, the CNN-layer has gradually deepened, and thus the network structure has become more and more complex [1–3]. Correspondingly, hardware implementation of CNN becomes power and area consuming. As a result, it is desired to design CNN hardware which can

© Springer Nature Singapore Pte Ltd. 2022
F. Sun et al. (Eds.): ICCSIP 2021, CCIS 1515, pp. 89–102, 2022.
https://doi.org/10.1007/978-981-16-9247-5_7

achieve high parallel computing capability and high efficiency of data transmission/storage.

The existing hardware platforms for implementing convolutional neural networks have their own advantages and disadvantages. The commonly used hardware platforms for performing CNN are central processing unit (CPU), application specific integrated circuit (ASIC), Graphic processing unit (GPU) and Field programming gate array (FPGA). Although the cost of traditional CPU is relatively low, it has disadvantages on low processing speed and high power consumption when performing deep learning algorithm. ASIC accelerates deep learning algorithms by customized hardware, but it has disadvantages including long design cycle, high cost, and low flexibility. GPU can realize the acceleration of deep learning algorithm through parallel computing, but its disadvantage is high power consumption. By contrast, FPGA can accelerate deep learning algorithm with reasonable power consumption. FPGA is reconfigurable chip and can achieve tradeoff between flexibility and efficiency. It is one of the mainstream hardware acceleration methods commonly used in deep learning algorithms. Therefore, we will study hardware acceleration method for convolutional neural network algorithms based on FPGAs.

In the past few years, a lot of hardware acceleration works have been proposed. The acceleration of convolution layer and full connection layer can be realized by mathematical transformation optimization method [4–8]. Parallel optimization [9] carries out parallel processing according to the dependence of data in convolutional neural network. Loop expansion [10] determines the utilization rate of data in on-chip cache by changing the way of data segmentation and mapping in on-chip cache. The cyclic block optimization [11] improves the computational communication ratio and reduces the access to off-chip memory, thus reducing the overall power consumption of the chip. Loop pipelining technology [12–14] uses deeper pipelining strategy to increase the speed of algorithm implementation. In recent years, to deal with the increasing amount data of large-scale deep CNN, more and more attention [15–17] has been paid to the algorithm acceleration based on FPGA cluster. Although these methods can perform algorithm acceleration, there exists several design difficulties on hardware such as efficient parallel computing and data storage/access scheme.

In this paper, we propose a novel 3D-CNN-array architecture to implement high-performance hardware acceleration platform. By partitioning data into different array nodes, the 3D-CNN-array can accelerate every single CNN convolution layer. In addition, it can calculate multi-layers convolution of CNN simultaneously via combining the overall array nodes of the architecture. Compared to conventional CNN acceleration method, the cost of the entire 3D-CNN-array architecture is lower. Moreover, the proposed architecture can achieve higher computing speed and larger memory size than convention method.

## 2  Background and Preliminaries

This section will introduce the architecture of multi-dimension array and the data partition strategy within parallel model.

## 2.1 Multi-dimensional Array Architecture

With the increase of convolution layers and the complexity of the network structure, the computing amount of the algorithm increase significantly. In order to improve the speed of reasoning and training, hardware platform with multi-dimensions architecture is used to accelerate the algorithm. The commonly used multi-dimensional topology is shown in Fig. 1.

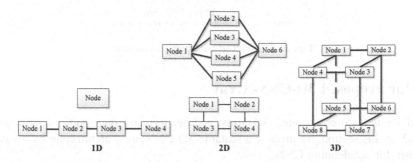

**Fig. 1.** Topology diagram of multi-dimensional FPGA.

At present, many researchers focus on convention architecture to accelerate deep learning algorithm. With the deepening of the network, higher performance is required for conventional hardware platform. The number of nodes in one-dimensional and two-dimensional architecture is limited by the transmission bandwidth between nodes. By contrast, the scalable three-dimensional (3D) array can broaden the transmission bandwidth. It can achieve higher performance by adding nodes in terms of specific algorithm requirements. When convolution is implemented by 3D array, the input data is partitioned and sent to array nodes. The input data can be broadcasted to multiple array nodes, which is determined by the specific data partition strategy and the algorithm.

## 2.2 Data Partition Strategy Within Parallel Model

Data parallelism and model parallelism are two common parallel models in distributed machine learning system [18]. Different devices, in data parallelism (Fig. 2a), have multiple copies of the same model. Different data is assigned to each device. The calculation results are obtained by combing the partial results of all devices. In model parallelism (Fig. 2b), different devices are responsible for different parts of the network model. For example, different network layers or different parameters in the same layer are assigned to different devices.

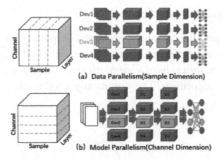

**Fig. 2.** Diagram of data partition strategy.

# 3  Our Proposed 3D-CNN-Array

Based on the aforementioned 3D array architecture and data partition strategy in Sect. 2, in this section, we propose a scalable 3D-CNN-array architecture by hardware platform for accelerating CNN.

Conventional hardware architecture, such as single node CNN architecture, can accelerate CNN with abundant resource such as high computing and storage capability. By contrast, the 3D-CNN-array architecture can accelerate CNN with resource-constrained devices. The 3D-CNN-array architecture is consisted of multiple nodes (Fig. 3). Data can only be transmitted between two adjacent nodes. The calculation results of last 3D-CNN-array layer can be sent to the first layer nodes. The end-to-end connection forms a ring-shaped 3D array with size of M * N * C. The number of M, N, and C in the 3D-CNN-array topology can be adjusted in terms of algorithm requirements, which enables the scalability of the architecture.

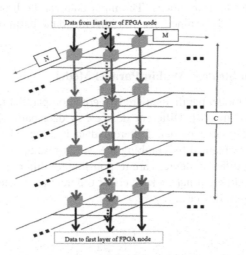

**Fig. 3.** Scalable 3D-CNN-array topology.

The CNN data is partitioned and mapped to each array node according to specific strategy. High-speed communication module between adjacent nodes is used to accelerate the data transmission. In this paper, the proposed architecture adopts the parallel model of data parallel and model parallel. Combined with data partition strategy, the scalable 3D-CNN-array architecture is fabricated.

## 3.1   Convolution on Single 3D-CNN-Array Node

A dedicated computing architecture is designed for each 3D-CNN-array node. It can effectively improve the efficiency of convolution by data reusage. The convolution computing architecture designed in this paper is based on the eyeriss [19–21] framework. The detail of this architecture is shown in Fig. 4.

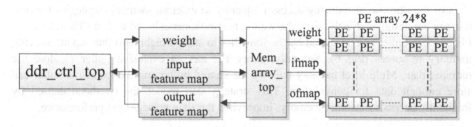

**Fig. 4.** System architecture of single node convolution calculation engine.

Convolution of single node involves DDR, memory, and PE array. The PE array is consisted of 192 PEs. In terms of characteristics of network and hardware resource, the size of the PE array can be adjusted to meet specific requirements. A single PE contains buffer module, DSP module, and control modules. The buffer module is employed to store data from CNN and temporary results. DSP module is mainly used for multiplication and addition of convolution operations. The control module is worked as a controller of PE.

The PE array is divided into 16 PE blocks to process convolution. Each PE block contains 3 * 3 PEs. In order to improve the data reusage, the input data such as weight, feature map, and partial sum are rearranged (Fig. 5). Both weight and feature map are broadcasted to every PE block. The same weight is sent to each PE in a row (Fig. 5a), while feature map is sent to PE along diagonal of PE block (Fig. 5b). The results of each PE will be sent to the adjacent PE for accumulation (Fig. 5c). Combing with 16 PE blocks, convolution is performed by a single 3D-CNN-array node. Similarly, the CNN is implemented by the cooperation of multi-nodes of 3D-CNN-array. The total memory size of all nodes in 3D-CNN-array is larger than conventional single high performance device. In addition, little volume data fed to each PE acquires limit hardware resource. Therefore, the design can meet the requirements of performance and storage by combing resource-constrained multi-nodes.

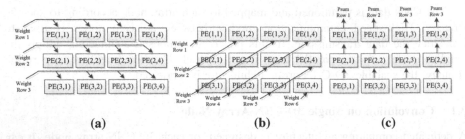

**Fig. 5.** The 3 * 4 PE array based on the eyeriss architecture for performing convolution operations (a) weights are broadcasted to PE in a row, (b) feature maps are sent to PE along the diagonal of PE block, (c) partial sum is transmitted to adjacent PE.

For the purpose of reducing access frequency to external memory, strategies for data reusage are designed. Firstly, since the weight is simultaneously fed to four PEs in a row of PE block, a buffer can be shared by the four PEs to store weight, and thus saving on-chip memory resources (Fig. 6). Secondly, every PE has an exclusive buffer to store the required data. Multi-level memory built by the shared buffer and the exclusive buffer can store enough data for convolution. This strategy can reduce the overhead caused by frequently access to external memory, improving the data reusage and performance.

| PE | Buf |   | PE | Buf |   | PE | Buf |   | PE | Buf |   |
|----|-----|---|----|-----|---|----|-----|---|----|-----|---|
| PE | Buf | B U F F | PE | Buf | B U F F | PE | Buf | B U F F | PE | Buf | B U F F |
| PE | Buf |   | PE | Buf |   | PE | Buf |   | PE | NM |   |
| PE | Buf |   | PE | Buf |   | PE | Buf |   | PE | NM |   |

**Fig. 6.** PE array with multi-level memory

According to the designed architecture, the partial results of each node should be transmitted to adjacent node. An optimization method is designed to achieve tradeoff between computing and data transmission. That is, computing and transmission can be performed simultaneously. During the process of convolution in a node, the partial results should be transmitted to adjacent node while the computing is ongoing. This method can share memory of a single node with other three nodes in a 3D-CNN-array layer, reducing the storage requirements for a single node.

## 3.2 Data Partition Strategy

In this paper, data partition strategy is based on the combined parallel model of data parallel and model parallel. Weight and feature map of each CNN layer is partitioned in terms of parallel model. In data parallel model, data partition can cause overhead on storage and transition, which decreases the performance of the entire system. Convolution of a single CNN layer will decrease the feature map size and increase the channel number. This will also lead to extra overhead on data transmission. In addition, the workload imbalance of will become severe. Therefore, the strategy that data parallel followed by model parallel is adopted in this work to improve the overall performance.

The transition of the partition strategy between data parallel and model parallel is aided by the high-speed communication module between nodes. The output of data parallel is stored in four 3D-CNN-array nodes which are numbered 1, 2, 3, and 4. The data in each node is divided into four blocks (a, b, c, d) along the channel direction. The transition process of partition strategy is shown in Fig. 7.

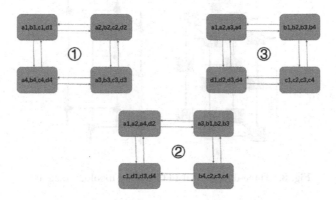

**Fig. 7.** Transformation process of data partition strategy

The transition is implemented with two steps. Firstly, partial data such as data block a2 and a4 is transmitted to adjacent node and reach an intermediate state 2. Secondly, the rest data such as data block a3 is transmitted. The output of the transition is sent to the corresponding nodes of adjacent 3D-CNN-array layer. This data partition strategy can perform convolution in four nodes simultaneously, which enables the scalability of the 3D-CNN-array architecture.

### 3.3 Contribution of the 3D-CNN-Array

The unique contribution of our proposed 3D-CNN-array architecture is summarized as follow. Firstly, the strategy of multilevel caches is employed to improve data reusage, and thus reducing the access frequency to external memory; Secondly, performance and throughout are balanced among 3D array nodes by using novel workload and weight partitioning schemes; Thirdly, computing and transmission are performed simultaneously, resulting in higher parallelism and lower hardware storage requirement; Finally, the efficient data mapping strategy is proposed for better scalability of the entire system. An appropriate hardware platform can be fabricated in terms of specific requirements of algorithms based on the scalability.

## 4  Hardware Implementation of Proposed 3D-CNN-Array

In the previous sections, the architecture of the proposed 3D-CNN-array has been presented in detail. In this section, we will introduce the hardware implementation of this architecture by FPGA.

Figure 8(a) is a neural network acceleration hardware platform based on FPGA. It is a three-dimensional structure with size of 2 * 2 * 3. According to the 3D-CNN-array, the results of the third layer nodes in FPGA array are sent to the first layer nodes for computing, thus forming a ring-shaped three-dimensional FPGA array.

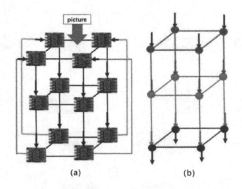

**Fig. 8.**  Three-dimensional FPGA array topology diagram

As shown in Fig. 8(b), the feature map is extracted from the data parallel and model parallel. The first and third layer of 3D-CNN-array architecture are connected via high-speed communication interfaces. The hardware system is consisted of 12 FPGA nodes and 24 high-speed optical fiber interfaces.

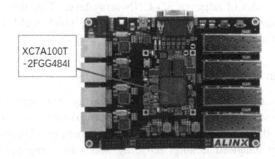

**Fig. 9.**  FPGA chip xc7a100t-2fgg484i on single node

In terms of the characteristics of the architecture, the desired FPGA should meet the following conditions: multiple high-speed communication interfaces, relatively low price, and essential resources. Finally, The XC7A100T of the Xilinx Aritix 7 series is chosen. The development board is shown in Fig. 9. Table 1 shows the main hardware resource of the XC7A100T-2FGG484I FPGA board.

**Table 1.** Parameters of XC7A100T-2FGG484I FPGA core board.

| GTPs | Block RAM | Distributed RAM | DSP | DDR3 | Differential crystal oscillator |
|---|---|---|---|---|---|
| 4 Ports | 4860 Kb | 1188 Kb | 240 | 512 MB * 2 | 125 MHz/200 MHz |

## 4.1 Implementation of Single Node Module

The improvement of ImageNet-based deep learning algorithms (or models) are mostly related to the model size. For one thing, the larger the model is, the higher network accuracy is. For another, larger networks may have better results. As the network becomes deeper and deeper, there are millions of parameters in a model. When floating-point is used, the required storage space is unaffordable for mobile hardware acceleration systems. In addition, the multiplication and addition of floating-point data can exhaust DSP resources. The calculation time consumed by floating-point computing is bottleneck for hardware acceleration. Therefore, to address this problem, the given CNN algorithm is transformed from floating-point 32 bits to 8 bits width. It mainly transforms the feature map, weights, and bias of pre-trained network model of the convolutional layer. The transform process involves mathematical statistics and mathematical operations, which do not need to retrain the transformed results. The 8-bit integer data is mapped to the original 32-bit data with little accuracy loss. The accuracy achieved by the transformed data can reach 95%.This method can achieve higher parallelism with limited DSP resource.

The implementation of single node is divided into several modules. It includes system control module, global cache module, DDR control module and PE array module. The system control module is the overall control of the single node. Its functions include fetching instruction set and parsing instruction set. The global buffer module is used to pre-store the input arrangement data and convolutional layer operation results, in which the communication module is also included. The DDR control module functions as the controller of DDR. The PE array module is of great importance in our design. It is consisted of weight buffer module, input buffer module, PE operation control module, PE multiplication and addition module, partial sum accumulation module, PE configuration module. It is used to arrange and control feature map, weight, bias, and partial sum. In addition, it is used to update input parameters of the convolution operation.

## 4.2 High Speed Communication Module Between Nodes

Considering the high-speed data transmission between nodes, GTP (Gigabit transceiver) high-speed communication interface supported by atrix-7 series FPGA is adopted. This interface is commonly used for data transmission of serial interface, and the maximum speed can reach 6.6 Gb/s. High speed transceivers support a variety of standard protocols. Here, Aurora, an open and free link layer protocol provided by Xilinx company, is used for point-to-point serial data transmission.

Due to the bit width of the internal interface of the protocol is 32 bits while the transmitted data is 8 bits, it is needed to combine 8 bits into 32 bits. If the data length is not integer times of four, it should be supplemented to an integer time of four before conversion. When the data transmission is received, the 32-bit data should be converted to 8-bit. According to the valid signal of the data, data integrity and accuracy can be ensured. The block diagram of the full-duplex communication diagram structure is shown in Fig. 10.

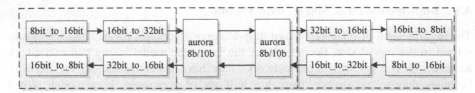

**Fig. 10.** Diagram of full-duplex high-speed communication

Communication transmission includes three modules: sending module, Aurora module and receiving module. The sending module includes a conversion module and a sending sub-module. The conversion module is used to convert 8-bit data to 32-bit. The sending sub-module is responsible for sending the data to the Aurora module. The receiving module includes a receiving sub-module and a reverse conversion module. The receiving sub-module is mainly used to buffer the data from Aurora module, and the reverse conversion module converts the data into a suitable bit width and sends it back to the internal buffer.

## 5  Experimental Results

To evaluate the performance of the proposed 3D-CNN-arry architecture, Tiny-YOLO convolution neutral network is selected for experiment. The Tiny-YOLO network is a simplified version of the YOLO network. It has 9 convolutional layers. The convolution kernels size of the first eight layers is 3 * 3, while the last layer of convolution kernels is 1 * 1. The detection principle of Tiny-YOLO is the same as YOLO, and its network structure is shown in Fig. 11. The size of the input image is 416 * 416, and the output of the last convolution layer consists of 125 feature images in which each image size is 13 * 13.

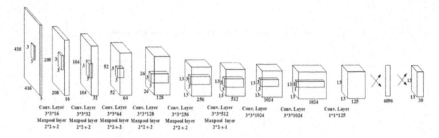

**Fig. 11.** The structure of Tiny-YOLO network.

The software Modelsim and Vivado are used to evaluate the performance of the single-layer Tiny-YOLO network with the system clock of 200 MHz. In the experiment, multiple FPGAs function as the nodes of the distributed system to accelerate network. Each FPGA has 240 DSPs for multiplication and addition operation. The size of PE array is a 24 * 8, the width of input and output data is 8 bits.

Table 2 shows the PE utilization used by each single Tiny-YOLO layer. The input channel number of first layer is 3, while it is 4 when data arrangement is completed. The PE utilization during operation is 75%. The convolution core size of the last layer is 1 * 1. Since only the first row of the PE array is used, the PE utilization by the last layer is 33.3% while the rest layers are 100%.

**Table 2.** Utilization ratio of PE array for each layer operation in Tiny-YOLO network.

| Tiny-YOLO | Conv 1 | Conv 2 | Conv 3 | Conv 4 | Conv 5 | Conv 6 | Conv 7 | Conv 8 | Conv 9 |
|---|---|---|---|---|---|---|---|---|---|
| Utilization rate | 75% | 100% | 100% | 100% | 100% | 100% | 100% | 100% | 33.3% |

Figure 12 shows the calculation time of the Tiny-YOLO network in a single FPGA node and a 2 * 2 FPGA array. Calculation time refers to the time that from input to convolution operation in a single FPGA, and the time for relu and max pooling. According to the data statistics in Fig. 12, the time consumed by 2 * 2 FPGA array to process single convolution layer is nearly 4 times as long as single FPGA. This is caused by boundary partition and padding. Therefore, based on these experimental results, it can be observed that the proposed 3D-CNN-array architecture can effectively improve system performance by combing multi-nodes with limited hardware resources.

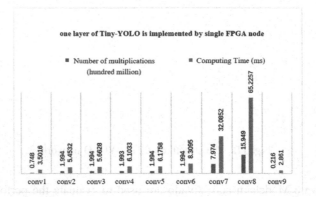

**(a)** Statistics of computing time and multiplication number of each layer of Tiny-YOLO obtained by only single FPGA node

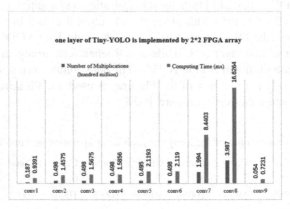

**(b)** Statistics of computing time and multiplication number of each layer of Tiny-YOLO obtained by FPGA array

**Fig. 12.** Statistics on the computational complexity and computing time that map the network to a single FPGA node and FPGA array.

Since FPGA based implementation of 3D-CNN-array architecture is ongoing, convolution cannot be performed on entire 3D FPGA array. However, simulation is implemented on CPU to perform convolution. Table 3 shows the consumed time on single CNN layer by 2D-CNN-array and 3D-CNN-array, respectively.

**Table 3.** Comparison of consumed time on single layer of Tiny-YOLO (unit: ms).

| Tiny-YOLO | Conv 1 | Conv 2 | Conv 3 | Conv 4 | Conv 5 | Conv 6 | Conv 7 | Conv 8 | Conv 9 |
|---|---|---|---|---|---|---|---|---|---|
| 2D array | 0.9391 | 1.4575 | 1.5675 | 1.5856 | 2.1193 | 2.119 | 8.4403 | 16.6264 | 0.7231 |
| 3D array | 0.7890 | 1.1018 | 0.9839 | 0.9070 | 2.281 | 1.7448 | 4.8900 | 7.6175 | 0.3678 |

Aa shown in Table 3, the time consumed by 3D-CNN-array is not in proportion to 2D-CNN-array on single layer. The reason may be that 3D array consumes less time on computing while more time is paid on data transmission.

# 6 Future Work

Due to the heavy workload of implementing the entire 3D-CNN array, only part of architecture is implemented (2 * 2 array is completed) at present, and the overall performance evaluation of 3D architecture will be implemented in the future work. Based on the simulation results on CPU, we will continue our work to complete the 3D array and analyze the actual performance.

# 7 Conclusion

In this paper, the novel 3D-CNN-array architecture is proposed and is analyzed. Moreover, the efficient parallel operation mode and the workload balance strategy of inter-/intra-node operation and transmission are discussed. The feasibility of the proposed architecture is verified by a popular CNN model Tiny-YOLO. The experimental results show that the parallelism of PE array of proposed 3D CNN array architecture is improved by 4 times, as compared to conventional single-node CNN architecture. The computational efficiency of FPGA array for single-layer network is nearly 4 times higher than that of a single FPGA. Simulation of 3D array is performed on CPU, and the performance is compared and analyzed. The high data reusage reduces the access frequency of external memory and speeds up the single node computing, which also reduces the overall power consumption of the system.

**Acknowledgement.** This work was supported by the Hundred Talents Program of Chinese Academy of Sciences under grant No. Y9BEJ11001. This research was primarily conducted at Suzhou Institute of Nano-Tech and Nano-Bionics (SINANO).

# References

1. Alex K., Ilya S., Geoffrey E.: ImageNet classification with deep convolutional neural networks. In: International Conference on Neural Information Processing Systems, vol. 25 (2012)
2. Karen, S., Andrew, Z.: Very deep convolutional networks for large-scale image recognition. Comput. Sci. **1409**, 1–14 (2014)
3. Kaiming, H., Xiangyu, Z., Shaoqing, R., Jian, S.: Deep residual learning for image recognition. In: Proceedings of the IEEE Conference on Computer Vision and Pattern Recognition CVPR 2016, pp. 770–778 (2016)
4. Adrian, M., Caulfield, E.S., Chung, A.P.: A cloud scale acceleration architecture. In: 49th Annual IEEE/ACM International Symposium on Microarchitecture (MICRO), p. 1. IEEE Computer Society (2017)

5. Jeremy, B., SungYe, K., Jeff, A.: clCaffe: OpenCL accelerated Caffe for convolutional neural networks. In: IEEE International Parallel and Distributed Processing Symposium Workshops (IPDPSW). IEEE (2016)
6. Jialiang, Z., Jing, L.: Improving the performance of OpenCL based FPGA accelerator for convolutional neural network. In: The ACM/SIGDA International Symposium (2017)
7. Chen, Z., Zhenman, F., Peichen, P.: Caffeine: towards uniformed representation and acceleration for deep convolutional neural networks. In: IEEE/ACM International Conference on Computer aided Design (2017)
8. Liqiang, L., Yun, L., Qingcheng, X.: Evaluating fast algorithms for convolutional neural networks on FPGAs. In: IEEE 25th Annual International Symposium on Field Programmable Custom Computing Machines (FCCM) (2017)
9. Lili, Z.: Research on the Acceleration of Tiny-yolo Convolution Neural Network Based on HLS. Chongqing University (2017)
10. Yufei, M., Yu, C., Sarma, V., Jae, S.: Optimizing loop operation and data ow in FPGA acceleration of deep convolutional neural networks. In: Proceedings of the ACM/SIGDA International Symposium on Field Programmable Gate Arrays FPGA 2017, pp 45–54 (2017)
11. Chen, Z., Peng, L., Guangyu, S., Yijin, G., Bingjun, X., Jason, C.: Optimizing FPGA based accelerator design for deep convolutional neural networks. In: Proceedings of the ACM/SIGDA International Symposium on Field Programmable Gate Arrays FPGA 2015, pp. 161–170 (2015)
12. Marimuthu, S., Jawahar, N., Ponnambalam, S.: Threshold accepting and ant-colony optimization algorithms for scheduling m-machine flow shops with lot streaming. J. Mater. Process. Technol. 209(2), 1026–1041 (2009)
13. YunChia, L., Mfatih, T., Quan, K.: A discrete particle swarm optimization algorithm for the no wait flowshop scheduling problem. Comput. Oper. Res. 35(9), 2807–2839 (2008)
14. Nicholas, G., Chelliah, S.: A survey of machine scheduling problems with blocking and no wait in process. Oper. Res. 44(3), 510–525 (1996)
15. Charles, E., Ekkehard, W.: GANGLION a fast field programmable gate array implementation of a connectionist classifier. IEEE J. Solid-State Circuits 27(3), 288–299 (1992)
16. Jocelyn, C., Steven, P., Francois, R., Boyer, P.Y.: An FPGA based processor for image processing and neural networks. In: Microneuro, p. 330. IEEE (1996)
17. Clement, F., Berin, M., Benoit, C.: NeuFlow: a runtime reconfigurable dataflow processor for vision. In: Computer Vision and Pattern Recognition Workshops (2011)
18. Geng, T., Wang, T., Li, A., Jin, X., Herbordt, M.: FPDeep: scalable acceleration of CNN training on deeply-pipelined FPGA clusters. Trans. Comput. 14(8), 1143–1158 (2020)
19. Motamedi, M., Gysel, P., Akella, V., Ghiasi, S.: Design space exploration of FPGA based deep convolutional neural networks. In: Proceedings of the Asia and South Pacific Design Automation Conference ASPDAC, pp. 575–580 (2016)
20. Jiang, L.I., Kubo, H., Yuichi, O., Satoru, Y.: A Multidimensional Configurable Processor Array Vocalise. Kyushu Institute of Technology (2014)
21. Chen, Y.H., Krishna, T., Emer, J.S., Eyeriss, S.V.: An Energy efficient reconfigurable accelerator for deep convolutional neural networks. IEEE J. Solid State Circuit 52, 127–138 (2016)

# Few-Shot Learning Based on Convolutional Denoising Auto-encoder Relational Network

Xinyu Xiang[1], Ping Zhang[1], Qiang Yuan[2], Renping Li[2],
Runqiao Hu[3], and Ke Li[3(✉)]

[1] State Grid Zhejiang Electric Power Co., Ltd., Hangzhou Power Supply
Company, Hangzhou 310000, China
[2] Hangzhou Xuntong Software Co., Ltd., Hangzhou 310000, China
[3] School of Aeronautic Science and Engineering, Beihang University,
Beijing 100191, China
like@buaa.edu.cn

**Abstract.** In this paper, we introduce the embedded learning idea in the learning model to design a few-shot learning algorithm based on convolution denoising auto-encoder relational network. The purpose is to solve the problem of high cost and small amount of data during the spacecraft's orbit operation. By building the end-to-end relationship network and learning relationships between each sample, we can diagnose the fault of the spacecraft thermal control system effectively with few samples. The experimental results show that the classification algorithm in this paper has a significant improvement in accuracy compared with traditional deep learning methods, and avoid overfitting problem effectively.

**Keywords:** Fault diagnosis · Few-short learning · CDAE

## 1 Introduction

During the spacecraft's in-orbit operation, the experimental simulation cannot fully simulate the actual operating conditions due to the complexity of the space environment. This leads to a small amount of data samples that rely on real experiments. Not only the data is costly, but also the data is very precious every time [1].

In order to maintain the safety, reliability and stability of spacecraft thermal control system, it is necessary to study the few-shot learning because of the huge economic resources of spacecraft's in-orbit operation. At present, the method of transfer learning is mainly used in few-shot learning [2], which transfers the prior knowledge from the source task to the few-short learning task. The few-shot learning model can be divided into four main categories: Multitask Learning, Embedding Learning, Learning with External Memory, Generative Modeling [3]. Among them, the embedding learning embeds each sample into a lower-dimensional space, so that similar samples are close in space, effectively distinguishing heterogeneous samples. Then, in the low-dimensional space, a hypothesis is reconstructed with only a small amount of samples for training. In this paper, we design a convolution denoising auto-encoder relational network based on embedding learning, effectively solve the problem of over-fitting and high-dimensional data noise for deep learning [4, 5].

© Springer Nature Singapore Pte Ltd. 2022
F. Sun et al. (Eds.): ICCSIP 2021, CCIS 1515, pp. 103–112, 2022.
https://doi.org/10.1007/978-981-16-9247-5_8

## 2   Network Structure

For the fault diagnosis with few examples, we build a convolution denoising auto-encoder relational network (CDAE), the network calculates sample's relationship scores for classification to meet the needs of identifying fault data with few samples.

This method can learn the metric relationship between different sample distributions, through the relationship network after training, query the relationship of the new category samples without continuing training [6]. As shown in Fig. 1, the network is mainly divided into three parts: feature extraction network, convolution denoising auto-encoder, and few-shot fault query recognition. The feature extraction network uses convolutional layers to extract and transmit features of spacecraft's fault data; The second part is to construct the convolution denoising auto-encoder relational network through the extracted features; The third part is to send samples into the relational network diagram, and finally get the classification of fault data by querying the relational score.

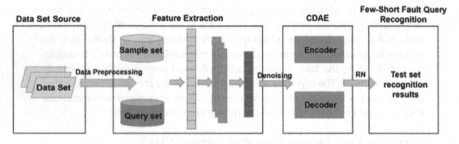

**Fig. 1.**  Convolutional denoising auto-encoder relational network.

### 2.1   Feature Extraction Network

The feature extraction network [7] adopts a sequential stacked convolutional neural network structure, convolutional layers and pooling layers after the activation function are stacked in sequence to form a sequential stacked structure network. Since the signals of the spacecraft thermal control system data set and the spacecraft power supply system data set are all time-series signals, the 1-D convolutional neural network is used. The feature extraction network structure is shown in Fig. 2.

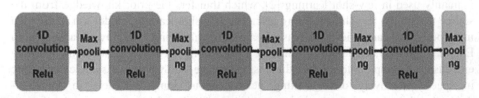

**Fig. 2.**  Structure of feature extraction network.

In order to obtain a suitable receptive field, the feature extraction network sets the size of the convolution kernel to 3 to ensure the convolution is reduced when the same receptive field is reached, thereby reducing the required parameters and the amount of calculation. The pooling part selects the max-pooling layer to achieve translational invariance, no matter where the target object is in the signal, it will not affect the recognition of the object, which improves the prediction ability of the model's recognition and detection.

## 2.2  Convolution Denoising Auto-encoder Relational Network

The convolutional denoising auto-encoder uses the unsupervised learning method of the traditional autoencoder [8]. We use the convolutional layer to replace the fully connected layer, combine with operations such as pooling to downsample the input features to achieve dimensionality reduction feature extraction, and finally implement a deep neural network through stacking [9, 10]. The convolutional layer can reduce the complexity of the network by the special structure of local weight sharing and make the layout closer to the actual biological neural network, especially the feature that the data of the multi-dimensional input vector can be directly input to the network, which avoids the feature extraction and classification process the complexity of data reconstruction in medium.

The convolutional denoising auto-encoder relational network is mainly divided into four parts: the denoising layer, the encoder, the decoder and the prediction network, as shown in Fig. 3. The input time- series signals are learned by the encoder's 1-D convolutional network, and the 1-D data structure features are reconstructed by the decoder's 1-D transposed convolution, and finally the input information of the reconstructed encoder is generated.

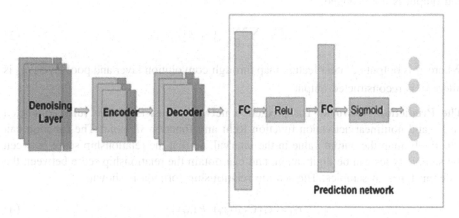

**Fig. 3.** Structure of convolutional denoising auto-encoder relational network.

**The Denoising Layer**

$$x = x_{original} + p(noise) \tag{1}$$

Where $x_{original}$ is the original sample input; $p(noise)$ is the noise introduced. It is used to create some "corrupted" input data, strengthen the robustness of the model, and make the features learned by the neural network be really useful. We can encode and decode the "corrupted" original data, and then restore it to the real original data. This method effectively enhances the generalization ability of the model, prevents the over-fitting problem, and makes the encoder more robust.

**Encoder.**

$$x_j^l = f\left(\sum\nolimits_{i \in M_j} x_i^{l-1} * k_{ij}^l + b_j^l\right) \tag{2}$$

Where $M_j$ is the collection of input data features; $x_j^l$ is feature of the $l$ convolutional layer, the former layer outputs feature sets for convolution summation and bias operations; $x_i^{l-1}$ is the output of the $i$ channel of the $l - 1$ layer of the convolution layer; $k_{ij}^l$ is convolution kernel matrix. The convolution kernel of each input feature set is different, and each convolution feature map corresponds to a bias $b_j^l$; $f$ is activation function, The activation function is the excitation layer, which maps the output of the convolutional layer nonlinearly.

**Decoder.** The decoder uses transposed convolution, which is also called deconvolution, it essentially changes the transposed convolution kernel to the transposition of the ordinary convolution kernel, and the element connection relationship between the input and output is not changed.

$$x_c^{i'} = \sum\nolimits_{k=1}^{K_1} z_k^i \oplus f_{k,c} \tag{3}$$

Where $z_k^i$ is output of latent feature map through convolution layer and pool layer; $f_{k,c}$ is filter; $x_c^{i'}$ is reconstructed output.

**The Prediction Network.** The prediction network consists of two fully connected layers and nonlinear activation function Relu and function *sigmoid*. The function can effectively map the output value in the interval, so that the relationship score between the sample types can be digitization, and can obtain the relationship score between the different types of samples. The scoring relationship formula is shown:

$$r_{i,j} = G\big(C\big(F(x_i), F(x_j)\big)\big) \tag{4}$$

Where $x_i$ and $x_j$ are two different sample data; $F(\cdot)$ is feature extraction network; $C(\cdot)$ is concat function between feature maps; $G(\cdot)$ is convolutional denoising auto-encoder relational network, the relationship score between samples can be finally obtained by it.

The convolutional denoising auto-encoder relational network's loss function is composed of the one-hot encoder mean square error and the divergence loss. Formula (5) is the mean square error of one-hot encoder, and formula (7) is the divergence loss.

$$L_{MSE} = \frac{1}{n}\sum\nolimits_{i=1}^{n}(y_i - \widehat{y}_i)^2 \tag{5}$$

Where $n$ is the number of samples, $y_i$ is the true one-hot encoder of the sample, $\widehat{y}_i$ is the one-hot encoder for predictive categories.

$$D_{kl}(p\|q) = \sum\nolimits_{i=1}^{n} p(x_i)\log\left(\frac{p(x_i)}{q(x_i)}\right) \tag{6}$$

$$D_{js}(p\|q) = \frac{D_{kl}(p\|\frac{p+q}{2})}{2} + \frac{D_{kl}(q\|\frac{p+q}{2})}{2}$$
$$= \frac{1}{2}\sum_{i=1}^{n}p(x_i)\log(\frac{2p(x_i)}{p(x_i) + q(x_i)}) + \frac{1}{2}\sum_{i=1}^{n}q(x_i)\log(\frac{2q(x_i)}{p(x_i) + q(x_i)}) \tag{7}$$

Where $p(x_i)$ is the probability distribution of the sample set; $q(x_i)$ is the probability distribution of query sets.

## 2.3   Network Model Framework

The convolutional denoising auto-encoder relational network model framework is shown in Fig. 4, the feature extractor in the framework is composed of 1-D convolutional layer (CN), batch normalization layer (BN) and max-pooling layer (P). The sample features obtained by the sample set through the feature extractor and the query features obtained by the query set are sent to the splicing function, and the query features are spliced at the same time. In Fig. 4, the orange arrow represents the data source query set, the blue arrow represents the data from the sample set, and the black arrow represents the data from the sample set and the query set. The convolutional denoising auto-encoder is mainly divided into droupout layer, encoder layer and decoder layer. Encoder is composed of 1-D convolutional layer (CN), batch normalization layer (BN) and max-pooling layer (P), the output of each layer is 31, 8, 2. Decoder is composed of 1-D transposed convolutional (TCN), the output of each layer is 5, 11, 23.

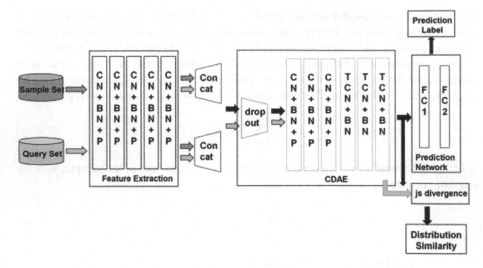

**Fig. 4.** Model framework of convolutional denoising auto-encoder relational network.

## 3 Experiment

### 3.1 Experiment Data

The data used for less sample fault detection is the digital signal of the spacecraft thermal control system.

In the process of spacecraft in-orbit test, the equipment operation in each period of the spacecraft thermal control system is recorded by real-time acquisition of sensors. Due to the complexity of the original data, it is necessary to preprocess the data, that is to clean up, divide and reduce the noise. Finally we can get 14 kinds of fault data signals, a total of 588 fault samples. Each data is time-series data with a length of 1000.

In the 588 sample data, 80% of each fault type was selected as the training set, and the remaining 20% data was used as the test set. During each iterative training, the sample set and the query set are formed by randomly selecting $c$ kinds of faults from the training set. The sample set is the $k$ labeled sample from each fault $S = \{(x_i, y_i)\}_{i=1}^{k*c}$, the query set comes from the remaining small part of the training set except the sample set $Q = \{(x_j, y_j)\}_{j=1}^{n}$.

### 3.2 Setting of Training Hyperparameters

Using *Adam* optimizer [11] in the training of few-shot classification model, it can deal with noise samples better and have natural annealing effect, and can deal with sparse gradient so the calculation is efficient and convenient. The initial learning rate is set to 0.001, the hyperparameter $\beta_1$ of the *Adam* optimizer is set to 0.9, the hyperparameter $\beta_2$ is set to 0.999, and the weight attenuation is set to 0.0001. *Adam* optimizer binds fixed-step attenuation learning rate, *step_size* is 1000 and *gamma* attenuation parameter is set to 0.5. In order to make the model learning effect better, we carry out a total of 30000 rounds of training, and the loss function tends to converge at this time. The test set is trained in 100 rounds per 1000 rounds of training set. The training hyperparameters involved in the model are shown in Table 1.

**Table.1.** Hyper-parameters of the convolutional denoising auto-encoder relational network.

| Hyperparameters | Value |
|---|---|
| Learning rate $lr$ | 0.001 |
| $\beta_1$ | 0.9 |
| $\beta_2$ | 0.999 |
| $Step\_size$ | 1000 |
| $Gamma$ | 0.5 |
| Training set $epoch$ | 30000 |
| Test set $epoch$ | 100 |
| Dropout probability | 0.2 |

## 4   Experiment Result

In the experiment training, we carry out four kinds of small sample data identification tests.

(1) Randomly select $c = 5$ fault types in the 14 types of faults, $k = 1$ labeled sample in sample set and $n = 19$ samples in query set.

(2) Randomly select $c = 5$ fault types in the 14 types of faults, $k = 5$ labeled sample in sample set and $n = 15$ samples in query set.

(3) Randomly select $c = 10$ fault types in the 14 types of faults, $k = 1$ labeled sample in sample set and $n = 9$ samples in query set.

(4) Randomly select $c = 10$ fault types in the 14 types of faults, $k = 5$ labeled sample in sample set and $n = 5$ samples in query set.

In order to measure the classification and recognition ability of convolutional denoising auto-encoder model, we compare the above four experiments with some traditional methods, like MANN [12], MN [13, 14], as a contrast method to evaluate the convolutional denoising auto-encoder relational network (CDAE-RN) algorithm. The results are shown in Table 2.

**Table.2.** Experiment results of the few-short learning algorithm about accuracy.

| Method | $c = 5$-accuracy | | $c = 10$-accuracy | |
|---|---|---|---|---|
| | $k = 1$ | $k = 5$ | $k = 1$ | $k = 5$ |
| MANN | 84.20% | 86.30% | 80.76% | 85.70% |
| MN | 87.53% | 89.86% | 84.35% | 87.42% |
| **CDAE-RN** | **91.72%** | **92.17%** | **87.44%** | **89.10%** |

Through the comparison of the above four experimental results, we can see that when the number of categories is 5, the accuracy of data classification is obviously higher than that of 10 categories, that means the fewer categories of small sample data sets, the higher accuracy can be learned; When under the same number of categories, the accuracy rate of the labeled sample number of 5 is significantly higher than the experimental accuracy rate of the labeled sample number 1.

Its recognition performance is better, and its performance in recognizing fewer sample types is more stable. When under the same number of categories, the accuracy rate of the labeled sample number of 5 is significantly higher than the experimental accuracy rate of the labeled sample number 1. Its recognition performance is better, and its performance in recognizing fewer sample types is more stable.

MANN and MN method have only 86.30% and 89.86% accuracy in the best case, because the few sample features learned by MANN depend very much on the characteristics of the sample itself, which leads to the learning of more unique features of fewer samples than associated common features. Although MN introduces attention mechanism on the basis of the original memory mechanism, the experimental effect is not ideal. Based on simplifying the network framework, the convolutional denoising auto-encoder relational network algorithm in this paper adopts the method of constructing sample relationship score, which significantly improves the accuracy of less sample recognition and classification, and its best recognition and classification can reach 92.17%.

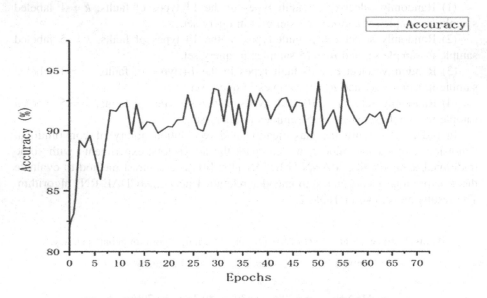

**Fig.6.** Diagnosis accuracy rate of spacecraft few-short fault data.

The accuracy of the less sample fault data for the spacecraft thermal control system is shown in Fig. 6, which is the accuracy result of experiment (2).

During the training period, the test set is tested for 500 epochs, and the accuracy of test recognition is obtained. By comparing these samples with the relational module to determine whether they come from the matching category, it is found that the test results are about 25 epochs, the accuracy of the test set is basically stable. The average accuracy can reach 92.17%. The relational atlas learns label prediction recognition and depth nonlinear js divergence measures for comparing query items and sample items. By periodic end-to-end training network, label discrimination and divergence measures are adjusted to achieve effective small learning. This method is more efficient than the traditional methods and can produce the best results.

## 5 Conclusion

In this paper, we propose a few-shot learning algorithm for the convolutional denoising auto-encoder relational network to solve the problem of over-fitting and difficult model training in spacecraft thermal control signals under traditional fault diagnosis methods due to the small number of samples.

Feature extraction uses the 1-D convolution model to extract and transmit features of spacecraft fault data. The convolutional denoising auto-encoder constructs the relational network by extracting the features, then sends the query samples into the relational network diagram, and finally obtains the discrimination of the fault data category by querying the relational score. Compared with traditional methods, the algorithm realizes high-resolution performance more quickly and effectively, and avoids the problem of over-fitting. The convolutional denoising auto-encoder relational network model is of great significance to solve the problem of constructing small sample data classification model.

**Acknowledgements.** This work are supported by the Chinese National Natural Science Foundation (No. 61773039), the Aeronautical Science Foundation of China (No. 2017ZDXX1043), and Aeronautical Science Foundation of China (No. 2018XXX).

## References

1. Johnson, S.B.: Introduction to system health engineering and management in aerospace. In: Proceedings of the First Integrated Systems Health Engineering and Management Forum (2005)
2. Pan, S.J., Yang, Q.: A survey on transfer learning. IEEE Trans. Knowl. Data Eng. **22**(10), 1345–1359 (2010)
3. Wang, Y., Yao, Q., Kwok, J.T., Ni, L.M.: Generalizing from a few examples: a survey on few-shot learning. ACM Comput. Surv. **1**, 34 (2020)
4. Zhou, J.T., Pan, S.J., Tsang, I.W.: A deep learning framework for hybrid heterogeneous transfer learning. Artif. Intell. **275**(OCT), 310–328 (2019)
5. Wen, L., Gao, L., Li, X.: A new deep transfer learning based on sparse auto-encoder for fault diagnosis. IEEE Trans. Syst. Man Cybern. Syst. **49**(1), 136–144 (2017)
6. Lei, H., Yang, Y.: CDAE: a cascade of denoising autoencoders for noise reduction in the clustering of single-particle Cryo-EM images. Front. Genet. **11**, 627746 (2021)

7. Wiatowski, T., Grohs, P., Blcskei, H.: Topology reduction in deep convolutional feature extraction networks. In: Society of Photo-Optical Instrumentation Engineers (SPIE) Conference Series (2017)
8. Wang, X., Ma, Y., Cheng, Y.: Domain adaptation network based on autoencoder. Chin. J. Electron. **27**(06), 1258–1264 (2018)
9. Ghifary, M., Kleijn, W.B., Zhang, M., Balduzzi, D., Li, W.: Deep reconstruction-classification networks for unsupervised domain adaptation. In: Leibe, B., Matas, J., Sebe, N., Welling, M. (eds.) ECCV 2016. LNCS, vol. 9908, pp. 597–613. Springer, Cham (2016). https://doi.org/10.1007/978-3-319-46493-0_36
10. Wang, Y., Zhou, P., Zhong, W., et al.: An optimization strategy based on hybrid algorithm of Adam and SGD. In: 2nd International Conference on Electronic Information Technology and Computer Engineering (2018)
11. Santoro, A., Bartunov, S., Botvinick, M., et al.: One-shot learning with memory-augmented neural networks. arXiv (2016)
12. Sewak, M., Sahay, S.K., Rathore, H.: An overview of deep-learning architectures of DNN & AE (ICIC-2018). In: 1st International Conference on Intelligent Computing (ICIC - 2018) (2018)
13. Vinyals, O., Blundell, C., Lillicrap, T., et al.: Matching networks for one shot learning. In: NeurIPS (2016)

# DICE: Dynamically Induced Cross Entropy for Robust Learning with Noisy Labels

Tianyu Liu[✉]

Institute for Artificial Intelligence, Tsinghua University (THUAI),
Beijing National Research Center for Information Science and Technology (BNRist),
State Key Lab on Intelligence Technology and Systems, Department of Computer
Science and Technology, Tsinghua University, Beijing, People's Republic of China
ty-liu19@mails.tsinghua.edu.cn

**Abstract.** Image classification has lead to the revolution of artificial intelligence in the past five years. However, image classification algorithms are significantly affected by the inherent variance in sensory input and noise in the labelled data in a real-world situation. Also, the class count of items in the real world is significantly larger than that of the typical experiment setup. How to speedily train/fine-tune a large scale model in giant label space with considerable noise is a recent interest of the machine learning community. This paper proposed a multi-stage training algorithm to fine-tune a pre-trained EfficientNet model on AliProducts large scale product classification dataset, which has a large label space (50030 classes) and severe label noise. Our method can generalize well on such a dataset while keeping the prior knowledge gained in the large-scale pretraining stage. With our novel Dynamically Induced Cross-Entropy(DICE) network loss and several other methods to tackle unbalanced datasets and improve model convergence, the model achieved 76.67% of Top-1 Accuracy and 85.42% of Top-5 accuracy, which are 3.63%/2.9% higher than symmetric cross-entropy and are significantly higher than the usual fine-tuning method with categorical cross-entropy loss(CCE).

**Keywords:** Robust loss · Noisy labels · Image classification

## 1 Introduction

Deep neural networks (DNNs) have achieved outstanding performance in recent years in open datasets such as ImageNet, CIFAR, and Cityscapes. However, the advancement relies on a large quantity of high-quality labeled data, which are expensive to annotate and hard to come by in real-world scenarios. Recent research [5] has also shown that more enormous datasets with noisier labels have better potential than cleaner, smaller datasets. Moreover, for larger dataset

This material is based upon work supported by TTAD-2021-03.

F. Sun et al. (Eds.): ICCSIP 2021, CCIS 1515, pp. 113–126, 2022.
https://doi.org/10.1007/978-981-16-9247-5_9

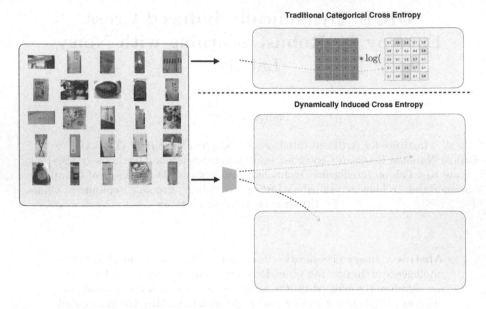

**Fig. 1.** Proposed dynamically induced Cross-Entropy.

such as JFT300M, its almost impossible to accurately label all 300 million label by hand, which would often result in 20% of noisy labels within [15]. Hence, dealing with label noise is essential when training bigger models and potentially providing us with a new paradigm in network training.

However, the current training routine does not adapt well to datasets with noisy labels, and there has been long-going research about label noise [1]. With the recent advancement in deep learning methods, label noise handling has gained more focus recently. However, existing methods either require hand-labeled *clean* dataset [20], or requires prior knowledge about the noise within [13], Hindering their real-world usability.

In general, real-world applications require us to take a pre-trained model trained on large open-source datasets and fine-tune them on explicit datasets. Typically, the old classification activation layer and the network's last layer are removed, and new classification heads are constructed and trained with (soft-max) Categorical Cross-Entropy (CCE). This method brought us two problems. Firstly, the new classification head would have an enormous parameter count when facing large label space, making it hard to train on a limited dataset and potentially increase the labeling cost, therefore hindering real-world application. Secondly, past studies [5,13] have shown that using the standard CCE to train deep models leads to serious over-fitting on noisy labels and could result in poor robustness of trained models.

Intrigued by the above situation and the challenges brought up by new datasets, we proposed a *Dynamically Induced Cross-Entropy (DICE)* loss as shown in Fig. 1, which is an easy to use loss function that can leverage the ability of trained backbone network to achieve better performance when facing label noise. And a new multi-stage training framework that requires minimal change for the training routine. Experiments show that combining these two methods results in robustness that is on par with the state-of-the-art method. Different from the methods that involve parameter estimation [4, 23], we took a more direct approach, making the method more fitted for large label space, and reduced the complexity of model training.

Our contribution are as follows:

- We proposed a Dynamically Induced Cross-Entropy (DICE) loss for robust classification.
- A multi-stage training method is adopted, in combination with the DICE loss, the model achieved leading robustness compared with various robust losses.
- We proved that our robust classification method, combined with label smoothing and negative sampling, can achieve state-of-the-art performance in the AliProducts dataset with large label space.

## 2  Recent Works

This section will briefly review existing works relating to our task regarding how to train a deep model on a noisy dataset robustly and how to adapt a pre-trained model on large label space efficiently. Recent year has seen various approaches toward this challenge, which can be divided into three varieties. The first is to estimate the noise and use it to train the model, and the second types try to design a more advanced robust loss function to mitigate the influence of noise. The third type tries to tackle this problem by novel training routines and learning methods.

**Noise Rate Estimation.** Early works, including [12–14], aim to estimate the label transition matrixes and use them for the training of target models. Noise rate estimation itself is a challenging task, especially when the dataset has a considerable number of classes. The poor performance of the upstream task will hinder the performance of the downstream training process[7, 19].

**Robust Loss Functions.** Recently, there has been extensive research about training losses that are robust to label noises. Early work shows that losses satisfying symmetric condition $l(z) + l(-z) = C$, where $C$ is a constant, are more robust to label noise (such as sigmoid and MAE) [5, 6]. However, recent work shows that these losses do not perform well on complicated datasets due to their limited convergence property and other optimization issues [24]. Giving rise to hybrid losses such as Generalized Cross-Entropy (GCE) [24], which is a combination of CCE and MAE regulated by a hyper-parameter $q$. And Symmetric Cross-Entropy [17] is a combination of CCE and Reverse Cross-Entropy (RCE). On the modification upon CCE, Partial Huberised Cross-Entropy (PHuber-CE) corrects CCE by gradient clipping [10]. Taylor Cross-Entropy (TCE) applies

Taylor Series to obtain the representation of CCE and regulate the training process by controlling the order of Taylor Series for CCE [3]. Above losses may be able to tackle the problem of label noise to some extent. They all require manual configuration of parameters according to noise situation and cannot exploit the potential of the trained network.

**Other Deep Learning Methods.** Some other approaches alter the procedure of training to tackle the problem of noisy labels [2,18,22]. More representative methods including the MetorNet [9] where the training of StudentNet is supervised with a sample weighting scheme. Co-teaching [8] on the other hand, trains two networks simultaneously and providing each other with the ability to discriminate noise. The DLDL [4] took the approach of estimating label ambiguity that achieved decent results, similar to that PENCIL [23] estimate the label distribution dynamically and achieved a better result. Some of these methods require a meticulously designed framework and training routine, making them slightly unfit for real-world deployment[21].

## 3    Methods

Previous research has shown that symmetric loss functions are robust to noisy labels. However, such an approach only leverages the loss function's ability and expects them to act in the means like a normalization method. The network, during training, gradually gains the ability to estimate noise and distinguish right and wrong labels. A unified loss throughout the whole training process could lead to overfitting in the early stage and hinder the end performance of the model.

In Sect. 3.1 we proposed Dynamically Induced Cross-Entropy to strike a dynamic balance between learning performance and learning robustness. In Sect. 3.2 we come up with a training method to better generate a weight for the loss function and fine-tune the model in noisy datasets without jeopardizing previously learned features. In Sect. 3.3, to minimize the impact of large label space and the problem of data imbalance, a negative sampling method inspired by that of NLP is used to reduce training cost and improve convergence speed. In Sect. 3.4, Label-smoothing is introduced to improve the robustness of the training process further.

### 3.1    Dynamically Induced Cross-Entropy

Traditional categorical cross-entropy is a different expression of KL-divergence. The KL-divergence(denoted as $KL(q||p)$, where $p$ and $q$ are two different distribution) can be expressed as:

$$KL(q||p) = H(q,p) - H(q), \tag{1}$$

where cross-entropy are denoted as $H(q,p)$. In typical classification practice, $H(q)$ is the entropy of given ground truth condition distribution $q = q(k|x)$, which is a constant for any given data distribution, therefore, are often omitted. Hence the cross-entropy loss takes the form of:

$$l_{ce} = -\sum_{k=1}^{K} q(k|\mathbf{x}) \log p(k|\mathbf{x}), \tag{2}$$

with the $p(k|\mathbf{x})$ as the probability of each label computed by the classifier. The overall dataset $\mathcal{D} = \{(\mathbf{x}, y)^{(i)}\}_{i=1}^{n}$ contains $K$ classes, $\mathbf{x}$ and $y$ are inputs and class labels respectively. The loss are constructed under the assumption of a single ground-truth label $y$, and $q(y|\mathbf{x}) = 1$ for correct classification($k = y$) and $q(y|\mathbf{x}) = 0$ for false classification($k \neq y$).

However, in the context of noisy labels, the distribution$q(k|\mathbf{x})$ does not subjectively represent the true class distribution. On the other hand, with the progression of training, the distribution $p(k|\mathbf{x})$ can gradually represent the true class distribution to some extent. To leverage the ability of $p(k|\mathbf{x})$, in addition to taken the $l_{ce}$ into account, we can also use the other direction of KL-divergence $KL(p\|q)$. Combining the two parts, the symmetric KL-divergence is:

$$SKL = KL(q\|p) + KL(p\|q). \tag{3}$$

and the Symmetric Cross-Entropy loss takes the form of:

$$l_{sce} = l_{ce} + l_{rce} \tag{4}$$

where:

$$l_{rce} = -\sum_{k=1}^{K} p(k|\mathbf{x}) \log q(k|\mathbf{x}). \tag{5}$$

It has been proven that the $l_{rce}$ are robust to label noise and $l_{ce}$ has better convergence property [5]. But previous symmetric loss [17] uses the same loss function throughout the training process, without leveraging the ability of the trained network.

In our practice, a weight factor $w_{ij}, i \in \{1, \cdots, K\}, j \in \{1, \cdots, |\mathbf{Q}_i|\}, \mathbf{Q}_i = \{(\mathbf{x}, y) \in \mathcal{D}|y = i\}$ for each data point $\mathbf{x}$ are calculated by previous network outputs, where $i$ is the class of given $\mathbf{x}$ , and $\mathbf{Q}_i$ is the set of data belonging to class $i$, with $j$ as ordering within the class. The proposed Dynamically Induced Cross-Entropy for sample $\mathbf{x}$ then takes the form of:

$$l_{dice} = \omega * l_{ce} + l_{rce} \tag{6}$$

The $\omega$ here act as a confidence parameter for $l_{ce}$, which are acquired at the end of each epoch by:

$$w_{ij} = \begin{cases} 1, & \text{if } p(i|x_j) > \sum_{m=i,n=1}^{n=|\mathbf{Q}_i|} p(m|x_n)/|\mathbf{Q}_i| \\ \frac{c}{t+c}, & \text{otherwise} \end{cases} \tag{7}$$

The loss of a given $\mathbf{x}$ will fall back to vanilla symmetric cross-entropy if the confidence values emitted by *softmax* layer are above the average of confidence value over each data $\mathbf{x}$ within class $i$. The value $t$ is the epoch count, and $c$ is a hyper-parameter set manually. With the progression of the training process, the $c/t + c$ part gradually approaches 0. Also, the condition serves as a precaution to prevent model collapse, since if the model is over-fitted to one data point, the average value will drop, the loss will then increase, forcing the network to predict as many positive instances within each class as possible.

Also, as the ground-truth conditional distribution $q(k|\mathbf{x})$ are now inside the logarithm of $l_{rce}$, which could cause $\log 0$ problem when calculating negative samples. To solve this and further improve robustness of training, the label smoothing technique is used, which is further described in Sect. 3.4.

## 3.2   Multi-stage Training Method

In order to fine-tune the pre-trained model on noisy datasets without jeopardizing previously learned knowledge, a multi-stage training method is adopted. The network is firstly all frozen except the last classification layer; after a period of training, the network is unfrozen block by block from back to front. Moreover, the learning rate is also reduced in the process to prevent gradient explosion.

---

**Algorithm 1:** Training process of proposed method

---

Reconstruct the network for the target domain;
Set trainable parameter according to trainable stage;
Set all $\omega_{ij}$ to 1;
**for** *Each epoch t* **do**
    **for** *Each batch* **do**
        Forward the network;
        Store each value $p(k|\mathbf{x})$;
        Back propagate with loss $l_{DICE}$;
    **end**
    **for** *Each class $i \in [1, k]$* **do**
        Calculate average value $\bar{p}_i$ over the class;
        **for** *Each item $j \in [1, |\mathbf{Q}_i|]$* **do**
            **if** $p(i|x_j) > \bar{p}_i$ **then**
                $\omega_{ij} = 1$;
            **else**
                $\omega_{ij} = c/t + c$;
            **end**
        **end**
    **end**
**end**

---

By doing so, the network is first adapted to the new dataset. While the network gradually gains the ability to tell the correct label from the wrong label, the loss function weights are being updated, and the network is also continuously refined during the training process.

The training process of our method are shown in Algorithm 1.

## 3.3 Negative Sampling

To classify each feature $h \in \mathbb{R}^m$ emitted by the backbone network into one of $K$ classes, a $O(m * K)$ size classification layer is needed. And the parameter count of this layer increases as the label size increases. Traditionally this will not be a problem, but as the label space reaches 50K in our case, each iteration of classification layer will take millions of FLOPs. In order to further reduce the sample size required for convergence and prevent the network from becoming too large and difficult to train, in the Word2Vec paper [11], the author adopted a negative sampling method. We took a similar approach to their negative sampling and made a little change for it to fit image classification task better.

In the process of training the network, each input of a sample means that the network weight must be adjusted so that the network can have better training results on this sample. Strengthen the correct part of its network, weaken the wrong part. When training a sample, we do not need to simultaneously update the weights of the remaining 50029 false negative samples in the 50030 part of the final fully connected layer. We only need to randomly sample them and update some of them. Which can significantly reduce the memory cost during training and speed up the training process.

In the case of batch training, the correct part of the batch is selected and the wrong sample randomly selected according to the category is attached for training. This method can not only reduce the parameters required in the training process, but also effectively adjust the sampling ratio. The weight of sample sampling can be determined by the following formula:

$$P(w_i) = \frac{f(w_i)^{0.75}}{\sum_{j=0}^{n} f(w_j)^{0.75}} \tag{8}$$

Among them, 0.75 is the experimentally determined hyperparameter, and f is the frequency of the sample and $n$ is number of classes.

## 3.4 Label-Smoothing

To tackle the log(0) problem in Sect. 3.1, and to further improve the convergence property of our model, label-smoothing is used to reduce the intra-class variance and increase the inter-class variance to prevent over-fitting.

Suppose that after a given picture, the model predicts that it belongs to category i with a score of $z_i$. After these scores are standardized by *softmax*, the probability $q_i$ of each category is obtained, and $q_i$ can be calculated as follows.

$$q_i = \frac{\exp(z_i)}{\sum_{j=1}^{K} \exp(z_j)} \tag{9}$$

When using cross-entropy as a loss function to minimize the distance between the true distribution and the model predicted distribution:

$$l(p,q) = - \sum_{i=1}^{K} p_i \log(q_i) = -z_y + \log(\sum_{i=1}^{K} \exp(z_i)) \qquad (10)$$

When the other part is small enough, the optimal solution $z$ approaches positive infinity. In other words, the loss function encourages the maximization of the difference between classes and may lead to severe over-fitting. When the dataset is too noisy to effectively maximize the difference between classes, the model is difficult to converge. The idea of label smoothing was first proposed in the training process of Inception-V2[16] and has been verified in many application scenarios. The idea is: when $i = y$, $q_i = 1 - \epsilon$ otherwise $q_i = \epsilon/(k-1)$, where K is the number of model categories, and $\epsilon$ is a small constant. When $\epsilon$ gradually becomes larger, the difference between classes becomes smaller. In this way, the tendency of the model to maximize the difference between classes can be effectively reduced, the convergence ability of the model under the noisy label can be enhanced, and the performance of the model can be improved eventually.

## 4    Experiments

### 4.1    Dataset

Ali-Products is a large-scale noisy product dataset, including 50030 categories of different products. Images are crawled from image search engine and online e-commerce sources using their produce SKU (Stock Keeping Unit) names. The dataset contains fine-grained labeled of different color, type, flavor, capacity and even batch of production of same kind of products. The similarity between categories making visually distinguishing them a really challenging task. The AliProducts dataset contains 2.5 million training images and 148K manually labeled validation set. Unlike other noisy datasets (e.g. Clothing 1M and Web-Vision), AliProducts contains massive fine-grained real-world noisy images that proposes the following challenges.

**Label Noise.** The left part of Fig. 1 are 25 image choosen from a same class, as we can see, there are severe labeling noise within them. By manually checking 20 random categories of 200 images, we estimated an average noise rate of about 37%, which are significantly higher than that of Clothing1M ($\tilde{2}$9%), and WebVision. Also unlike man-made noise (symmetric, paired, etc.) normally used in benchmarking, the innate similarity makes the training even harder.

**Limited Data Size.** Compared to other popular dataset, AliProduct has relatively limited data size. The ImageNet averages of over 700 images per categories, whilst the Aliproduct dataset averages 49 images per categories.

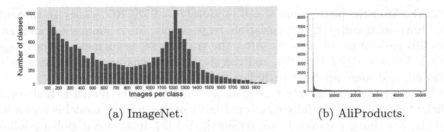

(a) ImageNet.                                    (b) AliProducts.

**Fig. 2.** Image count per category distribution of two datasets.

**Unbalanced Dataset.** Figure 2a shows the distribution of the number of images of each type of ImageNet, and Fig. 2b shows the distribution of the number of images of each type of product. It can be seen that the data set used this time has a severe long-tail effect. Among them, the categories with more than 100 images in each category account for only 8.9% of the dataset. More than half of the categories have less than 25 images, and 15% of the categories contain less than ten pictures. On the one hand, unbalanced data sets will make the model tend more on common categories. On the other hand, it will make it more challenging to train the model on a small sample class.

## 4.2   Experimental Setup

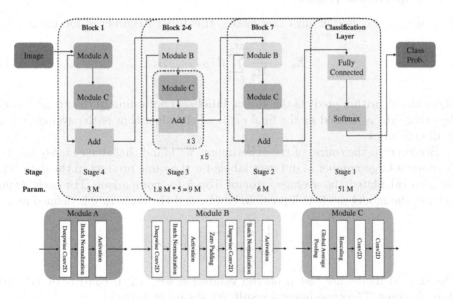

**Fig. 3.** Over all multi-stage experimental setup with network architecture.

Due to the limited amount of data, each picture in the training set is supplemented with data during the training process and then sent to the training network. After the pictures are scaled randomly by 95%–105%, they go through ±5% horizontal and vertical translation, respectively; 5% random shear and random flip are sent to the network. After the training set is augmented, the image is scaled to a scale of 224 * 224, and the transparent channel of some images is removed, and some products with damaged files are cleaned.

The overall model architecture is shown in Fig. 3. The model is built on a EfficientNet-B4, the last fully connected layer of the original model is removed, and the remaining parameters are retained. A 1024-dimensional global pooling layer are constructed and ReLU are used for activation. After that, a 50030-dimensional fully connected layer is constructed, eventually the random negative sampling Softmax, mentioned in Sect. 3.3, is used for activation.

The objective of the optimization is our DICE loss described in Sect. 3.1, and due to large-scale dataset, the $C$ is sat at 30. In our experiment, all multi-stage training consist of four stages, each stage are trained for 5 epochs. Stochastic Gradient Descent with momentum decay is used to maximize the model performance. The decay is set to $5e^{-3}$, the momentum is set to 0.9, the learning rate is set to 0.1 for the first stage, 0.03 for the second stage, 0.01 for the third stage, and 0.003 for the fourth stage.

The experiment is trained on a single *RTX-2080 Super* GPU, and each iteration takes 101 ms on average, and one epoch training is about 8 h. A total of 20 epochs in 4 stages took 4 days*card.

## 4.3   Experiment Result

Two metrics are used in our experiments, the Top-1 Accuracy is formulated as:

$$E_n = \frac{1}{M_n} \sum_{j=1}^{M_n} d\left(p\left(j\right), y_j\right), \tag{11}$$

where the algorithm predicts the unique label $p(j)$ according to the image $j$, and the error rate is defined as the final error of the algorithm is the average error of all categories.

However, in the course of the experiment, we found that due to noisy labels, there are a large number of different labels for the same product in the data set. We also calculated the average error of Top-5 for comparison. For each given picture, the model predicts 5 possible labels, and the error rate is defined as:

$$E_n = \frac{1}{M_n} \sum_{j=1}^{M_n} \sum_{i=1}^{5} d(p_i(j), y_{ij}) \tag{12}$$

The trained model are tested on the validation set, which consists of 170,000 clean pictures. The experimental result are shown in Table 1.

First, we observed that directly training with Categorical Cross-Entropy, MAE, could not yield satisfying results. The Cross-Entropy could not generalize well on noisy label space, and MAE/RCE can not handle complicated classification problems, coinciding with previous research statements.

The introduction of robust loss function dramatically increased the model accuracy, Our DICE loss achieved a Top-1 accuracy of 68.96% which are 1.73% above Symmetric Cross-Entropy (SCE). Proving the dynamically induced weight can effectively mitigate the instability caused by label noise. The addition of Multi-stage Training further improved our accuracy from 68.96% to 76.67%(+7.71%), widened the gap between SCE and DICE to 5.63%.

This experiment shows that the introduction of dynamically induced weight can improve the robustness on top of already robust symmetric cross-entropy, further improving the convergence and accuracy of the model.

**Table 1.** Ablation study and comparison between different setups.

| Backbone structure | Trainable Param. | Loss function | Multi-stage training | Top-1 Acc. | Top-5 Acc. |
|---|---|---|---|---|---|
| Inception V3 | 26M | Cross Entropy | | 34.19% | 47.27% |
| EfficientNet B4 | 51M | Cross Entropy | | 37.30% | 50.10% |
| EfficientNet B4 | 70M | MAE/RCE | | 37.84% | 51.82% |
| EfficientNet B4 | 70M | SCE | | 67.23% | 71.30% |
| EfficientNet B4 | 70M | DICE | | 68.96% | 72.82% |
| EfficientNet B4 | 70M | SCE | ✓ | 71.04% | 82.52% |
| EfficientNet B4 | 70M | DICE | ✓ | **76.67%** | **85.42%** |

Below are several visualized classification results. The leftmost image is the input 244 * 244 picture, and the right is Top-5 categories in confidence levels output by the level.

**Fig. 4.** Result of successfully recognized product.

As can be seen in Fig. 4, the model can successfully identify certain brand of beans in a bunch of similar products with a high degree of confidence.

124    T. Liu

**Fig. 5.** Example of how dataset noise could affect model performance.

Other work regarding noisy labels usually use synthetic noisy dataset with fixed noise rate for better evaluation. But Fig. 5 represents a label noise situation that would not exist in man-made noisy datasets. The input image contains multiple products, which is really common in online crawled dataset, which should be discussed further. For this instance, although, to the eye of human, it is obvious that the model prediction is correct, but two category may have other underlying differences causing a false classification.

**Fig. 6.** Our model successfully recognized similar products

As shown in Fig. 6, although the pictures of many health products are extremely similar, the model can identify a given product with a high degree of confidence (90.34%) based on the text and graphics of the product packaging.

## 5    Conclusion

This paper proposed a novel Dynamically Induced Cross-Entropy (DICE) loss by adding a weight factor, dynamically induced by the trained network, to discriminate noise in label space more accurately. Experiment shows that our loss function can address the under learning and over-fitting problem, which is common when training on noisy datasets simultaneously. Compared to other loss functions, our DICE loss can adapt during the training process and provide a better result when fine-tuning a pre-trained model. Compared to other tanning schemes, our solution has better simplicity making it easier to implement and deploy into real-world environments. Overall, we believe DICE is an attractive loss function for training robust deep structures against label noise, and proved that incorporating DICE loss with the multi-stage training scheme, is a promising framework to be used with other techniques for datasets with noisy labels.

# References

1. Angluin, D., Laird, P.: Learning from noisy examples. Mach. Learn. **2**(4), 343–370 (1988)
2. Berthon, A., Han, B., Niu, G., Liu, T., Sugiyama, M.: Confidence scores make instance-dependent label-noise learning possible. In: International Conference on Machine Learning, pp. 825–836. PMLR (2021)
3. Feng, L., Shu, S., Lin, Z., Lv, F., Li, L., An, B.: Can cross entropy loss be robust to label noise? In: IJCAI, pp. 2206–2212 (2020)
4. Gao, B.B., Xing, C., Xie, C.W., Wu, J., Geng, X.: Deep label distribution learning with label ambiguity. IEEE Trans. Image Process. **26**(6), 2825–2838 (2017)
5. Ghosh, A., Kumar, H., Sastry, P.: Robust loss functions under label noise for deep neural networks. In: Proceedings of the AAAI Conference on Artificial Intelligence, vol. 31 (2017)
6. Ghosh, A., Manwani, N., Sastry, P.: Making risk minimization tolerant to label noise. Neurocomputing **160**, 93–107 (2015)
7. Goldberger, J., Ben-Reuven, E.: Training deep neural-networks using a noise adaptation layer (2016)
8. Han, B., et al.: Co-teaching: robust training of deep neural networks with extremely noisy labels. arXiv preprint arXiv:1804.06872 (2018)
9. Jiang, L., Zhou, Z., Leung, T., Li, L.J., Fei-Fei, L.: MentorNet: learning data-driven curriculum for very deep neural networks on corrupted labels. In: International Conference on Machine Learning, pp. 2304–2313. PMLR (2018)
10. Menon, A.K., Rawat, A.S., Reddi, S.J., Kumar, S.: Can gradient clipping mitigate label noise? In: International Conference on Learning Representations (2019)
11. Mikolov, T., Chen, K., Corrado, G., Dean, J.: Efficient estimation of word representations in vector space. arXiv preprint arXiv:1301.3781 (2013)
12. Natarajan, N., Dhillon, I.S., Ravikumar, P.K., Tewari, A.: Learning with noisy labels. Adv. Neural. Inf. Process. Syst. **26**, 1196–1204 (2013)
13. Patrini, G., Rozza, A., Krishna Menon, A., Nock, R., Qu, L.: Making deep neural networks robust to label noise: a loss correction approach. In: Proceedings of the IEEE Conference on Computer Vision and Pattern Recognition, pp. 1944–1952 (2017)
14. Sukhbaatar, S., Fergus, R.: Learning from noisy labels with deep neural networks. arXiv preprint arXiv:1406.2080 (2014). vol. 2(3), p. 4
15. Sun, C., Shrivastava, A., Singh, S., Gupta, A.: Revisiting unreasonable effectiveness of data in deep learning era. In: Proceedings of the IEEE International Conference on Computer Vision, pp. 843–852 (2017)
16. Szegedy, C., Vanhoucke, V., Ioffe, S., Shlens, J., Wojna, Z.: Rethinking the inception architecture for computer vision. In: Proceedings of the IEEE Conference on Computer Vision and Pattern Recognition, pp. 2818–2826 (2016)
17. Wang, Y., Ma, X., Chen, Z., Luo, Y., Yi, J., Bailey, J.: Symmetric cross entropy for robust learning with noisy labels. In: Proceedings of the IEEE/CVF International Conference on Computer Vision, pp. 322–330 (2019)

18. Wei, H., Feng, L., Chen, X., An, B.: Combating noisy labels by agreement: a joint training method with co-regularization. In: Proceedings of the IEEE/CVF Conference on Computer Vision and Pattern Recognition, pp. 13726–13735 (2020)
19. Xia, X., et al.: Are anchor points really indispensable in label-noise learning? Adv. Neural. Inf. Process. Syst. **32**, 6838–6849 (2019)
20. Xiao, T., Xia, T., Yang, Y., Huang, C., Wang, X.: Learning from massive noisy labeled data for image classification. In: Proceedings of the IEEE Conference on Computer Vision and Pattern Recognition, pp. 2691–2699 (2015)
21. Yao, J., et al.: Deep learning from noisy image labels with quality embedding. IEEE Trans. Image Process. **28**(4), 1909–1922 (2018)
22. Yao, Q., Yang, H., Han, B., Niu, G., Kwok, J.: Searching to exploit memorization effect in learning from corrupted labels. arXiv preprint arXiv:1911.02377 (2019)
23. Yi, K., Wu, J.: Probabilistic end-to-end noise correction for learning with noisy labels. In: Proceedings of the IEEE/CVF Conference on Computer Vision and Pattern Recognition, pp. 7017–7025 (2019)
24. Zhang, Z., Sabuncu, M.R.: Generalized cross entropy loss for training deep neural networks with noisy labels. In: 32nd Conference on Neural Information Processing Systems (NeurIPS) (2018)

# ConWST: Non-native Multi-source Knowledge Distillation for Low Resource Speech Translation

Wenbo Zhu[✉], Hao Jin, JianWen Chen, Lufeng Luo, Jinhai Wang, Qinghua Lu, and Aiyuan Li

Foshan University, Foshan, China
zhuwenbo@fosu.edu.cn

**Abstract.** In the absence of source speech information, most end-to-end speech translation (ST) models showed unsatisfactory results. So, for low-resource non-native speech translation, we propose a self-supervised bidirectional distillation processing system. It improves speech ST performance by using a large amount of untagged speech and text in a complementary way without adding source information. The framework is based on an attentional Sq2sq model, which uses wav2vec2.0 pre-training to guide the Conformer encoder for reconstructing the acoustic representation. The decoder generates a target token by fusing the out-of-domain embeddings. We investigate the use of Byte pair encoding (BPE) and compare it with several fusion techniques. Under the framework of ConWST, we conducted experiments on language transcription from Swahili to English. The experimental results show that the transcription under the framework has a better performance than the baseline model, which seems to be one of the best transcriptional methods.

**Keywords:** End-to-End ST · wav2vec2.0 · Low resource · Self-supervised

## 1 Introduction

The data in many machine learning tasks that can be labeled is limited. The available labeled data of automatic speech recognition and ST is even more limited. Therefore, low-resource ASR and ST tasks are challenging. Data augmentation [18], knowledge refinement [19], and pre-training learning are the main techniques to overcome the problem of low-resource ASR. Multitask learning [1–3], pre-training of ASR data [2, 4–6], data augmentation [7–10], self-supervised pre-training [11, 12], self-training [13], or multilingual ST [14–18] have been used to address the problem of scarcity of source speech utterances in speech translation. In addition, labeled ASR, machine translation (MT), or ST data supplement (complement) multitask learning, pre-training, data augmentation, and multilingual ST.

End-to-end ST models can perform well when the source speech is sufficient. The latest end-to-end techniques can build cascade models and conduct joint training using ASR encoding and MT decoding. This cascade model helps simplify speech recognition and machine translation into subtasks, which will extract more speech and

F. Sun et al. (Eds.): ICCSIP 2021, CCIS 1515, pp. 127–141, 2022.
https://doi.org/10.1007/978-981-16-9247-5_10

language information embedding. In addition, the jointly trained model can give appropriate starting model parameters for finetuning the ST task in the next step [6, 20–22]. Moreover, the phoneme (phone) sequences of the source speech obtained from the word sequence output of a well-performing ASR system have been shown to be better in cascade approaches than the extracted word sequences in end-to-end ST [9, 23]. In other words, the phoneme quality will directly affect the performance of ST. Meanwhile, Salesky and Black [23] also showed that phoneme quality is very important for both cascade and end-to-end ST models in a low-resource context. Therefore, it is a challenge to improve the phoneme quality.

The excellent performance of end-to-end ST models in the past relied mainly on large amounts of labeled speech and text translation data, ASR transcriptions [24], or MT corpora [18]. As a result, the model performance tends to be bad for low-resource ST tasks. Traditional low-resource tasks go to optimize results only in a single modality. However, in low-resource non-native language scenarios, many labeled source speech and text data are lacking. Then, single modal optimization does not provide good performance. Therefore, it is a new challenge to optimize low-resource non-native language tasks from multiple modalities.

In this study, we propose a low-resource ST framework called ConWST. The framework combines self-supervised learning and a text pre-trained model. It can be combined with labeled audio and text embedding to improve the performance of low-resource ST tasks. The results show that the framework helps to get enhanced results in non-native ST with low source information. Our contributions are as follows.

- We propose a ConWST framework with a double teacher network.
- We performed phoneme encoding (characters or BPEs) for Swahili to English (Swa-EN) and tested different output granularities in practice.
- We analyze the effects of existing self-supervised learning approaches on speech translation and show that they significantly minimize labeled ASR requirements.
- We propose different MT pre-training models using decoder fusion methods, with the results showing that the best model can optimize the BLEU for non-native speech translation.

## 2   Related Work

**Sequence-Level Knowledge Distillation.** Sequence-level knowledge distillation (SeqKD) is a method for distilling knowledge from one model to another. SeqKD has been shown in recent studies to reduce the complexity of training data, making it easier to train student models. For example, Hirofumi Inaguma et al. proposed [29] non-autoregressive (NAR) [26–28] bidirectional SeqKD model, which focuses on text-based MT models from external sources. It demonstrates the effectiveness of SeqKD in end-to-end.

**Self-supervised.** Self-supervision [30–33] is a machine learning (ML) paradigm that involves unsupervised learning of structural patterns of data using contextual data. Self-supervision is particularly popular for problems involving a small amount of labeled data (for supervised training) and a large amount of unlabeled data (for self-supervised training). And in low-resource ASR [11], ST [34, 36], and multilingual ST [10], self-supervision has proven to be an effective pre-training process before fully supervised tasks. wav2vec 2.0 [37] is a self-supervised learning model that uses a contextual representation from the transformer model [38] to predict masked discrete speech encoding. In this paper, we investigate how self-supervised pre-training can be applied to labeled data of different sizes to improve the performance of low-resource ST models.

## 3 Proposed Method: ConWST

Traditional methods to solve low-resource tasks are usually optimized on a single model. But this method has a limited improvement. And it can only supplement data integrity in a single dimension. Since the low-resource ST task is performed as a bimodal transform task, performing multimodal data enhancement is a new challenge. It is one of the motivations of our study.

Therefore, this study proposes a dual-teacher network low resource ST framework. On the one hand, the acoustic representation is reconstructed and enriched by an out-of-domain audio reconstruction of the teacher network. On the other hand, the decoded text embedding is guided by introducing an out-of-domain text teacher network. It improves the low-resource task by enriching data integrity in multiple dimensions.

### 3.1 Problem Formulation

The E2E ST model is a direct result of the speech translation paradigm. Without creating a text vector as an intermediate output, $X_s = [x_1, x_2, \ldots, x_s]$ generates $Y_t = [y_1, y_2, \ldots, y_s]$. The input sequence of audio waveforms is represented by $X$, while $Y$ represents the associated translation vector for the target language translation. However, due to a lack of non-native voice, the end-to-end speech translation model is unable to learn the acoustic representation well. It also has an impact on how the target language is taught during the decoding process. As a result, optimizing non-native speech translation performance is essential (Fig. 1).

### 3.2 Encoder

Conformer approaches are often used in practical end-to-end speech recognition systems due to their excellent modeling capabilities. We introduce an audio teacher model at the audio encoder. This audio teacher model is combined with self-supervised learning to direct and rich the representation of source audio by learning labeled audio reconstructions in the out-of-domain. We use the wav2vec2.0 self-supervised model as the base structure of the teacher model.

**Audio Teacher Network.** The Wav2vec2.0 teacher network, which processes voice data in waveform, is the initial element of ConWST. Wav2vec2.0 [39] is a model that uses unlabeled audio data to learn a contextualized speech representation. It comprises a Transformer-based context encoder and a multi-layer convolutional feature encoder.

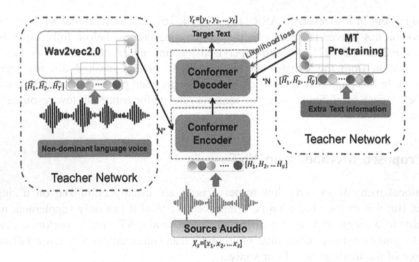

**Fig. 1.** The ConWST model structure.

The multi-layer convolutional encoder takes the raw audio signal as input $X \rightarrow Y$ maps the input features $X_s = [x_1, x_2, \ldots, x_s]$ to a latent embedding space. These embeddings are quantized by a vector quantization module $q : Z \rightarrow \widehat{Z}$. The embedded vectors $Z = [z_1, z_2, \ldots, z_t] \in Z$ are passed through a SpecAugment [44] module that randomly masks a portion of these embeddings to generate Zmasked. These masked embeddings are fed into a context network $g : Z \rightarrow C$ that Conformer encoder to generates a set of context representation $C = [c_1, c_2, \ldots, c_t]$. The model's audio presentation is well-initialized due to the self-supervised pre-trained contextual audio representation. Wav2vec2.0 learns an expression of speech audio during pre-training by solving a contrast loss $\mathcal{L}_c$ and a codebook diversity loss $\mathcal{L}_d$. The challenge is finding an adequately quantified underlying speech representation among a group of distractors obscured by the time step.

$$\mathcal{L} = \mathcal{L}_c + \alpha \mathcal{L}_d \tag{1}$$

where $\alpha$ is a tuned hyperparameter.

$$\mathcal{L}_c = -\log \frac{\exp(sim(c_t, q_t)/k)}{\sum_{\tilde{q} \sim Q_t} \exp(sim(c_t, \tilde{q})/k)} \tag{2}$$

where we compute the cosine similarity $sim(a, b) = a^T b / \parallel a \parallel \parallel b \parallel$ between context representations and quantized latent speech representations. A quantified candidate representation $\tilde{q} \in Q_t$, $k$ distractors, and a genuine quantified potential speech representation $q_t$ are the outputs of the contextual network.

$$\mathcal{L}_d = \frac{1}{GV} \sum_{g=1}^{G} -H(\overline{p}_g) = \frac{1}{GV} \sum_{g=1}^{G} \sum_{v=1}^{V} \overline{p}_{g,v} \log \overline{p}_g, v \tag{3}$$

The equal use of the $V$ entries in each of the $G$ codebooks by maximizing the entropy of the averaged softmax distribution one over the codebook entries for each codebook $\bar{p}_g$ across a batch of utterances.

We utilize raw 16-bit 16-kHz mono-channel audio as the audio input in the experiment, and we use a base configuration of wav2vec2.0, trained on audio data from Librispeech, which contains 10 min, 100 h, and 960 h pre-trained models with and without finetuning.

**Audio Student Network.** After Wav2vec 2.0, we utilized the Conformer encoding module with swish activation. It also leverages SpecAugment to improve the acoustic representation of the source speech by aligning the audio with the duration of the text sequence. To adjust the modeling scale, we set the kernel size of various CNNs to fit the acoustic representation of Wav2vec2.0.

We observe the baseline model and the self-attention weight heatmap of the encoder combined with the audio teacher network, which is finetuned with 10 min of labeled data as Figs. 2 and 3. The Figures represent the alignment relationship between the encoded audio input and the text output. The alignments of the inputs and outputs are directly related to the diagonal correlation of the weights (e.g., Figs. 2 and 3). Figure 3 shows that the alignment ability of the finetuned self-supervised encoder attention weights is enhanced compared to the baseline (e.g., Fig. 2). It suggests that it makes sense to have a teacher network integrated. The audio teacher network effectively enriches the acoustic representation by reconstructing the outer domain audio.

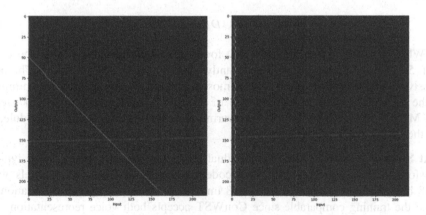

**Fig. 2.** It shows the alignment effect of the self-attentive mechanism for the audio input and text output of the baseline model. The audio heat map on the left shows a segment of the alignment relationship and shows that there is still a gap with the best results. The heat map on the right shows that the encoder does not learn the alignment relationship.

### 3.3    Decoder

We introduce a text teacher model on the text decoder terminal. This text teacher model is a pre-trained model for machine translation.

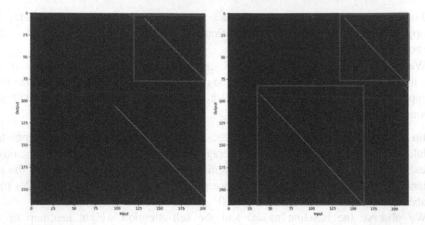

**Fig. 3.** It shows the alignment effect of a self-attention mechanism combining the audio input and text output of the audio teacher network. Compared to the baseline model, the heatmap on the left shows the two alignment relationships, and the alignment performance is close to diagonal. And the heatmap on the right shows the two-segment alignment relationship.

n tasks. The model contains much unlabeled out-of-domain text semantic information to guide and enrich the low resource text embedding.

**Text Teacher Network.** Using external MT data, we pre-train the conformer decoder module.

$$\mathcal{L}(\theta) = -E_{x,y} \in D \cup D_{MT-Pretext} \log P(y|x; \theta) \tag{4}$$

Where $\theta$ is the model parameters, D for target-language text, we have shown in Sect. 5.2 that the training tricks significantly affect translation performance. The progressive multitask training process is the most successful. We used the Adam optimizer in the experiment, with a learning rate of $2 \times 10^{-4}$ and a warm-up of 25k steps. The MT pre-training provides a decent warm-up for the shared transformer module, as per the results of the experiments.

**Text Student Network.** For the individual generating job, we leverage the typical transformer-based approach [40]. The decoder module has six Transformer levels, with 2048 being the most hidden of the 2048 units. We utilize pre-layer normalization to make the training comparable since ConWST accepts both voice representation and external text input.

We observe the baseline model of the text teacher network introduced on the decoding side and the heat map of the text self-attention weights, which shows the alignment relationship between the decoded text semantics, as in Figs. 4 and 5. The alignment relationship between the input and output is directly related to the diagonal correlation of the weights (as in Figs. 2 and 3). Figure 5 shows that the decoder's ability to align the attention weights is enhanced by introducing the MT pre-training model compared to the baseline. It indicates that the decoder has a better semantic learning ability. Also, it shows that the inclusion of the text teacher network is meaningful. It effectively enriches the text embedding by reconstructing the outer domain text.

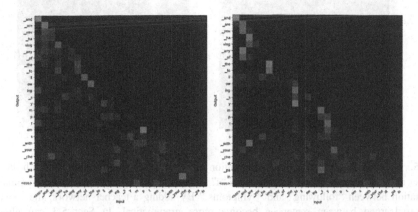

**Fig. 4.** It shows the probability of textual self-attention for the baseline model decoder. The color is more profound, indicating that the probability of attention between words is high, and better semantic features are acquired.

## 4    Experimental Setting

This section describes our dataset for speech translation (ST), text data preprocessing, acoustic features, and optimizer setup. Then, we describe in detail how to train our baseline model.

### 4.1    Datasets

The dataset consists of Source and Target. The source dataset includes a speech dataset of Swahili variants, a small speech dataset for both language pairings, and two parallel translated text corpora make up the source dataset. The target dataset includes a single English speech translation dataset. For details of the dataset, see Table 1.

**Data for wav2vec2.0 Teacher Models.** To investigate the effect of the amount of unlabeled data on pre-training and self-training, we used 10 min, 100 h, and 960 h of LibriSpeech data for wav2vec 2.0 pre-training and self-training. The XLSR model uses the following datasets for multilingual pre-training.

- MLS: Multilingual LibriSpeech (8 languages, 50.7k h): Dutch, English, French, German, Italian, Polish, Portuguese, Spanish
- CommonVoice (36 languages, 3.6k h): Arabic, Basque, Breton, Chinese (CN), Chinese (HK), Chinese (TW), Chuvash, Dhivehi, Dutch, English, Esperanto, Estonian, French, German, Hakh-Chin, Indonesian, Interlingua, Irish, Italian, Japanese, Kabyle, Kinyarwanda, Kyrgyz, Latvian, Mongolian, Persian, Portuguese, Russian, Sakha, Slovenian, Spanish, Swedish, Tamil, Tatar, Turkish, Welsh (see also finetuning splits from this paper).

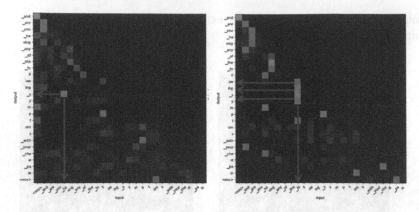

**Fig. 5.** It shows the probability of self-attention of the baseline model combined with the text teacher network. Learned additional "ha" and "s" relationships and instructed on the grammatical correlation between "following" and "symptoms." By adding a teacher network, the semantic features learned between sentences become more grammatical. In Sect. 5.3 can also be demonstrated to be effective by joining text the teacher network.

**Table 1.** Training datasets.

| Language pair | SWA-EN | |
| --- | --- | --- |
| | Train | Dev |
| Speech hours | 5.3 h | 1.9 h |
| Target tokens | 985 | – |
| Target utterances | 4.5K | 868 |

- Babel (17 languages, 1.7k h): Assamese, Bengali, Cantonese, Cebuano, Georgian, Haitian, Kazakh, Kurmanji, Lao, Pashto, Swahili, Tagalog, Tamil, Tok, Turkish, Vietnamese, Zulu

**Data for MT Pre-training Models.** We selected two different MT models for different language translation tasks for the comparison experiments. For the MT-pretraining model, we apply languid filtering, larger FFN and ensembling, reverse translation finetuning, ensembling, and reordering to the text to obtain the optimal model.

### 4.2    Training and Decoding Details

Our implementation is based on the ESPnet-ST toolkit [41]. In the following, we provide details for reproducing the results. The pipeline is identical for all experiments.

**Baseline Models.** All experiments use the same 12 layer encoder structure, with a 6-layer decoder structure, an embedding size of 256, 4 attention heads, and FFN dimension of 2048 based on the ConWST framework. For wav2vec 2.0 pre-training, we are using a small trained with 10 min of unlabeled librispeech. It comprises 24 self-attention blocks with model dimension 1024, inner dimension 4096, and 16 attention heads, resulting in about 300M parameters. In addition to the independent decoder model, we include an additional Teacher network to increase the effect of translation and to explore the impact on low-resource ST. The structure of the model has been described in Sects. 3.2 and 3.3. We save the checkpoint with the best BLEU on dev-set and average the last five checkpoints.

**Text Preprocessing.** Transcriptions and translations were normalized and tokenized using the Moses tokenizer. All sources are marked in lowercase with punctuation removed, and targets are marked in the true case for fair comparison BLEU.

**Speech Features.** We used Kaldi [42] to extract 83-dimensional features (80-channel log Mel filter-bank coefficients and 3-dimensional pitch features) normalized by the mean and standard deviation computed on the training set. For data augmentation, we used speed perturbation [43] with three factors of 0.9, 1.0, and 1.1 and SpecAugment [44] with three types of deterioration, including time warping (W), time masking (T), and frequency masking (F), where W = 5, T = 40, and F = 30.

**Optimization.** Following the training transformer's standard practice, we used the Adam optimizer [45] with the Noam learning rate schedule [9]. We set the initial learning rate to 1e−3 and the dropout rate of 0.1. We used a batch size of 32 sentences per GPU, with gradient accumulation of 2 and clipping gradient of 5. As for model initialization, we trained two separate teacher models and used their weights to initialize the conformer model. We also included this shared model in the experiments. Finally, for decoding, we used a beam size of 10 with a length penalty of 0.6

## 5  Main Results

This section described our experimental results obtained in Tables 2 and 3 and studied the fusion strategy of self-supervised learning with knowledge distillation techniques on end-to-end ST.

### 5.1  Baseline Work

The BLEU scores evaluated on the Swaziland-English corpus are shown in Table 1. We used the Conformer model as the baseline model, which was trained end-to-end without using any text resources of the source language. We choose the size of convolution kernels to evaluate the best baseline work results.

### 5.2  BPE Improving of Raw Phone Sequence

Byte pair encoding (BPE) is a technique that compresses phoneme sequences into syllable-like segmented sequences. Motivated by previous work that segmented speech into a phone sequence according to phone change boundaries [46], we applied BPE with BPE-Dropout of dropout-rate 0.1 [47, 53] to reduce the phone sequence length. As

**Table 2.** Compared baseline work to previous work.

| Method | Train | Dev | BLEU Δ |
|---|---|---|---|
| Transformer | 27.6 | 23.1 | – |
| Conformer kernel = 5 BPE 1k | 25.3 | 21.7 | −1.4 |
| Conformer kernel = 7 BPE 1k | 24.9 | 23.2 | +0.1 |
| Conformer kernel = 15 BPE 1k | **28.4** | **24.4** | **+1.3** |

the BPE unit inventory increases from 230 (the size of IPA) to 1k–64k, the phone sequence length can be reduced by about 30%–60%. We believe that combining BPE-based phone features will enable the model to have a deeper understanding of sentences.

To analyze the effect of BPE segmentation, we conducted experiments using different sizes of BPE ratios. As shown in Table 3, we compare the translation effects of different BPE sizes in the baseline model. "little flu" is mistranslated as "little flu viruses" in (cf. "Conformer kernel = 15 BPE = 16K"). Still, no such error occurs in (cf. "Conformer kernel = 15 BPE = 4k"). Fusing raw telephone qualities with acoustic features might be one cause. It may lead the model to focus too much on pronunciation while forgetting the meaning of the sentence, resulting in an incorrect translation. The phone features based on BPE segmentation regularly exceed the original phone features, as demonstrated in Table 4. When the BPE is more than 1K, the model's efficiency diminishes, which might be related to the excessive granularity of the segmentation. As a result, the succeeding model may struggle to learn the encoding efficiently.

**Table 3.** Compared to transcriptional sentences at different BPE. In this example, the text in green represents proper translations, and there are no missing words in other ways. In this example, the blue text represents proper translations, although other ways have missing words. The red text denotes incorrect translations.

| Method | Example 1 |
|---|---|
| Truth Text | well from my point of view it is a little flu |
| Transformer | well if my point of view it is from a little |
| Conformer kernel=15 BPE 1k | my point of view it is from a little well |
| Conformer kernel=15 BPE 4k | so my point of view it is from a little flu |
| Conformer kernel=15 BPE 16k | so that well from my point of it is a little flu viruses |

## 5.3    Improvements from Knowledge Distillation

In ST literature, it is acknowledged that the optimization of E2E-ST is more complicated than individually training. In this section, we use both self-supervised and knowledge distillation that can complement knowledge refinement to optimize the end-to-end ST.

**Table 4.** Compared to different BPE sizes.

| Method | BPE | Train | Dev | BLEU Δ |
|---|---|---|---|---|
| Transformer | 1K | 27.6 | 23.1 | – |
| Conformer kernel = 15 | 1K | **28.4** | **24.4** | **+1.3** |
| | 2K | 17.6 | 22.9 | −1.5 |
| | 4K | 15.7 | 22.6 | −1.8 |
| | 8K | 18.4 | 18.9 | −5.5 |
| | 10K | 20.2 | 20.1 | −4.3 |
| | 16K | 17.6 | 19.1 | −5.3 |
| | 32K | 13.1 | 12.3 | −12.1 |

**Improvements from Encoding.** We observe significant gains using the wav2vec 2.0 model compared to the previous baseline. These baselines were not pre-trained and did not use any additional other supervised speech translation data. The wav2vec 2.0 small model pre-trained with 10 min of Librilight data achieved an average of 25.3 BLEU, which is 2.2 BLEU points better than the baseline average. These results show that the acoustic representation learned by the wav2vec 2.0 model is beneficial beyond speech recognition and applicable to speech translation. And it shows that the two-teacher network combined with self-supervised learning proposed in this paper can improve the ST task with low source audio (Table 5).

**Table 5.** Compared different encoder teacher models to the baseline model.

| Method Enc | 10 min | | 100 h | | 960 h | | RTF/Latency (ms) |
|---|---|---|---|---|---|---|---|
| | Train | Dev | Train | Dev | Train | Tev | |
| E2E-Conformer ST | – | – | – | – | – | – | **3.153**/50731.3 |
| E2E-Conformer ST + Pre-wav2vec2.0-small | **31.7** | 20.6 | 30.2 | 24.3 | 29.5 | **25.3** | 3.099/48762.2 |
| E2E-Conformer ST + Pre-wav2vec2.0-large | 26.5 | 23.5 | 29.1 | 24.1 | 29.2 | 24.7 | 2.964/46634.7 |
| E2E-Conformer ST + Pre-wav2vec2.0-vox | 25.4 | 23.2 | 17.3 | 21.7 | 22.8 | 22.4 | 2.336/**36749.4** |

**Improvements from Decoding.** Self-training leverage additional unannotated speech data to improve performance. But self-training generates a noisy output which may lead the model to learn incorrect patterns. To inject more prior knowledge about the target language structure, a promising solution is to use the unannotated text in the target domain to train a teacher model and finetune the student model based on it. In this work, the pre-trained model is improved by using a text that has been additionally unlabeled in the language and using it to improve the generated decoding.

We use pre-trained models of external MT for different scales and different language translation tasks. It was used to evaluate the impact of external MT on BLEU scores in Table 6 (Second line). It Introducing external MT pre-training for the same language improves the BLEU by 1.8 BLEU with the baseline model. It shows that the external MT teacher model can improve the ST task performance. By introducing external MT pre-training in different languages to the baseline model, the results show that the MT task pre-training model in different languages also improves by 1.1 BLEU. Table 6 (Third line) indicates that the additional text decoding information in the same language versus different languages can help the ST task decoding learn the acoustic representation. The results show that the MT teacher model introduced in this paper at the decoding side can use the additional textual information to make the E2E ST decoder and improve the low resource ST task performance.

**Table 6.** Compared different decoder teacher models to the baseline model.

| Method Dec | Train | Dev | RTF/Latency (ms) | BLEU Δ |
|---|---|---|---|---|
| E2E-Conformer ST | 28.4 | 24.4 | 3.153/**50731.3** | – |
| E2E-Conformer ST + Pre-Ge-En | 30.7 | **26.2** | 3.340/52546.1 | +1.8 |
| E2E-Conformer ST + Pre-Ru-En | **31.9** | 25.1 | **3.532**/55568.9 | +1.1 |

### 5.4    Data Ablation for Encoder and Decoder Training

To better understand the contribution of each component, we performed an ablation study. The results are shown in Table 7. In the Second and Third lines, we perform a single task pre-training of the baseline work. When we add any of these, the performance goes up. It shows that both of our proposed two-teacher models are beneficial. We find that if a single teacher model does not achieve the best ST performance, the double teacher network is necessary for both ST tasks. It suggests that a two-stage pre-training paradigm is required. In the third line, we have instructed teachers who have adopted Russian. In this case, we observe that **0.8 BLEU** reduces it compared to the optimal performance. A plausible explanation is that these tasks do not match the semantic text features at the time of random initialization, which leads to degraded performance on the ST task.

**Table 7.** Mutil-teacher network ablation experiment.

| Method | Train | Dev | RTF/Latency | BLEU Δ |
|---|---|---|---|---|
| E2E-Conformer ST | 28.4 | 24.4 | 3.153/50731.3 | – |
| E2E-Conformer ST + wav2vec2.0 | – | – | – | – |
| + Pre-Ge-En | **33.6** | **27.9** | 3.074/47521.1 | **+3.5** |
| E2E-Conformer ST + wav2vec2.0 | – | – | – | – |
| + Pre-Ru-En | 32.1 | 23.6 | **2.841/44703.4** | −0.8 |

# 6  Discussion

Although this study combined with self-supervised training was shown to have improved performance on the low-resource ST task, there is no study showing the effectiveness of multilingual tasks on low resource ST on this basis. It is a challenge to explore the structure of multitasking with self-supervised learning throw.

# 7  Conclusion

We approach ST challenges by combining knowledge distillation and self-supervised learning approaches without using any extra source data. ConWST is a framework for end-to-end voice translation that we propose. On ST tasks in two languages, the framework improves earlier methods by an average of 2 BLEU. We also use ablation studies with a two-teacher network to show the complementarity and need for a two-teacher framework. Our study proposed innovative methods for end-to-end voice translation with low resources.

# References

1. Weiss, R.J., Chorowski, J., Jaitly, N., Wu, Y., Chen, Z.: Sequence-to-sequence models can directly translate foreign speech. arXiv preprint arXiv:1703.08581 (2017)
2. B'erard, A., Besacier, L., Kocabiyikoglu, A.C., Pietquin, O.: End-to-end automatic speech translation of audiobooks. In: Proceedings of ICASSP (2018)
3. Tang, Y., Pino, J., Wang, C., Ma, X., Genzel, D.: A general multitask learning framework to leverage text data for speech to text tasks. In: Proceedings of ICASSP (2021)
4. Bansal, S., Kamper, H., Livescu, K., Lopez, A., Goldwater, S.: Pre-training on high-resource speech recognition improves low-resource speech-to-text translation. In: Proceedings of NAACL (2019)
5. Stoian, M.C., Bansal, S., Goldwater, S.: Analyzing asr pre-training for low-resource speech-to-text translation. In: Proceedings of ICASSP (2020)
6. Wang, C., Wu, Y., Liu, S., Yang, Z., Zhou, M.: Bridging the gap between pre-training and finetuning for end-to-end speech translation. In: Proceedings of AAAI (2020)
7. Jia, Y., et al.: Leveraging weakly supervised data to improve the end-to-end speech-to-text translation. In: Proceedings of ICASSP (2019)
8. Pino, J., Puzon, L., Gu, J., Ma, X., McCarthy, A.D., Gopinath, D.: Harnessing indirect training data for end-to-end automatic speech translation: tricks of the trade. In: Proceedings of IWSLT (2019)
9. Salesky, E., Sperber, M., Black, A.W.: Exploring phoneme-level speech representations for end-to-end speech translation. In: Proceedings of ACL (2019)
10. McCarthy, A.D., Puzon, L., Pino, J.: Skinaugment: auto-encoding speaker conversions for automatic speech translation. In: Proceedings of ICASSP (2020)
11. Wu, A., Wang, C., Pino, J., Gu, J.: Self-supervised representations improve end-to-end speech translation. In: Proceedings of Interspeech (2020)
12. Nguyen, H., Bougares, F., Tomashenko, N., Estève, Y., Besaucier, L.: Investigating self-supervised pretraining for end-to-end speech translation. In: Proceedings of Interspeech (2020)

13. Pino, J., Xu, Q., Ma, X., Dousti, M.J., Tang, Y.: Self-training for end-to-end speech translation. In: Proceedings of Interspeech (2020)
14. Di Gangi, M.A., Negri, M., Turchi, M.: One-to-many multilingual end-to-end speech translation. In: Proceedings of ASRU (2019)
15. Inaguma, H., Duh, K., Kawahara, T., Watanabe, S.: Multilingual end-to-end speech translation. In: Proceedings of ASRU (2019)
16. Wang, C., Pino, J., Wu, A., Gu, J.: Covost: a diverse multilingual speech-to-text translation corpus. In: Proceedings of LREC (2020)
17. Wang, C., Wu, A., Pino, J.: Covost 2 and massively multilingual speech-to-text translation arXiv (2020)
18. Li, X., et al.: Multilingual speech translation with efficient finetuning of pretrained models. arXiv, abs/2010.12829 (2021)
19. Anastasopoulos, A., Chiang, D.: Tied multitask learning for neural speech translation. In: Proceedings of NAACL (2018)
20. Liu, Y., et al.: End-to-end speech translation with knowledge distillation. In: Proceedings of Interspeech (2019)
21. Chuang, S.-P., Sung, T.-W., Liu, A.H., Lee, H.-Y.: Worse WER, but better BLEU? Leveraging word embedding as intermediate in multitask end-to-end speech translation. In: Proceedings of ACL (2020)
22. Wang, C., Wu, Y., Liu, S., Zhou, M., Yang, Z.: Curriculum pre-training for end-to-end speech translation. In: Proceedings of ACL (2020)
23. Salesky, E., Black, A.W.: Phone features improve speech translation. In: Proceedings of ACL (2020)
24. Bansal, S., Kamper, H., Livescu, K., Lopez, A., Goldwater, S.: Pretraining on high-resource speech recognition improve the low-resource speech-to-text translation. In: Proceedings of NAACL (2019)
25. Kim, Y., Rush, A.M.: Sequence-level knowledge distillation (2016)
26. Zhou, C., Gu, J., Neubig, G.: Understanding knowledge distillation in non-autoregressive machine translation. In: Proceedings of ICLR (2019a)
27. Ren, Y., Liu, J., Tan, X., Zhao, Z., Zhao, S., Liu, T.Y.: A study of non-autoregressive model for sequence generation. In: Proceedings of the 58th Annual Meeting of the Association for Computational Linguistics (2020)
28. Schneider, S., Baevski, A., Collobert, R., Auli, M.: wav2vec: unsupervised pre-training for speech recognition. In: Proceedings of Interspeech, pp. 3465–3469 (2019)
29. Inaguma, H., Kawahara, T., Watanabe, S.: .Source and target bidirectional knowledge distillation for end-to-end speech translation. In: Proceedings of the 2021 Conference of the North American Chapter of the Association for Computational Linguistics: Human Language Technologies (2021)
30. Chen, T., Kornblith, S., Swersky, K., Norouzi, M., Hinton, G.E.: Big self-supervised models are strong semi-supervised learners. In: Advances in Neural Information Processing Systems, vol. 33 (2020)
31. Oord, A., Li, Y., Vinyals, O.: Representation learning with contrastive predictive coding. arXiv preprint arXiv:1807.03748 (2018)
32. Lan, Z., Chen, M., Goodman, S., Gimpel, K., Sharma, P., Soricut, R.: ALBERT: a lite BERT for self-supervised learning of language representations. In: International Conference on Learning Representations (2019)
33. Baevski, A., Zhou, Y., Mohamed, A., Auli, M.: wav2vec 2.0: a framework for self-supervised learning of speech representations. In: Larochelle, H., Ranzato, M., Hadsell, R., Balcan, M., Lin, H. (eds.) Proceedings of NeurIPS (2020)

34. Nguyen, H., Bougares, F., Tomashenko, N., Estève, Y., Besaucier, L.: Investigating self-supervised pre-training for end-to-end speech translation. In: Proceedings of INTER-SPEECH (2020)
35. Tran, C., Tang, Y., Li, X., Gu, J.: Cross-lingual retrieval for iterative self-supervised training. In: Larochelle, H., Ranzato, M., Hadsell, R., Balcan, M., Lin, H. (eds.) Proceedings of NeurIPS (2020)
36. Baevski, A., Zhou, Y., Mohamed, A.-R., Auli, M.: wav2vec2.0: a framework for self-supervised learning of speech representations. In: Advances in Neural Information Processing Systems, vol. 33 (2020)
37. Vaswani, A., et al.: Attention is all you need. In: Advances in Neural Information Processing Systems, pp. 5998–6008 (2017)
38. Baevski, A., Zhou, H., Mohamed, A., Auli, M.: Wav2vec 2.0: a framework for self-supervised learning of speech representations (2020)
39. Vaswani, A., Shazeer, N., Parmar, N., Uszkoreit, J., Jones, L., Gomez, A.N., et al.: Attention is all you need. arXiv (2017)
40. Koehn, P., et al.: Moses: open source toolkit for statistical machine translation. In: Proceedings of the 45th Annual Meeting of the ACL on Interactive Poster and Demonstration Sessions, pp. 177–180. Association for Computational Linguistics (2007)
41. Povey, D., et al.: The Kaldi speech recognition toolkit. In: IEEE 2011 workshop on automatic speech recognition and understanding. IEEE Signal Processing Society (2011)
42. Ko, T., Peddinti, V., Povey, D., Khudanpur, S.: Audio augmentation for speech recognition. In: Sixteenth Annual Conference of the International Speech Communication Association (2015)
43. Park, D.S.: Specaugment: a simple data augmentation method for automatic speech recognition. In: Kubin, G., Kacic, Z. (eds.) Interspeech 2019, 20th Annual Conference of the International Speech Communication Association, Graz, Austria, 15–19 September 2019, pp. 2613–2617. ISCA (2019)
44. Kingma, D.P., Ba, J.: Adam: a method for stochastic optimization. In: Bengio, Y., LeCun, Y. (eds.) 3rd International Conference on Learning Representations, ICLR 2015, San Diego, CA, USA, 7–9 May 2015, Conference Track Proceedings (2015)
45. Aswani, A.V., et al.: Attention is all you need. In: Advances in Neural Information Processing Systems, pp. 5998–6008 (2017)
46. Rico Sennrich, A.B., Haddow, B.: Neural machine translation of rare words with subword units. In: Proceedings of ACL (2016)
47. Provilkov, I., Emelianenko, D., Voita, E.: BPE-dropout: simple and effective subword regularization. In: Proceedings of ACL (2020)

# Functional Primitive Library and Movement Sequence Reasoning Algorithm

Ailin Xue, Xiaoli Li$^{(\boxtimes)}$, and Chunfang Liu

Department of Information, Beijing University of Technology, Beijing, China
lixiaolibjut@bjut.edu.cn

**Abstract.** Trajectory planning of manipulator is a popular research area. To allow the manipulator to have the knowledge of demonstrated skills and the intelligence to infer trajectories for new tasks, a new kind of imitation learning framework is proposed in this paper. Our framework builds up a Functional Primitives Library which is composed by three different types of elements: Event Primitive, Object Primitive and Relation Primitive. Event Primitive consists of action features extracted by Dynamic Movement Primitive and the functions of the actions which describe the state changes of operated objects monitoring by visual sensor. Object Primitive describes the objects involved in tasks. Relation Primitive is used to represent the relationship between objects. Besides, a state-movement reasoning algorithm based on dichotomy is raised to realize the inference of the complete movement sequence for a new task.

**Keywords:** Trajectory planning · Imitation learning · Movement primitives · Primitives library · Reasoning algorithm

## 1 Introduction

With the development of science and technology and the continuous improvement of human living standard, the demand for robot capability is expanding. Scholars works a lot on intelligent robots, especially manipulators for operational tasks.

It is a challenge research direction that robots can accomplish a given task with its own knowledge and without the instruction of human. In this situation, the robot should have the intelligence to perform a new task in a new environment on its own. To realize the autonomous planning, two problems have to be addressed: how to learn the knowledge and how to reason for a new condition.

Imitation learning is a direct way for robots to learn from teacher. The basic idea of imitation learning is to reproduce the demonstrated trajectories that a teacher provided [1]. In most cases, manipulator needs to capture the features of demonstrations and generate a new trajectory have these features but in different situations. Thus the learned knowledge should have generalization ability.

Considering the action repetition in different multi-action tasks, learning and saving all the movements is a waste of time and storage space when the

© Springer Nature Singapore Pte Ltd. 2022
F. Sun et al. (Eds.): ICCSIP 2021, CCIS 1515, pp. 142–155, 2022.
https://doi.org/10.1007/978-981-16-9247-5_11

number of tasks is large. Moreover, it is difficult to divide a complete action into several parts according to its function and combine them into a sequence that can complete a new task. Introducing the concept of primitive, store the basic skills and their functions is important. Moreover, the establishment of primitive library is also the focus of scholars' research.

In this paper, we propose an imitation learning framework to learn a primitive library which is composed by three kinds of basic functional elements: Event Primitive, Object Primitive and Relation Primitive. The DMPs learned from demonstrations are stored in Event Primitives, and functions are represented by the change of the object's states and relations. Object Primitive is used to describe the position and posture information of an object, tracked by the visual sensor Kinect. To simplify the problem, relations between objects are given by the human teacher.

In addition, a state-movement reasoning algorithm is raised to generate a sequence which can guide the motion of manipulators. This algorithm infers on the basic of continuity of states and matching of relations. In order to save the total time of searching primitives in the library, a binary search reasoning is adopted, that is, form the sequence from initial and goal state at the same time.

The main idea of this paper is shown in the Fig. 1.

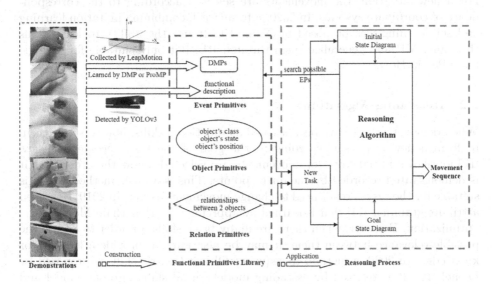

**Fig. 1.** Framework of the proposed model.

## 2    Related Work

### 2.1    Imitation Learning Framework

The concept of imitation learning was raised by Bandera [2], he concluded the structure of imitation learning is composed by perception system, system input, study strategy, motion mechanism, knowledge base and system output. There are many traditional imitation learning methods, such as, supervised learning, SEARN [3], feed forward training [4], etc.

In recent years, many imitation learning frameworks emerged. In 2006, Chella et al. [5] raised a cognitive system for imitation learning, which combined artificial vision and symbolic knowledge with conceptual spaces. The clusters of movements are constructed by their spatial pattern, however, in some situations the distribution of action execution space may be different from that of demonstration. In 2012, Lioutikov [6] introduced query points into the ProMP library learned by imitation, but functions of movements can not be indicated. Then Garam [7] proposed a kind of imitation learning framework based on PCA. The primitives in this paper focus more on how to generalize one movement, not complicated multi-movements tasks. Seyed et al. [8] proposed a method to learn actions' symbolic representations, which consists of three layers: Imitation Learning, Visuospatial Skill Learning and Symbolic Planning. They applied SIFT to match the objects and detect their changes in order to show the action's function, the problem is it can hardly be used on a new object. Scott [9] introduced a framework to learn skills from unstructured demonstrations. The movements are classified by the coordinate system the demonstrated trajectory belongs to. For a new situation, the movements are selected according to the correspondence of coordinate systems. In 2020, a framework combining imitation learning and self-learning was proposed by Nam [10]. It has the ability to learn skills through DMP and generalize them through RL, but only suitable for a single task: Peg-in-Hole.

### 2.2   Reasoning Algorithm

When demonstrations have been learned as functional skills, how to select them to form a new sequence according to the goal of the task becomes the key. In Lioutikov's initial work [6], movements are selected follow the order that it is demonstrated recorded by the query points. This is a basic method which is suitable for the tasks do not need to change movements' order. In 2019, He raised attribute grammar [11] that is learned by applying a Markov chain Monte Carlo optimization. However, when there are many basic skills, in order to ensure the possible relevance between them, it may be necessary to provide a lot of prior knowledge. In 2020, a method to sequence Object-Centric skills is proposed by Leonel [12]. It is realized by cascading models of all skills into one model and then choose action with the highest probability. The disadvantage is when there are many skills, it will cause the dimension disaster of the complete model.

## 3   Functional Primitives Library

In order to let the manipulator has the knowledge about human motions and provide the basis for the action sequence reasoning, the Functional Primitives Library (FPLib) that learned from demonstrations is introduced in this section.

The structure of FPLib consists of three kinds of basic primitives. Event Primitives combine Dynamic Movement Primitives (DMP) and functions of skills, Object Primitives represent objects involved in a task and Relation Primitives show the relationships between different Object Primitives.

For the accomplishment of basic industrial tasks, the initial FPLib contains seven basic skills: take, put, assemble, disassemble, pour, pull and push.

## 3.1 Learning from Demonstration

The movement skills are demonstrated by a human teacher, manipulator needs to learn it as its own knowledge. For the movement trajectory part, DMP are applied to learn the weights from demonstrations collected by LEAP MOTION. As for the features part, the relationships between objects are provided by teacher along with demonstration and the states of objects are recognized by YOLOv3.

**Data Acquisition.** To extract the position and posture information from demonstration shown by a human teacher, Leap Motion shown in Fig. 2(a) is applied in this work. Leap Motion can collect human hands positions and postures in the range of the distance is 10cm-60cm and the angle is 140–120°, which has the enough region and good accuracy for information collection of human hand movements. The interface of Leap Motion Controller is showed in Fig. 2(b).

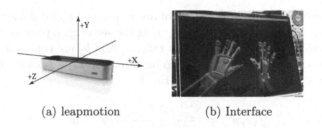

(a) leapmotion          (b) Interface

**Fig. 2.** Leap motion and its control interface

In order to meet the basic needs of most industrial tasks, seven basic skills are designed to compose our primitive library: take, put, assemble, disassemble, pour, pull and push. The diagrams of these movements demonstrated by a human teacher are illustrated in Fig. 3.

The corresponding trajectories of the six basic movements generated from the data that Leap Motion gathered are shown in Fig. 4.

**Dynamic Movement Primitive.** DMP is a method to fit the trajectories with a set of weights which is developed from second order spring damping model [13]. The characteristic of DMP is its nonlinear terms in the set of nonlinear differential functions. These nonlinear terms give DMP the power to generate

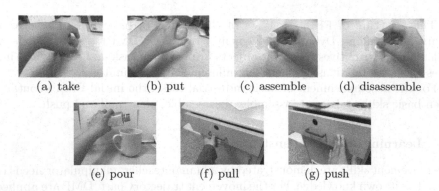

(a) take          (b) put          (c) assemble          (d) disassemble

(e) pour          (f) pull          (g) push

**Fig. 3.** Human demonstration of seven basic skills

new trajectories that has the same shape as the demonstrations, which is an advantage of DMP. The effect of DMP is as shown in Fig. 5, it can generate a new trajectory with a new start point(a), a new end point(b), or on a new scale(c).

The mathematical expression of DMP is shown below:

$$\tau \ddot{y} = a_y(b_y(y^* - y) - \hat{y} + f) \tag{1}$$

$$\tau \hat{x} = -a_x x \tag{2}$$

where $y$ represents the set of positions of an action and $\hat{y}$ and $\ddot{y}$ shows the speed and acceleration of motion respectively. $y^*$ is the set of goal positions. Moreover, $\tau$ is a time constant to adjust the decay rate, $a_y$ and $b_y$ are constant coefficients. $x$ is the phase variable which is meant to be zero. $f$ in Eq. 1 is called forced term, detailed representation is expressed in Eq. 3.

$$f(x, y^*) = \frac{\sum_{i=1}^N \psi_i(x)\omega_i}{\sum_{i=1}^N \psi_i(x)} x(y^* - y_0) \tag{3}$$

where $\psi(x)$ is the Gaussian basis function, detailed representation is expressed in Eq. 4. $N$ is the number of Gaussian basis functions and $y_0$ represents the system's initial state.

$$\psi_i = e^{-h_i(x-c_i)^2} \tag{4}$$

## 3.2   Skill Function Representation

The function of skill is an important basis for the choice of action. In this part, the function is represented by the change of objects' states and relationships. The states information is obtained from the demonstrations, through YOLOv3 algorithm. The relationships between objects is given by the teacher to simplify the problem.

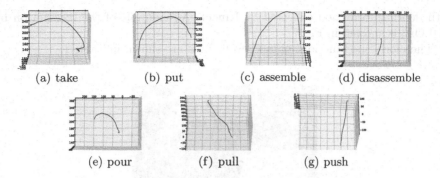

(a) take                (b) put                (c) assemble            (d) disassemble

(e) pour                (f) pull                (g) push

Fig. 4. Trajectories of seven basic skills collected by leap motion.

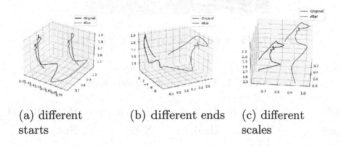

(a) different           (b) different ends      (c) different
starts                                          scales

Fig. 5. Effect of dynamic movement primitives.

YOLOv3 is the improvement of v1 and v2, which uses Darknet-53 network to extract image features, and uses three different scale feature maps to detect objects [14]. Darknet-53 contains 53 convolution layers, and set shortcut connections between some layers. The substructure of this network is called residual component, and it is illustrated in Fig. 6.

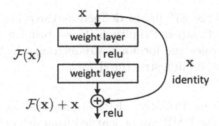

Fig. 6. The structure of residual component.

In this work, the YOLOv3 model is trained by multiple states of multiple objects. The states contains origin, open, close, held, etc. It is also requested to obtain the positions and angles of objects by combining the YOLOv3 result with depth information collected by Kinect. An example of the recognition by YOLOv3 is showed in Fig. 7.

Therefore, the functions of our seven skills are shown in Table.1.

**Fig. 7.** The recognition result of YOLOv3.

**Table 1.** Functions of seven skills.

| Skills | State_pre | State_post | Relation_pre | Relation_post |
|---|---|---|---|---|
| Take | None | Held | None | None |
| Put | Held | None | None | None |
| Assemble | Held | Held | A,B | A-link-B |
| Disassemble | Held | Held | A-link-B | A,B |
| Pour | Held | Held, lean | A-in-B | A-in-C |
| Pull | Closed | open | None | None |
| Push | Open | Closed | None | None |

### 3.3   Structure of Functional Primitive Library

The basic elements of the FPLib are defined as three kinds: Event Primitive, Object Primitive and Relation Primitive. These primitives can connect with each other with some rules and form a state diagram which can describe every scene in the demonstration in a structured way.

**Event Primitive.** Event Primitive (EP) is proposed to store the DMP of a skill and its function. The DMP can be learned from demonstration collected by Leap Motion. As for the skill's function, we define it as the change of states and relationships of objects.

The items in a EP are shown below:

– *dmp*: weight matrix of DMP learned from demonstration.
– *state_pre*: object's states before the movement.
– *state_post*: object's states after the movement.

– *relation_pre*: relationships between objects before the movement.
– *relation_post*: relationships between objects after the movement.

With the knowledge of skills, we can infer which skill to choose when we want an object to change its state to a goal state. It's realized by the match between objects' states in real-time and *state_pre* together with *relation_pre* stored in EPs and objects' states desired and *state_post* together with *relation_post*.

**Object Primitive.** In order to better describe the objects involved in a task, Object Primitive (OP) is introduced in this part. An OP contains basic states of an object, such as open or close, position and posture, class of the object, etc.
The items of OP are listed below:

– *class*: class of this object.
– *state*: states of object, like open, close, etc.
– *pos*: position and posture of object, expressed by quaternion.

It should be noted that the states and position changes with the process of the task.

**Relation Primitive.** Relation Primitive(RP) is used to indicate the relationship between objects. Relationships can exist between two or more objects. To simplify and unify the forms of different RPs, the relationships between more than three objects are transferred to that between two. The relationships are provided by the teacher.
The items of RP are shown as follows:

– *class*: class of this relationship.
– *obj_1*: One of the objects connected by this relationship.
– *obj_2*: Another object connected by this relationship.

**State Diagram.** State diagram is defined to show each scene in a video demonstration and can be understood by the robot better. It can be constructed by OPs and RPs described above.
It's transferred as an object-relation matrix in the computer. The row and column of the matrix represent all the OPs at that time, and the elements in the matrix are RPs. Therefore, object-relation matrix is a symmetric matrix whose diagonal elements are 0. For the example in Fig. 7, if there is a *book* and a *cup* on a *table*, the contents of the corresponding rows and columns of the matrix are *ons*; however, if the *book* has no relationship with a *cup*, the content will be 0. State diagram of this situation is shown in Fig. 8(b). The object-relation matrix of this example is shown in Fig. 8(c).
It should be noted that several state diagrams can be linked by EPs as a sequence to express a complete trajectory of a task.

150    A. Xue et al.

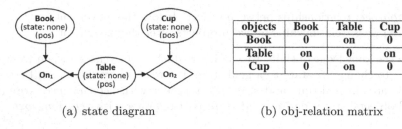

| objects | Book | Table | Cup |
|---------|------|-------|-----|
| Book | 0 | on | 0 |
| Table | on | 0 | on |
| Cup | 0 | on | 0 |

(a) state diagram                    (b) obj-relation matrix

**Fig. 8.** An example of state diagram

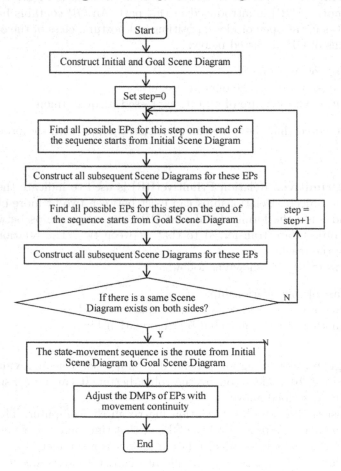

**Fig. 9.** Pipeline of the proposed reasoning algorithm.

# 4 Reasoning Algorithm

With the establishment of our FPLib, reasoning algorithm to generate a sequence of skills is devised in this section. The basic idea of reasoning is to use continuity of objects' states and manipulator's position to find a proper and reasonable skill sequence, which can change the initial states of objects to their goal states.

The reasoning algorithm can be departed into two parts, state continuous skill reasoning and information supplement of each movement. Now that we have a representation of the states and relationships of objects, we need to figure out how to associate skills with them.

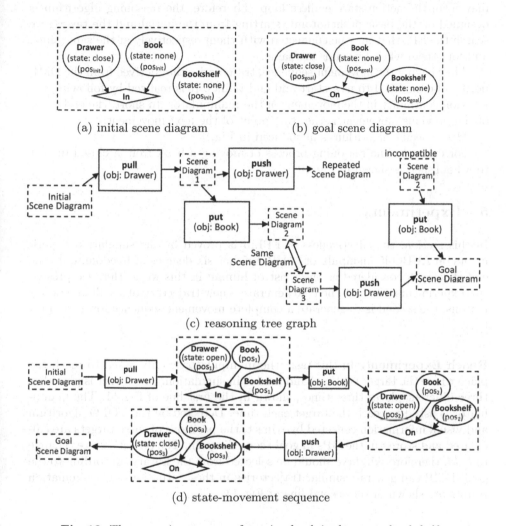

(a) initial scene diagram    (b) goal scene diagram

(c) reasoning tree graph

(d) state-movement sequence

**Fig. 10.** The reasoning process of moving book in drawer to bookshelf.

When given a new task, construct the initial and goal state diagrams first. Then, think about the definition of EP, each skill is described by its function, thus the states and relationships transformation when this action happens. For the previous state diagram, the possible skills next it are the EPs whose *state_pre* and *relation_pre* match the current states and relations; as for the next state diagram, the possible skills before it are the EPs whose *state_post* and *relation_post* match the goal states and relations. Besides, only one skill can be executed each moment, that is, only one state can be changed each moment.

Due to the uncertainty of movement sequence length, dynamic programming and decision tree are easy to cause the problem of search depth disaster, which may form the action-state endless loop. Therefore, the reasoning algorithm is designed on the basic of dichotomy, starting from the initial and the target, we search the EPs that may be connected with them respectively at the same time, and join them when two ends are same.

After having the movement sequence, trajectories that derived from the DMP need to be modified to new start and end points. It is realized by following the position continuity in the movement of the manipulator. In short, the end point of the previous movement is the start point of the next movement.

More specific algorithm is introduced in Fig. 9.

For example, the reasoning process of moving a book from a closed drawer to a bookshelf is shown in Fig. 10.

## 5    Experiments

In this section, the effectiveness of FPLib is proved by the simulation experiments on AUBO-i5 manipulator. AUBO-i5 has six degrees of freedom, only the end-effector is considered as the wrist of human in this work. Here we present two experiments, the first one is to generate a new trajectory of a skill in new situations; the second is to generate a complete movement sequence for a complex task.

**Reach Experiment.** In this task, the manipulator is only asked to reach the place where the target is placed and hold it in simulation. The target is placed at three different places three times, shown in the first line of Fig. 11. The manipulator is asked to reach the target each time. Detected by the YOLO algorithm and visual information collected by Kinect, the positions of these targets are calculated and stored in the OPs in goal scene diagram. The object's states change to *held*, therefore skill *take* should be selected from the library. According to the goal, DMP can generate similar trajectories in these situations. The simulation results are shown in the second line of Fig. 11.

**Complex Task Experiment.** In practical applications, most tasks need to perform multiple actions to complete. In this article, this kind of task is defined as a complex task. Here we consider a complex task of putting a glass of water on the shelf. For task like this, given only the initial and target scene is hard for work [8] to comprehend.

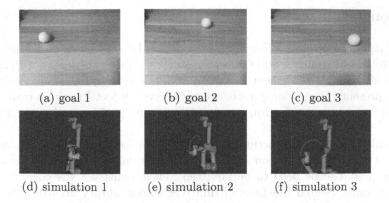

(a) goal 1          (b) goal 2          (c) goal 3

(d) simulation 1    (e) simulation 2    (f) simulation 3

**Fig. 11.** Different places that the target is placed and the corresponding simulation result.

The current and goal scene are shown in Fig. 12.

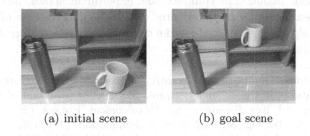

(a) initial scene          (b) goal scene

**Fig. 12.** The initial and goal scene of task: putting a glass of water on the shelf.

The generated skill sequence and corresponding simulated trajectories for each skill is illustrated in Fig. 13.

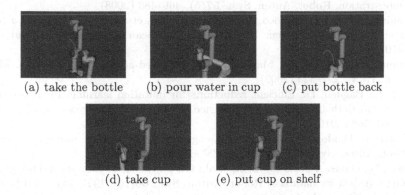

(a) take the bottle    (b) pour water in cup    (c) put bottle back

(d) take cup           (e) put cup on shelf

**Fig. 13.** The reasoning simulated movement sequence of this task.

# 6   Conclusion

In this paper, we propose a Functional Primitives Library based on Event Primitives, Relation Primitives and Object Primitives. Among them, Event Primitive consists of Dynamic Movement Primitive and its function; Relation Primitive is used to present the relationships between objects; Object Primitive is designed to stand for objects involved in a task, including its position and posture information.

In order to guide the action of manipulators for a new task, a sequence reasoning algorithm based on dichotomy is introduced. Firstly, the graph of initial and goal scene need to be inputted. Then, construct the corresponding state diagrams. Search the Event Primitives in our library according to state continuity and relation matching. When the global states have same nodes from both sides, a state-movement sequence from initial to target is delivered. The trajectories derived from Event Primitives in this sequence are revised according to position continuity and then form the movement sequence for this task.

The simulation results of reach experiment show the generalization ability of FPLib for a single action. The complex task experiment shows the capability of our FPLib when facing an unprecedented task. The effectiveness of our library and reasoning algorithm is proved for the obtained sequence can realize the goal of this task in simulation.

**Acknowledgment.** The work was jointly supported by the National Natural Science Foundation of China under Grant 61873006 and Grant 61673053, and in part by National Key Research and Development Project (2018YFC1602704, 2018YFB1702704), Beijing Natural Science Foundation (4212933) and Scientific Research Project of Beijing Educational Committee (KM202110005023).

# References

1. Argall, B.D., Sonia, C., Manuela, V., Brett, B.: A survey of robot learning from demonstration. Robot. Auton. Syst. **57**(5), 469–483 (2008)
2. Bandera, J.P., Molina-Tanco, L., Rodriguez, J.A., et al.: Architecture for a robot learning by imitation system. In: IEEE Mediterranean Electrotechnical Conference (2010)
3. Daumé, H., Langford, J., Marcu, D.: Search-based structured prediction. Mach. Learn. **75**(3), 297–325 (2009)
4. Ross, S., Bagnell, D.: Efficient reductions for imitation learning. In: Proceedings of the Thirtieth International Conference on Artificial Intelligence and Statistics, pp. 661–668 (2010)
5. Chella, A., Dindo, H., Infantino, I.: A cognitive framework for imitation learning. Robot. Auton. Syst. **54**(5), 403–408 (2006)
6. Forte, D., Gams, A., Morimoto, J., et al.: On-line motion synthesis and adaptation using a trajectory database. Robot. Auton. Syst. **60**(10), 1327–1339 (2012)
7. Park, G., Konno, A.: Imitation learning framework based on principal component analysis. Adv. Robot. **29**(9), 639–656 (2015)

8. Ahmadzadeh, S.R., Paikan, A., Mastrogiovanni, F., et al.: Learning symbolic representations of actions from human demonstrations. In: IEEE International Conference on Robotics and Automation ICRA, pp. 3801–3808 (2015)
9. Niekum, S., Osentoski, S., Konidaris, G., et al.: Learning grounded finite-state representations from unstructured demonstrations. Int. J. Robot. Res. **34**(2), 131–157 (2015)
10. Cho, N.J., Sang, H.L., Kim, J.B., et al.: Learning, improving, and generalizing motor skills for the peg-in-hole tasks based on imitation learning and self-learning. Appl. Sci. **10**(8), 2719 (2020)
11. Lioutikov, R., Maeda, G., Veiga, F., et al.: Learning attribute grammars for movement primitive sequencing. Int. J. Robot. Res. **39**(1), 21–38 (2020)
12. Rozo, L., Guo, M., Kupcsik, A.G., et al.: Learning and sequencing of object-centric manipulation skills for industrial tasks. In: IEEE International Conference on Intelligent Robots and Systems (IROS) (2020)
13. Schaal, S.: Dynamical movement primitives - a framework for motor control in humans and humanoid robotics. In: Kimura, H., Tsuchiya, K., Ishiguro, A., Witte, H. (eds.) Adaptive Motion of Animals and Machines. Springer, Tokyo (2006). https://doi.org/10.1007/4-431-31381-8_23
14. Redmon, J., Farhadi, A.: YOLOv3: an incremental improvement. ArXiv e-prints (2018)

# Constrained Control for Systems on Lie Groups with Uncertainties via Tube-Based Model Predictive Control on Euclidean Spaces

Yushu Yu[1]($\boxtimes$), Chuanbeibei Shi[1], Yuwei Ma[1], and Dong Eui Chang[2]

[1] School of Mechatronical Engineering, Beijing Institute of Technology, Beijing 100081, China
yushu.yu@bit.edu.cn

[2] School of Electrical Engineering, KAIST, Daejeon 31141, Korea
dechang@kaist.ac.kr

**Abstract.** In this paper, the constrained control of systems evolving on matrix Lie groups with uncertainties is considered. The proposed methodology is composed of a nominal Model Predictive Control (MPC), and a feedback controller. The previous work on the control of systems on manifolds is applied to design the nominal MPC, which generates the nominal trajectory. In the nominal MPC, the state and input constraints on the Lie group are transformed into the constraints on the Euclidean space. While to deal with uncertainties, the feedback control used to track the nominal trajectory is designed directly on the Lie group. The tracking error in the feedback control is proved to be bounded in invariant sets. Such invariant sets are further used to revise the constraints in nominal MPC. We prove that by using this methodology, the stability and safety of the system can be guaranteed simultaneously. The proposed methodology is applied to the constrained attitude control of rigid bodies. In the application example, the detailed mathematical proof and the numerical simulation are presented, illustrating the feasibility of the proposed methodology.

**Keywords:** Matrix lie group · Model predictive control · Robust control · Attitude control

## 1 Introduction

### 1.1 Motivation and Background

Many systems subject to constraints such as state and input constraints, and uncertainties. The state and input constraints are critical for safety. The uncertainties somehow may let the system violet the state and input constraints, hurting the safety of the system. How to address the state and input constraints under uncertainties in terms of safety is, therefore, a meaningful and challenging problem.

The tube-based MPC is a useful tool that can deal with the state and input constraints of a dynamic system with consideration of the disturbance. It has

© Springer Nature Singapore Pte Ltd. 2022
F. Sun et al. (Eds.): ICCSIP 2021, CCIS 1515, pp. 156–173, 2022.
https://doi.org/10.1007/978-981-16-9247-5_12

been applied to varieties of dynamic systems. Dimarogonas et al. investigated the decentralized control of uncertain nonlinear multi-agent systems using tube-based MPC [10,16]. They also studied the constrained control problem of under-water vehicles by tube-based MPC [12]. Chen et al. addressed the trajectory-tracking control problem for mobile robots by combining tube-based MPC [8]. Kobilarov et al. proposed a tube-based MPC whose tube is expressed by ellipsoids [11]. Yue et al. proposed a robust tube-based model predictive control for lane change maneuver of tractor-trailer vehicles [22]. Some researchers also applied tube-based MPC to the control problem of networks, e.g. [17].

On the other side, the state space of many systems is non-Euclidean manifold, e.g., the configuration of many mechanical systems. The motion control on non-Euclidean Lie group configuration space arouses great interests, which can mainly be categorized into two groups, the coordinate-based control and the geometric control [2,20]. The former method usually uses a local homomorphic map to obtain the local coordinates of the non-Euclidean Lie groups. Taking $SO(3)$ as an example, the local coordinates include Euler angle [24], exponential coordinate [18,20], quaternion [15], etc. While the latter normally builds the error function directly on the Lie group [13,21]. Because of the topological properties of the frequent Lie groups in mechanical systems, the global map between the Lie group and the Euclidean space usually does not exist [3,7,9]. To investigate the global control problem, some researchers adopt various methodologies, e.g., the hybrid system tools [14,19]. Also, the geometric control developed directly on the non-Euclidean Lie group can achieve almost global stability. However, non-linear control for complex systems with non-Euclidean Lie group configuration space is still a challenging problem.

Recent attempts to control of systems on manifolds include the method by embedding the manifold into ambient Euclidean space [5,6], where the design procedure is usually divided into two steps. First, the given manifold is embedded into the Euclidean space and the system dynamics is stably extended into the Euclidean space. Then the controller is designed on the ambient Euclidean space. As the system dynamics on the manifold is stably extended, the stability of the controlled system on the manifold can therefore be obtained. Such a methodology does not need a local coordinate chart on the manifold, thus can avoid frequent problems induced by the local coordinate chart. In the authors' previous work, the MPC on manifold via embedding is also considered [4]. By stably extending the system dynamics from manifold to ambient Euclidean space, the MPC on Euclidean space can be applied directly. However, the previous work does not consider the uncertainties of the system, which may make the actual trajectory differs from the nominal trajectory. In this way, the safety of the systems may be hurt. The constrained control problem of the system on the manifold is therefore a meaningful problem. It is noted that there are some significant challenges to address this problem for systems in non-Euclidean space. In order to guarantee the safety of the system, one may need to express the volume of the tube, i.e., the invariant set of the tracking error. However, it is difficult to express the tube if the manifold is embedded into the ambient Euclidean space, as the invariant set is not preserved anymore after the extension of the dynamics.

## 1.2  Contributions

In this paper, we aim to solve the constrained control problem for the systems evolving on the matrix Lie group. We will extend the previous methodology which embeds the matrix Lie group into ambient Euclidean space. Inspired by the methodology of tube-based MPC, we design the nominal trajectory of the tracking error dynamics on Euclidean space. And considering the disturbance, the tube on Euclidean space is defined. We will design the feedback controller directly on the Lie group by transferring the tube from the Euclidean space to the Lie group. We will show that in such a framework, the safety of the system can be ensured.

In summary, the contribution of this paper can be summarized as,

- We propose a framework to address the constrained control problem for systems on matrix Lie groups. The proposed methodology does not rely on any local coordinates of the Lie group and can apply the existing MPC technique on Euclidean spaces.
- The mathematical proof of the proposed methodology in terms of stability and safety is presented.
- The proposed methodology is applied to the attitude control of rigid bodies, demonstrating its feasibility.

This paper is organized into five sections. In Sect. 2, some background and the problem definition are presented. In Sect. 3, the framework of the tube-based MPC on the manifold is designed and analyzed. Section 4, the proposed methodology is applied to the constrained attitude control of rigid bodies.

## 1.3  Notation

Given a matrix Lie group $G$ and sets $S_1, S_2 \subset G$, we define the following set operations

$$S_1 \odot S_2 = \{s_1 s_2 : s_1 \in S_1, s_2 \in S_2\}$$
$$S_1 \oslash S_2 = \{s_1 : s_2 s_1 \in S_1, \forall s_2 \in S_2\}$$

Also we define the following set operations for sets in Euclidean spaces,

$$S_1 \oplus S_2 = \{s_1 + s_2 : s_1 \in S_1, s_2 \in S_2\}$$
$$S_1 \ominus S_2 = \{s_1 : s_2 + s_1 \in S_1, \forall s_2 \in S_2\} \tag{1}$$

Furthermore, let us define $\mathrm{Ad}_A B = ABA^{-1}$ for all $A \in \mathrm{GL}(n)$, $B \in \mathbb{R}^{n \times n}$. Then, $\mathrm{Ad}_g \xi \in \mathfrak{g}$ for all $g \in G$ and $\xi \in \mathfrak{g}$, where $\mathfrak{g}$ is the Lie algebra of $G$.

# 2    Background and Problem Formulation

## 2.1    System Dynamics and Preliminaries

Systems evolving on an $m$-dimensional matrix Lie group can be expressed by the following equation of motion (EOM),

$$\dot{g} = g\xi$$
$$\dot{\xi} = f(\xi, u) + d \tag{2}$$

where $g \in G$, $\xi \in \mathfrak{g}$, and $u \in \mathbb{R}^m$, $f(\cdot, \cdot)$ is the left-invariant vector field, $d \in \mathbb{R}^m$ is the disturbance induced by modeling uncertainties, and external disturbances. We suppose $d$ satisfies

$$\|d\| \leq b_1 \tag{3}$$

where $b_1$ is a positive constant.

Denote the reference trajectory of the system by

$$\mathbb{R} \ni t \mapsto (g_0(t), \xi_0(t)) \in G \times \mathfrak{g} \tag{4}$$

and the corresponding reference input of the system by,

$$\mathbb{R} \ni t \mapsto u_0(t) \in \mathbb{R}^m \tag{5}$$

We embed the matrix Lie group $G$ into the Euclidean space $\mathbb{R}^{n \times n}$. The tracking error trajectory can be defined on the Euclidean space as,

$$\mathbb{R} \ni t \mapsto (E(t), \Xi(t)) := (xg_0^{-1} - I, \xi - \xi_0) \in \mathbb{R}^{n \times n} \times \mathfrak{g} \tag{6}$$

If we let the trajectory of the system (2) track the reference trajectory, the tracking error dynamics of (2) can therefore be expressed as,

$$\dot{E} = (g_0 + Eg_0)\Xi g_0^{-1}$$
$$\dot{\Xi} = f(\Xi + \xi_0, u) - f(\xi_0, u_0) + d \tag{7}$$

It is noticed that the system (7) also evolves on the Lie group, not on the Euclidean space. By applying the technique of embedding the matrix Lie group $G$ into Euclidean space $\mathbb{R}^{n \times n}$, we can obtain the following equation evolving on $\mathbb{R}^{n \times n} \times \mathbb{R}^m$,

$$\dot{E} = (g_0 + Eg_0)\Xi g_0^{-1} - \alpha \nabla V (g_0 + Eg_0)g_0^{-1}$$
$$\dot{\Xi} = f(\Xi + \xi_0, u) - f(\xi_0, u_0) + d \tag{8}$$

where $E = xg_0^{-1} - I \in \mathbb{R}^{n \times n}$, and $V$ is a function $\mathbb{R}^{n \times n} \mapsto V(x) > 0$ satisfying

$$V^{-1}(0) = G$$
$$V(xg) = V(x), \forall x \in \mathbb{R}^{n \times n}, g \in G \tag{9}$$
$$\nabla^2 V(I)(y, y) > 0, \forall y \in \mathfrak{g}$$

In this way, we say that the system dynamics (2) is embedded into the Euclidean space stably.

## 2.2   Problem Formulation

In this paper we will consider the control problem of dynamic systems evolving on matrix Lie groups, under state constraints, input boundedness, and uncertainties. The control problem can therefore be expressed as follows.

**Problem 1.** *Consider the system evolving on matrix Lie groups governed by the EOM (2). Given specific configuration constraint $g \in \mathcal{X}$, and specific velocity constraint $V_0 \in \mathcal{V}$, input constraints $u \in U$, for reference state and input $(g_0, \xi_0) \in G \times \mathfrak{g}$, deign control input $u : t \mapsto (\tau, T)$ which forces $\|E(t)\| \leq \epsilon_1$ and $\|\Xi(t)\| \leq \epsilon_2$ as $t \to \infty$ with small positive constant $\epsilon_1$ and $\epsilon_2$ while fulfilling all the above constraints for all disturbance satisfying (3).*

The configuration error $E$ can further be divided into the parallel direction error and the transversal direction error as,

$$E \in \mathbb{R}^{n \times n} \mapsto E^{\perp} \in g^{\perp}, E \in \mathbb{R}^{n \times n} \mapsto E^{\|} \in g \qquad (10)$$

where $g^{\perp}$ is the orthogonal component of $g$ in Euclidean space $\mathbb{R}^{n \times n}$, under the Euclidean metric defined by $\langle A, B \rangle = trace(A^T B)$ for all $A, B \in \mathbb{R}^{n \times n}$.

Given the reference trajectory $g_0(t)$ satisfying $\alpha_1 I \leq g_0(t)g_0(t)^T \leq \alpha_2 I$ for all $t$, we linearize (8) along the reference trajectory, the tracking error dynamics can be expressed as,

$$
\begin{aligned}
\dot{E}^{\perp} &= -\alpha((\nabla^2 V(I) \cdot E^{\perp})(g_0 g_0^{\perp})^{-1})^{\perp} \\
\dot{E}^{\|} &= g_0 \Xi g_0^{-1} - \alpha(\nabla^2 V(I) \cdot E^{\perp})(g_0 g_0^T)^{-1})^{\|} \\
\dot{\Xi} &= \frac{\partial f}{\partial \xi}(\xi_0, u_0)\Xi + \frac{\partial f}{\partial u}\delta u + d
\end{aligned}
\qquad (11)
$$

where $\delta u = u - u_0$. As stated in [5], the first equation in (11) is exponentially stable at the origin. It is also possible to design control based on the linearized system (11). However, in order to solve Problem 1, we need to carefully consider the set of tracking errors, which may influence the admissible input and state set. As it is difficult to estimate the boundedness of the tracking error for the linearized system, we will therefore develop a methodology which generates the nominal trajectory based on (11), and tracks the nominal trajectory based on (2) directly.

## 3   Tube-Based MPC Design

### 3.1   Nominal MPC

By excluding the disturbance from the actual system, the nominal EOM of the system is given by,

$$
\begin{aligned}
\dot{\bar{g}} &= \bar{g}\bar{\xi} \\
\dot{\bar{\xi}} &= f(\bar{\xi}, \bar{u})
\end{aligned}
\qquad (12)
$$

where $\bar{*}$ represents the nominal value.

We will solve Problem 1 inspired by the idea of tube-based MPC. The tube-based MPC is composed of a nominal MPC and a feedback controller. The nominal MPC is designed from the nominal tracking error dynamics. By embedding the nominal EOM into Euclidean space, we design the nominal tracking error as $\bar{E} = \bar{X}g_0^{-1} - I \in \mathbb{R}^{n \times n}, \bar{\Xi} = \bar{\xi} - \xi_0$. Then excluding the disturbance from (11), the nominal tracking error dynamics embedded into the Euclidean space is obtained as,

$$\dot{\bar{E}}^{\perp} = -\alpha((\nabla^2 V(I) \cdot \bar{E}^{\perp})(g_0 g_0^{\perp})^{-1})^{\perp}$$
$$\dot{\bar{E}}^{\parallel} = g_0 \bar{\Xi} g_0^{-1} - \alpha(\nabla^2 V(I) \cdot \bar{E}^{\perp})(g_0 g_0^T)^{-1})^{\parallel} \qquad (13)$$
$$\dot{\bar{\Xi}} = \frac{\partial f}{\partial \xi}(\xi_0, u_0)\bar{\Xi} + \frac{\partial f}{\partial u}\bar{\delta}u$$

In the nominal MPC design, we define the initial tracking error $\bar{E} = E$ and $\bar{\Xi} = \Xi$, i.e., we let $\bar{g} = g$ and $\bar{\xi} = \xi$ at the initial time. The purpose of the nominal MPC is to let $\bar{E}^{\parallel}$ converge to the origin while satisfying the nominal input and state constraints.

To deal with the state and input constraints, we express the admissible set of the configuration and velocity error as $\bar{\mathcal{X}}$ and $\bar{\mathcal{V}}$ and the admissible control input as $\bar{\mathcal{U}}$. Therefore, the nominal MPC is expressed as,

$$\min_{\bar{\delta}u(s)} J(\bar{\zeta}, \bar{u}_0) = \quad V_r(\bar{\zeta}(t_k + \Gamma)) +$$
$$\int_{t_k}^{t_k + \Gamma} N_r(\bar{\zeta}(s), \bar{\delta}_u(s)) ds$$
$$s.t. \ \dot{\bar{E}}^{\parallel} = \bar{g}_0 \bar{\Xi} \bar{g}_0^{-1} - \alpha(\nabla^2 V(I) \cdot \bar{E}^{\perp})(\bar{g}_0 \bar{g}_0^T)^{-1})^{\parallel} \qquad (14)$$
$$\dot{\bar{\Xi}} = \frac{\partial f}{\partial \xi}(\xi_0, u_0)\bar{\Xi} + \frac{\partial f}{\partial u}\bar{\delta}_u$$
$$(\bar{E}^{\parallel}, \bar{\Xi}) \in \bar{\mathcal{X}} \times \bar{\mathcal{V}}, \bar{\delta}u(s) \in \bar{\mathcal{U}}$$

where $\zeta = (E^{\parallel}, \Xi)$ is the state, $V_r(\cdot)$ and $N_r(\cdot)$ are positive definite functions used to ensure the stability of the MPC. Notice that $\bar{\mathcal{X}}$, $\bar{\mathcal{V}}$, and $\bar{\mathcal{U}}$ will be given later, according to the actual admissible state and input set and the feedback controller.

## 3.2   Feedback Control for the Disturbed System on Matrix Lie Group

The nominal MPC can generate the nominal trajectory of the system on the matrix Lie group. Suppose the nominal error trajectory is given by $\mathbb{R} \ni t \mapsto (\bar{E}, \bar{\Xi})$, and the nominal input error trajectory is denoted by $\mathbb{R} \ni t \mapsto (\bar{\delta}_u)$. Then the nominal state trajectory is obtained as $\bar{g} = (\bar{E} + I)g_0, \bar{\xi} = \xi + \bar{\Xi}$, and the nominal input trajectory is obtained as $\bar{\tau} = \tau_0 + \delta_{\tau}$.

It is noted that using the nominal MPC, the generated nominal state trajectory is already restricted on the matrix Lie group. Therefore, we design the feedback control for the actual systems on the matrix Lie group directly.

For the actual system with uncertainties, it is necessary to design the tracking error carefully. We first define the tracking error between the nominal state and the actual state as $\tilde{E} = g\bar{g}^{-1} - I, \tilde{\Xi} = \xi - \bar{\xi}$. The feedback controller should ensure the boundedness of the tracking error $(\tilde{E}, \tilde{\Xi})$ and the input error $\tilde{\tau} = \tau - \bar{\tau}$ so that the constraints in the nominal MPC can be derived from the actual admissible input and state sets.

As the nominal trajectory always evolves on the matrix Lie group, the feedback controller can be designed in a cascaded format. Given the nominal trajectory generated by the NMPC, design the velocity $\xi_r$ which is the output of the outer loop controller such that

$$\text{Ad}_{\bar{g}}(\xi_r - \bar{\xi}) = -k_g(\tilde{E}^T\tilde{E} + \tilde{E}^T)^{\|} \tag{15}$$

where $k_g$ is a positive constant.

Then design the following control law of the inner loop to let $\xi$ track $\xi_r$,

$$u = u_r - k_\xi(\xi - \xi_r) \tag{16}$$

where $u_r = f^{-1}(\dot{\xi})$.

**Lemma 1.** [23] Given two vectors $x, y \in \mathbb{R}^n$ their convex hull is defined by $Co(x, y) := \{\xi : \xi = \theta x + (1 - \theta)y, 0 < \theta < 1\}$. Consider a vector-valued function $f : \mathbb{R}^n \mapsto \mathbb{R}^m$. Assume that $f$ is differentiable on an open set $S \subseteq \mathbb{R}^n$. Let $x, y$ two points of $S$ such that $Co(x, y) \subseteq S$. Then, there exist constant vectors $c_1, \cdots, c_m \in Co(x, y)$ such that,

$$f(x) - f(y) = \left[ \sum_{k=1}^{m} \sum_{j=1}^{n} l_m(k)l_n(j)^T \frac{\partial f_k(c_k)}{\partial x_j} \right] (x - y)$$

We define an intermediate tracking error $\xi_e := \xi - \xi_r$. From the second element of (2) and Lemma 1, there are $c_1, c_2, ..., c_m \in Co(u, u_r)$ such that,

$$
\begin{aligned}
\dot{\xi}_e &= f(\xi, u) - f(\xi_r, u) + f(\xi_r, u) - f(\xi_r, u_r) + d \\
&= f(\xi, u) - f(\xi_r, u) + \left[ \sum_{k=1}^{m} \sum_{j=1}^{n} l_m(k)l_n(j)^T \frac{\partial f_k(\xi_r, c_k)}{\partial x_j} \right] (u - u_r) + d
\end{aligned} \tag{17}
$$

where $L_1$ is the Lipschitz constant of the function $f(\cdot, u)$.

Defining $\varphi_1 = \frac{1}{2}\xi_e^T\xi_e$, we arrive at,

$$
\begin{aligned}
\dot{\varphi}_1 = \xi_e^T\dot{\xi}_e &\leq L_1\|\xi_e\|^2 - k_\xi \frac{J(\xi_r) + J^T(\xi_r)}{2}\|\xi_e\|^2 + \xi_e^T d \\
&\leq -(k_\xi J_{min}(\xi_e) - L_1)\|\xi_e\|^2 + \frac{1}{4\rho_g}\|\xi_e\|^2 + \rho_g b_1^2
\end{aligned} \tag{18}
$$

where $\rho_g$ is a positive constant. Then it is concluded that $\dot{\varphi}_1 < 0$ if $\|\xi_e\| > \frac{\rho_g}{k_\xi J_{min} - L_1 - \frac{1}{4\rho_g}} d_m$. As we let $\|\xi_e\| = 0$ at the initial instant, the velocity tracking error $\xi_e$ is bounded by

$$\|\xi_e\| \leq b_v := \frac{\rho}{k_\xi J_{min} - L_1 - \frac{1}{4\rho_g}} b_1 \tag{19}$$

Then we have the following Lemma.

**Lemma 2.** *Consider system (2). Suppose the nominal state and input trajectory are generated by solving (14), the control law (15) and (16) are used to track the nominal state. Then the tracking error $\tilde{E}$ and $\xi_e$ converge to the invariant set*
$$\tilde{\Omega}_E := \{\tilde{E} : \|(\tilde{E}^T \tilde{E} + \tilde{E}^T)^\| \| \leq \frac{\sqrt{2\rho_\xi} b_v}{\sqrt{2k_g - \frac{1}{2\rho_\xi}}}\}, \quad \tilde{\Omega}_\xi := \{\xi_e : \|\xi_e\| \leq b_v\}.$$

*Proof.* We define the candidate Lyapunov function as,

$$\varphi_2 = \|g\bar{g}^{-1} - I\|^2 = \langle g\bar{g}^{-1} - I, g\bar{g}^{-1} - I\rangle. \tag{20}$$

Then, taking the time derivative of $\varphi_2$ yields,

$$\begin{aligned}
\dot{\varphi}_2 &= 2\langle \tilde{E}, g(\xi - \bar{\xi})\bar{g}^{-1}\rangle \\
&= 2\langle \tilde{E}, g(\xi - \xi_r)\bar{g}^{-1}\rangle + 2\langle \tilde{E}, g(\xi_r - \bar{\xi})\bar{g}^{-1}\rangle \\
&= 2\langle \tilde{E}, g\bar{g}^{-1} \operatorname{Ad}_{\bar{g}} \xi_e\rangle + 2\langle \tilde{E}, g\bar{g}^{-1} \operatorname{Ad}_{\bar{g}}(\xi_r - \bar{\xi})\rangle \\
&= 2\langle \tilde{E}, (\tilde{E} + I) \operatorname{Ad}_{\bar{g}} \xi_e\rangle + 2\langle \tilde{E}, (\tilde{E} + I) \operatorname{Ad}_{\bar{g}}(\xi_r - \bar{\xi})\rangle \\
&= 2\langle \tilde{E}^T \tilde{E} + \tilde{E}, \operatorname{Ad}_{\bar{g}} \xi_e\rangle + 2\langle \tilde{E}^T \tilde{E} + \tilde{E}, \operatorname{Ad}_{\bar{g}}(\xi_r - \bar{\xi})\rangle \\
&= 2\langle (\tilde{E}^T \tilde{E} + \tilde{E})^\|, \operatorname{Ad}_{\bar{g}} \xi_e\rangle + 2\langle (\tilde{E}^T \tilde{E} + \tilde{E})^\|, \operatorname{Ad}_{\bar{g}}(\xi_r - \bar{\xi})\rangle
\end{aligned} \tag{21}$$

Substituting (15) into (21) and applying Young's inequality we have,

$$\begin{aligned}
\dot{\varphi}_2 &= -2k_g \|(\tilde{E}^T \tilde{E} + \tilde{E})^\|\|^2 + 2\langle (\tilde{E}^T \tilde{E} + \tilde{E})^\|, \operatorname{Ad}_{\bar{g}}(\xi_r - \bar{\xi})\rangle \\
&\leq -2k_g \|(\tilde{E}^T \tilde{E} + \tilde{E})^\|\|^2 + \frac{1}{2\rho_\xi} \|(\tilde{E}^T \tilde{E} + \tilde{E})^\|\|^2 + 2\rho_\xi \|b_v\|^2 \\
&\leq -(2k_g - \frac{1}{2\rho_\xi}) \|(\tilde{E}^T \tilde{E} + \tilde{E})^\|\|^2 + 2\rho_\xi b_v^2
\end{aligned}$$

where $\rho_\xi$ is a positive constant. It is seen that $\dot{\varphi}_2 \leq 0$ if $\|(\tilde{E}^T \tilde{E} + \tilde{E}^T)^\|\| \geq \frac{\sqrt{2\rho_\xi} b_v}{\sqrt{2k_g - \frac{1}{2\rho_\xi}}}$. Aslo we let $\tilde{E} = 0$ at the initial instant, it is then concluded that $\tilde{\Omega}_E := \{\|(\tilde{E}^T \tilde{E} + \tilde{E}^T)^\|\| \leq \frac{\sqrt{2\rho_\xi} b_v}{\sqrt{2k_g - \frac{1}{2\rho_\xi}}}\}$ is an invariant set for the closed-loop system under the control law (15) and (16).

## 3.3  Constraints Revision from Tube

The MPC synthesis should consider the revision of the admissible sets of state and control. As we have shown, the feedback control law is designed such that the tracking error and the input fall into the invariant set, the state and input constraints for the nominal system can be revised accordingly. In this way, the safety of the actual system is guaranteed in the presence of tracking error induced by the uncertainties.

From the configuration tracking error invariant set $\tilde{\Omega}_E$, the invariant set of $\tilde{g} = g\bar{g}^{-1}$ can be obtained as $\tilde{\Omega}_g = \tilde{\Omega}_E \oplus \{I\}$. Then the admissible set of $\bar{g}$ can be derived as $\bar{\mathcal{X}} = \mathcal{X} \oslash \tilde{\Omega}_g$, from which we can further derive the admissible set of the nominal parallel tracking error $\bar{\mathcal{X}}^{\|}$. And combining the results of the previous subsections, the constraints in the nominal MPC can therefore be revised as,

$$\bar{\mathcal{V}} = \mathcal{V} \ominus (\tilde{\Omega}_\zeta \oplus k_g \tilde{\Omega}_E), \bar{U} = U \ominus k_\xi \tilde{\Omega}_\xi \qquad (22)$$

# 4  Application Example

In this section, we will take the rotational motion of the rigid body as an application example to illustrate the theoretical results of this paper.

## 4.1  Rotational Dynamics of Rigid Body

The attitude control of the rigid body is started from the rotational motion of the rigid body, which is given by,

$$\begin{aligned} \dot{R} &= R\hat{\omega} \\ \dot{\omega} &= M^{-1}(\tau - \hat{\omega}M\omega) + d_r \end{aligned} \qquad (23)$$

where $R \in SO(3)$ is the rotation matrix of the rigid body, $\omega \in \mathbb{R}^3$ is the angular velocity, $M \in \mathbb{R}^{3\times3}$ is the inertia tensor, $\tau \in \mathbb{R}^3$ is the torque, and $d_r \in \mathbb{R}^3$ is the disturbance bounded by $\|d_r\| \leq b_r$ with positive constant $b_r$.

Given a reference trajectory,

$$\mathbb{R} \ni t \mapsto (R_0(t), \omega_0(t)) \qquad (24)$$

It is natural to derive that the error dynamics follows the following format,

$$\begin{aligned} R \ni t \mapsto (E(t), e(t)) &:= (X(t)R_0^{-1} - I, \omega(t) - \omega_0(t)) \\ &\in \mathbb{R}^{3\times3} \times \mathbb{R}^3 \end{aligned} \qquad (25)$$

By embedding the manifold into the Euclidean space, and splitting the tracking error $E$ into parallel error $E^{\|}$ and transversal error $E^{\perp}$, we have the following linearized tracking error dynamics,

$$\begin{aligned} \dot{E}^{\perp} &= -2\alpha E^{\perp} \\ \dot{E}^{\|} &= R_0 \hat{e} R_0^{-1} \\ \dot{e} &= M^{-1}(Me \times \omega_0 + M\omega_0 \times e) + M^{-1}\delta_\tau \end{aligned} \qquad (26)$$

It has been proved that the first error dynamics of (26) is stable, while the second and third dynamics can be stabilized to zeros. Therefore, we can design the MPC controller for the rotational dynamics (26).

The constraints on the attitude, angular velocity, and input are expressed as,

$$RR_0^T \in \mathcal{X}, \omega \in \mathcal{V}, \tau \in U \tag{27}$$

### 4.2  Feedback Control and Invariant Set of Tracking Error

For the system constraints (27), we can design the nominal error trajectory using MPC. Suppose the nominal error trajectory is given by $\mathbb{R} \ni t \mapsto (\bar{E}, \bar{\Xi})$, and the nominal input error trajectory is denoted by $\mathbb{R} \ni t \mapsto (\bar{\delta}_\tau)$. Then the nominal state and input trajectory is obtained as $\bar{R} = (\bar{E}+I)R_0, \bar{\omega} = \omega + \bar{\Xi}, \bar{\tau} = \tau_0 + \bar{\delta}_\tau$.

As shown in the previous section, we need to design a feedback control law to force the actual trajectory to track the nominal trajectory $(\bar{R}, \bar{\omega}, \bar{\tau})$, and the tracking error should be bounded in a robust invariant set, which is called the tube of the tracking error. A cascaded structure feedback controller will also be considered for this purpose.

First, we design the following reference angular velocity for the feedback attitude control. As the system dynamics always evolves on $SO(3)$, we design the angular velocity $\omega_r$ such that,

$$\mathrm{Ad}_{\bar{R}}(\hat{\omega}_r - \hat{\bar{\omega}}) = -k_1 \tilde{E}^{\|} \tag{28}$$

where $\tilde{E}^{\|} = R\bar{R}^T - I$ is the parallel error between $\bar{R}$ and $R$, $k_1$ is a positive constant. Note that $\bar{R}$ always evolves on $SO(3)$ for system (23).

Then design the body torque as,

$$\tau = \tau_r - k_2 e_\omega \tag{29}$$

where $e_\omega = \omega - \omega_r$, $\tau_r = M\dot{\omega}_r + \hat{\omega}_r M\omega_r$, and $k_2$ is a positive constant.

Let us consider the tracking error of the angular velocity of the rigid body. Substituting (28) into (23) yields,

$$\begin{aligned} \dot{e}_\omega &= M^{-1}\tau - M^{-1}\hat{\omega}M\omega - M^{-1}\tau_r + M^{-1}\hat{\omega}_r M\omega_r \\ &= M^{-1}(\tau - \tau_r) + M^{-1}\hat{\omega}_r M\omega_r - M^{-1}\hat{\omega}M\omega \end{aligned} \tag{30}$$

Define a function $\eta_1(\omega) : \{\omega \in \mathbb{R}^3 : \|\omega\| \leq \omega_m\} \ni \omega \mapsto M^{-1}\hat{\omega}M\omega \in \mathbb{R}^3$ with positive constant $\omega_m$, then we have,

$$\|\eta_1(\omega) - \eta_1(\omega_r)\| \leq L_2\|e_\omega\| \tag{31}$$

where $L_2$ is the Lipchitz constant of the function $\eta_1(\cdot)$.

In order to derive the results, we further define $\eta_2(\omega) : \{\omega \in \mathbb{R}^3 : \|\omega\| \leq \omega_m\} \ni \omega \mapsto \hat{\omega}M\omega \in \mathbb{R}^3$, hence we have

$$\|\eta_2(\omega_{0,r}) - \eta_2(\bar{\omega}_0)\| \leq L_3\|\omega_{0,r} - \bar{\omega}_0\| \leq L_3 k_1\|e_{\bar{R},0}\| \tag{32}$$

where $L_3$ is the Lipchitz constant of $\eta_2(\cdot)$.

**Proposition 1.** *Consider the system dynamics (23). The nominal state and input trajectory are represented by $\bar{R}(t), \bar{\omega}(t), \bar{\tau}(t)$. Suppose the control torque is determined by the feedback control law (29). If the positive constants $k_1$ and $k_2$ satisfy*

$$k_1 - \frac{1}{4\rho_1} > 0,$$

$$k_2\lambda(M)^{-1} - \rho_1 - \frac{1}{4\rho_2} - L_2 > 0$$

*then the state tracking error and the input of the closed-loop system falls into the following sets,*

$$E^{\|} \in \tilde{\Omega}_{E^{\|}} = \{E^{\|} : \|E^{\|}\| \leq \sqrt{\frac{\rho_2}{\min(\beta_1, \beta_2)}} b_r := L_R\}$$

$$\tilde{\omega} \in \tilde{\Omega}_\omega = \{\tilde{\omega} : \|\tilde{\omega}\| \leq (k_1 + 1)\sqrt{\frac{\rho_2}{\min(\beta_1, \beta_2)}} b_r\} \tag{33}$$

$$\tilde{\tau} \in \tilde{\Omega}_\tau = \{\tilde{\tau} : \|\tilde{\tau}\| \leq (\|M\|k_1(k_1 + 1) + L_3 k_1 + k_2)$$

$$b_r \sqrt{\frac{\rho_2}{\min(\beta_1, \beta_2)}} := \Delta_\tau\}$$

*where $k_5 = \frac{k_3}{k_4}$, $L_R = \sqrt{\frac{\rho_2}{\min(\beta_1, \beta_2)}} b_r$, $\beta_1 = k_1 - \frac{1}{4\rho_1}$, $\beta_2 = k_2\lambda(M)^{-1} - \rho_1 - \frac{1}{4\rho_2} - L_2$ with positive constants $\rho_1$, $\rho_2$, $\lambda(M)$ is the minimum eigenvalue of $M$.*

*Proof.* We define the following Lyapunov candidate as,

$$V = \text{tr}(I - R\bar{R}^T) + \frac{1}{2}e_\omega^T e_\omega \tag{34}$$

which is positive definite.

From (30), we can obtain the time derivative of $V$,

$$\begin{aligned}
\dot{V} &= \text{tr}\left[(\bar{R}R^T)^T \left(\text{Ad}_{\bar{R}}(\hat{\omega} - \hat{\bar{\omega}})\right)\right] + e_\omega^T \dot{e}_\omega \\
&= \text{tr}\left[(\bar{R}R^T)^T \left(\text{Ad}_{\bar{R}} \hat{e}_\omega\right)\right] \\
&\quad + \text{tr}\left[(\bar{R}R^T)^T \left(\text{Ad}_{\bar{R}}(\hat{\omega}_r - \hat{\bar{\omega}})\right)\right] \\
&\quad - k_2 e_\omega^T M^{-1} e_\omega + e_\omega^T[\eta_1(\omega_r) - \eta_1(\omega)] + e_\omega^T d_r \\
&= \left(\bar{R}\hat{e}_\omega \bar{R}^T\right)\left(R\bar{R}^T - \bar{R}R^T\right)^\vee \\
&\quad + \left(\bar{R}(\hat{\omega}_r - \hat{\bar{\omega}})\bar{R}^T\right)\left(R\bar{R}^T - \bar{R}R^T\right)^\vee \\
&\quad + -k_2 e_\omega^T M^{-1} e_\omega + e_\omega^T[\eta_1(\omega_r) - \eta_1(\omega)] + e_\omega^T d_r \\
&\leq - k_1\|\tilde{E}^{\|}\|^2 + \|\tilde{E}^{\|}\|\|e_\omega\| - k_2\lambda(M)^{-1}\|e_\omega\|^2 \\
&\quad + L_2\|e_\omega\|^2 + e_\omega^T d_r \\
&\leq - (k_1 - \frac{1}{4\rho_1})\|\tilde{E}^{\|}\|^2 - (k_2\lambda(M)^{-1} - \rho_1 \\
&\quad - \frac{1}{4\rho_2} - L_2)\|e_\omega\|^2 + \rho_2 b_r^2
\end{aligned} \tag{35}$$

Taking $\beta_1 = k_1 - \frac{1}{4\rho_1}$ and $\beta_2 = k_2\lambda(M)^{-1} - \rho_1 - \frac{1}{4\rho_2} - L_2$, if the parameters are selected such that $\beta_1 > 0$ and $\beta_2 > 0$, then

$$\dot{V} \leq -\min(\beta_1, \beta_2)\|(e_{\tilde{R}}^T, e_\omega^T)^T\|^2 + \rho_2 b_r^2 \tag{36}$$

It is seen that $\dot{V} < 0$ if $\|(\tilde{E}^T, e_\omega^T)^T\| > \sqrt{\frac{\rho_2}{\min(\beta_1,\beta_2)}}b_r$. The bound of $\tilde{E}$ and $e_\omega$ can be expressed as,

$$\|\tilde{E}\| \leq \|(e_{\tilde{R}}^T, e_\omega^T)^T\| \leq L_R$$
$$\|e_\omega\| \leq \|(e_{\tilde{R}}^T, e_\omega^T)^T\| \leq L_R \tag{37}$$

Recalling the definition of $e_\omega$ we arrive at,

$$\|\tilde{\omega}\| \leq k_1\|e_{\tilde{R}}\| + \|e_\omega\| \leq (k_1 + 1)L_R \tag{38}$$

Then we consider the boundedness of $\tilde{\tau} = \tau_d - \bar{\tau}$. From the control law, we have,

$$\tau_r - \bar{\tau} = M\dot{\omega}_r - M\dot{\bar{\omega}} + \eta_2(\omega_r) - \eta_2(\bar{\omega})$$
$$\leq Mk_1\|\dot{\tilde{E}}^\|\| + L_3k_1\|\tilde{E}^\|\| \tag{39}$$
$$\leq Mk_1\|\tilde{\omega}\| + L_3k_1\|\tilde{E}^\|\|$$

While from (29) it is concluded that $\tau_d - \tau_r = -k_2e_\omega$, hence combining (37) and (38) we have,

$$\|\tilde{\tau}\| \leq \|\tau_d - \tau_r\| + \|\tau_d - \bar{\tau}\|$$
$$\leq \|M\|k_1\|\tilde{\omega}\| + L_3k_1\|e_{\tilde{R}}\| + k_2\|e_\omega\| \tag{40}$$
$$\leq (\|M\|k_1(k_1 + 1) + L_3k_1 + k_2)b_r\sqrt{\frac{\rho_2}{\min(\beta_1, \beta_2)}}$$

This completes the proof.

## 4.3    Tube-Based MPC for Rotational Motion of Rigid Bodies

From the invariant set $\tilde{\Omega}_{E\|}$, we can define the invariant set of $\tilde{R} = R\bar{R}^T$ as $\tilde{\Omega}_R = \{\tilde{R} : \|\frac{(\tilde{R}-\tilde{R}^T)^\vee}{2}\| \leq L_R\}$. From the Rodrigues' formula, it is shown that,

$$\|\tilde{E}^\|\| = \sin\|\alpha\| \tag{41}$$

where $\alpha$ is the equivalent angle of the rotation matrix $\tilde{R}$. Then $R\bar{R}_0^T \in \mathcal{X}$ and $R\bar{R}^T \in \tilde{\Omega}_R$ implies $\bar{R}R_0^T \in \mathcal{X} \oslash \tilde{\Omega}_R$.

It is noted that there is a difference between $\bar{E}^\|$ and $\bar{R}R_0^T$. Therefore we need to derive the admissible set of $\bar{E}^\|$ from the admissible set of $\bar{R}R_0^T$. Suppose $\bar{E}^\| = (a_1, a_2, a_3)^T$, we can derive $\bar{R}R_0^T$ from $\bar{E}^\|$ as,

$$\bar{R}R_0^T = f_R(\bar{E}^\|) = \begin{bmatrix} r_{11} & r_{12} & r_{13} \\ r_{21} & r_{22} & r_{23} \\ r_{31} & r_{32} & r_{33} \end{bmatrix} \tag{42}$$

where

$$r_{11} = 1 - \frac{\left(a_2\,a_3 - a_2\,a_3\,\sqrt{-a_1{}^2 - a_2{}^2 - a_3{}^2 + 1}\right)\left(a_2{}^2 + a_3{}^2\right)}{a_2\,a_3\,(a_1{}^2 + a_2{}^2 + a_3{}^2)}$$

$$r_{12} = -a_3 - \frac{a_1\,a_2\left(\sqrt{-a_1{}^2 - a_2{}^2 - a_3{}^2 + 1} - 1\right)}{a_1{}^2 + a_2{}^2 + a_3{}^2}$$

$$r_{13} = a_2 - \frac{a_1\,a_3\left(\sqrt{-a_1{}^2 - a_2{}^2 - a_3{}^2 + 1} - 1\right)}{a_1{}^2 + a_2{}^2 + a_3{}^2}$$

$$r_{21} = a_3 - \frac{a_1\,a_2\left(\sqrt{-a_1{}^2 - a_2{}^2 - a_3{}^2 + 1} - 1\right)}{a_1{}^2 + a_2{}^2 + a_3{}^2}$$

$$r_{22} = 1 - \frac{\left(a_2\,a_3 - a_2\,a_3\,\sqrt{-a_1{}^2 - a_2{}^2 - a_3{}^2 + 1}\right)\left(a_1{}^2 + a_3{}^2\right)}{a_2\,a_3\,(a_1{}^2 + a_2{}^2 + a_3{}^2)}$$

$$r_{23} = -a_1 - \frac{a_2\,a_3\left(\sqrt{-a_1{}^2 - a_2{}^2 - a_3{}^2 + 1} - 1\right)}{a_1{}^2 + a_2{}^2 + a_3{}^2}$$

$$r_{31} = -a_2 - \frac{a_1\,a_3\left(\sqrt{-a_1{}^2 - a_2{}^2 - a_3{}^2 + 1} - 1\right)}{a_1{}^2 + a_2{}^2 + a_3{}^2}$$

$$r_{32} = a_1 - \frac{a_2\,a_3\left(\sqrt{-a_1{}^2 - a_2{}^2 - a_3{}^2 + 1} - 1\right)}{a_1{}^2 + a_2{}^2 + a_3{}^2}$$

$$r_{33} = \frac{(a_1{}^2 + a_2{}^2)\sqrt{-a_1{}^2 - a_2{}^2 - a_3{}^2 + 1} + a_3{}^2}{a_1{}^2 + a_2{}^2 + a_3{}^2}$$

From (42) the admissible set of $\bar{E}^{\parallel}$ can be derived from the admissible set of $\bar{R}R_0^T$. For example, if the admissible set of $\bar{R}R_0^T$ is given by $\mathcal{X} \oslash \tilde{\Omega}_R = \{R : C(\bar{R}R_0^T) \leq 0\}$, then we can express the admissible set of $\bar{E}^{\parallel}$ as $\bar{\mathcal{X}}^{\parallel} = \{\bar{E}^{\parallel} : C(f_R(\bar{E}^{\parallel})) \leq 0\}$, which is used to define the constraints in the nominal MPC.

Combining the previous results, we are now in the position to derive the nominal MPC for the rotational motion of the rigid body as,

$$\min_{\bar{\delta}_\tau(s)} J(\bar{\zeta}, \bar{\delta}_\tau) = \quad V_r(\bar{\zeta}(t_k + \Gamma)) + \int_{t_k}^{t_k + \Gamma} \left(N_r(\bar{\zeta}(s), \bar{\delta}_\tau(s))\right) ds$$

$$s.t. \quad \dot{\bar{E}}^{\parallel}(s) = R_0 \hat{\bar{e}} R_0^{-1}, \tag{43}$$

$$\dot{\bar{e}} = M^{-1}(M\bar{e} \times \omega_0 + M\omega_0 \times \bar{e}) + M^{-1}\bar{\delta}_\tau$$

$$(\bar{E}^{\parallel}, \bar{e}) \in \bar{\mathcal{X}}^{\parallel} \times \bar{\mathcal{V}}, \bar{\delta}_\tau \in \bar{U}$$

where $\zeta = (E^{\parallel}, e)$, the state constraint set $\bar{\mathcal{X}} = \mathcal{X} \oslash \tilde{\Omega}_R$, $\bar{\mathcal{V}} = \mathcal{V} \ominus \tilde{\Omega}_\omega$, $\bar{U} = U \ominus \tilde{\Omega}_\tau$.

We then synthesis the tube-based MPC as shown in Algorithm 1. As indicated by Theorem 1, Algorithm 1 combines the feedback control law and the nominal MPC, the constraints on the state/input of the rigid body with uncertainties can therefore be guaranteed to fulfill.

---

**Algorithm 1.** Synthesis of the tube-based MPC

---

**Initialization:** At time instant $t_0$, let $\zeta(0) = \bar{\zeta}(0)$.

1: At time instant $t_k$, solve the nominal MPC problem (43), obtain the nominal state and input $\bar{E}^{\parallel}(s), \bar{e}(s), \bar{\delta}_\tau(s), s \in [t_k, t_k + \Gamma)$.

2: Calculate $\bar{R}(s), \bar{\omega}, \bar{\tau}, s \in [t_k, t_k + \Gamma)$.

3: **for all** $s \in [t_k, t_{k+1})$ **do**

4:    Apply the actual control input $\tau(s)$ to the rigid body, according to (29).

5: **end for**

6: $\big(\zeta(t_k), \bar{\zeta}(t_k)\big) \leftarrow \big(\zeta(t_{k+1}), \bar{\zeta}(t_{k+1})\big)$, $t_k \leftarrow t_{k+1}$.

7: Go to step 1.

---

## 4.4   Simulation

During the simulation, the inertia tensor of the rigid body is $M = \text{diag}(2.263, 2.47,$ $4.7235) kg \cdot m^2$, the initial attitude of a rigid body is set to $R(0) = \exp(0.65[\frac{\sqrt{2}}{2},$ $\frac{\sqrt{2}}{2}, 0]^T)$, and the reference attitude is set to $R_0 = \exp(-0.6[\frac{\sqrt{2}}{2}, \frac{\sqrt{2}}{2}, 0]^T)$. The angular velocity of the rigid body is under the constraint $\|\omega\| < 1 \text{rad/s}$. While the attitude constraint of the rigid body is given by $0.65 \le e_3^T R R_0^T R_0 e_3 \le 0.95$. The disturbance acting on the rigid body is assumed to uniform distribution $d_r \sim U(-1.75, 1.75)$. The Lipchitz constants are calculated according to the EOM as $L_2 = 1.39$ and $L_3 = 3.34$. The open-source ACADO is adopted to solve the MPC problem [1]. In the simulation, the prediction horizon is set to 0.7 s, and the sampling time is 0.1 s.

From Proposition 1, the tube along the nominal attitude trajectory is calculated as $\{\tilde{E}^{\parallel} : \|\tilde{E}^{\parallel}\| \le 0.1563\}$, from which the constraint for $\bar{R}R_0^T$ is revised as $0.7608 \le e_3^T \bar{R}R_0^T R_0 e_3 \le 0.8895$. And the admissible set for $\bar{E}^{\parallel}$ is further revised as $\{\bar{E}^{\parallel} : 0.7608 \le e_3^T f_R(\bar{E}^{\parallel}) R_0 e_3 \le 0.8895\}$ in the nominal MPC.

The simulation results are shown in Figs. 1, 2, 3 and 4. The attitude of the rigid body expressed in Euler angles is shown in Fig. 1. It is seen that the attitude of the system evolves from the initial attitude to the reference attitude. The attitude constraint of the rigid body is expressed in Fig. 3, from which it is seen that the attitude constraint is satisfied using the proposed control algorithm, in the presence of uncertainties. It is also noted that because of the attitude constraint, the rotational trajectory from the initial attitude to the desired attitude does not follow the geodesics on $SO(3)$. The angular velocity of the rigid body is depicted in Fig. 2. It is seen that the constraints on the angular velocity are also fulfilled. While the input torque under the proposed control algorithm is presented in Fig. 4. These two figures also show that the velocity and the input torque are all in the admissible sets. From the simulation results, the feasibility of the proposed methodology on attitude control of the rigid body is verified.

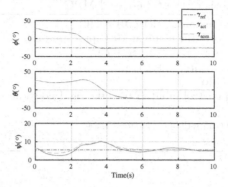

**Fig. 1.** The nominal and actual attitude expressed in Euler angles. The dot-dashed line represents the reference value. The solid line represents the actual value. While the virtual line represents the nominal value.

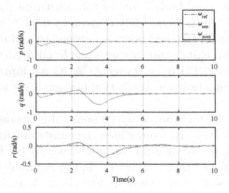

**Fig. 2.** The reference and actual angular velocity.

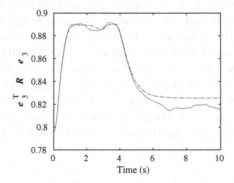

**Fig. 3.** The attitude constraints in one test trial.

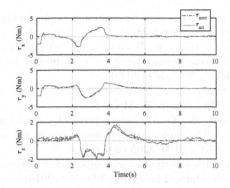

**Fig. 4.** The actual and nominal input of the vehicle in one test trial.

## 5   Conclusions

In this paper, we have developed a methodology to design a controller that deals
with the state and input constraints for systems on the matrix Lie groups with
uncertainties. The methodology is inspired by the Tube-based MPC. By embedding the manifold into Euclidean space, the nominal MPC has been designed on
the Euclidean space. As the generated nominal trajectory is restricted on the
Lie group, the feedback controller used to track the nominal trajectory has been
designed on the manifold directly. The results of the simulation showed that the
tracking error in the feedback controller can be bounded into robust invariant
sets, which can be used to revise the constraints in the nominal MPC expressed
in the Euclidean space. In this way, the nominal MPC in the Euclidean space
and the feedback controller on the Lie group can be combined together. Therefore, the proof for the safety of the overall system evolving on the manifold has
been obtained. The application example of the proposed methodology on the
rotational motion of the rigid body has been presented. The proposed methodology does not rely on any local coordinates of the Lie group and can apply the
existing MPC techniques on the Euclidean space.

## References

1. ACADO Toolkit Homepage (2009–2013)
2. Bharadwaj, S., Osipchuk, M., Mease, K.D., Park, F.C.: Geometry and inverse
   optimality in global attitude stabilization. J. Guidance Control Dyn. **21**(6), 930–
   939 (1998)
3. Bhat, S.P., Bernstein, D.S.: A topological obstruction to continuous global stabilization of rotational motion and the unwinding phenomenon. Syst. Control Lett.
   **39**(1), 63–70 (2000)
4. Chang, D.E., Phogat, K.S., Choi, J.: Model predictive tracking control for invariant
   systems on matrix lie groups via stable embedding into Euclidean spaces. IEEE
   Trans. Autom. Control **65**(7), 3191–3198 (2020)

5. Chang, D.E.: On controller design for systems on manifolds in Euclidean space. Int. J. Robust Nonlinear Control **28**(16), 4981–4998 (2018)
6. Chang, D.E.: Globally exponentially convergent continuous observers for velocity bias and state for invariant kinematic systems on matrix lie groups. IEEE Trans. Autom. Control **66**(7), 3363–3369 (2020)
7. Chaturvedi, N.A., Sanyal, A.K., McClamroch, N.H.: Rigid-body attitude control. IEEE Control Syst. Mag. **31**(3), 30–51 (2011)
8. Chen, Y., Li, Z., Kong, H., Ke, F.: Model predictive tracking control of nonholonomic mobile robots with coupled input constraints and unknown dynamics. IEEE Trans. Industr. Inf. **15**(6), 3196–3205 (2019)
9. Dai, J.S.: Euler-CRodrigues formula variations, quaternion conjugation and intrinsic connections. Mech. Mach. Theory **92**, 144–152 (2015)
10. Filotheou, A., Nikou, A., Dimarogonas, D.V.: Robust decentralised navigation of multi-agent systems with collision avoidance and connectivity maintenance using model predictive controllers. Int. J. Control **93**(6), 1470–1484 (2020)
11. Garimella, G., Sheckells, M., Moore, J., Kobilarov, M.: Robust obstacle avoidance using tube NMPC, pp. 1–9 (2018)
12. Heshmati-Alamdari, S., Nikou, A., Dimarogonas, D.V.: Robust trajectory tracking control for underactuated autonomous underwater vehicles in uncertain environments. IEEE Trans. Autom. Sci. Eng. **18**(3), 1–14 (2020)
13. Lee, T.: Geometric tracking control of the attitude dynamics of a rigid body on SO(3). In: Proceedings of American Control Conference, pp. 1200–1205, San Francisco, CA, June 2011
14. Mayhew, C.G., Sanfelice, R.G., Teel, A.R.: Quaternion-based hybrid control for robust global attitude tracking. IEEE Trans. Autom. Control **56**(11), 2555–2566 (2011)
15. Naldi, R., Furci, M., Sanfelice, R.G., Marconi, L.: Robust global trajectory tracking for underactuated VTOL aerial vehicles using inner-outer loop control paradigms. IEEE Trans. Autom. Control **62**(1), 97–112 (2017)
16. Nikou, A., Dimarogonas, D.V.: Decentralized tube-based model predictive control of uncertain nonlinear multi-agent systems. Int. J. Robust Nonlinear Control **29**(10), 2799–2818 (2019)
17. Yan, H., Duan, Z.: Tube-based model predictive control using multi-dimensional Taylor network for nonlinear time-delay systems. IEEE Trans. Autom. Control **18**, 1288–1301 (2020)
18. Yu, Y., Yang, S., Wang, M., Li, C., Li, Z.: High performance full attitude control of a quadrotor on SO(3). In: Proceedings of IEEE International Conference on Robotics and Automation (ICRA), pp. 1698–1703, Seattle, Washington, May 2015
19. Yushu, Yu., Ding, X.: A global tracking controller for underactuated aerial vehicles: design, analysis, and experimental tests on quadrotor. IEEE/ASME Trans. Mechatron. **21**(5), 2499–2511 (2016)
20. Yu, Y., Ding, X., Jim Zhu, J.: Attitude tracking control of a quadrotor UAV in the exponential coordinates. J. Franklin Inst. Eng. Appl. Math. **350**(8), 2044–2068 (2013)
21. Yushu, Yu., Li, P., Gong, P.: Finite-time geometric control for underactuated aerial manipulators with unknown disturbances. Int. J. Robust Nonlinear Control **30**(13), 5040–5061 (2020)
22. Yue, M., Hou, X., Zhao, X., Xiangmin, W.: Robust tube-based model predictive control for lane change maneuver of tractor-trailer vehicles based on a polynomial trajectory. IEEE Trans. Syst. Man Cybern. Syst. **50**(12), 5180–5188 (2020)

23. Zemouche, A., Boutayeb, N., Bara, G.: Observers for a class of Lipschitz systems with extension to H-infinity performance analysis. Syst. Control Lett. **57**(1), 18–27 (2008)
24. Zhao, B., Xian, B., Zhang, Y., Zhang, X.: Nonlinear robust adaptive tracking control of a quadrotor UAV via immersion and invariance methodology. IEEE Trans. Industr. Electron. **62**(5), 2891–2902 (2015)

**Vision**

Vision

# Social-Transformer: Pedestrian Trajectory Prediction in Autonomous Driving Scenes

Hanbing Sun and Fuchun Sun$^{(\boxtimes)}$

Institute for Artificial Intelligence, Tsinghua University (THUAI), Beijing National Research Center for Information Science and Technology (BNRist), State Key Lab on Intelligence Technology and Systems, Department of Computer Science and Technology, Tsinghua University, Beijing, People's Republic of China
sunhb19@mails.tsinghua.edu.cn, fcsun@tsinghua.edu.cn

**Abstract.** This article introduces pedestrian trajectory prediction, which is a crucial step in the perception of autonomous driving. The controller system should predict the person's motion before making a decision. Pedestrian trajectory prediction can be divided into two sub-problems: modeling historical trajectories and modeling pedestrian social relationships. Both of these two points are factors that have a vital influence on the future location. However, most of the previous works cannot make good use of historical track information and have more deviation as the forecast period is longer, or they will have more calculations in modeling human-human interaction. In this paper, we propose Social-Transformer, a Transformer-based model that uses an encoder module to model historical trajectories, uses the decoder part to decode future positions, and uses the hidden vector in the middle to establish social relationships among pedestrians. As a result, our model can maintain a relatively stable error during the long trajectory prediction process and will not deviate more due to the predicted trajectory side length. At the same time, our social modeling is more straightforward and more effective. Therefore, we can reduce the number of model parameters while improving the effect. In addition, our model has a 2% to 50% improvement both on ADE and FDE metrics on the public datasets, ETH [19] and UCY [13].

**Keywords:** Trajectory prediction · Social interaction · Autonomous driving

## 1 Introduction

Predicting the future trajectory of humans in dynamic scenarios is a crucial point of autonomous driving, which supplies vital information for the downstream decision-making process. In autonomous driving, accurate pedestrian trajectory prediction enables the system to plan the vehicle's movement in advance in an

---

Supported by organization Toyota Motor Technical Research and Service.

F. Sun et al. (Eds.): ICCSIP 2021, CCIS 1515, pp. 177–190, 2022.
https://doi.org/10.1007/978-981-16-9247-5_13

aggressive environment. For example, in the driver's view, the trajectory of the pedestrian will affect his next decision, whether to go straight or wait for him to pass. Similarly, in driving assistance systems, the controller must predict the trajectory of pedestrians before making a decision.

**Fig. 1.** The goal of this paper is to predict the future trajectory of pedestrian. This can be divided into two sub-problems: historical trajectories modeling and social interaction modeling. We use an encoder-decoder framework to solve this problem.

However, trajectory prediction is challenging because two crucial points should to be considered during the prediction. One is that the historical trajectory of pedestrians will affect the future positions, and the other is that the complex relationship among pedestrians will affect each other and even their future decisions. First, it is obvious that the past locations of pedestrians contain information for judging future positions. However, how to model the historical course is a intricate problem. Second, the interaction among pedestrians is mainly driven by common sense and social customs. This requires understanding the complex relationship and modeling them in a proper way. Meanwhile, the complexity of pedestrian trajectory prediction comes from different social behaviors, such as parallel walking with others in a group, avoiding collisions, and entering a specific point in different directions. This paper refers to the various behaviors of pedestrians mentioned above as social interaction and proposes a way to describe them.

Since this field is crucial, this encouraged researchers in this area to focus on modeling social interactions and propose deep networks. Yet, there are still many problems with current solutions. Such as Social-Force-based models [9, 12] concentrate on modeling human interaction by handcraft, although it is easy to calculate in simple scenarios, manual modeling cannot handle complex scenarios. Since the rapid development of deep learning, many previous works have used LSTM [1,8,16,29] to solve the problem of pedestrian trajectory modeling. As a neural memory network, LSTM can use hidden layer vectors to express social relationships among pedestrians while modeling their trajectories. However, when LSTM models long sequences, there will be more and more deviation as time increases. In addition, some previous work [21,25] uses the Attention mechanism to perform social modeling based on the LSTM network, which has certain improvements on open datasets. Recent years, Graph-Neural-Network-based models [10,17,22] have been promoted in this field to model human interactions. But these methods generally require a lot of calculations and need more time to obtain the results. In total, the previous methods have problems in two aspects: First, LSTM is mostly used for trajectory modeling, but LSTM has the characteristic of unstable long-sequence modeling; that is, as the prediction time increases, the deviation error becomes more significant; Second, most previous works used more complex social relationship modeling, although they achieved relatively good results, the amount of calculation is enormous, and it is not suitable for real-time systems for autonomous driving.

As shown in Fig. 1, this paper proposes a new type of encoder-decoder framework that uses Transformer to solve this historical trajectory modeling problem. We designed Social-Transformer to overcome the two aforementioned limitations.

Experiments on multiple pedestrian trajectory prediction datasets have proved the improvement of our model. Our contributions are as follows:

1. We propose a Transformer-based model, a novel model structure for pedestrians modeling, we use an encoder module to model the historical trajectories and a decoder part decode the future locations. In addition, the middle hidden layer vector is used to model the social relationship. Since the Transformer itself has the advantage of dealing with long sequences, with the increase of time, the stability of our prediction sequence has also been greatly improved. At the same time, Transformer can perform parallel computing, so the efficiency is much higher than LSTM.
2. We are the first one to use the Attention mechanism in the hidden vector of Transformer-based model to build human interactions. In this way, we need few parameters, but the effect is very good. The calculation speed is increased while reducing the amount of calculation, which can be applied to the real-time system of unmanned driving.
3. We conduct experiments on two open datasets and able to achieve about 2% to 50% improvement comparing with other methods.

## 2   Related Work

Due to the importance of the trajectory prediction problem, many researchers now propose solutions in this field. In this section, we will give a brief view of different methods.

**Human Trajectory Prediction in Deep Models.** With the development of deep learning, many researchers search a proper model to solve prediction problem. Social-LSTM [1] is one of the first deep models to solve pedestrian trajectory prediction. It uses a recurrent neural network to model the historical trajectory of each pedestrian, then uses a pooling mechanism to aggregate the hidden states and then predict the trajectory. Subsequently, social-GAN [7] used the GAN model for packaging the LSTM model framework and improved performance on this basis. Only considering the coordinate trajectory of pedestrians alone obviously has great limitations for prediction. Later works such as Sophie [21], SR-LSTM [29] and Peek Into The Future (PIF) [14] added visual features into models and applied new pooling mechanisms to improve prediction accuracy. It is innovative that Sophie using an attentive GAN to modeling the interaction among people. The attention mechanism lets the person in one scene notice the other people and calculate the influence weights on him. Similarly, SR-LSTM also weighs the contribution of each pedestrian to others via an original weighting mechanism but not named attention. Differently, Peeking into the future use a two-stream model which modeling both trajectories and behaviors of pedestrians during training steps. It achieves better performance, because the two tasks can complement each other. Since Graph CNNs were introduced by [11] which added CNN concepts into graphs, many previous work, such as Social-STGCNN [17], STGAT [10] and Recursive Social Behavior Graph (RSBG) [22], used Graph Neural Network to build human interactions and promoted better performance on predicting. Social-STGCNN substitutes the need of aggregation methods by modeling the interactions as a graph. STGAT models the spatial interactions captured by the graph attention mechanism at each time-step and adopts an extra LSTM to encode the temporal correlations of interactions.

**Encoder-Decoder Model.** Encoder-Decoder framework was first promoted by [23]. It was promoted to map a fixed-length input into a fixed-length output, where the two lengths may be different. The Encoder-Decoder model and its variants are considered as the best solution for many complex tasks, for example, machine translation [26], speech recognition [20] and video captioning [23]. Similarly, our problem is to predict the future trajectories of all pedestrians given the historical trajectories and the input and output sequence lengths may be inconsistent. At the same time, the Encoder-Decoder model is designed to generate new sequences based on existing sequences, which is just suitable for our problem. Thus, we adopt Encoder-Decoder framework as our prominent architecture.

**Recent Advancements in Transformer.** Transformer was first promoted by [24] and caused a great sensation. It has achieved great results in many downstream tasks. It groundbreakingly uses the Attention mechanism to notice all the information in the entire sequence. At the same time, it combines the encoder and decoder with the cross attention so that the decoder module can also pay attention to the information encoded by the former when decoding. Natural language processing models such as Bert [5] and GPT [6] using Transformer structure have sound effects in many fields such as translation, text generation, and sentiment analysis. Besides in the field of natural language processing, Transformer also has many excellent applications in the computer vision direction.

For example, DETR [4] uses the Transformer framework in image detection on COCO 2017 detection and panoptic segmentation datasets, and Segformer [27] and SETR [30] achieve the best results in image segmentation. Transformer overcomes the shortcoming of LSTM that the error will increase over time when predicting long sequences. It ensures that while the sequence can be calculated in parallel, it can calculate the part of the sequence that currently has the most significant influence according to the actual situation. For our problem, the transformer can be used to model the historical trajectory, and at the same time, use the hidden layer vector in the middle to model the social relationship so that the two limitations mentioned above can be solved. First, as time goes by, the error will not deviate significantly, and secondly, the use of simple social modeling methods can significantly reduce the amount of calculation and meet the real-time needs in autonomous driving scenarios.

## 3   Method

Our goal is to predict the future trajectories of the pedestrians in a scene. Obviously, a person's historical trajectory is an essential factor in determining their future positions. In addition, social relationships also plays an important role. For example, a person could alter his/her path to avoid collision with other people. Therefore, this problem can be converted into two sub-problems: modeling the historical trajectory of every pedestrian and modeling the social interaction relationship of all pedestrians in one scene.

In this section, we present our Social-Transformer model (as shown in Fig. 2). Our model has three components: a Transformer-based module for taking the pedestrians' historical trajectory as input, we call it the encoder part, a Social-Attention-based module for capturing the spatial correlations of interactions, and a Transformer-based module for output the predicted trajectory of every pedestrian, which is a decoder part.

### 3.1   Problem Definition

Trajectory prediction can be equivalent to a sequence generation problem, which estimating all pedestrians' states in the future based on the given past information. First, we assume that each scene has been preprocessed to obtain the spatial coordinates of every pedestrian. Previous work also follows this conventions [1,2,7,15]. Then, we suppose there are $N$ pedestrians in one scene, represented as $p_1, p_2, ..., p_N$. At last, at time-instant $\tau$, we could assume that every pedestrian's trajectory is represented by his/her spatial positions, that is to say, $xy$-coordinates $traj_i^\tau = (x_i^\tau, y_i^\tau)$. Therefore, the past and current trajectory of pedestrian $i$ at time $\tau$ is represented as by the ordered set as:

$$traj_i^\tau = \{(x_i^\tau, y_i^\tau | \tau \in t_0, t_1, ..., t_{pred}\} \ \forall i \in N \qquad (1)$$

Throughout the paper, we use $t_0$ to $t_{obs}$ as the past time, and $t_{obs+1}$ to $t_{pred}$ as the future time. We observe all pedestrians' $xy$-coordinates from $t_0$ to $t_{obs}$, take

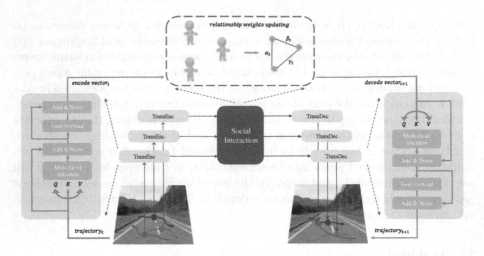

**Fig. 2.** Overview of our Social-Transformer method. The framework is based on an encoder-decoder model and consists of 3 parts: The encoder part takes the historical trajectories of pedestrians as input. The Social-Interaction module models the social relationship among people. The decoder module generates the predicted locations of pedestrians.

these sequences into a model with params $W^*$, and predict the $xy$-coordinates of them from $t_{obs+1}$ to $t_{pred}$.

$$traj_{1:N}^{t_{obs+1} : t_{pred}} = f(traj_{1:N}^{t_0 : t_{obs}} ; W^*) \tag{2}$$

## 3.2   Model Description

The Social-Transformer model consists of three main parts: a Transformer-based module for modeling the pedestrian's historical trajectories, we call it encoder part, a Social-Attention-based module for modeling the social interaction for all pedestrians in one scene, and a similar Transformer-based module for predicting the future trajectories of all pedestrian which is decoder module (as shown in Fig. 2).

First, the encoder module takes sequences of all pedestrians in one scene as input, $traj_{1:N}^{t_0 : t_{obs}}$, and then output their extracted features from the historical trajectories. Second, the Social-Attention-based module takes the outcome of the previous module and models the social interaction of all pedestrians in one scene. This module concentrates on the most critical information, builds a social interaction graph, and updates the relationship weight for every pedestrian in one scene. Then, the historical trajectories and social interaction information are included in the input for the last decoder module (the Transformer-based module). Finally, the decoder module compares its input with ground truth and reconstructs the trajectories of all pedestrians. In the following sections, we elaborate each module in detail.

**Historical Trajectory Modeling.** Each pedestrian has his/her own motion states, including preferred speed, acceleration, and so on. Previous works mostly use LSTM for memorizing the historical motions [1,7,10]. Still, in recent years, people use Transformer instead of LSTM to deal with sequence generation problems [24] because Transformer shows better performance in many tasks and more stable speed in calculating. However, no one has tried to use Transformer as a backbone to modeling the past motions of pedestrians. Therefore, we will introduce how to modify the model backbone to fit our problem.

Transformer is mostly used in NLP tasks, which has two parts of the input: token embedding and position embedding. Token embedding is defined as the embedding vector of the input sequences, which has the shape of $[B, L, C]$. Where $B$ represents the batch size, $L$ represents the length of a sequence, and $C$ represents the sequence dim at time $\tau$. In our problem, we first compute the relative position of each pedestrian to the previous time step:

$$\Delta x_i^\tau = x_i^\tau - x_i^{\tau-1} \tag{3}$$

$$\Delta x_i^\tau = y_i^\tau - y_i^{\tau-1} \tag{4}$$

Then we use a linear layer to project the input relative position into high dimension space and use vector $e_i^\tau$ to present the embedded trajectory (token embedding) of pedestrian $i$ at time $\tau$:

$$e_i^\tau = \phi(\Delta x_i^\tau, \Delta y_i^\tau; W^e) \tag{5}$$

which $\phi$ is an embedding function, $W^e$ is the embedding weight.

Position embedding shows the temporal information for every pedestrian from $t_0$ to $t_{obs}$, since Transformer does not have the function of inputting in chronological order like LSTM, it needs a positional embedding to encode timing information. For example, $t_0$ is represented by number 0, and $t_1$ is represented by number 1. In Transformer, there is a sine cosine formula $PE$ to compute the position embedding for each time $\tau$, which take $pos \in \{1 : T\}$ and model dim $i$ as inputs:

$$p_i^\tau - PE(pos, i) \tag{6}$$

Through this function we can calculate a fix position embedding for each sequence at each time $\tau$. In this paper, we use $p_i^\tau$ to represent the position embedding as an input of Transformer. In summary, we define the input of encoder module as:

$$input_i^\tau = e_i^\tau + p_i^\tau \tag{7}$$

After that, the Transformer can be used to encode the input and generate the encoded hidden layer vector.

$$y_i^{t_{obs}} = Trans_{encoder}(input_i; W_{trans_{encoder}}) \tag{8}$$

**Pedestrian Interaction Modeling.** Naive use of one Transformer module does not capture the interaction between people. However, an accurate trajectory prediction must take into account the social relationship resume. For example, when pedestrians appear in different positions in a crowd, their focus is also different. People walking on the road concentrate on the information of vehicles and traffic lights, and pedestrians walking in the crowd pay close attention to the movement of pedestrians in front of them. Therefore, we hope that every pedestrian in the scene can pay more attention to the person who has the most significant influence on him.

To achieve this, we use the attention mechanism to model the social connection and take the encoded historical trajectories of pedestrians in one scene as the input of the Social-Attention module. We first established a relationship matrix $M \in \mathbb{R}^{N \times N}$ about pedestrians. Each pedestrian is represented by the encoded historical trajectory information. In this relationship matrix, the $ith$ row and $jth$ column represent the weight of the relationship between the two pedestrian $i$ and $j$. Take $y_i$ as the encoded trajectory of pedestrian $i$,and $y_{i/N}$ as the historical trajectories of other pedestrians except the pedestrian $i$:

$$y_i^{'} = ATT_{social}(y_{1:N/i}^{\tau}; W_{social}), \ \tau \in \{t_0 : t_{obs}\} \tag{9}$$

Using the attention mechanism, each pedestrian will pay attention to other pedestrians in the whole scene, and calculate the influence of other pedestrians on himself, thereby generating the weight matrix $M$, and then update his/her own encoded history trajectory, so in this way, the historical trajectory information is included social relations. We will next use the updated vector $y_i^{'}$ to represent every pedestrian and decode his/her future trajectory.

**Future Trajectory Prediction.** We hope that our model can output a reasonable trajectory range for trajectory prediction but not an actual location. Most previous works [1, 3, 25] reflect the uncertainty by predicting the Gaussian distribution's parameter values and then obtaining the exact future location sampled from the Gaussian distribution. In this paper, we also take this measure to calculate loss during training.

Similar to the encoder module for the historical trajectory modeling, the prediction module is based on the decoding part of the Transformer. In this module, we take the previous vector as input which includes the historical trajectory and social relationship, and output the two-dimensional Gaussian distribution parameters of $t_{obs+1}$ to $t_{pred}$. Then we sample the specific coordinate values from such Gaussian distribution parameters and compute a negative log-Likelihood loss with ground truth.

$$result_i^{t_{obs+1}:t_{pred}} = Trans_{decoder}(y_i^{'}; W_{trans_{decoder}}) \tag{10}$$

Which $W_{trans_{decoder}}$ is the parameters of this decoder module, $y_i^{'}$ is the vector which includes the information of historical trajectory and social interaction of pedestrian $i$.

**Implementation Details.** Since our datasets are relatively small, we use a lightweight Transformer with fewer parameters to make predictions. We use an embedding for dimension 32 for token embedding before using the positions as input of the Transformer module. We set the parameters in the Transformer module as follows; the model dim is 64, the fully connected layer's dimension is 128, the number of layers is 6, the query dim is 24, the value dim is 24, the number of multi-head attention is 4. During the training step, we use a learning rate of 0.001 and Adam for an optimizer. The Social-Transformer model was trained on a single GPU.

## 4 Experiments

In this section, we first introduce two datasets that are commonly used in pedestrian trajectory prediction. Then we compare our model's performance against other baselines on these two datasets. At last, we present a qualitative analysis of our model in some special situations.

### 4.1 Datasets and Evaluation Metrics

We compare with other baselines on two public pedestrian datasets. The two public datasets are ETH [19] and UCY [13], which include the trajectory of pedestrians in the open scene and the social relationships among the crowd. The trajectories are sampled every 0.4 s. The ETH dataset is divided into two scenarios, ETH and HOTEL, and the UCY dataset is divided into three scenarios ZARA01, ZARA02, and UNIV. In total, we trained and tested our model on these five datasets. Like Social-LSTM [1], we observed the trajectories of 3.2 s with correspond of 8 frames and predicts the trajectories of 4.8 s which are 12 frames. These datasets include a lot of challenging behaviors: suddenly turning, gathering together, suddenly disappearing in certain scenes, etc.

We use two indicators to measure the model's performance: the average displacement error (ADE) [18] and the final displacement error (FDE) [1]. ADE is used to measure the average prediction performance in the process of trajectory prediction, and FDE is used to measure the final trajectory prediction accuracy at the endpoints. The output of our model is a two-dimensional Gaussian distribution. By sampling in the Gaussian distribution, we calculate the ADE and FDE between the sampled $xy$-coordinates and the standard value.

$$ADE = \frac{\sum_{i \in N} \sum_{\tau \in t_{pred}} ||tr\hat{a}j_i^{\tau} - traj_i^{\tau}||^2}{N \times t_{pred}} \tag{11}$$

$$FDE = \frac{\sum_{i \in N} ||tr\hat{a}j_i^{\tau} - traj_i^{\tau}||^2}{N}, \tau = t_{pred} \tag{12}$$

### 4.2 Quantitative Analysis

In this section, we will introduce the quantitative analysis of our model.

**Table 1.** Quantitative results of all the baselines and our model. All models take as input of 8 frames and predict the next 12 frames, our model has the best performance on ETH, HOTEL, UNIV datasets on both ADE and FDE.

| Metric | Datasets | LSTM | S-LSTM [1] | Social Attention [25] | CIDNN [28] | STGAT [10] | Social-Transformer (Ours) |
|--------|----------|------|------------|------------------------|------------|------------|----------------------------|
| ADE | ETH | 1.09 | 1.09 | 1.39 | 1.25 | 0.88 | **0.52** |
| | HOTEL | 0.86 | 0.79 | 2.51 | 1.31 | 0.56 | **0.50** |
| | UNIV | 0.61 | 0.67 | 1.25 | 0.90 | 0.52 | **0.51** |
| | ZARA1 | 0.41 | 0.47 | 1.01 | 0.50 | **0.41** | 0.49 |
| | ZARA2 | 0.52 | 0.56 | 0.88 | 0.51 | **0.31** | 0.53 |
| **AVG** | | 0.70 | 0.72 | 1.41 | 0.89 | 0.54 | **0.51** |
| FDE | ETH | 2.41 | 2.35 | 2.39 | 2.32 | 1.66 | **0.53** |
| | HOTEL | 1.19 | 1.76 | 2.91 | 2.36 | 1.15 | **0.51** |
| | UNIV | 1.31 | 1.40 | 2.54 | 1.86 | 1.13 | **0.52** |
| | ZARA1 | 0.88 | 1.00 | 2.17 | 1.04 | 0.91 | **0.52** |
| | ZARA2 | 1.11 | 1.17 | 1.75 | 1.07 | 0.68 | **0.55** |
| **AVG** | | 1.52 | 1.54 | 2.35 | 1.73 | 1.11 | **0.53** |

**Performances on Datasets.** The performance of Social-Transformer is compared with other models on ADE/FDE metrics in Table 1. In total, our model performs the best on ETH, HOTEL, UNIV datasets both on ADE and FDE. For the ADE indicator, the best baseline method that has the lowest average prediction error is STGAT. However, our model has made significant progress compared to STGAT, especially on the ETH dataset, which has a 40% reduction. At the same time, on the HOTEL and UNIV datasets, our model also has an error reduction of 2% to 10%. For the FDE indicator, the results show that our model outperforms all compared methods on all datasets. Compared with STGAT, our model in most datasets has a drop of more than 50%.

These results show that our model has advantages compared to other methods, especially on the final displacement error. It shows that the Social-Transformer is more stable when predicting the sequence. There is no such thing as the longer the sequence, the greater the deviation.

**Ablation Study.** In this section, our purpose is to test the rationality of social modeling. The Table 2 shows the values of ADE and FDE on five datasets after adding and removing social modeling in our model. After adding social modeling, on the five datasets, the value of ADE is reduced by about 9.25% to 12% compared with the model without social modeling. At the same time, the FDE indicator changes more obviously. Almost on every dataset final displacement error has dropped by more than 15%. On the ZARA01 dataset, the improvement of FDE is undeniable, from 0.89 to 0.55. The improvement shows that the social interaction modeling plays an important role in predicting the future locations of pedestrians, especially in the FDE metric.

**Table 2.** Ablation study of the Social-Transformer model. The study are tested on the five datasets

| Dataset | Without social interaction (ADE/FDE) | With social interaction (ADE/FDE) |
|---------|--------------------------------------|-----------------------------------|
| ETH | 0.59/0.71 | **0.52/0.53** |
| HOTEL | 0.56/0.64 | **0.50/0.51** |
| UNIV | 0.60/0.64 | **0.51/0.52** |
| ZARA1 | 0.54/0.60 | **0.49/0.52** |
| ZARA2 | 0.79/0.89 | **0.53/0.55** |

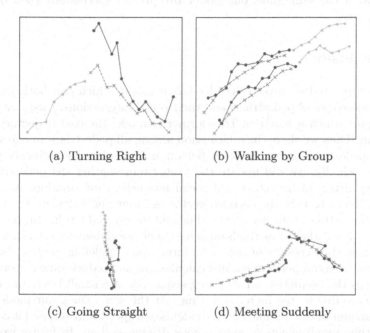

(a) Turning Right         (b) Walking by Group

(c) Going Straight         (d) Meeting Suddenly

**Fig. 3.** Visualization results of our model. The coordinate points of the triangle in the figure represent the historical trajectory of the pedestrian, the cross point represents the actual future trajectory of the pedestrian, and the circular point represents the predicted value of our model. We chose four representative scenes, (a)–(d).

## 4.3 Qualitative Analysis

Visualization results are shown in Fig. 3. The coordinate points of the triangle in the figure represent the historical trajectory of the pedestrian, the cross point represents the actual future trajectory of the pedestrian, and the circular point represents the predicted value of our model. We chose four representative scenes in all results.

Figure 3(a) shows that our model successfully predicted the turning behavior of the pedestrian. In this scene, there is only one pedestrian. By mainly judging his historical trajectory, our Social-Transformer model made a correct prediction of a turn right.

Figure 3(b) shows a complex communicative behavior, two pedestrians walking side by side. In this case, the target pedestrian obviously pays more attention to his nearest friend rather than others. Our model also notices this and predicts a similar path for them.

Figure 3(c) shows a simple scene. It shows that our model accurately predicts the future trajectory and direction of pedestrians.

Figure 3(d) shows a complex social scene. In the swarming and collision avoiding scene, target person show a strong tendency to separate their walking directions. And at the same time, our model also predict successfully their different walking paths.

## 5   Conclusions

We have presented a encoder-decoder based model which can both learn historical trajectories of pedestrians and their social interactions. First, we use the encoder part which is based on Transformer to model the past trajectory of one pedestrian. Then we share the information among all pedestrians in one scene to let every pedestrian notice the other person and calculate the influence weights on others. Finally, we will update the vector representing the pedestrian and combining historical trajectory and social interaction information. At last, we use the decoder to take the encoded vector as input and calculate the variance between the output of the decoder module and the ground truth. Our model outperforms state-of-the-art methods on two publicly available datasets. In addition, we also show the necessity of the social interaction modeling module. Based on Transformer, we can perform parallel calculations and reduce time consumption, which keeps the prediction error of long sequences at a small level, and will not deviate more due to the increase in time. At the same time, our model has a smaller amount of calculation, and the calculation speed is faster, and it can meet the real-time requirements of autonomous driving system. In future work, due to the complex traffic environment will also affect pedestrian prediction, we will extend our work to multi-class agents, such as bicycles, vehicles, and pedestrians, to pay attention to each other and complete more complicated social interaction modeling. In addition, visual information is also very important in prediction. Many pedestrians decide the next step based on the surrounding environment. So we will consider the influence of the environment, including traffic lights, road type, and weather factors.

## References

1. Alahi, A., Goel, K., Ramanathan, V., Robicquet, A., Fei-Fei, L., Savarese, S.: Social LSTM: human trajectory prediction in crowded spaces. In: Proceedings of the IEEE Conference on Computer Vision and Pattern Recognition, pp. 961–971 (2016)

2. Alahi, A., Ramanathan, V., Fei-Fei, L.: Socially-aware large-scale crowd forecasting. In: Proceedings of the IEEE Conference on Computer Vision and Pattern Recognition, pp. 2203–2210 (2014)
3. Antonini, G., Bierlaire, M., Weber, M.: Discrete choice models of pedestrian walking behavior. Transp. Res. Part B: Methodol. **40**(8), 667–687 (2006)
4. Carion, N., Massa, F., Synnaeve, G., Usunier, N., Kirillov, A., Zagoruyko, S.: End-to-end object detection with transformers. In: Vedaldi, A., Bischof, H., Brox, T., Frahm, J.-M. (eds.) ECCV 2020. LNCS, vol. 12346, pp. 213–229. Springer, Cham (2020). https://doi.org/10.1007/978-3-030-58452-8_13
5. Devlin, J., Chang, M.W., Lee, K., Toutanova, K.: BERT: pre-training of deep bidirectional transformers for language understanding. arXiv preprint arXiv:1810.04805 (2018)
6. Floridi, L., Chiriatti, M.: GPT-3: its nature, scope, limits, and consequences. Minds Mach. **30**(4), 681–694 (2020). https://doi.org/10.1007/s11023-020-09548-1
7. Gupta, A., Johnson, J., Fei-Fei, L., Savarese, S., Alahi, A.: Social GAN: socially acceptable trajectories with generative adversarial networks. In: Proceedings of the IEEE Conference on Computer Vision and Pattern Recognition, pp. 2255–2264 (2018)
8. Hasan, I., Setti, F., Tsesmelis, T., Del Bue, A., Galasso, F., Cristani, M.: MX-LSTM: mixing tracklets and vislets to jointly forecast trajectories and head poses. In: Proceedings of the IEEE Conference on Computer Vision and Pattern Recognition, pp. 6067–6076 (2018)
9. Helbing, D., Molnar, P.: Social force model for pedestrian dynamics. Phys. Rev. E **51**(5), 4282 (1995)
10. Huang, Y., Bi, H., Li, Z., Mao, T., Wang, Z.: STGAT: modeling spatial-temporal interactions for human trajectory prediction. In: Proceedings of the IEEE/CVF International Conference on Computer Vision, pp. 6272–6281 (2019)
11. Kipf, T.N., Welling, M.: Semi-supervised classification with graph convolutional networks. arXiv preprint arXiv:1609.02907 (2016)
12. Koppula, H.S., Saxena, A.: Anticipating human activities using object affordances for reactive robotic response. IEEE Trans. Pattern Anal. Mach. Intell. **38**(1), 14–29 (2015)
13. Lerner, A., Chrysanthou, Y., Lischinski, D.: Crowds by example. In: Computer Graphics Forum, vol. 26, pp. 655–664. Wiley (2007)
14. Liang, J., Jiang, L., Niebles, J.C., Hauptmann, A.G., Fei-Fei, L.: Peeking into the future: predicting future person activities and locations in videos. In: Proceedings of the IEEE/CVF Conference on Computer Vision and Pattern Recognition, pp. 5725–5734 (2019)
15. Luber, M., Stork, J.A., Tipaldi, G.D., Arras, K.O.: People tracking with human motion predictions from social forces. In: 2010 IEEE International Conference on Robotics and Automation, pp. 464–469. IEEE (2010)
16. Manh, H., Alaghband, G.: Scene-LSTM: a model for human trajectory prediction. arXiv preprint arXiv:1808.04018 (2018)
17. Mohamed, A., Qian, K., Elhoseiny, M., Claudel, C.: Social-STGCNN: a social spatio-temporal graph convolutional neural network for human trajectory prediction. In: Proceedings of the IEEE/CVF Conference on Computer Vision and Pattern Recognition, pp. 14424–14432 (2020)
18. Pellegrini, S., Ess, A., Schindler, K., Van Gool, L.: You'll never walk alone: modeling social behavior for multi-target tracking. In: 2009 IEEE 12th International Conference on Computer Vision, pp. 261–268. IEEE (2009)

19. Pellegrini, S., Ess, A., Van Gool, L.: Improving data association by joint modeling of pedestrian trajectories and groupings. In: Daniilidis, K., Maragos, P., Paragios, N. (eds.) ECCV 2010. LNCS, vol. 6311, pp. 452–465. Springer, Heidelberg (2010). https://doi.org/10.1007/978-3-642-15549-9_33
20. Prabhavalkar, R., Rao, K., Sainath, T.N., Li, B., Johnson, L., Jaitly, N.: A comparison of sequence-to-sequence models for speech recognition. In: Interspeech, pp. 939–943 (2017)
21. Sadeghian, A., Kosaraju, V., Sadeghian, A., Hirose, N., Rezatofighi, H., Savarese, S.: SoPhie: an attentive GAN for predicting paths compliant to social and physical constraints. In: Proceedings of the IEEE/CVF Conference on Computer Vision and Pattern Recognition, pp. 1349–1358 (2019)
22. Sun, J., Jiang, Q., Lu, C.: Recursive social behavior graph for trajectory prediction. In: Proceedings of the IEEE/CVF Conference on Computer Vision and Pattern Recognition, pp. 660–669 (2020)
23. Sutskever, I., Vinyals, O., Le, Q.V.: Sequence to sequence learning with neural networks. arXiv preprint arXiv:1409.3215 (2014)
24. Vaswani, A., et al.: Attention is all you need. arXiv preprint arXiv:1706.03762 (2017)
25. Vemula, A., Muelling, K., Oh, J.: Social attention: modeling attention in human crowds. In: 2018 IEEE International Conference on Robotics and Automation (ICRA), pp. 4601–4607. IEEE (2018)
26. Wu, Y., et al.: Google's neural machine translation system: bridging the gap between human and machine translation. arXiv preprint arXiv:1609.08144 (2016)
27. Xie, E., Wang, W., Yu, Z., Anandkumar, A., Alvarez, J.M., Luo, P.: SegFormer: simple and efficient design for semantic segmentation with transformers. arXiv preprint arXiv:2105.15203 (2021)
28. Xu, Y., Piao, Z., Gao, S.: Encoding crowd interaction with deep neural network for pedestrian trajectory prediction. In: Proceedings of the IEEE Conference on Computer Vision and Pattern Recognition, pp. 5275–5284 (2018)
29. Zhang, P., Ouyang, W., Zhang, P., Xue, J., Zheng, N.: SR-LSTM: state refinement for LSTM towards pedestrian trajectory prediction. In: Proceedings of the IEEE/CVF Conference on Computer Vision and Pattern Recognition, pp. 12085–12094 (2019)
30. Zheng, S., et al.: Rethinking semantic segmentation from a sequence-to-sequence perspective with transformers. In: Proceedings of the IEEE/CVF Conference on Computer Vision and Pattern Recognition, pp. 6881–6890 (2021)

# GridPointNet: Grid and Point-Based 3D Object Detection from Point Cloud

Quanming Wu[1], Yuanlong Yu[1(✉)], Tao Luo[2], and Peiyuan Lu[2]

[1] College of Mathematics and Computer Science, Fuzhou University,
Fujian 350116, China
yu.yuanlong@fzu.edu.cn
[2] China North Vehicle Research Institute, Beijing 100072, China

**Abstract.** In this paper, we propose a framework called GridPointNet that uses only point clouds for 3D object detection. There are two important branches in the research of 3D object detection, one is grid-based method and the other is point-based method. These two methods have their own advantages and disadvantages, and many previous works have also tried to merge these two methods. In this paper, we also use this idea to integrate the two methods into a object detection framework. Specifically, we use a grid-based method to divide the point cloud into voxels, and then use 3D sparse convolution to learn voxel features from the point cloud and generate 3D region proposals. At the same time, we use an improved point cloud sampling method to sample a small number of key points from the entire scene, and then aggregate multi-level voxel features based on the point method. After getting all the features, a method called RoI-Grid pooling is used to aggregate the features. Finally, the size and position of the frame are obtained through 3D proposal refinement. Our experiments on the KITTI dataset show that our framework has superior performance.

**Keywords:** 3D object detection · Point Cloud · RPN

## 1 Introduction

Autonomous driving is a hot research field in recent years, designed to help humans drive vehicles better and safer, and reduce the burden of drivers. 3D object detection is an important part of it, the goal is to detect and classify object categories in the scene. The point cloud is a kind of data generated by the reflection of the lidar that can store 3D information. The point cloud can make up for the shortcomings of the traditional RGB camera that only has 2D information and cannot effectively perform 3D object detection. Therefore, many methods currently exploit point clouds for 3D object detection. However, due to the disorder and irregularity of point clouds, it is difficult to directly apply traditional object detection methods.

This work supported by National Natural Science Foundation of China (NSFC) under grant 61873067.

Some works perform 3D object detection [1,12,19] with a monocular image, though such methods have lower performance, it can reduce the cost of the expensive laser radar sensor. some works convert a sparse point cloud into Bird's Eye View(BEV) representation [3,7,23]. The idea is intuitive and simple for the sake of leveraging CNNs and standard 2D detection pipeline. Another idea is to divide the 3D space into many grids called voxels [8,22,26], and then extend the 2D convolutional network method to 3D. Both of these methods need to divide the point cloud into grids, so they are collectively referred to as grid-based method. In 2017, Qi et al. proposed PointNet [14], which enables the network to directly consume raw point clouds and learn 3D representations from a point cloud for classification and segmentation. Hence, a series of point-based methods [13,17,20,25] sprang up for 3D object detection on the basis of PointNet due to its generalizability to complex scenes. PV-RCNN [16] employ both 3D CNN and point-based method to learn more features.

In this paper, we propose a 3D object detection framework called GridPoint-Net. As [16], we first generate high-quality 3D region proposals by grid-based methods. Then we applied a PointNet++ [15] variants on the voxels to extract rich context features. In other words, the operation object of PointNet++ is changed from points to voxels divided by grids.

Our contributions are as follows. (1) We propose a grid and point-based 3D object detection framework called GridPointNet. (2) We have improved the method of point cloud sampling. (3) We use a novel PointNet++ variant to aggregate the features extracted by the Voxel Feature Encoding (VFE) layer. (4) Our experiments on the KITTI dataset show that our proposed framework has superior performance.

## 2    Related Work

### 2.1    Image-Based 3D Object Detection

Some previous works directly employed only RGB images for 3D object detection. [1] utilized the constraints of the contact between the object and the ground plane, a method with the smallest energy value is proposed to extract the 3D candidate object frame. [12] combines 3D object attributes with the geometric constraints of the 2d bounding box to generate a 3D bounding box. [19] predicts the 6D pose estimation of the object from an RGB image. Mono3D-PLiDAR [21] lifts the input image into 3D camera coordinates, namely, pseudo-LiDAR points, via monocular depth estimation, then a 3D object detector is applied with the pseudo-LiDAR. Image-based 3D object detection is sub-optimal, but it provides a lot of inspiration for later researchers.

### 2.2    Grid-Based 3D Object Detection

The research of 3D object detection take the advantage of many previous 2D object detection works. The key point is to convert the LIDAR point cloud into a 2D representation. MV3D [3] transform point cloud to bird's eye view (BEV) and then apply 2D detection method to BEV for object location. To improve the small object detection performance of MV3D, AVOD [7] adopt a FPN [10] as backbone to extract full resolution feature map. ContFuse [9] extract multi-scale features from image and LiDAR BEV map with ResNet, then perform a multi-scale fusion of images and projection onto BEV map. We note that Pixor [23] took on-stage method rather than the two-stages method to perform 3D object detection in the LiDAR BEV map. VoxelNet [26] employs a series of Voxel Feature Encoding (VFE) layers to extract voxel features. SECOND [22]uses 3D sparse convolution to greatly increase the speed of convolution operations.

## 2.3   Point-Based 3D Object Detection

PointNet [14] can directly learn the features of the point cloud, exploit the input invariance of symmetric function to deal with the disorder of point cloud and combine local features and global features for instance segmentation. However, PointNet lacks the processing of local features, which led to the proposed of PointNet++ [15]. The core point of the paper is to propose a multi-level feature extraction structure. Based on the work of PointNet and PointNet++, many 3D object detection methods have been proposed.

F-PointNet [13] uses PointNet as the backbone to perform 3D object detection with the help of a mature 2D object detector. Based on F-PointNet, F-ConvNet [20] generates richer features by sliding on frustum. PointRCNN [17] uses only the raw point cloud as input and generate point-wise proposals from the point cloud top to down. STD [25] generates 3D region proposals based on spherical anchors.

## 3   GridPointNet

In this paper, we propose a 3D object detection framework called GridPointNet that combines the advantage of grid-based methods and point-based methods. The framework takes only point clouds as input, and it is a two-stage detection method. The overall architecture of the network is shown in Fig. 1.

### 3.1   3D Proposal Generation

First, we discretize the input point cloud into voxels with a resolution of $L \times W \times H$. In [16], the features of voxels are calculated as the average of the coordinates and reflection intensity of all points in each non-empty voxel. We adopt the VFE layer from [26] to get more features of voxels. First, the fully connected layer is used to extract the point-wise features in the voxels, and then all the point features are aggregated through the max pooling operation to obtain the voxel features.

In many previous methods, 3D convolution is applied to voxels, which requires a lot of calculations, resulting in the slow speed of this method. Point

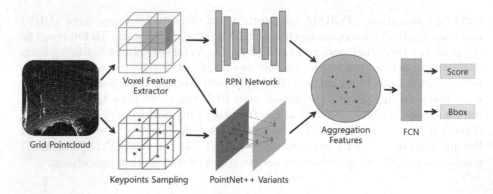

**Fig. 1.** The overview of GridPointNet proposed in this paper. First input the point cloud divided into voxels, extract the voxel features and sample a small number of key points. Then the 3D proposals generated by the RPN network and the features extracted by the PointNet++ variant are fused using RoI-Grid pooling. Finally, the 3D bounding box and confidence are output through the fully connected network.

cloud data is a very sparse data format, about 97% of the space in KITTI is empty. Therefore, the use of 3D sparse convolution can greatly reduce the computational complexity of the convolution operation. In [22], 3D sparse convolution is used to achieve better performance. In this paper, we also use 3D sparse convolution to generate features.

Specifically, we will use a sparse convolution with a size of $3 \times 3 \times 3$. Each convolution operation is equivalent to a 2× down-sampling of the point cloud, and finally we will get an 8× down-sampled feature map. Previous work has shown that using a 2D bird's-eye view to generate proposals will get better performance. Therefore, the feature map output by the 3D sparse convolution is converted into a bird's-eye view, that is, the sparse convolution is used to down-sample in the Z-axis direction, and the height of the feature is compressed, and finally the BEV feature similar to the 2D image is obtained.

For the generation of the proposals, we use the same RPN network as [22], which has a similar architecture to SSD [11]. Since the generated feature map is down-sampled, the detection performance for small objects is poor, so the three down-sampled feature maps will be up-sampled to the same size as the input feature, and then connected into a feature map. Finally, an anchor-based strategy is used to generate proposals.

## 3.2   Features Aggregation

In [15], Set Abstraction is proposed to capture the local structure of the point cloud. The method is to iteratively use pointnet in the local area and then use the generated few new points to represent the entire point cloud. The idea is similar to the backbone of extracting the entire point cloud.

In [15,16], Furthest-Point-Sampling (FPS) algorithm is used for point cloud sampling, the computational complexity is relatively high since each sampling must calculate the distance between the current point and all the remaining points. This paper uses a combination of grid sampling and random sampling because we have previously discretized the point cloud into grids, so only a small amount of calculation is required. Specifically, we randomly select a point from each non-empty voxel as keypoints. To control the number of sampling points, given a keypoints set $P_k = \{p_1, ..., p_n\}$, if $n < p^{max}$, $p^{max} - n$ points will be sampled from the remaining points. If $n > p^{max}$, $n - p^{max}$ points will be randomly deleted from the point set $P_k$.

After sampling the key points, a Set Abstraction variant called Voxel Set Abstraction (VSA) from [16] is used to aggregate multi-scale semantic features. SA operation is used to learn point features around key points, while VSA operation is used to learn voxel features around key points. Since the voxel features already contain local features, this approach can better capture the local structure of the point cloud.

Finally we aggregate the features obtained above via the RoI-Grid Pooling operation. The specific method is to divide each proposal with grids, and then use the center of each grid point to aggregate the features of the surrounding key points. This method can get more context information, and the subsequent proposal refinement can have better performance.

### 3.3    Proposal Refinement

The proposal refinement network takes proposal features as input. In order to get more accurate results, the network outputs the residuals of size and position relative to the input proposal.

For the training loss of the network, our approach is the same as [22]. Two boxes are actually the same box when the angle of the two boxes is different by $\pi$, but in many previous works, this will cause a greater loss. Therefore, an angle classification loss is used here:

$$L_{cls-\theta} = -\alpha_t(1 - p_t)^\gamma \log(p_t) \qquad (1)$$

Where $p_t$ is the model's estimated probability, the values of the two constants are $\alpha = 0.25$ and $\gamma = 2$ and the regression loss of the angle is:

$$L_{reg-\theta} = SmoothL1(sin(\theta_p - \theta_t)) \qquad (2)$$

Where $\theta_p$ is the angle of the prediction box, and $\theta_t$ is the angle of the ground truth box.

Therefore, the multitasking loss of the box refinement branch is:

$$L_{total} = \beta_1 L_{cls} + \beta_2(L_{reg-\theta} + L_{reg}) + \beta_3 L_{cls-\theta} \qquad (3)$$

Where $L_{cls}$ is the classification loss of the box, and $L_{reg}$ is the regression loss of the position and size of the box. The values of the three hyperparameters are $\beta_1 = 1.0$, $\beta_2 = 2.0$ and $\beta_3 = 0.2$.

The network also has a branch output prediction confidence as follows:

$$score = \min(\max(0, 2IoU - 0.5), 1) \qquad (4)$$

where $IoU$ refers to the 3D IoU between proposal and ground truth.

## 4 Experiments

### 4.1 Dataset

The KITTI [4,5] data set is an algorithm evaluation data set in an autonomous driving scenario. We use the 3D object detection benchmark provided by KITTI. The goal of this benchmark is to train a 3D object detectors for "car", "pedestrian" and "cyclist". The benchmark contains 7481 training samples and 7518 test samples. As with other object detection methods, we follow [2] to split the KITTI training set into two parts, of which 3712 samples are used for training and 3769 samples are used for validation. Then, we take the split training set to train the 3D object detection framework in this paper, the validation set for test and evaluate the results.

### 4.2 Results

We use KITTI to verify the performance of the proposed 3D object detection algorithm. The results show that our method has better performance overall than the previous method. The results of the "Car" category on the KITTI val set are shown in Table 1. As you can see, our method has improved on "Easy" and "Hard" compared to previous works.

**Table 1.** 3D detection AP on KITTI val set of our model for "Car" compared with other methods.

| Methods | Modality | Easy | Moderate | Hard |
|---------|----------|------|----------|------|
| MV3D [3] | LiDAR+RGB | 71.29 | 62.68 | 56.56 |
| F-PointNet [13] | LiDAR+RGB | 83.76 | 70.92 | 63.65 |
| AVOD-FPN [7] | LiDAR+RGB | 84.41 | 74.44 | 68.65 |
| F-ConvNet [20] | LiDAR+RGB | 89.02 | 78.80 | 77.09 |
| VoxelNet [26] | LiDAR | 81.97 | 65.46 | 62.85 |
| SECOND [22] | LiDAR | 87.43 | 76.48 | 69.10 |
| PointRCNN [17] | LiDAR | 88.88 | 78.63 | 77.38 |
| STD [25] | LiDAR | 89.7 | 79.8 | 79.3 |
| 3D-SSD [24] | LiDAR | 89.71 | 79.45 | 78.67 |
| SA-SSD [6] | LiDAR | 90.15 | 79.91 | 78.78 |
| PV-RCNN [16] | LiDAR | 92.57 | **84.83** | 82.69 |
| Ours | LiDAR | **92.66** | 83.91 | **82.93** |

The results of the "Pedestrian" and "Cyclist" category on the KITTI val set are shown in Table 2. There are only a few works that show the results of the "Pedestrian" and "Cyclist" on the KITTI val set. At present, the detection of "Pedestrian" and "Cyclist" lags behind the "Car" category. As can be seen in Table 2, the 3D AP of the "Pedestrian" category at the hard level is less than 58%. Partly because of the sample size, the sample size of the "Car" category is much larger than the other two.

**Table 2.** 3D detection AP on KITTI val set of our model for "Pedestrian" and "Cyclist" compared with other methods.

| Methods | Pedestrian | | | Cyclist | | |
|---|---|---|---|---|---|---|
| | Easy | Moderate | Hard | Easy | Moderate | Hard |
| F-PointNet [13] | 70.00 | 61.32 | 53.59 | 77.15 | 56.49 | 53.37 |
| Part-$A^2$ [18] | 70.73 | 64.13 | 57.45 | 88.18 | 73.35 | 70.75 |
| STD [25] | **73.9** | **66.6** | 52.9 | **88.5** | 72.8 | 67.9 |
| Ours | 70.48 | 64.92 | **57.83** | 87.82 | **73.67** | **71.02** |

We selected some of the results and visualized the results on the point cloud, and also projected them into the 2D image to make the results more intuitive as shown in Fig. 2

**Fig. 2.** Results of detection on the KITTI validation set.

## 5 Conclusion

In this paper, we present a 3D object detection framework that uses only point cloud data. GridPointNet uses a grid-based method to extract voxel features and 3D sparse convolution to generate 3D proposals. Then a point-based method is used to extract local features based on key points and voxel features. In order to aggregate features, a novel pooling method called RoI-Grid Pooling is used, which can obtain richer context information. Finally, we conducted experiments on the KITTI dataset, and the results showed that our method surpassed the previous method in many aspects.

# References

1. Chen, X., Kundu, K., Zhang, Z., Ma, H., Fidler, S., Urtasun, R.: Monocular 3D object detection for autonomous driving. In: Proceedings of the IEEE Conference on Computer Vision and Pattern Recognition, pp. 2147–2156 (2016)
2. Chen, X., et al.: 3D object proposals for accurate object class detection. In: Advances in Neural Information Processing Systems, pp. 424–432 (2015)
3. Chen, X., Ma, H., Wan, J., Li, B., Xia, T.: Multi-view 3D object detection network for autonomous driving. In: Proceedings of the IEEE Conference on Computer Vision and Pattern Recognition, pp. 1907–1915 (2017)
4. Geiger, A., Lenz, P., Stiller, C., Urtasun, R.: Vision meets robotics: the KITTI dataset. Int. J. Robot. Res. **32**(11), 1231–1237 (2013)
5. Geiger, A., Lenz, P., Urtasun, R.: Are we ready for autonomous driving? The KITTI vision benchmark suite. In: 2012 IEEE Conference on Computer Vision and Pattern Recognition, pp. 3354–3361. IEEE (2012)
6. He, C., Zeng, H., Huang, J., Hua, X.S., Zhang, L.: Structure aware single-stage 3D object detection from point cloud. In: Proceedings of the IEEE/CVF Conference on Computer Vision and Pattern Recognition, pp. 11873–11882 (2020)
7. Ku, J., Mozifian, M., Lee, J., Harakeh, A., Waslander, S.L.: Joint 3D proposal generation and object detection from view aggregation. In: 2018 IEEE/RSJ International Conference on Intelligent Robots and Systems (IROS), pp. 1–8. IEEE (2018)
8. Li, B.: 3D fully convolutional network for vehicle detection in point cloud. In: 2017 IEEE/RSJ International Conference on Intelligent Robots and Systems (IROS), pp. 1513–1518. IEEE (2017)
9. Liang, M., Yang, B., Wang, S., Urtasun, R.: Deep continuous fusion for multi-sensor 3D object detection. In: Ferrari, V., Hebert, M., Sminchisescu, C., Weiss, Y. (eds.) ECCV 2018. LNCS, vol. 11220, pp. 663–678. Springer, Cham (2018). https://doi.org/10.1007/978-3-030-01270-0_39
10. Lin, T.Y., Dollár, P., Girshick, R., He, K., Hariharan, B., Belongie, S.: Feature pyramid networks for object detection. In: Proceedings of the IEEE Conference on Computer Vision and Pattern Recognition, pp. 2117–2125 (2017)
11. Liu, W., et al.: SSD: single shot MultiBox detector. In: Leibe, B., Matas, J., Sebe, N., Welling, M. (eds.) ECCV 2016. LNCS, vol. 9905, pp. 21–37. Springer, Cham (2016). https://doi.org/10.1007/978-3-319-46448-0_2
12. Mousavian, A., Anguelov, D., Flynn, J., Kosecka, J.: 3D bounding box estimation using deep learning and geometry. In: Proceedings of the IEEE Conference on Computer Vision and Pattern Recognition, pp. 7074–7082 (2017)
13. Qi, C.R., Liu, W., Wu, C., Su, H., Guibas, L.J.: Frustum PointNets for 3D object detection from RGB-D data. In: Proceedings of the IEEE Conference on Computer Vision and Pattern Recognition, pp. 918–927 (2018)
14. Qi, C.R., Su, H., Mo, K., Guibas, L.J.: PointNet: deep learning on point sets for 3D classification and segmentation. In: Proceedings of the IEEE Conference on Computer Vision and Pattern Recognition, pp. 652–660 (2017)
15. Qi, C.R., Yi, L., Su, H., Guibas, L.J.: PointNet++: deep hierarchical feature learning on point sets in a metric space. In: Advances in Neural Information Processing Systems, pp. 5099–5108 (2017)
16. Shi, S., et al.: PV-RCNN: point-voxel feature set abstraction for 3D object detection. In: Proceedings of the IEEE/CVF Conference on Computer Vision and Pattern Recognition, pp. 10529–10538 (2020)

17. Shi, S., Wang, X., Li, H.: PointRCNN: 3D object proposal generation and detection from point cloud. In: Proceedings of the IEEE Conference on Computer Vision and Pattern Recognition, pp. 770–779 (2019)
18. Shi, S., Wang, Z., Shi, J., Wang, X., Li, H.: From points to parts: 3D object detection from point cloud with part-aware and part-aggregation network. IEEE Trans. Pattern Anal. Mach. Intell. **43**, 2647–2664 (2020)
19. Tekin, B., Sinha, S.N., Fua, P.: Real-time seamless single shot 6D object pose prediction. In: Proceedings of the IEEE Conference on Computer Vision and Pattern Recognition, pp. 292–301 (2018)
20. Wang, Z., Jia, K.: Frustum ConvNet: sliding frustums to aggregate local point-wise features for amodal. In: 2019 IEEE/RSJ International Conference on Intelligent Robots and Systems (IROS), pp. 1742–1749. IEEE (2019)
21. Weng, X., Kitani, K.: Monocular 3D object detection with pseudo-lidar point cloud. In: Proceedings of the IEEE/CVF International Conference on Computer Vision Workshops, pp. 857–866 (2019)
22. Yan, Y., Mao, Y., Li, B.: SECOND: sparsely embedded convolutional detection. Sensors **18**(10), 3337 (2018)
23. Yang, B., Luo, W., Urtasun, R.: PIXOR: real-time 3D object detection from point clouds. In: Proceedings of the IEEE Conference on Computer Vision and Pattern Recognition, pp. 7652–7660 (2018)
24. Yang, Z., Sun, Y., Liu, S., Jia, J.: 3DSSD: point-based 3D single stage object detector. In: Proceedings of the IEEE/CVF Conference on Computer Vision and Pattern Recognition, pp. 11040–11048 (2020)
25. Yang, Z., Sun, Y., Liu, S., Shen, X., Jia, J.: STD: sparse-to-dense 3D object detector for point cloud. In: Proceedings of the IEEE International Conference on Computer Vision, pp. 1951–1960 (2019)
26. Zhou, Y., Tuzel, O.: VoxelNet: end-to-end learning for point cloud based 3D object detection. In: Proceedings of the IEEE Conference on Computer Vision and Pattern Recognition, pp. 4490–4499 (2018)

# Depth Image Super-resolution
# via Two-Branch Network

Jiaxin Guo[1,2,3], Rong Xiong[1,3], Yongsheng Ou[1,2,3]([✉]), Lin Wang[1],
and Chao Liu[1,3]

[1] Shenzhen Institutes of Advanced Technology Chinese Academy of Sciences,
Shenzhen 518055, China
[2] Guangdong Provincial Key Laboratory of Robotics and Intelligent System,
Shenzhen Institute of Advanced Technology, Chinese Academy of Sciences,
Shenzhen, China
ys.ou@siat.ac.cn
[3] Guangdong-Hong Kong-Macao Joint Laboratory of Human-Machine
Intelligence-Synergy Systems (#2019B121205007), Shenzhen, China

**Abstract.** With the continuous development of sensors, a number of
inexpensive and effective depth cameras have shown up, which have
greatly contributed to the development of autonomous driving and 3D
reconstruction technologies. However, the depth images captured by low-
cost depth cameras are low-resolution, which is difficult to meet the needs
of practical applications. We propose a two-branch network to achieve
depth map super-resolution with high-resolution guidance image, which
can be viewed as a prior to guide the low-resolution depth map to restore
the missing high-frequency details of structures. To emphasize the guidance role of high-resolution images, we use spatially-variant kernels based
on the guidance feature map to replace the original convolution kernels.
In addition, in order to extract the feature maps of the depth images
more effectively, we add the channel attention mechanism between convolution layers. Our network is trained end-to-end, supporting various
sizes of input images because the network backbone uses full convolution
and no fully connected layers. The proposal model is trained only on a
certain dataset under three super-resolution factors and utilized directly
on other datasets without fine-tuning. We show the effectiveness of our
model by comparing it with state-of-art methods.

**Keywords:** Computer vision · Convolutional neural networks · Depth
map super-resolution

National Key Research and Development Program of China under Grant
2018AAA0103001.
National Natural Science Foundation of China (Grants No. U1813208, 62173319,
62063006).
Guangdong Basic and Applied Basic Research Foundation (2020B1515120054).
Shenzhen Fundamental Research Program (JCYJ20200109115610172).

F. Sun et al. (Eds.): ICCSIP 2021, CCIS 1515, pp. 200–212, 2022.
https://doi.org/10.1007/978-981-16-9247-5_15

# 1   Introduction

In recent years, with the continuous development of depth sensor technology, many inexpensive and effective depth cameras have emerged, such as ASUS Xtion Pro, Microsoft Kinect, etc. The depth information of the scene has become widely used in various practical projects, such as robot vision [1], autonomous driving assistance [2,3,27], virtual reality [4], and 3D reconstruction [5]. However, due to the limitation of hardware conditions, the depth image obtained by depth cameras is generally low-resolution, which is challenging to meet the demand of practical applications. For example, Microsoft's Kinect camera only provides 640 × 480 resolution depth image. Depth map super-resolution via improving the quality of hardware would be expensive. Therefore the resolution of depth images is usually improved by algorithmic processing (Fig. 1).

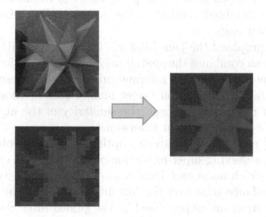

**Fig. 1.** The basic principle of guided depth map super-resolution is to predict the high-resolution image corresponding to a low-resolution depth map, with the guidance of high-resolution images in additional modality (e.g., RGB image captured by the regular camera)

Color maps are accessible to capture, and obtain more clear edges than depth maps. Theoretically, it is possible to use the precise edges of the color map to restore the edge information in the depth map, but this is not a simple task because of the inconsistency between the color map and the depth map. For example, there is a lot of texture information in the color map, which can cause texture artifacts when guiding the depth map super-resolution.

Therefore, we propose a new depth map guided super-resolution method based on CNN networks. The network can recover the sensitive parts of image edges well and avoid texture artifacts. Our main contributions are as follows:

- Compared with other methods, our method effectively uses spatially-variant kernels in the network instead of just traditional convolutional kernels. And the channel attention module is added to optimize the network efficiency.

- Our model learns the residuals between the interpolated depth map and the corresponding high-resolution depth map, with the aim of allowing the network to focus specifically on the missing high-frequency information. Learning the residuals avoids the repeated learning of flat areas in the images, which both speeds up the training and better preserves the original information of the image.
- Due to the above improvements, our method achieves fine results on several datasets. And we also get good results when used on practical data.

## 2    Related Work

**Local-Based Method:** The local methods are used to establish the relationship between the depth map and the color map by using image filters. It is based on the basic assumption that pixel points with similar colors in a specific region tend to have similar depth values. The pixel values of the filtered output image are obtained by a weighted average of the corresponding pixel values on the depth map and color map.

Kopf et al. [6] proposed the joint bilateral upsampling (JBU), based on joint bilateral filter, which combines the spatial information of the low-resolution target image and the value domain information of the high-resolution guidance image to obtain the high-resolution target image. This method considers both the smoothness of the depth map and the similarity of the high intensity map but may produce a certain gradient inversion.

Yang et al. [7] used bilateral filter to optimize the cost volume to obtain a smooth and edge-preserving super-resolution depth image. He et al. [8] proposed the guided filter, which assumes a local linear relationship between the output image and the guidance image on the filtering window. If the guidance image has an edge, the output image processed by the guided filter also keeps the edge unchanged.

**Global Methods:** Global methods formulate the depth image super-resolution as an optimization problem, thus maintaining more global structured information. The loss function of the optimization problem consists of two main items: the data fidelity term and the regularization term. The former focused on the similarity between the output image and the target image, and the latter ensures that the output image and the guidance image have similar structures.

Diebel et al. [9] were the first to propose the use of Markov random field (MRF) formulation to solve the problem of structural mismatch in the depth map and the guided map, but the output image of this method is too smooth. Park et al. used nonlocal mean filter to compute the weight of the edges in the guided map as the central part of the regularization term [10]. Ferstl et al. [11] treated the problem as a convex optimization problem using an anisotropic diffusion tensor to adjust the depth upsampling. Aodha et al. [12] proposed a block-based approach to match the image block information of the depth map with the candidate block information in the guidance image to transform the problem into a MRF labeling problem.

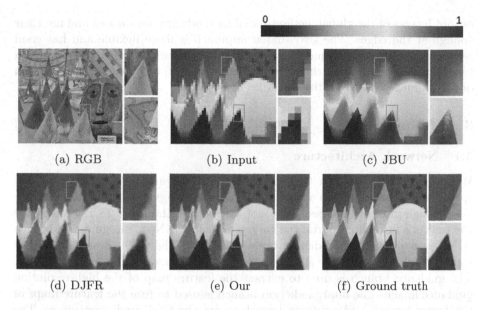

**Fig. 2.** Results of comparing our model with other methods when upsampling factor is 8. (a) high-resolution RGB guidance image; (b) input low-resolution depth image; (c) use JBU [6]; (d) use DJFR [19]; (e) our model; (f)ground truth. Our method has smooth and clear edges and few texture artifacts.

**CNN-Based Methods:** Convolutional neural networks (CNNs) have access the great success in high-level computer vision tasks. In recent years, CNNs have also been used to solve some low-level computer vision-related problems, such as image super-resolution [13], noise removal [14], image defogging [15], image restoration [16], etc. CNN-based depth map SR algorithms can be divided into single-image super-resolution and super-resolution with guidance images.

The most classical study of single-image super-resolution is SRCNN, proposed by Dong et al. [13], which uses end-to-end CNN to recover texture and edge information of the object. It contains three processes, patch extraction and representation, non-linear mapping, and reconstruction (Fig. 2).

Super-resolution with guidance images performs joint filter in the form of two-branching networks, considering the feature of both target map and guided map. Li et al. [18] proposed a learning-based joint filter method. It uses two subbranches to extract the feature maps of the high-resolution guidance image and the low-resolution depth image, respectively. Next, fuse them to obtain the final high-resolution depth image. Hui et al. [17] proposed a multiscale guided convolutional network (MSGNet), whose main feature is that the guidance image is dynamic and guides the upsampling process of the depth map at multiple scales.

Comparing the above methods, although the local-based methods can be real-time, they all use the guide image directly to enhance the depth map and focus less on the consistency between the depth image and the guide image. Thus, it will result in severe texture artifacts in the image. Most of the final output images of the global method-based methods are too smooth and not clear enough at the edges. The CNN-based approach is more flexible and has good results in maintaining boundaries and reducing texture artifacts. We propose a two-branch network with the attention mechanism for guided super-resolution of depth images based on the structure of Li [19].

## 3   Method

### 3.1   Network Architecture

We propose a two-branch CNN network with the attention mechanism and spatially-variant kernels to obtain super-resolution depth images with the guidance of high intensity images. We adopt a structure similar to [18,19] and divide the network into three parts: the target branch ($CNN_T$), the guidance branch ($CNN_G$), and the final prediction branch ($CNN_F$). The target branch is used as a sub-branch to extract the feature map of the input low-resolution depth image. The guidance branch is used to extract the feature map of the high-resolution guidance image. The final prediction branch is used to fuse the feature maps of the target branch and guidance branch to get the final prediction image. The structure of the whole network is depicted in Fig. 3.

**Guidance Branch:** The input to the guidance branch is a high-resolution image ($H \times W \times C$), where $H$, $W$, $C$ is the height, width, channels of the image separately. $CNN_G$ uses three convolution modules to extract the feature map of the guidance image-each module including a conventional convolution layer and followed by an activation function ReLU. We apply the same padding to the convolution modules to keep the image size constant.

**Target Branch:** The low-resolution depth image $D_L$ ($\frac{H}{r} \times \frac{W}{r} \times 1$, where $r$ is the upsampling factor, which can be 4, 8, 16 in our work), is interpolated by bilinear into the upsampled low-resolution depth image $\uparrow D_L$ ($H \times W \times 1$), which has the same resolution as the guidance image, and will be used as the input of this sub-branch. The structure of the target branch is basically the same as that of the guidance branch, but the channel attention module is added between each two convolution layers. The use of channel attention helps the network learn the correlation between channels and adaptively re-calibrate the feature response of the channels. It can increase the important features and decreasing the unimportant ones, thus making the extracted features more representational. We use the SEnet [20] as our channel attention module. After each convolution operation, a global average pooling is acted upon all channels. Assuming that the current layer after convolution is $U$ ($H \times W \times C$), where C is the number of channels, a new vector $z_c$ ($1 \times 1 \times C$) will be formed after global average pooling:

$$\mathbf{z}_c = \frac{1}{W \times H} \sum_{i=1}^{W} \sum_{j=1}^{H} \mathbf{U}_{i,j}, \tag{1}$$

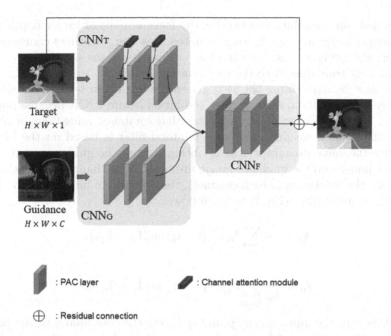

: PAC layer          : Channel attention module

⊕   : Residual connection

**Fig. 3.** Network design: our network has two sub-branches: $\text{CNN}_T$ and $\text{CNN}_G$. The input of $\text{CNN}_T$ is the upsampled low-resolution image via bilinear interpolation, and the input of $\text{CNN}_G$ is the high-resolution guidance image. The size of all convolution filters of the two sub-branches is $5 \times 5$, and the number of them to layers is 16-16-16. The difference between $\text{CNN}_T$ and $\text{CNN}_G$ is that the channel attention module is added in $\text{CNN}_T$. The $\text{CNN}_F$ are used to fuse the feature map of $\text{CNN}_T$ and $\text{CNN}_G$. The first layer of $\text{CNN}_F$ is a PAC layer; others are convolution layers. The filter size of these layers is $5 \times 5$, and the number of them to layers is 32-32-32-1. The output map is added with the input low-resolution image to generate the final prediction image.

where $\mathbf{U}_{i,j}$ is the value of vector at $(i, j)$ in $\mathbf{U}$. The $\mathbf{z}_c$ is next input of the FCN-ReLU-FCN mini-network, which is acted as a process of extraction. The first FCN (Fully Connected Layer) transfers the number of channels $C$ to $C/l$ to reduce the computational cost. So the current layer's shape is $1 \times 1 \times C/l$, and we take $l$ to be 16. The next layer is the ReLU layer, which acts as a nonlinear activation function. The second FCN layer restores channels from $1 \times 1 \times C/l$ to $1 \times 1 \times C$. Following the FCN-ReLU-FCN mini-network, the sigmoid layer makes the output weights non-linearly distributed on 0 to 1, which is the attention weight of each channel after the channel attention mechanism. Multiply this weight with the channels after the convolution module is used as the input of the next convolution module.

**Final Prediction Branch:** We fuse the output feature map of the target depth image from $\text{CNN}_T$ and the output feature map of the guidance image from $\text{CNN}_G$ as the input to the final prediction branch. In [17–19] and other most commonly used guided super-resolution networks, the feature maps of target depth image and guidance image are directly concatenated. However, the direct concatenation considers the guidance and the target as two inputs of the same nature, which is not entirely consistent with the meaning of "guidance".

The joint bilateral filter [26] is a general image filter, which had achieved relatively good results in guided super-resolution before CNNs became popular. Bilateral filter is an edge-preserving filter that combines value-domain weights and spatial-domain weights. The joint bilateral filter is based on the bilateral filter, but the value domain weight is obtained from the guidance map. When the input image and the guidance image are both single channel (multi-channels images are the overlaying of each channel), the equation of bilateral filter (Eq. 2) and joint bilateral filter (Eq. 3) are as follows:

$$J_{\mathbf{p}} = \frac{1}{k_{\mathbf{p}}} \sum_{\mathbf{q} \in \omega} \mathbf{I_q} f(\|\mathbf{p} - \mathbf{q}\|) g(\|\mathbf{I_p} - \mathbf{I_q}\|), \tag{2}$$

$$J_{\mathbf{p}} = \frac{1}{k_{\mathbf{p}}} \sum_{\mathbf{q} \in \omega} \mathbf{I_q} f(\|\mathbf{p} - \mathbf{q}\|) g(\|\tilde{\mathbf{I}}_{\mathbf{p}} - \tilde{\mathbf{I}}_{\mathbf{q}}\|), \tag{3}$$

where $\mathbf{I}$ denotes the input image, $\mathbf{p}$ and $\mathbf{q}$ denote the coordinates of the pixel in the original image, $\tilde{\mathbf{I}}_{\mathbf{p}}$ and $\tilde{\mathbf{I}}_{\mathbf{q}}$ in the guidance image. $J$ denotes the output, and $f$ and $g$ are the weight distribution functions, which are normalized Gaussian functions.

Hang Su et al. [25] proposed the PAC module by transferring the idea of joint bilateral filter into CNN networks. We adopt the PAC module to $\text{CNN}_F$ and use the feature map gained from $\text{CNN}_G$ to calculate a guidance weight kernel $K$. $K$ is added to the conventional convolution method to form a fused feature map. The standard convolution formula is Eq. 4, and the convolution formula with guided weight kernel $K$ is Eq. 5:

$$\mathbf{v}_i' = \sum_{j \in \Omega(i)} \mathbf{W}_j \mathbf{v}_j + \mathbf{b}, \tag{4}$$

$$\mathbf{v}_i' = \sum_{j \in \Omega(i)} K(\mathbf{f}_i, \mathbf{f}_j) \mathbf{W}_j \mathbf{v}_j + \mathbf{b}. \tag{5}$$

Supposing $\mathbf{p}_i$ is a certain location $(x_i, y_i)$ in the feature map. $\mathbf{W}_j$ is the corresponding weight value of $\mathbf{p}_j$ in $\mathbf{W}$ with $\mathbf{p}_i$ as the center point. $\mathbf{v}_i \in \mathbb{R}^c$ is the value of location $\mathbf{p}_i$ on the feature map, and $C$ is the number of channels in the feature map. $K$ is the guided kernel, $\mathbf{f}_i$ is the vector value of $\mathbf{p}_i$ at the corresponding position in the feature map of the guidance image, and in our experiments $K$ is used as a fixed Gaussian function:

$$K(\mathbf{f}_i, \mathbf{f}_j) = \exp\left(-\frac{1}{2}(\mathbf{f}_i, \mathbf{f}_j)^{\mathsf{T}}(\mathbf{f}_i, \mathbf{f}_j)\right) \tag{6}$$

After PAC, we add three convolution modules for final result prediction. Note that our network learns the high-frequency information missing in the upsampling process, which can be viewed as the residual part. Thus it needs to be summed up with the original input image pixel-wisely. This approach allows the network to focus better on extracting high-frequency information and not to change flat low-frequency regions.

**Loss Function:** We denote the result of the final obtained depth map super-resolution as $I_{SR}$ and the ground truth as $I_{GT}$. We learn the network parameters by minimizing the summed squared loss:

$$loss = \|I_{GT} - I_{SR}\| \tag{7}$$

## 4 Experiment

We acquire the target low-resolution image by using bilinear to downsample the high-resolution depth map to $1/4$, $1/8$, $1/16$ of the original size. For some test images whose sizes are not divisible by the above upsampling factor, we crop the original high-resolution depth map and the guidance image so that they are just divisible by scale. Since pixel-level mapping from low-resolution to high-resolution images is complex and computationally intensive, direct upsampling of low-resolution images allows mapping pixels with less deviation. Thus, we upsample the low-resolution depth map by bilinear and use it as the input of $CNN_T$.

**Table 1.** Our model compared with other methods in terms of average RMSE. Following [18,19], the average RMSE is measured in centimeters for the NYU v2 dataset [21]. For other datasets, we compute RMSE with upsampled depth maps scaled to the range [0, 255]. Bolded numbers represent the best, and underlined numbers represent the second best.

| Dataset | NYU v2 | | | MPI sintel | | | Lu | | | Middlebury | | |
|---------|--------|--------|--------|--------|--------|--------|--------|--------|--------|--------|--------|--------|
| Scale | 4× | 8× | 16× | 4× | 8× | 16× | 4× | 8× | 16× | 4× | 8× | 16× |
| Bicubic | 8.57 | 14.53 | 23.98 | 6.54 | 8.80 | 12.17 | 5.07 | 9.22 | 14.27 | 4.44 | 7.58 | 11.87 |
| GF | 7.44 | 13.78 | 22.26 | 6.10 | 8.22 | 11.22 | 4.87 | 8.85 | 14.09 | 4.01 | 7.22 | 11.71 |
| JBU | 4.94 | 8.52 | 13.61 | 5.88 | 7.63 | 10.97 | 2.99 | 5.06 | 7.78 | 2.44 | 5.18 | 8.13 |
| DJF | 2.93 | 5.37 | 9.52 | 4.77 | _6.39_ | 9.38 | 2.54 | 4.23 | _7.66_ | 2.14 | 4.16 | 7.38 |
| DJFR | _2.63_ | _5.21_ | _9.18_ | **4.58** | 6.41 | _9.21_ | _2.25_ | _4.06_ | **7.07** | **2.07** | _4.06_ | **7.12** |
| Ours | **2.52** | **4.89** | **8.89** | _4.69_ | **6.13** | **8.81** | **1.91** | **3.87** | 7.92 | _2.09_ | **3.16** | _7.37_ |

**Training Details:** The NYUv2 [21] dataset consists of 1449 labeled RGB-D images acquired by Microsoft Kinect, and as in [19], we selected the first 1000 as the training set and the last 449 as the test set. We set the epoch to 2500 rounds, and the learning rate divided by ten at 1000 and 2000 rounds (the initial learning rate is 0.0001). All code is implemented by PyTorch.

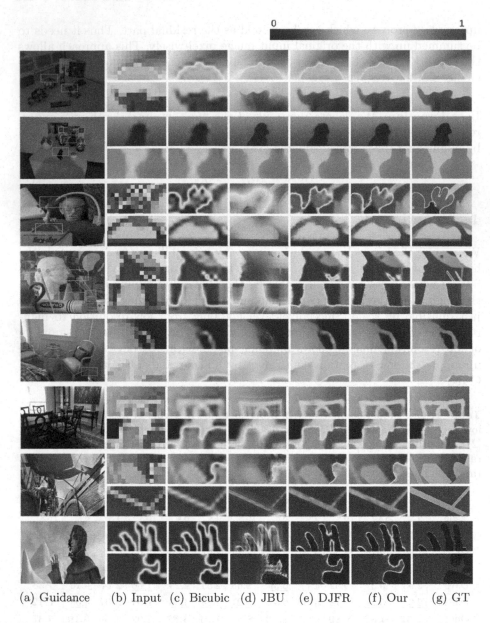

(a) Guidance    (b) Input  (c) Bicubic    (d) JBU    (e) DJFR    (f) Our    (g) GT

**Fig. 4.** Comparison of our method with other methods while upsampling factor is 8. We selected every two images from Lu, Middlebury, NYUv2, and MPI Sintel datasets. (a) high-resolution RGB guidance image; (b) input low-resolution depth image; (c) use bicubic interpolation; (d) use JBU [6]; (e) use DJFR [19]; (f) our model; (g) ground truth.

**Test Details:** We compare the proposal model with the state-of-art approaches, using RMSE as the metric for comparison, and test it on four datasets. The results are shown in Table 1. Note that our model only used the first 1000 images of NYUv2 as training and did not do fine-tune when tested on other datasets.

**Datasets:** We use four RGB-D datasets:

- NYUv2 [21]: It includes 1449 labeled RGB-D images acquired by Microsoft Kinect. We choose the first 1000 as the training set and the last 449 as the test set.
- MPI Sintel [23]: This RGB-D dataset contains depth maps generated from a manually created 3D animation movie. We selected the RGB images in the "clean" directory as the guidance images and the depth maps in the "depthrviz" directory as the target images. We discard those frames without depth maps and select 864 image pairs out of 1064 as test images.
- Middlebury [22]: We select 30 RGB-D images from the 2001–2006 datasets, where the missing holes in depth were filled by Lu et al. [24]
- Lu [24]: This provides 6 RGB-D image pairs acquired by the ASUS Xtion Pro camera.

As shown in Fig. 4, our method has better restoration ability at the edges, which have clearer curves and fewer holes. Also, our method has good prediction for some complex structures with disapparent features in the guidance image (e.g., the tiny elephant toy in the first image). The resulting image obtained by our method has fewer texture artifacts, for example, our result compared with JBU on the fourth image. This is because our approach is more effective in extracting the feature map of depth image and more reasonable in predicting the edges in combination with the guidance map,

Our results outperform the other methods on most of the datasets but do not perform particularly well with upsampling factor = 16 on the Lu and Middlebury datasets, which can be seen in Table 1. This might be because our network cannot avoid the disappearance of gradients, when the upsampling factor became higher. It is not hard to recognize that when the image is reduced to 1/16 of its original size, most of high-frequency details will disappear. Therefore, $CNN_T$ may be ineffective due to lack of a solution to maintaining the gradient of the image.

**The Residuals Result:** We visualized the residuals of the network, and the result is shown in Fig. 5. Because the residuals have both positive and negative values, before visualizing them, we first add the absolute value of the largest negative number to all the values, so that all the values are above zero.

As can be seen in the Fig. 5, our results has bare texture artifacts appearing in the flat areas, and retaining their original information well. At the edges, the curves of the contours are clearly reproduced. However, some "bilateral" curves rise at the edges, such as the right contours of the book. This is because our model is smart to learn the position of the edges, but unsatisfactory to predict the accurate value and width of the edges.

(a) RGB                    (b) Input              (c) Ground truth

(d) Our output          (e) Our residual

**Fig. 5.** Results of comparing our residual when upsampling factor is 8.

## 5    Conclusion

We propose a two-branch CNN network for depth map super-resolution with guidance. The model can be trained end-to-end, with a fully convolutional network so that all sizes of images can be input into it. The two branches of the network, $CNN_T$, $CNN_G$, extract the feature maps of the low-resolution target image and the high-resolution guidance image, respectively. $CNN_F$ performs final reconstruction. Our model combines the channel attention mechanism and spatially variant kernels. The former is used to enhance the effectiveness of extracting feature information from low-resolution depth maps. The latter emphasizes the guidance role of the guided map to reduce texture artifacts and obtain smoother edges compared to direct stitching and fusion. Our proposed model is trained on the NYUv2 dataset only and test well under other datasets without fine-tuning. Comparing with other current methods, our model achieves better results on several datasets, verifying the effectiveness of our model on guided depth super-resolution. In future work, we will further explore the efficacy of joint image guidance under multiple tasks, such as denoising and image fusion tasks.

## References

1. Endres, F., Hess, J., Engelhard, N., Sturm, J., Cremers, D., Burgard, W.: An evaluation of the RGB-D SLAM system. In: 2012 IEEE International Conference on Robotics and Automation, pp. 1691–1696 (2012)
2. Qu, Y., Ou, Y.: LEUGAN: low-light image enhancement by unsupervised generative attentional networks. arXiv preprint arXiv:2012.13322 (2020)
3. Qu, Y., Chen, K., Liu, C., et al.: UMLE: unsupervised multi-discriminator network for low light enhancement. arXiv preprint arXiv:2012.13177 (2020)

4. Guo, K., Xu, F., Yu, T., Liu, X., Dai, Q., Liu, Y.: Real-time geometry, Albedo, and motion reconstruction using a single RGB-D camera. ACM Trans. Graph. **36**(4), 1 (2017). Article 44a

5. Zollhöfer, M., Nießner, M., Izadi, S., et al.: Real-time non-rigid reconstruction using an RGB-D camera. ACM Trans. Graph. **33**(4), 1–12 (2014). Article 156

6. Kopf, J., Cohen, M.F., Lischinski, D., et al.: Joint bilateral upsampling. ACM Trans. Graph. **26**(3), 96 (2007)

7. Yang, Q., Yang, R., Davis, J., et al.: Spatial-depth super resolution for range images. In: Proceedings of 2007 IEEE Computer Society Conference on Computer Vision and Pattern Recognition, Minneapolis, Minnesota, USA, 18–23 June 2007 (2007)

8. He, K., Sun, J., Tang, X.: Guided image filtering. IEEE Trans. Pattern Anal. Mach. Intell. **35**(6), 1397–1409 (2013)

9. Diebel, J., Thrun, S.: An application of Markov random fields to range sensing. In: NIPS (2005)

10. Park, J., Kim, H., Tai, Y.W., Brown, M., Kweon, I.: High quality depth map upsampling for 3D-TOF cameras. In: ICCV, pp. 1623–1630 (2011)

11. Ferstl, D., Reinbacher, C., Ranftl, R., Rüther, M., Bischof, H.: Image guided depth upsampling using anisotropic total generalized variation. In: ICCV, pp. 993–1000 (2013)

12. Mac Aodha, O., Campbell, N.D.F., Nair, A., Brostow, G.J.: Patch based synthesis for single depth image super-resolution. In: Fitzgibbon, A., Lazebnik, S., Perona, P., Sato, Y., Schmid, C. (eds.) ECCV 2012. LNCS, vol. 7574, pp. 71–84. Springer, Heidelberg (2012). https://doi.org/10.1007/978-3-642-33712-3_6

13. Dong, C., Loy, C.C., He, K., Tang, X.: Learning a deep convolutional network for image super-resolution. In: Fleet, D., Pajdla, T., Schiele, B., Tuytelaars, T. (eds.) ECCV 2014. LNCS, vol. 8692, pp. 184–199. Springer, Cham (2014). https://doi.org/10.1007/978-3-319-10593-2_13

14. Dong, C., Deng, Y., Loy, C.C., et al.: Compression artifacts reduction by a deep convolutional network. In: Proceedings of 2015 IEEE International Conference on Computer Vision, ICCV, Santiago, Chile (2015)

15. Eigen, D., Krishnan, D., Fergus, R.: Restoring an image taken through a window covered with dirt or rain. In: Proceedings of IEEE International Conference on Computer Vision, ICCV 2013, Sydney, Australia (2013)

16. Ren, J.S., Xu, L., Yan, Q., et al.: Shepard convolutional neural networks. In: Proceedings of Advances in Neural Information Processing Systems 28: Annual Conference on Neural Information Processing Systems, Montreal, Quebec, Canada, 7–12 December 2015 (2015)

17. Hui, T.-W., Loy, C.C., Tang, X.: Depth map super-resolution by deep multi-scale guidance. In: Leibe, B., Matas, J., Sebe, N., Welling, M. (eds.) ECCV 2016. LNCS, vol. 9907, pp. 353–369. Springer, Cham (2016). https://doi.org/10.1007/978-3-319-46487-9_22

18. Li, Y., Huang, J.-B., Ahuja, N., Yang, M.-H.: Deep joint image filtering. In: Leibe, B., Matas, J., Sebe, N., Welling, M. (eds.) ECCV 2016. LNCS, vol. 9908, pp. 154–169. Springer, Cham (2016). https://doi.org/10.1007/978-3-319-46493-0_10

19. Li, Y., Huang, J.B., Ahuja, N., Yang, M.H.: Joint image filtering with deep convolutional networks. IEEE Trans. Pattern Anal. Mach. Intell. **41**(8), 1909–1923 (2019)

20. Hu, J., Shen, L., Sun, G.: Squeeze-and-excitation networks. In: Proceedings of the IEEE Conference on Computer Vision and Pattern Recognition (CVPR), pp. 7132–7141 (2018)

21. Silberman, N., Hoiem, D., Kohli, P., Fergus, R.: Indoor segmentation and support inference from RGBD images. In: Fitzgibbon, A., Lazebnik, S., Perona, P., Sato, Y., Schmid, C. (eds.) ECCV 2012. LNCS, vol. 7576, pp. 746–760. Springer, Heidelberg (2012). https://doi.org/10.1007/978-3-642-33715-4_54

22. Hirschmuller, H., Scharstein, D.: Evaluation of cost functions for stereo matching. In: Proceedings of IEEE Conference on Computer Vision and Pattern Recognition (2007)

23. Butler, D.J., Wulff, J., Stanley, G.B., Black, M.J.: A naturalistic open source movie for optical flow evaluation. In: Fitzgibbon, A., Lazebnik, S., Perona, P., Sato, Y., Schmid, C. (eds.) ECCV 2012. LNCS, vol. 7577, pp. 611–625. Springer, Heidelberg (2012). https://doi.org/10.1007/978-3-642-33783-3_44

24. Lu, S., Ren, X., Liu, F.: Depth enhancement via low-rank matrix completion. In: Proceedings of IEEE Conference on Computer Vision and Pattern Recognition (2014)

25. Su, H., Jampani, V., Sun, D., Gallo, O., Learned-Miller, E., Kautz, J.: Pixel-adaptive convolutional neural networks. In: Proceedings of the IEEE/CVF Conference on Computer Vision and Pattern Recognition (CVPR), pp. 11166–11175 (2019)

26. Tomasi, C., Manduchi, R.: Bilateral filtering for gray and color images. In: Sixth International Conference on Computer Vision (IEEE Cat. No. 98CH36271), pp. 839–846 (1998)

27. Qu, Y., Ou, Y., Xiong, R.: Low illumination enhancement for object detection in self-driving. In: IEEE International Conference on Robotics and Biomimetics (ROBIO), vol. 2019, pp. 1738–1743 (2019)

# EBANet: Efficient Boundary-Aware Network for RGB-D Semantic Segmentation

Ruiquan Wang[✉], Qingxuan Jia, Yue Shen, Zeyuan Huang,
Gang Chen, and Junting Fei

Beijing University of Posts and Telecommunications, Beijing, China
wangruiquan@buptrobot.com

**Abstract.** Semantic segmentation is widely used in robot perception and can be used for various subsequent tasks. Depth information has been proven to be a useful clue in the semantic segmentation of RGB-D images for providing a geometric counterpart to the RGB representation. At the same time, considering the importance of object boundaries in the robot's perception process, it is very necessary to add attention to the boundaries of the objects in the semantic segmentation model.

In this paper, we propose Efficient Boundary-Aware Network (EBANet) which relies on both RGB and depth images as input. We design a boundary attention branch to extract more boundary features of objects in the scene and generate boundary labels for supervision by a Canny edge detector. We also adopt a hybrid loss function fusing Cross-Entropy (CE) and structural similarity (SSIM) loss to guide the network to learn the transformation between the input image and the ground truth at the pixel and patch level. We evaluate our proposed EBANet on the common RGB-D dataset NYUv2 and show that we reach the state-of-the-art performance.

**Keywords:** RGB-D semantic segmentation · Boundary attention · Hybrid loss

## 1 Introduction

For autonomous and intelligent robots, accurate scene perception is necessary. Semantic segmentation is well suited for such an initial step, as it provides precise pixel-wise information that can be used for numerous subsequent tasks.

Besides exploiting various contextual information from the visual cues [1–6], depth data have recently been utilized as supplementary information to RGB data to achieve improved segmentation accuracy [7–14]. Depth data naturally complements RGB signals by providing the 3D geometry to 2D visual information, which is robust to illumination changes and helps better distinguishing various objects. Especially in the environments where robots work, cluttered scenes may impede semantic segmentation. Incorporating depth images can alleviate this effect by providing complementary geometric information, as shown in [15–17].

Furthermore, in robot tasks, the accurate distinction of the boundaries of objects in the scene is more important than the accuracy of the overall cognition of the scene. However, in many studies of semantic segmentation, among the multitude of papers

© Springer Nature Singapore Pte Ltd. 2022
F. Sun et al. (Eds.): ICCSIP 2021, CCIS 1515, pp. 213–224, 2022.
https://doi.org/10.1007/978-981-16-9247-5_16

contributing to the impressive 86% relative improvement in pixel accurancy (e.g., [18–22]), only a few address mask boundary quality.

Based on these insights we propose our Efficient Boundary-Aware Network (EBANet) which relies on both RGB and depth images as input. We design a boundary attention decoder branch to extract more boundary features of objects in the scene. A Canny edge detector is used to generate boundary-labeled images from the original segmentation labels for supervising the boundary attention branch. We also adopt a hybrid loss function fusing Cross-Entropy (CE) and structural similarity (SSIM) loss inspired by BASNet [23]. The hybrid loss guides the network to learn the transformation between the input image and the ground truth at the pixel and patch level, which helps the optimization to focus on the boundary. Our EBANet shows better performance than the state-of-the-art RGB-D segmentation methods as shown by our experiments (see Fig. 1).

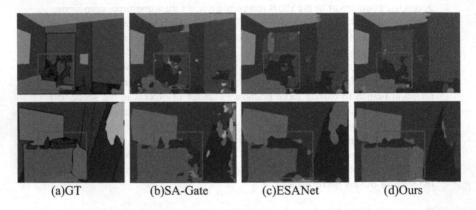

(a)GT          (b)SA-Gate          (c)ESANet          (d)Ours

**Fig. 1.** Sample result of our method (EBANet) compared to SA-Gate [24] and ESANet [25]. Column (a) shows the ground truth (GT). (b), (c) and (d) are results of SA-Gate, ESANet and ours.

The main contributions of this paper are:

- A novel boundary-aware RGB-D semantic segmentation network: EBANet, which is a deeply supervised encoder-decoder architecture with dual decoder branches of semantic segmentation branch and boundary attention branch.
- A hybrid loss that fuses CE and SSIM to supervise the training process at the pixel and patch level to make the network focus on the boundary while training.
- A evaluation of the proposed method with a comparison with 2 state-of-the-art methods on the common RGB-D dataset NYUv2. Our method achieves state-of-the-art results in terms of mean Intersection over Union (mIoU).

## 2 Related Work

### 2.1 RGB-D Semantic Segmentation

With the development of depth sensors, recently there is a surge of interest in leveraging depth data for the semantic segmentation task, dubbed as RGB-D semantic segmentation [7–9, 26–28]. Depth images provide complementary geometric information to RGB images and, thus, improve segmentation [15, 16].

Incorporating depth information into RGB segmentation architectures is challenging as depth introduces deviating statistics and characteristics from another modality. The majority of approaches for RGB-D segmentation simply use two branches, one for RGB and one for depth data. Each branch can focus on extracting modality-specific features in this way. For example, the RGB branch extracts color and texture features while the depth branch extracts geometric and illumination-independent features. Then the feature representations are fused in the network. It leads to stronger feature representations to fuse these modality-specific features. [15] shows that if the features are fused at multiple stages, the segmentation performance increases. Typically, the features are fused once at each resolution stage with the last fusion at the end of both encoders. FuseNet [15], RedNet [16] and ESANet [25] fuse the depth features into the RGB encoder, which follows the intuition that the semantically richer RGB features can be further enhanced using complementary depth information. SA-Gate [24] combines RGB and depth features and fuses the recalibrated features back into both encoders. In order to make the two encoders independent of each other, ACNet [17] uses an additional, virtual, third encoder that obtains modality-specific features from the two encoders and processes the combined features. Instead of fusing in the encoder, the modality-specific features can also be used to refine the features in the common decoder via skip connections as in RDFNet [7], SSMA [29] and MMAF-Net [30].

In addition, the introduction of depth data has increased the scale of the network and the requirements for hardware. In [31], depth information is used to project the RGB images into a 3D space. However, it leads to significantly higher computational complexity to process the resulting 3D data. [8, 32–35] design specifically tailored convolutions, taking into account depth information, which often lack optimized implementations for hardware. [25] builds a light-weight network named Efficient Scene Analysis Network (ESANet) by exchanging the basic block in all ResNet layers with more efficient blocks and using a decoder that utilizes a novel learned upsampling. ESANet achieves the state-of-the-art performance with using fewer hardware resources than other methods. Following ESANet, we further improve the performance of the network at object boundaries by the attention mechanism.

### 2.2 Attention Mechanism

Attention mechanisms have been widely utilized in kinds of computer vision tasks, serving as the tools to spotlight the most representative and informative regions of input signals [2, 36–40]. For example, to improve the performance of the image/video classification task, SENet [36] introduces a self recalibrate gating mechanism by model importance among different channels of feature maps. Based on similar spirits, SKNet

[37] designs a channel-wise attention module to select kernel sizes to adaptively adjust its receptive field size based on multiple scales of input information. [38] introduces a non-local operation that explores the similarity of each pair of points in space. For the segmentation task, a well-designed attention module could encourage the network to learn helpful context information effectively. For instance, DFN [39] introduces a channel attention block to select the more discriminative features from multi-level feature maps to get more accurate semantic information. DANet [2] proposes two types of attention modules to model the semantic inter-dependencies in spatial and channel dimensions respectively. BANet [40] introduces a boundary feature mining branch to generate boundary feature maps which help the network focus on boundary area and extract low-level features selectively. However, BANet is an RGB-only network for the task of portrait segmentation and its boundary feature mining branch is not suitable for an RGB-D semantic segmentation network architecture. In our work, we design a boundary attention branch that extracts boundary features from both RGB and depth information as well as make the boundary features are fused with segmentation maps at multiple stages.

## 3   Method

This section starts with the architecture overview of our proposed EBANet. We describe the details of our designed boundary attention branch in Sect. 3.2. The formulation of our hybrid loss is presented in Sect. 3.3.

### 3.1   Overview

The proposed EBANet is a deeply supervised encoder-decoder architecture as shown in Fig. 2.

The RGB and depth encoder both use a ResNet architecture [41] as the backbone. Each $3 \times 3$ convolution is replaced by a $3 \times 1$ and a $1 \times 3$ convolution with a ReLU in-between, called Non-Bottleneck-1D-Block (NBt1D), which is shown that can simultaneously reduce inference time and increases segmentation performance in ESANet [25]. At each of the five resolution stages in the encoders (see Fig. 2), depth features are fused into the RGB encoder. The features from both modalities are first reweighted with a Squeeze and Excitation (SE) module [36] and then summed element-wisely. Using this channel attention mechanism, the model can learn which features of which modality to focus on and which to suppress, depending on the given input. Due to the limited receptive field of ResNet [42], a context module is used to incorporate context information by aggregating features at different scales by several branches.

Our decoder contains two branches with the similar structure, one is used to output the result of semantic segmentation, and the other is used to output the result of boundary detection. Each decoder uses the structure in ESANet which extends the one of SwiftNet [43], but different loss functions are used for supervision (See Sect. 3.3). 512 channels in the first decoder module are used and the number of channels in each $3 \times 3$ convolution is decreased as the resolution increases. Three additional Non-Bottleneck-1D-blocks are incorporated to further increase segmentation performance. Finally, the feature maps are unsampled by a factor of 2. A light-weight learned upsampling method is used. In addition, skip connections from encoder to decoder stages of the same resolution are used. We will further introduce how the boundary attention branch works in Sect. 3.2.

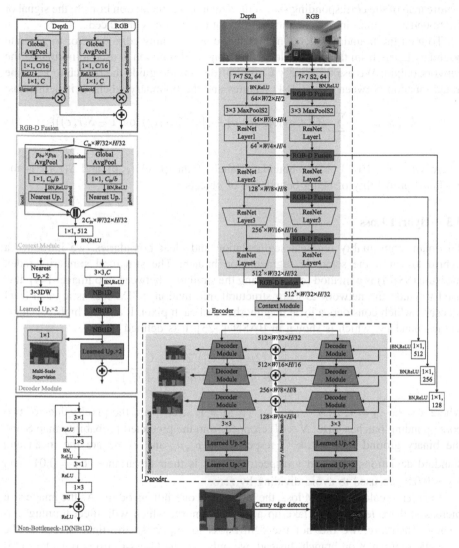

**Fig. 2.** Overview of our proposed EBANet.

## 3.2 Boundary Attention Branch

Our boundary attention branch is designed to introduce an attention mechanism to the boundaries of objects for the network. The boundary attention branch can be regarded as a copy of the original semantic segmentation branch. The difference is that the boundary attention branch only outputs a prediction of a single category, that is, it is judged whether a certain pixel belongs to the object boundaries or not. It doesn't care what kind of object the pixel belongs to. Thus, after training, the boundary attention branch can further extract boundary features from the RGB-D features that output from the encoder. By adding the output of each decoder module of the boundary attention branch to the feature map of the corresponding size of the semantic segmentation branch, the signal of the boundary feature in the semantic segmentation branch is enhanced.

To train the boundary attention branch, we use a Canny edge detector to generate boundary labels from the original labels. The sigmoid function is used to normalize the network output. We use the Binary Cross-Entropy loss to guide the branch to learn the transformation between the RGB-D features and the boundary labels. It is defined as:

$$l_{boundary} = -\sum_{(r,c)} [G(r,c)\log(S(r,c) + (1 - G(r,c))\log(1 - S(r,c))] \tag{1}$$

where $G(r,c) \in \{0,1\}$ is the boundary label of the pixel $(r,c)$ and $S(r,c)$ is the predicted probability of being boundaries of objects.

### 3.3  Hybrid Loss

To obtain high-quality regional segmentation and clear boundaries, we introduce a hybrid loss into the semantic segmentation branch. The structural similarity index measure (SSIM) is a method for measuring the similarity between two images [44]. It is used to guide the network to learn structural information. SSIM loss is a patch-level measure, which considers a local neighborhood of each pixel. It assigns higher weights to the boundary, which is shown in BASNet [23]. It is defined as:

$$l_{SSIM} = 1 - \frac{(2\mu_x\mu_y + C_1)(2\sigma_{xy} + C_2)}{(\mu_x^2 + \mu_y^2 + C_1)(\sigma_x^2 + \sigma_y^2 + C_2)} \tag{2}$$

where $x = \{x_j : j = 1, ..., N^2\}$ and $y = \{y_j : j = 1, ..., N^2\}$ are the pixel values of two corresponding patches (size: $N \times N$) cropped from the predicted probability map S and the binary ground truth mask G respectively. $\mu_x, \mu_y$ and $\sigma_x, \sigma_y$ are the mean and standard deviations of $x$ and $y$ respectively, $\sigma_{xy}$ is their covariance, $C_1 = 0.01^2$ and $C_2 = 0.03^2$ are used to avoid dividing by zero.

In order to calculate SSIM loss, the labels need one-hot encoding. As the image size increases, these tensors will take up a lot of memory, which will affect training efficiency. Therefore, we did not use SSIM loss to supervise the final output of the semantic segmentation branch. Instead, we only use the Cross-Entropy (CE) loss [45] at the final output, and use the CE and SSIM loss at each decoder module in semantic segmentation. All these losses are summed to get the loss of the segmentation branch, which is defined as:

$$l_{segmentation} = l_{final} + \sum_i^n l_i \tag{3}$$

where $l_{final}$ is the loss of the final output and $l_i$ is the loss of the i-th decoder module output. Losses of the decoder module output is defined as:

$$l_{decoder} = l_{CE} + l_{SSIM} \qquad (4)$$

where $l_{CE}$ is the CE loss. Our training loss is defined as the summation of all outputs:

$$l_{total} = \alpha \cdot l_{segmentation} + \beta \cdot l_{boundary} \qquad (5)$$

where $\alpha, \beta$ are hyperparameters for adjusting the weights of the two branches.

## 4 Experiments

We evaluate our approach on the commonly used RGB-D dataset NYUv2 [46] and present an ablation study to essential parts of our network.

### 4.1 Datasets and Implementation Details

NYUv2 contains 1,449 indoor RGB-D images, of which 795 are used for training and 654 for testing. We used the common 40-class label setting. We used a network input resolution of 640 × 480 and applied median frequency class balancing [47]. As the input to the context module has a resolution of 20 × 15 due to the downsampling of 32, we used $b = 2$ branches, one with global average pooling and one with a pooling size of 4 × 3.

We trained our networks using PyTorch [48] for 500 epochs with batches of size 8. We use 2 RTX 2080ti GPU cards (with 11 GB memory) for both training and testing. For optimization, we used both SGD with momentum of 0:9 and Adam [49] with learning rates of {0.00125; 0.0025; 0.005; 0.01; 0.02; 0.04} and {0.0001; 0.0004}, respectively, and a small weight decay of 0:0001. We adapted the learning rate using PyTorch's onecycle learning rate scheduler. To further increase the number of training samples, we augmented the images using random scaling, cropping, and flipping. For RGB images, we also applied slight color jittering in HSV space. We used 0.9–1.1 times for jittering H and S while [−25, +25] for jittering V randomly. The best models were chosen based on the mIoU. And we get our best model when $\alpha = 1, \beta = 1.2$ in the total loss.

### 4.2 Results on NYUv2

Table 1 lists the results of our RGB-D approach for NYUv2 dataset. We compared the proposed EBANet with the current state-of-the-art methods, SA-Gate and ESANet. Our model achieves leading performance. According to the results, the performance of SA-Gate is far from the results given in the paper (52.4% for mIoU). The success of SA-Gate is due to a larger batch size during training. And this is difficult to reproduce under our existing hardware conditions. Instead, we only use about a quarter of the hardware resources to achieve similar results. The effectiveness of our proposed method can be proven by the results.

**Table 1.** Mean intersection over union of our ESANet compared to state-of-the-art methods on NYUv2. The results in the table are produced in the environment we use. (*: SA-Gate achieved 51.4% mIoU using 8 NVIDIA TITAN V GPU cards with batches of size 16 according to the paper. For our 2 cards we can only training with batches of size 8.)

| Method | BackBone | mIoU (%) | Pixel Acc. (%) |
|--------|----------|----------|----------------|
| SA-Gate* | 2 × ResNet101 | 48.94 | 75.80 |
| ESANet | 2 × ResNet50 | 50.00 | 75.93 |
| **EBANet (ours)** | 2 × ResNet50 | **51.51** | **76.82** |

**Table 2.** Ablation study for the proposed parts on NYUv2 test set.

| Model | Boundary Attention | Hybrid Loss | mIoU (%) |
|-------|--------------------|-------------|----------|
| Baseline (ESANet) | / | / | 50.00 |
| Hybrid-loss-only | / | √ | 50.48 |
| Boundary-attention-only ($\alpha$=1, $\beta$=1.2) | √ | / | 49.69 |
| EBANet ($\alpha$=1, $\beta$=1.2) | √ | √ | **51.51** |

## 4.3   Ablation Study on NYUv2

Further, we perform ablation studies on the NYUv2 dataset under the same hyperparameters. Table 2 shows the study results for the proposed parts of our network architecture. ESANet is used as the baseline. There is no boundary attention branch in the hybrid-loss-only experiment, and only CE loss at the final output without hybrid loss is used in the boundary-attention-only experiment. According to the results, it can be seen that the improvement of network performance by using only hybrid loss is slight. However, using only boundary attention branch may have harmful effects on network performance. This is caused by hyperparameters $\alpha, \beta$. The hyperparameters that achieve better performance in EBANet may not be suitable for networks that do not use hybrid loss. At present, we have not studied their selection extensively, which will be one of our next research directions. However, the performance of EBANet, which uses both the boundary attention branch and the hybrid loss, has greatly improved. The results can show that boundary attention branch and hybrid loss play a mutually reinforcing role.

# 5   Conclusion

In this paper, we have presented a boundary-aware RGB-D segmentation approach, called EBANet, which is characterized by the boundary attention decoder branch and the hybrid loss function fusing Cross-Entropy (CE) and structural similarity (SSIM) loss to make the network extract more boundary features. On the common RGB-D dataset NYUv2, our EBANet achieves state-of-the-art results in terms of mIoU. Thus, it provides new possibilities for the application of semantic segmentation in robots.

**Acknowledgment.** This work was supported by Major Project of the New Generation of Artificial Intelligence (No. 2018AAA0102900).

# References

1. Long, J., Shelhamer, E., Darrell, T.: Fully convolutional networks for semantic segmentation. In: IEEE Conference on Computer Vision and Pattern Recognition, CVPR 2015, Boston, MA, United States, pp. 431–440. IEEE Computer Society (2015)
2. Fu, J., et al.: Dual attention network for scene segmentation. In: 32nd IEEE/CVF Conference on Computer Vision and Pattern Recognition, CVPR 2019, Long Beach, CA, United States, pp. 3141–3149. IEEE Computer Society (2019)
3. He, J., Deng, Z., Qiao, Y.: Dynamic multi-scale filters for semantic segmentation. In: 17th IEEE/CVF International Conference on Computer Vision, ICCV 2019, Seoul, Republic of Korea, pp. 3561–3571. Institute of Electrical and Electronics Engineers Inc., United States (2019)
4. Fu, J., et al.: Adaptive context network for scene parsing. In: 17th IEEE/CVF International Conference on Computer Vision, ICCV 2019, Seoul, Republic of Korea, pp. 6747–6756. Institute of Electrical and Electronics Engineers Inc., United States (2019)
5. Cheng, B., et al.: SPGNet: semantic prediction guidance for scene parsing. In: 17th IEEE/CVF International Conference on Computer Vision, ICCV 2019, Seoul, Republic of Korea, pp. 5217–5227. Institute of Electrical and Electronics Engineers Inc., United States (2019)
6. Zhang, F., et al.: ACFNet: attentional class feature network for semantic segmentation. In: 17th IEEE/CVF International Conference on Computer Vision, ICCV 2019, Seoul, Republic of Korea, pp. 6797–6806. Institute of Electrical and Electronics Engineers Inc., United States (2019)
7. Lee, S., Park, S.J., Hong, K.S.: RDFNet: RGB-D multi-level residual feature fusion for indoor semantic segmentation. In: 16th IEEE International Conference on Computer Vision, ICCV 2017, Venice, Italy, pp. 4990–4999. Institute of Electrical and Electronics Engineers Inc., United States (2017)
8. Wang, W., Neumann, U.: Depth-aware CNN for RGB-D segmentation. In: Ferrari, V., Hebert, M., Sminchisescu, C., Weiss, Y. (eds.) ECCV 2018. LNCS, vol. 11215, pp. 144–161. Springer, Cham (2018). https://doi.org/10.1007/978-3-030-01252-6_9
9. Zhang, Z., Cui, Z., Xu, C., Yan, Y., Sebe, N., Yang, J.: Pattern-affinitive propagation across depth, surface normal and semantic segmentation. In: 32nd IEEE/CVF Conference on Computer Vision and Pattern Recognition, CVPR 2019, Long Beach, CA, United States, pp. 4106–4115. IEEE Computer Society (2019)

10. Chen, Y., Mensink, T., Gavves, E.: 3D neighborhood convolution: learning depthaware features for RGB-D and RGB semantic segmentation. In: 7th International Conference on 3D Vision, 3DV 2019, Quebec, QC, Canada, pp. 173–182. Institute of Electrical and Electronics Engineers Inc., United States (2019)

11. He, Y., Chiu, W.C., Keuper, M., Fritz, M.: STD2P: RGBD semantic segmentation using spatio-temporal data-driven pooling. In: 30th IEEE Conference on Computer Vision and Pattern Recognition, CVPR 2017, Honolulu, HI, United States, pp. 7158–7167. Institute of Electrical and Electronics Engineers Inc. (2017)

12. Li, Z., Gan, Y., Liang, X., Yu, Y., Cheng, H., Lin, L.: LSTM-CF: unifying context modeling and fusion with LSTMs for RGB-D scene labeling. In: Leibe, B., Matas, J., Sebe, N., Welling, M. (eds.) ECCV 2016. LNCS, vol. 9906, pp. 541–557. Springer, Cham (2016). https://doi.org/10.1007/978-3-319-46475-6_34

13. Cheng, Y., Cai, R., Li, Z., Zhao, X., Huang, K.: Locality-sensitive deconvolution networks with gated fusion for RGB-D indoor semantic segmentation. In: 30th IEEE Conference on Computer Vision and Pattern Recognition, CVPR 2017, Honolulu, HI, United States, pp. 1475–1483. Institute of Electrical and Electronics Engineers Inc. (2017)

14. Hung, S.W., Lo, S.Y., Hang, H.M.: Incorporating luminance, depth and color information by a fusion-based network for semantic segmentation. In: 26th IEEE International Conference on Image Processing, ICIP 2019, Taipei, Taiwan, pp. 2374–2378. IEEE Computer Society (2019)

15. Hazirbas, C., Ma, L., Domokos, C., Cremers, D.: FuseNet: incorporating depth into semantic segmentation via fusion-based CNN architecture. In: Lai, S.-H., Lepetit, V., Nishino, K., Sato, Y. (eds.) ACCV 2016. LNCS, vol. 10111, pp. 213–228. Springer, Cham (2017). https://doi.org/10.1007/978-3-319-54181-5_14

16. Jiang, J., Zheng, L., Luo, F., Zhang, Z.: RedNet: residual encoder-decoder network for indoor RGB-D semantic segmentation. arXiv preprint arXiv:1806.01054 (2018)

17. Hu, X., Yang, K., Fei, L., Wang, K.: ACNet: attention based network to exploit complementary features for RGBD semantic segmentation. In: 26th IEEE International Conference on Image Processing, ICIP 2019, Taipei, Taiwan, pp. 1440–1444. IEEE Computer Society (2019)

18. Zhu, X., Hu, H., Lin, S., Dai, J.: Deformable ConvNets v2: more deformable, better results. In: 32nd IEEE/CVF Conference on Computer Vision and Pattern Recognition, CVPR 2019, Long Beach, CA, United States, pp. 9300–9308. IEEE Computer Society (2019)

19. Cai, Z., Vasconcelos, N.: Cascade R-CNN: delving into high quality object detection. In: 31st Meeting of the IEEE/CVF Conference on Computer Vision and Pattern Recognition, CVPR 2018, Salt Lake City, UT, United States, pp. 6154–6162. IEEE Computer Society (2018)

20. Bodla, N., Singh, B., Chellappa, R., Davis, L.S.: Soft-NMS - improving object detection with one line of code. In: 16th IEEE International Conference on Computer Vision, ICCV 2017, Venice, Italy, pp. 5562–5570. Institute of Electrical and Electronics Engineers Inc., United States (2017)

21. Huang, Z., Huang, L., Gong, Y., Huang, C., Wang, X.: Mask scoring R-CNN. In: 32nd IEEE/CVF Conference on Computer Vision and Pattern Recognition, CVPR 2019, Long Beach, CA, United States, pp. 6402–6411. IEEE Computer Society (2019)

22. Li, Z., Zhuang, Y., Zhang, X., Yu, G., Sun, J.: COCO instance segmentation challenges 2018: winner (2018). http://presentations.cocodataset.org/ECCV18/COCO18-Detect-Megvii.pdf

23. Qin, X., Zhang, Z., Huang, C., Gao, C., Dehghan, M., Jagersand, M.: BASNet: boundary-aware salient object detection. In: 32nd IEEE/CVF Conference on Computer Vision and Pattern Recognition, CVPR 2019, Long Beach, CA, United States, pp. 7471–7481. IEEE Computer Society (2019)

24. Chen, X., et al.: Bi-directional cross-modality feature propagation with separation-and-aggregation gate for RGB-D semantic segmentation. In: Vedaldi, A., Bischof, H., Brox, T., Frahm, J.-M. (eds.) ECCV 2020. LNCS, vol. 12356, pp. 561–577. Springer, Cham (2020). https://doi.org/10.1007/978-3-030-58621-8_33

25. Seichter, D., Köhler, M., Lewandowski, B., Wengefeld, T., Gross, H.: M Efficient RGB-D semantic segmentation for indoor scene analysis. arXiv preprint arXiv:2011.06961

26. Kong, S., Fowlkes, C.: Recurrent scene parsing with perspective understanding in the loop. In: 31st Meeting of the IEEE/CVF Conference on Computer Vision and Pattern Recognition, CVPR 2018, Salt Lake City, UT, United States, pp. 956–965. IEEE Computer Society (2018)

27. Lin, D., Chen, G., Cohen-Or, D., Heng, P.A., Huang, H.: Cascaded feature network for semantic segmentation of RGB-D images. In: 16th IEEE International Conference on Computer Vision, ICCV 2017, Venice, Italy, pp. 1320–1328. Institute of Electrical and Electronics Engineers Inc., United States (2017)

28. Chen, X., Lin, K., Qian, C., Zeng, G., Li, H.: 3D sketch-aware semantic scene completion via semi-supervised structure prior. In: 2020 IEEE/CVF Conference on Computer Vision and Pattern Recognition, CVPR 2020, Virtual, Online, United States, pp. 4192–4201. IEEE Computer Society (2020)

29. Valada, A., Mohan, R., Burgard, W.: Self-supervised model adaptation for multimodal semantic segmentation. Int. J. Comput. Vision 128(5), 1239–1285 (2020)

30. Fooladgar, F., Kasaei, S.: Multi-modal attention-based fusion model for semantic segmentation of RGB-depth images. arXiv preprint arXiv:1912.11691 (2019)

31. Zhong, Y., Dai, Y., Li, H.: 3D geometry-aware semantic labeling of outdoor street scenes. In: 24th International Conference on Pattern Recognition, ICPR 2018, Beijing, China, pp. 2343–2349. Institute of Electrical and Electronics Engineers Inc., United States (2018)

32. Xing, Y., Wang, J., Chen, X., Zeng, G.: 2.5D convolution for RGB-D semantic segmentation. In: 26th IEEE International Conference on Image Processing, ICIP 2019, Taipei, Taiwan, pp. 1410–1414. IEEE Computer Society (2019)

33. Xing, Y., Wang, J., Zeng, G.: Malleable 2.5D convolution: learning receptive fields along the depth-axis for RGB-D scene parsing. In: Vedaldi, A., Bischof, H., Brox, T., Frahm, J.-M. (eds.) ECCV 2020. LNCS, vol. 12364, pp. 555–571. Springer, Cham (2020). https://doi.org/10.1007/978-3-030-58529-7_33

34. Chen, L., Lin, Z., Wang, Z., Yang, Y.L., Cheng, M.M.: Spatial information guided convolution for real-time RGBD semantic segmentation. IEEE Trans. Image Process. 30 (2021), 2313–2324 (2021)

35. Chen, Y., Mensink, T., Gavves, E.: 3D neighborhood convolution: learning depth-aware features for RGB-D and RGB semantic segmentation. In: 7th International Conference on 3D Vision, 3DV 2019, Quebec, QC, Canada, pp. 173–182. Institute of Electrical and Electronics Engineers Inc., United States (2019)

36. Hu, J., Shen, L., Albanie, S., Sun, G., Wu, E.: Squeeze-and-excitation networks. IEEE Trans. Pattern Anal. Mach. Intell. 42(8), 2011–2023 (2020)

37. Li, X., Wang, W., Hu, X., Yang, J.: Selective kernel networks. In: 32nd IEEE/CVF Conference on Computer Vision and Pattern Recognition, CVPR 2019, Long Beach, CA, United States, pp. 510–519. IEEE Computer Society (2019)

38. Wang, X., Girshick, R., Gupta, A., He, K.: Non-local neural networks. In: 31st Meeting of the IEEE/CVF Conference on Computer Vision and Pattern Recognition, CVPR 2018, Salt Lake City, UT, United States, pp. 7794–7803. IEEE Computer Society (2018)

39. Yu, C., Wang, J., Peng, C., Gao, C., Yu, G., Sang, N.: Learning a discriminative feature network for semantic segmentation. In: 31st Meeting of the IEEE/CVF Conference on Computer Vision and Pattern Recognition, CVPR 2018, Salt Lake City, UT, United States, pp. 1857–1866. IEEE Computer Society (2018)

40. Chen, X., Qi, D., Shen, J.: Boundary-aware network for fast and high-accuracy portrait segmentation. arXiv preprint arXiv:1901.03814

41. He, K., Zhang, X., Ren, S., Sun, J.: Deep residual learning for image recognition. In: 29th IEEE Conference on Computer Vision and Pattern Recognition, CVPR 2016, Las Vegas, NV, United states, pp. 770–778. IEEE Computer Society (2016)

42. Zhao, H., Shi, J., Qi, X., Wang, X., Jia, J.: Pyramid scene parsing network. In: 30th IEEE Conference on Computer Vision and Pattern Recognition, CVPR 2017, Honolulu, HI, United states, pp. 6230–6239. Institute of Electrical and Electronics Engineers Inc., United States (2017)

43. Orsic, M., Kreso, I., Bevandic, P., Segvic, S.: In defense of pre-trained imagenet architectures for real-time semantic segmentation of road-driving images. In: 32nd IEEE/CVF Conference on Computer Vision and Pattern Recognition, CVPR 2019, Long Beach, CA, United states, pp. 12599–12608. IEEE Computer Society (2019)

44. Wang, Z., Simoncelli, E.P., Bovik, A.C.: Multiscale structural similarity for image quality assessment. In: The Thrity-Seventh Asilomar Conference on Signals, Systems & Computers, vol. 2, no. 2003, pp. 1398–1402 (2003)

45. Murphy, K.P.: Machine Learning: A Probabilistic Perspective. MIT Press, Cambridge (2012)

46. Silberman, N., Hoiem, D., Kohli, P., Fergus, R.: Indoor segmentation and support inference from RGBD images. In: Fitzgibbon, A., Lazebnik, S., Perona, P., Sato, Y., Schmid, C. (eds.) ECCV 2012. LNCS, vol. 7576, pp. 746–760. Springer, Heidelberg (2012). https://doi.org/10.1007/978-3-642-33715-4_54

47. Eigen, D., Fergus, R.: Predicting depth, surface normals and semantic labels with a common multi-scale convolutional architecture. In: 15th IEEE International Conference on Computer Vision, ICCV 2015, Santiago, Chile, pp. 2650–2658. Institute of Electrical and Electronics Engineers Inc., United States (2015)

48. Paszke, A., et al.: PyTorch: an imperative style, high-performance deep learning library. In: Advances in Neural Information Processing Systems, vol. 32, no. 2019, pp. 8024–8035 (2019)

49. Kingma, D.P., Ba, J.L.: Adam: a method for stochastic optimization. In: 3rd International Conference on Learning Representations, ICLR 2015, San Diego, CA, United states (2015)

# Camouflaged Object Segmentation with Transformer

Haiwen Wang[1], Xinzhou Wang[2], Fuchun Sun[1(✉)], and Yixu Song[1]

[1] Institute for Artificial Intelligence, Tsinghua University (THUAI),
Beijing National Research Center for Information Science and Technology (BNRist),
State Key Lab on Intelligent Technology and Systems, Department of Computer
Science and Technology, Tsinghua University, Beijing, People's Republic of China
wanghw19@mails.tsinghua.edu.cn, fcsun@tsinghua.edu.cn,
songyx@mail.tsinghua.edu.cn
[2] School of Electronic and Information Engineering, Tongji University,
Shanghai, China

**Abstract.** The Vision Transformer (ViT) [6] directly applies a Transformer architecture to image classification and achieves an impressive result compared with convolutional networks. This paper presents a new ViT-base camouflaged object segmentation method, called COS Transformer, which aims to identify and segment objects concealed in a complex environment. The high intrinsic similarities between object and surrounding makes the task challenging than salient object detection. Most recent camouflaged object segmentation methods(e.g., EGNet [29], PraNet [10] and SINet [9]) adopt convolutional network with an encoder-decoder architecture and focused on increasing the receptive field, which is limited by the depth of the network. In camouflaged object segmentation (COS) task, the camouflage is mainly relied on contrast of the whole surrounding instead of the local information. We introduce transformer with global context awareness in this paper, for self-attention allowing COS Transformer to aggregate features globally even in the lowest layers. Specifically, the architecture is composed of a transformer-based encoder and a multi-layers feature aggregation refinement module. After training on the COD10K [9] dataset, COS Transformer attains excellent results compared to state-of-the-art convolutional networks, e.g. 11.7% improvement of $E_\phi$ [8] on the COD10K contrasted to SINet.

**Keywords:** Camouflaged object · Segmentation · Transformer

## 1 Introduction

Camouflage is an attempt to conceal the texture of a foreground object into the background by combination of color, illumination, or material. Identifying and spotting camouflaged objects is challenging for both humans and artificial

---

X. Wang—Equal contributions.

F. Sun et al. (Eds.): ICCSIP 2021, CCIS 1515, pp. 225–237, 2022.
https://doi.org/10.1007/978-981-16-9247-5_17

intelligence while the technology of camouflaged objects segmentation could be used in many areas in the future, such as search and rescue work, detection of agricultural pests, medical imaging or the military environment (e.g., search-and-rescue mission and rare species discovery) [18].

Camouflaged objects are divided into two types: wildlife, insects or aquatic life seamlessly embedded in surroundings to protect themselves from predators, and artificially camouflaged objects such as snipers and artillery under camouflage net. The purpose of camouflage is to destroy the outline of the target and deceiving the visual perceptual system of the observer utilizing complex texture and color blending with surrounding. To demonstrate how challenging to identify camouflaged objects, we collect few examples from dataset CAMO [13] (see Fig. 1).

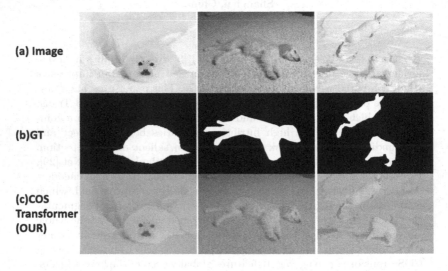

**Fig. 1.** Examples of camouflaged objects, ground truth and prediction of our model

COS task has long been dominated by convolutional neural networks (CNNs) applying an encoder-decoder architecture [9,13,18,20] with ingenious and complicated decoder to obtain the global information of images, which is of vital importance for COS task. Nevertheless, it is tricky to lever the cost of computation resource and the depth of the network, which directly determine the reception field of the network. To address the limitation of reception field, inspired by the predators, most machine learning based camouflaged object segmentation methods [9,13,18] could be divided into two stages: searching and recognition. We address this issue from another perspective: transformer. Segmentation transformer [31], on the other hand, builds hierarchical feature maps and enable even the lowest level to aggregate features globally and locally. Transformer is far more flexible than CNN [6], while lack some of the inductive biases inherent to CNN, including translation equivariance and locality, which limits the generalization performance of transformer when trained on insufficient amounts of training samples. Fortunately, recent works offered abundant datasets COD10K [9].

The overall contribution of this paper is that we redefine the camouflaged object segmentation problem as a foreground and background segmentation from a sequence-to-sequence viewpoint, instead of the dominating CNN model architecture. Thus, we replace the loss function of segmentation of the structure loss [20,26]. Finally, our COS Transformer achieve state-of-the-art performance on three benchmark datasets: CHAMELEON [22], CAMO [13] and COD10K [9].

## 2 Related Work

**Camouflaged Object Segmentation:** Camouflaged object segmentation has attracted researchers attention in a long history. Biologists analyzed the camouflaged models in the animal kingdom since 100 years ago [23]. Before the machine learning methods are introduced into the field of image processing, elaborate handcrafted low-level feature filters has tremendous impact on distinguishing foreground and background. To obtain more information from the scene, spatial features [19] and temporal features [14] are also token into account. Recently, encoder-decoder architecture with deep CNNs push COS to a new era and set new state-of-the-art. Most of them are composed of a coarsely search stage and a identify stage to aggregate multi-level feature and refine the feature map [9,13,18,20,26]. To strengthen the ability to distinguish the target and background more precisely, recurrent methods are also employed [25]. The amount and scale of camouflaged object segmentation datasets is deficient in the early years. To address this issue, COD10K is introduced with 10,000 images and became the largest COS dataset to date with the richest annotations.

**Vision Transformer:** The attention mechanism is first introduced in [1], which is called alignment model in this paper. Recent years, transformer became the defacto mainstream approach in Natural Language Processing (NLP) field. However, its deployment in computer vision was limited until Google came up with ViT, the Vision transformer [6]. It convinced researchers that computer vision methods could even achieve relatively higher performance without CNNs. To convert images into sequences, ViT splits an image into several patches and feed them info a linearly projection layer with position embedding. Though the idea of adopting transformer into computer vision is nothing new [4], transformer will not outperform CNNs without abundant training data and computational resource, for transformer is lack some of the inductive biases inherent to CNN, including translation equivariance and locality.

Though transformer have revolutionized the object detection task, encoder-decoder based fully-convolutional network (FCN) remains unchanged in semantic segmentation field until SETR [31]. It is a pure transformer maintaining the resolution during the image processing process. With the ability to capture global context information, transformer provide a high-performance encoder, which could be beneficial in semantic segmentation tasks. It provides direct inspiration to exploit a transformer-based encoder for COS task. Compared to semantic segmentation, COS requires more global context information to identify which region is concealed and transform could exactly enlarge the reception field as depicted in Fig. 2.

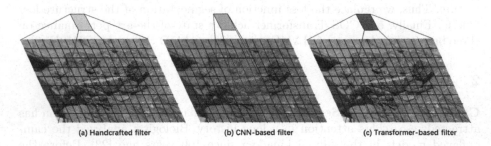

(a) Handcrafted filter                (b) CNN-based filter                (c) Transformer-based filter

**Fig. 2.** Reception field of handcrafted-filter, CNN and transformer. Handcrafted-filter lacks diversity of filters and CNN is limited by reception field. The transformer, on the other hand, has ability to capture global contextual information.

## 3 Methodology

### 3.1 COS Transformer Encoder

The camouflaged objects is defined as the objects attempting to conceal the texture of themselves into the background by combination of color, illumination, or material [9]. For human's visual system, the first step to identify the camouflaged object is learning a global recognition of the surrounding. The overall color as well as the texture of surroundings could be beneficial to detect the targets, which has local similarity as well as global distinction when compared to environment. When we take a close look at the boundary of the concealed object, it would be a tough task to give a clear judgement of which area belongs to target. But from another perspective, when we give a global sight of the whole scene, the target will appear dramatically in sight. The fact implies that global context modeling is of tremendous importance on context based tasks especially COS task. This inspire us to take a strategy of strengthening the global connection of the image to locate the target.

**Image Split:** The application of transformer in NLP achieved revolutionary success, which suggest that the transformer can play a role of encoder in COS task [5]. However, the input of NLP is a series of sentences to be converted into embedded vectors, and images can not be embedded directly without transformation. The spatial dimension of the images is $X \in \mathbb{R}^{n \times H \times W \times 3}$, where n is batch size, H and W are sizes of images, while in NLP transformer, the feature embeddings $Z \in \mathbb{R}^{n \times L \times C}$, where L is the length of embedded vectors. To mimic the NLP's sequential inputs, an intuitive method is to flatten one image into a vector. However, the length of flatten vector will suffer from a dimensional disaster. For instance, a $512 \times 512 \times 3$ image will have a length of 786,432, which outnumbers the total number of English vocabulary. Considering the quadratic time complexity of self-attention, the computational cost will be catastrophic. To address this issue, image is reshaped into a sequence of patches with a size of $p \in \mathbb{R}^{n \times P^2 \times 3}$ and the complexity of self-attention will decrease by a factor of $P^4$, where P is the size of each patch and P is 16 in this paper. The image is divided into $\frac{H}{16} \times \frac{W}{16}$ patches and then passed into a linear projection to convert the flatten vector into a $D$ dimension latent vector [6]. To retain the geometrical relationship among pixels in neighbourhood which is destroyed while splitting images in to flatten vectors, we introduce a learnable embedding called positional embedding trained on ImageNet [21] dataset and added it directly to the projected vectors. With this positional embedding, we retain the spatial information in spite of turning a 2-D relationship into sequential. In order to give transformer a warm up, we prepared an extra class token with learnable parameters.

**Multi-head Self Attention:** Multi-head Self Attention (MSA) plays a role of backbone in this paper. In NLP tasks, multi-head self attention is in vogue due to its' ability to connect the current processing vector with all passed vectors, which captures the short-term as well as long-term information. When transferred to computer vision tasks, this merit turns into global reception field. The self-attention mechanism is introduced with three critical vectors: the query vector $Q$, the key vector $K$ and the value vector $V$. The calculation of these vectors is as followed:

$$Q = XW^Q, K = XW^K, V = XW^V \tag{1}$$

where $W^Q, W^K, W^V$ are weight matrices. To give a better understanding of the meaning of $Q, K$ and $V$, We can think of self-attention as being analogous to the process of search: Assuming that we are search a paper, we will search the keywords of this paper instead of typing in the entire article. The words for searching is $Q$, the keywords in the best matching paper is $K$ and the value of the target paper is $V$. As depicted in Fig. 3, the calculation mainly followed the path of "Scaled Dot-Product Attention" [6]:

$$Attention(Q, K, V) = softmax(\frac{QK^T}{\sqrt{d_k}}V) \tag{2}$$

where $d_k$ stands for the dimension of $K$. Softmax function is introduced to obtain the weights from the attention score of each pair of tokens and the rescaling factor $\sqrt{d_k}$ is to counteract the effect of gradients disappear when $QK^T$ is extremely large. Since the ability of one single attention function in semantic comprehending is limited, we introduce Multi-Head Attention mechanism to enhance the information exchange in separated feature maps. Each head process $Q, K, V$ simultaneously and the output matrix is multiplied by $W^O$ after concatenating:

$$MultiHead(Q, K, V) = Concat(Attention_1, ..., Attention_h)W^O$$
$$Attention_i = Attention(QW_i^Q, KW_i^K, VW_i^V)$$

(3)

Where $W^O, W_i^Q, W_i^K$ and $W_i^V$ are projection matrices. The entire procedure is depicted in the Fig. 3.

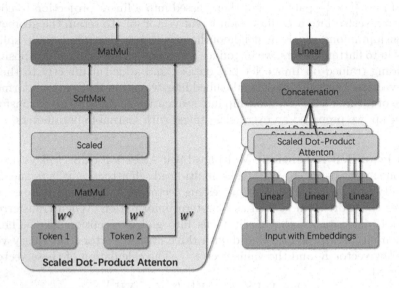

**Fig. 3.** Multi-Head Attention: multiple scaled Dot-Product Attention calculating simultaneously

**Transformer:** The encoder is mainly consist of several transformer encoders. Concretely, the Transformer, as depicted in Fig. 4, receives the tokens from linear projection layer with pre-trained position embedding. The tokens are passed into Mult-Head Attention after layer normalized and then transformed by Multi-Layer Perceptron (MLP) with residual skip:

$$Z^i = MultiHead(Z^{i-1}) + MLP(MSA(Z^{i-1}))$$

(4)

where $Z^i$ denote the output of the i-th transformer. Taking into account the training difficulties caused by the network, deep supervised training is adopted for middle layers of transformers and the total loss is composed of weighted auxiliary loss and the final loss.

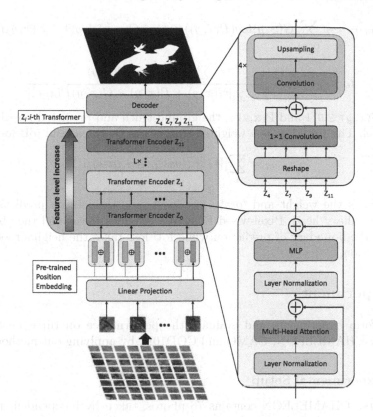

**Fig. 4.** Schematic illustration of the proposed COS Transformer

## 3.2 Decoder Module

Receiving the high level feature maps from the encoder, the main goal of decoder is to generate a semantic comprehension based on the context information passed by encoder. First, we extract the feature maps from several layers of transformer with the same resolution, which is differ from previous work using pyramid shape. Then a $1 \times 1$ convolution is deployed to augment the number of channels and an element-wise addition after the convolution, playing a role of multi-layer feature map fusion, enhancing the ability of representation of the global context information. Based on the enhanced global context information of the input image, the decoder, denoted as MLF (multi-layer fusion), progressively restore the output to the full image resolution along with four combination operations consisted of convolution and upsampling. The overview of the decoder is depicted in Fig. 4.

## 3.3 Loss Function

The definition of the loss function is identical to the structure loss in [20] and [26]. The structure loss is composed of two basic loss function: binary cross entropy (BCE) loss and IoU loss:

$$loss_{BCE} = -\sum_{(x,y)} [G(x,y)log(P(x,y)) + (1 - G(x,y))log(1 - P(x,y))] \quad (5)$$

$$loss_{IoU} = 1 - \frac{\sum_{(x,y)} G(x,y)P(x,y)}{\sum_{(x,y)} [G(x,y) + P(x,y) - G(x,y)P(x,y)]} \quad (6)$$

where $G(x,y) \in 0,1$ and P(x,y) is the ground truth and predicted possibility of each pixel. The total loss is a weighted sum of the BCE loss and IoU loss.

$$loss_{total} = \sum_i [W_i \times (loss^i_{BCE} + loss^i_{IoU})] \quad (7)$$

where $W_i$ is the weight and $loss^i_{BCE} + loss^i_{IoU}$ is the loss on prediction and several auxiliary head. Pixel-wised BCE loss provides the model the ability to finetune the boundary of prediction while IoU loss takes the neighborhood into consideration.

## 4   Experiments

We perform experiments and evaluate the performance on three benchmark datasets: CHAMELEON, CAMO and COD10K, by applying out method.

### 4.1   Experimental Setup

**Datasets:** CHAMELEON contains 76 photos, taken by independent photographers who marked these as good examples of camouflaged animals from the Internet, selected by Google image search with the keyword "camouflaged animal". And the counterpart object-level ground truths were crafted manually by authors' five fellow students. CAMO is a image dataset of camouflaged objects consisted of 1250 images covered eight categories, where 1000 images are for training, and the others are for testing. COD10K comprises 5066 camouflaged images, 3040 of which are used for training and 2026 for testing, covering 69 object categories. In order to compare fairly with the previous work, we use 3040 images of COD10K training set and 1000 images of CAMO as the training set and others as testing sets.

**Implementation Details:** Our network adopts the input linear projection layer and the transformer part of ViT [6] pretrained by the method DeiT [24] as the encoder network, which the number of transformer layers, multi-heads and the embedding dimension of linear projection layer is 12, 12, 768, respectively. The remained modules are the decoder network randomly initialized. Whether training or testing, the shape of input image is adjusted to $352 \times 352 \times 3$, before feeding into our network. Then, some data augmentations are applied to the resized image, such as random flip with ratio 0.5, photometric distortion and normalization. Our implementation is based on the public codebase mmsegmentation [3], while the initial learning rate is $1e - 2$ and adopting SGD optimizer

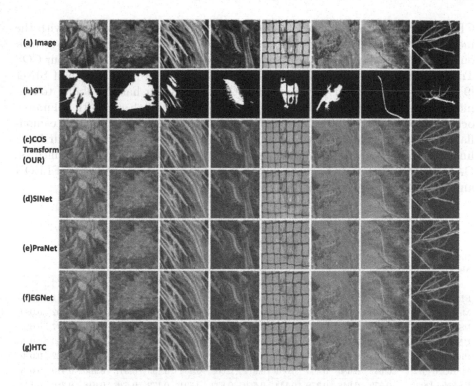

**Fig. 5.** Qualitative comparison between COS Transformer and other top-performing models on three benchmark datasets. Best viewed in color and zoom in (Color figure online).

with a polynomial learning policy. We set the batch size as 8 and the total iteration of training is 80000 along with 0.9 momentum without weight decay. As PSPNet [28], the auxiliary segmentation loss is beneficial to train the model. We add an auxiliary loss for the 4-th transformer layer with a 2-layer convolution network. The platform for training and inference is Intel®Xeon®CPU E5-2620 2.10 GHZ ×31 and GeForce RTX 2080Ti GPU.

**Evaluation Metrics:** Following the metrics of SINet [9], we employs four widely evaluation metrics to compare the performance of the camouflaged object segmentation, including S-measure [7], Mean E-measure [8], Mean F-measure [17] and Mean Absolute Error denoted as $S_\alpha$, $E_\phi$, $F_\beta^W$, $\mathcal{M}$, respectively.

### 4.2  Comparison with the State-of-the-Arts

Table 1 compares our segmentation results with the 14 SOTA baseline models on three benchmark datasets: CHAMELEON, CAMO, COD10K. Our COS Transformer achieves a new state of the art on all datasets across all four metrics. For example, our method improves $E_\phi$ by 6.6%, 16.2%, and 11.7% on the

CHAMELEON, CAMO, and COD10K dataset, separately comparing with the method SINet [9]. Furthermore, in order to understand the performance of various methods intuitively, Fig. 5 presents qualitative comparisons among our COS Transformer and four baselines-HTC [2], EGNet [29], PraNet [10] and SINet [9]. It demonstrates that our approach COS Transformer has the ability to segment precisely the fine details of edge(e.g., 1-st, 2-nd, 4-th and 6-th columns), occluded camouflaged objects(e.g., 3-rd and 5-th columns), and small camouflaged objects(e.g., the last two columns), while the output of other four baselines are more coarse and inaccurate. Since the ANet-SRM model trained on CAMO does not public implementation code, so the results of CHAMELEON and COD10K are not obtained, denoted by '-'.

**Table 1.** Quantitative comparison on three benchmark datasets

| Baseline Models | CHAMELEON [22] | | | | CAMO-Test [13] | | | | COD10K-Test [9] | | | |
|---|---|---|---|---|---|---|---|---|---|---|---|---|
| | $S_\alpha \uparrow$ | $E_\phi \uparrow$ | $F_\beta^W \uparrow$ | $\mathcal{M} \downarrow$ | $S_\alpha \uparrow$ | $E_\phi \uparrow$ | $F_\beta^W \uparrow$ | $\mathcal{M} \downarrow$ | $S_\alpha \uparrow$ | $E_\phi \uparrow$ | $F_\beta^W \uparrow$ | $\mathcal{M} \downarrow$ |
| FPN [15] | 0.794 | 0.783 | 0.590 | 0.075 | 0.684 | 0.677 | 0.483 | 0.131 | 0.697 | 0.691 | 0.411 | 0.075 |
| MaskRCNN [11] | 0.643 | 0.778 | 0.518 | 0.099 | 0.574 | 0.715 | 0.430 | 0.151 | 0.613 | 0.748 | 0.402 | 0.080 |
| PSPNet [28] | 0.773 | 0.758 | 0.555 | 0.085 | 0.663 | 0.659 | 0.455 | 0.139 | 0.678 | 0.680 | 0.377 | 0.080 |
| UNet++ [32] | 0.695 | 0.762 | 0.501 | 0.094 | 0.599 | 0.653 | 0.392 | 0.149 | 0.623 | 0.672 | 0.350 | 0.086 |
| PiCANet [16] | 0.769 | 0.749 | 0.536 | 0.085 | 0.609 | 0.584 | 0.356 | 0.156 | 0.649 | 0.643 | 0.322 | 0.090 |
| MSRCNN [12] | 0.637 | 0.686 | 0.443 | 0.091 | 0.617 | 0.669 | 0.454 | 0.133 | 0.641 | 0.706 | 0.419 | 0.073 |
| PFANet [30] | 0.679 | 0.648 | 0.378 | 0.144 | 0.659 | 0.622 | 0.391 | 0.172 | 0.636 | 0.618 | 0.286 | 0.128 |
| CPD [27] | 0.853 | 0.866 | 0.706 | 0.052 | 0.726 | 0.729 | 0.550 | 0.115 | 0.747 | 0.770 | 0.508 | 0.059 |
| HTC [2] | 0.517 | 0.489 | 0.204 | 0.129 | 0.476 | 0.442 | 0.174 | 0.172 | 0.548 | 0.520 | 0.221 | 0.088 |
| ANet-SRM [13] | – | – | – | – | 0.682 | 0.685 | 0.484 | 0.126 | – | – | – | – |
| EGNet [29] | 0.848 | 0.870 | 0.702 | 0.050 | 0.732 | 0.768 | 0.583 | 0.104 | 0.737 | 0.779 | 0.509 | 0.056 |
| F3Net [26] | 0.854 | 0.899 | 0.749 | 0.045 | 0.779 | 0.840 | 0.666 | 0.091 | 0.786 | 0.832 | 0.617 | 0.046 |
| PraNet [10] | 0.860 | 0.907 | 0.763 | 0.044 | 0.769 | 0.824 | 0.663 | 0.094 | 0.789 | 0.861 | 0.629 | 0.045 |
| SINet [9] | 0.869 | 0.891 | 0.740 | 0.044 | 0.751 | 0.771 | 0.606 | 0.100 | 0.771 | 0.806 | 0.551 | 0.051 |
| OURs (FCN) | 0.869 | 0.940 | 0.822 | 0.031 | 0.808 | 0.888 | 0.759 | 0.062 | 0.791 | 0.896 | 0.677 | 0.036 |
| OURs (PUP) | 0.876 | 0.946 | 0.835 | 0.029 | 0.786 | 0.870 | 0.728 | 0.069 | 0.775 | 0.881 | 0.651 | 0.040 |
| OURs (MLF) | **0.885** | **0.950** | **0.850** | **0.025** | **0.813** | **0.896** | **0.776** | **0.060** | **0.798** | **0.901** | **0.693** | **0.035** |

### 4.3  Ablation Study

From the previous comparison, we can see the fact that the ability of our transformer encoder for feature representation is better than CNNs. We adopt some simpler designs of decoder architecture than previous camouflaged object segmentation methods, such as SINet, PraNet or EGNet, explaining the effectiveness of the transformer encoder. Table 1 show the results of three variant decoder designs, which FCN decoder simply upsampling by bilinear to the original image size have a relatively competitive performance to the SINet, further verifying the function of the transformer encoder. Instead of the FCN decoder, the PUP decoder adopts progressively upsampling policy to recover the full resolution of the input image. But the performance of the PUP decoder is slightly better than the FCN decoder only on the CHAMELEON, while inferior on CAMO and COD10K. One possible cause of the PUP decoder for inferior performance on the other two datasets is that multiple convolutions could not decode better. Obviously, the multi-layers feature fusion decoder, denoted by MLF, achieves the best performance among all the variants on three benchmark datasets, demonstrated that it is beneficial to fuse multiple feature of different transformer layers.

## 5 Conclusion

Our work explored the possibility of utilizing ViT [6]-base backbone to segment camouflaged object concealed in a complex environment, called COS Transformer. The camouflaged object segmentation task is not defined on specific catalog, but on the global feature contrast. We supposed that transformer, with global context awareness, could strive to embrace challenges towards the camouflaged object segmentation and our experimental result confirms the conjecture. Compared to ViT, we introduced multi-layer feature aggregation as decoder to give a deeper understanding of the semantic information. Additionally, deep supervised training is adopted for middle layers of transformers and the total loss is composed of weighted auxiliary loss and the final loss. Each loss consists of two parts: binary cross entropy loss and IoU loss. By employing transformer as encoder and multi-layer feature aggregation as decoder, denoted by MLF, we surpassed the state-of-the-art models. Our results indicate the promising application of transformer in camouflaged object segmentation task, but further research shall focus on the intrinsic reasons of global contextual information awareness of transformer as well as specific failure cases.

## References

1. Bahdanau, D., Cho, K., Bengio, Y.: Neural machine translation by jointly learning to align and translate. arXiv preprint arXiv:1409.0473 (2014)
2. Chen, K., et al.: Hybrid task cascade for instance segmentation. In: Proceedings of the IEEE/CVF Conference on Computer Vision and Pattern Recognition, pp. 4974–4983 (2019)
3. Contributors, M.: MMSegmentation: Openmmlab semantic segmentation toolbox and benchmark (2020). https://github.com/open-mmlab/mmsegmentation
4. Cordonnier, J.B., Loukas, A., Jaggi, M.: On the relationship between self-attention and convolutional layers (2019)
5. Devlin, J., Chang, M.W., Lee, K., Toutanova, K.: Bert: Pre-training of deep bidirectional transformers for language understanding. arXiv preprint arXiv:1810.04805 (2018)
6. Dosovitskiy, A., et al.: An image is worth 16 × 16 words: Transformers for image recognition at scale. arXiv preprint arXiv:2010.11929 (2020)
7. Fan, D.P., Cheng, M.M., Liu, Y., Li, T., Borji, A.: Structure-measure: a new way to evaluate foreground maps. In: Proceedings of the IEEE International Conference on Computer Vision, pp. 4548–4557 (2017)

8. Fan, D.P., Gong, C., Cao, Y., Ren, B., Cheng, M.M., Borji, A.: Enhanced-alignment measure for binary foreground map evaluation. arXiv preprint arXiv:1805.10421 (2018)
9. Fan, D.P., Ji, G.P., Sun, G., Cheng, M.M., Shen, J., Shao, L.: Camouflaged object detection. In: Proceedings of the IEEE/CVF Conference on Computer Vision and Pattern Recognition, pp. 2777–2787 (2020)
10. Fan, D.-P., et al.: PraNet: parallel reverse attention network for polyp segmentation. In: Martel, A.L., et al. (eds.) MICCAI 2020, Part VI. LNCS, vol. 12266, pp. 263–273. Springer, Cham (2020). https://doi.org/10.1007/978-3-030-59725-2_26
11. He, K., Gkioxari, G., Dollár, P., Girshick, R.: Mask R-CNN. In: Proceedings of the IEEE International Conference on Computer Vision, pp. 2961–2969 (2017)
12. Huang, Z., Huang, L., Gong, Y., Huang, C., Wang, X.: Mask scoring R-CNN. In: Proceedings of the IEEE/CVF Conference on Computer Vision and Pattern Recognition, pp. 6409–6418 (2019)
13. Le, T.N., Nguyen, T.V., Nie, Z., Tran, M.T., Sugimoto, A.: Anabranch network for camouflaged object segmentation. Comput. Vis. Image Underst. **184**, 45–56 (2019)
14. Hou, J.Y.Y.H.W., Li, J.: Detection of the mobile object with camouflage color under dynamic background based on optical flow. Procedia Eng. **15**, 2201–2205 (2011)
15. Lin, T.Y., Dollár, P., Girshick, R., He, K., Hariharan, B., Belongie, S.: Feature pyramid networks for object detection. In: Proceedings of the IEEE Conference on Computer Vision and Pattern Recognition, pp. 2117–2125 (2017)
16. Liu, N., Han, J., Yang, M.H.: PiCANet: learning pixel-wise contextual attention for saliency detection. In: Proceedings of the IEEE Conference on Computer Vision and Pattern Recognition, pp. 3089–3098 (2018)
17. Margolin, R., Zelnik-Manor, L., Tal, A.: How to evaluate foreground maps? In: Proceedings of the IEEE Conference on Computer Vision and Pattern Recognition, pp. 248–255 (2014)
18. Mei, H., Ji, G.P., Wei, Z., Yang, X., Wei, X., Fan, D.P.: Camouflaged object segmentation with distraction mining. In: Proceedings of the IEEE/CVF Conference on Computer Vision and Pattern Recognition, pp. 8772–8781 (2021)
19. Pan, Y., Chen, Y., Fu, Q., Zhang, P., Xu, X.: Study on the camouflaged target detection method based on 3D convexity. Mod. Appl. Sci. **5**(4), 152–157 (2011)
20. Qin, X., Zhang, Z., Huang, C., Gao, C., Dehghan, M., Jagersand, M.: BASNet: boundary-aware salient object detection. In: Proceedings of the IEEE/CVF Conference on Computer Vision and Pattern Recognition, pp. 7479–7489 (2019)
21. Russakovsky, O., et al.: ImageNet large scale visual recognition challenge. Int. J. Comput. Vis. **115**(3), 211–252 (2015). https://doi.org/10.1007/s11263-015-0816-y
22. Skurowski, P., Abdulameer, H., Błaszczyk, J., Depta, T., Kornacki, A., Kozieł, P.: Animal camouflage analysis: Chameleon database. **2**(6), 7 (2018). Unpublished Manuscript
23. Thayer, G.: Concealing-Coloration in the Animal Kingdom: An Exposition of the Laws of Disguise Through Color and Pattern: Being a Summary of Abbott H. Thayer's. Macmillan, New York (1909)
24. Touvron, H., Cord, M., Douze, M., Massa, F., Sablayrolles, A., Jégou, H.: Training data-efficient image transformers & distillation through attention. arXiv preprint arXiv:2012.12877 (2020)
25. Wang, W., Shen, J., Cheng, M.M., Shao, L.: An iterative and cooperative top-down and bottom-up inference network for salient object detection. In: CVPR19 (2019)

26. Wei, J., Wang, S., Huang, Q.: F$^3$net: fusion, feedback and focus for salient object detection. In: Proceedings of the AAAI Conference on Artificial Intelligence, vol. 34, pp. 12321–12328 (2020)
27. Wu, Z., Su, L., Huang, Q.: Cascaded partial decoder for fast and accurate salient object detection. In: Proceedings of the IEEE/CVF Conference on Computer Vision and Pattern Recognition, pp. 3907–3916 (2019)
28. Zhao, H., Shi, J., Qi, X., Wang, X., Jia, J.: Pyramid scene parsing network. In: Proceedings of the IEEE Conference on Computer Vision and Pattern Recognition, pp. 2881–2890 (2017)
29. Zhao, J.X., Liu, J.J., Fan, D.P., Cao, Y., Yang, J., Cheng, M.M.: EGNet: edge guidance network for salient object detection. In: Proceedings of the IEEE/CVF International Conference on Computer Vision, pp. 8779–8788 (2019)
30. Zhao, T., Wu, X.: Pyramid feature attention network for saliency detection. In: Proceedings of the IEEE/CVF Conference on Computer Vision and Pattern Recognition, pp. 3085–3094 (2019))
31. Zheng, S., et al.: Rethinking semantic segmentation from a sequence-to-sequence perspective with transformers. In: Proceedings of the IEEE/CVF Conference on Computer Vision and Pattern Recognition, pp. 6881–6890 (2021)
32. Zhou, Z., Rahman Siddiquee, M.M., Tajbakhsh, N., Liang, J.: UNet++: a nested U-Net architecture for medical image segmentation. In: Stoyanov, D., et al. (eds.) DLMIA/ML-CDS -2018. LNCS, vol. 11045, pp. 3–11. Springer, Cham (2018). https://doi.org/10.1007/978-3-030-00889-5_1

# DGrid: Dense Grid Network for Salient Object Detection

Yuxiang Cai[1,2], Xi Wu[2], Zhiyong Huang[3] iD, Yuanlong Yu[3(✉)] iD, Weijie Jiang[3], Weitao Zheng[2], and Renjie Su[2]

[1] Shanghai Jiao Tong University, 800 Dongchuan Road, Shanghai 200240, China
caiyuxiang@sjtu.edu.cn
[2] State Grid Fujian Information and Telecommunication Company, Fuzhou 350001, China
[3] College of Mathematics and Computer Science, Fuzhou University, Fuzhou 350002, China
yu.yuanlong@fzu.edu.cn

**Abstract.** The performance of salient object detection has been significantly advanced by using fully convolutional networks (FCN). However, it still remains nontrivial to take full advantage of the multi-level convolutional features for salient object detection. In this paper, a dense grid network framework (denoted **DGrid**) is proposed to solve the above problem, which mainly consists of the backbone module, extended module and fusion module. Specifically, **DGrid** utilizes a multi-branch refinement mechanism for saliency detection. First, the backbone module is used to generate a coarse prediction map. Then, the extended module, which contains four branches, is used to improve the resolution and precision of the prediction map gradually from coarse to fine. Moreover, we proposed the densely connected strategy to fully fuse features at different levels. Finally, the fusion module densely fuses the highest level features of all branches to achieve the final saliency map. Experimental results on five widely used benchmark datasets demonstrate that **DGrid** can improve the accuracy of detection by maintaining a high-resolution feature branch, and it outperforms state-of-the-art approaches without any post-processing.

**Keywords:** Salient object detection · Dense grid network · Refinement · Convolutional features

## 1 Introduction

Salient object detection (SOD), which aims to locate the most visually conspicuous objects in an image, has become an important intermediate step for many applications, including visual tracking [1], image segmentation [2], etc.

This work supported by Science and Technology Project of State Grid Fujian Electric Power Co., Ltd. under grant 52130M19000X and National Natural Science Foundation of China (NSFC) under grant 61873067.

F. Sun et al. (Eds.): ICCSIP 2021, CCIS 1515, pp. 238–246, 2022.
https://doi.org/10.1007/978-981-16-9247-5_18

A large number of SOD methods have been developed based on different ideas [3,7–9,11,17,19,20,22–25]. Earlier SOD methods, inspired by cognitive studies of visual attention, mostly employed handcrafted features [7,22,25] (e.g., color, texture and contrast). Although these methods are computationally efficient, they are far from satisfactory in complex scenarios due to the lack of high-level semantic knowledge. Recently, Convolutional neural networks (CNN) have demonstrated state-of-the-art performance in SOD field. The early CNN based SOD methods operate on image blocks [8,9], i.e., these methods first divide the image into small image blocks, and then use CNN to predict the saliency score of each image block. Although these methods have great performance improvements compared with traditional methods, it is time-consuming by using region-based strategy. Fully convolutional networks (FCNs) [12] have demonstrated impressive performance in many dense labeling tasks, so FCNs based SOD methods have become increasingly popular in SOD field [3,11,17,19,20,23,24]. Wang et al. [20] propose a stage-wise refine strategy to generate predictions. Liu et al. [23] propose a pixel-wise contextual attention network to hierarchically embed global and local context information. However, these methods do not achieve a fine edge detail. To solve this problem, edge or contour constraints were introduced into the SOD methods and experimental results verify the effectiveness of the addition of auxiliary edge information [14,18].

To improve performance, most SOD methods have proposed multi-level feature fusion strategies [5,13,23], but these fusion strategies currently cannot fully integrate features, e.g., DSS [5] only considers the effect of deep-level features on low-level features, but ignores the effect of low-level features on high-level features. Besides, some methods have proposed stagewise architectures in order to better predict saliency [5,17,20], but these stagewise architectures are not yet powerful and robust, e.g., CPD [20] only designs two branches, and the performance will depend heavily on the coarse branch. To solve the above problems, this paper proposes a dense grid network architecture for SOD (**DGrid**), which contains the backbone module, extended module and fusion module. To solve the dense prediction problem more effectively, we design the extended module, which contains four branches, to improve the resolution and precision of the prediction map gradually from coarse to fine. To fully fuse multi-level features, we design a dense fusion strategy inspired by Densenet [6] to fuse the features of adjacent branches of the extended network, i.e., the next branch network constantly fuses the features of all levels of the previous branch. Finally, the fusion module fuses the highest-level features to further improve performance. Experimental results verify the effectiveness and efficiency of the proposed **DGrid** method.

The remainder of this paper is organized as follows. Section 2 introduces the architecture of the proposed DGrid method. Section 3 illustrates the experimental results.

## 2  The Proposed Method

As shown in Fig. 1, our proposed DGrid consists of three modules: the backbone module, extended module and fusion module. Here we can use VGG [15] or Resnet [4] (truncate fully connected layers) as the components of the backbone module. To fully fuse multi-level features, we design the extended module with the densely connected strategy, so it can be seen from Fig. 1 that DGrid can form a $4 \times 5$ dense grid structure through both the backbone module and extended module. Finally, we use the fusion module to achieve the final saliency map. Note that the fourth branch of the extended module maintains high-resolution feature maps, which can contribute to achieving better accuracy of detection. In the following, we will introduce the extended module, fusion module and model training in detail.

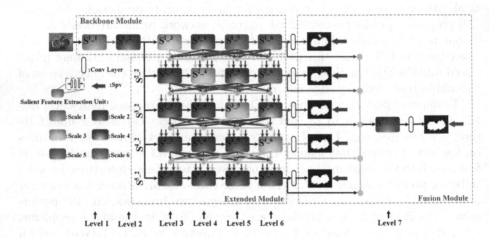

**Fig. 1.** Framework of the proposed DGrid method.

### 2.1  Extended Network Module

The extended module is the core of DGrid. As shown in Fig. 1, the entire extended module includes four branches, and the resolution of the saliency map is gradually improved by continuously reducing the number of downsampling operation in each branch. The salient feature extraction (SFE) unit as the basis of the extended module which is used to continuously enhances the features, i.e., increases the score of the salient region while suppressing the score of the background region. It can be seen from Fig. 1 that SFE unit in this module not only fuses the output features of the previous SFE unit of the current branch (i.e., the single connection in the horizontal direction), but also fuses the features of all levels of the previous branch (i.e., the dense connection in the vertical direction). Specifically, each SFE unit in the extended module includes two successive steps: feature fusion and feature enhancement. The feature fusion step fuses the output of the previous SFE unit of the same branch with the output of all SFE units of the previous branch to form a fusion feature, the feature enhancement step further enhances the fusion feature to form an enhanced feature.

The output feature matrix of feature fusion step in the $i$th branch, $j$th level SFE unit can be denoted by $\mathbf{F}^{i\text{-}j}$, where $i \in \{2, \ldots, 5\}$, $j \in \{3, \ldots, 6\}$. The details of feature fusion step can be computed by Eq. (1):

$$\mathbf{F}^{i\text{-}(j+1)} = R[C_{1\times1}(\mathbf{S}^{i\text{-}j})] \oplus R[C_{1\times1}(\mathbf{S}^{(i-1)\text{-}3})] \oplus \cdots \oplus R[C_{1\times1}(\mathbf{S}^{(i-1)\text{-}6})], \quad (1)$$

where $C_{1\times1}$ denotes the convolution operation with $1 \times 1$ kernel size, which is used to change the number of channels of the feature to the same. R denotes the bilinear interpolation operation, $\mathbf{S}^{i\text{-}j}$ denotes the output feature matrix of feature enhancement step in the $i$th branch, $j$th level SFE unit (i.e., the output of the $i$th branch, $j$th level SFE unit). $C_{1\times1}$ is essentially used for weighted fusion of features, i.e., the contribution of each level feature in the current SFE unit can be adaptively controlled by $C_{1\times1}$.

The feature enhancement step includes a two-layer convolution operation. Inspired by the architecture of ResNet [4], we reuse activations from a previous layer by utilizing skip connections. The details of feature enhancement step can be computed by Eq. (2):

$$\mathbf{S}^{i\text{-}j} = \mathbf{Relu}[\mathbf{F}^{i\text{-}j} \oplus C_{w\times w}[\mathbf{Relu}[C_{w\times w}(\mathbf{F}^{i\text{-}j})]]], \quad (2)$$

Note that we set the number of feature channels to 32, 64, 128 and 256 at scale 2, scale 3, scale 4 and scale 5, respectively. The experimental results in Sect. 3 show that DGrid will better balance performance and efficiency under this channel setting.

## 2.2  Fusion Module

Finally, we use the fusion module to fuse the last level feature of each branch (including the backbone module) to predict the final result $\mathbf{O}_{\text{final}}$ as shown in Eq. 3. Specifically, we first use the convolution operation $C_{1\times1}$ (kernel size is 1) to change the number of channels of the output feature of each branch to 128 and use bilinear interpolation operation to resize the features to the maximum resolution, then we use the convolution operation $C_{5\times5}$ (kernel size is 5) to enhance the fusion feature which is fused by addition operation, and finally use convolution operation $C_{3\times3}$ (kernel size is 3) to achieve the final saliency.

$$\mathbf{O}_{\text{final}} = C_{3\times3}\mathbf{Relu}[C_{5\times5}[R[C_{1\times1}(\mathbf{S}^{1\text{-}6})] \oplus \cdots \oplus R[C_{1\times1}(\mathbf{S}^{5\text{-}6})]]]]. \quad (3)$$

## 2.3  Model Training

We use the cross-entropy loss to train our DGrid, so the total loss can be denoted as:

$$\mathbb{L} = \alpha_f \mathcal{L}_f(\mathbf{W}, w_f) + \sum_{l=1}^{L} \alpha_l \mathcal{L}_l(\mathbf{W}, w_l), \quad (4)$$

where $\mathfrak{L}_f$ denotes the loss of the fusion module, $\mathfrak{L}_l$ denotes the loss of each branch of the backbone module and extended module. $L = 5$, $\alpha_f$ and $\alpha_l$ are used to balance each loss term and we set $\alpha_f = \alpha_l = 1$ in this paper.

# 3   Experiments

## 3.1   Datasets and Evaluation Metrics

Five public benchmark datasets are adopted to evaluate the performance of DGrid: DUT-O [22], ECSSD [21], HKU-IS [9], PASCAL-S [10], DUTS [16]. We adopt two widely metrics to evaluate the performance of all methods, i.e., $F_{measure}(F_\beta)$, Mean Absolute Error (MAE). We use the maximum of F-measure, and $\beta^2$ is set to be 0.3.

## 3.2   Implementation Details

We follow most recent works [3,11,14,20] to train DGrid on the DUTS-TR dataset [16]. DGrid is implemented by PyTorch on a PC equipped with an Intel i7-4790 CPU and a NVIDIA TiTan XP GPU. For a fair comparison, VGG [15] and ResNet [4] are used as backbone networks, respectively (denoted as DGrid-V and DGrid-R, respectively). All the weights of new convolutional layers are initialized with a truncated normal ($\sigma$). We do not use any data augmentation strategy during training. Stochastic gradient descent (SGD) is used to train the model, and hyper-parameters, including the momentum, learning rate, and weight decay, are set to be 0.9, $5e-5$, and 0.0005, respectively. All images are resized to $356 \times 356$, and the batchsize is set to 5 and the maximum epoch is set to 30. We divide the learning rate by 10 after 15 epochs. During the inference, DGrid-R can run at 33 fps.

## 3.3   Ablation Analysis

To demonstrate the advantages of densely connected strategy, we compare DGrid-R with a variant (Single-F) as shown in Table 1. Single-F model just uses a single fusion strategy to fuse the same level features between adjacent branches. It can be seen from Table 1 that DGrid-R achieves a noticeable performance increase especially on $F_{measure}$ metric, so we can confirm the importance of the multi-level features fusion in the saliency detection and the effectiveness of the proposed densely connected strategy. To demonstrate the performance of different channel settings, we show the results of different channel settings in Table 1. It can be seen that $F_{measure}$ and MAE goes up with the increase of channels number until it reaches a peak value at 64 (Channel 64). However, the performance improvement between DGrid-R (Channel 32) and Channel 64 is minimal. Table 1 also lists the parameters and computations of DGrid-R and variants. From these results, we can see that the computational complexity of Channel-64 is much higher than DGrid-R. Thus, the number of channel setting of DGrid-R can balance the performance and computational efficiency.

**Table 1.** Ablation analyses on DUT-O, HKU-IS and DUTS-TE.

| | DUT-O | | HKU-IS | | DUTS-TE | | FLOPs/G | Params/k |
|---|---|---|---|---|---|---|---|---|
| | $F\uparrow$ | $M\downarrow$ | $F\uparrow$ | $M\downarrow$ | $F\uparrow$ | $M\downarrow$ | | |
| Single-F | .777 | .060 | .919 | .033 | .858 | .039 | | |
| DGrid-R | .781 | .052 | .924 | .032 | .866 | .038 | | |
| Chanal 8 | .777 | .061 | .918 | .034 | .855 | .041 | 27.49 | 26.55 |
| Chanal 16 | .781 | .059 | .920 | .033 | .862 | .039 | 32.04 | 27.98 |
| DGrid-R | .781 | .052 | .924 | .032 | .866 | .038 | 47.01 | 33.16 |
| Chanal 64 | .778 | .052 | .927 | .030 | .870 | .038 | 100.34 | 52.80 |

### 3.4 Comparison with the State-of-the-Art

On the five benchmarks, we compare the proposed DGrid against 11 methods in terms of $F_{measure}$, MAE as shown in Table 2. It can be seen from Table 2 that DGrid performs favorably against the state-of-the-art methods in terms of both metrics on most of the datasets especially on the relative large datasets (HKUIS, DUTS-TE, DUT-OMRON). Specially, DGrid-R outperforms the sub-optimal method (CPD-R) 0.26 in terms of $F_{measure}$ on DUTS-TE dataset. We also visually compare our DGrid-R with other methods on some representative images in Fig. 2. From these results, we can see that DGrid-R performs well in most challenging scenarios. It demonstrates that the proposed multi-branch refinement mechanism and densely connected strategy can thorough fuse multi-level complementary salient features. Specially, DGrid-R can produce more accurate edges compared with other methods (row 4), which indicates the effectiveness of maintaining a high-resolution feature branch.

**Table 2.** Performance comparison with 11 state-of-the-art methods over 5 datasets. The best three results are shown in red, blue and green, respectively.

| | ECSSD | | DUT-O | | PASCAL-S | | HKU-IS | | DUTS-TE | |
|---|---|---|---|---|---|---|---|---|---|---|
| | $F\uparrow$ | $M\downarrow$ | $F\uparrow$ | $M\downarrow$ | $F\uparrow$ | $M\downarrow$ | $F\uparrow$ | $M\downarrow$ | $F\uparrow$ | $M\downarrow$ |
| **Traditional methods** | | | | | | | | | | |
| DRFI [7] | .751 | .170 | .623 | .150 | .639 | .207 | .745 | .145 | .600 | .155 |
| wCtr [25] | .684 | .165 | .541 | .171 | .599 | .196 | .695 | .138 | .522 | .176 |
| **VGG based methods** | | | | | | | | | | |
| BDMP [23] | .917 | .045 | .734 | .064 | .836 | .074 | .910 | .039 | .827 | .049 |
| PAGR [24] | .904 | .061 | .707 | .071 | .819 | .089 | .897 | .048 | .817 | .056 |
| PiCANet [11] | .919 | .047 | .759 | .068 | .845 | .078 | .908 | .042 | .826 | .054 |
| MLMSNet [19] | .917 | .045 | .734 | .064 | .836 | .074 | .910 | .039 | .828 | .049 |
| CPD [20] | .923 | .040 | .747 | .057 | .842 | .075 | .909 | .033 | .839 | .043 |
| AFNet [3] | .924 | .042 | .759 | .057 | .845 | .070 | .910 | .036 | .838 | .046 |
| DGrid-V | .925 | .041 | .769 | .055 | .847 | .075 | .917 | .034 | .855 | .042 |
| **Resnet based methods** | | | | | | | | | | |
| SRM [17] | .905 | .054 | .725 | .069 | .823 | .084 | .893 | .046 | .798 | .059 |
| DGRL [18] | .916 | .043 | .741 | .063 | .830 | .074 | .902 | .037 | .805 | .050 |
| PiCANet-R [11] | .925 | .047 | .770 | .065 | .844 | .077 | .906 | .043 | .839 | .050 |
| CPD-R [20] | .926 | .037 | .754 | .056 | .839 | .071 | .911 | .034 | .840 | .043 |
| BASNet [14] | .931 | .037 | .779 | .056 | .841 | .076 | .919 | .032 | .838 | .048 |
| DGrid-R | .935 | .037 | .781 | .052 | .848 | .072 | .924 | .032 | .866 | .038 |

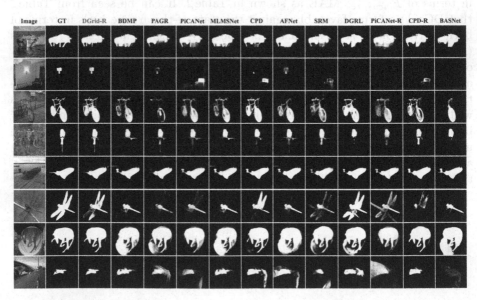

**Fig. 2.** Representative results of different methods on some challenging images.

# 4 Conclusion

In this paper, we aim to aggregate multi-level convolutional features effectively and efficiently. Inspired by the design of Desnet [6], we propose a dense grid network framework (DGrid) that adapts a multi-branch refinement mechanism for saliency detection. DGrid consists of three modules: backbone module, extended module and fusion module. Specifically, DGrid can improve the resolution and precision of the prediction map gradually from coarse to fine through an extended module. Meanwhile, DGrid uses the densely connected strategy to fully fuse features at different levels. Experimental results show that DGrid performs favorably against state-of-the-art methods. By visualizing the representative results on some challenging images, we also verify that DGrid can improve the accuracy of detection by maintaining a high-resolution feature branch.

# References

1. Borji, A., Frintrop, S., Sihite, D.N., et al.: Adaptive object tracking by learning background context. In: Proceedings of the IEEE Conference on Computer Vision and Pattern Recognition Workshop, pp. 23–30. IEEE, Piscataway (2012)
2. Donoser, M., Urschler, M., Hirzer, M., et al.: Saliency driven total variation segmentation. In: Proceedings of the IEEE International Conference on Computer Vision, pp. 817–824. IEEE, Piscataway (2009)
3. Feng, M., Lu, H., Ding, E.: Attentive feedback network for boundary-aware salient object detection. In: Proceedings of the IEEE Conference on Computer Vision and Pattern Recognition, pp. 1623–1632. IEEE, Piscataway (2019)
4. He, K., Zhang, X., Ren, S., et al.: Deep residual learning for image recognition. In: Proceedings of the IEEE Conference on Computer Vision and Pattern Recognition, pp. 770–778. IEEE, Piscataway (2016)
5. Hou, Q., Cheng, M., Hu, X., et al.: Deeply supervised salient object detection with short connections. In: Proceedings of the IEEE Conference on Computer Vision and Pattern Recognition, pp. 3203–3212. IEEE, Piscataway (2017)
6. Huang, G., Liu, S., Van, D., et al.: CondenseNet: an efficient DenseNet using learned group convolutions. In: Proceedings of the IEEE International Conference on Computer Vision and Pattern Recognition, pp. 2752–2761. IEEE, Piscataway (2018)
7. Jiang, H., Wang, J., Yuan, Z., et al.: Salient object detection: a discriminative regional feature integration approach. In: Proceedings of the IEEE Conference on Computer Vision and Pattern Recognition, pp. 2083–2090. IEEE, Piscataway (2013)
8. Lee, G., Tai, Y., Kim, J.: Deep saliency with encoded low level distance map and high level features. In: Proceedings of the IEEE Conference on Computer Vision and Pattern Recognition, pp. 660–668. IEEE, Piscataway (2016)
9. Li, G., Yu, Y.: Visual saliency based on multiscale deep features. In: Proceedings of the IEEE Conference on Computer Vision and Pattern Recognition, pp. 5455–5463. IEEE, Piscataway (2015)
10. Li, Y., Hou, X., Koch, C., et al.: The secrets of salient object segmentation. In: Proceedings of the IEEE Conference on Computer Vision and Pattern Recognition, pp. 280–287. IEEE, Piscataway (2014)

11. Liu, N., Han, J., Yang, M.H.: PiCANet: learning pixel-wise contextual attention for saliency detection. In: Proceedings of the IEEE Conference on Computer Vision and Pattern Recognition, pp. 3089–3098. IEEE, Piscataway (2018)
12. Long, J., Shelhamer, E., Darrell, T.: Fully convolutional networks for semantic segmentation. In: Proceedings of the IEEE Conference on Computer Vision and Pattern Recognition, pp. 3431–3440. IEEE, Piscataway (2015)
13. Luo, Z., Mishra, A., Achkar, A., et al.: Non-local deep features for salient object detection. In: Proceedings of the IEEE Conference on Computer Vision and Pattern Recognition, pp. 6609–6617. IEEE, Piscataway (2017)
14. Qin, X., Zhang, Z., Huang, C., et al.: BASNet: boundary-aware salient object detection. In: Proceedings of the IEEE Conference on Computer Vision and Pattern Recognition, pp. 7479–7489. IEEE, Piscataway (2019)
15. Simonyan, K., Zisserman, A.: Very deep convolutional networks for large-scale image recognition. In: IEEE International Conference on Learning Representations, pp. 1–14 (2013)
16. Wang, L., Lu, H., Wang, Y., et al.: Learning to detect salient objects with imagelevel supervision. In: Proceedings of the IEEE Conference on Computer Vision and Pattern Recognition, pp. 136–145. IEEE, Piscataway (2017)
17. Wang, T., Borji, A., Zhang, L., et al.: A stagewise refinement model for detecting salient objects in images. In: Proceedings of the IEEE International Conference on Computer Vision, pp. 4019–4028. IEEE, Piscataway (2017)
18. Wang, T., Zhang, L., Wang, S., et al.: Detect globally, refine locally: a novel approach to saliency detection. In: Proceedings of the IEEE Conference on Computer Vision and Pattern Recognition, pp. 3127–3135. IEEE, Piscataway (2018)
19. Wu, R., Feng, M., Guan, W., et al.: A mutual learning method for salient object detection with intertwined multi-supervision. In: Proceedings of the IEEE Conference on Computer Vision and Pattern Recognition, pp. 8150–8159. IEEE, Piscataway (2019)
20. Wu, Z., Su, L., Huang, Q.: Cascaded partial decoder for fast and accurate salient object detection. In: Proceedings of the IEEE Conference on Computer Vision and Pattern Recognition, pp. 3907–391. IEEE, Piscataway (2019)
21. Yan, Q., Xu, L., Shi, J., et al.: Hierarchical saliency detection. In: Proceedings of the IEEE Conference on Computer Vision and Pattern Recognition, pp. 1155–1162. IEEE, Piscataway (2013)
22. Yang, C., Zhang, L., Lu, H., et al.: saliency detection via graph-based manifold ranking. In: Proceedings of the IEEE Conference on Computer Vision and Pattern Recognition, pp. 3166–3173. IEEE, Piscataway (2013)
23. Zhang, L., Dai, J., Lu, H., et al.: Salient object detection: a discriminative regional feature integration approach. In: Proceedings of the IEEE Conference on Computer Vision and Pattern Recognition, pp. 1741–1750. IEEE, Piscataway (2018)
24. Zhang, X., Wang, T., Qi, J., et al.: Progressive attention guided recurrent network for salient object detection. In: Proceedings of the IEEE Conference on Computer Vision and Pattern Recognition, pp. 714–722. Piscataway, NJ:IEEE (2018)
25. Zhu, W., Liang, S., Wei, Y., et al.: Saliency optimization from robust background detection. In: Proceedings of the IEEE Conference on Computer Vision and Pattern Recognition, pp. 2814–2821. IEEE, Piscataway (2014)

# A Multi-frame Lane Detection Method Based on Deep Learning

Jinyuan Liu$^{(\boxtimes)}$ and Yang Gao$^{(\boxtimes)}$

School of Automobile, Chang'an University, Xi'an, China

**Abstract.** In recent years, many lane detection methods have been proposed. However, most of them lead to unsatisfactory performance in handling some extreme difficult driving scenes such as shadows, wireless and dark night. Aiming at this problem, a multi-frame lane detection method based on UNET_CLB was proposed. This method introduced multi-frame information of continuous driving scenes for lane detection on the basis of traditional deep learning. Convolutional neural network (CNN) is combined with convolutional long short-term memory network (CONVLSTM) and deep densely connected convolutional networks (DENSE_NET), a deep advanced semantic extraction network was proposed. The experimental results on the public datasets show that this method achieves an F1-score of 92.391% on the TuSimple dataset, and the F1-score on the CULane dataset is up to 13.6% higher than the existing method. The simulation results based on the Webots platform also show that the method proposed in this paper has a good effect on lane detection in wireless, shadow and shadow environments.

**Keywords:** Lane detection · Deep learning · Autonomous vehicle

## 1 Introduction

Lane detection, as one of the important technologies of assisted driving and unmanned driving in the road environment perception module, has attracted widespread attention in the academic and industrial circles. With the development and successful application of deep learning technology, there exists a multitude of deep learning based lane detection methods [1]. The current lane detection methods based on deep learning are mainly divided into four categories [2]: 1) Encoder-decoder CNN. An end-to-end codec lane detection model was proposed by KIM [3] et al., which was based on the segmentation task of road scenes and was trained on the ImageNet dataset through transfer learning, and good detection accuracy was obtained. A network called LaneNet was proposed by Neven [4] et al. The network was based on the SegNet [5] network to construct a backbone, and two decoders were used at the same time. One outputs a binary image mask to distinguish the foreground and background of the lane, and the other outputs a high-dimensional embedded lane vector through clustering. Considering that the network output was a feature map and the inverse perspective conversion matrix parameters are changed for the up and downhill vehicle pitch angle changes. Finally, a network called H-NET was designed to learn bird's-eye image inverse perspective conversion matrix parameters, and then the curve is used to fit the lane line.

© Springer Nature Singapore Pte Ltd. 2022
F. Sun et al. (Eds.): ICCSIP 2021, CCIS 1515, pp. 247–260, 2022.
https://doi.org/10.1007/978-981-16-9247-5_19

2) Fully convolutional network (FCN [6]), this type of network extracts more image features through convolution, and is not connected to the fully connected layer at the end, which can avoid the problem of losing image spatial information. A dual-view CNN (DVCNN) framework was proposed by He [7] et al. to process top-view and front-view images. A weighted hat-like filter was applied to the top view to find lane candidates. Then the front view was combined to obtain the fused lane features through full convolution. For the purpose of multi-task learning, a network called VPGNet was proposed by LEE [8] et al., which designed a shared feature extraction layer followed by four branches. At the same time, the optimization algorithm based on clustering and resampling was used to finish lane detection, lane marking recognition and vanishing point extraction. 3) CNN+RNN. Considering that road lane is continuous on the pavement, a method combining CNN and RNN was presented by Li [9]. In order to obtain continuous lane features, a complete single road image was divided and CNN was used for feature extraction, and then RNN was used to predict the complete lane feature. The results show that this method can achieve better results than using only CNN. However, the RNN in this method can only model time series features in a single frame of image, and RNN and CNN are two independent modules that need to be trained separately. 4) GAN model. The generative adversarial network (GAN [10]), which consists of a generator and a discriminator, is also employed for lane detection. For example, an embedding-loss GAN (EL-GAN) was proposed by Ghafoorian [11] for semantic segmentation of driving scenes, where the lanes were predicted by a generator based on the input image, and judged by a discriminator with shared weights.

The above-mentioned deep learning based methods are mostly used in environments with uniform illumination changes, and have high accuracy and robustness. However, in some extreme difficult driving scenes such as shadows, wireless and dark night, the performance is often severely degraded. At the same time, it is more difficult to produce datasets in difficult driving scenarios, which further hinders the development of lane detection technology in such scenarios. Since the lane is a continuous linear structure, the position of lanes in the neighboring frames are highly related. Furthermore, the lane features that cannot be detected in the current frame can be inferred by merging the information of the previous frame. Therefore, this characteristic of lane is used in this paper, and CNN as well as Long Short-Term Memory (LSTM) network are combined to propose a lane detection network called UNET_CLB, which combines spatio-temporal information and deep information. Continuous multi frame information are used to improve the detection rate of lane in difficult scenes.

## 2 Lane Detection Network

### 2.1 Spatiotemporal Information Fusion Network Model UNET_CL

The network called U-Net [12] was proposed in 2015. A codec structure of skip connection was adopted, which can combine the deep and shallow information of the image to effectively extract image features. As shown in Fig. 1, inspired by U-Net, a spatiotemporal information fusion network model called UNET_CL is proposed. The overall network structure is composed of encoder, CONVLSTM and decoder. The encoder is responsible for extracting the lane features in the continuous monocular image. The CONVLSTM [13] is used to fuse the multi-frame semantic information of the corresponding channels of the encoder and the decoder. The decoder is responsible for restoring the semantic information of the target according to the extracted lane features.

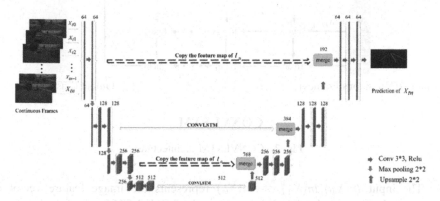

**Fig. 1.** UNET_CL network model architecture

The specific layers include:

(1) The input of network: The lane image vector of consecutive frames, that is: $X_{tn}(t = 0, 1, \cdots, n)$. $t_1, t_2 \ldots t_n$ represent different moments.

(2) Encoder structure: The encoder consists of 4 layers and 4 blocks. From top to bottom, it is 1th to 4th layers. Each block includes two convolutional layers. Each convolutional layer is composed of two-dimensional convolution (Conv2D), batch normalization (BN) and activation function (rectified linear unit, ReLU). After each layer, maxpooling is used to downsample the feature map.

(3) CONVLSTM: In the original U-Net network, the information fusion of the corresponding layer is carried out by copy and crop, so that in the process of matching the size of the feature map of the corresponding layer of the encoder and the decoder, the feature map needs to be trimmed, which will lose a lot of edge information. In order to ensure the integrity of the lane features, the spatial and temporal features of the lane itself are combined on the basis of skip connection, that is, the features extracted by the encoder are connected to the decoder through CONVLSTM. Classical LSTM as a general unit of spatiotemporal prediction model can save long-term information. Its biggest disadvantage is the loss of spatial information. Therefore, on the basis of LSTM, convolution operation is used instead of matrix multiplication in LSTM to obtain CONVLSTM. The specific structure as shown in Fig. 2. The specific structure is shown in Fig. 2.

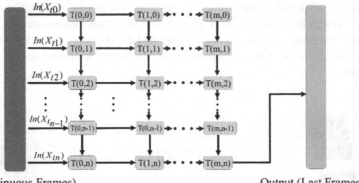

Input (Continuous Frames)                                          Output (Last Frames)

## CONVLSTM

**Fig. 2.** CONVLSTM architecture

The input $In(X_{t0}), In(X_{t1}), \cdots, In(X_{tm})$ represents the image feature vector of output by the encoder. $T(m, n)$ represents the CONVLSTM unit of the layer $m$ at time $n$, and the activation output of the CONVLSTM unit at time $t$ can be expressed as:

$$C_t = f_t \circ C_{t-1} + i_t \circ \tanh(W_{xc} * In(X_t) + W_{hc} * H_{t-1} + b_c),$$
$$f_t = \sigma(W_{xf} * In(X_t) + W_{hf} * W_{t-1} + W_{cf} \circ C_{t-1} + b_f),$$
$$o_t = \sigma(W_{xo} * In(X_t) + W_{ho} * W_{t-1} + W_{co} \circ C_{t-1} + b_o), \qquad (1)$$
$$i_t = \sigma(W_{xi} * In(X_t) + W_{hi} * W_{t-1} + W_{ci} \circ C_{t-1} + b_i),$$
$$H_t = o_t \circ \tanh(C_t),$$

Among them: $C_t, H_t, C_{t-1}, H_{t-1}$ respectively represent the cell state and activation output value of the CONVLSTM unit at time $t$ and time $t-1$. $C_t, f_t, o_t, i_t$ respectively represent the cell state, forget gate, output gate and input gate at time $t$. $W_{xi}$ represents the weight matrix of the input through the input gate. $W_{hi}$ represents the weight matrix of the input gate for the cell state. $b_i$ represents the deviation matrix for the input gate. The meaning of other $W$ and $b$ can be inferred from the above rule. $\sigma(\cdot)$ represents the sigmoid activation function. $\tanh(\cdot)$ represents the hyperbolic tangent nonlinear activation function. $*$ represents convolution operation, and $\circ$ represents Hadamard product.

(4) Decoder structure: The decoder is composed of 4 layers. From bottom to top, the output of the fourth layer of the encoder is extracted by CONVLSTM, then the image is amplified by upsample and then superimposed with the output of the third layer of the copied encoder. After two convolutions, it is used as the input of the third layer of the decoder. The same is true for each subsequent layer. Finally, after successively passing through the convolution of the first block of the first layer of the decoder, the semantic segmentation prediction map is output.

It can be seen from Fig. 1 that the model chooses to perform feature fusion in the first layer and the third layer by direct copying, and the second and fourth layers choose to perform feature fusion after the CONVLSTM. Regarding the performance difference caused by the fusion of the skip connection, the following will be experimentally verified.

## 2.2 The Network Model UNET_CLB Based on the Fusion of Spatiotemporal Information and Deep Information

In the UNET CL structure, the output of the fourth layer of the encoder may repeatedly learn redundant features after a series of continuous convolutions, which not only increases the amount of network parameters, but also reduces the readability of high-dimensional semantic information. Therefore, this structure is optimized to design the network called UNET_CLB based on the fusion of spatiotemporal information and deep information. The network structure is shown in Fig. 3.

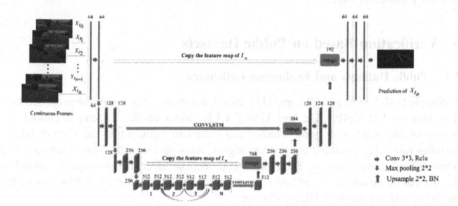

**Fig. 3.** UNET_CLB network model architecture

Inspired by Dense_NET [14], we adjust the series of convolution layers at the bottom to convolution blocks. That is, every two convolutions are regarded as a block. Each block needs the output of all the previous blocks as input. The specific connection method is shown in Fig. 4.

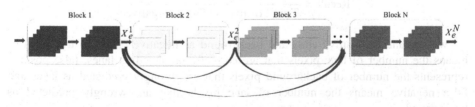

**Fig. 4.** Dense_NET architecture

Each color represents a convolution block composed of $n$ convolution layers. $X_e^i$ represents the output of the i-th block, $i \in \{1, 2, \cdots, N\}$. The i-th block receives the cascade of all previous convolutional blocks as input. That is: $[X_e^1, X_e^2, \cdots, X_e^{i-1}] \in \mathbb{R}^{(i-1)T \times C_l \times W_l \times H_l}$. $T$ represents the number of consecutive frames input by the network. $C_l, W_l, H_l$ respectively represent the number of channels, width and height of the output of the l-th layer. Then the output of the i-th block is: $X_e^i \in \mathbb{R}^{T \times C_l \times W_l \times H_l}$.

It can be found that this connection method can make the final block benefit from the features output by all previous blocks, and the previous layer directly participates in the back propagation of the final gradient, which can avoid the problem of gradient disappearance of the model. Different from ResNet [15], feature multiplexing is used by Dense_NET to enhance the ability of the network to use features. The parallel mapping of learned features at different layers increases the input changes of subsequent layers and improves efficiency, meanwhile due to feature multiplexing, the number of parameters of the network is greatly reduced, which means the structure is simpler. However, too many Dense_NET blocks will also affect the efficiency of feature multiplexing. Therefore, a comparative experiment is designed to select the optimal parameters later.

## 3   Verification Based on Public Datasets

### 3.1   Public Datasets and Evaluation Indicators

TuSimple [16] dataset and CULane [17] dataset are choosed to verify the proposed lane detection models UNET_CL and UNET_CLB. Most of the TuSimple dataset are photos of highways with good weather and sufficient light, while the Culane dataset includes rainy days, vehicle congestion, nights, missing lanes, lane line occlusion and other difficult environments. Therefore, the detection effect of the proposed model in the normal environment is verified on the TuSimple dataset, and the robustness of the model is verified on the CULane dataset.

The task of lane detection is a serious imbalance classification task. The pixels of the lane are much smaller than the pixels of the background, and the ratio between them is about 1/50. Therefore, it is not enough to evaluate with accuracy alone. The more reasonable indicators are precision and racall, as shown in Formula 2 and Formula 3.

$$\text{Pr ecision} = \frac{\text{True Positive}}{\text{True Positive} + \text{False Positive}} \tag{2}$$

$$\text{Recall} = \frac{\text{True Positive}}{\text{True Positive} + \text{False Negative}} \tag{3}$$

we set lane as positive class and background as negative class. So true positive means the number of lane pixels that are correctly predicted as lanes, false positive represents the number of background pixels that are wrongly predicted as lanes and false negative means the number of lane pixels that are wrongly predicted as background.

The precision represents the proportion of pixels that are predicted to be correct among all pixels predicted to be lane lines, and the recall represents the proportion of pixels that are correctly predicted to the pixels of the entire lane line. Considering that the precision and recall only represent the performance of lane detection in a certain aspect, F1-score is introduced as an overall evaluation, as shown in formula 4. F1-score achieves a balanced opposition by integrating precision and recall.

$$F1 \text{ - } score = 2 \cdot \frac{Precision \cdot Recall}{Precision + Recall} \tag{4}$$

The experiments are implemented on a computer equipped with a Xeon E5 2620 with 16 cores and 32 threads, and GPUs are one GTX2080ti and one GTX1080ti. The deep learning environment is: CUDA10.0; CUDNN7.3.1; Pytorch1.6.0; Python3.7 and other related dependent libraries.

## 3.2    Contrast Experiment of Network the Number of Input Frame Based on UNET_CL Network Model

This group of experiments is designed to compare the performance of the model when using different number of frames. Table 1 shows the performance of the UNET_CL with different input frames. Among them, Val_acc represents the accuracy of the network on the validation set; Test_acc represents the accuracy on the test set, Precision, Recall, and F1-score respectively represent the precision, recall and F1-score of the network on the test set.

**Table 1.** Comparative experiment of input frame number based on UNET_CL model

| The number of frames | Val_acc (%) | Test_acc (%) | Precision (%) | Recall (%) | F1-score (%) |
|---|---|---|---|---|---|
| 1 | 96.46 | 96.54 | 79.000 | 98.500 | 87.679 |
| 2 | 97.23 | 97.25 | 83.21 | 96.875 | 89.524 |
| 3 | 97.57 | 97.52 | 84.546 | 96.000 | 89.909 |
| 4 | 97.76 | 97.57 | 85.32 | 95.88 | 90.298 |
| 5 | 97.81 | 97.60 | 85.50 | 95.76 | 90.339 |

It can be seen from Table 1 that when the number of input frames is five, the model obtains a higher comprehensive evaluation F1-score value, but at this time the increase of accuracy and precision has been lower than 0.2%. It is because that if too many previous frames are used, the outcome may be not good as lane situations in far former frames are sometimes significantly different from the current frame. The improvement of the model is saturated, and when the number of frames is five, the training time of the model increases significantly. Considering comprehensively, the number of model input frames is uniformly set to three.

### 3.3 Contrast Experiment of Layer Skip Connection Method Based on UNET_CL Network Model

This group of experiments is designed to compare the performance of the model when the direct copy method and the CONVLSTM method are used for feature fusion at different layers. Table 2 shows the performance of the UNET_CL network model when different skip connection methods are used. The model UNET_CL$_{14}$ indicates that the CONVLSTM method is used to merge in the first and fourth layers, and the direct copy method is used to merge in the second and third layers. The other models are the same.

**Table 2.** Comparative experiment of layer jump connection based on UNET_CL model

| Model | Val_acc (%) | Test_acc (%) | Precision (%) | Recall (%) | F1-score (%) |
|---|---|---|---|---|---|
| UNET_CL$_{14}$ | 97.06 | 96.97 | 81.673 | 97.653 | 88.951 |
| UNET_CL$_{24}$ | 97.66 | 97.54 | 86.000 | 96.379 | 90.894 |
| UNET_CL$_{34}$ | 96.32 | 96.09 | 74.338 | 97.641 | 84.411 |
| UNET_CL$_4$ | 97.57 | 97.52 | 84.546 | 96.000 | 89.909 |
| UNET | 96.46 | 96.54 | 79.000 | 98.500 | 87.679 |

It can be seen from Table 2 that when the CONVLSTM is used to merge in the second and fourth layers, the accuracy on the verification set and test set is the highest. This is because when the CONVLSTM fusion method is adopted, the model can merge the lane details of the previous frames through the low level fusion, and the low abstraction information of the lanes of the previous frames (larger receptive fields, easy to obtain larger contour information) through the advanced fusion, which makes the whole model better save all the valid information of the picture and filter invalid information.

### 3.4 Contrast Experiment on the Number of Dense_NET Blocks Based on UNET_CLB Network Model

This group of experiments is designed to study the effect of different numbers of Dense_NET blocks. Table 3 shows the performance of different numbers of Dense_-NET blocks based on the UNET_CLB network model. Among them, the model UNET_CL$_4$_B$_3$ represents the UNET_CLB model with three Dense_NET blocks in the 4th layer, and the rest of the models are the same.

**Table 3.** Contrast experiment on the number of DenseNET blocks based on UNET_CLB model

| Model | Val_acc (%) | Test_acc (%) | Precision (%) | Recall (%) | F1-score (%) |
|---|---|---|---|---|---|
| UNET_CL$_4$_B$_3$ | 97.67 | 97.59 | 85.381 | 97.896 | 91.211 |
| UNET_CL$_4$_B$_4$ | 97.03 | 96.82966 | 76.366 | 96.805 | 85.379 |
| UNET_CL$_4$_B$_5$ | 96.98 | 96.88822 | 80.308 | 97.507 | 88.076 |

It can be seen from Table 3 that too many Dense_NET blocks will decrease the performance of the model. When the number of Dense_NET blocks is 3, the evaluation indexes of the model are all the highest.

### 3.5    Contrast of UNET_CLB Network Model and Existing Models

In order to further verify the performance of the lane detection model proposed in this paper, UNET_CL$_{24}$, UNET_CL$_4$_B$_3$ and UNET_CL$_{24}$_B$_3$ are compared with UNET, MRFNet, ResNet and other existing models on public datasets. Table 4 and Table 5 show each model's performance on the TuSimple dataset and CULane dataset.

**Table 4.** Comparison of different network models on the TuSimple dataset

| Model | Val_acc (%) | Test_acc (%) | Precision (%) | Recall (%) | F1-score (%) |
|---|---|---|---|---|---|
| UNET | 96.46 | 96.54 | 79.000 | 98.500 | 87.679 |
| MRFNet | 97.36 | 97.23 | 82.153 | 97.420 | 89.137 |
| ResNet | 97.45 | 97.37 | 83.899 | 96.689 | 89.841 |
| UNETCL$_{24}$ | 97.66 | 97.54 | 86.000 | 96.379 | 90.894 |
| UNET_CL$_4$_B$_3$ | 97.67 | 97.59 | 85.381 | 97.896 | 91.211 |
| UNET_CL$_{24}$_B$_3$ | 97.89 | 97.65 | 87.283 | 98.135 | 92.391 |

It can be seen from Table 4 that compared with the existing model, the precision of model UNET_CL$_{24}$ is increased by up to 7%, and the recall is reduced by up to 1.121%. Compared with the existing model, the precision of model UNET_CL$_4$_B$_3$ is increased by up to 6.381%, and the recall is reduced by up to 0.604%. It can be seen that the use of multi-frame input and CONVLSTM helps to improve the accuracy of the model, and the Dense_NET blocks help to maintain the recall of the model. Compared with the existing model, the optimal model UNET_CL$_{24}$_B$_3$ has a precision increase of up to 8.282%, a recall of up to 0.365%, and a comprehensive evaluation F1-score of up to 92.391%. Experiments show that the lane detection method proposed has a greater improvement than the existing methods under normal circumstances.

**Table 5.** Comparison of different network models on the CULane dataset

| Model | Scene | | |
|---|---|---|---|
| | Dark night (F1-score%) | Wireless (F1-score%) | Shadow (F1-score%) |
| UNET | 56.5 | 35.7 | 56.8 |
| MRFNet | 61.3 | 37.2 | 59.3 |
| ResNet | 65.9 | 41.7 | 64.6 |
| UNET_CL$_{24}$_B$_3$ | 70.1 | 45.9 | 69.5 |

It can be seen from Table 5 that in the dark environment, the F1-score of the model called UNET_CL$_{24}$_B$_3$ increases by up to 13.6. In the wireless environment, the F1-score increases by up to 10.2%. In shadow environment, the F1-score increases by up to 12.7%. Therefore, the method proposed in this paper is more conducive to extracting the missing features of the lane in difficult environments (dark night, wireless, shadow), and has higher robustness.

The recognition effect on the CULane dataset is shown in Fig. 5.

**Fig. 5.** Recognition effect on CULane dataset

# 4 Simulation Verification

## 4.1 Simulation Environment and Simulation Dataset

Based on the webots simulation platform, a city night simulation environment and an integrated model car are built to verify that the proposed model can have a good recognition effect in difficult environments such as dark night, shadow and wireless. A monocular camera is installed on the roof of the vehicle to obtain information on the road environment while the vehicle is traveling, and a GPS is installed under the vehicle to obtain vehicle coordinates. As shown in Fig. 6.

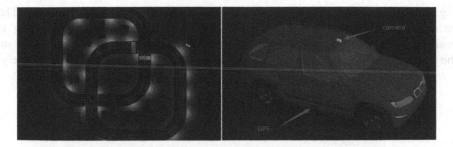

**Fig. 6.** Simulation environment and simulation model vehicle

By controlling the driving of the simulated vehicle, we collected a total of 6000 lane line images in the dark night environment to make a lane simulation dataset by labelme software. As shown in Fig. 7 from left to right images are the original lane images, semantic segmentation images and instance segmentation images respectively.

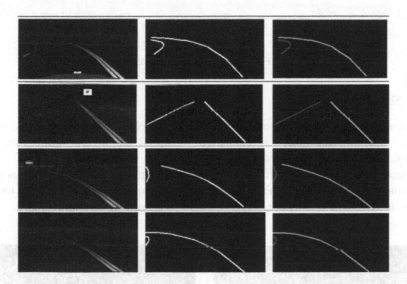

**Fig. 7.** Simulation datasets

## 4.2 Training Result

First, we divide the lane simulation dataset into training set: validation set: test set according to the ratio of 7:1:2. Then we set the input of the UNET_CLB model to three consecutive images, batch size to 8, total training epochs to 3000, optimizer to adam, learning rate to 0.001, and loss function to CrossEntropy which weight ratio is settled to 0.02:0.99:0.99:0.99:0.99. The error curve of UNET_CLB model training is shown in

Fig. 8. It can be seen from the figure that the model loss rapidly at the 100th epoch. The error remains basically unchanged at the 500th epoch, and the model training is basically fitted. After the training, the error percentages of the UNET_CLB model on the training set, validation set, and test set are 5.33%, 8.17%, and 5.69% respectively.

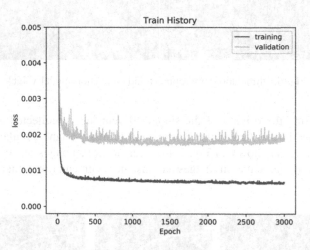

**Fig. 8.** Training loss curve

## 4.3 Simulation Result

The lane detection model trained in Sect. 4.2 is transplanted to the simulation model vehicle, and the lane detection simulation is carried out in the built urban night environment.

Figure 9 shows the recognition result of the lane line by the UNET_CLB model at the corner of the simulated vehicle in the dark environment. Because there are too few pixels on the left lane line, the UNET_CLB model has a worse fitting effect.

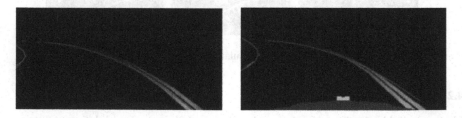

**Fig. 9.** Recognition results of simulation vehicles at dark night

Figure 10 and Fig. 11 shows the UNET_CLB model recognition results of the simulation model car driving at difficult scenes full of shadows and no lane lines respectively. It can be seen that the UNET_CLB model fits the lane line well.

**Fig. 10.** Recognition results of simulation vehicles at shadow

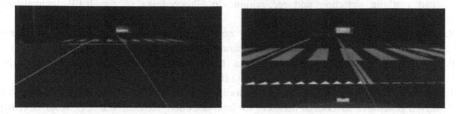

**Fig. 11.** Recognition results of simulation vehicles at wireless

## 5 Conclusion

Aiming at the problem of poor lane detection in difficult scenes such as dark night, shadow and wireless. A lane detection model UNET_CL that combines multi-frame input with CONVLSTM is designed. Further a deep advanced semantic extraction network model called UNET_CLB is designed. The optimal parameters of the model are selected by contrast experiment. Then the proposed method is compared with the existing method based on the public dataset, and the results show that the detection effect of this method is good in both robustness and recognition accuracy. Lastly based on the Webots simulation platform, a simulation scenario that meets difficult environments such as dark night, shadow and wireless is built, and a simulation dataset is made to train the UNET_CLB model. The results show that the UNET_CLB model can complete lane recognition well in difficult environments.

## References

1. Jigang, T., Songbin, L., Peng, L.: A review of lane detection methods based on deep learning. Pattern Recognit. **111**, 107623 (2021)
2. Zou, Q., Jiang, H., Dai, Q., et al.: Robust lane detection from continuous driving scenes using deep neural networks. IEEE Trans. Veh. Technol. **69**(1), 41–54 (2019)
3. Kim, J., Park, C.: End-to-end ego lane estimation based on sequential transfer learning for self-driving cars. In: Proceedings of the IEEE Conference on Computer Vision and Pattern Recognition Workshops (2017)
4. Neven, D., De Brabandere, B., Georgoulis, S., et al.: Towards end-to-end lane detection: an instance segmentation approach. In: Proceedings of the 2018 IEEE Intelligent Vehicles Symposium (IV). IEEE (2018)

5. Badrinarayanan, V., Kendall, A., Cipolla, R.: Segnet: a deep convolutional encoder-decoder architecture for image segmentation. IEEE Trans. Pattern Anal. Mach. Intell. **39**(12), 2481–2495 (2017)
6. Long, J., Shelhamer, E., Darrell, T.: Fully convolutional networks for semantic segmentation. In: Proceedings of the IEEE Conference on Computer Vision and Pattern Recognition (2015)
7. He, B., Ai, R., Yan, Y., et al.: Accurate and robust lane detection based on dual-view convolutional neutral network. In: IEEE Intelligent Vehicles Symposium, pp. 1041–1046 (2016)
8. Lee, S., Kim, J., Shin Yoon, J., et al.: Vpgnet: vanishing point guided network for lane and road marking detection and recognition. In: Proceedings of the IEEE International Conference on Computer Vision (2017)
9. Li, J., Mei, X., Prokhorov, D., et al.: Deep neural network for structural prediction and lane detection in traffic scene. IEEE Trans. Neural Netw. Learn. Syst. **28**(3), 690–703 (2016)
10. Goodfellow, I., Pouget-Abadie, J., Mirza, M., et al.: Generative adversarial nets. Adv. Neural. Inf. Process. Syst. **27**, 2672–2680 (2014)
11. Ghafoorian, M., Nugteren, C., Baka, N., Booij, O., Hofmann, M.: EL-GAN: embedding loss driven generative adversarial networks for lane detection. In: Leal-Taixé, L., Roth, S. (eds.) ECCV 2018. LNCS, vol. 11129, pp. 256–272. Springer, Cham (2019). https://doi.org/10.1007/978-3-030-11009-3_15
12. Ronneberger, O., Fischer, P., Brox, T.: U-net: convolutional networks for biomedical image segmentation. In: Proceedings of the International Conference on Medical Image Computing and Computer-Assisted Intervention. Springer (2015)
13. Shi, X., Chen, Z., Wang, H., et al.: Convolutional LSTM network: a machine learning approach for precipitation nowcasting. In: Proceedings of the 29th Annual Conference on Neural Information Processing Systems (NIPS), Montreal, Canada, 2015 (2015)
14. Huang, G., Liu, Z., Van Der Maaten, L., et al.: Densely connected convolutional networks. In: Proceedings of the IEEE Conference on Computer Vision and Pattern Recognition (2017)
15. He, K., Zhang, X., Ren, S., et al.: Deep residual learning for image recognition. In: Proceedings of the IEEE Conference on Computer Vision and Pattern Recognition (2016)
16. Cheng, W., Luo, H., Yang, W., et al.: DET: a high-resolution DVS dataset for lane extraction. In: Proceedings of the IEEE Conference on Computer Vision and Pattern Recognition Workshops (2019)
17. Shirke, S., Udayakumar, R.: Lane datasets for lane detection. In: Proceedings of the 2019 International Conference on Communication and Signal Processing (ICCSP). IEEE (2019)

# Ensemble Deep Learning Based Single Finger-Vein Recognition

Chongwen Liu[1], Huafeng Qin[1(✉)], Gongping Yang[2], Zhengwen Shen[3], and Jun Wang[3]

[1] School of Computer Science and Information Engineering, Chongqing Technology and Business University, Chongqing 400067, China
liuchongwen@ctbu.edu.cn
[2] School of Software Engineering, Shandong University, Jinan 250101, China
gpyang@sdu.edu.cn
[3] China University of Mining and Technology, Xuzhou 221116, Jiangsu, China

**Abstract.** Finger-vein biometrics has been extensively investigated for personal verification. Single sample per person (SSPP) finger-vein recognition is one of the open issues in finger-vein recognition. In this paper, a deep ensemble learning method is proposed for SSPP finger-vein recognition. To the best of our knowledge, this is the first work proposed for finger-vein identification with single finger-vein sample per person. First, we generate different feature maps from an input image, based on which multiple independent deep learning based classifiers are proposed for finger-vein identification. Second, a shared learning scheme is investigated among classifiers to improve their feature representation captivity. Third, an approach is proposed to adjust learning speed of weak classifiers, so that all classifiers achieve best performance at the same time. Finally, a deep ensemble learning method are proposed by combing all weak classifiers. The experimental results on two public finger-vein databases show that our approach outperforms its all classifiers and existing approaches, and achieves the state-of-the-art recognition results.

**Keywords:** Finger-vein recognition · One-shot learning · Ensemble learning

## 1 Introduction

With wide application of Internet, the information security becomes more and more important. Traditional personal identification technique such as key and password is difficult to meet people's needs. For example, the key is easy to be copied and missed and password is usually forgotten, especially for old people. Biometric technique as a

This work was supported in part by the National Natural Science Foundation of China under Grant 61976030, and Science Fund for Creative Research Groups of the Chongqing University under Grant CXQT21034, in part by the Natural Science Foundation Project of Chongqing under Grant cstc2018jcyjAX0095, and in part by the Scientific and Technological Research Program of Chongqing Municipal Education Commission under Grant KJQN201900848 and KJQN202000841.

F. Sun et al. (Eds.): ICCSIP 2021, CCIS 1515, pp. 261–275, 2022.
https://doi.org/10.1007/978-981-16-9247-5_20

solution has been widely investigated in past years. Compared to traditional identification approach, using physiological characteristics to identify or verify a person has following advantages [1]. (1) difficult to be missed; (2) difficult to be forged; (3) easy to use; (4) easy to carry. Currently, various traits such as face, iris, fingerprint, vein have been employed for personal recognition and are broadly split in two categories [27]. (1) extrinsic characteristics e.g. face, iris and fingerprint. (2) intrinsic characteristics e.g. finger-vein, hand-vein and palm-vein. Extrinsic characteristics are suspect to be copied and forged, and their fake version have successfully employed to attack the recognition system [11].

## 1.1 Related Work

Despite the recent advances in finger-vein biometric recognition, it is still changeable task in practical application because the vein capturing is affected many factors e.g. illumination, environment temperature, behavior of user and so on. In general, the factors can not avoid during capturing process, so there are many low quality finger-vein images, which result the reduction of recognition accuracy. To achieve robust recognition, various approaches are proposed for vein recognition in pasted years, such as local binary pattern (LBP) [10,13], Gabor filter [5,34]. Some researchers brought deep learning based approaches into finger-vein recognition, for example, deep learning approaches are employed for vein image segmentation [20], quality assessment of vein image [19], and finger-vein recognition [3,8,30].

## 1.2 Motivation

In finger-vein recognition, it is impossible to capture a lots of vein sample from same finger, so the training sample of each class is generally limited. For example, the samples form each finger is less than twelve in existing databases [6,17,18]. Specially, there is only one single sample per finger for SSPP (single sample per person) problem when considering their limited storage and privacy policy. Therefore, it becomes particularly intractable for such a identification system with SSPP when within-class information is not available to predict the unknown variations in query samples. Currently, various approaches have been proposed for boimetrics identification with SSPP such as face recognition [28,29], palmprint [25] and fingerprint [4]. Similarly, the corresponding finger-vein recognition systems still suffer SSPP problem due to the following facts: (1) There is only one enrollment sample in some recognition systems, such as credit card and large-scale recognition, because of the limitation of storage capability. (2) To achieve online identification, the recognition systems usually only store one sample per subject to improve processing speed and time. (3) Some users are not willing to cooperatively capture sufficient samples in order to protect personal privacy. Obviously, providing one enrollment sample is convenient, simple and acceptable for users. It is not surprising that the finger-vein recognition suffers from same SSPP problem.

As described in previous works, the deep learning techniques show a powerful capacity for feature representation, but they generally require sufficient training samples to train a large number of network parameters. Therefore, their learning capacity may have not been well exploited for finger-vein SSPP due to the limited training data of each class (a person or subject) for SSPP. Besides, the deep learning model is easy to suffer from over-fitting on small amount dataset. As a result, deep learning based vein identification approaches may not achieve high performance for finger-vein SSPP.

Ensemble Learning aims at combining multiple learners to obtain a more robust representation of object, and it is successfully applied for boimetrics e.g. classification tasks such as fingerprint classification [32], palm-vein recognition [9], and face recognition [7]. As the features from different learners can achieve complementary representations for input image, their combination performs well for identification. In this paper, we proposed a deep ensemble learning approach for finger-vein identification, to deal with finger-vein SSPP.

## 2  Proposed Method System and Our Contributions

Motivated by the success of ensemble learning, and driven by the SSPP finger-vein recognition, we propose a ensemble deep neural network to learn robust representation from a single sample for SSPP finger-vein recognition. In our work, multiple deep learning classifiers are employed to extract robust features from different feature maps generated from a original input image and then a robust deep ensemble learning approach is generated by combining all weak classifiers. To further improve the performance of our approach, a shared learning approach is investigated during the training process. Besides, we proposed a learning speed adjustment approach so that all weak classifiers can achieve best performance at same time. As each classifier can capture robust features, our ensemble learning approach produces a more complete representation of finger-vein image for identification. The main contributions of this paper are summarized as follows: (1) This work makes the first attempt for SSPP finger-vein identification. (2) We proposed a shared learning scheme to share representations from multiple feature maps. Generally, the classifier of CNN is easily overfitting for SSPP problem, so a shared learning scheme is employed to improve their performance. We employ a feature map to train a classifier. In this way, multiple classifiers are obtained to extract feature. (3) We develop a dynamic speed adjustment scheme to automatically control learning speed of each classifier. The learning speeds of all classifiers are generally different, so it is difficult for them to achieve best performance at same time, which results in poor performance for ensemble classifier. To solve this problem, a learning speed adjustment approach are proposed to improve the performance of our deep assemble learning approach.

The frame work of our work is shown in Fig. 1. First, we generate feature maps from a input image based on several baselines. With the resulting map and input image, we train several weak classifiers separately. We use CNN models as weak classifiers. Second, we ensemble all classifiers to obtain one ensemble classifier for identification. After training, an input image is subject to prepossessing base on baselines and the resulting maps are taken as input of our deep learning ensemble mode to compute its probability of being to a class.

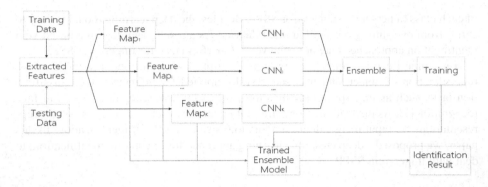

**Fig. 1.** Framework.

# 3  Ensemble Learning for SSPP Finger-Vein Recognition

## 3.1  Feature Extraction

To achieve robust performance in SSPP problem, it is necessary to generate multiple feature maps from the single training sample of each class. The feature maps represent different aspects of the object, so their combination can achieve better performance [14]. Here, three baselines (e.g. CNN [6], Gabor filters [33], and LBP [10]) have achieved promising performance for finger-vein recognition, so we employ them to produce feature maps which are taken as input of ensemble model for classification.

**Finger-Vein Images.** Generally, the vein vessel is difficult to be observed in visible light, but it is captured by near infrared light with 760 nm wavelength. The vein pattern appears darker than the other regions of the finger, because only the blood vessels absorb the infrared rays. The finger-vein image sample is shown in Fig. 2(a).

**Segmentation.** As shown in Fig. 2(a), the contrast of vein pattern in original finger-vein image is poor, which results low recognition accuracy. Image segmentation as a solution have been employed for feature extraction and shows good performance in works [18,26], and [21]. In recent years, deep learning based methods have shown more robust capacity of feature representation compared to handcrafted approaches. So, some researches bring it to vein segmentation [20,21]. To train good weak classifier, the CNN based model is used to extract robust vein texture patterns, which are input into weak classifier. First, a CNN based approach is developed to predict the probability of pixels to belong to veins or to background by learning a deep feature representation. Then, a CNN is trained to extract the vein patterns from any image region. Second, to improve the performance, and then an original method based on a FCN to recover missing finger-vein patterns in the binary image. Figure 2(b) is segmentation image from a gray-scale image.

**LBP.** The LBP describes the relationship between the neighborhood points and the corresponding center point, with the features of constant rotation and gray scale. LBP has been widely used to extract finger vein features and shows good performance [10, 13]. Therefore, we employ LBP to local information of finger-vein images. LBP patterns extracted from original image and segmented image are shown in Fig. 2(c) and Fig. 2(d).

**Gabor.** The Gabor filter is a type of wavelet, it has a good time-domain and frequency-domain transform characteristics. Gabor functions are used to construct filters with different scaling directions caused by different parameters (e.g., spatial position, frequency, phase, and direction). Furthermore, the Gabor filter is widely used to capture texture information, it adapts to extract feature from finger-vein image. In finger vein recognition, there have been more works using gabor as a feature, such as work [5, 34].

For the practical application of finger-vein recognition, the real part of the Gabor filter is used. In work [33], Garbo filter is used to extract texture information of finger-vein image. The Gabor feature of original image and segmented image are shown in Fig. 2(e) and Fig. 2(f).

We employ the three baselines to extract 5 different features from original images. Including the original finger-vein images, there are totally 6 feature maps, as shown in Fig. 2 and Table 1.

**Table 1.** Feature maps

| Input | Preprocessing 1 | Preprocessing 2 | Feaure map |
|---|---|---|---|
| Original image | Null | Null | 1st feaure map |
| Original image | Segmentation | Null | 2nd feaure map |
| Original image | Null | LBP | 3rd feaure map |
| Original image | Segmentation | LBP | 4th feaure map |
| Original image | Null | Gabor | 5th feaure map |
| Original image | Segmentation | Gabor | 6th feaure map |

## 3.2 Convolutional Neural Networks

Ensemble learning model is constructed from the combination of weak classifiers [24]. The choice of weak classifier affects the performance of the ensemble model. In previous work, CNNs have been widely used in finger vein recognition and achieved good recognition performance, such as work [3, 8], and [30]. In this work, we choose CNN model as independent weak classifier, and each CNN is trained by one feature map, as shown in Fig. 1. Each trained CNN model describe one aspect of finger-vein. The CNN is a multi-layer perception network with hidden layers. A traditional recognition model for classifier can be formulated by minimizing the error function. During training deep network, the gradient descent method is used to update network parameters. The details of network structure are shown in Table 2.

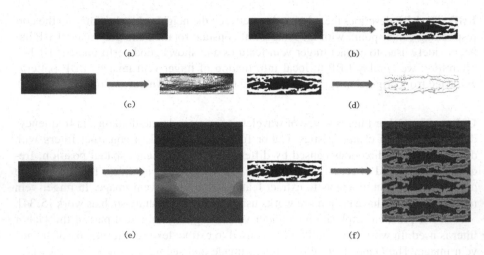

**Fig. 2.** Samples of 6 different feature maps. (a) 1st feature map, (b) 2nd feature map, (c) 3rd feature map, (d) 4th feature map, (e) 5th feature map, (f) 6th feature map.

**Table 2.** CNN parameters

| Feature maps | Layer type | Number of filter | Size of kernel | Number of stride | Number of padding | Dropout |
|---|---|---|---|---|---|---|
| Feature Map 1 and 2 | CL1 (Convolutional layer-1) | 64 | $2 \times 2$ | $1 \times 1$ | $0 \times 0$ | – |
| | M1 (Max-Pooling Layer-1) | 1 | $2 \times 2$ | $2 \times 2$ | $0 \times 0$ | – |
| | CL2 (Convolutional layer-2) | 64 | $2 \times 2$ | $1 \times 1$ | $0 \times 0$ | – |
| | M2 (Max-Pooling Layer-2) | 1 | $2 \times 2$ | $2 \times 2$ | $0 \times 0$ | – |
| | CL3 (Convolutional layer-3) | 64 | $2 \times 2$ | $1 \times 1$ | $0 \times 0$ | – |
| | M3 (Max-Pooling Layer-3) | 1 | $2 \times 2$ | $2 \times 2$ | $0 \times 0$ | – |
| | CL4 (Convolutional layer-4) | 128 | $2 \times 2$ | $1 \times 1$ | $0 \times 0$ | – |
| | M4 (Max-Pooling Layer-4) | 1 | $2 \times 2$ | $2 \times 2$ | $0 \times 0$ | – |
| | CL5 (Convolutional layer-5) | 256 | $2 \times 2$ | $1 \times 1$ | $0 \times 0$ | – |
| | M5 (Max-Pooling Layer-5) | 1 | $2 \times 2$ | $2 \times 2$ | $0 \times 0$ | – |
| | R1 (ReLu Layer-1) | – | – | – | – | 0.5 |
| | Softmax Layer | – | – | – | – | – |
| Feature Map 3-6 | CL1 (Convolutional layer-1) | 64 | $2 \times 2$ | $1 \times 1$ | $0 \times 0$ | – |
| | M1 (Max-Pooling Layer-1) | 1 | $2 \times 2$ | $2 \times 2$ | $0 \times 0$ | – |
| | CL2 (Convolutional layer-2) | 64 | $2 \times 2$ | $1 \times 1$ | $0 \times 0$ | – |
| | M2 (Max-Pooling Layer-2) | 1 | $2 \times 2$ | $2 \times 2$ | $0 \times 0$ | – |
| | CL3 (Convolutional layer-3) | 64 | $2 \times 2$ | $1 \times 1$ | $0 \times 0$ | – |
| | M3 (Max-Pooling Layer-3) | 1 | $2 \times 2$ | $2 \times 2$ | $0 \times 0$ | – |
| | CL4 (Convolutional layer-4) | 128 | $2 \times 2$ | $1 \times 1$ | $0 \times 0$ | – |
| | M4 (Max-Pooling Layer-4) | 1 | $2 \times 2$ | $2 \times 2$ | $0 \times 0$ | – |
| | CL5 (Convolutional layer-5) | 128 | $2 \times 2$ | $1 \times 1$ | $0 \times 0$ | – |
| | M5 (Max-Pooling Layer-5) | 1 | $2 \times 2$ | $2 \times 2$ | $0 \times 0$ | – |
| | CL6 (Convolutional layer-6) | 256 | $2 \times 2$ | $1 \times 1$ | $0 \times 0$ | – |
| | M6 (Max-Pooling Layer-6) | 1 | $2 \times 2$ | $2 \times 2$ | $0 \times 0$ | – |
| | R1 (ReLu Layer-1) | – | – | – | – | 0.5 |
| | Softmax Layer | – | – | – | – | – |

## 3.3 Shared Learning

If the feature maps are correlative, we can utilize the knowledge from other weak classifiers to improve current classifier [15]. In general, features with higher correlation provides positive knowledge, which improve weak classifier. So we compute the similarity of feature map firstly. In work [31], a feature similarity index (FSIM) is proposed to similarity of feature maps. We compute FSIM of $feature_1(image)$ and $feature_2(image)$ to express the correlation of feature 1 and feature 2 of current image. We use $F_j$ $S_t(F_i, F_j)$ to express the feature map similarity of feature map i($F_i$) and feature map j($F_j$), which is compute as follow:

$$S_t(F_i, F_j) = \frac{\sum FSIM(I_i, I_j)}{n} \tag{1}$$

where $n$ is the number of training samples, and $I_i$ and $I_j$ are feature maps in $F_i$ and $F_j$ respectively, but generate from the same finger-vein image.

We divide the training process of weak classifier into $K$ steps, and each step contains $P$ epochs. After training current classifier in each step, the training samples from other feature maps are used to adjust the parameter by shared learning. In this work, we use the feature map similarity $S_t(F_i, F_j)$ to compute the number of epochs used in shared learning $Ec_{F_i,F_j}$. The $Ec_{F_i,F_j}$ is set as follow:

$$Ec_{F_i,F_j} = 2^{\lfloor \frac{P}{4} \times S_t(F_i,F_j) \rfloor - 1} \tag{2}$$

The performance can be improved by sharing knowledge when high feature correlation [16]. In training process, one train step of $CNN_i$, the data of $feature_i$ are used to train $CNN_i$ by $P$ epochs, and then the data of $feature_j$ are used to train $CNN_i$ by $Ec_{F_i,F_j}$ epochs, as shown in Fig. 3. After the data of all high correlative features are used to train $CNN_i$ by shared learning, $CNN_i$ enter next train step.

## 3.4 Learning Speed Adjustment

During training weak classifiers, the learning speeds of classifiers are different, because the input data are different. When all weak classifiers achieve their best performance, the ensemble model is best. We propose a learning speed adjustment method to control learning speeds of weak classifiers. The parameter $\alpha$ is used to adjust the learning speed of each classifier. The whole training process is divided into $K$ steps, and $P$ epochs in each step. The parameter $\alpha_{i,u}$ is used to adjust the number of epochs dynamically for $classifier_i$ of train step $u$. When the classifier had achieve well performance, the number of epochs will decrease in next step. The $\alpha_{i,u}$ computes as follow:

$$\alpha_{i,u} = \frac{1}{1 + e^{-L_{i,u-1}}} \tag{3}$$

Where the $L_{i,u-1}$ is the loss function value after train step $u - 1$. The number of epochs $p_{i,u}$ for train step $u$ of $classifier_i$ is:

$$p_{i,u} = \begin{cases} 1, & \lfloor \alpha_{i,u} \cdot P \rfloor < 1 \\ \lfloor \alpha_{i,u} \cdot P \rfloor, & other. \end{cases} \tag{4}$$

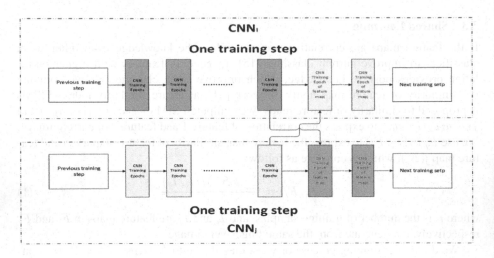

**Fig. 3.** Shared learning by high correlative feature maps.

### 3.5 Ensemble Classifier

We use an access weight can be set to increase the weight of good classifier and decrease the weight of pool classifier during ensemble weak classifiers. We use $E^+$ and $E^-$ to express positive weight and negative weight of classifiers. The $E^+$ is compute as:

$$E_{i,u}^+ = \frac{\dfrac{1}{1 + exp(-Score_{i,u})}}{\sum_{i=1}^{K} \dfrac{1}{1 + exp(-Score_{i,u})}} \qquad (5)$$

where $Score_{i,u}$ is the close test accuracy of each $classifier_i$ after train step $u$. The $E^-$ is compute as:

$$E_{i,u}^- = \frac{\dfrac{1}{1 + exp(-L_{i,u})}}{\sum_{i=1}^{K} \dfrac{1}{1 + exp(-L_{i,u})}} \qquad (6)$$

Where $L_{i,u}$ is the loss function value after train step $u$.
The ensemble weight $W$ of after train step $u$ is updated as:

$$W_{i,u}^* = \begin{cases} \dfrac{|E_{i,u}^+ - E_{i,u}^-|}{\sum_{i=1}^{K} |E_{i,u}^+ - E_{i,u}^-|}, & E_{i,u}^+ \geq 0.5 \\ 0, & E_{i,u}^+ < 0.5 \end{cases} \qquad (7)$$

Where $K$ is the number of classifiers. The ensemble weight $W$ is updated after each train step. Consider the efficiency of ensemble model, if the classifier plays poor performance, this classifier could not join the ensemble step. Where $K$ is the number of classifiers. The ensemble weight $W$ is updated after each train step. In our model, if the close test score more than 0.5, this classifier will join the ensemble step, vice versa.

### 3.6  Structure of Train Process

The training process is divided into 3 stages, which shown as train part in Fig. 1. Three different train networks are proposed in this paper. (1) **Basic approach** We extract feature maps as described in Sect. 3.1, then we train weak classifier(CNN) as described in Sect. 3.2, finally we ensemble all classifier by vote as describe in Sect. 3.5. Although this approach simply train classifier separately, when ensemble all classifier by vote weight during training, both positive contribution and negative effect are considered by employing Eq. (5–7). To avoid the poor weak classifier play gadfly in ensemble model, we set a threshold to accept the classifiers, the vote weight by employing Eq. (7) is used to ensemble model. This structure is shown in Fig. 4(a). (2) **Shared learning method** The shared learning method inherits the basic approach. During training classifiers, other feature maps are used to train classifiers in different 'levels' in each train step. This 'levels' of correlative by employing Eq. (1). The train network structure of shared learning is shown in Fig. 4(b). (3) **Shared learning + Adjust learning speed method** The third method inherits the second one which shared learning high relative feature maps, in addition, we add the parameter of adjust learning speed. The parameter of learn speed adjustment by employing Eq. (3) to determine the number of epoch of next train step by employing Eq. (4). This parameter update at the end of each train step, and feedback to train classifiers before next train step. The train network structure of shared learning + Adjust learning speed method is shown in Fig. 4(c).

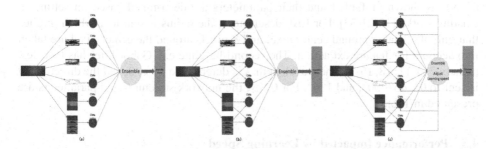

**Fig. 4.** Training network structures. (a) Training structure of Basic approach. (b) Training structure of shared learning method. (c) Training structure of shared learning + Adjust learning speed method.

## 4   Experiments

To estimate the performance of our approach, we carry out experiments on two public finger-vein databases, namely the Hong Kong Polytechnic University (HKPU) [12], the University Sains Malaysia (FV-USM) [2]. In experiments, we show the experimental results of each classifiers and objective task, respectively.

## 4.1    Finger-Vein Database

In this paper, we take experiment on HKPU database and FV-USM database. The HKPU finger-vein image database [12] consists of images from 156 male and female volunteers. The FV-USM database [2] is from University Sains Malaysia. It consists of left and right hand index and middle fingers' vein images from 123 subjects. The details of both datasets are described in Table 3.

**Table 3.** Finger-vein databases

| Database | Subject | Number of fingers | Images per finger | Sessions | Image size | Total images |
|----------|---------|-------------------|-------------------|----------|------------|--------------|
| HKPU     | 156     | 2                 | 12                | 2        | 513 * 256  | 3132         |
| FV-USM   | 123     | 4                 | 12                | 2        | 640 * 480  | 5904         |

## 4.2    Experiment Setup

We aim at solving finger-vein SSPP problem, so the first image from first session is selected for training and the three images from second session is employed for testing. As a result, there are 210 samples in training set and 630 samples (1260 fingers × 6 samples) in test set for HKPU database. Similarly, there are 246 training samples and 1476 samples (246 fingers × 6 samples) for FV-USM database. We compute the identification accuracy on the test set to estiamte the performance of proposed method.

In our work, the 6 feature maps are generated by three baselines (e.g. LBP, Gabor, CNN), as shown in Table 1 and their parameters are determined based on setting in existing works [10,21,33]. For LBP descriptors, the radius is sent to 1 which implies that only the 1 layer around center pixel and 8 pixels around the center pixel are taken into account for feature ext action. The second baseline e.g. Gabor filter has 6 scales, namely $7, 9, 11, 13, 15, 17$, the wavelength $\lambda$ is determined by $\pi/2$, and the directions $\theta$ is sent to $0°, 45°, 90°$, and $135°$. For CNN, the network structures and parameters are presented in Table 2.

## 4.3    Performance Impacted by Learning Speed

As described in subsection, our approach is proposed by combining six weak classifiers. In general, the learning speed of each classifier is different. Therefore, the object task can achieve highest identification accuracy only if each classifier achieves optimal performance at same time. In this section, the experiments are carried to evaluate how to impact the performance of object task by employing Eq. (3) and Eq. (4) to adjust the learning speed of each classifier. Figure 5 (a) and Fig. 5 (b)show the identification accuracy of six classifiers and our approach on HKPU database before and after adjusting the learning speed. In Fig. 5(a), the performance of all approaches is improved when the number of the iteration step is less than 30. However, two classifiers achieve significant degradation of identification accuracy after 35 iterations. The reason is that two classifiers have higher speed than remaining classifiers so that they can not achieve optimal performance at same time. Therefore, it is difficult for object task to achieve good performance. By contrast, the learning speed of the all weak classifiers is adjusted dynamically, they show the best performance after about 50 iterations(as shown in Fig. 5(b)), which results improvement of objection classifier. Therefore, our approach achieves higher identification accuracy after employing Eq. (3) and Eq. (4) for learning sped adjustment. The experiments on FV-USM (as shown in Fig. 5(c) and Fig. 5(d)) show consistent trends that all weak classifiers can achieve optimal performance at same time (about 40 iterations). Also, observed training curves (Fig. 5(a), Fig. 5(c), Fig. 5(b), and Fig. 5(d)), we see that all approaches show good stability after employing learning speed adjustment scheme.

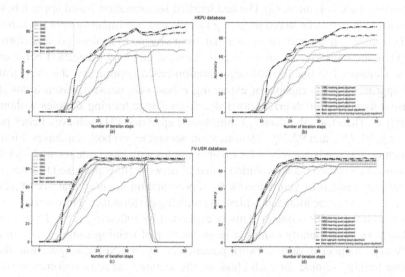

**Fig. 5.** Performance of various classifiers with learning speed adjustment. (a) The performance of all our approaches on HKPU database without adjust learning speed. (b) The performance of all our approaches+adjust learning speed on HKPU database. (c) The performance of all our approaches on FV-USM database without adjust learning speed. (d) The performance of all our approaches+adjust learning speed on FV-USM database.

## 4.4 Performance Comparisons

In this section, we compare our approach with existing approaches to evaluate the performance of our method in terms of improving identification accuracy. In experiments, the state-of-art methods such as [6, 12, 26], is employ for finger-vein identification with a single training sample per finger. As described in Sect. 4.2, we select first image as training and 6 images collected in second session for testing. The identification accuracies of various approaches have been listed in Table 4 for comparison. From the experimental results, we can see that the proposed approach (basic approach + shared learning + learning speed adjustment) outperforms the existing approaches and achieves highest identification accuracy, e.g. 92.11% and 94.17% on HKPU database and FV-USM database. Also, we observed that the hand-crated approaches [12,22,26], considered our work achieve less that 91.00% identification accuracy on both databases. Such a poor performance may be attributed following facts. (1) The handcrafted segmentation-based approaches assume that the cross-sectional profile of a vein pattern show a valley [18] or line-like texture [17] and proposed various mathematical model to extract vein patterns. However, the vein pixels create more complex distributions instead of valley or strait line and the pixels in non-vein region also show valley or line-like attributes, so their performance is limited. (2) The handcrafted segmentation-based approaches usually match vein networks stored in testing sample and enrolment sample for identification. Therefore, it is difficult for such a matching scheme to achieve good performance when there are larger variations such as rotation, scaling and translation between two images. Compared to handcrafted segmentation-based approaches, the deep learning based approach [21] is capable of extracting robust vein networks from a law image because it harnesses a rich prior knowledge from a huge training samples without any assumption. Therefore, the deep learning based approach [21] achieves better performance e.g. 91.75% and 92.29% identification accuracies on both databases. Similarly, its matching scheme is not robust for image samples with large rotation and translation variations. As a solution, a convolutional neural network [6] is proposed to extract high level features instead of vein network by representation learning that are objectively related to vein identification and achieves promising performance. However, it does not perform well for SSPP problem. This is explained by following facts. Deep learning based approaches generally require a large number of training samples to estimate a usually huge number of deep network parameters. In the SSPP configuration, there is only one training sample for each class, so the learning capacity becomes weak, and subject to string overfitting, which leads to low identification performance. Ensemble learning is a solution of SSPP problem because it can exploit the knowledge from different feature maps to improve identification accuracy. Therefore, our basic approach + shared learning achieves 85.63% and 92.31% accuracies on both datasets, which are further improved to 92.11% and 94.17% by adjusting the learning speed of all weak classifiers. Such a good performance may be attributed to this facts. Each classifier includes different discriminate features. As own in Table 4, the relative feature maps can make positive contribution for classification, so the knowledge related to classification is transferred among feature maps by shared learning, which effectively improves the feature representation capacity of object task. Meanwhile, the learning speed adjustment ensures each classifier to achieve best performance at the same time so that the object task performs best representation for vein identification.

**Table 4.** Performance comparisons with state-of-art methods

| Method | Database | |
|---|---|---|
| | HKPU | FV-USM |
| Rig Das et al. [6] | 82.19% | 91.75% |
| MC [18] | | 90.34% |
| RLT [17] | | 78.28% |
| Qin [21] | 91.75% | 92.29% |
| Gabor filters [12] | 77.78% | 86.96% |
| Difference-curvature [22] | 73.97% | 83.91% |
| Mean-curvature [26] | 88.89% | 87.01% |
| Region-growth [23] | 82.29% | 86.62% |
| Basic approach | 78.73% | 91.03% |
| Basic approach + shared learning | 85.63% | 92.31% |
| Basic approach + learning speed adjustment | 82.6% | 92.1% |
| Basic approach + shared learning+ learning speed adjustment | 92.11% | 94.17% |

## 5  Conclusion

This paper proposed a new deep ensemble learning approach for SSPP finger-vein recognition. First, we generate feature maps from training images. Second, we propose a shared learning scheme during training weak classifiers. Third, an approach is proposed to adjust learning speed of weak classifiers. In the experiment part, we compare our performance of our method with the state-of-the-art method. The final result of whole model can achieve the state-of-the-art recognition results.

## References

1. Albrecht, T., Lüthi, M., Vetter, T., Chen, H., Houmani, N.: Encyclopedia of Biometrics (2009)
2. Asaari, M.S.M., Suandi, S.A., Rosdi, B.A.: Fusion of band limited phase only correlation and width centroid contour distance for finger based biometrics. Expert Syst. Appl. **41**(7), 3367–3382 (2014)
3. Avci, A., Kocakulak, M., Acir, N.: Convolutional neural network designs for finger-vein-based biometric identification. In: 2019 11th International Conference on Electrical and Electronics Engineering (ELECO), pp. 580–584 (2019)
4. Chatterjee, A., Bhatia, V., Prakash, S.: Anti-spoof touchless 3D fingerprint recognition system using single shot fringe projection and biospeckle analysis. Opt. Lasers Eng. **95**, 1–7 (2017)
5. Cho, S.R., et al.: Enhancement of finger-vein image by vein line tracking and adaptive gabor filtering for finger-vein recognition. Appl. Mech. Mater. **145**, 219–223 (2012)
6. Das, R., Piciucco, E., Maiorana, E., Campisi, P.: Convolutional neural network for finger-vein-based biometric identification. IEEE Trans. Inf. Forensics Secur. **14**(2), 360–373 (2019)

7. Ding, C., Tao, D.: Trunk-branch ensemble convolutional neural networks for video-based face recognition. IEEE Trans. Pattern Anal. Mach. Intell. **40**(4), 1002–1014 (2018)
8. Gumusbas, D., Yildirim, T., Kocakulak, M., Acir, N.: Capsule network for finger-vein-based biometric identification. In: 2019 IEEE Symposium Series on Computational Intelligence (SSCI), pp. 437–441 (2019)
9. Joardar, S., Chatterjee, A., Bandyopadhyay, S., Maulik, U.: Multi-size patch based collaborative representation for palm dorsa vein pattern recognition by enhanced ensemble learning with modified interactive artificial bee colony algorithm. Eng. Appl. Artif. Intell. **60**, 151–163 (2017)
10. Kang, W., Chen, X., Qiuxia, W.: The biometric recognition on contactless multi-spectrum finger images. Infrared Phys. Technol. **68**, 19–27 (2015)
11. Khan, S.H., Akbar, M.A., Shahzad, F., Farooq, M., Khan, Z.: Secure biometric template generation for multi-factor authentication. Pattern Recognit. **48**(2), 458–472 (2015)
12. Kumar, A., Zhou, Y.: Human identification using finger images. IEEE Trans. Image Process. **21**(4), 2228–2244 (2012)
13. Lee, E.C., Jung, H., Kim, D.: New finger biometric method using near infrared imaging. Sensors **11**(3), 2319–2333 (2011)
14. Li, Q., et al.: A multi-task learning based approach to biomedical entity relation extraction. In: 2018 IEEE International Conference on Bioinformatics and Biomedicine (BIBM), pp. 680–682 (2018)
15. Lou, Y., Fu, G., Jiang, Z., Men, A., Zhou, Y.: Improve object detection via a multi-feature and multi-task CNN model. In: 2017 IEEE Visual Communications and Image Processing (VCIP), pp. 1–4 (2017)
16. Misra, I., Shrivastava, A., Gupta, A., Hebert, M.: Cross-stitch networks for multi-task learning. In: 2016 IEEE Conference on Computer Vision and Pattern Recognition (CVPR) (2016)
17. Miura, N., Nagasaka, A., Miyatake, T.: Feature extraction of finger-vein patterns based on repeated line tracking and its application to personal identification. Mach. Vis. Appl. **15**(4), 194–203 (2004)
18. Miura, N., Nagasaka, A., Miyatake, T.: Extraction of finger-vein patterns using maximum curvature points in image profiles. ICE Trans. Inf. Syst. **90**(8), 1185–1194 (2007)
19. Qin, H., El-Yacoubi, M.A.: Deep representation for finger-vein image-quality assessment. IEEE Trans. Circuits Syst. Video Technol. **28**(8), 1677–1693 (2018)
20. Qin, H., El Yacoubi, M.A., Lin, J., Liu, B.: An iterative deep neural network for hand-vein verification. IEEE Access **7**, 34823–34837 (2019)
21. Qin, H., El-Yacoubi, M.A.: Deep representation-based feature extraction and recovering for finger-vein verification. IEEE Trans. Inf. Forensics Secur. **12**(8), 1816–1829 (2017)
22. Qin, H., Qin, L., Xue, L., He, X., Chengbo, Yu., Liang, X.: Finger-vein verification based on multi-features fusion. Sensors **13**(11), 15048–15067 (2013)
23. Qin, H., Qin, L., Chengbo, Yu.: Region growth-based feature extraction method for finger-vein recognition. Opt. Eng. **50**(5), 214–229 (2011)
24. Sagi, O., Rokach, L.: Ensemble learning: a survey. Wiley Interdiscip. Rev. Data Min. Knowl. Discov. **8**(5), e1249 (2018)
25. Shao, H., Zhong, D.: One-shot cross-dataset palmprint recognition via adversarial domain adaptation. Neurocomputing **432**, 288–299 (2021)
26. Song, W., et al.: A finger-vein verification system using mean curvature. Pattern Recognit. Lett. **32**(11), 1541–1547 (2011)
27. Vodinh, T.: Biomedical Photonics Handbook, 2nd edn (2012)
28. Wang, L., Li, Y., Wang, S.: Feature learning for one-shot face recognition. In: 2018 25th IEEE International Conference on Image Processing (ICIP), pp. 2386–2390 (2018)

29. Wu, Z., Deng, W.: One-shot deep neural network for pose and illumination normalization face recognition. In: 2016 IEEE International Conference on Multimedia and Expo (ICME), pp. 1–6 (2016)
30. Zhang, J., Lu, Z., Li, M., Wu, H.: Gan-based image augmentation for finger-vein biometric recognition. IEEE Access 7, 183118–183132 (2019)
31. Zhang, L., Zhang, L., Mou, X., Zhang, D.: FSIM: a feature similarity index for image quality assessment. IEEE Trans. Image Process. 20(8), 2378–2386 (2011)
32. Zhang, L., Zhang, L., Zhang, D., Zhu, H.: Ensemble of local and global information for finger-knuckle-print recognition. Pattern Recognit. 44(9), 1990–1998 (2011). Computer Analysis of Images and Patterns
33. Zhang, Y., Li, W., Zhang, L., Lu, Y.: Adaptive gabor convolutional neural networks for finger-vein recognition. In: 2019 International Conference on High Performance Big Data and Intelligent Systems (HPBD IS), pp. 219–222 (2019)
34. Zhang, Y., Li, W., Zhang, L., Ning, X., Sun, L., Lu, Y.: Adaptive learning gabor filter for finger-vein recognition. IEEE Access 7, 159821–159830 (2019)

# Hand-Dorsa Vein Recognition Based on Local Deep Feature

Yuqing Wang[1], Zhengwen Shen[2], Jun Wang[2(✉)], Gongping Yang[3], and Huafeng Qin[4]

[1] Jiang Su Sheng Tong Shan Zhong Deng Zhuan Ye Xue Xiao, Xuzhou 221116, Jiangsu, China
[2] China University of Mining and Technology, Xuzhou 221116, Jiangsu, China
[3] School of Software Engineering, Shandong University, Jinan 250101, China
gpyang@sdu.edu.cn
[4] School of Computer Science and Information Engineering, Chongqing Technology and Business University, Chongqing 400067, China

**Abstract.** Deep Neural Network (DNN), which has been paid considerable attention in the last several years, has an outstanding ability of feature representation in the large-scale image task. However, due to the sufficient hand vein database, it is difficult to apply the DNN model to the vein recognition task. Therefore, according to vein specific-distribution traits which are only composed of vessels, a novel training strategy that we use the large-scale hand vein patches database instead of the small-scale hand database to train the DNN model is proposed to solve this problem. Local deep feature (LDF) is obtained by using the DNN model trained on the large-scale hand vein patches database to extract features of vein patches. Several fusion ideas are used to fuse local deep features to form the global feature vector of the whole vein image, and PCA (principal component analysis) is introduced to relieve secondary vein information and speed up the training of SVM. Rigorous experiments with our lab-made hand vein database are conducted to demonstrate the effectiveness of proposed LDF.

**Keywords:** Hand-Dorsa vein recognition · Training strategy · Local deep feature · Principal component analysis

## 1 Introduction

With the development of information technology, biometric authentication has been paid considerable attention in the last several decades, because it provides significant merits over traditional manners like uniqueness, reliability, and difficulty of falsification. Biometric identification is based on the distinctive information in human biometric features such as face [1], finger vein [2], iris [3], palmprint [4]. Among them, vein recognition, which is not introduced until 1990 by MacGregor and Welford [5], has become one of the most popular biometric identification methods with the advantage of unique, portable, and inherent properties.

© Springer Nature Singapore Pte Ltd. 2022
F. Sun et al. (Eds.): ICCSIP 2021, CCIS 1515, pp. 276–285, 2022.
https://doi.org/10.1007/978-981-16-9247-5_21

Commonly, the vein recognition technique involves image acquisition, vein image preprocessing, vein image feature extraction and representation, classifier design and vein recognition [6]. The most important and difficult part, in reality, is the feature extraction methods design, many efforts have been contributed to develop an effective feature extraction method towards vein recognition. The related work can be classified into three groups. The methods in the first group, which refers to the repeated line tracking method [7], the maximum curvature point method [8], the mean curvature [9], and the Gabor filter [10], are based on observation on the geometric shape or topological structure of the vein image. In these methods, the vein network is segmented firstly, and then the topological feature of the vein network is extracted for matching. However, the results of the geometrical models are usually unsatisfactory since the segmentation results of low-quality images are often inaccurate. Vein texture descriptors based on the binary code are adopted in the second group, which covers the local binary pattern (LBP) [11], the local line binary pattern (LLBP) [12], the discriminative local binary pattern (DLBP) [13], the personalized best bit map (PBBM) [14], etc. These methods transform the image matrix to a 1-D or 2-D feature matrix. The characteristic of being sensitive to the translation and rotation of input images, however, would result in bad recognition performance. To overcome these problems, a multimodal biometric system is employed in the last group, which combines the evidence obtained from hand vein and other traits. Yang and Zhang proposed the supervised local-preserving canonical correlation analysis method (SLPCCAM) to generate fingerprint-vein feature vectors in feature-level fusion [15]. Finger vein and finger dorsal texture were fused using the proposed holistic fusion and non-linear fusion methods at the score level in [10]. Kang and Park [16] integrated finger vein and finger geometry through SVM-based score level fusion. However, along with the higher accuracy, a variety of limitations appear in multimodal biometric systems, such as the longer recognition time, the higher cost for multiple high-quality sensors, and the more inconvenience to the user. All the methods mentioned above, hand-crafted feature representation models, can't ensure the discriminative representation, high performance.

In recent years, Deep Neural Network, which can learn more discriminative and robust representation, has acquired high performance in the large-scaled image recognition task. In the light of their powerful capacity for feature representation, some researchers brought them into biometrics. Several deep learning models such as in [17–19] have been built for face verification and have shown great success on the LFW face dataset. However, Thanks to a sufficient hand vein database, it is difficult to exploit DNN to learn discriminative features of hand vein information. Therefore, according to vein specific-distribution traits which are only composed of vessels, a novel training strategy that we use the large-scaled hand vein patches database instead of the small-scaled hand database to train the DNN model is proposed to solve this problem. Then we use the DNN model trained on the large-scaled hand vein patches database to extract deep features of vein patches. Several fusion ideas are an attempt to fuse local deep features to form a final feature vector, and before feeding into SVM to classify hand vein information. PCA is adopted to relieve secondary vein feature information and speed up the training of SVM. The procedure of the proposed LDF is as shown in Figs. 1 and 2.

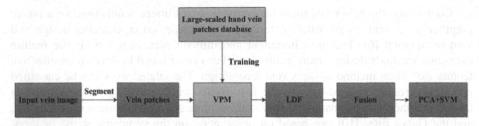

**Fig. 1.** The procedure of the proposed LDF

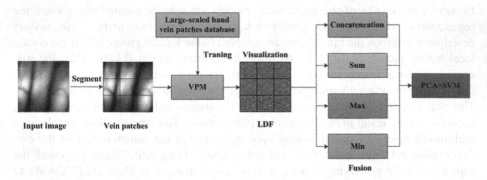

**Fig. 2.** Example showing a series of steps to generate a LDF for a hand-dorsa vein ROI image representation.

The paper is organized as follows: The design of the proposed hand-dorsa vein capturing device is introduced in Sect. 2. Section 3 gives the detailed procedures of the LDF. The identity and gender experimental results and discussion is described in Sect. 4. Finally, we summarize the paper and conclude the future work in Conclusions.

## 2   Lab-Made Hand Vein Database

To obtain persuasive and satisfactory classification results, we realized a lab-made hand-dorsa vein database with a total of 2000 images with the proportion of male and female are respectively 100 and each person with 10 right hand-dorsa vein images captured. All hand-dorsa vein images in the database were acquired in two specifically set sessions separated by a time interval of more than 10 days, and at each time, five samples were acquired from each subject at the wavelength of 850 nm. To the fullest of the dorsal vein information, we set the size of the images as 460*680 with extremely high quality. Figure 3 shows some samples of the home-made database. The ROI extraction [20] process specifically designed for this database is conducted followed by the grey and size normalization. To overcome the problem of insufficient trainset, we cut 100000 vein image patches that contain vessels to establish a large-scaled hand-vein patches database which is used to train the DNN model to obtain the extractor of local deep feature, and the patches size is set as 64*64. Figure 4 shows some image patches in the large-scaled hand-dorsa vein patches database.

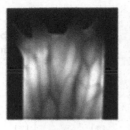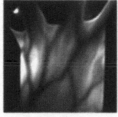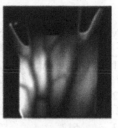

**Fig. 3.** Samples of our home-made hand vein database.

**Fig. 4.** Samples of our home-made large-scale hand vein patches database.

# 3 Local Deep Feature

**Table 1.** The configuration of our VP.

| Layer Type | Number of Filters | Size of Feature Map | Size of Kernel | Number of Stride | Number of Padding |
|---|---|---|---|---|---|
| Image input layer | 224*224*3 | | | | |
| Conv1_1 Relu1_1 | 64 | 224*224*64 224*224*64 | 3*3 | 1*1 | 1*1 |
| Con1_2 Relu1_2 Pool1 | 64 | 224*224*64 224*224*64 112*112*64 | 3*3 2*2 | 1*1 2*2 | 1*1 0*0 |
| Con2_1 Rclu2_1 | 128 | 112*112*128 112*112*128 | 3*3 | 1*1 | 1*1 |
| Conv2_2 Relu2_2 Pool2 | 128 | 112*112*128 112*112*128 56*56*128 | 3*3 2*2 | 1*1 2*2 | 1*1 0*0 |
| Conv3_1 Relu3_1 | 256 | 56*56*256 56*56*256 | 3*3 | 1*1 | 1*1 |
| Conv3_2 Relu3_2 | 256 | 56*56*256 56*56*256 | 3*3 | 1*1 | 1*1 |
| Conv3_3 Relu3_3 Pool3 | 256 | 56*56*256 56*56*256 28*28*256 | 3*3 2*2 | 1*1 2*2 | 1*1 0*0 |

(*continued*)

**Table 1.** (*continued*)

| Layer Type | Number of Filters | Size of Feature Map | Size of Kernel | Number of Stride | Number of Padding |
|---|---|---|---|---|---|
| Conv4_1 Relu4_1 | 512 | 28*28*512 28*28*512 | 3*3 | 1*1 | 1*1 |
| Conv4_2 Relu4_2 | 512 | 28*28*512 28*28*512 | 3*3 | 1*1 | 1*1 |
| Conv4_3 Relu4_3 Pool4 | 512 | 28*28*512 28*28*512 14*14*512 | 3*3 2*2 | 1*1 2*2 | 1*1 0*0 |
| Conv5_1 Relu5_1 | 512 | 14*14*512 14*14*512 | 3*3 | 1*1 | 1*1 |
| Conv5_2 Relu5_2 | 512 | 14*14*512 14*14*512 | 3*3 | 1*1 | 1*1 |
| Conv5_3 Relu5_3 Pool5 | 512 | 14*14*512 14*14*512 7*7*512 | 3*3 2*2 | 1*1 2*2 | 1*1 0*0 |
| FC6 Relu6 Dropout6 | 4096*1 4096*1 4096*1 | | | | |
| Relu7 FC7 Dropout7 | 4096*1 4096*1 4096*1 | | | | |
| FC8 Softmax layer Output layer | 200*1 200*1 200*1 | | | | |

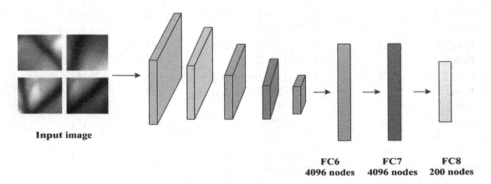

**Fig. 5.** Samples of our home-made hand vein database.

## 3.1 Vein Patches Model (VPM)

In this paper, we adopt one of the most popular VGG Net-16 [21] to train the large-scaled hand vein database instead of the small-scaled hand vein database, and the obtained model is named as vein patches model (VPM). VPM which is as shown in Fig. 5 and Table 1 is composed of 13 convolution layers, 5 pooling layers, and 3 fully connected layers. The input image size is set as 224*224 and 64 filters of 3*3 whose stride and padding are set as 1 are used in 1st convolution layers. Therefore, the size of the feature map is 224*224* 64 in 1st convolution layer, where 224 and 224 are the height and width of the feature map respectively. The rectified linear unit (Relu) Layer can be expressed as follows [22, 23]:

$$Y = max(0, X) \tag{1}$$

Where x and Y are the input and output value of the Relu function, respectively. The feature maps obtained by passing the Relu layer (Relu1_1) pass the 2nd convolution layer and the Relu layer (Relu1_2) before passing the max pooling layer (Pool1). The aforementioned contents is the 1st group convolution layers and the detailed procedures of other convolution layers is as shown in Fig. 2 and Table 1. After the input vein images pass the 13 convolution layers, feature maps of 7*7*512 is finally obtained. Besides, in our model, the numbers of output nodes the 1st, 2nd, 3rd full connected convolution layers are 4096, 4096, and 200, respectively. The features of the 2nd full connected layers are regarded as the representation of vein patches.

LDF is produced by adopting the output of the second fully connected layer in the VPM which has highly discriminative and robust representation. Unlike [24] that adopts coarse-to-fine transfer learning strategy to acquire discriminative task-specific feature representation, our training strategy that directly train VGG on the large-scaled hand vein patches database to obtain task-specific local deep feature is more simple and feasible.

Caffe deep Neural Network framework is adopted for re-training VGG model and extracting the second full connected layer feature as local deep feature. In our training experiment, mini-batch size is set to 5 and the maximum of iterations is 9000. The learning rate is set to 0.001 and we use a weight decay of 0.0005.

## 3.2 Fusion

In our experiment, hand vein ROI images are divided into non-overlapping m*m sub-images. If m is large, the sub-image cannot reflect the detailed vein information. However, if m is small, the sub-image can be affected by noise. Therefore, combining with prior knowledge, we set 64*64 as the size of the sub-image and m as 3.

VPM is utilized to extract the local deep feature of vein patches, and the feature vector of whole vein image is formed by concatenating local deep features, which is defined as:

$$I = \{I_1, I_2, \ldots, I_i, \quad i = 1, 2, \ldots, m * m\} \tag{2}$$

Where I indicates the feature vector of the whole vein image, I_i is the local feature vector of vein patches. Due to the size of local feature is 4096 which is also the feature numbers of the second full connected layer in VPM, the size of global feature is m*m*4096. Besides, other fusion strategies [25] such as 'sum','max','min' are also attempted to use fuse the local feature vector, and the recognition result of different fusion idea is illustrated in Sect. 4.

## 4 Experiments and Analysis

### 4.1 Identity Recognition of Hand-Dorsa Vein Information

In our experiment, to evaluate the effectiveness of the proposed LDF, we perform the rigorous experiment on our lab-made hand vein database with several fusion ideas such as 'sum', 'max', 'min'. The global feature composed of LDF is a high dimension feature, which can increase the training time of SVM. Therefore, to relieve the secondary vein feature information and speed up the training of SVM, PCA is proposed to reduce the dimension of the global feature vector. The specific classification accuracy with a different set of dimensions is as shown in Fig. 6.

We can come clearly to the conclusion from Fig. 5 that this fusion idea which is by concatenating LDF is high performance. Moreover, when the size of the global feature is 50 in this fusion strategy, the highest recognition rate is 98.1%. Comparing with other fusion ideas, this fusion strategy can acquire high accuracy because it has the spatial position information of vein images.

### 4.2 Comparison with State of the Art Local Feature Models

In order to further demonstrate the high performance of the proposed model, we conduct rigorous experiments on our self-established hand vein database with the representative local feature extraction algorithms which are including LBP, LDP and LTP. And such local feature representation model is widely applied for biometric identification because it can provides competitive performance. The final comparison result is as shown in Fig. 7.

It can be concluded from Fig. 7 that performing rigorous experiments with the different local feature representations the proposed LDF model gains the highest performance, which also further demonstrates the representation capability of the proposed model.

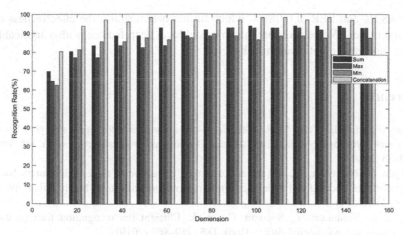

**Fig. 6.** Trend of different fusion methods' recognition rate with number of global features change.

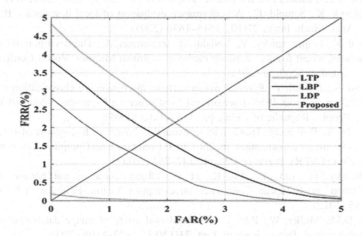

**Fig. 7.** Comparison with other local feature representation methods.

## 5 Conclusions

In this paper, a novel training strategy that we use the large-scaled hand vein patches database instead of the small-scaled hand database to train the DNN model is proposed to acquire the extractor of the local deep feature. The local deep feature is obtained by exploiting the DNN model trained on the large-scaled hand vein patches database to the discriminative feature of vein patches. Moreover, several fusion ideas are used to fuse local deep features to form final feature vectors, and it should be noted that before feeding the final discriminative feature vector into SVM, PCA is incorporated to improve the classification performance and speed up the training of SVM by discarding the secondary feature information. The experimental results on the lab-made hand-dorsa hand vein database with the proposed local deep feature realize the recognition rate of 98.1% and EER of 0.089%, which further demonstrates the effectiveness of the proposed model. We believe that the proposed local deep feature is also applicable for another biometric identification task.

# References

1. Gao, G., Yu, Y.B., Yang, M.D., et al.: Cross-resolution face recognition with pose variations via multilayer locality-constrained structural orthogonal procrustes regression. Inf. Sci. **506**, 19–36 (2020)
2. Miura, N., Nagasaka, A., Miyatake, T.: Feature extraction of finger-vein pattern based on repeated line tracking and its application to personal identification. Mach. Vis. Appl. **15**(4), 194–203 (2004)
3. Vyas, R., Kanumuri, T., Sheoran, G., et al.: Efficient iris recognition through curvelet transform and polynomial fitting. Optik **185**, 859–867 (2019)
4. Jia, W., Hu, R.X., Lei, Y.K., Zhao, Y., Gui, J.: Histogram of oriented lines for Palmprint recognition. IEEE Trans. Syst. Man Cybern. A Syst. Hum. **44**(3), 385–395 (2014)
5. Morgan, M.J.: Features and the primal sketch. Vis. Res. **51**(7), 738–753 (2011)
6. Mikolajczyk, K., Schmid, C.: A performance evaluation of local descriptors. IEEE Trans. Pattern Anal. Mach. Intell. **27**(10), 1615–1630 (2005)
7. Chatfield, K., Lenmtexpisky, V., Vedaldi, A., Zisserman, A.: The devil is in the details: an evaluation of recent feature encoding methods in British Machine Vision Conference Univ Dundee, Dundee, Scotland (2011)
8. Grauman, K., Darrell, T.: Pyramid match kernels: discriminative classification with sets of image feature. In: 10th IEEE International Conference on Computer Vision (ICCV 2005), Beijing, Peoples Republic of China, pp. 1458–1465 (2005)
9. Kobayashi, T: BoF meets HOG: feature extraction based on histograms of oriented p.d.f gradients for image classification. In: 26th IEEE Conference on Computer Vision and Pattern Recognition (CVPR), Portland, OR, pp. 747–754 (2011)
10. Russakovsky, O., Lin, Y., Yu, K., et al.: Object-centric spatial pooling for image classification. In: European Conference on Computer Vision, Florence, Italy, vol. 7573, pp. 1–15 (2012)
11. Squire, D.M., Muller, W., Pun, T.: Content-based query of image databases: inspirations from text retrieval. Pattern Recogn. Lett. **21**(13/14), 1193–1198 (2000)
12. Lazebnik, S., Schmid, C., Ponce, J.: Beyond bags of features: spatial pyramid matching for recognizing natural scene categories. In: IEEE Conference on Computer Vision and Pattern Recognition (2006)
13. Wang, J., Wang, G.: Quality-specific hand vein recognition system. IEE Trans. Inf. Forens. Secur. **12**(11), 2599–2610 (2017)
14. Yang, J., Yu, K., Gong, Y., et al.: Linear spatial pyramid matching using sparse coding for image classification. In: IEEE Conference on Computer Vision and Pattern Recognition (2009)
15. Wang, J., Yang, J., Yu, K.: Locality-constrained linear coding for image classification. In: IEEE Conference on Computer Vision and Pattern Recognition, San Francisco, pp. 13–18 (2010)
16. Fan, R., Chang, K., Hsieh, C., et al.: LIBLINEAR: a library for large linear classification. J. Mach. Learn. Res. **9**, 1871–1874 (2008)

17. Taigman, Y., Yang, M., Ranzato, M., Wolf, L.: DeepFace: closing the gap to human-level performance in face verification. In: Computer Vision & Pattern Recognition, pp. 1701–1708 (2015)
18. Sun, Y., Wang, X., Tang, X.: Deeply learned face representations are sparse, selective, and robust. In: Computer Vision & Pattern Recognition, pp. 2892–2900 (2015)
19. Sun, Y., Liang, D., Wang, X., Tang, X.: DeepID3: face recognition with very deep neural networks (Feb. 2015). https://arxiv.org/abs/1502.00873
20. Wang, J., Wang, G., Li, M., Wang, K., Tian, H.: Hand vein recognition based on improved template matching. Int. J. Bioautomat. 18(4), 337–348 (2014)
21. Christian, S., et al.: Going deeper with convolutions. In: 2015 IEEE Conference on Computer Vision and Pattern Recognition, pp. 1–9 (2015)
22. Heaton, J.: Artificial Intelligence for Humans, Volume 3: Deep Learning and Neural Networks. Heaton Research, Inc., St. Louis (2015)
23. Nair, V., Hinton, G.E.: Rectified linear units improve restricted Boltzmann machines. In: Proceedings of the 27th International Conference on Machine Learning, Haifa, Israel, 21–24, pp. 807–814 (2010)
24. Lu, Y., Wu, S., Fang, Z., et al.: Exploring finger vein based personal authentication for secure IoT. In: Future Generation Computer Systems (2017)
25. Wang, G., Zaiyu Pan, J.W.: Bimodal vein recognition based task-specific transfer learning. E100-D(7) (2017)

# Detection Method of Apple Based on Improved Lightweight YOLOv5

Zhijun Li, Xuan Zhang(✉), Xinger Feng, Yuxin Chen, Ruichen Ma,
Weiqiao Wang, and Shu Zhao

Tsingzhan AI Research Institute, Nanjing 211100, China
Xuan.Zhang@tsingzhan.com

**Abstract.** In order to improve the accuracy of apple detection, this essay proposes a detection method based on improved lightweight YOLOv5. By replacing the Depth Separable Convolution, the YOLOv5 algorithm goes through a lightweight modification. A visual attention mechanism model is additionally proposed, which is embedded in YOLOv5 to solve non-attention preference and parameter redundancy when extracting features in the network. The detection accuracy is therefore increased, and the computational burden brought by network parameters is reduced. Compared with the original algorithm, the detection speed can be increased optimally by 13.51%, and the average mAP can reach 95.03%. This method can basically fulfill the apple fruit identification on trees in natural environments.

**Keywords:** Apple · Deep learning · Object detection · YOLOv5

## 1  Introduction and Related Works

China is a big apple-planting country. The total national output of apples was 42.455 million tons in 2019 [1]. In many areas in Shanxi, Shandong and other provinces, apple planting has become a local industrial pillar, dually increasing agricultural economic benefits and the income of local farmers [2]. However, apple harvesting mainly relies on manual plucking at this juncture, which appears to be labor-intensive and time-consuming [3]. With the continuous advancement of agricultural equipment, fruit picking robots have been widely applied in the agricultural field [4–7]. The robot system is mainly divided into two sub-systems, including the vision system and the manipulator system. Among them, the vision system is responsible for detecting and positioning the fruit [8], and the manipulator system is in charge of separating the fruit from the fruit tree [9]. Therefore, the key to success is how the vision system can quickly and accurately detect the fruits on the tree [10].

F. Sun et al. (Eds.): ICCSIP 2021, CCIS 1515, pp. 286–294, 2022.
https://doi.org/10.1007/978-981-16-9247-5_22

The target detection algorithm based on deep learning can quickly detect the number of targets and related positions. This algorithm is mainly divided into two categories, one is the first-stage detection algorithm represented by the YOLO series [10–13] and the SSD series [14–16]; this type of algorithm has a faster detection speed, but its accuracy is relatively low. According to the growth characteristics of roxburgh rose fruit in the natural environment, YAN J W et al. [17] used the YOLOv3 neural network with residual module to train the roxburgh rose fruit recognition model. The average accuracy rate of various types of recognition is 88.5%, the average recall rate is 91.5%, and the recognition rate is about 20 f/s. The other type is a second-stage detection algorithm represented by the RCNN series [18–20], which has high detection accuracy but fails at real-time performance. JING W B et al. [21] used the Faster-RCNN model to identify and count apples and the average recognition accuracy reached 95.53%. Under unsatisfactory conditions such as low light, dense distribution of apples, and long shooting distances, the recognition accuracy also reached more than 90%. Good stability, showing good stability. For picking robots, the algorithm should be taken into account to ensure the detection accuracy and detection speed. YOLOv5 has received favor from researchers due to its advanced detection speed and accuracy [22, 23]. Specifically YOLOv5 adds Mosaic data augmentation, adaptive anchor frame calculation, adaptive image scaling, and other operations at the data input level; the feature extraction network is CSPDarknet53 based on CSPNet [24], which can reduce memory loss within a certain range; the processing output part adopts FPN [25] and PANet [26] structure, which can speed up the information flow between various levels.

We take apple as the research object, utilizing Depth Separable Convolution and visual attention mechanism to improve the YOLOv5 detection algorithm via the lightweight modification to provide a technical reference for intelligent agricultural equipment in the modern orchard environment.

## 2  Improved Lightweight YOLOv5

The YOLOv5 model originates from YOLO. The YOLO algorithm returns to the coordinates of the target frame and its category in the output layer, possessing a good detection speed. The core idea of the YOLO algorithm is to divide the input image into $S \times S$ grids, and the grid where the target center is located is responsible for predicting the target. Each grid is in charge of predicting $B$ target frames, the target frame returns to position coordinates and confidence value for the prediction. Setting a confidence threshold, filtering out target frames with low confidence, and performing Non-Maximum Suppression (NMS) processing on the retained frames will result in the final prediction effect, as shown in Fig. 1.

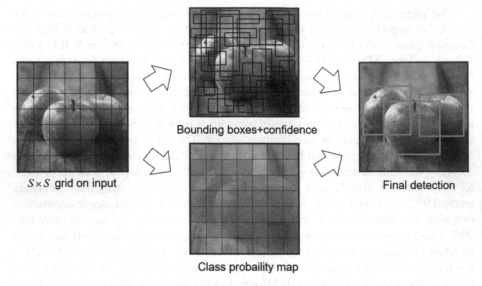

**Fig. 1.** YOLO object detection model

## 2.1    Alter Depth Separable Convolution

Depth Separable Convolution was first proposed by Sifre et al. [27] for neural network image classification. Its core conception is to divide the standard convolution operation into Depthwise Convolution and Pointwise Convolution operations. The most significant advantage of using Depth Separable Convolution is that this method can greatly reduce related parameter calculations while keeping the actual accuracy rate unchanged. We replaced the standard convolution in the feature extraction part of YOLOv5 with Depth Separable Convolution, aiming to effectively reduce the parameter calculation of the algorithm and improve the lightweight degree of algorithm without lowering the accuracy.

## 2.2    Embedding Attention Mechanism Module

In the traditional deep neural network, the algorithm processes all the features of the image equivalently and does not partially focus on a particular area in the visual receptive field, which will cause irrelevant information in the network to participate in a large number of calculations, thus increasing platform memory loss. Targeting the non-attention preference problem during the feature extraction process of the YOLOv5 network, in other words, adopting the same weighting method for features of different degrees of significance, we propose a self-attention mechanism module based on Depth Separable Convolution. It is named Global Pooling Attention Module (GPAM), as shown in Fig. 2. And we add this module to the YOLOv5 feature extraction network to solve the above problems. The GPAM module possesses the advantages of simple structure, convenient utilization, and great versatility. By establishing the interdependence between the channels, the GPAM module can realize the purpose of adaptively calibrating the corresponding characteristics between channels.

In order to reduce the computational complexity of the network, we choose Depth Separable Convolution instead of standard convolution. First of all, the algorithm performs the deep separable convolution operation for the input feature map. It processes the calculated feature map with global maximum pooling, global average pooling, and global hybrid pooling based on maximum pooling and average pooling. By adopting different global pooling methods in different channels, the diversity of module attention extraction can be improved. This operation converts the two-dimensional feature in a single channel into a real number so that the output feature map is no longer limited to a specific receptive field, and context information outside the partial range zone can be used to obtain sufficient information to analyze the relationship between channels. After global pooling, the module concentrates partially on the feature map in a single channel, making it easier for the network to extract essential features and eliminate useless features. Secondly, dimensionality expansion is performed on the feature maps after receiving global pooling respectively, and the spatial resolution after being expanded is consistent with the original input feature maps, followed by the processing of Sigmoid operation. The above feature map and the original input feature map are multiplied by element so that each feature channel can be redistributed with a specific weight according to its significance. Finally, the results calculated by the three branches are combined to complete the feature recalibration in the channel dimension, and a new set of feature mapping is obtained, as shown in the Fig. 2. The GPAM module utilizes compression and expansion sequentially to perform reinforcement learning of the critical points sampled by the shallow features. We introduce a structure to the module, which resembles the residual unit, to ensure that the vanishing or exploding gradient problems will not appear in the case of a deeper network. For the visual attention mechanism module, we propose the GPAM module; since it can help the neural network to improve its key feature extraction capability in image information processing to a certain extent.

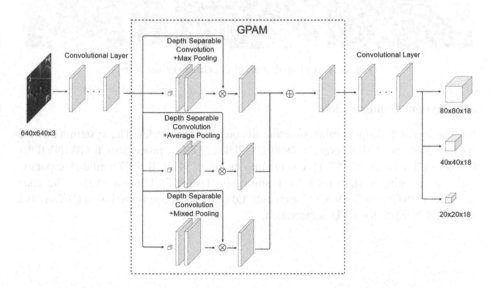

**Fig. 2.** Block diagram of the improved YOLOv5 algorithm with GPAM module

We use Depth Separable Convolution to improve the algorithm's degree of light-weight, use the Global Pooling Attention Module to enhance the algorithm's accuracy, and merge it to form a new module embedded in the YOLOv5 network structure. The combined network structure can extract the shallow feature maps obtained by the convolution calculation into deep feature maps with more critical information and further extract the crucial information to improve the overall detection effect of the algorithm.

## 3   Experiment Statistics and Algorithm Test

### 3.1   Experiment Statistics

Since there are a large number of apple-related pictures from the web, we developed an image crawler based on Python to download these pictures in batches, reducing the cost of data collection while improving the efficiency of data collection. The primary sources of pictures are Baidu and Google. We performed data cleaning on the collected data to reduce the interference of repeated, blurred, and unqualified pictures on the results. After cleaning, 1,000 pictures were retained in total. We used picture labeling software to data-annotate these pictures and utilize random rotation, random cropping, random brightness, random noise, and other methods to perform data enhancement. The training set and test set are divided and referred to the ratio of 8:2, and some pictures are shown in Fig. 3.

**Fig. 3.**   Part of apple images crawled from the web

### 3.2   System Configuration

We use PyTorch deep learning structure to construct the model. The system hardware configuration is AMD Ryzen7 4800H CPU@2.9 GHz processor, 6 GB NVIDIA GeForce GTX 1660Ti GPU, 16 GB running memory, 512 GB SSD hard disk capacity, and the operating system used for training and testing is Ubuntu 18.04. The code compiler is PyCharm 2019.3.3 Community Edition and is configured with CUDA 10.2 and cuDNN 7.6.5 for GPU acceleration.

## 3.3    Algorithm Test

In order to verify the feasibility of the improved YOLOv5 fruit detection algorithm proposed in this paper, it is necessary to conduct comparative testing between the YOLOv5 algorithm with individually replaced Depth Separable Convolution, embedded Global Pooling Attention Module, integrated Depth Separable Convolution, and the Global Pooling Attention Module in the feature extraction network and the unimproved original YOLOv5 algorithm.

### 3.3.1    Speed Detection Algorithm Testing

This paper records the speed of the algorithm for detecting multiple images and takes the average value. The comparative experimental results are shown in Table 1. The value in parentheses indicates the relative improvement rate of different revised versions of the algorithm based on the detection speed of the original algorithm. YOLOv5s, YOLOv5m, YOLOv5l, and YOLOv5x are four network structures of YOLOv5 with different depths and widths and their parameter quantities increase sequentially [28]. The improved network parameters are reduced by 15.49%, 13.24%, 10.52%, and 8.27% respectively with different structures compared with those before the improvement.

**Table 1.** Comparison experiment results of the detection speed of the algorithm before and after the improvement

| Algorithm before and after improvement | | YOLOv5s | YOLOv5m | YOLOv5l | YOLOv5x |
|---|---|---|---|---|---|
| Algorithm before improvement | | 37.16 ms (0.00) | 84.87 ms (0.00) | 152.33 ms (0.00) | 310.53 ms (0.00) |
| Algorithm after improvement | Separately replace Depth Separable Convolution | 31.12 ms (−16.25%) | 72.08 ms (−15.07%) | 132.77 ms (−12.84%) | 277.33 ms (−10.69%) |
| | Separately Embedded Attention Mechanism Module | 38.19 ms (+2.74%) | 87.52 ms (+3.12%) | 157.77 ms (+3.57%) | 323.51 ms (+4.18%) |
| | Fusion Depth Separable Convolution and Attention Mechanism Modules | 32.14 ms (−13.51%) | 74.73 ms (−11.95%) | 138.21 ms (−9.27%) | 290.31 ms (−6.51%) |

Separately replacing Depth Separable Convolution can significantly increase the detection speed of the algorithm by 10.69% to 16.25%. Embedding the attention mechanism module singly will exert a certain but small extent of impact on the calculation speed, and the detection speed of the YOLOv5 algorithm remains basically unchanged before and after the improvement. After combining Depth Separable Convolution and attention mechanism modules, compared with singly replacing Depth Separable Convolution, the algorithm will partially increase the computational burden and reduce the detection speed; the fastest detection speed is 32.14 ms, maximally 13.51% higher than before the improvement. The above results demonstrate that individually replacing Depth Separable Convolution brings a more significant increase in calculation speed; after combining the attention mechanism module, it still possesses the advantage of a faster detection speed compared with the original algorithm.

### 3.3.2  Average Accuracy Rate Algorithm Testing

This paper records the algorithm's detection of *mAP* of multiple pictures. The comparison experiment results are shown in Table 2. The value in parentheses indicates the absolute improvement rate of different revised versions of the algorithm based on the average accuracy of the algorithm before the improvement.

**Table 2.** Comparison experiment results of the mAP (mean Average Precision) before and after the improvement

| Algorithm before and after improvement | | YOLOv5s | YOLOv5m | YOLOv5l | YOLOv5x |
|---|---|---|---|---|---|
| Algorithm before improvement | | 88.51% (0.00) | 90.38% (0.00) | 91.86% (0.00) | 92.32% (0.00) |
| Algorithm after improvement | Separately replace Depth Separable Convolution | 87.19% (−1.32%) | 89.23% (−1.15%) | 90.94% (−0.92%) | 91.49% (−0.83%) |
| | Separately Embedded Attention Mechanism Module | 91.23% (+2.72%) | 93.35% (+2.97%) | 95.12% (+3.26%) | 95.86% (+3.54) |
| | Fusion Depth Separable Convolution and Attention Mechanism Modules | 89.91% (+1.40%) | 92.20% (+1.82%) | 94.20% (+2.34%) | 95.03% (+2.71) |

The average accuracy rates of the original YOLOv5 algorithm under different structures are 88.51%, 90.38%, 91.86%, and 92.32%. Except for YOLOv5s, which is less than 90%, the detection accuracy of the rest of the structures is all above 90%. This result illustrates that YOLOv5 has a good model structure, detection effect, and good applicability for apple detection in natural environments. Changing Depth Separable Convolution separately will lead to the loss of the algorithm's accuracy. Compared with that which was improved before, the loss rate of the algorithm is controlled within 2%. Compared with the previous improvement, the detection accuracy can be improved by 3.54% and 3.125% on average after the attention mechanism is embedded separately. Embedding the attention mechanism module in the algorithm structure is beneficial for processing the shallow feature maps obtained by convolution calculations into deep feature maps with essential information, learning about the correlation between channels, enhancing the significant features in the feature maps, weakening the secondary features, further extracting the critical information, and thus effectively improving the overall detection effect of the algorithm. The detection accuracy of YOLOv5x after fusion exceeds 95%, which is the highest result of the test. The detection results of some samples are shown in Fig. 4.

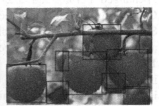

**Fig. 4.** Detection effect of some apple pictures

## 4 Conclusion

In order to improve the apple detection effect in the natural environment, the YOLOv5 algorithm goes through lightweight improvement based on replacing Depth Separable Convolution, and we additionally propose a visual attention mechanism module, which is embedded in YOLOv5 to solve the attention preference and parameter redundancy problems in the network's feature extraction. The test results showed that the improved YOLOv5 detection algorithm can enhance accuracy while improving the degree of lightweight. Compared with the original algorithm, the detection speed can be increased optimally by 13.51%, and the average mAP can reach 95.03%. In future work, we sincerely hope to collect more sample pictures on the spot for algorithm training and testing and classify the quality of different fruits, such as dividing them into three levels: good, medium, and poor, in order to form a complete set of visual detecting system.

## References

1. China Fruit Marking Association. Apple Market Forecast and Operational Recommendations. Hebei Science and Technology News, 13 October 2020 (003) (2020)
2. Zhang, J.: Empirical Analysis of Regional Differences of Apple's Planting Cost and Benefit in China. Inner Mongolia Agricultural University (2018)
3. Papageorgiou, E.I., Aggelopoulou, K.D., Gemtos, T.A., et al.: Yield prediction in apples using fuzzy cognitive map learning approach. Comput. Electron. Agric. **91**, 19–29 (2013)
4. Yang, X.H.: Research on visual navigation path method of kiwi fruit picking robot. Technol. Wind **15**, 23–24 (2021)
5. Wan, J.Q., Fan, S.Z., Gong, L., et al.: Research status and development direction of design and control technology of fruit and vegetable picking robot system. Smart Agricult. **2**(04), 17–40 (2020)
6. Zhao, D., Shen, T., Chen, Y., et al.: Fast tracking and recognition of overlapping fruit for apple harvesting robot. Trans. Chin. Soc. Agricult. Eng. **31**(2), 22–28 (2015)
7. Fan, Y.Y., Zhang, Z.M., Chen, G.P., et al.: Application of vision sensor in the target fruit recognition system of picking robot. J. Agricult. Mechaniz. Res. **41**(05), 210–214 (2019)
8. Feng, W., Zhao, D.A.: Fast tracking and recognition of target fruit of apple picking robot. Inf. Technol. **05**, 5–9 (2018)
9. Su, M., Han, H.M.: Research on new equipment for fruit picking controlled by robot and manual assistance. Pract. Electron. **Z1**, 86–87 (2020)
10. Redmon, J., Divvala, S., Girshick, R., et al.: You only look once: unified, real-time object detection. In: The IEEE Conference on Computer Vision and Pattern Recognition, pp. 779–788. IEEE, Piscataway (2016)
11. Redmon, J., Farhadi, A.: YOLO9000: better, faster, stronger. In: The IEEE Conference on Computer Vision and Pattern Recognition, pp. 7263–7271. IEEE, Piscataway (2017)
12. Redmon, J., Farhadi, A.: YOLO v3: an incremental improvement [EB/OL] (2018). https://arxiv.org/abs/1804.02767
13. Bochkovskiy, A., Wang, C., Liao, H.: YOLOv4: optimal speed and accuracy of object detection [EB/OL] (2020). https://arxiv.org/abs/2004.10934
14. Liu, W., Anguelov, D., Erhan, D., et al.: SSD: single shot multibox detector. In: European Conference on Computer Vision, pp. 21–37. Springer, Cham (2016)

15. Zhang, S., Wen, L., Bian, X., et al.: Single-shot refinement neural network for object detection. The IEEE Conference on Computer Vision and Pattern Recognition, pp. 4203–4212. IEEE, Piscataway (2018)
16. Wang, D., Zhang, B., Cao, Y., et al.: SFSSD: shallow feature fusion single shot multibox detector. In: International Conference in Communications, Signal Processing, and Systems, pp. 2590–2598. Springer, Singapore (2019)
17. Yan, J.W., Zhao, Y., Zhang, L.Y., et al.: Recognition of prickly pear fruit in natural environment based on residual network. J. Chin. Agricult. Mechaniz. **41**(10), 191–196 (2020)
18. Girshick, R., Donahue, J., Darrell, T., et al.: Rich feature hierarchies for accurate object detection and semantic segmentation. In: The IEEE Conference on Computer Vision and Pattern Recognition, pp. 580–587. IEEE, Piscataway (2014)
19. Girshick, R.: Fast R-CNN. In: Proceedings of the IEEE International Conference on Computer Vision, pp. 1440–1448. IEEE, Piscataway (2015)
20. Ren, S., He, K., Girshick, R., et al.: Faster R-CNN: towards real-time object detection with region proposal networks. IEEE Trans. Pattern Anal. Mach. Intell. **39**(6), 1137–1149 (2017)
21. Jing, W.B., Hu, H.T., Cheng, C., et al.: Ground apple recognition and counting based on deep learning. Jiangsu Agricult. Sci. **48**(05), 210–219 (2020)
22. Zhou, W.H., Zhu, S.L.: Research on the application of smart examination room solutions based on deep learning technology. Construct. Budget Inf. Technol. Informatiz. **12**, 224–227 (2020)
23. Wang, F.: Artificial intelligence detection and recognition algorithm for masks and helmets based on improved YOLOv5. Construct. Budget **11**, 67–69 (2020)
24. Wang, C.Y., Liao, H.Y.M., Yeh, I.H., et al.: CSPNet: a new backbone that can enhance learning capability of CNN. In: The IEEE/CVF Conference on Computer Vision and Pattern Recognition Workshops, pp. 390–391. CVPRW, Seattle (2020)
25. Lin, T.Y., Dollar, P., Girshick, R., et al.: Feature pyramid networks for object detection. In: The IEEE Conference on Computer Vision and Pattern Recognition, pp. 2117–2125. IEEE, Piscataway (2017)
26. Liu, S., Qi, L., Qin, H., et al.: Path aggregation network for instance segmentation. In: The IEEE Conference on Computer Vision and Pattern Recognition, pp. 8759–8768. IEEE, Piscataway (2018)
27. Sifre, L., Mallat, S.: Rigid-motion scattering for texture classification. Comput. Sci. **3559**, 501–515 (2014)
28. Shu, L., Zhang, Z.J., Lei, B.: Research on Dense-Yolov5 algorithm for infrared target detection. Opt. Optoelectron. Technol. **19**(01), 69–75 (2021)

# Scene Graph Prediction with Concept Knowledge Base

Runqing Miao[✉] and Qingxuan Jia

Beijing University of Posts and Telecommunications, Beijing, China
tsingm@bupt.edu.cn

**Abstract.** Image understanding is an emerging research direction in computer vision, and scene graphs are the most mainstream form of understanding. A scene graph is a topological graph with objects in the scene as nodes and relationships as edges, used to describe the composition and semantic association of objects in an image scene. Scene graph prediction requires not only object detection, but also relationship prediction.

In this work, we propose a scene graph prediction method based on a conceptual knowledge base, which uses the condensed human understanding stored in the knowledge base to assist the generation of the scene graph. We designed a simple model to fuse image features, label features and knowledge features. Then the data filtered by the model is used as the input of the classic scene graph generation model, and better prediction results are obtained. Finally, we analyzed the reasons for the slight increase in the results, and summarized and prospected.

**Keywords:** Scene graph · Scene graph prediction · Knowledge graph

## 1 Introduction

Computer vision has always been an important branch of artificial intelligence research. Classic tasks like image recognition [6] and object detection [19] have a variety of models and methods. As far as we know, such tasks can be classified as intuitive regression problems, which is predicted directly by the model trained from labeled supervised data. Due to the subjectivity of human cognition, there are still many deficiencies in subjective image comprehension tasks such as image captioning [7,28] and VQA(visual question answering) [20,26].

The scene description corresponding to the image must be constructed accurately, not just the discrete marks of objects in the image in image understanding tasks. Therefore, scene graph prediction as an intermediate task has gradually become a new direction in the field of computer vision. If we define it mathematically, a node $(G)$ in the scene graph stands for an object $(O)$ in the visual

Supported by Major Project of the New Generation of Artificial Intelligence (No. 2018AAA0102900).

scene, and the node contains the object's classification label $(L)$ and the visual feature bounding box $(B)$. While edges stand for the cognitive relationships $(R)$ between objects, which is mainly divided into the following three types: spatial, relationships and logical relationships. At the same time, because the scene graph has the network structure of the topology graph, it is very similar to the knowledge graph [9], both are often closely related to graph neural network [24] when modeling.

While scene graph prediction [5,10,23,25] have a number of methodological studies as a field, on the contrary almost no related datasets, only Visual Genome [11] has been widely recognized because of the hard work of annotation on relation between objects. Visual Genome has 1.3 million objects and 1.5 million relations in 108k images. Among them, 21 objects, 17 relations, 16 attributes are marked in every image. Although this dataset has a huge amount of data scale, there is a clear long-tail distribution in the labeling of relationships, the most common relationships, Including "on", "has", "in" and "wearing" accounted for more than 80% of the total relationship notes. Another problem is that there are some unlabeled or duplicate relationships in the data set. Several state-of-the-art networks such as Neural Motifs [29] accurately match the Visual Genome from the perspective of data fitting. Although this scheme can obtain satisfactory recall rate, due to the limitation of bias of data set annotation itself, it is not accurate and consistent with human cognition, and the real relationship in the image can be incorporated into the scene graph.

In order to remedy the inaccurate scene graph prediction caused by Visual Genome dataset bias, some work has been pointed out and modification schemes have been proposed, which mainly include two parts. The first is to improve the prediction model to correct the interference caused by "blind guessing" [22], that is, to predict the relationship between objects directly from the labels of objects without the visual features of objects. By means of causal reasoning, the normal predicted relationship can be subtracted from the part directly predicted by the label. The second is the optimization of dataset [16], that is, filtering and modifying the annotated relations in Visual Genome to reduce bias. An attempt was made on VG150 [25], a simplified version of Visual Genome, to identify and eliminate part of the tag directly predictive relationship through a simple network.

The above two different methods are both scene graph prediction tasks from the perspective of pure vision and try to solve the problem of ignoring image features caused by data set BIAS with different ideas. However, there are still some problems in data set Bias that are not mentioned in the above methods, such as missing and duplication of relation annotations. At the same time, we have access not only to Visual Genome or similar scene graph datasets, but also to lots of wild-world knowledge bases [1,4,15,21] in research fields such as knowledge engineering and recommendation system. These knowledge bases store common-sense concepts and relationships that conform to human cognition. If the knowledge base is introduced into the scene graph prediction, it will help us to predict more cognitive relationships for the scene graph [13].

Our method proposes a more comprehensive scenario relation annotation based on existing data, using common sense knowledge provided by ConceptNet to modify Visual Genome data sets to improve the reliability of scenario graph predictions. It mainly includes: using knowledge relation to filter out repeated or unreasonable relation annotations, strengthen the relationship annotations that conform to the description of the knowledge base and give this type of annotations a higher degree of confidence. Our experiments show that the new Visual Genome, which incorporates knowledge information from ConceptNet, performs better in scene prediction tasks than the original dataset.

The structure of this paper is as follows: The second section introduces relevant references. The third section introduces the method of dataset modification. The fourth section introduces the scene graph prediction experiment. The last section summarizes and prospects (Fig. 1).

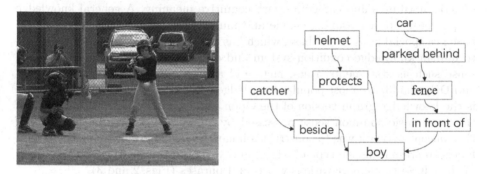

**Fig. 1.** Example of annotation from Visual Genome. A scene graph attempts to mark the objects in the image, including people and entities, as nodes of the graph (red), and then mark their relationships as edges between nodes (green). (Color figure online)

## 2 Related Works

### 2.1 Scene Graph Prediction

Scene graph [10,12,17,25] is a concept from computer vision. It is a visual understanding form of graph structure that expresses the high level of current scene, which is primarily used to describe the objects in current scene. This is meaningful to visual comprehension tasks, like image retrieval [18], image question answering [8], image or video captioning [7,28], and human-object relation detection [30] and image prediction [31].

In the early years, scene graph prediction [25] mainly used the message transmission of graph neural network, and iterated continuously to fuse the feature of adjacent nodes and edges. Yang et al. [27] purposed RPN and Attention Graph Convolution Network on basis. Zeller et al. [29] analysed hidden priori information in Action Genome. Then a method for deep matching of data sets is proposed, which has greatly improved the effect.

However, this goal-directed over-fitting of datasets does not necessarily predict a truly meaningful scene graph that conforms to human cognition. After Tang et al. [22] uses the model to predict, the part that directly maps from the object label to the relationship is reduced, so as to achieve the original intention of correcting the deviation of the dataset. Liang et al. [14] considered from Visual Genome, which used a simple network filtering and fitting relationship annotation to improve the quality of the dataset.

## 2.2 Knowledge Graph in Computer Vision

Knowledge Graph is a concept from natural language process, which is a kind of semantic network that composed of entities, relationships and attributes, usually used to represent the structure of facts [9]. Entities can be real-world abstract and figurative objects. Semantic descriptions of entities and their relationships include attributes and categories with cognitive meaning. A general knowledge graph consist of a reasoning engine and multi-layer database [9]. A knowledge base is a special kind of database, which has topological structure corresponding to human knowledge cognition system and contains different types of common sense such as statements, rules, facts and axioms. WordNet [15], Freebase [2] and DBpedia [3] are most popular knowledge bases these years. ConceptNet [21] is the knowledge graph version of the Open Mind strategy, a knowledge base of the most basic common sense possessed by humans. The original intention of the concept network was to construct a huge knowledge graph, using edges with labels (representing the type of edges) and weights (representing the credibility of the edges) to connect various words and phrases (Figs. 2 and 3).

## 3    Methodology

### 3.1    Problem Definition

Given an image $I$, the first step is using Faster R-CNN, which is a widely used target detection algorithm with excellent detection speed. In fact, Faster RCNN can be divided into four main contents: Conv layers, Region Proposal Networks, Roi Pooling and Classification. Faster RCNN can directly output bounding-box and tag of objects in the image:

$$[O_1, O_2, ..., O_N] = f_{fasterrcnn}(I) \tag{1}$$

where $f_{fasterrcnn}$ corresponds to the Faster R-CNN module, and $O_1, O_2, ..., O_N$ are $N$ object proposals in the image, which have a bounding box and a label. Formally, we can write:

$$O = (B, L) = [[x, y, w, h], l] \tag{2}$$

where $x$ and $y$ is the top-left coordinates of the bounding-box, $w$ and $h$ stand for width and height of the bounding-box. The next step is to apply $(B_m, L_m)$

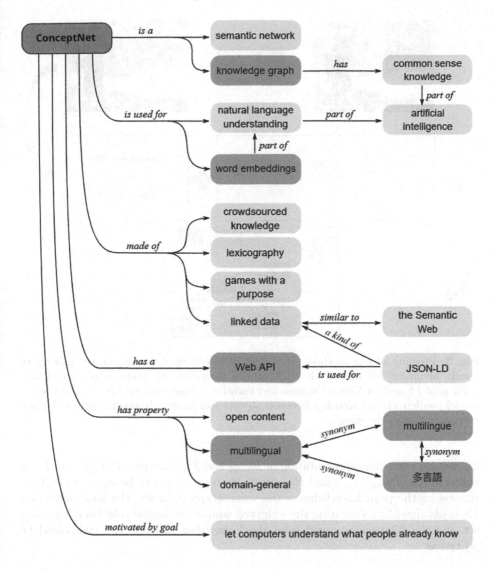

**Fig. 2.** Structure of ConceptNet.

and $(B_n, L_n)$ to predict the relation $R_{m,n}$ between object $O_m$ and $O_n$. To sum up, we could write this step as:

$$R_{m,n} = f((B_m, L_m), (B_n, L_n)) \tag{3}$$

In knowledge graph such as ConceptNet, the triples can be summarized as:

$$E_{tail} - E_{head} = R_{head \rightarrow tail} \tag{4}$$

where $E_{head}$ and $E_{tail}$ sign for the entity of head and tail. Vector differential between the two is $R$. Rather than high dimensional vector space or structured

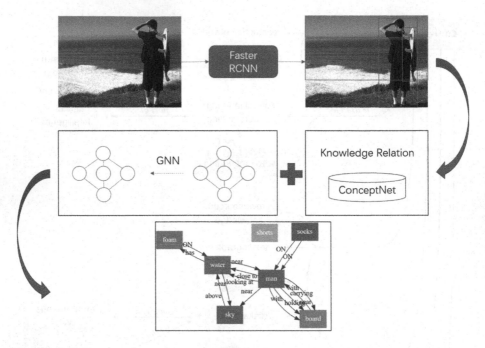

**Fig. 3.** Pipeline of our method. a) Faster RCNN is used for object recognition to obtain bounding-box and labels of objects in the scene. b) Train graph neural network model based on Visual Genome and knowledge base ConceptNet. c) The trained model predicts the relationship between objects and finally obtains the scene diagram corresponding to the image.

knowledge base, the representation of $E_{head}$ and $E_{tail}$ are equal to $L_m$ and $L_n$ in vision graph. $R_{head->tail}$ and $R_{m,n}$ can also be assumed to be equivalent. After possessing the prior knowledge of the scene graph data set, the final prediction $R*$ is obtained by calculating the weighted sum of the initial relation of the data set and the relation retrieved from the knowledge base. So the task could be writed as:

$$R*_{m,n} = f_{visualgenome}((B_m, L_m), (B_n, L_n)) + f_{conceptnet}(E_m, E_n) \qquad (5)$$

## 3.2  Data Source

ConceptNet is combined with word embedding (for example, word2vec) to facilitate word relevance evaluation (making the embedding of related words closer).

ConceptNet 5.5 was built from the following sources:

- Facts from Open Mind Common Sense (OMCS) and sister projects in other languages
- Use a custom parser ("Wikiparsec") to extract information from parsing Wiktionary in multiple languages

- Purposeful games designed to gather common sense
- Open multilingual WordNet [15], Linked data representation for WordNet and its parallel multilingual project
- JMDict, A Multilingual Japanese dictionary
- OpenCyc, the upper word hierarchy provided by Cyc, represents common sense knowledge of the logic of systematic predicates
- A subset of DBpedia [3], is the fact web extracted from the Wikipedia infobox.

Combining these resources, ConceptNet contains 21 million edges and more than 8 million nodes. Its English vocabulary contains approximately 1,500,000 nodes, and it contains 83 languages, each of which contains at least 10,000 nodes.

Wiktionary is the largest input source for ConceptNet. It provides 18.1 million edges and is responsible for its vast multilingual vocabulary. However, most of the features of ConceptNet come from OMCS and a variety of purposeful games that express many different relationships between terms, Examples include PartOf ("A wheel is part of a car") and UsedFor ("A car is used for driving").

### 3.3  Data Fusion

Given an image $I$, use Faster-RCNN for target recognition, abstract $N$ objects in current scene with bounding-box and label. Then pair them to $N * (n - 1)$ pairs. $(O_m, O_n)$ and $(O_n, O_m)$ have different meanings because of the difference between subject and object. These combinations are then entered into the extracted ConceptNet for knowledge search one by one. The retrieved relations are used to enhance or correct the original relations. Combined with the existing Visual Genome scene graph, a simple prediction model was used to output a new scene graph relationship based on knowledge base.

In Fig. 4, The input of the predictive model mainly consists of two parts. The first part comes from Visual Genome, including visual features of objects from bounding-box boxes $I_m, I_n$ and text features of object labels $V_m, V_n$. The second part comes from the knowledge base, which features the knowledge $K$ provided by ConceptNet. These features are transformed into high-dimensional vectors as the input of a multi-layer perceptron neural network, which outputs predictive relational label $R*$. The network is trained on new data sets annotated according to the rules described above.

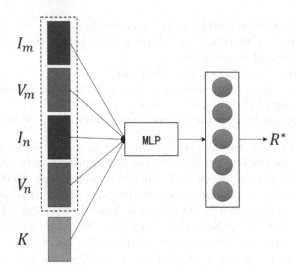

**Fig. 4.** Structure of visual and knowledge prediction model. $I_m$ and $I_n$ represent the image characteristics of subject and object. $V_m$ and $V_n$ represent the word vector of subject and object. $K$ represents the relation searched from ConceptNet.

## 4 Experiments

### 4.1 Data Preparation

Visual Genome data system consists of the following types of files:

1. 108k pictures. (5.4 Million Region Descriptions, 1.7 Million Visual Question Answers, 3.8 Million Object Instances, 2.8 Million Attributes, 2.3 Million Relationships)
2. image_data.json - hyperlink and size of every image.
3. scene_graphs.json - All descriptions of scene graph in every image.
4. region_descriptions.json - Semantic relationship description in every images.

Then we batch process the data with pictures as the unit, and mark scene graph annotations in scene_graphs.json into .json files. Convert the pictures one by one according to the number. We also implemented two meaningful visualization components: graphviz-based scene diagrams and matplotlib-based natural language annotations.

### 4.2 Scene Graph Generation

There are three main types of scene map prediction tasks at present. As shown in Table 1, Predicate Classification (PredCls)'s input are real labels and bounding-box. Scene Graph Classification (SGCls) using unlabeled ground reality bounding-box while Scene Graph Detection(SGDet) only take the image itself

**Table 1.** Scene graph tasks.

| Task | Recall | Input | Output |
|---|---|---|---|
| Predicate classification | PredCls | Image, Box, Object | Relation |
| Scene graph classification | SGCls | Image, Box | Object, Relation |
| Scene graph prediction/Generation | SGGen | Image | Box, Object, Relation |

as input. We have verified Visual Genome and our new version under the three types of recall: R@20, R@50, and R@100.

The results of Table 2 show that the effect of the model based on the new data set is improved to some extent, because the annotation combined with knowledge is more reasonable and more consistent with human cognition. However, because of change of both train and test set, the improvement effect is not obvious, and the advantages of the new dataset are not fully reflected in the scene graph prediction index. However, this should not be taken to mean that the real quality of scenario diagram predictions is not refined, and we will verify downstream tasks in future work.

**Table 2.** Result of scene graph prediction.

| Visual genome | | | | | | | | |
|---|---|---|---|---|---|---|---|---|
| SGGen | | | SGCls | | | PredCls | | |
| R@20 | R@50 | R@100 | R@20 | R@50 | R@100 | R@20 | R@50 | R@100 |
| 25.38 | 32.56 | 37.25 | 35.36 | 38.98 | 39.89 | 59.16 | 65.59 | 67.37 |
| Ours | | | | | | | | |
| SGGen | | | SGCls | | | PredCls | | |
| R@20 | R@50 | R@100 | R@20 | R@50 | R@100 | R@20 | R@50 | R@100 |
| 25.49 | 32.78 | 37.66 | 35.63 | 39.12 | 40.27 | 59.86 | 66.39 | 68.02 |

## 4.3 Environment

In scene graph prediction, our hardware environment is consist of NVIDIA GeForce GTX 2080. There are 8 steps in training, each step takes about 8 h.

## 5 Conclusion

In this paper, we propose a method to combine knowledge base information with scene graph data. The original data and the knowledge base data are sent in and out of an MLP network at the same time to generate new scene graph data. The prediction accuracy of scene graphs combined with knowledge has been improved to a certain extent. However, because this improvement in conformity with the cognitive significance is not directly presented in the data set fitting, in the future we plan to verify the effect of our method on more downstream tasks such as image captioning and visual question answer. On the other hand, we will also try to integrate more different types and domains of knowledge bases into the scene graph data, looking forward to further performance improvements.

**Acknowledgement.** This work was supported by Major Project of the New Generation of Artificial Intelligence (No. 2018AAA0102900).

# References

1. Auer, S., Bizer, C., Kobilarov, G., Lehmann, J., Cyganiak, R., Ives, Z.: DBpedia: a nucleus for a web of open data. In: Aberer, K., et al. (eds.) ASWC/ISWC -2007. LNCS, vol. 4825, pp. 722–735. Springer, Heidelberg (2007). https://doi.org/10. 1007/978-3-540-76298-0_52
2. Berant, J., Chou, A., Frostig, R., Liang, P.: Semantic parsing on freebase from question-answer pairs. In: Proceedings of the 2013 Conference on Empirical Methods in Natural Language Processing, pp. 1533–1544 (2013)
3. Bizer, C., et al.: DBpedia-a crystallization point for the web of data. J. Web Semant. **7**(3), 154–165 (2009)
4. Bollacker, K., Evans, C., Paritosh, P., Sturge, T., Taylor, J.: Freebase: a collaboratively created graph database for structuring human knowledge. In: Proceedings of the 2008 ACM SIGMOD International Conference on Management of Data, pp. 1247–1250 (2008)
5. Cohen, W.W., Sun, H., Hofer, R.A., Siegler, M.: Scalable neural methods for reasoning with a symbolic knowledge base. arXiv preprint arXiv:2002.06115 (2020)
6. Dhingra, B., Zaheer, M., Balachandran, V., Neubig, G., Salakhutdinov, R., Cohen, W.W.: Differentiable reasoning over a virtual knowledge base. arXiv preprint arXiv:2002.10640 (2020)
7. Gao, L., Wang, B., Wang, W.: Image captioning with scene-graph based semantic concepts. In: Proceedings of the 2018 10th ICML, pp. 225–229 (2018)
8. Goyal, Y., Khot, T., Summers-Stay, D., Batra, D., Parikh, D.: Making the V in VQA matter: elevating the role of image understanding in visual question answering. In: Proceedings of the IEEE Conference on Computer Vision and Pattern Recognition, pp. 6904–6913 (2017)
9. Ji, S., Pan, S., Cambria, E., Marttinen, P., Philip, S.Y.: A survey on knowledge graphs: representation, acquisition, and applications. IEEE Trans. Neural Netw. Learn. Syst. (2021)
10. Johnson, J., et al.: Image retrieval using scene graphs. In: Proceedings of the IEEE Conference on Computer Vision and Pattern Recognition, pp. 3668–3678 (2015)
11. Krishna, R., et al.: Visual genome: connecting language and vision using crowd-sourced dense image annotations. arXiv preprint arXiv:1602.07332 (2016)
12. Li, Z., Ding, X., Liu, T.: Constructing narrative event evolutionary graph for script event prediction. arXiv preprint arXiv:1805.05081 (2018)
13. Liang, X., Hu, Z., Zhang, H., Lin, L., Xing, E.P.: Symbolic graph reasoning meets convolutions. Adv. Neural. Inf. Process. Syst. **31**, 1853–1863 (2018)
14. Liang, Y., Bai, Y., Zhang, W., Qian, X., Zhu, L., Mei, T.: VRR-VG: refocusing visually-relevant relationships. In: Proceedings of the IEEE/CVF ICCV, pp. 10403–10412 (2019)

15. Miller, G.A.: Wordnet: a lexical database for English. Commun. ACM **38**(11), 39–41 (1995)
16. Narasimhan, M., Lazebnik, S., Schwing, A.G.: Out of the box: reasoning with graph convolution nets for factual visual question answering. arXiv preprint arXiv:1811.00538 (2018)
17. Pan, B., et al.: Spatio-temporal graph for video captioning with knowledge distillation. In: Proceedings of the IEEE/CVF Conference on Computer Vision and Pattern Recognition, pp. 10870–10879 (2020)
18. Qi, M., Wang, Y., Li, A.: Online cross-modal scene retrieval by binary representation and semantic graph. In: Proceedings of the 25th ACM International Conference on Multimedia, pp. 744–752 (2017)
19. Ren, H., Hu, W., Leskovec, J.: Query2box: reasoning over knowledge graphs in vector space using box embeddings. arXiv preprint arXiv:2002.05969 (2020)
20. Shih, K.J., Singh, S., Hoiem, D.: Where to look: focus regions for visual question answering. In: Proceedings of the 2019 CVPR, pp. 4613–4621 (2016)
21. Speer, R., Chin, J., Havasi, C.: Conceptnet 5.5: an open multilingual graph of general knowledge. In: Thirty-First AAAI Conference on Artificial Intelligence (2017)
22. Tang, K., Niu, Y., Huang, J., Shi, J., Zhang, H.: Unbiased scene graph generation from biased training. In: Proceedings of the IEEE/CVF CVPR, pp. 3716–3725 (2020)
23. Wan, H., Luo, Y., Peng, B., Zheng, W.-S.: Representation learning for scene graph completion via jointly structural and visual embedding. In: IJCAI, Stockholm, Sweden, pp. 949–956 (2018)
24. Wu, Z., Pan, S., Chen, F., Long, G., Zhang, C., Philip, S.Y.: A comprehensive survey on graph neural networks. IEEE Trans. Neural Netw. Learn. Syst. **32**(1), 4–24 (2020)
25. Xu, D., Zhu, Y., Choy, C.B., Fei-Fei, L.: Scene graph generation by iterative message passing. In: Proceedings of the IEEE Conference on Computer Vision and Pattern Recognition, pp. 5410–5419 (2017)
26. Xu, K., Li, J., Zhang, M., Du, S.S., Kawarabayashi, K.I., Jegelka, S.: What can neural networks reason about? arXiv preprint arXiv:1905.13211 (2019)
27. Yang, J., Lu, J., Lee, S., Batra, D., Parikh, D.: Graph R-CNN for scene graph generation. In: Proceedings of the ECCV, pp. 670–685 (2018)
28. You, Q., Jin, H., Wang, Z., Fang, C., Luo, J.: Image captioning with semantic attention. In: Proceedings of the IEEE Conference on Computer Vision and Pattern Recognition, pp. 4651–4659 (2016)
29. Zellers, R., Yatskar, M., Thomson, S., Choi, Y.: Neural motifs: scene graph parsing with global context. In: Proceedings of the CVPR, pp. 5831–5840 (2018)
30. Zhang, M., Liu, X., Liu, W., Zhou, A., Ma, H., Mei, T.: Multi-granularity reasoning for social relation recognition from images. In: 2019 IEEE International Conference on Multimedia and Expo (ICME), pp. 1618–1623. IEEE (2019)
31. Zhao, B., Meng, L., Yin, W., Sigal, L.: Image generation from layout. In: Proceedings of the 2019 CVPR, pp. 8584–8593 (2019)

# A Discussion of Data Sampling Strategies for Early Action Prediction

Xiaofa Liu[1], Xiaoli Liu[2], and Jianqin Yin[2(✉)]

[1] School of Modern Post (School of Automation), BUPT, Beijing 100876, China
[2] School of Artificial Intelligence, BUPT, Beijing 100876, China
jqyin@bupt.edu.cn

**Abstract.** Action prediction aims to predict an ongoing activity from an incomplete video, which is an important branch of human activity analysis with the important application in a number of fields, such as security surveillance, human-machine interaction, automatic driving, etc. Due to time continuity, there are a large number of redundant frames in video action sequences, which often brings challenges such as low computational efficiency and noise for action prediction. Most of the existing works levarage dense sampling or sparse sampling for processing video frames and characterize actions. On the one hand, the dense sample-based method often introduces redundant noise for predictions, easily causing confusing of the action semantics. On the other hand, although sparse sample-based method can alleviate the problem of redundant noise to a certain extent, it ignores the impact of sampling rate on action representation. In this paper, we combine the two-stream network framework and the teacher-student network framework to build an action prediction model, and discuss the influence of action representation under different sampling rates for partial or full videos. In this way, we can select more appropriate frames for video representation and thus achieve more accurate action prediction. The method proposed in this paper has achieved the current state-of-the-art performance on the standard dataset, i.e., UCF101, which verifies the effectiveness of our method.

**Keywords:** Action prediction · Teacher-student framework · Data sampling

## 1 Introduction

Early action prediction aims to recognize the semantic information of the action an ongoing video. With the development of deep network in image classification and video understanding, methods based deep learning has become the mainstream methods in the field of action prediction in recent years [1–7].

As shown in Fig. 1, it is a challenging task to accurately and quickly recognize the semantics of current actions from an incomplete video, especially when the actions are performed at very early stages. At the same time, the motion information contained in partial videos with different observation rates is also very different, even for the same action. How to extract robust features from these incomplete videos while reducing the

© Springer Nature Singapore Pte Ltd. 2022
F. Sun et al. (Eds.): ICCSIP 2021, CCIS 1515, pp. 306–314, 2022.
https://doi.org/10.1007/978-981-16-9247-5_24

influence of redundant noise caused by the temporal continuity of video frames is very important to the problem of video action prediction.

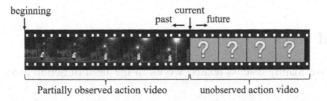

**Fig. 1.** Early action prediction, which predicts action label given a partially observed video.

Many works have been proposed for early action prediction. For instance, Kong et al. [1] extended marginalized stacked autoencoder (MSDA) to sequential data, which utilizes rich sequential context information to better capture the appearance evolution and temporal structure of the full action videos. To avoid the effect of noise caused by the background of the RGB frames as much as possible, Chen et al. [2] used the skeletal data to model and analyze actions. Liu et al. [3] also used the human skeletal sequence and introduced dilated convolutional network to model motion dynamics via a sliding window over the time axis. Gammulle et al. [5] proposed to use a GAN to generate future action descriptors and then classify them. Based on the idea of knowledge distillation, Wang et al. [6] used teacher network for action recognition to guide student network for prediction tasks, thus improving the accuracy of the prediction network. The above-mentioned works use sparse sampling strategies, i.e., a fixed number of frames are sampled for a video regardless of its length. This data sampling method alleviates the redundancy and noise problems caused by using all video frames to a certain extent, and fully utilizes the temporal information of the action sequence. But another problem is that different frame rates of sampling may affect the performance of early action prediction, which is ignored by the previous work. For example, key motion information is missing from few frames, while reductant noise from all video frames is disturbing the network.

In this work, we explore the impact of different data sampling rates on early human action prediction, aiming to provide a guiding significance for subsequent related works. Firstly, we sample different numbers of video frames for partial and full videos. Secondly, the pre-trained BN-Inception network on Kinetic-400 is used to extract features of partial and full videos, respectively. The teacher-student network framework proposed in [6] is used as the pipeline for early action prediction. We evaluate the performance on UCF101 dataset and obtain the current start-of-the-art (SOTA) performance, verifying the effectiveness of the proposed method. The experimental results show that it is unnecessary to use all frames for early action prediction, and different framerates have limited affect for predictions.

In summary, the main contributions of our work in this article are as follows:

- For data sampling, we discuss the efficiency of different data sampling rates on early action prediction, and provide a novel guidance significance for subsequent works.

- The proposed method is evaluated on the UCF101 dataset and achieves the state-of-the-art performance, verifying the influence of different sampling rates on early action prediction.

## 2 Related Work

In this part, we mainly discuss related works in the field of action prediction.

### 2.1 Action Recognition

Early action recognition mainly relied on manual features extracted from video (such as 3DHOG [8], SIFT [9], etc.) to model action appearance information and motion information. In recent years, as the progress of deep learning for a series of vision tasks, deep network has developed into the main methods for action recognition, which mainly includes Convolutional Neural Networks (CNN) [10–12] and Two-Stream networks [4, 13], which achieves state-of-the-art recognition results on UCF101[15], Kinetics [16] and other datasets. Tran et al. [17] proposed the deep 3-dimensional convolutional networks (C3D) model, which used 3D ConvNets to model the spatio-temporal and motion information of video actions. The author verified that the linear classifier with C3D feature achieves the best effect in various video analysis tasks. However, the increasing depth of the network is limited due to the expensive computational cost and memory requirements of 3D ConvNets. Qiu et al. [17] proposed to decouple the 3D convolution into a 2D convolution for spatial modeling and a 1D convolution for temporal modeling. Therefore, the author built a Pseudo-3D Residual Networks (P3D) network to simulate 3D ConvNets to learn the spatio-temporal representation of videos, and verified the effectiveness and generalization of its spatio-temporal representation on five commonly used datasets. Different from 2D CNN and 3D CNN, Simonyan et al. [14] proposed the two-stream network that uses two parallel networks. One of which uses still images as input to obtain the appearance information of video actions, and the other uses multi-frame dense optical flow as input to obtain the motion information of the video actions. The two kinds of information are merged at the end to realize the final action classification. In order to use the information of the entire video without being limited by the length of time, Wang et al. [12] proposed Temporal Segment Networks (TSN) for long-term modeling. Firstly, the full video was divided into K segments, then each segment passes through the two-stream network to obtain the action representation and category scores. Finally, the two networks are merged to achieve video-level prediction. Because the spatial background of the video and the occurrence of actions often do not change synchronously, Feichtenhofer et al. [19] proposed a SlowFast network, which also uses two paths. One pathway is designed to capture semantic information that can be given by images or a few frames, which operates at low frame rates and slow refreshing speed. The other pathway is responsible for capturing rapidly changing motion by operating at fast refreshing speed and high temporal resolution. The two pathways are fused by lateral connections.

## 2.2 Action Prediction

For video action prediction, many methods based on deep learning have emerged in recent years. Kong et al. [1] proposed a Deep Sequential Context Networks (DeepSCN) for early action prediction. The author believed that the confidence of prediction increases with the number of observed frames. In [1], the author directly used the C3D features [17] generated by video frames through a structured support vector machines (SVM) to capture the time structure of human behavior. Chen et al. [2] extracted human skeleton points under the framework of deep reinforcement learning to characterize the human body structure. Their proposed method activated the action-related parts of the feature to capture action-related information and suppress the influence of noise. To solve the different duration of different actions, Liu et.al. [3] proposed a time scale selection network Scale Selection Network (SSNet), which adaptively selects the number of frames for prediction according to the duration of the action. In this way, the author can suppress the influence of noise. To make full use of the global information of the video, Wang et al. [6] proposed to distill some useful knowledge from the teacher model to facilitate the student prediction model. Although the above works [1–6] did not use all frames of the video, they have not discussed and explored the impact of different number of the videos for early action prediction. Therefore, in this paper, we discuss the influence of different sampling rates on action representation in action prediction.

## 3 Methodology

In this section, we introduce in detail how our manuscript performs data sampling strategies and feature extraction. First, we introduce the overall framework of the network. Then we introduce the sampling method and feature extraction method in our framework.

As shown in Fig. 2, in our work, we divide a full video into $N(N = 10)$ sub-segments of equal length. The first $n$ sub-segments are defined as the progress level $n$ with an observation rate of $n/N$. We use $x_n$ to represent the feature of the sub-segment of the progress level $n$.

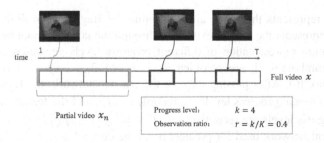

**Fig. 2. Definition of some concepts.** Taking the progress level of 4 as an example, this figure shows the division of video, the definition of the progress level, and the representation of features in motion prediction.

## 3.1  Overview

In this work, we use the teacher-student network framework proposed in [6] as the basic model. The overall network framework is shown in Fig. 3.

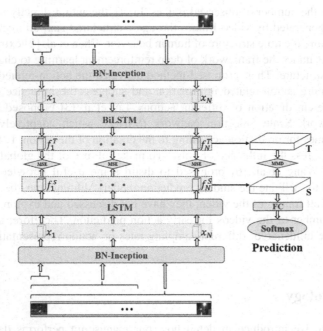

**Fig. 3.  Overall framework.** The overall structure of the network based on the framework of the teacher-student network in [6].

Given the currently observed partial action video, our goal is to predict the action semantic label $y$ of the video.

The teacher network can be defined as:

$$F_T = T(C(X)) \tag{1}$$

Where $X$ represents the frame after sampling the fragments of different progress levels. $C(\cdot)$ represents the feature extraction through the convolutional neural network [20]. The feature representation of different progress levels generated after the convolutional neural network are recorded as $x_i, i = (1, 2, \ldots, N)$. $T(\cdot)$ represents the teacher network [6]. After passing through the teacher network, the feature representation under different progress levels are recorded as $f_i^T$, and the feature representation under all progress levels are recorded as $T, T = \{f_1^T, f_2^T, \ldots, f_N^T\}$.

The student network used for prediction can be defined as:

$$F_S = S(C(X)) \tag{2}$$

$$y = V(L(F_S)) \tag{3}$$

Where $X$ and $C(\cdot)$ indicate the same as the teacher network in formula (1). $S(\cdot)$ represents the student network [6]. After passing through the student network, the feature representation under different progress levels are recorded as $f_i^S$, and the feature representation under all progress levels are recorded as $S, S = \{f_1^S, f_2^S, \ldots, f_N^S\}$. The feature $F_S$ obtained by the student network passes through the linear layer $L(\cdot)$ and the final Softmax layer $V(\cdot)$ to finally obtain the predicted label.

The teacher-student network is the same as [6]. In the following sections we will further describe the feature extraction and data sampling strategies.

### 3.2 Feature Processing

To explore the number of frames of partial and full videos for early action prediction, we represent the human action under different sampling rates for early action prediction. Our detailed implementation for feature extraction is as follows. Firstly, we extract the dense optical flow characterization $A$ from the full video. Then we use a sliding window with a size of 5 and a stride of 1 to sample a number of frames on $A$, and the sampled frames are used as the input of BN-Inception [20] for feature extraction. Finally, we obtain the feature representation of the full video, denoting by B.

### 3.3 Data Sampling Strategies

To obtain the feature representation of different progress levels for prediction, we obtain the feature representation for different partial videos from the feature representation $B$ of the full video. Finally, we use different sampling rates to sample the features of the partial videos or full videos, and the final features are obtained by mean pooling operation, denoting by $x_i, i = (1, 2, \ldots, N)$, where $x_i$ is a one-dimensional feature vector with a size of 1024.

## 4 Experiments

We test our proposed method on a benchmark dataset, i.e., UCF-101[15]. Below, we will analyze the experimental details and results.

### 4.1 Implementation Details

We use the same experimental settings as in [6] on the RGB dataset UCF101. To generate feature representation for teacher and student network learning, we use the pre-trained BN-Inception network on Kinetic-400 [16] to extract the features of the partial video and the full video, respectively. For the partial video and the full video, we use a stride length of 5 to sample L frames, ranging from 10 to 60, to form the video representation.

## 4.2    Experiments on the UCF-101 Dataset

The UCF101 dataset [15] contains 101 categories and a total of 13,320 videos. The video duration is about a few seconds of length.

The detailed experimental results are shown in Table 1. Compared with the baselines that use all frames, the accuracy of our method is the best regardless of the sampling rates. The experimental results show that it is unnecessary to use all frames for early action recognition. Proves that using all frames may cause redundant noise for accurate prediction. As shown in Table 1, the performance of different sampling rates is similar. And the sampling rate ranging from 15 to 20 works the best. When the number of sampling frames continues to increase, it will introduce more irrelevant information for the action, which easily cause misclassification, especially using all video frames for the prediction.

**Table 1.** Prediction results (%) on the UCF101 set.

| Observation ratio | 10% | 30% | 50% | 70% | 100% | Mean |
|---|---|---|---|---|---|---|
| Baseline | 75.34 | 90.28 | 93.26 | 93.92 | 94.87 | 91.04 |
| L = 10 | 86.39 | 91.25 | 93.45 | 94.38 | 95.30 | 92.68 |
| L = 15 | 86.42 | 91.61 | 93.56 | 94.79 | 95.36 | 92.88 |
| L = 20 | 86.37 | 91.39 | 93.59 | 94.41 | 95.25 | 92.75 |
| L = 25 | 86.26 | 91.25 | 93.59 | 94.49 | 95.38 | 92.79 |
| L = 30 | 86.12 | 91.50 | 93.40 | 94.43 | 95.22 | 92.67 |
| L = 35 | 86.34 | 91.55 | 93.51 | 94.68 | 95.46 | 92.79 |
| L = 40 | 86.04 | 91.47 | 93.35 | 94.46 | 95.33 | 92.68 |
| L = 45 | 86.50 | 91.31 | 93.56 | 94.51 | 95.19 | 92.68 |
| L = 50 | 86.58 | 91.44 | 93.35 | 94.51 | 95.46 | 92.75 |
| L = 55 | 86.18 | 91.44 | 93.37 | 94.51 | 95.46 | 92.75 |
| L = 60 | 86.01 | 91.44 | 93.43 | 94.35 | 95.33 | 92.67 |

## 5    Conclusion

In this paper we discuss the redundancy of videos in the field of video action prediction, and verified the influence of action representation under different sampling rates on the accuracy of action prediction. We have empirically shown that it is unnecessary to use all frames of the video for early action prediction, and different sampling rates of the videos show similar performance, but 15–20 frames are the more proper sampling rates. We hope that the discussion in this paper will provide guiding significance for future work in the field of video action prediction. How to make full use of the limited information while reducing the impact of video redundancy and noise has further research significance for action representation and predictive performance.

# 6 Future Work

If necessary, to obtain detailed experimental support, we plan to use more backbones for verification on more datasets.

**Acknowledgement.** This work was supported partly by the National Natural Science Foundation of China (Grant No. 62173045, 61673192), and partly by the Fundamental Research Funds for the Central Universities (Grant No. 2020XD-A04-2).

# References

1. Kong, Y., Tao, Z., Fu, Y.: Deep sequential context networks for action prediction, In: CVPR, 2017, pp. 1473–1481 (2017)
2. Chen, L., Lu, J., Song, Z., Zhou, J.: Part-activated deep reinforcement learning for action prediction. In: Ferrari, V., Hebert, M., Sminchisescu, C., Weiss, Y. (eds.) ECCV 2018. LNCS, vol. 11207, pp. 435–451. Springer, Cham (2018). https://doi.org/10.1007/978-3-030-01219-9_26
3. Liu, J., Shahroudy, A., Wang, G., Duan, L.Y., Kot, A.C.: SSNet: scale selection network for online 3D action prediction, In: CVPR, pp. 8349–8358 (2018)
4. Zhao, H., Wildes, R.P.: Spatiotemporal feature residual propagation for action prediction, In: ICCV, pp. 7003–7012 (2019)
5. Gammulle, H., Denman, S., Sridharan, S., Fookes, C.: Predicting the future: a jointly learnt model for action anticipation, In: ICCV, pp. 5562–5571 (2019)
6. Wang, X., Hu, J. F., Lai, J. H., Zhang, J., Zheng, W.S.: Progressive teacher-student learning for early action prediction, In: CVPR, pp. 3556–3565 (2019)
7. Scarafoni, D., Essa, I., Ploetz, T.: PLAN-B: predicting likely alternative next best sequences for action prediction, arXiv preprint arXiv:2103.15987 (2021)
8. Alexander K., Marcin M., Cordelia S.: A spatio-temporal descriptor based on 3d-gradients, In: British Machine Vision Conference, pp. 275–281 (2008)
9. Scovanner, P., Ali, S., Shah, M.: A 3-dimensional sift descriptor and its application to action recognition, In: ACM International Conference on Multimedia, pp. 357–360 (2007)
10. Carreira, J., Zisserman, A.: Quo vadis, action recognition? a new model and the kinetics dataset, In: CVPR, pp. 4724–4733 (2017)
11. Hara, K., Kataoka, H., Satoh, Y.: Learning spatio-temporal features with 3d residual networks for action recognition, In: ICCV, p. 4 (2017)
12. Wang, L., et al.: Temporal segment networks: towards good practices for deep action recognition. In: Leibe, B., Matas, J., Sebe, N., Welling, M. (eds.) ECCV 2016. LNCS, vol. 9912, pp. 20–36. Springer, Cham (2016). https://doi.org/10.1007/978-3-319-46484-8_2
13. Zhu, Y., Lan, Z., Newsam, S., Hauptmann, A.: Hidden two-stream convolutional networks for action recognition. In: Jawahar, C.V., Li, H., Mori, G., Schindler, K. (eds.) ACCV 2018. LNCS, vol. 11363, pp. 363–378. Springer, Cham (2019). https://doi.org/10.1007/978-3-030-20893-6_23
14. Simonyan, K., Zisserman, A.: Two-stream convolutional networks for action recognition in videos, In: NIPS, pp. 568–576 (2014)
15. Soomro, K., Zamir, A.R., Shah, M.: Ucf101: a dataset of 101 human actions classes from videos in the wild, CoRR (2012). abs/1212.0402
16. Kay, W., et al.: The kinetics human action video dataset, CoRR (2017). arXiv preprint arXiv: 1705.06950

17. Tran, D., Bourdev, L., Fergus, R., Torresani, L., Paluri, M.: Learning spatiotemporal features with 3d convolutional networks, In: ICCV, pp. 4489–4497 (2015)
18. Qiu, Z., Yao, T., Mei, T.: Learning spatio-temporal representation with pseudo-3d residual networks, In: ICCV, pp. 5533–5541 (2017)
19. Feichtenhofer, C., Fan, H., Malik, J., et al.: SlowFast networks for video recognition, In: ICCV, pp. 6202–6211 (2019)
20. Ioffe, S., Szegedy, C.: Batch normalization: accelerating deep network training by reducing internal covariate shift. In: International Conference on Machine Learning. PMLR, pp. 448–456 (2015)

# Sensor Fusion Based Weighted Geometric Distance Data Association Method for 3D Multi-object Tracking

Zhen Tan[1,3]($\boxtimes$), Han Li[2], and Yang Yu[3]

[1] Technische Universität München, München, Germany
[2] LiangDao AI, Beijing, China
[3] College of Intelligence Science and Technology, National University of Defense Technology, Changsha 410073, China

**Abstract.** In the field of autonomous driving, 3D multi-object tracking (MOT) plays an important role as one of the key tasks in the overall perception system, which ensures efficient and safe vehicle navigation and motion planning. Most of the existing MOT methods are based on detection, i.e. tracking by detection (TBD), and use only a single depth sensor such as LiDAR (light and detection ranging) to detect and track the target. However, the very sparse point cloud at long distances leads to the inability of these methods to generate very accurate detection results, which subsequently affects the tracking results. Therefore, in this paper, we propose a 3D MOT method based on sensor fusion by using the detection results from both LiDAR and cameras. First, we combine and match the results from the 2D and 3D detection. Second, the target state is predicted using the Kalman Filter. Next, to associate the prediction and detection results, we design a data association method based on weighted-geometric distance. Finally, the matched detection and prediction results are updated by the Kalman Filter. Through quantitative evaluation and test validation, it is proved that this sensor fusion-based 3D MOT method we propose indeed outperforms most of the 3D MOT algorithms at this stage.

**Keywords:** 3D MOT · Data association · Kalman Filter · Sensor fusion · Weighted-geometric distance

## 1 Introduction

In the field of autonomous driving, 3D MOT plays an important role as one of the key tasks in the overall perception system, which ensures efficient and safe vehicle navigation and motion planning [1]. As autonomous driving technology becomes more popular and plays an increasingly important role in urban smart

This work was supported by the National Key Research and Development Program (2018YFB1305101).

© Springer Nature Singapore Pte Ltd. 2022
F. Sun et al. (Eds.): ICCSIP 2021, CCIS 1515, pp. 315–327, 2022.
https://doi.org/10.1007/978-981-16-9247-5_25

transportation systems, safety has become a primary concern. By using target detection and multi-target tracking to better understand the vehicle's surroundings, and to understand and predict the trajectory of surrounding targets, the vehicle can be driven more safely [2].

The autonomous driving perception system is often divided into two important tasks: detection and tracking [3]. There have been some recent end-to-end frameworks [4] that handle both parts simultaneously, but the performance and stability of these approaches are still under discussion. At this stage, detection-based tracking remains the main method of 3D MOT, and due to the great improvement of 3D object detection algorithms such as PointRCNN [6], PointRGNN [7], and CenterPoint [4] in recent years, the tracking results have also improved tremendously. However, the accuracy of these results is still limited by the characteristics of the sensor itself. In 3D MOT, we often use LiDAR (light detection and ranging) [37] as our sensor to obtain data. However, the point cloud obtained by LiDAR is often very sparse at long distances (>80 m) due to the limitation of the line bundles and distance, so the dimension or label of the object is often difficult to be accurately detected and located. On the other hand, image-based detection can obtain high-quality detection results, even at long distances, due to the very high pixel resolution of the camera. In addition, the 2D detector at this stage can solve the problem of occlusion well. Therefore, it is of great significance to study 3D MOT methods based on sensor fusion [8].

At this stage in 3D MOT, there are various challenges [9] such as the problem of occlusion between targets and the problem of losing targets at long distances. These problems can be solved to some extent by the multi-sensor fusion scheme proposed above [10]. In addition, a reasonable motion model design [11] is also a good solution. Another challenge in 3D MOT is how to associate data between the predicted states and the observed data; that is, to find the correspondence between the observed and the predicted state quantities by establishing the cost function between them. Most of the 3D MOT frameworks tend to use the intersection over union (IoU) between 3D boxes for data association [12], which is indeed a straightforward and effective approach. However, by doing so, it is easy to ignore the connection between other features, and furthermore, some scenarios may occur where there are no overlapping regions. Therefore, some approaches have also been proposed for data association based on Euclidean distance [14] or Mahalanobis distance [13], combined with the Hungarian algorithm [15] or the greedy algorithm [16].

In this paper, we propose a 3D MOT method based on sensor fusion and weighted geometric distance data association (WGDMOT). Specifically, we fuse the 3D MOT detection results of LiDAR and cameras, and use the weighted geometric distance as the data association method. The method takes EagerMOT [17] as the baseline, first projecting the 3D detection onto the 2D image plane using perspective projection, then matching and fusing the 2D and 3D detection using 2D IoU to find both the well-matched 3D detection and the unmatched 2D detection. Lastly, the previous trajectory is used to get the predicted 3D object using the Kalman Filter on the current trajectory. The predicted results and the matched detection results are matched in 3D space using our proposed data association method based on the weighted geometric feature cost distance. Then, the unsuccessful predictions from the first step become the input to the second step for the second data association in the 2D image plane. Finally, the state is updated based on the data association results.

We evaluated our proposed tracker based on the NuScenes [18] tracking dataset. Our proposed method has significantly improved the performance based on the baseline EagerMOT [17], especially in tracking pedestrians. The main contributions of our paper are as follows:

1) we design a new cost distance based on weighted geometric features for data association, which is able to exploit the relationship between different geometric features and thus improve the accuracy of data association.
2) we performed a comparison with baseline EagerMOT [17] and had a significant improvement in pedestrian tracking, and ablation experiments were performed on the weights of the proposed cost distance.

## 2   Related Work

### 2.1   2D MOT

At this stage, most of the research work in 2D MOT still concentrates on detected-based tracking, where the two most important aspects are actually detection and data association methods. The idea of some methods is to find a better detector, and based on such detectors like the RCNN family [20–22], YOLO [23,24], SSD [25], and RetinaNet [26], it becomes clear that it is possible to outperform many previous 2D MOT methods without making very large changes. Other methods focus on designing a robust cost distance for data association, such as [27,28] that use the Hungarian for data association, and [16] that uses the greedy algorithm.

With the further development of deep learning research, researchers have also started to focus not only on a single detection, and there are some approaches that propose end-to-end [19,29] methods to train detection and tracking as a whole and then output the results. Nevertheless, the robustness and generalization are still under discussion.

### 2.2   3D MOT

Many of the first 3D MOT methods are based on traditional clustering detection methods [30], such as the use of downsampling, ground point segmentation, and non-ground point clustering. However, these methods are very susceptible to the impact of noise, as they rely on the calculation of the bounding box process to get detection results. Moreover, the accuracy and estimation of the dimensions of the bounding box are very true values with a relatively large error. With the emergence of end-to-end detection methods [7,31] and the continuous improvement of their effectiveness, the detection component of 3D MOT has been gradually replaced by the end-to-end method. Recently, [32] proposed a very simple 3D MOT framework, AB3DMOT [32], which uses 3D IoU as the cost distance for data association and is able to achieve very high FPS. Nevertheless, this method is very dependent on the results of the 3D detector and is vulnerable to occlusion. Subsequently, [33] proposed using Mahalanobis distance instead of 3D IoU as a cost distance based on AB3DMOT [32], thus solving the case that there is no overlapping region. This is a relatively big improvement on AB3DMOT [32], but it is still limited by the 3D detector. Since there are always relatively large limitations in single sensor detection, [17] proposed fusion methods for LiDAR and cameras, respectively, proposing to associate the predicted trajectory and fused detection results by a scaled distance. However, both Mahalanobis distance and scaled distance do not consider the weighted relationship between different variables. Therefore, we propose a new cost distance that takes into account the weighted relationship between different geometric features and can effectively improve the tracking performance of small objects.

## 3   Method

We propose the WGFMOT method based on the recent EagerMOT [17] architecture. Our method first fuses the detection results of 2D and 3D detection and then performs two-stage data association based on the fusion results and the results predicted by the Kalman filter [34]. The first stage of data association is performed on 3D space, where we propose using the weighted-geometry feature as cost distance for data association, and the second stage is performed on a 2D image plane, using projection transformation and 2D IoU for secondary matching and lastly, the tracking trajectory is updated. The method is able to take full advantage of the detection results from the camera and LiDAR: (1) the camera can provide comparative 2D detection results, thus reducing the chance of false detection in 3D detection; (2) the LiDAR can provide more accurate 3D detection object position information; (3) using our proposed weighted-geometry feature distance, we can consider the weighted relationship between different geometric features to achieve better tracking performance.

### 3.1   2D and 3D Object Detection

In this module, we primarily use the results of different 2D and 3D detectors as input for the detection part of our method. In our experiments, we use the NuScenes [18] dataset as experimental data, and our detection results are based on the output of the 3D deep learning detector, CenterPoint [4], and the 2D deep learning detector, MMdetection [5].

### 3.2   Fusion

Fusion is generally divided into pre-fusion and late-fusion, where pre-fusion is to use a combination of different sensor data as input in order to output a

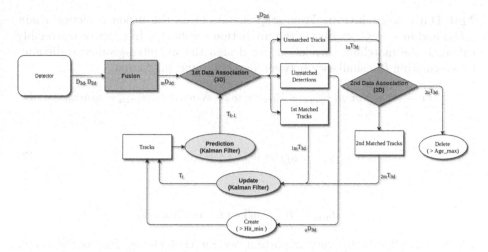

**Fig. 1.** Architecture overview. We considered the results obtained by detector as observations. In each frame, fusion - state prediction - 1st data association - 2nd data association - update is performed. In the 1st data association stage, we propose to use weighted-geometric distance to calculate the similarity of prediction and detection.

detection result. In our proposed method, we use the late-fusion method, which fuses the results of different detections instead. This fusion method is simpler and more effective than pre-fusion, and does not require additional transformation of the original data. As shown in Fig. 1, based on the detection results $D_{2d}$ and $D_{3d}$ from Section A, we first project the 3D bounding box onto the 2D image plane. We then compute the 2D IoU for matching and output the matched result $_mD_{3d}$ to the first data association section, while the unmatched detection $_uD_{2d}$ is output to the second data association section. Doing so partially solves the problem of FP (False Positive), because the 3D detector is more prone to false detection than the 2D detector.

### 3.3   State Initialization and Prediction

MOT is essentially a multivariate state estimation problem, i.e., the prediction of the state of the object at the present stage by using the previous object state and motion model. To simplify our model, we propose using the constant velocity model (CA) and the Kalman Filter (KF) [34] to predict the state $S_t$ $(x_i, y_i, z_i, l_i, w_i, h_i, theta_i, vx_i, vy_i, vz_i)$ of the 3D object in our method. Where t denotes the $t_{th}$ frame, i denotes the $i_{th}$ object of this frame.

### 3.4   Data Association

In our proposed method, the data association is divided into two stages. The first stage is in 3D space, where the cost is calculated using our proposed weighted-geometric distance, and the second stage is in the 2D image plane, where we use the 2D IoU with the Hungarian algorithm [15].

**\*1st Data Association.** From step B, we obtain the fusion detection result $_mD_{3d}$ and in step C, we obtain the prediction result $P_{3d}$. In order to reasonably calculate the matching correlation, we design the weighted-geometric distance for calculating the similarity between detection and prediction:

$$H1 = w1 * Norm(P_{pred} - P_{det}) + w2 * Norm(dims_{pred} - dims_{det}) \quad (1)$$

$$\theta_{diff} = |\theta_{pred} - \theta_{det}| \quad (2)$$

$$cost_{dist} = H1 + w3 * (1 - cos(\theta_{diff})) \quad (3)$$

where $(w1, w2, w3)$ are very important weight coefficients, $P_{det}$ is the center coordinates $(xi, yi, zi)$ of the 3D bounding box of the detection part, $P_{pred}$ is the center coordinates of the prediction, and $dims_{det}$ $(l, w, h)$ is the dimensional information of the 3D bounding box of the detection part, $dims_{pred}$ denotes the dimensional information of the predicted part, and $(\theta_{pred}, \theta_{det})$ denotes the yaw of the predicted and detected emergent. $Norm()$ denotes normalization.

The scaling distance proposed by EagerMOT [17] considers dimensions and coordinates to have the same weight (importance), but in fact, different attributes are different for tracking, so the dimensions and coordinates should not bear equal weight. Our proposed cost distance adjusts their importance by adjusting the size of $w1, w2$ and $w3$, which leads to a significant improvement in the object tracking of small targets. Our cost distance also outperforms the 3D IoU-based and Euclidean distance-based methods. By doing this step, we get the detection and prediction results on association $(D_{3d}^i, T_{3d}^j)$, which are input to the update stage, and the prediction results without association $_uT_{3d}$, which are input to the second stage of data association.

**2nd Data Association.** The unsuccessful matched $D_{2d}$ is further matched with the $_uT_{3d}$ output in the first stage, which is performed by projecting the $_uT_{3d}$ onto the 2D image plane using a simple 2D IoU and Hungarian algorithm. This process is mainly used to perform additional association for the FN (False Negative) case. This step can solve the missed cases caused by partial occlusion and further increase the stability of tracking. The matching prediction $_{2m}T_{3d}$ is output to the update stage, while the remaining predictions that cannot be associated are sent to the Birth and Death stage for judgment.

## 3.5  State Update

Given the matched pairs of detections and predictions driven from data association, we can use the Kalman Filter to update the trajectories in this frame. The main updated state quantities are [x, y, z, theta, l, w, h, vx, vy, vz].

## 3.6  Birth and Death

The Birth and Death mechanism is mainly used to deal with the generation and deletion of the trajectory. $_uD_{3d}$, which failed to be associated in the first data association stage, uses $Hit_{min}$ to determine whether to generate a new trajectory; while $_{2u}T_{3d}$, which failed to be associated in both association stages, uses $Age_{max}$ to determine whether to delete the trajectory. This means that we have not been able to find the corresponding object from the detection in consecutive $Age_{max}$ frames, possibly because the object has disappeared from the field of view, or is completely obscured.

# 4  Experimental Evaluation

## 4.1  Dataset

We evaluate our method based on NuScenes. NuScenes contains 1000 scenes, each 20 s long, and is fully annotated using 3D bounding boxes with 23 classes and 8 attributes [18]. The dataset uses a frequency 2 Hz to sample key frames (images, LiDAR) and annotate each target in each key frame using semantic categories, attributes (visibility, activity, and pose), and rectangles (containing x, y, z, width, length, height, and yaw) for each of the 23 object classes.

## 4.2  Evaluation Metrics

In this paper, we follow the NuScenes Tracking Challenge [18] and evaluate our method by the following indicators:

- AMOTA (Average Multi-Object Tracking Accuracy) [32]: main evaluation metric. Average over the MOTA [35] metric (see below) at different recall thresholds
- AMOTP (Average Multi-Object Tracking Precision) [32]
- MOTA (multi object tracking accuracy) [35]: This measure combines three error sources: false positives, missed targets and identity switches.
- MOTP (multi object tracking precision) [35]: The misalignment between the annotated and the predicted bounding boxes.
- FP (number of false positives): The total number of false positives.
- FN (number of false negatives): The total number of false negatives (missed targets).
- IDS (number of identity switches): The total number of identity switches.

## 4.3  Quantitative and Ablation Experiments

In our experiments, we first compared our proposed method with the baseline EagerMOT [17] on the NuScenes validation dataset. We used 3D detections provided by CenterPoint [4] and 2D detections provided by Cascade R-CNN [5,36]. The tracking results are shown in Table 1.

**Table 1.** Performance of our method with EagerMOT [17] on pedestrians and cars on NuScenes dataset

|     | Method | AMOTA↑ | AMOTP↑ | MOTA↑ | MOTP↑ | FP↓ | FN↓ | IDs↓ |
|-----|--------|--------|--------|-------|-------|-----|-----|------|
| Car | EagerMOT [17] | **0.778** | 0.444 | 0.694 | **0.272** | 418 | **366** | 51 |
|     | Ours | 0.777 | **0.486** | **0.706** | 0.268 | **335** | 434 | **33** |
| Ped | EagerMOT [17] | 0.797 | **0.371** | 0.689 | 0.28 | 195 | 242 | 20 |
|     | Ours | **0.814** | 0.329 | **0.752** | **0.305** | **118** | **233** | **14** |

The arrows in the table indicate how good or bad the metric is for Tracking. An upward-pointing arrow indicates a higher value for a better result, and vice versa. We compare the results in our experiments mainly for pedestrian and car tracking, as these two categories appear much more frequently in the data than the others. By comparing the sensor fusion framework, EagerMOT [17], In terms of car tracking, our proposed method was able to effectively reduce the number of ID switches (from 51 to 33), the number of False Positive cases was also greatly reduced, and all other metrics (except False Negative) were very close to the performance of EagerMOT, with the only problem being the increase in the number of FNs (Missed). In terms of pedestrian tracking, our method has a significant advantage, with all metrics (except AMOTP) improving, with MOTA improving by more than 0.05 and FP reducing even by almost 40% (from 195 to 118).

It can be found that our proposed method is able to reduce the ID switches and FP cases well, and more importantly, since we use different weights to measure the attributes of the target in the data association, our algorithm is more able to take into account the small changes of the object. Therefore, we can also see that the performance in small target tracking (e.g. pedestrian) is much better than the baseline EagerMOT [17].

**Table 2.** Ablation experiments for weighted geometric distance weighting coefficients on pedestrian tracking

| Weights (w1, w2, w3) | AMOTA↑ | MOTA↑ | MOTP↑ | FP↓ | FN↓ | IDs↓ |
|----------------------|--------|-------|-------|-----|-----|------|
| 1.0, 1.0, 0 | 0.819 | 0.714 | 0.233 | 168 | 240 | 13 |
| 1.0, 1.0, 0 + angular | 0.813 | 0.731 | 0.259 | 186 | 189 | 21 |
| 0.75, 1.0, 0 | 0.814 | 0.752 | 0.305 | 118 | 233 | 14 |
| 0.75, 1.0, 0 + angular | 0.814 | 0.75 | 0.304 | 121 | 233 | 14 |
| 0.75, 0.75, 0 | 0.821 | 0.762 | 0.259 | 104 | 230 | 16 |
| 0.5, 1.0, 0 | 0.824 | 0.745 | 0.305 | 93 | 269 | 13 |
| 0.5, 1.0, 0.25 | 0.818 | 0.737 | 0.328 | 119 | 247 | 20 |
| 0.5, 1.0, 0.5 | 0.826 | 0.721 | 0.281 | 169 | 233 | 8 |

**Ablation Test on Different Weight.** We have verified through the above experimental results that our proposed method of measuring different categories of geometric information with different weights can improve the performance on small target tracking, and we want to figure out how the proportion and size of the weights affects the result. Therefore, we test the effect of different weights on pedestrian tracking by ablation test. The test results are shown in Table 2.

**Table 3.** Comparison of different data association methods on NuScenes dataset

|                    | AMOTA↑ | Recall↑ | MOTA↑ | MOTP↑ | IDs↓ |
|--------------------|--------|---------|-------|-------|------|
| 3D IoU             | 0.472  | 0.644   | 0.424 | 0.302 | 84   |
| Euclidean distance | 0.716  | 0.754   | 0.658 | **0.265** | **60** |
| Ours               | **0.725** | **0.766** | **0.667** | 0.276 | 61   |

According to the weighted geometric distance equation we proposed in Sect. 3.4, it can be seen from Eq. (1) that the weights of $w1$ and $w2$ are used to balance the point center distance and the dimension distance. And it can be found in Eq. (3) that the magnitude of the $w3$ value is used to control the degree of influence of the angle in the data association.

Based on our experiments in Table 2, It can be found that the different weights of different geometric categories do affect the tracking performance. Keeping the weight $w2$(dims) constant, decreasing the weight of $w1$(position) will not affect the tracking results for cars, but can improve the tracking results for pedestrians. The influence of $w3$ in small target tracking is relatively small, probably because the randomness of motion of small targets (especially pedestrians) is very large, so it leads to a lower accuracy of angle estimation, so if we take the angle into account in our model, we must first evaluate the accuracy of target angle estimation. In addition, we tried to take into account the angular as a variable into Kalman Filter, however, the results showed that angular has a small and even negative effect on the improvement of tracking performance.

Furthermore, we compared different data association methods, and the comparison results (for all categories) are shown in Table 3, which shows that our association method is indeed more stable. In addition, we also visualized the tracking results to visually compare the tracking performance of several data association methods. From Fig. 2, we can find that our method can overcome the shortcomings of other methods to some extent.

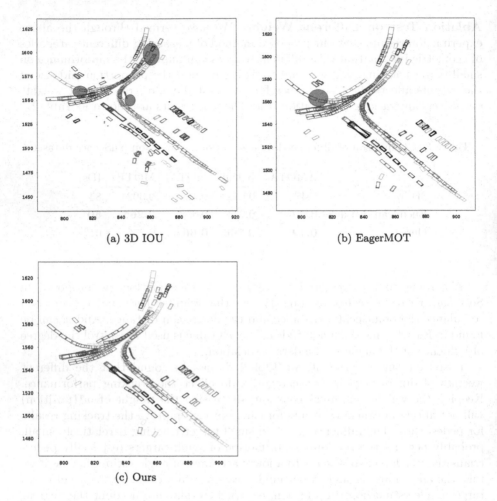

(a) 3D IOU

(b) EagerMOT

(c) Ours

**Fig. 2.** Using different data association methods, each color indicates an ID, In 3d IOU based data association method, the same object have many different colors, indicating poor tracking, and compared with the EagerMOT, there is a missing issue in the red circle while our method track well in this case (red circle: bad tracking cases). (Color figure online)

## 5    Conclusion

In this paper, we propose a WGDMOT method that combines the detection advantages of different sensors and uses weighted-geometric distance as the approach to data association. Based on the NuScenes dataset for testing, we can indeed find a significant improvement in the effectiveness of this method compared to 3D IOU-based and Euclidean distance-based data associations. It is also more robust compared with the baseline EagerMOT [17] and performs better than the baseline in pedestrian tracking. However, the appearance feature is not taken into account in this experiment, and future research will consider more dimensional information to improve the performance of tracking.

**Acknowledgement.** This work was supported by the National Key Research and Development Program (2018YFB1305101).

# References

1. Romeas, T., Guldner, A., Faubert, J.: 3D-multiple object tracking training task improves passing decision-making accuracy in soccer players. Psychol. Sport Exerc. **22**, 1–9 (2016)
2. Menouar, H., Guvenc, I., Akkaya, K., Uluagac, A.S., Kadri, A., Tuncer, A.: UAV-enabled intelligent transportation systems for the smart city: applications and challenges. IEEE Commun. Mag. **55**(3), 22–28 (2017)
3. Shi, W., Alawieh, M.B., Li, X., Yu, H.: Algorithm and hardware implementation for visual perception system in autonomous vehicle: a survey. Integration **59**, 148–156 (2017)
4. Yin, T., Zhou, X., Krahenbuhl, P.: Center-based 3D object detection and tracking. In: Proceedings of the IEEE/CVF Conference on Computer Vision and Pattern Recognition, pp. 11784–11793 (2021)
5. Chen, K., et al.: MMDetection: open mmlab detection toolbox and benchmark. arXiv preprint arXiv:1906.07155 (2019)
6. Shi, S., Wang, X., Li, H.: Pointrcnn: 3D object proposal generation and detection from point cloud. In: Proceedings of the IEEE/CVF Conference on Computer Vision and Pattern Recognition, pp. 770–779 (2019)
7. Shi, W., Rajkumar, R.: Point-GNN: graph neural network for 3D object detection in a point cloud. In: Proceedings of the IEEE/CVF Conference on Computer Vision and Pattern Recognition, pp. 1711–1719 (2020)
8. Kocić, J., Jovičić, N., Drndarević, V.: Sensors and sensor fusion in autonomous vehicles. In: 2018 26th Telecommunications Forum (TELFOR), pp. 420–425. IEEE, November 2018
9. Luo, W., Xing, J., Milan, A., Zhang, X., Liu, W., Kim, T.K.: Multiple object tracking: a literature review. Artif. Intell. **293**, 103448 (2020)
10. Burlet, J., Dalla Fontana, M.: Robust and efficient multi-object detection and tracking for vehicle perception systems using radar and camera sensor fusion. In: IET and ITS Conference on Road Transport Information and Control (RTIC 2012), pp. 1–6. IET, September 2012
11. Naidu, V.P.S., Gopalaratnam, G., Shanthakumar, N.: Three model IMM-EKF for tracking targets executing evasive maneuvers. In: 45th AIAA Aerospace Sciences Meeting and Exhibit, p. 1204 (2007)
12. Weng, X., Wang, Y., Man, Y., Kitani, K.: Graph Neural Networks for 3D Multi-Object Tracking. arXiv preprint arXiv:2008.09506 (2020)
13. Mark, H.L., Tunnell, D.: Qualitative near-infrared reflectance analysis using Mahalanobis distances. Anal. Chem. **57**(7), 1449–1456 (1985)
14. Danielsson, P.E.: Euclidean distance mapping. Comput. Graphics Image Process. **14**(3), 227–248 (1980)
15. Mills-Tettey, G.A., Stentz, A., Dias, M.B.: The dynamic hungarian algorithm for the assignment problem with changing costs. Robotics Institute, Pittsburgh, PA, Technical report, CMU-RI-TR-07-27 (2007)

16. Pirsiavash, H., Ramanan, D., Fowlkes, C.C.: Globally-optimal greedy algorithms for tracking a variable number of objects. In: CVPR 2011, pp. 1201–1208. IEEE, June 2011
17. Kim, A., Ošep, A., Leal-Taixé, L.: EagerMOT: 3D Multi-Object Tracking via Sensor Fusion. arXiv preprint arXiv:2104.14682 (2021)
18. Caesar, H., et al.: nuScenes: a multimodal dataset for autonomous driving. In: Proceedings of the IEEE/CVF Conference on Computer Vision and Pattern Recognition, pp. 11621–11631 (2020)
19. Zhang, Z., Cheng, D., Zhu, X., Lin, S., Dai, J.: Integrated object detection and tracking with tracklet-conditioned detection. arXiv preprint arXiv:1811.11167 (2018)
20. Girshick, R.: Fast R-CNN. In: Proceedings of the IEEE International Conference on Computer Vision, pp. 1440–1448 (2015)
21. Girshick, R., Donahue, J., Darrell, T., Malik, J.: Rich feature hierarchies for accurate object detection and semantic segmentation. In: Proceedings of the IEEE Conference on Computer Vision and Pattern Recognition, pp. 580–587 (2014)
22. He, K., Gkioxari, G., Dollár, P., Girshick, R.: Mask R-CNN. In: Proceedings of the IEEE International Conference on Computer Vision, pp. 2961–2969 (2017)
23. Redmon, J., Farhadi, A.: YOLO9000: better, faster, stronger. In: Proceedings of the IEEE Conference on Computer Vision and Pattern Recognition, pp. 7263–7271 (2017)
24. Tian, Y., Yang, G., Wang, Z., Wang, H., Li, E., Liang, Z.: Apple detection during different growth stages in orchards using the improved YOLO-V3 model. Comput. Electron. Agric. **157**, 417–426 (2019)
25. Liu, W., et al.: SSD: single shot MultiBox detector. In: Leibe, B., Matas, J., Sebe, N., Welling, M. (eds.) ECCV 2016. LNCS, vol. 9905, pp. 21–37. Springer, Cham (2016). https://doi.org/10.1007/978-3-319-46448-0_2
26. Wang, Y., Wang, C., Zhang, H., Dong, Y., Wei, S.: Automatic ship detection based on RetinaNet using multi-resolution Gaofen-3 imagery. Remote Sens. **11**(5), 531 (2019)
27. Sahbani, B., Adiprawita, W.: Kalman filter and iterative-hungarian algorithm implementation for low complexity point tracking as part of fast multiple object tracking system. In: 2016 6th International Conference on System Engineering and Technology (ICSET), pp. 109–115. IEEE, October 2016
28. Qin, Z., Shelton, C.R.: Improving multi-target tracking via social grouping. In: 2012 IEEE Conference on Computer Vision and Pattern Recognition, pp. 1972–1978. IEEE, June 2012
29. Peng, J., et al.: Chained-tracker: chaining paired attentive regression results for end-to-end joint multiple-object detection and tracking. In: Vedaldi, A., Bischof, H., Brox, T., Frahm, J.-M. (eds.) ECCV 2020. LNCS, vol. 12349, pp. 145–161. Springer, Cham (2020). https://doi.org/10.1007/978-3-030-58548-8_9
30. Ćesić, J., Marković, I., Jurić-Kavelj, S., Petrović, I.: Detection and tracking of dynamic objects using 3D laser range sensor on a mobile platform. In: 2014 11th International Conference on Informatics in Control, Automation and Robotics (ICINCO), vol. 2, pp. 110–119. IEEE, September 2014
31. Shi, S., Wang, X., Li, H.P.: 3D object proposal generation and detection from point cloud. In: Proceedings of the IEEE Conference on Computer Vision and Pattern Recognition, Long Beach, CA, USA, pp. 16–20, June 2019
32. Weng, X., Wang, J., Held, D., Kitani, K.: 3D multi-object tracking: a baseline and new evaluation metrics. In: 2020 IEEE/RSJ International Conference on Intelligent Robots and Systems (IROS), pp. 10359–10366. IEEE, October 2020

33. Chiu, H.K., Prioletti, A., Li, J., Bohg, J.: Probabilistic 3D multi-object tracking for autonomous driving. arXiv preprint arXiv:2001.05673 (2020)
34. Welch, G., Bishop, G.: An introduction to the Kalman filter (1995)
35. Bernardin, K., Elbs, A., Stiefelhagen, R.: Multiple object tracking performance metrics and evaluation in a smart room environment. In: Sixth IEEE International Workshop on Visual Surveillance, in conjunction with ECCV, vol. 90, no. 91. Citeseer, May 2006
36. Cai, Z., Vasconcelos, N.: Cascade R-CNN: delving into high quality object detection. In: Proceedings of the IEEE Conference on Computer Vision and Pattern Recognition, pp. 6154–6162 (2018)
37. Reutebuch, S.E., Andersen, H.E., McGaughey, R.J.: Light detection and ranging (LIDAR): an emerging tool for multiple resource inventory. J. Forest. **103**(6), 286–292 (2005)

# Multiple Granularities with Gradual Transition Network for Person Re-identification

Jialin Lu, Qingjie Zhao$^{(\boxtimes)}$, and Lei Wang

Beijing Institute of Technology, Beijing 100081, China
zhaoqj@bit.edu.cn

**Abstract.** Person re-identification (Re-ID) is a challenging task in computer vision, which aims at retrieving a target pedestrian from a gallery of person images captured from various cameras. Recent part-based methods, which employ horizontal splitting to integrate global and local information as final person representation, are not efficient enough in cases where the discriminative information near the splitting boundary is missing or incomplete due to partition. To address this issue, we proposed a novel method called Multiple Granularities with Gradual Transition Network (MGGTN) to fully mine fine-grained features at each part level and make the person representation more discriminative and robust. Our model introduces multi-branch network architecture to extract features with multiple granularities and uses a gradual transition strategy to obtain partial regions instead of easily partitioning the feature map into several stripes. Experimental results demonstrate the effectiveness of our method for Re-ID task. Especially, we achieve the new state-of-the-art results on both DukeMTMC-ReID and CUHK03 datasets and obtain the top rank1 result on Market1501 dataset.

**Keywords:** Person re-identification · Multi-branch network · Different granularities feature learning

## 1 Introduction

Person re-identification (Re-ID) is regarded as a sub-task of target retrieval, with the purpose of re-identifying a given person from lots of pedestrian images captured by multiple cameras at different moments and places, which is shown in Fig. 1. It is very challenging due to varying human poses and camera views [16], as well as complex environmental conditions like background clutter [26], occlusion [12,15,22,32], and camera types, etc. To this end, most of the existing methods concentrate on learning robust features to these large variations, which contains global features [19,41,43], local features [7,29], and other auxiliary features learned from some auxiliary information, such as semantic attributes [20,27,34], domain information [31,37], and GAN generation [24,41,42], etc. And there are

© Springer Nature Singapore Pte Ltd. 2022
F. Sun et al. (Eds.): ICCSIP 2021, CCIS 1515, pp. 328–342, 2022.
https://doi.org/10.1007/978-981-16-9247-5_26

Query Image                          Gallery Images

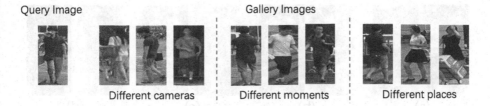

Different cameras  ┊  Different moments  ┊  Different places

**Fig. 1.** Some examples of images based on Market1501 dataset. They are the query image and the gallery images from different cameras, moments, and places.

also some methods [3,5,6,9,14,21] prone to designing metric losses for computing the similarities of person, which can enable the network to learn features useful for similarity metrics [13].

Previous Re-ID methods commonly using deep networks to extract a global feature of a human image. The global feature can account for some between-class changes, like image styles, pedestrian spatial location variations, and the whole appearance changes. However, it ignores some discriminative detail information (e.g., bags, hats), interference information (e.g., complex background, occlusion), and intra-class differences (e.g., camera view variations, human poses). In contrast, the local feature can handle this limitation.

Motivated by such observations, recent part-based methods and attention mechanisms are proposed to combine local features with global features, which show the effectiveness of enhancing the representation ability of person features, and they have made remarkable advances. Attention mechanism methods [25,26,30,36] learns features from salient regions of interest (ROI), which are the high activations in feature maps, so it can reduce the interference of clutter background information. For part-based methods, some part located approaches based on human body semantic information (e.g., head, arm, leg) are employed to Re-ID tasks, such as pose estimator [1], region proposal method, etc. These external strategies contribute to matching the misaligned human parts but are not robust when body parts are missing or the poses are erroneously estimated. Moreover, it can't be overlooked that such non-end-to-end methods [7,35,39] increase the complexity of feature learning. Compared with localizing body regions, some other studies [11,29] obtain parts by equally slicing a person image into several horizontal stripes instead of specific semantic parts, which not only are easy but also achieve better performance, for the network can focus on the fine-grained and discriminative feature of the small fixed region. However, the humans are not well aligned caused by pose and camera view variations, thus the discriminative information is not always contained in the pre-defined partition stripes. If the important features are located in the area near the split boundary, they can be lost or incomplete due to division. Several illustration examples are shown in Fig. 2.

In this paper, we propose Multiple Granularities with Gradual Transition Network (MGGTN) to effectively cover more discriminative information and reduce the negative influences caused by horizontal splitting. The backbone of

**Fig. 2.** The illustration of the proposed problem: (a) (b) Different person with similar appearance, (c) (d) The same person but looking different. The examples show that some discriminative features are broken by horizontally partitioning.

MGGTN is ResNet-50 [13] and it contains one global branch for the coarsest feature and two local branches for finer information. In local branches, the number of stripes is different for various fine level information and the local feature is extracted independently from the stripe parts. In particular, the stripe parts are divided by a gradual transition strategy, which introduces transition parts between each pair of adjacent parts.

The contributions of this paper can be summarized as follows: 1) The gradual transition strategy effectively improves the robustness and discrimination of the person representation. 2) With the purpose of maximally taking advantage of classification loss and metric loss, we combine them together and assign appropriate weights to balance their roles in training. 3) Extensive experiments show that our method not only exceeds the advanced methods on both DukeMTMC-ReID [41] and CUHK03 [17] datasets but also outperforms the best rank1 on Market1501 [40] dataset.

## 2    Related Work

In this section, we review some of the most representative studies related to our work in recent years as below.

**Part-Based Algorithms.** Before 2017, many researchers have done a lot of work in human pose estimation and landmark detection, which achieve great performance. Then these methods are applied in Re-ID tasks to locate human body parts. Zhao et al. [39] and Su et al. [7] focus on dividing multiple part areas of the human body by using pose estimation algorithms to locate the pedestrian key points, which can address the pose variance problem. Compare with [7,39], Wei et al. [35] use the same tool to extract local features with a fewer number of body parts, which further improves Re-ID performance. However, the gap between Re-ID datasets and pose estimation datasets can introduce possible noises when directly utilizing the pose estimation model in Re-ID tasks. To achieve end-to-end models, some methods [2,4,18] introduce an attention mechanism, which allows the network to decide where to focus by itself. Zhang et al. [38] propose alignment matching of part features, which achieves an impressive improvement in Re-ID work. Sun et al. [29] introduce a Part-based Convolutional Baseline (PCB), which easily divides the feature map into six horizontal stripe areas of the same size and uses a refined part pooling to reassign the outliers. PCB not only effectively improves the classification accuracy but also provides a strong baseline for Re-ID tasks. After that, Wang et al. [33] design an MGN network, a further development based on PCB, which designs a multi-branch network and combines multi-level features. HPM [11] explores the networks referring pyramid idea to get many stripe-based features and they are integrated with the local feature. To address the confusion that different pedestrians may have similar features in corresponding parts, Park et al. [23] propose a network based on PCB to learn the relation information between each stripe and the rest of them.

**Loss Functions.** Loss functions are used to measure the gap between ground truth and predictive labels and supervise the feature learning process of the deep network. In Re-ID works, the most commonly used loss functions can be divided into two categories: classification losses and metric losses. Previous Re-ID works either used classification losses or metric losses individually. Recently, many works have combined them together in training. They share the same network and promote each other, which achieves a great improvement in performance.

Generally speaking, softmax loss is the most common classification loss for Re-ID task because it can be easily combined with other losses. For metric losses, typically, triplet loss is to reduce the distance of intra-class and enlarge the inter distance. But it is possible to limit the generalization ability when the triple samples randomly picked are easy to discriminate for the network. To address this issue, Hermans et al. [14] proposed a modified triplet loss changing the random triples to hard triples, which pushes the network to explore hard positive pairs (images with the same label but large distance) and hard negative pairs (images with different identities but looking similarly). And there are also some other variants [5,6] based on triplet loss proposed to improve the traditional triplet loss in metric learning. Metric losses help the network better understand what is the same person and improve the discrimination capacity.

## 3  Proposed Method

In this section, we propose MGGTN model, which can extract discriminative and robust features and address the problem of losing detail information near the split boundary when dividing local regions. The framework of our model is shown in Fig. 3.

Randomly select $P \times K$ pedestrian images from given training datasets as the input of the model, where the P is the total amount of person ID in one batch and the K is the number of images for each ID. Here we use ResNet-50 as the backbone with some modifications following the previous work [29]. In detail, we remove the average pooling layer and the fully connected layer. In our model, there are 3 branches after conv4_1, one global branch with $12 \times 4 \times 2048$

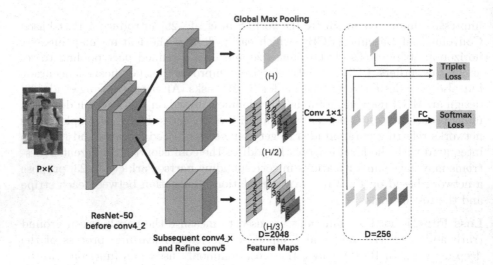

**Fig. 3.** Overview of our Multiple Granularities with Gradual Transition Network. There are 3 branches following the ResNet-50 backbone after conv4_1. We assume that the output feature maps in two local branches are divided into 6 stripes in order to show the moving stride between parts. The global and local features are extracted from these parts independently. For testing, we concatenate all the 12 features together to be the final person representation. For a better layout, we show the three-dimensional feature vectors as two-dimensional slices. Notice that we use non-share $1 \times 1$ convolution layers for reduction and non-share fully connected layers.

output feature map and two local branches with $24 \times 8 \times 2048$ output feature maps, for the stride of convolution in conv5_1 is set to 1 in two local branches, which are referring the method in [33]. The branches are all the subsequences of ResNet-50 after conv4_1. Then, we use a gradual transition module to obtain four and five local horizontal parts respectively from the output feature map in each local branch. For each local part and global region, a global max pooling operation is used to extract features, following a $1 \times 1$ convolution layer with batch normalization and Relu to reduce the feature dimension from 2048 to 256. After that, the triplet loss [14] is employed to three 256-dim global features. And all the features reduced to 256-dim, including 3 global features and 9 local ones, are fed into 12 corresponding classifiers using a fully connected layer to predict person ID, which is used to compute softmax loss. During testing, we concatenate all the 12 features together as the final pedestrian feature representation.

## 3.1   Multiple Granularities Architecture

In Re-ID tasks, the multi-branch deep network architecture is commonly used to extract pedestrian features. Considering [33], whose network structure shows superior performance in multiple granularity feature learning, we employ the similar basic framework of [33] on our model.

Specifically, a larger feature map provides more detail information. Thus, increasing the size of the feature map of local branches can help the network extract more fine-grained features. On the other hand, the local regions with smaller sizes can focus on more fine-grained features. Therefore, the partitions in two local branches are also with various scales to push different local branches concentrating on learning different granularities. Besides, each local branch also takes the global feature into account, because the global region in different branches may focus on different coarse-grained information. It should be noted that we employ the three global features after reduction on softmax loss rather than the features before reduction, which is different from [33].

## 3.2 Gradual Transition Module

Due to the misalignment problem in Re-ID, the regions near the pre-defined split boundary are very likely to contain some discriminative information. We argue that there is some useful information at split boundary lost or broken due to partition. To cope with this issue, we propose a gradual transition method to divide each feature map, from which more discriminative features can be covered. It can promote the discrimination of learned features by adding transition parts between two adjacent horizontal regions. More introduction will be given in the following.

Each local branch contains two kinds of local parts called the non-transition part and transition part marked bold in Table 1. In MGGTN, there is one global branch $b_1$ and two local branches $b_2$, $b_3$. The feature maps are divided into 2, 3 parts in each local branch. So if the size of the output feature map in $b_2$, $b_3$ is $H \times W \times C$, the height of part in each local branch is $h_2(=\frac{1}{2}H)$, $h_3(=\frac{1}{3}H)$, respectively. We define the moving stride of transition parts between each pair of adjacent non-transition parts as L. It is set to $4(=\frac{1}{6}H)$ in our method, which is the greatest common divisor of $h_2$ and $h_3$.

Therefore, there are two transition parts in the second branch and one transition part between each pair of adjacent non-transition parts in the third branch. Finally, we can obtain four and five parts in the second and third branches, respectively. More details of each part are shown in Table 1.

**Table 1.** Comparison of the settings in each branch. Part No. denotes the number of parts in each branch. G denotes the global part and L denotes the local part. Part size denotes the scale of the global and local feature maps. Location in Map shows that where each local part is in the original global feature map on H. dimension.

| Branch | Part No. | Part Size(H×W) | Location in Map |
|---|---|---|---|
| Branch 1 (Global) | 1(G) | 12 × 4 | 1–12 |
| Branch 2 (Local) | 1(G)+4(L) | 24 × 8, 12 × 8 (×4) | 1–24, 1–12, **5–16**, **9–20**, 13–24 |
| Branch 3 (Local) | 1(G)+5(L) | 24 × 8, 8 × 8 (×5) | 1–24, 1–8, **5–12**, 9–16, **13–20**, 17–24 |

### 3.3  Loss Function

Person re-identification is usually regarded as a multi-classification task. Therefore, we use softmax loss to predict the label of each person. We use a set of fully connected layers with non-shared weights as the classifier. Each feature vector $f_i$ of the image is fed into the corresponding classifier, and following by a softmax function to predict its label $\hat{y}_i$. We employ it to all the learned feature vectors after $1 \times 1$ convolution reduction and then calculate the Cross Entropy loss individually. The loss for each image is the average of these losses instead of the sum. Therefore, the softmax loss function can be formulated as:

$$L_{softmax} = \sum_{n=1}^{N} \frac{1}{P} \sum_{i=1}^{P} CE\left(\hat{y}_i^{\,n}, y^n\right) \tag{1}$$

where N is the total number of images in a batch, P denotes the number of learned feature vectors for each image, CE is the Cross Entropy loss, $\hat{y}_i^{\,n}$ is the predictive result of feature vector $f_i$ on image $n$, $y^n$ denotes the real label of the image $n$.

In order to improve the discrimination capacity of the network, we employ the batch-hard triplet loss [14] on three global features after reduction, which can reduce the distance of intra-class and enlarge the inter distance between classes. During training, we use the average loss of the three triplet losses as the final loss of the input image. The batch-hard triplet loss is defined as:

$$L_{triplet} = \sum_{p=1}^{P} \sum_{k=1}^{K} \left[ \alpha + \max_{j=1...K} d\left(f_k^p, f_j^p\right) - \min_{\substack{n=1...P \\ m=1...K \\ n \neq p}} d\left(f_k^p, f_m^n\right) \right]_+ \tag{2}$$

where P denotes the number of person identities in a batch, and K means there are K images from each identification label in the batch, so the batch size is $P \times K$. $[x]_+$ is $\max(x, 0)$. $\left(f_k^p, f_j^p, f_m^n\right)$ is a triplet of samples. $d\left(f_k^p, f_j^p\right)$ and $d\left(f_k^p, f_m^n\right)$ denote the distance between positive sample pairs and that between negative sample pairs, respectively. $\alpha$ is a margin hyper-parameter to control the distances between the same identity and different identity sample pairs in feature space.

Finally, to learn discriminative feature representations, we define the final loss of our model as the sum of softmax loss and batch-hard triplet loss, and they are balanced by two parameters $\lambda$ and $\mu$ to maximally taking advantage of classification loss and metric loss. The final loss function can be written as:

$$L = \lambda L_{softmax} + \mu L_{triplet} \tag{3}$$

## 4  Experiments

### 4.1  Implementation

**Experimental Details.** We refer to some works [11,29] and resize all the input images into $384 \times 128$ in order to capture enough information. The backbone of our network is ResNet50 pre-trained on ImageNet [8]. The difference is that we remove the fully connected layer and average pooling layer in the last of ResNet50 and set the stride of the convolution layer in conv5_1 block from 2 to 1 for the two local branches. For the training datasets augment, we deploy random horizontal flipping, normalization, and random erasing. To train our model, we set the mini-batch size to 16 for each iteration, which is sampled by randomly selected P identities and K images for each identity, and the P and K are both set to 4. The margin parameter for batch-hard triplet loss is 1.2. For the learning rate, we set the initial learning rate to 0.0002, and it decays to 2e-5 and 2e-6 after 320 and 380 epochs. 500 epochs are used for the training process. The optimizer we used for updating parameters is Adam with the weight decay factor of 0.0005. During the evaluation, all the features after reduction are concatenated together as the final feature representation. The features of the original image and horizontally flipped image are both normalized and added up as the query and gallery features. All experiments follow the same settings as above.

**Protocols.** To evaluate the performance of our proposed method and compare the results with the existing advanced Re-ID methods, we adopt the Cumulative Matching Characteristics (CMC) at rank 1 and mean Average Precision (mAP) on 3 datasets. And all of our experiment results reported are under a single-query setting.

### 4.2  Datasets

**Market1501.** It consists of 32668 images of 1501 different persons captured by six cameras in different views and places with bounding boxes annotated by the pedestrian detector of Deformable Part Model (DPM) [10]. And it is divided into the training set including 12936 person images of 751 individuals and the testing set including 750 individuals with 3368 images for query and 19732 images for the gallery.

**DukeMTMC-ReID.** It is a subset of DukeMTMC dataset for Re-ID task. It offers 36411 images of 1812 identities from eight cameras in total. The training set and testing set contain 702 identities respectively, which are sampled randomly from the overall images. Specifically, there are 16522 images for training, and for testing, it provides 2228 query images and 17661 gallery ones.

**CUHK03.** It contains 14097 images of 1467 identities from five camera groups and provides two types of annotating bounding boxes: Manually labeled and detected by the DPM detector [10]. More concretely, it offers 7368 training images, 1400 query images, and 5328 gallery ones for the labeled dataset, while the detected dataset includes 7365 person images for training, 1400 images for query, and 5332 ones for the gallery. Besides, there are 767 identities for the training set and the other 700 identities for the testing, which following the new protocol [8].

**Table 2.** Comparison with state-of-the-art methods on Market1501, DukeMTMC-ReID, CUHK03 datasets in a single query setting. "∗", "Δ", "o", "†" denotes the methods related to stripes, attention, pose or body semantics, other approaches, respectively.

| Method | Market1501 | | DukeMTMC-ReID | | CUHK03 | | | |
|--------|------------|------|---------------|------|--------|------|--------|------|
| | | | | | Labeled | | Detected | |
| | rank1 | mAP | rank1 | mAP | rank1 | mAP | rank1 | mAP |
| PN-GAN [24] (ECCV 18)o† | 89.43 | 72.58 | 73.58 | 53.20 | - | - | 79.76 | - |
| HA-CNN [18] (CVPR 18)Δ | 91.20 | 75.70 | 80.50 | 63.80 | 44.40 | 41.00 | 41.70 | 38.60 |
| PCB [29] (ECCV 18)∗ | 92.30 | 77.40 | 81.80 | 66.10 | - | - | 61.30 | 54.20 |
| VPM [28] (CVPR 19)† | 93.00 | 80.80 | 83.60 | 72.60 | - | - | - | - |
| PCB+RPP [29] (ECCV 18)∗ | 93.80 | 81.60 | 83.80 | 69.20 | - | - | 63.70 | 57.50 |
| HPM [11] (AAAI 19)∗ | 94.20 | 82.70 | 86.60 | 74.30 | - | - | 63.90 | 57.50 |
| DG-Net [42] (CVPR 19)† | 94.80 | 86.00 | 86.60 | 74.80 | - | - | - | - |
| MGN [33] (ACM MM 18)∗ | 95.70 | 86.90 | 88.70 | 78.40 | 68.00 | 67.40 | 66.80 | 66.00 |
| ABD-Net [4] (ICCV 19)Δ | 95.60 | 88.28 | 89.00 | 78.59 | - | - | - | - |
| Relation [23] (AAAI 20)∗ | 95.20 | 88.90 | 89.70 | 78.60 | 77.90 | 75.60 | 74.40 | 69.60 |
| **MGGTN (Ours)** | **95.90** | 88.14 | **90.73** | **80.59** | **79.53** | **77.56** | **75.46** | **72.72** |

## 4.3  Comparison with State-of-the-Art Methods

In this section, we compare the proposed method MGGTN with current state-of-the-art methods on the three datasets, including Market1501, DukeMTMC-ReID, and CUHK03 to show the robustness and competitive performance of our method. It should be noted that we do not conduct any re-ranking algorithm like [43]. Results are shown in Table 2.

**Market1501.** The table shows that our method achieves the best rank1 accuracy of 95.90% and the competitive mAP performance of 88.14%, which both significantly surpass the closest competitor PCB, MGN, and HPM. The MGN methods achieve the best rank1 result of 95.70%, while our MGGTN exceeds that by 0.2% in rank1 accuracy. Compared with all the method results reported in the table, our model has a considerable competitive advantage on mAP, which surpasses all the methods except Relation but it is similar to that of the Relation method.

**DukeMTMC-ReID.** This dataset is challenging for the reason that the pedestrian images are captured from eight different cameras and there are dramatical variances of bounding box size among multiple camera views. However, we do not utilize any post-processing and we can see that our method still achieves the best scores on both rank1 and mAP, which are the most outstanding results on this dataset. Meanwhile, the results also demonstrate the robustness of our method on human pose and camera view variances. Among all the compared methods, although the result of the Relation method is the closest to our model, our MGGTN exceeds the performances of Relation by 1.03% on rank1 and 1.99% on mAP. Note that our MGGTN is the first method achieving above 80% on mAP and 90% on rank1.

**CUHK03.** Compared with the above two datasets, CUHK03 is a more challenging dataset because it provides fewer images for training and more camera view variations. From the table, we can see that all methods work not well on both two annotations. However, MGGTN achieves the most outstanding performance on the two datasets with different annotations. Furthermore, our method improves Relation/HPM/MGN of 3.12%/15.22%/6.72% on mAP and 1.06%/11.56%/8.66% on rank1 in detected datasets, which are clear gaps. Therefore, it can be concluded that our method has obvious superiority in challenging issues.

## 4.4    Ablation Studies

To further investigate the effectiveness of every component and setting of the proposed method MGGTN, we conduct several ablation studies with different settings on Market1501 dataset, which contain different numbers of network branches, with and without considering transition parts, different pooling strategies, and the different weight ratio of two losses. The experiment results are shown in Table 3 and Table 4. Notice that the rest unrelated settings in each comparative experiment are the same as the default ones in MGGTN.

**Multiple Branches for Multiple Granularities.** We use fewer branches and split levels to achieve better performance. We conduct 4 comparative experiments to verify the effectiveness on multiple granularities of the three-branch architecture by removing or adding branches, which can be observed in rows 1, 2, 3, and 4 of Table 3. We can find that when we remove branch 3, the mAP and rank1 drop obviously from 87.37% and 95.34% to 84.33% and 94.06%. One reason is that using only one level to split the global feature maps is hard to cope with the unaligned outliers, which is similar to PCB [29]. However, learning two different level partial features from coarse to fine can enhance the robust ability of the final feature. The other reason is that two different partitions with overlap can provide some correlation information between them helping to learn different discriminative features. In addition, when the network only preserves the global branch, the mAP and rank1 drop more, which are from 84.33% and 94.06% to 68.24% and 87.68%. It powerfully demonstrates the effectiveness of multiple granularities for learning discriminative feature representation. We also compare the model by adding branch 4. We can find that adding branch 4 does not bring significant improvement, and a bottleneck begins to appear in the boost of performance. Meanwhile, the global information of a person may be underestimated if too many local parts, and if the local branches are not enough, it is difficult to extract multiple and discriminative local features. Therefore, the three-branch is optimal for our method.

**Effectiveness of Transition Method.** We argue that there may be some discriminative information lost or broken at the split boundary when dividing the feature maps and introducing the gradual transition method can address this issue, from which more discriminative features can be learned. In order to verify the effectiveness of the transition method, we add two group comparative

**Table 3.** Ablation study with different settings of sub-models and pooling strategies on Market1501 datasets. Here w/o denotes the model is without the setting and w/denotes the model is with the setting. B1, B2, B3, B4 refers to the first, second third and fourth branch, respectively. The pooling here refers to global pooling.

| Model | rank1 | mAP |
| --- | --- | --- |
| B1(branch) | 87.68 | 68.24 |
| B1+B2 w/o transition parts | 94.06 | 84.33 |
| B1+B2+B3 w/o transition parts | 95.34 | 87.37 |
| B1+B2+B3+B4 w/o transition parts | 95.37 | 87.99 |
| B1+B2 w/transition parts | 95.07 | 86.14 |
| B1+B2+B3 w/transition parts | **95.90** | **88.14** |
| Avg pool | 95.04 | 86.93 |
| Avg pool + Max pool | 95.22 | 88.05 |
| Max pool | **95.90** | **88.14** |

**Table 4.** Results with different weight parameters of the two losses on Market1501 dataset. Here the $\lambda$ denotes the weight for softmax loss and $\mu$ for triplet loss in formula (3).

| $\lambda$ | $\mu$ | rank1 | mAP |
| --- | --- | --- | --- |
| 1 | 1 | 95.16 | 86.72 |
| 1 | 2 | 94.95 | 86.59 |
| 1 | 3 | 94.54 | 86.35 |
| 2 | 1 | 95.58 | 88.14 |
| 2.5 | 1 | 95.61 | 87.99 |
| 3 | 1 | **95.90** | **88.14** |
| 3.5 | 1 | 95.31 | 87.74 |
| 4 | 1 | 95.01 | 87.27 |

experiments, which are shown in Table 3. It can be found that with the help of transition parts, there is a 1.01%/1.81% improvement on rank1/mAP when the network only contains the global branch and the first local branch. And the performance is further improved by 0.56%/0.77% of rank1/mAP when there are all three branches, which proves the effect of the transition method on supplementing discriminative information. We also argue that the transition parts can introduce some relation information between two adjacent parts, which assists the network in exploring multiple fine-grained features.

**Pooling Strategies.** We design three different pooling strategies in all experiments, including the global average pooling, the global max pooling, and the integration of them, whose performances are shown in Table 3. We can see that the global max pooling performs the best among the 3 strategies. The reason is that max pooling only takes the maximum response value of a specific local part into account, which can suppress the interference of irrelevant information in the region. In contrast, the global average pooling operation preserves all locations of the fixed partial view and the contributions of all the locations to the final local feature presentation are the same. The integration of them can weaken the advantage of max pooling for bringing the unrelated features of the background, which reduces the discriminative ability of the feature presentation. Thus, the experiment results show that the global max pooling is the better choice in our MGGTN method.

**Weight Parameters of Loss.** Table 4 presents the experimental results of the ablation study on different weight parameters of softmax loss and triplet loss. The parameter assignment can be regarded as a ratio problem between the two losses. Therefore, we fix one parameter to 1 and change the other one in order to adjust the ratio value. The trend of rank1 and mAP with the change of weight parameters for two losses is shown in Fig. 4. Firstly, when $\lambda/\mu \leq 1$, the performance decreases by 0.62%/0.37% on rank1/mAP with the increase of $\mu$ from 1 to 3. Then, we set $\mu = 1$ and make $\lambda$ larger than $\mu$. It can be observed that with $\lambda$ increasing, the mAP and rank1 of MGGTN increase firstly and then decline. And note that the MGGTN method achieves 95.90% on rank1 and 88.14% on mAP when $\lambda$ is set to 3, which is the best performance in the process of changing $\lambda$. We believe that it is because the number of features employed on softmax loss is larger than that on triplet loss. Therefore, the weight for softmax loss in final loss should be larger than the weight of triplet loss with the purpose of promoting the effect of the network on learning discriminative features to achieve higher performance on classification and reach a balance between the two losses.

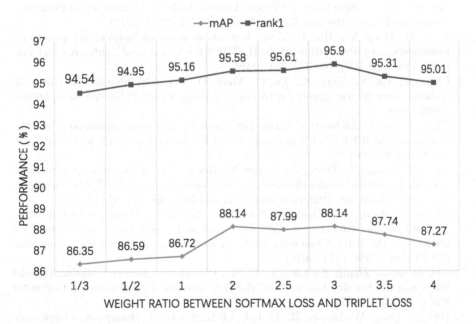

**Fig. 4.** The trend of rank1 and mAP with the change of weight parameters for two losses. The weight ratio is $\lambda/\mu$. And $\lambda$ is the weight parameter for softmax loss and $\mu$ is for triplet loss.

## 5   Conclusion

In this work, we propose a novel coarse-to-fine method called Multiple Granularities with Gradual Transition Network (MGGTN) to learn more discriminative representation for the person re-identification task. Different from previous part-based works, our method considers the information at partition boundary and uses a gradual transition strategy, which reduces the loss of features caused by horizontal splitting. Therefore, it can cover more discriminative information on each part level and further improve the robustness of the final feature. Furthermore, our method optimizes the combination of classification loss and metric loss by introducing parameters as a kind of ratio to balance them rather than simply summing. In this way, their advantages can be better exploited and the performance of feature learning is further improved. Extensive experiments demonstrate that our method remarkably exceeds the previous methods on 2 popular benchmarks. What is more, it outperforms the best rank1 results on Market1501 dataset.

# References

1. Cao, Z., Simon, T., Wei, S.E., Sheikh, Y.: Realtime multi-person 2D pose estimation using part affinity fields. In: Proceedings of the IEEE Conference on Computer Vision and Pattern Recognition (CVPR), pp. 7291–7299 (2017)
2. Chen, B., Deng, W., Hu, J.: Mixed high-order attention network for person re-identification. In: Proceedings of the IEEE/CVF International Conference on Computer Vision (ICCV), pp. 371–381 (2019)
3. Chen, M., Ge, Y., Feng, X., Xu, C., Yang, D.: Person re-identification by pose invariant deep metric learning with improved triplet loss. IEEE Access **6**, 68089–68095 (2018)
4. Chen, T., et al.: Abd-net: attentive but diverse person re-identification. In: Proceedings of the IEEE/CVF International Conference on Computer Vision (ICCV), pp. 8351–8361 (2019)
5. Chen, W., Chen, X., Zhang, J., Huang, K.: Beyond triplet loss: a deep quadruplet network for person re-identification. In: Proceedings of the IEEE Conference on Computer Vision and Pattern Recognition (CVPR), pp. 403–412 (2017)
6. Cheng, D., Gong, Y., Zhou, S., Wang, J., Zheng, N.: Person re-identification by multi-channel parts-based CNN with improved triplet loss function. In: Proceedings of the IEEE Conference on Computer Vision and Pattern Recognition (CVPR), pp. 1335–1344 (2016)
7. Chi, S., Li, J., Zhang, S., Xing, J., Qi, T.: Pose-driven deep convolutional model for person re-identification. In: 2017 IEEE International Conference on Computer Vision (ICCV) (2017)
8. Deng, J., Dong, W., Socher, R., Li, L.J., Li, K., Fei-Fei, L.: Imagenet: a large-scale hierarchical image database. In: 2009 IEEE Conference on Computer Vision and Pattern Recognition (CVPR), pp. 248–255. IEEE (2009)
9. Deng, W., Zheng, L., Ye, Q., Kang, G., Yang, Y., Jiao, J.: Image-image domain adaptation with preserved self-similarity and domain-dissimilarity for person re-identification. In: Proceedings of the IEEE Conference on Computer Vision and Pattern Recognition (CVPR), pp. 994–1003 (2018)
10. Felzenszwalb, P., McAllester, D., Ramanan, D.: A discriminatively trained, multi-scale, deformable part model. In: 2008 IEEE Conference on Computer Vision and Pattern Recognition (CVPR), pp. 1–8. IEEE (2008)
11. Fu, Y., et al.: Horizontal pyramid matching for person re-identification. In: Proceedings of the AAAI Conference on Artificial Intelligence (AAAI), vol. 33, pp. 8295–8302 (2019)

12. Gao, S., Wang, J., Lu, H., Liu, Z.: Pose-guided visible part matching for occluded person ReID. In: 2020 IEEE/CVF Conference on Computer Vision and Pattern Recognition (CVPR) (2020)
13. He, K., Zhang, X., Ren, S., Sun, J.: Deep residual learning for image recognition. In: Proceedings of the IEEE Conference on Computer Vision and Pattern Recognition (CVPR), pp. 770–778 (2016)
14. Hermans, A., Beyer, L., Leibe, B.: In defense of the triplet loss for person re-identification. arXiv preprint arXiv:1703.07737 (2017)
15. Huang, H., Li, D., Zhang, Z., Chen, X., Huang, K.: Adversarially occluded samples for person re-identification. In: 2018 IEEE/CVF Conference on Computer Vision and Pattern Recognition (CVPR) (2018)
16. Karanam, S., Yang, L., Radke, R.J.: Person re-identification with discriminatively trained viewpoint invariant dictionaries. In: IEEE International Conference on Computer Vision (ICCV) (2015)
17. Li, W., Zhao, R., Xiao, T., Wang, X.: Deepreid: deep filter pairing neural network for person re-identification. In: Proceedings of the IEEE Conference on Computer Vision and Pattern Recognition (CVPR), pp. 152–159 (2014)
18. Li, W., Zhu, X., Gong, S.: Harmonious attention network for person re-identification. In: Proceedings of the IEEE Conference on Computer Vision and Pattern Recognition (CVPR), pp. 2285–2294 (2018)
19. Liang, Z., Zhang, H., Sun, S., Chandraker, M., Qi, T.: Person re-identification in the wild. In: 2017 IEEE Conference on Computer Vision and Pattern Recognition (CVPR) (2017)
20. Lin, Y., et al.: Improving person re-identification by attribute and identity learning. Pattern Recogn. **95**, 151–161 (2019)
21. Liu, H., Feng, J., Qi, M., Jiang, J., Yan, S.: End-to-end comparative attention networks for person re-identification. IEEE Trans. Image Process. **26**(7), 3492–3506 (2017)
22. Miao, J., Wu, Y., Liu, P., Ding, Y., Yang, Y.: Pose-guided feature alignment for occluded person re-identification. In: 2019 IEEE/CVF International Conference on Computer Vision (ICCV) (2019)
23. Park, H., Ham, B.: Relation network for person re-identification. In: Proceedings of the AAAI Conference on Artificial Intelligence (AAAI), vol. 34, pp. 11839–11847 (2020)
24. Qian, X., et al.: Pose-normalized image generation for person re-identification. In: Proceedings of the European Conference on Computer Vision (ECCV), pp. 650–667 (2018)
25. Si, J., et al.: Dual attention matching network for context-aware feature sequence based person re-identification. In: Proceedings of the IEEE Conference on Computer Vision and Pattern Recognition (CVPR), pp. 5363–5372 (2018)
26. Song, C., Yan, H., Ouyang, W., Liang, W.: Mask-guided contrastive attention model for person re-identification. In: 2018 IEEE/CVF Conference on Computer Vision and Pattern Recognition (CVPR) (2018)
27. Su, C., Zhang, S., Xing, J., Gao, W., Tian, Q.: Deep attributes driven multi-camera person re-identification. In: Leibe, B., Matas, J., Sebe, N., Welling, M. (eds.) ECCV 2016. LNCS, vol. 9906, pp. 475–491. Springer, Cham (2016). https://doi.org/10.1007/978-3-319-46475-6_30
28. Sun, Y., et al.: Perceive where to focus: learning visibility-aware part-level features for partial person re-identification. In: Proceedings of the IEEE/CVF Conference on Computer Vision and Pattern Recognition (CVPR), pp. 393–402 (2019)

29. Sun, Y., Zheng, L., Yang, Y., Tian, Q., Wang, S.: Beyond part models: person retrieval with refined part pooling (and a strong convolutional baseline). In: Proceedings of the European Conference on Computer Vision (ECCV), pp. 480–496 (2018)
30. Wang, C., Zhang, Q., Huang, C., Liu, W., Wang, X.: Mancs: a multi-task attentional network with curriculum sampling for person re-identification. In: Proceedings of the European Conference on Computer Vision (ECCV), pp. 365–381 (2018)
31. Wang, G., Lai, J.H., Liang, W., Wang, G.: Smoothing adversarial domain attack and p-memory reconsolidation for cross-domain person re-identification. In: 2020 IEEE/CVF Conference on Computer Vision and Pattern Recognition (CVPR) (2020)
32. Wang, G., et al.: High-order information matters: Learning relation and topology for occluded person re-identification. In: Proceedings of the IEEE/CVF Conference on Computer Vision and Pattern Recognition (CVPR), pp. 6449–6458 (2020)
33. Wang, G., Yuan, Y., Chen, X., Li, J., Zhou, X.: Learning discriminative features with multiple granularities for person re-identification. In: Proceedings of the 26th ACM International Conference on Multimedia (ACM MM), pp. 274–282 (2018)
34. Wang, J., Zhu, X., Gong, S., Li, W.: Transferable joint attribute-identity deep learning for unsupervised person re-identification. In: Proceedings of the IEEE Conference on Computer Vision and Pattern Recognition (CVPR), pp. 2275–2284 (2018)
35. Wei, L., Zhang, S., Yao, H., Gao, W., Tian, Q.: Glad: global-local-alignment descriptor for pedestrian retrieval. In: Proceedings of the 25th ACM International Conference on Multimedia (ACM MM), pp. 420–428 (2017)
36. Xu, J., Zhao, R., Zhu, F., Wang, H., Ouyang, W.: Attention-aware compositional network for person re-identification. In: Proceedings of the IEEE Conference on Computer Vision and Pattern Recognition (CVPR), pp. 2119–2128 (2018)
37. Zhai, Y., et al.: Ad-cluster: augmented discriminative clustering for domain adaptive person re-identification. In: Proceedings of the IEEE/CVF Conference on Computer Vision and Pattern Recognition (CVPR), pp. 9021–9030 (2020)
38. Zhang, X., et al.: Alignedreid: surpassing human-level performance in person re-identification. arXiv preprint arXiv:1711.08184 (2017)
39. Zhao, H., et al.: Spindle net: person re-identification with human body region guided feature decomposition and fusion. In: Proceedings of the IEEE Conference on Computer Vision and Pattern Recognition (CVPR), pp. 1077–1085 (2017)
40. Zheng, L., Shen, L., Tian, L., Wang, S., Wang, J., Tian, Q.: Scalable person re-identification: a benchmark. In: Proceedings of the IEEE International Conference on Computer Vision (ICCV), pp. 1116–1124 (2015)
41. Zheng, Z., Liang, Z., Yi, Y.: Unlabeled samples generated by GAN improve the person re-identification baseline in vitro. In: IEEE Computer Society (2017)
42. Zheng, Z., Yang, X., Yu, Z., Zheng, L., Yang, Y., Kautz, J.: Joint discriminative and generative learning for person re-identification. In: Proceedings of the IEEE/CVF Conference on Computer Vision and Pattern Recognition (CVPR), pp. 2138–2147 (2019)
43. Zhong, Z., Zheng, L., Cao, D., Li, S.: Re-ranking person re-identification with k-reciprocal encoding. IEEE Computer Society (2017)

# Robotics & Application

# Generative Adversarial Networks and Improved Efficientnet for Imbalanced Diabetic Retinopathy Grading

Kaifei Zhao[1], Wentao Zhao[1], Jun Xie[2], Binrong Li[2], Zhe Zhang[1], and Xinying Xu[1(✉)]

[1] College of Electrical and Power Engineering, Taiyuan University of Technology, Taiyuan 030024, China
{zhaokaifei0312, zhaowentao0376}@link.tyut.edu.cn,
{zhangzhe, xuxinying}@tyut.edu.cn
[2] College of Information and Computer, Taiyuan University of Technology, Jinzhong 030600, China
xiejun@tyut.edu.cn, libinrong0384@link.tyut.edu.cn

**Abstract.** Diabetic retinopathy (DR) is a complication of diabetes and one of the causes of blindness and visual impairment. Automated and accurate DR grading is of great significance for timely and effective treatment of fundus diseases. At present, traditional convolutional neural networks (CNNs) will pay too much atteneion to the DR level with a lot of samples because of the unbalanced data distribution. So unbalanced data distribution will affect the classification ability of the model. In This paper, Double-Generator-Efficientnet Network (DGENet) based on Efficientnet is proposed to effectively improve the grading ability of DR, which consists of the following: (1) The first network classifies No DR and DR to solve the problem that No DR occupies most of the data distribution. (2) The second network divides the DR in the first network into mild, moderate, severe non-proliferative DR (NPDR) and proliferative DR(PDR). The second add the generative network from Deep Convolutional Generative Adversarial Networks (DCGAN) for data enhancement to solve the problem of imbalanced data in the four levels of DR. (3) Add attention mechanism modules to the four-level network. Experimental results show that the proposed DGENet outperforms some new methods in the publicly available Kaggle and Messidor-2 fundus image datasets, especially on the four levels of DR1 to DR4.

**Keywords:** Diabetic Retinopathy Grading · Unbalanced data · Generative adversarial networks · Efficientnet

## 1 Introduction

Diabetic Retinopathy (DR) is a complication of diabetes and has become one of the major diseases threatening human health [1, 2]. According to estimates by the World Health Organization (WHO) and the International Diabetes Federation (IDF), the number of diabetic patients in the world will exceed 590 million by 2035. Among them, there will be more than 140 million diabetic patients in my country, but there are only 30,000 ophthalmologists in China. Therefore, there are a lot of DR patients, which

F. Sun et al. (Eds.): ICCSIP 2021, CCIS 1515, pp. 345–359, 2022.
https://doi.org/10.1007/978-981-16-9247-5_27

has caused a huge burden on a limited number of ophthalmologists. Many clinical studies in recent years have shown that rapid and accurate DR classification is important to doctors and patients. It reveals DR severity levels to improve the selection of the appropriate therapeutic options.

DR grading can be classified through the type, number and size of the lesions in the fundus image [3]. According to the International Diabetic Retinopathy Classification Standard [4], the severity of DR can be divided into five types: no abnormality (No DR), mild NPDR, moderate NPDR, severe NPDR and PDR [5]. According to the characteristics of different periods, patients with DR need to be checked regularly.

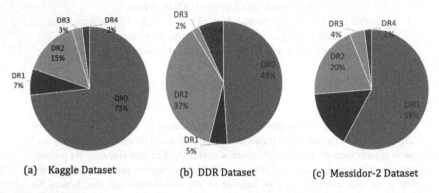

(a)　Kaggle Dataset          (b) DDR Dataset          (c) Messidor-2 Dataset

**Fig. 1.** The imbalanced data distribution of three DR grading datasets: EyePACS, DDR and Messidor-2 datasets.

CNN is a cognitive method for image processing [6, 7]. CNNs have made great progress in recent years and have been widely used in the field of computer vision [8, 9]. Image classification is the process of extracting needed feature from the processing. Medical image analysis is achieved from the extracted features from the cognitive computation method [10]. Due to the powerful feature extraction capabilities of CNNs, they have also been widely used in medical image tasks [11]. CNNs have achieved good results in the classification of DR, but due to the complexity of the task, it is still challenging in clinical practice. The colors and contours of most of the pixels in the five levels of DR are similar, so they are easy to confuse. The area of a single lesion in the fundus image is small and contains few pixels, so it is easy to ignore it when extracting features by CNNs, which leads to the failure of important features to be extracted, which reduces the accuracy of the classification results. The DR data distribution of different levels is extremely imbalanced (AS shown in Fig. 1). For example, the Kaggle fundus dataset contains 35126 fundus images [24], it has 25810(73.48%) images in DR0, 2443(6.95%) images in DR1, 5292(15.07%) images in DR2, 873(2.49%) images in DR3, 708(2.02%) images in DR4. Messidor-2 fundus dataset contains 1744 fundus images [26], it has 1017(58.31%) images in DR0, 270(15.48%) images in DR1, 347 (19.90%) images in DR2, 75(4.30%) images in DR3, 35(2.01%) images in DR4. Among them, the data distribution of the non-abnormal grade (DR0) occupies a large proportion in the dataset, while the other abnormal grades only occupy a small proportion of the distribution.

The imbalance of the data will cause the model to pay too much attention to the DR level with more samples and ignore the DR level with fewer samples. It will affect the generalization ability of the model. Therefore, in response to the above problems, our contributions are summarized as follows:

(1) Use two networks to train the dataset. The first 2-classification network is used to classify DR and No DR. The second 4-classification network classify DR grading. The double networks training removes no abnormal fundus images in the 4-classification network, which can reduce the impact of the classification effect due to the excessive proportion of the no abnormal level (DR0) data.

(2) Add the generative network from the DCGAN to data enhancement for the 4-classification network. It can alleviate the impact caused by imbalanced data on the base of removing the impact of the DR0 level.

(3) The attention mechanism module is added to the 4-classification network, which can effectively highlight the characteristics of lesions, suppress irrelevant information, and effectively improve the classification performance of the network.

## 2 Related Work

In recent years, remarkable progress has been made in the field of medical analysis through the use of deep learning algorithms. Deep learning provides powerful support for DR grading [12–14]. Specifically, Van Grinsven et al. [15] proposed a selective sampling method, which speeds up the training speed of bleeding detection in color fundus images by dynamically selecting misclassified negative samples during the training process. Zhou et al. [16] designed the Multi-Cell architecture to gradually increase the depth of the CNN and the resolution of the input image, effectively reducing the computational complexity and alleviating the impact of the disappearance of the gradient. Gulshan et al. [17] applied the Inceptionv3 architecture to automatically detect diabetic retinopathy and diabetic macular edema in retinal fundus images. Previous studies have shown that methods based on deep learning are effective DR grading tasks.

Goodfellow et al. [18] proposed a generative adversarial network (GAN). The adversarial network can be composed of a generative model (generator) and a discrimination model (discriminator). During the training process, two networks are optimized in turn until the two networks reach dynamic equilibrium. Through counter learning, the algorithm can directly learn the distribution of data. However, it is difficult to learn its pixel distribution without supervision for complex data. Face-book AI team [19] proposed Deep Convolutional Generative Adversarial Network (DCGAN). DCGAN adds deep neural networks into neural networks, not only speeds up the training process of neural networks, but also makes the training process more stable. Generative adversarial networks have been used to medical image processing, and have achieved good results. Xue et al. [20] proposed a new end-to-end medical image segmentation method based on the network architecture SEGAN. SEGAN uses a new multi-scale L1 loss function to evaluate the experimental results. Shankaranarayana et al. [21] combined FCN and GAN to automatically segment the fundus optic disc to assist in the diagnosis of glaucoma. This method is superior to existing methods in all evaluation indicators. Lahiri et al. [22] used the semi-supervised semantic segmentation method of generative adversarial network to segment blood vessels from fundus images.

## 3   Methodology

### 3.1   Overview of DGENet

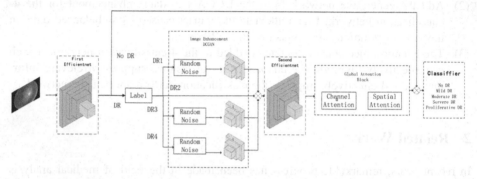

**Fig. 2.** The DGENet structure proposed in this article. The backbone network is composed of two Efficientnets. First Efficientnet is a 2-classification network and Second Efficientnet is a 4-classification network. The input image first passes through First Efficientnet, and outputs DR or No DR. The DR part is enhanced by DCGAN data as the input of Second Efficientnet and the probability value of each DR level is output through Global Attention Block in the last layer of Second Efficientnet.

The structure of DGENet is shown in Fig. 2. DGENet takes fundus images as input and uses all the Kaggle datasets to train the First Efficientnet. First Efficientnet loads ImageNet's pre-trained model and its output results are DR and No DR. The No DR part in First Efficientnet will be used as the evaluation content of the final No DR of DGENet. The data of the DR part will use the label value as the analyzing conditions and generate random noise according to the weight $w_i$ of each category. Random noise is used as input and sent to the trained DCGAN network corresponding to each label for image generation. The generated image is used as data enhancement. The generated images and the original data are used as input to the Second Efficientnet for 4-class training. Second Efficientnet loads ImageNet's pre-trained model and adds Global Attention Block to the last layer. The input of Global Attention Block is the feature map $F \in R^{H \times W \times C}$ of the convolutional layer of the last layer of Second Efficientnet, where H, W, and C represent the height, width and number of channels in the feature map, respectively. The Global Attention Block is subjected to a global average pooling

(GAP) and a fully connected layer (FC) to perform the classification task, and the four types of prediction results of DR1-DR4 are obtained.

## 3.2 Deep Convolutional Generative Adversarial Networks

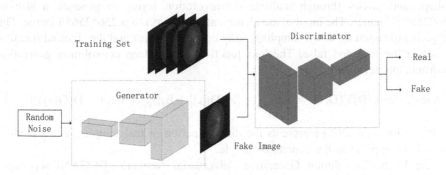

**Fig. 3.** The basic structure diagram of the deep convolutional generation confrontation network

The structure of the deep convolution generation confrontation network is shown in Fig. 3. The entire network is composed of two parts: the generator G and the discriminator D. The generator G accepts a random distribution generated according to a certain probability distribution as noise and generates a picture that is as similar as possible to the real data. The discriminator D is responsible for distinguishing true and false from the real dataset and the generated images.

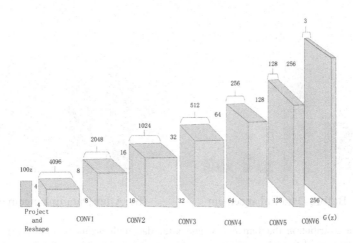

**Fig. 4.** The structure of generator G in DCGAN. We need to generate 256*256*3 resolution images, but the basic generator G can only generate 64*64*3 resolution images. So we have extended it.

The DCGAN is improved to generate images with the resolution of 256\*256\*3. The improved network structure of the generator G is shown in Fig. 4. The generator network inputs a random noise z and generates an image G(z) through upsampling layer. The upsampling layer uses the deconvolution algorithm. G accepts a random noise z. The noise z is transformed into a 4\*4\*1024 feature map through Project and reshape and passes through multiple deconvolution layers to generate a size of 256\*256\* 3 images. The input of the identification network is a 256\*256\*3 image. The image is processed by down-sampling, fully connected layer and the sigmoid function to output the true and false. The loss function of the deep convolution generation confrontation network is:

$$\min(G)\ \max(D)V(D,G) = E_{x \sim p_{data}(x)}[\log D(x)] + E_{z \sim p_z(z)}[\log(1 - D(G(z)))] \quad (1)$$

In the formula, D(X) represents the discrimination of real samples. z is a random input. G (z) represents the generated sample.

The Deep Convolution Generative Adversarial Network (DCGAN) separately trains DR1, DR3, and DR4 according to the proportion of each level of DR in the Kaggle dataset. During the training process, according to the generator in every n cycles Inception Score of the model, extract the three generator models and weights with the highest Inception Score in each level.

The three generator models are added to the data preprocessing part of the second network of DGENet. In the data preprocessing part, each level uses the corresponding generator network to generate $(w_i - 1) * x_i$ image data for the training of the four-classification network. $w_i$ is the weight of each level. After the data enhancement of DCGAN, the data volume of each level before and after comparison is shown in Fig. 5.

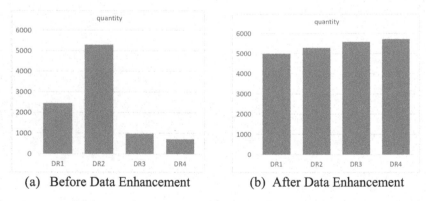

(a)  Before Data Enhancement          (b)  After Data Enhancement

**Fig. 5.** Data distribution diagram before and after data enhancement. Figure (a) is the data distribution before data enhancement, and Figure (b) is the data distribution after data enhancement.

### 3.3  Efficientnet

CNN can expand the convolutional network by adjusting the width and depth of the network and the resolution of the input image. In the previous research work of Efficientnet, a lot of research work only attempts to expand one of the dimensions, and rarely makes comprehensive adjustments to the three dimensions.

Google researchers proposed a compound expansion method, the principle of which is to scale CNN with a more structured idea according to certain restrictions and proportions [23]. This method sets a set of basic scaling factors w, d and r to uniformly scale the width, depth and resolution respectively. The proportional coefficient satisfies:

$$d = a^{\varnothing}, \ w = \beta^{\varnothing}, \ r = \gamma^{\varnothing} \tag{2}$$

Where $\varnothing$ is the compound coefficient determining the network size and computational resource. For any new $\varnothing$, the total resource cost will increase by $2^{\varnothing}$. The above parameters still need to be met:

$$\alpha * \beta^2 * \gamma^2 \approx 2, \ \alpha \geq 1, \ \beta \geq 1, \ \gamma \geq 1. \tag{3}$$

The structure of EfficientNet-b0(see Fig. 6) is improved on the base of mobilenet v2, using Inverted Residuals and Linear Bottlenecks, and combining SE modules. And set:

$$\alpha = 1.2, \ \beta = 1.1, \ \gamma = 1.15 \tag{4}$$

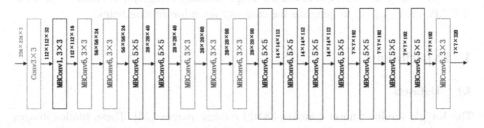

**Fig. 6.** The architecture of EfficientNet-B0.

### 3.4  Global Attention Block

GAB is composed of channel attention and spatial attention. The structure is shown in Fig. 7. GAB adopts simplified feature $F_{reduce} \in \mathcal{R}^{H \times W \times C'}$ as input to learn global attention feature mapping independent of category.

First, we calculate the channel attention feature maps $F_{c\_att} \in \mathcal{R}^{H \times W \times C'}$ by the following formula:

$$F_{c\_att} \in (\sigma(Conv2(GAP(F_{GAB-IN})))) \otimes F_{GAN-IN} \qquad (5)$$

$\sigma$ denotes the Sigmoid function, GAP is the global average pooling layer, Conv2 indcates two $1 \times 1$ convolutional layers, $F_{GAB-IN}$ is the $F_{reduce}$, and $\otimes$ denotes elmentwise multiplication.

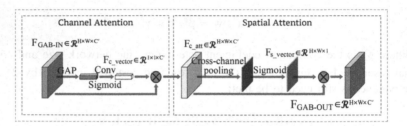

**Fig. 7.** The structure of the Global Attention Block

Then, we calculate the output of GAB, the spatial attention feature maps $F_{GAB-OUT}$, by the following formula:

$$F_{GAB-OUT} = F_{c\_att} \otimes (\sigma(C\_GAP(F_{c\_att}))) \qquad (6)$$

C_GAP denotes the cross channel average pooling. $F_{GAB-OUT}$ is taken as the input of CAB, i.e. $F_{CAB-IN}$, to generate the category attention feature maps.

## 4 Experiments

### 4.1 Datasets

The Kaggle fundus dataset contains 88400 fundus images [24]. These fundus images are provided through EyePACS [25]. EyePACS is a free retinopathy screening platform. Each experimental subject provides the left and right visual field of the human eye. It contains 35126 training images and 53576 test images, but only 35126 training images are marked with a DR level from 0 to 4, so we only use 35126 training images for the experiment.

Messidor dataset [26]: Messidor contains two datasets, namely Messidor and Messidor-2. Messidor divides the DR levels into 4 categories, which are inconsistent with international standards. We do not use the Messidor dataset. Messidor-2 contains 874 examinations. Each examination contains fundus images of the left and right eyes, so it contains 1748 images. Messidor-2 has an improvement over Messidor. In addition to including the DME label, the DR level is in accordance with international standards. It is divided into 5 categories. So Messidor-2 will be used in the next experiment.

## 4.2  The Experiment of DCGAN

We use the Kaggle dataset to train the DCGAN network. The Inception Score (IS(G)) is one of the quantitative indicators for the DCGAN:

$$IS(G) = \exp\left(\frac{1}{N}\sum_{i=1}^{N} D_{KL}(p(y|x^{(i)})\|p(y))\right) \qquad (7)$$

p(y|x) represents the probability distribution of the image x belonging to each category. P(y) represents the edge distribution of all images generated by the generator in all categories. $D_{KL}$ represents the KL divergence of p(y|x) and p(y).

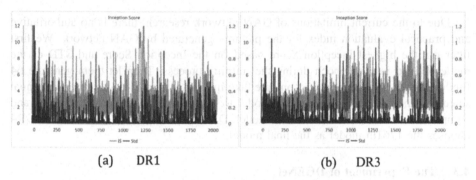

(a)    DR1                              (b)    DR3

**Fig. 8.** The figure shows the evaluation parameters of DR1and DR3 in each cycle during the training process. The red line represents the Inception Score, which corresponds to the left axis, and the blue line represents the standard deviation STD, which corresponds to the right axis. (Color figure online)

We extract the three levels of DR1, DR3 and DR4 images in Kaggle and use three networks for training. The three models are trained for 2000 rounds with the Adam optimizer and cross-entropy loss function. In each round of training, the model will be used to randomly generate 1000 images. Images are sent to inception_v3 trained with Imagenet for testing and get the Inception Score of each round. The model with the highest comprehensive score will be an indicator for selecting generator G.

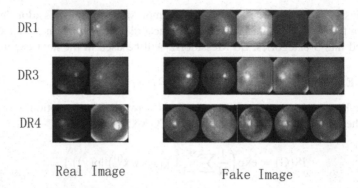

Real Image                     Fake Image

**Fig. 9.** Fundus images generated using the final selected generator model. The two columns on the left are real images in Kaggle. The five columns on the right are images generated by the model. The first line is the DR1 level image. The second line is the DR3 level image. The third line is the DR4 level image.

Due to the current limitations of GAN network research, there is no authoritative and practical evaluation index for the pictures generated by GAN network. We first filter out the highest Inception Score based on the Inception Score and STD of the model trained in each epoch during the training process. Then let them generate 64 fundus images respectively. We compare fake images with real images through manual screening methods and screen out a model to be the final model. After analysis and comparison, DR1 chooses the 1232th model, DR3 chooses the 1200th model and DR4 chooses the 1761th model as the final model.

### 4.3    The Experiment of DGENet

Accuracy (Acc), sensitivity (Sen) and F1 score are used to evaluate the performance of the proposed method. We will get a score for each type of result to reflect the performance of data enhancement and GAB.

Kaggle dataset is divided into a training set and a validation set. Messidor-2 dataset as the test set. According to the number and proportion of each level of DR in the Kaggle dataset, 1750 images (350 images of each level) are used as the validation set and 33376 images are used as the training set. The experiment is as follows: (1) Use Efficientnet-b0 and Efficientnet-b1 to perform five-classification training tasks. Then the model with the best performance on the validation set (has the minimum loss) is selected as the final model. The evaluation index of the final model on the validation set and the test set is calculated to be the baseline score. (2) Use efficientnet-b0 and efficientnet-b1 to perform two-classification training task respectively. Select the final model and calculate the performance index of DR0. (3) Remove all DR0 data and labels in the Kaggle dataset and use efficientnet-b0 and efficientnet-b1 to perform a four-classification training task for images of DR1 to DR4 respectively. (4) On the basis of the third data processing, use the trained DCGAN for data enhancement and repeat the third experiment content. (5) Add GAB to efficientnet-b0 and efficientnet-b1 and repeat the third and fourth experiments.

**Table 1.** Experiments on Kaggle validation dataset

| Structure | Grade | Acc | Sen | F1 |
|---|---|---|---|---|
| Efn-b0(5) | DR0 | 0.9046 | 0.8457 | 0.7800 |
| | DR1 | 0.9091 | 0.7686 | 0.7719 |
| | DR2 | 0.8983 | 0.7914 | 0.7569 |
| | DR3 | 0.9149 | 0.7514 | 0.7793 |
| | DR4 | 0.9354 | 0.7486 | 0.8226 |
| | Average | 0.9125 | 0.7811 | 0.7821 |
| Efn-b1(5) | DR0 | 0.9097 | 0.8600 | 0.7921 |
| | DR1 | 0.9137 | 0.7800 | 0.7834 |
| | DR2 | 0.9029 | 0.8029 | 0.7676 |
| | DR3 | 0.9189 | 0.7600 | 0.7893 |
| | DR4 | 0.9400 | 0.7600 | 0.8352 |
| | Average | 0.9170 | 0.7926 | 0.7935 |
| Efn-b0(2) | DR0 | 0.9091 | 0.8457 | 0.7883 |
| + Efn-b1(4) | DR1 | 0.9143 | 0.7857 | 0.7857 |
| | DR2 | 0.9034 | 0.8114 | 0.7707 |
| | DR3 | 0.9200 | 0.7629 | 0.7923 |
| | DR4 | 0.9406 | 0.7629 | 0.8370 |
| | Average | 0.9175 | 0.7937 | 0.7948 |
| Efn-b1(2) | DR0 | 0.9120 | 0.8600 | 0.7963 |
| + Efn-b1(4) | DR1 | 0.9149 | 0.7857 | 0.7868 |
| | DR2 | 0.9046 | 0.8114 | 0.7728 |
| | DR3 | 0.9206 | 0.7629 | 0.7935 |
| | DR4 | 0.9411 | 0.7629 | 0.8383 |
| | Average | 0.9186 | 0.7966 | 0.7975 |
| Efn-b1(2) | DR0 | 0.9120 | 0.8600 | 0.7963 |
| + Efn-b1(4) | DR1 | 0.9177 | 0.7914 | 0.7937 |
| + GAN | DR2 | 0.9063 | 0.8057 | 0.7747 |
| | DR3 | 0.9229 | 0.7743 | 0.8006 |
| | DR4 | 0.9446 | 0.7771 | 0.8487 |
| | Average | 0.9207 | 0.8017 | 0.8028 |
| DGENet | DR0 | 0.9120 | 0.8600 | 0.7963 |
| (Efn-b1(2) | DR1 | 0.9200 | 0.7971 | 0.7994 |
| + Efn-b1(4) | DR2 | 0.9091 | 0.8114 | 0.7813 |
| + GAN | DR3 | 0.9257 | 0.7800 | 0.8077 |
| + GAB) | DR4 | 0.9457 | 0.7829 | 0.8523 |
| | Average | 0.9225 | 0.8063 | 0.8074 |

**Table 2.** Experiments on Messidor-2 dataset

| Structure | Grade | Acc | Sen | F1 |
|---|---|---|---|---|
| Efn-b0 | DR0 | 0.8412 | 0.8299 | 0.8590 |
| | DR1 | 0.8589 | 0.6037 | 0.5699 |
| | DR2 | 0.8893 | 0.7550 | 0.7308 |
| | DR3 | 0.9507 | 0.5067 | 0.4691 |
| | DR4 | 0.9805 | 0.5429 | 0.5278 |
| | Average | 0.8610 | 0.7603 | 0.7654 |
| Efn-b1 | DR0 | 0.8509 | 0.8427 | 0.8683 |
| | DR1 | 0.8635 | 0.6148 | 0.5825 |
| | DR2 | 0.8939 | 0.7666 | 0.7420 |
| | DR3 | 0.9541 | 0.5200 | 0.4937 |
| | DR4 | 0.9834 | 0.5714 | 0.5797 |
| | Average | 0.8685 | 0.7729 | 0.7770 |
| DGENet | DR0 | 0.8521 | 0.8427 | 0.8692 |
| (Efn-b1(2) | DR1 | 0.8693 | 0.6370 | 0.6014 |
| + Efn-b1(4) | DR2 | 0.9008 | 0.7781 | 0.7574 |
| + GAN | DR3 | 0.9593 | 0.6000 | 0.5590 |
| + GAB) | DR4 | 0.9874 | 0.6857 | 0.6857 |
| | Average | 0.8718 | 0.7844 | 0.7884 |

**Table 3.** Comparative experiment with other methods on the Kaggle dataset

| Method | Acc | Sen | F1 |
|---|---|---|---|
| Kwasigroch et al. [27] | 0.8170 | 0.8475 | 0.8248 |
| Qummar et al. [28] | 0.9067 | 0.7509 | 0.8533 |
| DRCNN [29] | 0.9064 | 0.7399 | 0.7994 |
| Cabinet [30] | 0.8668 | – | – |
| CF-DRNet [31] | 0.8310 | 0.5399 | – |
| Recep E. Hacisoftaoglu et al. [32] | 0.9210 | 0.8650 | – |
| DGENet | 0.9225 | 0.8063 | 0.8074 |

The experimental results of Kaggle validation set are shown in Table 1 and the experimental results of Messidor-2 dataset are shown in Table 2. DGENet performed very well on the Kaggle dataset. Compare with the evaluation index of Efficientnet-b0, the accuracy of DGENet reached 92.25% (an increase of 1%), the sensitivity reached 80.63% (an increase of 2.52%), F1 score reached 80.74% (an increase of 2.53%). This paper pays more attention to the sensitivity of each category. The experimental results show the overall classification performance of the model has been improved after adding the depth, the width and the resolution to Efficientnet. The classification performance of DR1, DR3 and DR4 have been improved after adding DCGAN for enhancement, but the classification performance of DR2 has declined. The classification performance of each category has been improved after adding the GAB. As shown in Table 2, the experimental results of the Messidor-2 dataset have improved in all aspects compared to Efficientnet-b0. We compare other methods on the Kaggle dataset.

As shown in Table 3. The experimental results show that DGENet has the highest accuracy. DGENet focus on unbalanced data issues. So DGENet has higher sensitivity and F1 score on DR1, DR3 and DR4 than other method. DGENet has higher average sensitivity and F1 score compared with other methods. In general, DGENet has a strong classification performance in the Diabetic Retinopathy grading methods in recent years.

## 5    Conclusion and Discussion

This paper proposes a Diabetic Retinopathy Grading network (DGENet) based on Efficientnet. DGENet reduce the effect of DR0 on the result by the first Efficientnet that classifies DR and NoDR. According to the proportion of data, the image is generated by DCGAN for the balance of the data volume of the four levels of DR1-DR4. We also improved the four-level Efficientnet (add the attention mechanism) to improve the classification performance of abnormal DR.

The experimental results on the Kaggle and Messidor-2 datasets show that the classification performance of abnormal data has been improved. On the one hand, the current ubiquitous phenomenon is that in addition to normal fundus images, not enough fundus images and the diversity is not high. We plan to study that how to generate high-quality and practical the strong fundus image that can be used to further solve the problem of data imbalance in the future. On the other hand, because the current DR classification accuracy rate cannot be applied to reality, we will try the new networks and improved it according to the characteristics of the fundus image, so as to further improve the grading performance of DR.

**Acknowledgments.** This work was supported by the Natural Science Foundation of Shanxi Province (201801D121144) and the Natural Science Foundation of Shanxi Province (201901D211079).

## References

1. Cho, N.H., Shaw, J.E., Karuranga, S., et al.: IDF Diabetes Atlas: Global estimates of diabetes prevalence for 2017 and projections for 2045. Diab. Res. Clin. Pract. **138**, 271–281 (2018)
2. Ding, J., Wong, T.Y.: Current epidemiology of diabetic retinopathy and diabetic macular edema. Curr. Diab. Rep. **12**(4), 346–354 (2012)
3. Usman Akram, M., Khalid, S., Tariq, A., Khan, S.A., Azam, F.: Detection and classification of retinal lesions for grading of diabetic retinopathy. Comput. Biol. Med. **45**(1), 161–171 (2014)
4. Haneda, S., Yamashita, H.: International clinical diabetic retinopathy disease severity scale. Nippon rinsho. Jpn. J. Clin. Med. **68**(9), 228–235 (2010)
5. Wilkinson, C.P., et al.: Proposed international clinical diabetic retinopathy and diabetic macular edema disease severity scales. Ophthalmology **110**(9), 1677–1682 (2003)
6. Zhou, J., et al.: Improved softmax loss for deep learning based face and expression recognition. Cogn. Comput. Syst. **1**(4), 97–102 (2019)

7.  Long, D., Zhang, S., Zhang, Y.: Performance prediction based on neural architecture features. Cogn. Comput. Syst. 2(2), 80–83 (2020)
8.  Xu, X., Li, G., Xie, G., et al.: Weakly supervised deep semantic segmentation using CNN and ELM with semantic candidate regions. Complexity 2019, 1–12 (2019)
9.  Zhou, J., Zhao, W., Guo, L., Xu, X., Xie, G.: Real time detection of surface defects with inception-based MobileNet-SSD detection network. In: Ren, J., et al. (eds.) BICS 2019. LNCS, vol. 11691, pp. 510–519. Springer, Cham (2020). https://doi.org/10.1007/978-3-030-39431-8_49
10. Wang, G.: A perspective on deep imaging. IEEE Access 4, 8914–8924 (2017)
11. Jeyaraj, P.R., Nadar, E.: Deep Boltzmann machine algorithm for accurate medical image analysis for classification of cancerous region. Cogn. Comput. Syst. 1(3), 85–90 (2019)
12. Gargeya, R., Leng, T.: Automated identification of diabetic retinopathy using deep learning. Ophthalmology 124(7), 962–969 (2017)
13. Zhang, W., et al.: Automated identification and grading system of diabetic retinopathy using deep neural networks. Know. Bas. Syst. 175, 12–25 (2019)
14. Jordi, D.L.T., Alls, A.V., Puig, D.: A deep learning interpretable classifier for diabetic retinopathy disease grading. Neurocomputing 396, 465–476 (2019)
15. Van Grinsven, M., Van Ginneken, B., Hoyng, C., Theelen, T., Sanchez, C.: Fast convolutional neural network training using selective data sampling: application to hemorrhage detection in color fundus images. IEEE Trans. Med. Imag. 35(5), 1273–1284 (2016)
16. Zhou, K., et al.: Multi-cell multi-task convolutional neural networks for diabetic retinopathy grading. In: Proceedings of the Annual International Conference of the IEEE Engineering in Medicine and Biology Society, EMBS (2018)
17. Gulshan, V., et al.: Development and validation of a deep learning algorithm for detection of diabetic retinopathy in retinal fundus photographs. JAMA 316(22), 2402–2410 (2016)
18. Goodfellow, I.J., Pouget-Abadie, J., Mirza, M., et al.: Generative adversarial nets. In: International Conference on Neural Information Processing Systems. MIT Press, pp. 2672–2680 (2014)
19. Radford, A., Metz, L., Chintala, S.: Unsupervised representation learning with deep convolutional generative adversarial networks. Computer Science. arXiv:1511.06434v2 (2015)
20. Rezaei, M., et al.: A conditional adversarial network for semantic segmentation of brain tumor. In: Crimi, A., Bakas, S., Kuijf, H., Menze, B., Reyes, M. (eds.) BrainLes 2017. LNCS, vol. 10670, pp. 241–252. Springer, Cham (2017). https://doi.org/10.1007/978-3-319-75238-9_21
21. Shankaranarayana, S.M., Ram, K., Mitra, K., Sivaprakasam, M.: Joint optic disc and cup segmentation using fully convolutional and adversarial networks. In: Jorge Cardoso, M., Arbel, T., Melbourne, A., Bogunovic, H., Moeskops, P., Chen, X., Schwartz, E., Garvin, M., Robinson, E., Trucco, E., Ebner, M., Yanwu, Xu., Makropoulos, A., Desjardin, A., Vercauteren, T. (eds.) FIFI/OMIA -2017. LNCS, vol. 10554, pp. 168–176. Springer, Cham (2017). https://doi.org/10.1007/978-3-319-67561-9_19
22. Lahiri, A., Ayush, K., Biswas, P.K., et al.: Generative adversarial learning for reducing manual annotation in semantic segmentation on large scale miscroscopy images: automated vessel segmentation in retinal fundus image as test case. In: 2017 IEEE Conf Comp Vision Pattern Recog Workshops (CVPRW) Workshops (CVPRW), pp. 794–800 (2017)
23. Tan, M., Le, Q.V.: EfficientNet: rethinking model scaling for convolutional neural networks. In: ICML (2019)

24. Gulshan, V., et al.: Development and validation of a deep learning algorithm for detection of diabetic retinopathy in retinal fundus photographs. JAMA - J. Am. Med. Assoc. **316**(22), 2402–2410 (2016)
25. Sun, Y., Chen, Y., Wang, X., Tang, X.: Deep learning face representation by joint identification-verification. In: Advances in Neural Information Processing Systems, pp. 1988–1996 (2017)
26. Decenciere, E., et al.: Feedback on a publicly distributed image database: the messidor database. Image Anal. Stereol. **33**(3), 231–234 (2014)
27. Kwasigroch, A., Jarzembinski, B., Grochowski, M.: Deep CNN based decision support system for detection and assessing the stage of diabetic retinopathy. In: 2018 International Interdisciplinary PhD Workshop (IIPhDW); IEEE, pp.111–116 (2018)
28. Qummar, S., Khan, F.G., Shah, S., Khan, A., Shamshirband, S., Rehman, Z.U., et al.: A deep learning ensemble approach for diabetic retinopathy detection. IEEE Access **7**, 150530–150539 (2019)
29. Li, X., Song, Y., Squirrell, D., et al.: Towards implementation of AI in New Zealand national diabetic screening program: cloud-based, robust, and bespoke. PLoS ONE **15**(4), e0225015 (2020)
30. He, A., Li, T., Li, N., et al.: CABNet: category attention block for imbalanced diabetic retinopathy grading. IEEE Trans. Med. Imag. **40**(1), 143–153 (2020)
31. Wu, Z., Shi, G., Chen, Y., et al.: Coarse-to-fine classification for diabetic retinopathy grading using convolutional neural network. Artif. Intell. Med. **108**, 101936 (2020)
32. Hacisoftaoglu, R.E., Karakaya, M., Sallam, A.B.: Deep learning frameworks for diabetic retinopathy detection with smartphone-based retinal imaging systems. Patt. Recog. Lett. **135**, 409–417 (2020)

# Sample-Efficient Reinforcement Learning Based on Dynamics Models via Meta-policy Optimization

Guoyu Zuo[1,2]([✉]) [iD], Zhipeng Tian[1,2], Shuai Huang[1,2], and Daoxiong Gong[1,2]

[1] Faculty of Information Technology, Beijing University of Technology,
Beijing 100124, China
{zuoguoyu,gongdx}@bjut.edu.cn, {tiantiant,huangshuai}@emails.bjut.edu.cn
[2] Beijing Key Laboratory of Computing Intelligence and Intelligent Systems,
Beijing 100124, China

**Abstract.** Model-based reinforcement learning (RL) can acquire remarkable sample efficiency, which makes it a suitable choice for applications where experiment data is hard to collect. However, it is difficult to learn an accurate dynamics model fully matched with the real-world, and the accuracy of the model usually affects the agent's final performance. In this paper, we propose a novel model-based RL approach called Meta-policy Optimization method with branched rollouts (MPOBR), which gets rid of strong dependency on an accurate model. In MPOBR, meta-learning is used to train a policy prior on an ensemble of learned dynamics models, so that this prior can be rapidly adapted to the environment when combined with environment rollouts. To reduce the affect of model compounding bias, short model-generated rollouts branched from real data are used to update the meta-policy. The experiments on simulated robotic tasks are designed to verify the effectiveness of our method. Results show that our approach can achieve the same asymptotic performance of state-of-the-art model-free algorithms while significantly reducing sample complexity.

**Keywords:** Robot learning · Model-based reinforcement learning ·
Meta-learning · Model bias

## 1 Introduction

Reinforcement learning (RL) provides a general framework for sequential decision problems, in which the agent can learn how to realize the set task by exploiting trial-and-error mechanism. Past successes in simulated domains have verified the effectiveness and generality of model-free reinforcement learning algorithms

Supported by National Natural Science Foundation of China (61873008 and 61773022), the Beijing Natural Science Foundation (4192010) and the National Key R & D Plan (2018YFB1307004).

F. Sun et al. (Eds.): ICCSIP 2021, CCIS 1515, pp. 360–373, 2022.
https://doi.org/10.1007/978-981-16-9247-5_28

such as playing video games [1] and board-games [2]. However, due to ten millions of interaction between the agent and the environment, model-free reinforcement learning algorithms are difficult to be applied in complex robotic tasks.

A common alternative for effectively alleviating sample complexity is model-based reinforcement learning. These methods can improve sample efficiency since they firstly acquire predictive dynamics models during interaction with the environment, then the agent can learn an improved policy from interactions with these models, reducing samples from the real-world. Different model architectures [3,4] and loss functions [5,6] have been used for fitting dynamics models. And many excellent dynamic programming algorithms can also be adapted to search for an improved policy.

The simplest model parameterization is linear models, which are data efficient and many optimal control methods can be applied to the following policy optimization. However, such models have limited expressiveness, which hinders their applications in complex nonlinear dynamics and high-dimensional state spaces. Another widely used probabilistic non-parametric approach is modelling the dynamic model by Gaussian processes (GPs) [3]. These models can effectively provide uncertainty over the predictions. However, their applications are also limited to relatively low-dimensional tasks.

In recent years, many methods have been proposed to utilize neural networks to determine the dynamics models for complicated tasks [4,7]. However, it's difficult to learn a dynamics model that absolutely accurately represents the real environment, even equipped with a high-capacity model. And the accuracy of the learned model often affects the agent's asymptotic performance. So, model-based methods can be sample-efficient, but the final performance is inferior to their model-free counterparts [8].

Some methods attempt to narrow the gap between model-based and model-free RL methods. In [9], Kurutach et al. proposed to employ neural network ensembles to represent the uncertainty in models and Gal et al. employed Bayesian deep dynamics models in [10]. Although these approaches improve the asymptotic performance of model-based methods, recent research have shown that it's still difficult for them to achieve the same performance as state-of-the-art model-free methods robustly [11].

In this paper, we put forward a novel model-based RL algorithm that avoids strong dependency on an accurate learned model. The idea of our method is to extend model-based algorithm to the meta-learning framework, so that a policy prior can be learned to quickly switch to the optimal policy for the real environment after one or several policy gradient steps. Firstly, an improved method of learning dynamics models is presented to alleviate the influence of subjective uncertainty and aleatoric uncertainty. In order to improve sample efficiency, we sample environment trajectories with meta-policy instead of adapted policies. Then, a special way of inferring model trajectories is introduced in the meta-learning framework to reduce model compounding bias. In the end, we introduce how a policy prior can be learned via meta-learning. To verify the proposed method, three experiments on robotic benchmark tasks were performed. The results show that our approach can efficiently complete the given tasks with less environment samples and outperform other model-based methods.

The remainder is structured as follows. First, we review model-based reinforcement learning and meta-reinforcement learning in the background section. Then we detailedly introduce our method in the method section. In the next part, experiments on simulation robotic tasks are designed to verify our algorithm's effectiveness. Finally, the conclusion is given in the last section.

## 2  Background

### 2.1  Preliminaries

In reinforcement learning, the interactive process between an agent and the environment can be formulated as a Markov decision process (MDP) $\mathcal{M}$, defined by the tuple $(\mathcal{S}, \mathcal{A}, p, r, \gamma, H)$. Here, $\mathcal{S}$ is a series of states, $\mathcal{A}$ is a series of actions, $p\,(s_{t+1} \mid s_t, a_t)$ denotes the state transition distribution, $r : \mathcal{S} \times \mathcal{A} \to \mathbb{R}$ represents the rewards function, $\gamma \in [0, 1]$ is a discount factor and $H$ is the horizon length. An optimal policy $\pi^*$ that maps a state to an action $\pi : \mathcal{S} \to \mathcal{A}$ is expected to be learned, which can be infered by maximizing the expected long-term reward:

$$\pi^* = \mathrm{argmax}_\pi \, E_{\tau \sim \pi(\tau)}[r(\tau)] \tag{1}$$

where, $r(\tau)$ is the cumulative reward of the trajectory, denoted by $r_\tau = \sum_{i=1}^{N} \gamma^{i-1} r_i$.

In model-free reinforcement learning, the state transition distribution is considered to be unknown. For model-based reinforcement learning, they firstly build a model of the state transition distribution, also known as dynamics model, using data collected from interaction with the environment. Once learned, the dynamics model is used to infer the distribution over state-trajectories after applying a series of actions. By calculating the expected return over state trajectories, we can assess several candidate action sequences, and choose the optimal action sequence. In recent years, a series of policy gradient algorithms are proposed to get an optimal policy for continuous control tasks.

### 2.2  PPO

Proximal Policy Optimization (PPO) [12] is an on-policy policy gradient algorithm proposed to solve the problem that it's is not easy to determine the learning rate of policy gradient algorithms. As an actor-critic method, PPO maintains an actor network $\pi_\theta\,(s_t)$ with the parameters $\theta$, and a critic network $Q_\phi\,(s_t, a_t)$ with the parameters $\phi$.

For the critic part, its goal is to assess the value of the current state, so as to help the actor network to choose the optimal action. Assuming a one-step state transition sequence, the loss function of the critic network can be defined as:

$$L = \frac{1}{N} \sum \left(r(s, a) + V(s') - V(s)\right)^2 \tag{2}$$

For the actor part, its purpose is to learn a policy to maximize the expected long-term reward. The actor parameters can be updated using the policy gradient:

$$\theta = \theta + \alpha \nabla_\theta J(\theta) = \theta + \alpha \mathbb{E}_{\pi_\theta} \left[ \nabla_\theta \log \pi_\theta(a \mid s)(r(s,a) + V(s') - V(s)) \right] \quad (3)$$

## 2.3 Meta Reinforcement Learning

Meta learning is also called "learning to learn", which aims to utilize past learning experience to accelerate the learning of the target task. In reinforcement learning, the target of few-shot meta-learning is to make the agent to quickly learn an optimal policy $\pi_\theta(a \mid s)$ for a new task $T$ drawn from a distribution $\rho(T)$. Our approach is built on gradient-based meta-learning framework model-agnostic meta-learning (MAML) [13]. The meta-objective for MAML can be written as:

$$\min_\theta \sum_{T_i \sim \rho(T)} L_{T_i}(f_{\theta_i}) = \sum_{T_i \sim \rho(T)} L_{T_i}\left(f_{\theta - \alpha \nabla_\theta L_{T_i}(f_\theta)}\right) \quad (4)$$

According to the Eq. 4, the whole learning process can be divided into two parts. Firstly, a small number of training data on multiple tasks $T_i$ is sampled and the model parameters for each task $T_i$ can be updated by:

$$\theta'_i = \theta - \alpha \nabla_\theta L_{T_i}(f_\theta) \quad (5)$$

where $L_{T_i}$ is the inner objective loss, and it is usually optimized by vanilla policy gradient (VPG) [14] for the adaptation step.

After that, MAML recalculates the inner objective loss using updated model parameters, and the sum of which is the meta-objective. By minimizing the meta-objective, initialization parameters $\theta$ are learned, so that for any task $T_i \sim \rho(T)$ the policy can quickly adapt it after one or several policy gradient steps.

In original MAML RL, the loss function of task $T_i$ and model $f_\theta$ is defined as follows:

$$L_{T_i}(f_\theta) = -\mathbb{E}_{x_t, a_t \sim f_\theta, q(T_i)} \left[ \sum_{t=1}^{H} R_i(x_t, a_t) \right] \quad (6)$$

where $R_i(x_t, a_t)$ is the reward function of the target task. A policy gradient algorithm named TRPO is used to maximize the total reward of all tasks $T_i \sim \rho(T)$ in the outer optimization of MAML.

## 3   Method

In this section, we detailedly introduce our method MPOBR, which aims to combine model-based reinforcement learning with model-agnostic meta-learning [13]. As a model-based reinforcement learning method, we firstly describe how these models are learned. Then we introduce our method to infer model trajectories. Moreover, we introduce how a policy prior can be learned via meta-learning framework, so that it can quickly switch to the optimal policy after several policy gradient steps. Finally, an overall algorithm is presented to obtain an intuitive grasp of our method.

## 3.1  Model Learning

In model-based reinforcement learning, the key is to learn an accurate dynamics model. However, due to the influence of subjective uncertainty and aleatoric uncertainty, the learned model is hard to absolutely represent the process between the agent and the real environment. We overcome it by learning a distribution of dynamics models $\{f_{\phi_1}, \ldots, f_{\phi_K}\}$, in the form of an ensemble, of the real environment dynamics. In our experiments, each member of the ensemble $f_{\phi_k}(s_t, a_t)$ is modeled as a probabilistic neural network which can be denoted as: $f_{\phi_k}(s_{t+1} \mid s_t, a_t) = \mathcal{N}(\mu_{\phi_k}(s_t, a_t), \Sigma_{\phi_k}(s_t, a_t)))$. The output is a Gaussian distribution, where $\mu_{\phi_k}(s_t, a_t)$ is the mean and $\Sigma_{\phi_k}(s_t, a_t)$ denotes the diagonal covariance. In the following content, we introduce how the dynamics models can be learned.

Collecting training data: We collect training data by sampling initial state $s_1 \sim p(s_1)$, executing actions according to policy at each timestep, and recording the corresponding trajectories $\tau = (s_1, a_1, \ldots, s_{T-1}, a_{T-1}, s_T)$ of length $T$. In order to improve sample efficiency, we sample environment trajectories with meta-policy instead of adapted policies although the data collected by adapted policies is more diverse. We slice the trajectories $\tau$ into a series of state-action tuples $(s_t, a_t, s_{t+1})$ which are then stored in the dataset $D$. In order to address the distributional shift caused by the policy change along with the meta-optimization, we continually collect interaction data with real environment under the current policy, aggregate them with the previous data, and retrain the dynamics models with warm starts.

Training the model: In our work, we use a bootstrap ensemble of dynamics models $\{f_{\phi_1}, \ldots, f_{\phi_K}\}$ to approximate the dynamics of the true environment. In order to decorrelate the models, each model differs in its random initialized, and is trained with a different randomly selected subsets $D_k$ of the collected real environment samples. We train each model $f_{\phi_k}$ in the ensemble using the negative log prediction probability loss: $\sum_{n=1}^{T} -\log f_{\phi_k}(s_{t+1} \mid s_t, a_t)$.

## 3.2  Trajectory Inference

Once dynamics models $\{f_{\phi_1}, \ldots, f_{\phi_K}\}$ are learned, we can use them to replace the real environment dynamics to generate model trajectories. A common practice is to imagine model trajectories under the dynamics model starting from the initial state distribution, which can be used for the following policy optimization or planning procedure. However, if the dynamics model is inaccurate, the predicted state distribution is different from the actual one and the errors would accumulate for multi-step rollouts, leading to degraded performance. According to the idea in [15], a simple procedure of using short model-generated rollouts branched from real data can effectively alleviate the error. In MPOBR, we begin a rollout from a state which has been experienced in real environment and imagine short steps $T_k$ according to policy $\pi_\theta$ under the learned model $f_{\phi_k}$. The whole procedure is as follows:

$$T_k = \{s_1, \ldots s_{t-1}, a_{t-1}, s_t \ldots, s_h\} \quad with \quad s_t \sim f_{\phi_k}(s_t \mid s_{1:t-1}, a_{1:t-1}) \quad (7)$$

where $\{a_1 \ldots a_{t-1}\}$ is a sequence of actions guided by policy $a_t = \pi(s_t)$ starting from state $s_1 \in D$ and $h$ is the length of the trajectory. Even if the length of steps is short, many such short rollouts can be executed to generate a mass of model samples for policy optimization.

### 3.3 Policy Learning on Model Trajectories

Unlike common model-based reinforcement learning algorithms which tend to learn an accurate dynamics model with high predictive power, our core idea is to learn a policy prior which can quickly adapt to any one of these learned dynamics models. To learn this prior, we exploit one gradient-based meta rein-forcement learning structure named MAML. In MAML, an initialization policy $\pi_\theta$ is learned, and for any task $T_i \sim \rho(T)$ it can quickly switch to the opti-mal policy after one or several gradient steps. So, we can construct a task dis-tribution by embedding these learned dynamics models into different MDPs $\mathcal{M}_k = (\mathcal{S}, \mathcal{A}, f_{\phi K}, r, \gamma, H)$. The meta-objective of our method is as follows:

$$\max_\theta \frac{1}{K} \sum_{k=1}^{K} J_k(\boldsymbol{\theta}_k') \quad s.t. \quad \boldsymbol{\theta}_k' = \boldsymbol{\theta} + \alpha \nabla_\theta J_k(\boldsymbol{\theta}) \tag{8}$$

According to Eq. (8), the whole training process can be divided into two parts: inner optimization and outer optimization. The inner objective is defined as follows:

$$J_k(\boldsymbol{\theta}) = \mathbb{E}_{a_t \sim \pi_\theta(a_t|s_t)} \left[ \sum_{t=1}^{H} r(s_t, a_t) \mid s_{t+1} = \hat{f}_{\phi_k}(s_t, a_t) \right] \tag{9}$$

where, $J_k(\theta)$ is the expected return under the policy $\pi_\theta$ and the estimated dynamics model $f_{\phi_k}$. In order to estimate the expectation in Eq. (9), we imagine model trajectories by employing the above-mentioned method and compute the corresponding reward by evaluating the reward function $r(s_t, a_t)$. In our imple-mentation, vanilla policy gradient (VPG) [14] is used for the adaptation step, and the policy can be updated by $\boldsymbol{\theta}_k' = \boldsymbol{\theta} + \alpha \nabla_\theta J_k(\boldsymbol{\theta})$. In the outer optimization, the meta goal is to maximize the cumulative reward of adapted policies for all dynamics models, which can be written as:

$$\max_\theta \frac{1}{K} \sum_{k=0}^{K} J_k(\boldsymbol{\theta}_k') \tag{10}$$

To calculate the meta-objective, imaginary trajectory $T_k'$ is rolled out with the adapted policy $\pi_{\theta_k'}$ for the model $f_{\phi_k}$. In our experiments, Proximal Policy Opti-mization (PPO) [12] is used to maximize the meta-objective.

### 3.4 Algorithm

As shown in Algorithm 1, we summarize the overall learning process of our method. The final goal of our algorithm is to acquire the prior knowledge on the real environment through meta-learning on an ensemble of dynamics models.

---

**Algorithm 1:** Our method

---

1  Require Inner and outer step size $\alpha, \beta$
2  Initialize the policy $\pi_\theta$, the models $f_{\phi_1}, f_{\phi_2}, \ldots, f_{\phi_K}$ and $\mathcal{D} \leftarrow \emptyset$
3  **for** $N$ *epochs* **do**
4      Sample trajectories from the real environment with policy $\pi_\theta$. Add them to $\mathcal{D}$.
5      Train all models using $\mathcal{D}$.
6      **for** *all models* $f_{\phi_k}$ **do**
7          Sample many states $S$ uniformly from $\mathcal{D}$
8          Perform model rollouts $T_k$ according to policy $\pi_\theta$ separately starting from state $s \in S$
9          Compute adapted parameters $\theta'_k = \theta + \alpha \nabla_\theta J_k(\theta)$ using trajectories $T_k$
10         Roll-out model trajectories $T'_k$ starting from state $s \in S$ according to the adapted policy $\pi_{\theta'_k}$
11     Update $\theta \rightarrow \theta - \beta \frac{1}{K} \sum_k \nabla_\theta J_k(\theta'_k)$ using the trajectories $T'_k$
12 Return optimal pre-update parameters $\theta^*$

---

First, we initialize the policy and the models with different random weights. Then, we continue to sample trajectories from the real environment for the purpose of model learning. At the first iteration, a random policy is used to collect data from the real world, and store it in a replay buffer $D$. At subsequent iterations, trajectories are collected with meta-policies $\pi_\theta$, and then aggregated with previous trajectories stored in dataset $D$. All the ensemble of models are trained with the aggregated real-environment samples as introduced in Model learning. The algorithm proceeds to imagine trajectories from each model of the ensemble $\{f_{\phi_1}, \ldots, f_{\phi_K}\}$ using policy $\pi_\theta$. In order to reduce model compounding error, all the imagined trajectories are starting from state $s$ which has been experienced in real-world. These short trajectories are used to execute the inner adaptation policy gradient step, generating the adapted policies $\{\pi_{\theta'_1}, \ldots, \pi_{\theta'_K}\}$. Finally, we generate imaginary trajectories under the adapted policy $\pi_{\theta'_k}$ and model $f_{\phi_k}$, and exploit the meta-objective to optimize the meta policy. We repeat these process until desired performance is reached.

## 4 Experimental Evaluation

To test the effectiveness of our approach, we implemented three robotic experiments on standard benchmark locomotion tasks. First, we describe the experimental environment and tasks in detail. Then, training details and network architecture are detailedly explained. Finally, three types of experimental tasks are designed in the robot simulation environment to answer the following questions:

- How does our method compare against model-free methods in terms of asymptotic performance?

– How does our method compare against model-based methods in terms of sample complexity?
– Does our meta learning method effectively adapt to the situations when dynamics models are difficult to learn?

## 4.1 Experimental Setup

We test our method on three robot simulation tasks provided by OpenAI Gym [16,17], using the MuJoCo physics engine [18], as shown in Fig. 1. The goal of different experimental tasks is to train the agent to move in a way that satisfies given movements, such as walking, running, crawling. They need to learn the forward-moving gait as fast as possible. In Table 1, we briefly summarize the dimensionality of observation space and action space of these task environments. For all continuous control benchmark tasks, we set the length of horizon as 200. It is noted that average return on three random seeds was used to assess the performance of all methods.

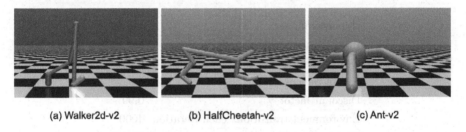

(a) Walker2d-v2            (b) HalfCheetah-v2            (c) Ant-v2

**Fig. 1.** Mujoco environments used in our experiments. Form left to right: Walker2D, Half-cheetah, Ant

**Table 1.** Parameters for task environments.

| Task | Dimension of observation space | Dimension of action space | Horizon |
|------|-------------------------------|---------------------------|---------|
| Ant-v2 | $R^{28}$ | $R^8$ | 200 |
| Walker2d-v2 | $R^{17}$ | $R^6$ | 200 |
| HalfCheetah-v2 | $R^{23}$ | $R^6$ | 200 |

## 4.2 Training Details

In this section, we detailedly describe the training process of our algorithm, including environment trajectory collection, dynamics model learning and policy learning.

In our experiments, 20 environment trajectories in an algorithm iteration are collected and split into 4000 environment transitions, which are then used to train dynamics models. Similarly, 200,000 imaginary model transitions are sampled to optimize the meta-optimization.

For model learning, we use 5 fully connected neural networks to predict the next state given a state and an action. The model networks are designed with 3 hidden layers, containing of 512 *ReLU* neurons in each layer. We use weight normalization to avoid overfitting and the Adam optimizer with a batch-size of 500 to optimize one-step prediction error. During training, we frequently compute the validation loss of neural network dynamics models and early stop training once the loss no longer decreases.

We use a neural network to represent the Gaussian policy $\pi_\theta(a \mid s) = \mathcal{N}\left(a \mid \mu(a)_{\theta_\mu}, \sigma_{\theta_\sigma}\right)$, which receives the current state $s$ as an input, and outputs the corresponding action. It is designed to contain two fully connected hidden layers with 32 neurons in each layer, using *tanh* nonlinearity, and outputs the mean and variance of Gaussian distribution. For convenience, all the parameters mentioned above are summarized in Table 2.

**Table 2.** Hyperparameters used in our method.

| Hyperparameter | Value |
|---|---|
| Inner learning rate $\alpha$ | 0.001 |
| Outer learning rate $\beta$ | 0.001 |
| Size of the ensemble | 5 |
| Discount factor $\gamma$ | 0.99 |
| Environment transitions each iteration | 4000 |
| Model transitions each iteration | 200,000 |

### 4.3   Comparison to Model-Free Reinforcement Learning Algorithms

In this experiment, the asymptotic performance is used for assessing the final performance of our algorithm, in which four state-of-the-art model-free reinforcement learning algorithms serve as baselines, covering Proximal Policy Optimization (PPO) [12], Deep Deterministic Policy Gradient (DDPG) [19], Trust Region Policy Optimization (TRPO) [20], and Actor Critic using Kronecker-Factored Trust Region (ACKTR) [21]. In the case of PPO, we contrast the advantage of incorporating model-based reinforcement learning and meta-learning, as our method uses PPO policy gradient algorithm for policy learning as well. Figure 2 show the results on the Ant, HalfCheetah and Walker2d tasks. The horizontal axis, in log-scale, indicates the number of time steps of real environment and the vertical axis is the average return. The solid curve represents the variation of average return along with time steps, and the shaded area represents the range of the corresponding average return with three random seeds.

For all three experiment tasks, our method can reach maximum final performance while significantly reducing the demand of samples, revealing excellent

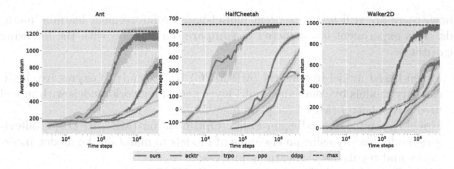

**Fig. 2.** Learning curves of our method and model-free baselines on robotic task with a horizon of 200.

asymptotic performance and sample efficiency of our algorithm. For example, MPOBR's average return on the Ant task at 360 thousand time steps is the same as that of ACKTR at 4 million steps. For the challenging Walker task, MPOBR can obtain final performance at 2 million time steps, while the best of four baselines, PPO, takes 25 million time steps to achieve the final performance.

**Table 3.** The performance and real-world samples in the Ant, HalfCheetah and Walker2D tasks compared with model-free baselines.

| Method | Ant | | HalfCheetah | | Walker2D | |
|--------|-----|--|-------------|--|----------|--|
| | Return | Real-world | Return | Real-world | Return | Real-world |
| TRPO | 935 | 54 million | 645 | 3.6 million | 875.33 | 80 million |
| PPO | 981.32 | 19.5 million | 464 | 2.2 million | 893.42 | 25 million |
| DDPG | 464.21 | 4.85 million | 239 | 5.6 million | 419.23 | 7.3 million |
| ACKTR | 961.33 | 4.6 million | 614 | 4.7 million | 655.34 | 2.5 million |
| Ours | 1188 | 0.7 million | 643 | 0.241 million | 949.83 | 2 million |

Table 3 summarizes the asymptotic performance and real-world samples of different algorithms in the Ant, HalfCheetah and Walker2D tasks. We can see that our method can reach the same even better final performance using at least 6.5 times less data. In HalfCheetah task, our method achieves comparable asymptotic performance with about 15 times less real-world samples. All of these reveal outstanding asymptotic performance of our method.

### 4.4 Comparison to Model-Based Reinforcement Learning Algorithms

In the front experiment, we have proved that our method can effectively learn a near optimal policy and significantly alleviate the need of excess samples. As we know, there are still many excellent model-based reinforcement learning methods. This experiment is conducted to compare our method with the following algorithms:

- Model-based model-free hybrid (MB-MPC) [7]: extends to expressive, high-capacity models by combining multi-layer neural network models with model predictive control (MPC) for planning.
- Model-Ensemble Trust-Region Policy Optimization (ME-TRPO) [9]: alleviates model bias by using an ensemble of models to maintain the model uncertainty and regularize the learning process.
- Model-Based Meta-Policy-Optimization (MB-MPO) [22]: meta-learns a policy on dynamics models with a different way of sampling environment trajectories and inferring model rollouts.

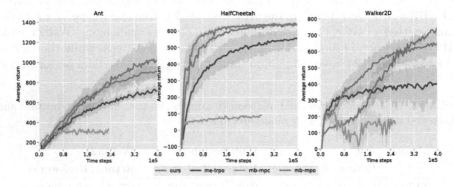

**Fig. 3.** Learning curves of our method and model-based baselines on robotic task with a horizon of 200.

The results in Fig. 3 highlight the advantage of our method. Whilst MB-MPO can quickly converge to the final performance, it usually lags behind our method in terms of asymptotic performance, showing the effectiveness of model trajectory inferring of our method. Due to the short-horizon characteristic of the MPC, MB-MPC struggles to perform well on all tasks and tends to learn a sub-optimal policy. In contrast, ME-TRPO can learn better policies, but the final performance on the three tasks is worst when compared to MPOBR and MB-MPO. Furthermore, the convergence speed of ME-TRPO is slower.

In Table 4, we summarize the convergence speed and asymptotic performance of these methods. For the challenging Walker2D task, MPOBR has the best asymptotic performance. In the Ant task, it can achieve the same average return of MB-MPO at 501 thousand time steps, confirming the effect of our method of sampling environment trajectories. Moreover, our method can obtain similar performance to MB-MPO in HalfCheetah task.

**Table 4.** The performance and real-world samples in the Ant, HalfCheetah and Walker2D tasks compared with model-free baselines.

| Method | Ant | | HalfCheetah | | Walker2D | |
|---|---|---|---|---|---|---|
| | Return | Real-world | Return | Real-world | Return | Real-world |
| ME-TRPO | 742 | 390 thousand | 572 | 325 thousand | 396 | 268 thousand |
| MB-MPC | 310 | 68 thousand | 89 | 172 thousand | 0 | 0 thousand |
| MB-MPO | 1023.67 | 632 thousand | 644 | 232 thousand | 802 | 996 thousand |
| Ours | 1188 | 705 thousand | 643 | 241 thousand | 949.83 | 2 million |

## 4.5   Ablation Study

We conduct an ablation study to test how the meta-training on an ensemble of dynamics models improves the asymptotic performance. As a comparison, we set the inner learning rate $\alpha$ to zero, which denotes the case without meta-learning. Figure 4 show the experiment results.

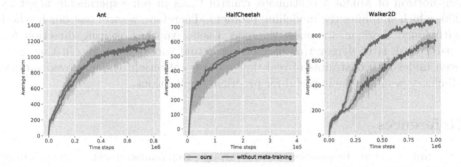

**Fig. 4.** Learning curves with or without meta-training on an ensemble of dynamics models on robotic tasks with a horizon of 200.

We can see that there is slight difference between with and without meta-training in the Ant and HalfCheetah tasks, but for the Walker2d task our method observably outperforms the other one with respect to sample efficiency and asymptotic performance. This is because it's difficult to represent the real-world in Walker2d task by an ensemble of dynamics models, so that the policy learned on dynamics models is hard to behave well in real environment. For our method, the purpose is to learn a policy prior, not a final policy, getting ride of strong dependency on accurate dynamics models. We can see that even if meta-learning does not obviously improve the convergence speed of our method in relatively simple task, the asymptotic performance of our method is unaffected. In conclusion, our method not only has good performance on relatively simple tasks, but also improves the convergence speed and asymptotic performance on complex tasks.

# 5   Conclusion

In this paper, we propose a simple and effective model-based RL algorithm, MPOBR, which can quickly learn policies across different challenging domains with less environment samples. In our method, an ensemble of dynamics models are trained in order to reduce the impact of subjective uncertainty, and a policy prior is expected to adapt the real environment with one or several policy gradient steps in order to get rid of heavy dependence on a precise dynamics model. We achieve this goal by meta-learning a policy over an ensemble of learned dynamics models, and use probabilistic neural network to capture aleatoric uncertainty. Moreover, we exploit short model-generated rollouts branched from real data to reduce the influence of model compounding bias. Therefore, the MPOBR algorithm has the final performance rivaling state-of-the-art model-free algorithms, and can reach the similar convergence speed to other model-based methods. Furthermore, the experiment results of ablation study prove that our method has advantage in more challenging tasks.

Our method can achieve the same asymptotic performance of state-of-the-art model-free algorithms with significantly more efficient convergence. However, the horizon of MuJoCo continuous control tasks in our experiments is set as 200, which simplifies the modelling problem. Therefore, we will test our method with longer horizon and more complex tasks. Another exciting direction for future work is to deploy this method on actual robotic systems. In this case, even under the constraints of real-time sample collection, the improved sample efficiency would make it useful for practical applications.

# References

1. Mnih, V., et al.: Human-level control through deep reinforcement learning. Nature **518**(7540), 529–533 (2015)
2. Silver, D., et al.: Mastering the game of go without human knowledge. Nature **550**(7676), 354–359 (2017)
3. Deisenroth, M., Rasmussen, C.E.: PILCO: a model-based and data-efficient approach to policy search. In: Proceedings of the 28th International Conference on machine learning (ICML 2011), pp. 465–472 (2011)
4. Depeweg, S., Hernández-Lobato, J.M., Doshi-Velez, F., Udluft, S.: Learning and policy search in stochastic dynamical systems with Bayesian neural networks, arXiv preprint arXiv:1605.07127 (2016)
5. Farahmand, A.-M.: Iterative value-aware model learning. In: NeurIPS, pp. 9090–9101 (2018)
6. Wu, Y.-H., Fan, T.-H., Ramadge, P.J., Su, H.: Model imitation for model-based reinforcement learning, arXiv preprint arXiv:1909.11821 (2019)
7. Nagabandi, A., Kahn, G., Fearing, R.S., Levine, S.: Neural network dynamics for model-based deep reinforcement learning with model-free fine-tuning. In: 2018 IEEE International Conference on Robotics and Automation (ICRA), pp. 7559–7566. IEEE (2018)
8. Moerland, T.M., Broekens, J., Jonker, C.M.: Model-based reinforcement learning: a survey, arXiv preprint arXiv:2006.16712 (2020)

9. Kurutach, T., Clavera, I., Duan, Y., Tamar, A., Abbeel, P.: Model-ensemble trust-region policy optimization, arXiv preprint arXiv:1802.10592 (2018)
10. Gal, Y., McAllister, R., Rasmussen, C.E.: Improving PILCO with Bayesian neural network dynamics models. In: Data-Efficient Machine Learning Workshop, ICML, vol. 4, no. 34, p. 25 (2016)
11. Wang, T., et al.: Benchmarking model-based reinforcement learning, arXiv preprint arXiv:1907.02057 (2019)
12. Schulman, J., Wolski, F., Dhariwal, P., Radford, A., Klimov, O.: Proximal policy optimization algorithms, arXiv preprint arXiv:1707.06347 (2017)
13. Finn, C., Abbeel, P., Levine, S.: Model-agnostic meta-learning for fast adaptation of deep networks. In: International Conference on Machine Learning, pp. 1126–1135. PMLR (2017)
14. Peters, J., Schaal, S.: Policy gradient methods for robotics. In: 2006 IEEE/RSJ International Conference on Intelligent Robots and Systems, pp. 2219–2225. IEEE (2006)
15. Janner, M., Fu, J., Zhang, M., Levine, S.: When to trust your model: Model-based policy optimization, arXiv preprint arXiv:1906.08253 (2019)
16. Brockman, G., et al.: OpenAI gym. https://github.com/openai/gym
17. Plappert, M., Andrychowicz, M., Ray, A., Mcgrew, B., Zaremba, W.: Multi-goal reinforcement learning: challenging robotics environments and request for research, arXiv preprint arXiv:1802.09464 (2018)
18. Todorov, E., Erez, T., Tassa, Y.: Mujoco: a physics engine for model-based control. In: 2012 IEEE/RSJ International Conference on Intelligent Robots and Systems, pp. 5026–5033. IEEE (2012)
19. Lillicrap, T.P., et al.: Continuous control with deep reinforcement learning, arXiv preprint arXiv:1509.02971 (2015)
20. Schulman, J., Levine, S., Abbeel, P., Jordan, M., Moritz, P.: Trust region policy optimization. In: International Conference on Machine Learning, pp. 1889–1897. PMLR (2015)
21. Wu, Y., Mansimov, E., Liao, S., Grosse, R., Ba, J.: Scalable trust-region method for deep reinforcement learning using kronecker-factored approximation, arXiv preprint arXiv:1708.05144 (2017)
22. Clavera, I., Rothfuss, J., Schulman, J., Fujita, Y., Asfour, T., Abbeel, P.: Model-based reinforcement learning via meta-policy optimization. In: Conference on Robot Learning, pp. 617–629. PMLR (2018)

# From Human Oral Instructions to General Representations of Knowledge: A New Paradigm for Industrial Robots Skill Teaching

Shiyu Chen[1], Yongjia Zhao[1,2(✉)], Xiaoyong Lei[1], Tao Qi[1], and Kan Liu[1]

[1] State Key Laboratory of Virtual Reality Technology and Systems, Beihang University, Beijing, People's Republic of China
zhaoyongjia@buaa.edu.cn
[2] Jiangxi Research Institute, Beihang University, Beijing, Jiangxi, People's Republic of China

**Abstract.** Converting human oral instructions into general representations of knowledge which robots can understand, can realize more advanced behaviors for unmanned driving, drones, robots and other fields. This paper presents a novel paradigm based on two-stage structure that transforms human oral instructions into general representations of operating knowledge. Firstly, a Speech-to-Text module is used to realize automatic speech recognition, which results in a text expression for the input oral instruction. In the second stage, a Text-to-Knowledge module is used to realize natural language understanding, which introduces and visualizes task-related knowledge graphs converted from the text expression. To validate this paradigm, the task of computer motherboard assembly was chosen as an example, and a low-cost monophonic speech corpus named PC-CORPUS was built. This PC-CORPUS, is 3 h 44 min long and has 2278 wave audios. 14 speakers from different accent areas in China were invited in the recording. Then experiments were designed and carried out on this paradigm with PC-CORPUS. The average edit distance of this paradigm is 10.87%, comparing the triples of final visual knowledge representations with the ones were labeled by the experts.

**Keywords:** Knowledge graph · Computer assembly · Natural language understanding

## 1 Introduction

No doubt that intellectualization is the trend of information technology. In various industries like service and manufacturing, or on the assembly line in factories, there already has been more and more "smart" devices, which can replace human in repetitive, monotonous tasks. Currently, robots can be used to perform a fixed sequence of operations in complete tasks, mainly relying on online programming (or namely lead-through programming) [1, 2] and offline programming (OLP, or namely hard programming) [3, 4] methods. Although the programming methods mentioned above can reduce the labor intensity to a certain extent, for complex and scalable tasks, the

F. Sun et al. (Eds.): ICCSIP 2021, CCIS 1515, pp. 374–388, 2022.
https://doi.org/10.1007/978-981-16-9247-5_29

trajectory sequence generated by hard programming is far from expressing the complex operation intentions of humans. It is better to use human oral expressions or other multi-modal expressions. Robots need to obtain knowledge from human teachings, to achieve higher-level behaviors. Some of the knowledge comes from structured, semi-structured or unstructured data [5–7], some comes from action demonstrations [8–10]. As one of the most important mediums of human communication, the collection of human oral instructions is more convenient than data or actions. Therefore, it is a much easier way to acquire human knowledge through voice commands than collecting data from Internet and recording action demonstrations.

Human oral instructions are a natural teaching material for the teaching of robotic skills, which can make robots more human-like while handling complex tasks. Consequently, a paradigm that transforms human oral instructions into general representations of operating knowledge is needed.

Voice technology is one of the most important branches of computer multimedia technology. Like Siri of Apple and XiaoAI of Xiaomi, Internet corporations have developed smart voice assistant based on Automatic Speech Recognition (ASR). With the development of artificial intelligence, not only in the Internet industry, but ASR technology has been becoming widely used in education, manufacturing and military. Natural language understanding (NLU) analyzes the input to get specific intentions and other information. In manufacturing industry, NLU is often limited to task-oriented dialog systems and applications that understand human input, in other words, intent understanding and slot filling (or entity recognition). Apart from ASR and NLU, information about the environment, tasks, operations and robots' own skills are needed when robots performing tasks. Knowledge graph (KG) which formally proposed to improve the search quality by Google in 2012, using semantic retrieval to collect information from multiple sources, can save information mentioned above as structured data.

Via ASR, NLU and KG technology, we established a two-stage architecture, which converts human verbal instructions into general representations of knowledge. This architecture supports robots to perform a series of operations in various task scenarios to complete complex tasks, that is, to complete complex operation tasks in a dynamic environment.

Our contributions are three folds:

1) We construct an overall paradigm from human oral instructions to general representations of operating knowledge. The paradigm uses ASR technology to convert human speeches into unstructured texts, and then uses NLU to convert texts into knowledge. If there is information or knowledge in the speech input that is not in the knowledge base, the knowledge base will be automatically updated accordingly.
2) We propose a domain-related knowledge expression form, which is different from general knowledge expressions. This form only contains information such as the behavior, tools, and artifacts of the operation task, but does not include common-sense information.
3) We construct a Chinese speech corpus, in which utterance contains computer architecture and computer motherboard assembly tasks. The speech input instructions are set as the computer motherboard assembly task so that we can verify the effectiveness of the paradigm. The corpus is recorded according to the corresponding document which will be introduced afterwards.

# 2 Related Work

## 2.1 Automatic Speech Recognition

Recent research has studied ASR models based on deep learning with great recognition accuracy. DeepSpeech [11, 12], is a Chinese end-to-end ASR system developed by Baidu, using Mel Cepstral Coefficient (MFCC) to extract spectrograms as audio features in the speech input, and then using recurrent neural network (RNN) to convert an input sequence into a sequence of character probabilities for the transcription. PyTorch-Kaldi [13] has built a bridge chain between PyTorch and Kaldi [14] to develop a modern speech recognition system, suing Kaldi for feature extraction and label solving, and PyTorch for neural network training. SpeechBrain [15] is an all-in-one speech toolkit with multiple functions including ASR, we choose Transformer [16] as the main neural work structure with CTC loss function.

## 2.2 Automatic Knowledge Graph Construction

Automatic knowledge graph construction seeks to build a knowledge graph from unstructured text [17]. Apart from multiple teams who have participated the ICDM knowledge graph contest, many researchers [18] aim to build a whole process converting text information into knowledge. In [19], an automatic knowledge graph construction from speech to knowledge has been built. When a user speaks, the system will convert the speech input into knowledge graphs. Inspired by this work, we consider to extract key information of only operation tasks, instead of other information. Besides, we consider verbal instructions as the input, which may reduce the typing procedures, simplifying it to the speech input.

## 2.3 Expressions of the Operational Intent

Most industrial fields use online programming (lead-through programming) methods or offline programming (OLP) methods to let robots perform a fixed sequence of operation steps to complete the task. In [1], An expert welder is required to move the robot end effector to complete a welding process, at the same time, the position and speech information are recorded for robots to replicate the task. Similarly, [2] uses the lead through teaching method to obtain the guiding points to generate the robot program. The exploitation of offline programming methods improves the robotic deburring process of aerospace components [3]. Apart from CAD-based and digitizer-based offline programming methods, [4] allows the integrations of virtual reality technology and OLP. Many tools based on online and offline programming methods have been developed to make robots perform tasks, but these tools are not suitable for robots to complete complex operation tasks in a dynamic environment.

There are some characteristics of complex operation tasks: 1) Complex operation tasks are usually composed of multiple subtask sequences; 2) The ontology and environment during the task execution process are dynamic, which requires multi-sensor fusion to obtain ontology and environment information as input conditions for task execution; 3) There are complex space, time and event-driven interactions with the operating objects.

For related research on teaching robots to complete complex operation tasks, the existing methods still have the following problems: 1) Although the task operation and the task scenario are relatively fixed, the existing methods do not make full use of the existing scenario knowledge; 2) Language is an important medium for human communication. Humans teaching relys mainly on action demonstrations and structured data, instead of flexible human verbal instructions; 3) The operational knowledge can be dynamically generated, but there is no domain-specific knowledge representation form.

# 3 Architecture

We present a novel paradigm based on two-stage structure that transforms human oral instructions into general representations of operating knowledge. The paradigm consists two parts, the text generation structure and the knowledge representation structure. The whole structure of this paradigm is shown in Fig. 1.

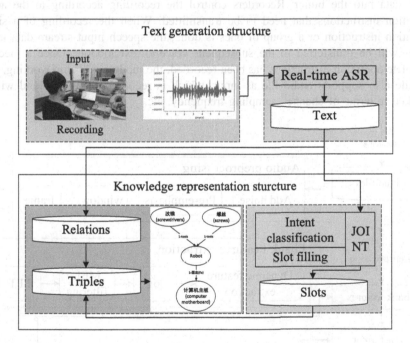

**Fig. 1.** The whole structure of our paradigm. The blue part shows recording module of the text generation structure, the green part shows the voice-to-text module. The orange part shows the text-to-slot module of the knowledge representation structure, and the purple one shows the slot-to-knowledge module. The recording module inputs the audio files by volunteers. The voice-to-text module outputs texts through speech recognition. After syntactic analysis and text-to-slot module, texts are converted into triples, which are visualized in the slot-to-knowledge module. (Color figure online)

In the text generation structure, the human oral instructions are input into the recording module, which sends them to the voice-to-text module for speech recognition. The structure outputs the text representations of the verbal instructions.

The knowledge representation structure is composed of text-to-slot and slot-to-knowledge modules. The text-to-slot module uses the intent classification and slot filling joint training model to convert the text output by the text generation structure into slots. The slots are then converted and visualized into domain-related knowledge representations through the slot-to-knowledge module.

## 3.1  Text Generation Based on Automatic Speech Recognition

The following modules are designed to convert the speech input into texts. The speech input can be recorded through a variety of devices, supporting mono voice streams and audio files.

Recording module. The real-time speech input is recorded and transferred to the computer via PyAudio. Recording module monitors the input voice stream, saves the input data into the buffer. Recorders control the recording according to the actual operation instructions that need to be transmitted. When the recording of a single operation instruction or a group of ones is done, the speech input stream data in the buffer will be transferred to the subsequent voice-to-text module. Once a piece of complete operation instructions has been recorded, the module will stop working. This module also supports audio file as input, which is recorded previously and will be checked in terms of channel, sampling frequency, etc.

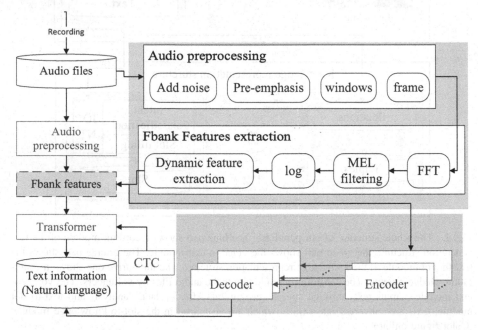

**Fig. 2.** Automatic Speech Recognition module. After audio preprocessing, audio files are converted into FBank feature, which has the required feature vector size, through the linear change of the layer normalization. Then it is delivered into Transformer to obtain the output sequence and probability.

Voice-to-Text module (Fig. 2). This module, pre-trained by AiShell-1 [14], a Chinese Mandarin voice database, has then been trained by self-made low-cost database named PC-CORPUS. Mono speech input data received from the above module will be converted into text information. While the speech input is recorded according to the word order expressed by humans, the text information output by this module is correspondingly segmented into separate parts, saved to the input file which is prepared for the next phase.

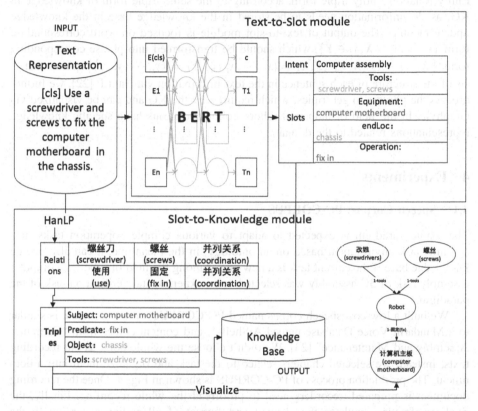

**Fig. 3.** Knowledge representation structure. The text information (Natural language) is further processed to obtain the intent and slots. Then the slots are converted into the triple form of "entity-relation-entity" and visualized via Graphviz.

## 3.2    Knowledge Representation Based on Natural Language Understanding

The following modules (Fig. 3) are designed to convert text information into slot information.

Text-to-Slot module. The intent classification task is a classification problem of predicting labels; the slot filling task is a problem of predicting sequence labels. This module is based on JointBert [20], a joint intent classification and slot filling model based on Bert [21]. We use a single sentence $X = (x_1, x_2, \ldots, x_T)$, which is the output as a part of text information by the above modules, as input, a label $y$, as the output of the intent classification, and a sequence of slot labels $Y = (y_1, y_2, \cdots, y_T)$, as the output of the slot filling.

Slot-to-Knowledge module. This module converts the slot information into an Entity-Relation-Entity triple form, according to the same triple form of knowledge in KG, as slot information needs to be stored in the knowledge base in the knowledge update module. The output of text-to-slot module is focused on word corresponding form $\{x_t : y_t, x_t \in X, y_t \in Y\}$, which should be transformed into phrase corresponding form $\left\{ X_k : Y_k, X_k {\subseteq} X, Y_k {\subseteq} Y, X_k = (x_t, \cdots, x_{t+n}), Y_k = \left(y_t, \cdots, y_{t+n}\right)\right\}$. After analysis of the structure of each sentence in the text information via HanLP [22], we further process the phrases to get triples, which required by the KG and can be visualized via Graphviz. In the field of industrial robots, robot operations have specific knowledge representations related to the domain.

# 4   Experiments

## 4.1   Speech Corpus: PC-CORPUS

The whole paradigm is expected to adapt to various complex operation tasks in a dynamic task environment based on an ontology, in the meantime, it can also update knowledge base if the current task is a new one. Among the field of robotics, computer assembly task of 3C assembly was selected as an experimental verification task of the paradigm.

We built a low-cost speech corpus named PC-CORPUS, whose structure is similar to a Mandarin Voice Database named AiShell-1, and content comes from "Computer Assembly and Maintenance" [23]. We didn't choose the whole book as our recording texts, instead, we selected chapters related to the task and organize them into a document. The production process of PC-CORPUS is shown in Fig. 4. Once the recording document is prepared, recorders need to proofread the while recording. Finally, the final proofreader regulates the channel and format of all audios according to the experiment requirements, and proofread all audio files and content files one more time.

IOS system phones or tablets, Android system phones, and computers are used as the recording devices. 14 speakers, of different genders, from different accent areas in China, were invited to participate in the recording. The distribution of recorders can be seen in Fig. 5.

PC-CORPUS contains 3h44 min of Mandarin speech data and over 8000 words. we set a blank space "blank" between every phrase. Including "blank", there are 839 new words and 1277 new phrases stored in the dictionary apart from repeating ones. Then we created PC-CORPUS in which there are 2278 mono wave audios, sampling frequency being 16 kHz. The longest duration of a single audio is 30.2 s, the shortest duration is 1.34 s, the total duration of all audios is 3 h 44 min.

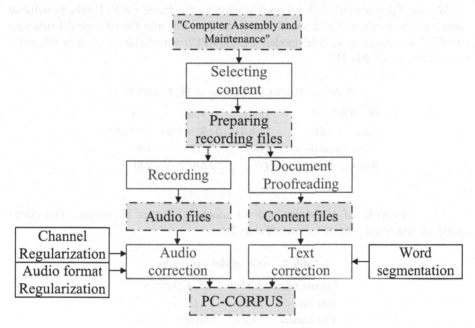

**Fig. 4.** The production process of PC-CORPUS.

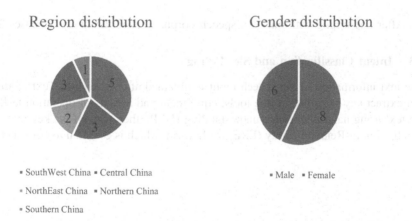

**Fig. 5.** Region distribution and gender distribution of 14 recorders. The recorders come from five of the seven geographic regions of China. Although the recordings are all in Mandarin, most of the recorders have local accent habits. Apart from that, Recorders of different genders have different pitches while recording.

## 4.2   Automatic Speech Recognition

Automatic Speech Recognition (ASR) is used to convert the speech input stream data received from the recording module into text information with "blank". Considering speech data in the field of specific operation tasks may not be efficient in open-source speech corpus in actual applications, we further fine-tuned the model using PC-CORPUS after pretrained by AiShell-1.

We use SpeechBrain [15], an open-source toolkit based on PyTorch, to achieve speech-to-text module. We choose Transformer [16] Encoder-Decoder model structure and CTC loss function as ASR model. PC-CORPUS was divided into train set, valid set and test set (Table 1):

**Table 1.** Dataset distribution of PC-CORPUS

| PC-CORPUS | Train | Valid | Test |
|---|---|---|---|
| Data Size (kB) | 250691170 | 54567594 | 55856384 |
| Voice Duration (sec) | 4986 | 1198 | 1269 |
| Number of Audios | 971 | 240 | 240 |

After 50 epochs of pretraining and 50 epochs of further fine-tuning, The corresponding test results are as follows (Table 2):

**Table 2.** ASR model test results

| Dataset name | AiShell-1 | PC-CORPUS |
|---|---|---|
| Test loss | 5.88 | 3.23 |
| Test accuracy | 93.2% | 96.8% |
| Test CER | 6.05 | 5.2 |

After fine-tuning with our own speech corpus, the test accuracy increases 3.6%.

## 4.3   Intent Classification and Slot Filling

The text information of the speech input is obtained after Speech-to-Text module, we can extract key information like tools, equipment and actions of operation tasks from the text using natural language understanding (NLP), then convert the key information into the Entity-Relation-Entity (ERE) triple form, which is essential to construct a KG.

There is a close relationship and dependency between intent classification task and slot filling task. For example, when the intent is "book a movie ticket", the corresponding slots are "movie name", "cinema name", "movie time", etc. when the slots are "flight" and "destination", the corresponding intent is "booking air tickets". Therefore, there is a joint training method between the two tasks named JointBert, a joint model of intent classification and slot filling task. JointBert adds a soft-max to predict intent and slot labels based on Bert.

An example of the input and output of this module is shown in the Fig. 6 below.

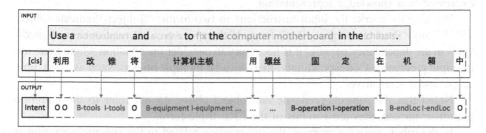

**Fig. 6.** An example of intent classification and slot filling joint task.

According to PC-CORPUS, we further constructed a low-cost dataset named PC-Joint based on FewJoint [24], and then started training on the JointBert model. The training results are as follows (Table 3):

**Table 3.** Intent classification and slot filling test results

| Model | Intent accuracy | Slot filling F1 |
|---|---|---|
| JointBert (10 Epochs) | 97.0% | 88.8% |
| JointBert + CRF (10 Epochs) | 97.2% | 88.3% |

### 4.4 Slot Information Visualization and Storage

When we get slot information from Text-to-Slot module, we should convert it from the word correspondence form $\{x_t : y_t, x_t \in X, y_t \in Y\}$ to the phrase correspondence form $\{X_k : Y_k, X_k \subseteq X, Y_k \subseteq Y, X_k = (x_t, \cdots, x_{t+n}), Y_k = (y_t, \cdots, y_{t+n})\}$ before further processes. Like the example in Fig. 6, we can get the following phrase information:

$$\{'screwdriver' : tools,' computer\ motherbard' : equipment, \atop 'screws' : tools,' fix' : operations,' chassis' : endLoc\} \qquad (1)$$

From the phrase information, tools, equipment, operations and endLoc respectively correspond to the required operating tools, operating equipment, operations and operating positions during the operation. It is enough to drive the robot to perform operations once we get these slots information. However, in the implementation process, to allow the operator to supervise the entire process, the information needs to be expressed in a knowledge representation.

We roughly restrict the input instructions in two forms: "Subject-Predicate-Object (SPO)" and "Predicate-Object (PO)" form. If there is a parallel relationship of predicates in the dependency parsing, it is necessary to consider the situation where there are multiple predicates. Correspondingly, there will be multiple objects, such as `pick up a screw and a screwdriver'.

Noted that the subject, predicate and object above do not refer to the common grammar, instead, they are variants of the ERE triple form.

In the robot operation process, the information related to the specific operation is regarded as key information that needs to be visualized and stored. Different from other general knowledge representations, this experiment needs to discuss the relationship of slots in the input verbal instructions. When there is tool information in the slots, the tool information is generally regarded as a complement, such as `install the computer motherboard with screws', but if the object is missing in the verbal instructions, the tool information should be regarded as the object, such as `robot picks up screws'.

Like the example in Fig. 6, we can see the input instruction as SPO form, and further convert it to "computer motherboard–fix in–chassis" with screwdrivers and screws as tools, that is, "computer motherboard" is seen as the subject, "fix in" the predicate, "chassis" the object and "screwdrivers", "screws" the supplementary information. There may be more complicated situations during the actual applications. We use the Chinese NLP tool HanLP to deal with possible situations.

After we get the triple information, they can be visualized via Graphviz (Figs. 7, 8 and 9):

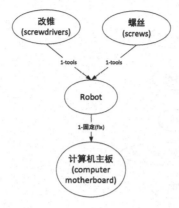

**Fig. 7.** Legend-A single input instruction: "Use a screwdriver and screws to fix the computer motherboard."

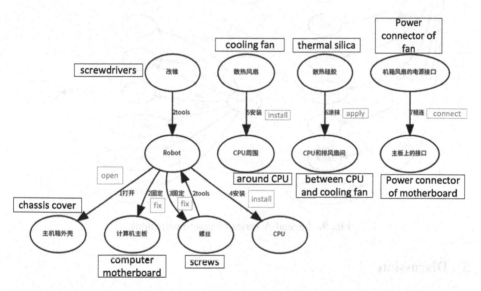

**Fig. 8.** Legend-A series of input instructions: "Open the chassis cover, then use a screwdriver and screws to fix the computer motherboard. Fix the screws near the power socket, then install CPU, apply some thermal silica between CPU and cooling fan, finally connect the power connector of the fan to the connector on the motherboard."

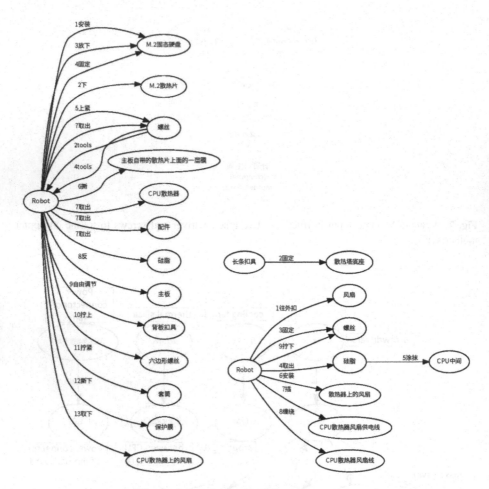

**Fig. 9.** Legend-A series of input instructions

## 5  Discussion

The paradigm is judged by the evaluation process in the ICDM knowledge graph contest [17]. The evaluation is mainly to judge whether the knowledge representation obtained by the paradigm is consistent with the human-labeled knowledge representation (correct representations) under the supervision of experts. If the results are the same, the score is 0. If not, the score is positively correlated with the edit distance between the obtained result and the correct result. Referring to this scoring standard, the average edit distance of the paradigm is 10.87%.

The influence of the speech recognition module (from speech to text module) on the entire paradigm is also discussed consider that our paradigm adds an ASR module (text generation structure) compared with other general models. Our paradigm provides the text output by the text generation module, which should be regarded as recognition results instead of natural language. During the experiment, it was found that although there are recognition errors in ASR module, but after the text-to-slot module, information that is irrelevant with the operation task will be eliminated, and the impact of the problems in speech recognition on the follow-up process will be reduced accordingly.

There is still considerable room for improvement: 1) How to effectively divide the actions through NLP tools when there are multiple action prompts in the verbal instructions; 2) When the operation information is incorrectly recognized in the ASR module, how to correct it through interactions with the knowledge base. The follow-up work will continue.

## 6 Conclusion

In this paper, we have constructed a paradigm, which converts human speech input into intentions and operations, which can be further saved and visualized as knowledge. Among the whole process, ASR, NLP and KG technology are used. The knowledge obtained differs from other automatic knowledge graph system, it only includes essential operations, equipment, tools and position information during the operation tasks, so that robots can easily follow the input instructions to complete complexed tasks.

For further improvement, the interaction between the knowledge base and the system can be more detailed and real-time, so that the recognition rate and the visualization effect of speech input can be improved.

**Acknowledgements.** This work is supported by the National Key Research & Development Program of China (No. 2018AAA0102902).

## References

1. Ali, M.H.M., Atia, M.R.: A lead through approach for programming a welding arm robot using machine vision. Robotica, pp. 1–11 (2021)
2. Pan, Z., Zhang, H.: Robotic machining from programming to process control: a complete solution with force control. Ind. Robot: An Int. J. **35**(5), 400–409 (2008)
3. Leali, F., Pellicciari, M., Pini, F., Berselli, G., Vergnano, A.: An offline programming method for the robotic deburring of aerospace components. In: Neto, P., Moreira, A.P. (eds.) WRSM 2013. CCIS, vol. 371, pp. 1–13. Springer, Heidelberg (2013). https://doi.org/10.1007/978-3-642-39223-8_1
4. Bolano, G., Roennau, A., Dillmann, R., Groz, A.: Virtual reality for offline programming of robotic applications with online teaching methods. In: 2020 17th International Conference on Ubiquitous Robots (UR) (2020)
5. Zangeneh, P., Mccabe, B.: Ontology-based knowledge representation for industrial megaprojects analytics using linked data and the semantic web. Adv. Eng. Inf. **46**(6), 101164 (2020)

6. Roberto, W., Adiel, M., Renato, F., Luiz, S.A.: Capture and visualisation of text understanding through semantic annotations and semantic networks for teaching and learning. J. Inf. Sci. (2020)
7. Yu, H., Li, H., Mao, D., Cai, Q.: A relationship extraction method for domain knowledge graph construction. World Wide Web **23**(2), 735–753 (2020). https://doi.org/10.1007/s11280-019-00765-y
8. Yang, Y., Fermüller, C., Aloimonos, Y.: A cognitive system for human manipulation action understanding. Adv. Cogn. Syst. **2014**(3), 67–86 (2014)
9. Yang, Y., Yi, L., Fermüller, C., Aloimonos, Y.: Robot learning manipulation action plans by " watching" unconstrained videos from the world wide web. In: The Twenty-Ninth AAAI Conference on Artificial Intelligence (AAAI-15). AAAI Press (2015)
10. Tsagarakis, N.G., Caldwell, D.G., Negrello, F., et al.: Walk-man: a high-performance humanoid platform for realistic environments. J. Field Robot. **34**(7), 1225–1259 (2017)
11. Hannun, A.: Deep Speech: Scaling up end-to-end speech recognition. ArXiv abs/1412.5567 (2014)
12. Amodei, D., et al.: Deep speech 2: end-to-end speech recognition in English and Mandarin. In: Proceedings of the 33nd International Conference on Machine Learning, ICML 2016, pp. 173–182. New York City, NY, USA, June 19–24, 2016, ser. JMLR Workshop and Conference Proceedings, vol. 48. JMLR.org (2016)
13. Ravanelli, M., Parcollet, T., Bengio, Y.: The pytorch-kaldi speech recognition toolkit. In: ICASSP 2019 - 2019 IEEE International Conference on Acoustics, Speech and Signal Processing (ICASSP), pp. 6465–6469 (2019)
14. Povey, D., et al.: The Kaldi speech recognition toolkit. In: IEEE 2011 Workshop on Automatic Speech Recognition and Understanding (No. EPFL-CONF192584). IEEE Signal Processing Society (2011)
15. Mirco, R., et al.: {SpeechBrain}: A General-Purpose Speech Toolkit. arXiv preprint arXiv: 2106.04624 (2021)
16. Vaswani, A., et al.: Attention is all you need. arXiv preprint arXiv:1706.03762 (2017)
17. Wu, X., Wu, J., Fu, X., Li, J., Zhou, P., Jiang, X.: Automatic knowledge graph construction: A report on the 2019 icdm/icbk contest. In: 2019 IEEE International Conference on Data Mining (ICDM), pp. 1540–1545. IEEE (2019)
18. Chen, P., Lu, Y., Zheng, V.W., Chen, X., Li, X.: An automatic knowledge graph construction system for K-12 education. In: Proceedings of the Fifth Annual ACM Conference on Learning at Scale, pp. 1–4 (2018)
19. Fu, X., et al.: A speech-to-knowledge- graph construction system. In: Proceedings of the Twenty-Ninth International Joint Conference on Artificial Intelligence (IJCAI-20) Demonstrations Track, pp. 5303–5305 (2020)
20. Chen, Q., Zhu, Z., Wen, W.: BERT for joint intent classification and slot filling. ArXiv abs/1902.10909 (2019)
21. Devlin, J., Ming-Wei, C., Kenton L., Kristina T.: BERT: Pre-training of Deep Bidirectional Transformers for Language Understanding. NAACL-HLT (2019)
22. Han He: HanLP: Han Language Processing (2020). https://github.com/hankcs/HanLP
23. Dark Horse Programmer: Computer Assembly and Maintenance. People's Posts and Telecommunications Press, Beijing (2019)
24. Hou, Y., Mao, J., Lai, Y., Chen, C., Liu, T.: Fewjoint: a few-shot learning benchmark for joint language understanding. arXiv preprint arXiv:2009.08138 (2020)

# 3D Grasping Pose Detection Method Based on Improved PointNet Network

Jiahui Chen⬛, Yunhan Lin, Haotian Zhou, and Huasong Min(✉)⬛

Wuhan University of Science and Technology,
Wuhan 430080, People's Republic of China
mhuasong@wust.edu.cn

**Abstract.** In this paper, a 3D grasping pose detection method based on improved PointNet network was proposed. We introduced a skip connection into the backbone layer of PointNet network and compared the collocation of the latest different activation functions and loss functions to solve the problem that the lightweight PointNet network did not consider the local geometric information of the point cloud. This method effectively ensured the geometric information of the original point cloud, realized feature reuse, and made the transfer of features and gradients more effective. We applied the improved PointNet to robotics grasping, and our proposed method could directly deal with the original point clouds obtained by sensors. Compared with similar algorithms GPD and PointNetGPD, experiment results showed that the proposed grasping pose detection method had improved the test accuracy on the data set and the actual success rate of grasping.

**Keywords:** Point clouds · Grasping pose detection · PointNet · Activation functions · Loss functions

## 1 Introduction

Robotic grasping was a basic skill of intelligent robot which was widely used in industry, medical industry, family service. The comprehensive algorithm of grasping was mainly divided into three categories: the grasping algorithm for known objects, familiar objects, and unknown objects [1]. To apply robotics grasping operation to more complex work, the research focuses gradually turned to how to grasp unknown objects. The reference [2] had solved the grasping of known objects very well. The purpose of grasping familiar objects was to generate a grasping strategy without relying on the complete model by making use of the shape similarity between the target object and the previously checked object [3, 4]. The maturity of the methods of grasping

This work was supported by the National Key R&D Program of China (grant No.: 2017YFB1300400), National Natural Science Foundation of China (grant No.: 62073249), Major Project of Hubei Province Technology Innovation (grant No.: 2019AAA071), Scientific Research Program Foundation for Talents from Department of Education of Hubei Province (grant No.: Q20191108) and Youth Project of Hubei Natural Science Foundation (grant No.: 2020CFB116).

F. Sun et al. (Eds.): ICCSIP 2021, CCIS 1515, pp. 389–402, 2022.
https://doi.org/10.1007/978-981-16-9247-5_30

unknown objects and familiar objects laid the foundation for the algorithm of grasping unknown objects. This paper mainly studied the grasping methods of unknown objects.

For unknown object grasping, the accuracy of perceived environment is especially important. According to the input data, the robotic grasping pose detection was divided into the method based on 2D images and the method based on 3D point clouds. Grasping based on 2D image limited the application scene of robotic grasping. References [5] and [6] were deep learning methods based on the Cornell dataset with RGB images as input. In 2017, Mahler [7] proposed DexNet2.0 which could segment the corresponding depth map of the target object and generate hundreds of candidates grasping poses based on the depth map.

Compared with the above methods, the method based on 3D point cloud could get abundance of geometric information. The early related researches estimated the pose information by designing complex point cloud feature descriptors [8]. There had been mainly three methods for deep learning using point cloud data: multi-view projection, voxel-based and direct processing of point clouds. Literature [9] put forward that the original point cloud data was projected into multiple multi-view depth maps with the help of Multi-view CNN. This method strongly depended on the accurate CAD model. Reference [10] introduced a method to improve the analysis ability of geometric information by convolution of voxel point clouds with the help of 3D-CNN network.

How to directly deal with 3D data to achieve robotics grasping became a focus. In 2017, the author of [11] proposed PointNet to directly deal with 3D point clouds for object recognition and segmentation. PointNet could overcome the problem of point cloud disorder and ensure the geometric information of the target. The idea of Grasp Pose Detection in Point Clouds (GPD) proposed by ten et al. [12] designed an evaluation model of grasping quality based on CNN. But when the input point cloud was sparse GPD had serious problems such as over-fitting and performance degradation, which was related to the fact that GPD takes the projection features of the normalized point clouds as input. Inspired by the recent work of PointNet and GPD, Liang et al. [13] proposed a method of detecting grasp configurations from point sets. Different from the previous method of grasping pose estimation using Multi-view CNN [9] or 3D-CNN [10], PointNetGPD directly dealt with the raw point clouds inside the gripper, and PointNet was used to estimate the grasping quality. PointNetGPD can maximize the geometric information of the original point cloud, fully considered the 3D geometric information, and inferred the grasping quality more effectively. However, the PointNet network cannot capture the local feature of the point cloud very well, so the performance of lightweight network PointNetGPD in grasping quality assessment network still had room for improvement.

To summarize, our key contributions are as follows:

(1) This paper introduces a skip connection into the PointNet network structure which effectively collects the geometric information of the raw point cloud, reuses different levels of features, and improves the feature extraction ability of the network while adding few network parameters.

(2) By comparing three activation functions of feature extraction layer: ReLU, Swish [14] and Mish [15] and two loss functions of output layer: Softmax loss and L-Softmax [16] loss, this paper proposes a network structure that optimizes the

generalization and convergence speed of the network, which makes the transmission of features and gradients more effective to improve the accuracy of grasping detection and classification.

(3)  The network training is carried out in the data set provided by PointNetGPD. The results show that, this paper achieves better results in the accuracy of grasping pose detection compared with the two methods of PointNetGPD and GPD. This method is also tested on the actual grasping platform, and the grasping success rate is also better than the former two methods.

## 2  Related Work

PointNet provided an excellent solution for 3D point clouds processing. The basic PointNet network architecture is shown in Fig. 1.

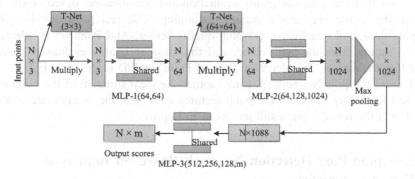

**Fig. 1.** Architecture of basic PointNet [11] network.

The PointNet network is represented as:

$$f(x_1, x_2, \cdots, x_n) = w\left\{\max_{i=1,2,\cdots,n}[h(x_i)]\right\} \tag{1}$$

$(x_1, x_2, \cdots, x_n)$ is an input disordered point cloud, and continuous functions $w$ and $h$ represent Multilayer Perceptron (MLP). Shown in Fig. 1, the 3D coordinates of the 3D point cloud containing $N$ points are input, and a 3D spatial transformation matrix is introduced to predict the network T-Net. According to the distribution of the input point cloud, a rotation matrix is fitted, and the input point cloud achieve data alignment. The aligned data finishes feature extraction through a MLP model (64, 64), and 64-dimensional features are extracted from each point. Then a three-layer MLP (64, 128, 1024) is used to extract features in units of feature points. At this time, the network has extracted 1024-dimensional deep features of each point from the original $N$ 3D points, and then the maximum pooling layer (Max pooling) solves the problem of point cloud disorder. When the global features are obtained, these features are sent into a three-layer fully connected network. Finally, the classifier is trained to output the scores of $m$ categories to achieve classification.

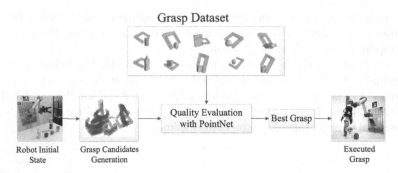

**Fig. 2.** PointNetGPD algorithm flow [13].

PointNetGPD [13] is the representative of the mainstream grasping classification thought. This method can be divided into two independent parts: grasping candidate pose generation and grasping quality evaluation and classification. Based on the YCB dataset, the author generates a dataset containing 350k real point clouds, gripper grasping pose, and quantitative grasping quality scores. And PointNet is selected to extract features from the point cloud, and the grasping quality evaluation model is trained on the dataset. The algorithm flow of PointNetGPD is shown in Fig. 2.

Because the PointNet network can't capture the local structure of the point cloud well and the ability to extract the point features is limited, the success rate of Point-NetGPD in the actual capture still has room to improve.

## 3  Grasping Pose Detection Network Based on Improved PointNet Network

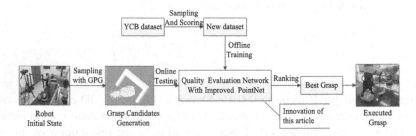

**Fig. 3.** The overall architecture diagram of this paper. Firstly, the network model is trained offline through the dataset. The original RGB-D data obtained by the sensor is converted to 3D point cloud during online grasping. Then, according to the given geometric constraints, some candidate grasping poses are sampled. For each candidate, the point cloud inside the gripper is clipped and transformed into the local coordinate system gripper. Finally, the candidate grasp is input into the grasping quality evaluation network based on improved PointNet, and the scores are obtained. The candidate grasp pose with the highest score is adopted.

In this paper, by introducing a skip connection, the PointNet network structure is improved to realize feature reuse. Then, we compare three activation functions of ReLU, Swish and Mish in the feature extraction layer and the Softmax loss and L-Softmax loss in the output layer. Then, the improved PointNet network is applied to the grasping pose detection network to realize the end-to-end grasp quality evaluation. The overall scheme structure is shown in Fig. 3. This chapter introduces the sampling and scoring of the data set before network training and each part of improved network.

## 3.1    Generation of Grasping Dataset

The generation of grasping data includes two parts: sampling grasping pose and grading grasping quality. For a given object $o$, the friction force between the object and the gripper is $\gamma$, the geometric center of the object $M_o$, the 6D pose of the object $W_o$, the grasping problem is anthemically described as:

$$s = (W_o, M_o, \gamma) \tag{2}$$

$s$ represents the state of an object $W_o \in \mathbb{R}^6$. This paper denotes a grasping configuration in 3D space as:

$$g = (p, r) \in \mathbb{R}^6 \tag{3}$$

$$p = (x, y, z) \in \mathbb{R}^3, r = (r_x, r_y, r_z) \in \mathbb{R}^3 \tag{4}$$

$p$ and $r$ represent grasping position and orientation respectively. Point clouds of $N$ points collected by the camera are denoted as $P \in \mathbb{R}^{3 \times N}$, the grasping quality $Q(s, g)$. Given the grasp g of a gripper and the observed p of the sensor, our aim is to learn a measure of the grasping quality $Q_\theta(P, g) \in \{c_0, c_1, \cdots\}$, where $\theta$ defines the parameters of grasping quality evaluation network and $\{c_0, c_1, \cdots\}$ represents the tag of grasp $p$. These categories can be assigned by $Q(s, g)$. The specific operation is divided into the following two steps: sampling and scoring.

Sample on the precise grid of the given object in YCB data set to generate candidate grasping pose. First, two surface points $p_1$ and $p_2$ are randomly selected as the contact points of the gripper. A grasping angle of 0 to 90° is specified to construct the grasping pose as follows:

$$g = ((p_1 + p_2)/2, r) \tag{5}$$

Secondly, by judging whether the gripper will collide with the grid after the grasping action is executed, the inappropriate grasping is removed. Finally, the remaining candidates are transformed from the grid coordinate system to the point cloud coordinate system, and the transformation matrix is obtained by ICP operation on the grid and the corresponding registration point cloud.

For given sampling grasp $g$ and object state $s$, two different robust grasp quality metrics are used to mark the grasp. One of them is a force-closure metric $Q_{fc}$, and it requires the coefficient of friction $\gamma$ and only provides a binary outcome that indicates whether the grasp is force-closure or not. The other grasp metric $Q_{gws}$ is based on Grasp Wrench Space (GWS) analysis [17]. Compared to $Q_{fc}$, GWS analysis proposes to use the radius of GWS as a quantitative score of grasp quality. The weighted and combined the two metrics are used to generate the grasping pose score:

$$Q(s,g) = \alpha Q_{fc}(s,g) + \beta Q_{gws}(s,g) \qquad (6)$$

Where $Q_{gws}$ is much larger than $Q_{fc}$, thus we choose $(\alpha, \beta) = (1.0, 0.01)$. The grasping pose was sampled according to the above method, and the grasping quality was scored and manual annotation was completed.

## 3.2 Improved PointNet Network Architecture

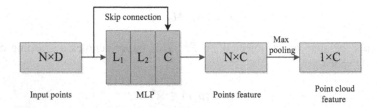

**Fig. 4.** Improved PointNet network architecture. The input to the network is $N$ points of dimension $D$, and each point in the whole point cloud is input into the MLP network. The input dimension of the first layer MLP is $D$ and the output dimension is $L_1$. The second level of MLP has an input dimension of $L_1$ and an output dimension of $L_2$. After the introduction of skip connection, the input of the third layer is composed of the output of the second layer connected with the network input $D + L_2$, and the output dimension is C. The MLP network can extract the C-dimensional features of each point, and then obtain the C-dimensional features of the global point cloud through the maximum pooling layer.

**Skip Connection.** To solve the problem that the original Pointnet network loses the geometric information in the process of feature extraction, this article propose that a skip connection is introduced between the input of Pointnet network and the maximum pooling layer. As can be seen from Fig. 2. PointNet uses shallow multilayer perceptron and shallow spatial converter network for feature extraction and mapping, which is a lightweight network with few parameters. Increasing the depth of Pointnet directly to improve the performance of the network will lead to the problem of gradient disappearance or gradient explosion, which makes the whole network difficult to train, and the network performance will decline. Shown in Fig. 4, the skip connection combines low-level original features and high-level abstract features to realize feature reuse and make full use of features at different levels. It can make feature and gradient transfer more effective and lightweight network training simpler in the case of almost no increase in training time, so it is suitable for application scenarios of grasping.

**Activation Function.** Each layer of the original network MLP network is characterized by Batch Normalization, and then ReLU is used as the activation function.

Literature [18] points out that the classification accuracy obtained by the BN algorithm and different activation functions is related to the specific network structure. Therefore, in order to further improve the generalization performance and gradient transfer efficiency of the model, Swish and ReLU were compared in this paper. The expression of the ReLU function:

$$f(x) = \begin{cases} 0 & x < 0 \\ x & x \geq 0 \end{cases} \tag{7}$$

ReLU function solves the problem that the gradient of sigmoid and tanh function disappears. However, when the input value is less than 0, the output is simply set to 0, resulting in that the neuron is no longer activated and the parameters cannot be updated, which may cause many effective features to be transmitted and blocked.

Swish [14] function was proposed by the Google team in 2017. It is a smooth and non-monotonic function, and its function expression is:

$$f(x) = \frac{x}{1 + e^{-\lambda x}} \tag{8}$$

Where $\lambda$ can be set as a constant or as a trained parameter, Swish function is a smooth function between the linear function and ReLU function, and it can still output valid values when the input is negative, avoiding the situation that the gradient parameter cannot be updated when the neuron is not activated.

The Mish [15] function was proposed in 2019 and has the following function expression:

$$f(x) = x * \tanh(\ln(1 + \exp(x))) \tag{9}$$

This function has the same characteristics as Swish function, such as no upper bound and lower bound, non-monotone, etc., but its smoothness is slightly better than Swish, and it achieves better performance than the two commonly used activation functions mentioned above on many benchmark data sets.

In the following experiment, different activation functions are applied to the network designed in this paper for comparison.

**Loss Function.** The output layer of the original network uses the cross-entropy loss function based on Softmax function to train the classifier, and the Softmax loss function is widely used in single-label multi-classification tasks. For a K-classified task, the loss function expression is as follows:

$$L_i = -\log\left(\frac{e^{\|W_{y_i}\|\|x_i\|\cos(\theta_{y_i})}}{\sum_j e^{\|W_j\|\|x_j\|\cos(\theta_j)}}\right) \tag{10}$$

Softmax function is simple and efficient, but it cannot effectively learn the features of compactness within the class and dispersion between classes. The L-Softmax (Large-Margin Softmax Loss) is introduced a positive integer variable $m$ to generate a margin of the decision boundary. The expression is as follows:

$$L_i = -\log\left(\frac{e^{\|W_{y_i}\|\|x_i\|\phi(\theta_{y_i})}}{e^{\|W_{y_i}\|\|x_i\|\phi(\theta_{y_i})} + \sum_{j\neq y_i} e^{\|W_j\|\|x_j\|\cos(\theta_j)}}\right), \phi(\theta) = \begin{cases} \cos(m\theta), 0 \leq \theta \leq \frac{\pi}{m} \\ D(\theta), \frac{\pi}{m} \leq \theta \leq \pi \end{cases} \quad (11)$$

When the boundary distance of classification $m$ is larger, the learning difficulty will be higher.

In the following part of the experiment, the combination of activation function and loss function mentioned above is compared and different combination comparison experiments are carried out to obtain the network model with the best performance.

### 3.3    Grasping Quality Evaluation Network Based on Improved PointNet Network

In this paper, a lightweight grasping quality evaluation network based on improved Pointnet network is proposed. By introducing a skip connection, optimizing activation function and classification loss function of output layer, the performance of feature extraction and gradient transfer of the network is improved.

Eventually, this paper realizes the end-to-end grasping object classification and outputs grasping pose with the highest grasping. This network is different from Dex-Net2.0 [7] which takes the whole point cloud as input, but first transforms the 1000 points sampled from the closed region inside the gripper into the unified local grabbing coordinates introduced in Fig. 5. The red represents the point cloud of the closed region inside the gripper.

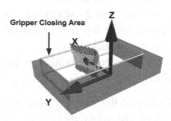

**Fig. 5.** Grasp representation in local gripper coordinates. (Color figure online)

As is shown in Fig. 6, the input unordered point set first normalized the point cloud through the first T-Net, then added a multi-layer perceptron to extract 64-dimensional features of each point. Then the second T-Net line up the extracted point features to solve the problem of invariance of point cloud transformation. The feature dimension is increased to 1024 by the second MLP, which includes three convolution layers and three full connection layers. The data transfer is nonlinear by Mish activation function, and the 1024-dimensional point feature integrating the input feature and the output is used as the input of the maximum pooling layer. At the end of the network, the full connection is used to match the global features of the point cloud with the correct label in the class $C$ labels. The binary output is used as the basis for judgment, and the L-Softmax loss function is used as the classification constraint. The subsequent classification is completed, which means that the best grasping pose with the highest $Q(s, g)$ value is successfully obtained.

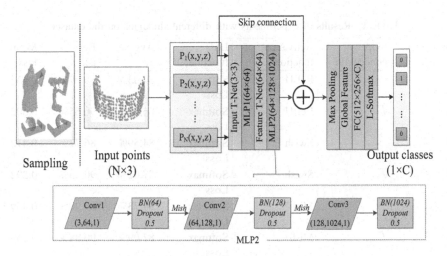

**Fig. 6.** The grasping quality evaluation network in this paper.

## 4   Experiments and Discussion

In this paper, the improved grasping quality evaluation network is tested on the data set and the actual robot grasping platform. The test of the data set mainly focuses on the performance of the grasping quality classification task, while the grasping experiment of the robot platform mainly investigates whether the overall scheme can have good grasping effect in practical application.

### 4.1   Simulation Experiments and Discussion

The simulation environment is carried out on a sever with GPU of NVIDA GeForce RTX 2080 Ti, and the network is implemented by PyTorch framework. The data set of 350K real point cloud containing 47 objects provided by PointNetGPD [13] is selected to provide single-view point cloud for each network input, and the metric value of grasping quality is set as 1/0.6. As the standard metric of good grasp pose and unqualified grasp pose in binary classification task, greater than 1/0.6 is considered as good grasp. $C$ -class L-Softmax cross entropy loss is used as the target of the classifier for network training. The whole network was optimized by Adam [19] optimizer and parameters are initialized by Gaussian distribution with an average value of 0. The training time of grasping classification network is about 5 h. The initial learning rate is set as 0.005, and then it decays exponentially according to the rules. A total of 200 epochs are learned.

The combined comparison experiment mainly investigates the introduction of skip connection in the backbone layer and the influence of ReLU, Swish or Mish activation functions in the feature extraction layer with Softmax loss or L-Softmax loss in the output layer on the network performance. The results of 12 sets of comparison experiments are shown in the Table 1.

**Table 1.** Results of experiments with different strategies on the dataset

| Strategies | Skip connection | Activation function | Loss function | Avg acc | Best acc | Mean loss |
|---|---|---|---|---|---|---|
| 1 | × | ReLU | Softmax Loss | 84.03% | 86.09% | 0.437 |
| 2 | √ | ReLU | Softmax Loss | 86.75% | 90.65% | 0.302 |
| 3 | × | Swish | Softmax Loss | 84.59% | 86.77% | 0.472 |
| 4 | √ | Swish | Softmax Loss | 87.02% | 90.23% | 0.292 |
| 5 | × | Mish | Softmax Loss | 84.73% | 86.90% | 0.459 |
| 6 | √ | Mish | Softmax Loss | 87.09% | 90.88% | 0.269 |
| 7 | × | Mish | L-Softmax Loss | 85.06% | 86.99% | 0.369 |
| 8 | √ | Mish | L-Softmax Loss | **87.23%** | **91.34%** | **0.223** |
| 9 | × | Swish | L-Softmax Loss | 84.96% | 86.90% | 0.383 |
| 10 | √ | Swish | L-Softmax Loss | 87.13% | 91.04% | 0.253 |
| 11 | × | ReLU | L-Softmax Loss | 84.47% | 86.33% | 0.396 |
| 12 | √ | ReLU | L-Softmax Loss | 86.92% | 90.86% | 0.244 |

Analyze the above Table 1: Firstly, by comparing two adjacent strategies, such as strategy 2 with strategy 1, strategy 4 with strategy 3 and totally six groups of comparisons, the skip connection improved the classification accuracy of the network in the test set by 2.17%–2.72%, and reduced the average loss value by 0.130–0.190 under the same combination of activation function and loss function. The validity of skip connection is proved. Then, by comparing the collocation of activation function and loss function in the singular strategy set and the even strategy set, the combination with the best average classification accuracy and average loss value is Mish + L-Softmax Loss. It is proved that Mish + L-Softmax Loss has a better optimization effect than the other five collocations. Among the 12 groups of strategies, strategy 8 performed best in all indicators, 3.20% higher than strategy 1 before improvement in Avg acc index and 0.214 lower than Mean loss index. It can be concluded that the farther away the loss function is, the more difficult it is to update the gradient of the network layer. The introduction of skip connection in the input layer effectively improves the transmission of gradient and feature. Meanwhile, the Mish activation function itself is smoother than ReLU and Swish, allowing information to better penetrate the neural network. L-SoftMax Loss displays better feature discrimination, which also helps strategy 8 network structure to achieve optimal performance.

In this paper, strategy 8 is referred to as SC + Mish + L-Softmax and compared with PointNetGPD and the benchmark algorithm GPD. GPD selects the 12-channel version with better effect. Figure 7 is the comparison of classification accuracy curve and loss value curve on the test set. More quantitative results can be found in Table 2.

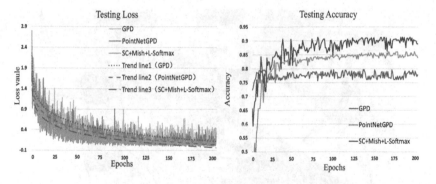

**Fig. 7.** The test accuracy and loss curve of the three algorithms on single views. The abscissa of the left figure represents the iteration times of epoch, which is divided into 200 epochs in total, and the ordinate represents the loss value. The abscissa of the right figure represents the number of iterations of epoch, and the ordinate represents the classification accuracy. Qualitative analysis shows that the improved network structure declines faster on the curve performance of the loss value and reaches a relatively lower stable value with better convergence performance. The average value on the curve of classification accuracy is also higher.

**Table 2.** Algorithm comparison results on the dataset

| Method | Avg accuracy | Mean loss |
|---|---|---|
| GPD | 78.90% | 0.456 |
| PointNetGPD | 84.03% | 0.327 |
| SC + Mish + L-Softmax | 87.23% | 0.223 |

As shown in Table 2: PointNetGPD directly processing the point cloud is 5.87% higher than the average classification accuracy of the GPD input by the depth map, and the loss value is reduced by 0.129. In this paper, the improved PointNetGPD with SC + Mish + L-Softmax can improve the average classification accuracy of the test set by 3.2% compared with the previous PointNetGPD. The average loss value is reduced by 0.104. Therefore, the proposed Pointnet improved by introducing a skip connection and selecting the combination of Mish and L-Softmax to detect grasping pose network architecture has the best performance effect on the test set.

### 4.2  Actual Robotic Experiments and Discussion

The experimental platform as shown in Fig. 8. It is built to verify the effectiveness of the improved method in the actual grasping experiment. This paper carries out on the AUBO-i5 robotic arm equipped with a two-finger gripper, and the Kinect2 camera provides a single-view point cloud.

**Fig. 8.** Grasping experimental platform

The single-object grasping dataset contains three known objects including banana, water cup and pineapple and two unknown objects including wide tape and pen container. This paper compares the success rate of grasping a single object for ten times. The strategy 8 with the best effect in Table 1 is compared with GPD and PointNetGPD. The comparison results of the three models are presented in Table 3.

**Table 3.** Single object grasping experiment results in real world

| Method | Avg | Banana | Pine apple | Cup | Wide tape | Pen holder |
|---|---|---|---|---|---|---|
| GPD | 46.00% | 30.00% | 40.00% | 70.00% | 30.00% | 60.00% |
| PointNetGPD | 76.00% | 80.00% | 70.00% | 80.00% | 50.00% | 70.00% |
| SC + Mish + L-Softmax | 82.00% | 90.00% | 80.00% | 90.00% | 70.00% | 80.00% |

From the overall average grasping success rate, the method proposed in this paper can reach 82.00%, 6.00% higher than PointNetGPD. For unknown objects, the success rate of the wide tape and the pen holder in the proposed method is higher than the other two methods, which indicates that the improved network proposed in this paper has better generalization. Our method can better adapt to real-world grasping.

## 5  Conclusion

In this paper, a lightweight grasping quality evaluation network based on improved Pointnet network is proposed. This paper introduces a skip connection and selects Mish function and L-Softmax loss. The experimental results show that the improved method can extract features directly from the original point cloud data, effectively guarantee the geometric information of the original point cloud, realize the reuse of features, and make the transfer of features and gradients more effective. Finally, compared with other methods, our grasping pose detection method achieves the best results in both the test accuracy and the success rate of actual grasping.

## References

1. Schaub, H., Schttl, A.: 6-DOF Grasp detection for unknown objects. In: ACIT 2020 (10th International Conference on Advanced Computer Information Technologies). IEEE(2020)
2. Przybylski, M., Asfour, T., Dillmann, R.: Planning grasps for robotic hands using a novel object representation based on the medial axis transform. In: 2011 IEEE/RSJ International Conference on Intelligent Robots and Systems, pp. 1781–1788. IEEE (2011)
3. Bohg, J., Kragic, D.: Grasping familiar objects using shape context. In: 2009 International Conference on Advanced Robotics, pp. 1–6. IEEE (2009)
4. Bohg, J., Kragic, D.: Learning grasping points with shape context. Robot. Auton. Syst. **58** (4), 362–377 (2010)
5. Lenz, I., Lee, H., Saxena, A.: Deep learning for detecting robotic grasps. Int. J. Robot. Res. **34**(4–5) (2013)
6. Redmon, J., Angelova, A.: Real-Time Grasp detection using convolutional neural networks. In: Proceedings IEEE International Conference on Robotics & Automation (2014)
7. Mahler, J., Liang J., Niyaz, S., et al.: Dex-Net 2.0: deep learning to plan robust grasps with synthetic point clouds and analytic grasp metrics (2017)
8. Savarese, S., Li, F. F.: 3D generic object categorization, localization and pose estimation. In: IEEE 11th International Conference on Computer Vision, ICCV 2007, Rio de Janeiro, Brazil, October, pp. 14–20. IEEE (2007)
9. Zeng, A., Yu, K.T., Song, S., et al.: Multi-view self-supervised deep learning for 6D pose estimation in the Amazon Picking Challenge. In: 2017 IEEE International Conference on Robotics and Automation (ICRA). IEEE (2017)
10. Varley, J., Dechant C., Richardson, A., et al.: Shape Completion Enabled Robotic Grasping. IEEE (2017)
11. Qi, C. R., Su, H., Mo, K., et al.: PointNet: deep learning on point sets for 3D classification and segmentation. In: The 2017 IEEE Conference on Computer Vision and Pattern Recognition, pp.77–85. IEEE (2017)

12. Ten Pas, A., Gualtieri, M., Saenko, K., et al.: Grasp pose detection in point clouds. Int. J. Robot. Res. **36**(13–14), 1455–1473 (2017)
13. Liang, H., Ma, X., Li, S., et al.: PointNetGPD: Detecting grasp configurations from point sets (2018)
14. Ramachandran, P., Zoph, B., Le. Q.V.: Searching for activation functions (2017)
15. Misra, D.: Mish: A self regularized non-monotonic neural activation function. arXiv Preprint (4). arXiv:1908.08681(2019)
16. Liu, W., Wen, Y., Yu, Z., et al.: Large-margin softmax loss for convolutional neural networks. In: ICML, vol. 2, no.3, p. 7 (2016)
17. Siciliano, Bruno, Khatib, et al.: Springer handbook of robotics. Springer-Verlag, New York, Inc. (2007)
18. Ioffe, S., Szegedy, C.: Batch normalization: accelerating deep network training by reducing internal covariate shift. JMLR.org (2015)
19. Kingma, D., Ba J.: Adam: a method for stochastic optimization. Computer Science (2014)

# MCTS-Based Robotic Exploration for Scene Graph Generation

Fangbo Zhou[1], Huaping Liu[2(✉)], Xinghang Li[2], and Huailin Zhao[1]

[1] School of Electrical and Electronic Engineering, Shanghai Institute of Technology, Shanghai, China
[2] Department of Computer Science and Technology, Tsinghua University, Beijing, China
hpliu@tsinghua.edu.cn

**Abstract.** Many researchers have used scene graphs to improve performance in some tasks in recent years, such as complete image matching, image generation, and visual questions answers. However, the current scene graph generation mainly constructs a single picture or a scene graph of a part of the scene. To construct a scene graph of the entire room, the agent needs to explore the entire room autonomously. We propose a scene graph generation method based on Monte Carlo Tree Search (MCTS). In the agent's exploration of the room, the agent uses MCTS to select a reliable location among the locations that the agent can reach in the next step. After multiple searches, the agent can find most or all objects in the room. Experiments show that our method helps the agent finds more objects in a fixed step size than the agent's random exploration of the room. The agent can create a complete scene graph because it sees most of the objects in the room.

**Keywords:** MCTS · Scene graph generation · Object search

## 1 Introduction

Semantic understanding of images needs to clarify the relationship between objects in the image, and automatically generate a semantic graph structure (called scene graph [1,2]) to represent the image. The object in the image corresponds to the graph node. The relationship between the objects corresponds to the graph edge. Compared with semantic maps [3], scene graphs can indicate the relationships between objects, which can apply to many tasks, such as image matching [4] and image generation [5], visual questions answers [6].

In embodied tasks, the scene graph has been applied [7]. However, the agent understands the surrounding environment more effectively and build a scene graph is still a problem. As shown in Fig. 1, assuming that the agent perceives the environment at one location only, the agent's obtained room information is incomplete. The agent must explore the room to discover new objects and corresponding spatial locations and then understand the complete scene information [8–10].

How the agent explores one path to find more objects in the room? Suppose the starting point of the agent is the zeroth level of the tree. In that case, all the possibilities of each step of the agent are regarded as the tree's nodes. If the room is small, the

© Springer Nature Singapore Pte Ltd. 2022
F. Sun et al. (Eds.): ICCSIP 2021, CCIS 1515, pp. 403–415, 2022.
https://doi.org/10.1007/978-981-16-9247-5_31

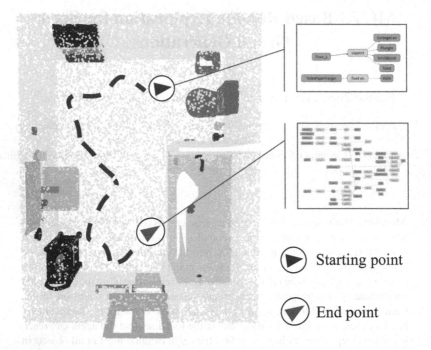

**Fig. 1.** The agent only observes a few objects in a fixed position. After exploring the room, the agent gradually builds a complete scene graph in the room.

agent can enumerate all possible paths. However, if there are many navigable locations in the room, the search space will be huge. Based on this, we use Monte Carlo Tree Search (MCTS) [11, 12] to help the agent search path in the room. MCTS is a tree-based data structure that can balance exploration and exploitation, algorithm that still can be effective in the huge search space.

In the search process, the agent uses the MCTS algorithm to select the next action space to be executed at each step, reaching a position with the highest quality. After executing a certain number of action sequences, the agent can find many or even all objects in the room on the walking route. This method enables the agent to explore the environment more effectively and builds a complete scene graph.

In summary, the main contributions of this paper are as follows:

- We propose an environment exploration method that the agent with the visual object detector uses the MCTS to design a path;
- A complete scene graph is generated, based on the agent finding most of the objects in the room;
- We conducted experiments in the AI2Thor simulation environment to verify that our proposed method is better than random selection and greedy algorithms.

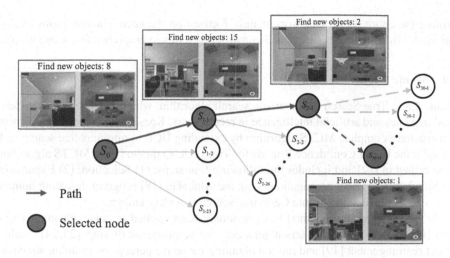

**Fig. 2.** Based on the MCTS-based objective search process, $S_0$ represents the initial position of the agent, and $S_{30-6}$ represents the sixth action selected when the agent walks on the 30th step (described in Sect. 3.3 agent's action space). The corresponding state of the agent for each node is shown in the blue box. The left side is the first view of the agent and the result of object detection, and the right side is the top view and the path that the agent walks. (Color figure online)

## 2 Related Work

In this section, we briefly introduce the related works of scene graph generation and Monte Carlo Tree Search.

### 2.1 Scene Graph Generation

Johnson et al. [4] introduced the scene graph and pointed out that a scene graph is a data structure used to describe a scene, and apply it to semantic retrieval tasks. A scene graph contains instances of objects, attributes of objects, and associations between objects. With the Visual Genome dataset [13] introduction, a large-scale dataset that annotates scene graphs on images has attracted many scholars to focus on scene graph tasks [1, 14]. Images and edges portray the pairwise relationship between objects. Compared with previous text-based visual scene representations, scene graph representations provide much contextual information about relative geometry and semantics. The research on scene graphs can be divided into two categories: 1) scene graph generation [15]; 2) scene graph application [7]. The scene graph generation algorithm's focus is to generate an accurate scene graph in a given visual scene. A wide range of visual tasks, such as semantic image retrieval [4], generate new images [5] manipulate existing images [16], embodied scene description [17] and visual question and answer [7], all have used scene graphs to improve performance.

The related work of scene graph generation mainly focused on a single picture or part of the scene. However, to construct a scene graph of the entire room, the agent needs to explore the entire room. Our work mainly focused on the agent's autonomous exploration, discovering more objects, and constructing a more comprehensive scene graph.

## 2.2 Monte Carlo Tree Search

Monte Carlo Tree Search is a heuristic search algorithm, which has been most widely used in games and artificial intelligence in recent years. Kocsis and Szepervari [11] first constructed a complete MCTS algorithm by extending UCB to minimax tree search and named it the Upper Confidence Bounds for Trees (UCT) method. The MCTS algorithm is described in [12] and includes the following four steps: (1) Selection: (2) Expansion (3) Simulation (4) Backpropagation. With the AlphaGo [18] program defeating human professional players, the Monte Carlo tree search is widely known.

In recent years, this method has previously been applied to robot planning tasks [19–24], such as advanced action selection for autonomous driving [23,24], multi-object rearrangement [19] and motion planning for active perception in unknown environments [25]. Our task is different from these applications, the agent needs to discover as many objects as possible, and the agent automatically explores the room.

## 3  Framework

### 3.1  Overview

This work aims to develop a method to help the agent discover as many objects as possible within a certain period, thereby improving the quality of scene graph generation. Precisely, the agent is placed in a random starting position in the room and continues to explore the room for a certain amount of steps. The object detection method is used to obtain the object category and position, and the number of objects found by the agent is required as much as possible. It is worth noting that our work can improve the quality of scene graph generation and be widely applied to other tasks, such as Manipulation Question Answering [26] and Scene Captioning [27].

Figure 2 shows the problem of autonomous scene object search. At the initial position $S_0$, the agent can only observe some objects. Starting from the current location, the agent uses the MCTS algorithm to select a location with the highest quality among the locations that can be reached next as the starting location for the next exploration. By means of repeating the above process, the agent can continuously discover new objects until the specified exploration time expires. The agent can discover most or all of the objects in the room.

### 3.2  Scene Graph Generation

The agent can obtain more information in the scene by observing as many objects as possible, which plays an important role in constructing the room's scene graph. The agent searches for objects to obtain the category, position, and instance mask of the scene object. We first map the object mask observed by the agent at the initial position to the depth map to obtain the point cloud.

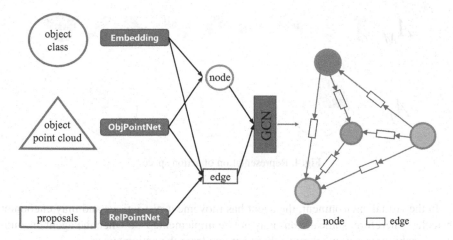

**Fig. 3.** Scene graph generation, The visual extractor extracts the class of the object, the point cloud and the proposals edges of the perspective to obtain the node and edge, which are then further processed by GCN to obtain the scene map.

Following [4], as shown in the Fig. 3, we use a learning method based on Point-Net [28] and Graph Convolutional Networks (GCN) [29] to predict the scene graph. Take the objects and proposal edges in the agent's current view as input to obtain the local scene graph and continuously update the point cloud during movement of the agent. Due to the consistency of multiple views, the agent can align the same object under each viewpoint to achieve node alignment and the local scene graph's fusion to the global scene graph.

### 3.3 Object Detector

Mask R-CNN [30] can effectively detect objects while outputting high-quality instance segmentation masks. We use the form of the backbone network Resnet50 + FPN. Furthermore, we use the pre-trained weights on the CoCo dataset to retrain the objects in AI2Thor.

### 3.4 Action Space

As shown in Fig. 4, the action space that the agent can take at the position $(x, y, \theta)$ consists of a movement and a rotation, Allowing the agent to perform a rotation after the movement can better perceive the entire scene.

- **Movement**: Agent can move in 8 directions, corresponding to coordinate changes: $x - 0.25m$, $x + 0.25m$, $y - 0.25m$, $y + 0.25m$, $x - 0.25m$ and $y - 0.25m$, $x - 0.25m$ and $y + 0.25m$, $x + 0.25m$ and $y - 0.25m$, $x + 0.25m$ and $y + 0.25m$. In addition, the agent can maintain this position and only rotate.
- **Rotation**: Agent can rotate left and right at a fixed angle $\Delta_R$, corresponding to: $\theta - 90$, no rotation, $\theta + 90$.

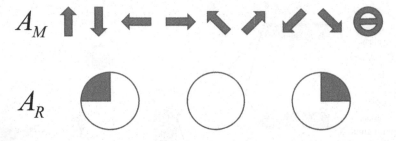

**Fig. 4.** Representation of action space

In the virtual environment, the agent has movement restrictions and may encounter obstacles. Therefore, some actions may not be implemented, so when the agent encounters an inability to act, we remove these actions from the action space.

## 4   Algorithm

The agent uses the MCTS algorithm of heuristic search to explore a path that can find as many objects as possible. It does a partial exploration of the traversable path instead of searching the entire room for all alternative paths. When the agent chooses the next action to be performed in the action space, it will reach a different position or orientation and then observe different objects. Therefore, the agent needs to use the MCTS algorithm to select the most reliable action in the action space to be executed next.

Whenever the agent acts, it will reach a position and get a certain reward. In our work, the reward depends on the number of new objects the agent finds. The MCTS algorithm can be divided into four steps.

- **Selection:** The agent acts as the current position to reach a position that is most worth exploring. The general strategy is first to reach a position that has not been explored before, and if it has explored all of it, select the position with the largest UCB value.
- **Expansion:** The agent takes the previously selected position as the current position and chooses an action execution in its action space. The general strategy is that the agent chooses an action to arrive at the corresponding position randomly.
- **Simulation:** The agent performs object detection at the location of the new expansion, obtains the currently observed objects, compares them with the previously observed objects, and uses the number of newly observed objects as a reward for this position.
- **Backpropagation:** It is a step that agent feedback the reward corresponding to the previous expansion position to all the previous positions passed and update the quality value and visit times of these nodes.

**Algorithm 1.** The MCTS algorithm

1: **function** PATH_GENERATION($l_0$)
2:     $PATH_0 \leftarrow l_0$
3:     current location $l_c \leftarrow$ starting point $l_0$
4:     **while** Max steps **do**
5:         $l_{c+1} \leftarrow$ MCTS_SEARCH($l_c$)
6:         $PATH_{c+1} \leftarrow l_{c+1}$
7:     **end while**
8:     **return** $PATH$
9: **end function**
10: **function** MCTS_SEARCH($l_c$)
11:     root node $v_0 \leftarrow$ current location $l_c$
12:     **while** within computational budget **do**
13:         $v_l \leftarrow$ TREE_POLICY($v_0$)
14:         $\Delta \leftarrow$ DEFAULT_POLICY($s(v_l)$)
15:         BACKUP($v_l, \Delta$)
16:     **end while**
17:     **return** BEST_CHILD($v_0, 0$)
18: **end function**
19: **function** TREE_POLICY($v$)
20:     **while** $v$ is nonterminal **do**
21:         **if** $v$ not fully expanded **then**
22:             **return** EXPAND($v$)
23:         **else**
24:             $v \leftarrow$ BEST_CHILD($v, Cp$)
25:         **end if**
26:     **end while**
27:     **return** $v$
28: **end function**
29: **function** BEST_CHILD($v, c$)
30:     **return** $\underset{v' \in \text{ children of } v}{\arg\max} \frac{Q(v')}{N(v')} + c\sqrt{\frac{2\ln N(v)}{N(v')}}$
31: **end function**

The agent repeats the above steps until the computational budget is reached. In a huge search space and limited computing power, this heuristic search can help the agent choose the most reliable action more intensively and with greater probability. After the agent executes 15 or 30 steps, the reached position will form a path. The agent can observe more objects by selecting this path through the MCTS algorithm.

The Algorithm 1 is the pseudocode implementation of the paper, the TREE_POLICY realizes the two stages of Selection and Expansion, DEFAULT_POLICY realizes the Simulation stage, and BACKUP realizes the Backpropagation stage. The definition of a computational budget is a constant used to limit the number of searches or search time. In our work, the limit can only be searched down to 200 times. According to Auer et al. [31], we use UCB1 to calculate the reward, as shown in line 30 of Algorithm 1, where $v'$ represents the current tree node, $v$ represents the parent node, $Q$ represents the cumulative quality value of this tree node, and $N$ represents the visit of this tree node number of times, $C$ is a constant parameter (it can control the weight of exploitation and exploration).

**Table 1.** Comparison of different methods and detectors

| Method | Detector | Kitchen | | Living room | | Bedroom | | Bathroom | | Avg | |
|---|---|---|---|---|---|---|---|---|---|---|---|
| | | $SoP_{15}$ | $SoP_{30}$ | $SoP_{15}$ | $SoP_{30}$ | $SoP_{15}$ | $SoP_{30}$ | $SoP_{15}$ | $SoP_{30}$ | $SoP_{15}$ | $SoP_{30}$ |
| Random | Mask R-CNN | 0.50 | 0.56 | 0.56 | 0.62 | 0.59 | 0.67 | 0.52 | 0.59 | 0.54 | 0.61 |
| | GT | 0.53 | 0.61 | 0.65 | 0.70 | 0.59 | 0.70 | 0.64 | 0.72 | 0.60 | 0.68 |
| Greedy | Mask R-CNN | 0.66 | 0.68 | 0.65 | 0.65 | 0.73 | 0.73 | 0.67 | 0.67 | 0.68 | 0.68 |
| | GT | 0.74 | 0.76 | 0.78 | 0.78 | 0.86 | 0.89 | 0.83 | 0.84 | 0.80 | 0.82 |
| MCTS | Mask R-CNN | 0.78 | 0.88 | 0.76 | 0.80 | 0.84 | 0.88 | 0.81 | 0.84 | 0.79 | 0.85 |
| | GT | 0.87 | 0.98 | 0.80 | 0.93 | 0.96 | 0.99 | 0.93 | 0.99 | 0.89 | 0.97 |

## 4.1  Environment and Evaluation Metrics

We conduct our experiments at AI2Thor [32] (The House Of inteRactions), a realistic and interactive framework for AI agents composed of indoor scenes. An agent is a capsule shaped entity that can navigate within scenes and interact with objects. There are 4 scene categories, kitchen, living room, bedroom, bathroom, there are 30 rooms in each category. For time reasons, we use the first room of each scene, namely FloorPlan1, FloorPlan201, FloorPlan301, FloorPlan401. We use each position in the room as the starting point of the path, and the starting direction is randomly set.

To evaluate the agent's performance using different methods, we design the evaluation index Score of the path ($SoP$), can be expressed as follows:

$$SoP_n = \frac{\sum_{i=0}^{n} N_i}{C_{all}} \tag{1}$$

$N_i$ represents the new object observed at the $i$th node on the path, and $C_{all}$ represents the number of all objects in the room. $n$ represents the length of the path, which contains $SoP_{15}$ and $SoP_{30}$, corresponding to the path length of 15 steps and 30 steps.

## 4.2  Comparison and Analysis of Results

Agent randomly selects (Random) in the action space as our baseline for each agent's step. Besides, we still use the Greedy algorithm to participate in the comparison, that is, choose a position that can see the most objects among the positions that the agent can reach in the next step. If the number of objects seen in each position is equal, the agent randomly chooses a position. On this basis, we use MCTS to select the most reliable action. Besides, we also use the detection results of GT and Mask R-CNN for these two methods and compare their performance.

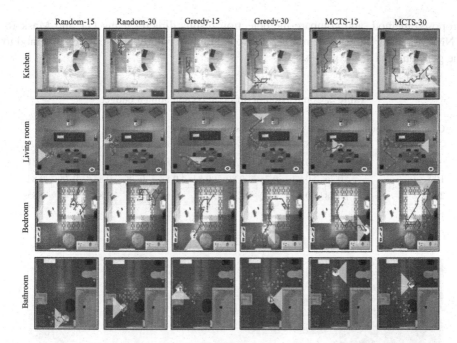

**Fig. 5.** Visualization examples of four scenarios in AI2Thor simulation environment. Red indicates the search path, and the green arrow indicates the direction of the agent. Random-15 means the path generated by walking 15 steps using random selection. (Color figure online)

Table 1 shows the experiments we have done in detail. Compared with the randomly selected path, we use the MCTS method to improve the four scenarios greatly. Especially in the bedroom and bathroom scenarios, the $SoP_{30}$ indicator reaches 0.99, which indicates that the agent can almost find the room after 30 steps. When using GT as the detection result, compared to random selection, the object search of scenes using MCTS has achieved an improvement of 0.29 on both the $SoP_{15}$ and $SoP_{30}$ indicators.

It can be seen from Table 1 that when the agent uses the Greedy algorithm for path search, its $SoP_{15}$ and $SoP_{30}$ are very close. We analyze this because the greedy algorithm only considers the local optimum and does not consider the global path planning. MCTS allows the agent to explore forward multiple times before making a selection.

Using the object detector Mask R-CNN will cause a decrease of about 0.1 in $SoP$ compared to using GT. Still, we believe that this error is acceptable, and we hope to apply MCTS to real-world object search.

## 5   Experiment

In this section, we first briefly introduce the dataset and evaluation method. In order to verify that our proposed framework can find most objects within a certain step, we use the agent to randomly select the action space as the baseline, compare with our proposed method, and compare the detection results directly using GT and Mask R-CNN. Moreover, show some representative examples. Finally, we apply this method to the generation of scene graphs.

**Table 2.** Comparison of different computational budget

| Computational budget | Kitchen | | Living room | | Bedroom | | Bathroom | | Avg | |
|---|---|---|---|---|---|---|---|---|---|---|
| | $SoP_{15}$ | $SoP_{30}$ | $SoP_{15}$ | $SoP_{30}$ | $SoP_{15}$ | $SoP_{30}$ | $SoP_{15}$ | $SoP_{30}$ | $SoP_{15}$ | $SoP_{30}$ |
| 50 | 0.74 | 0.75 | 0.72 | 0.78 | 0.81 | 0.87 | 0.75 | 0.83 | 0.76 | 0.81 |
| 100 | 0.76 | 0.87 | 0.75 | 0.80 | 0.84 | 0.88 | 0.78 | 0.84 | 0.78 | 0.84 |
| 200 | 0.78 | 0.88 | 0.76 | 0.80 | 0.84 | 0.88 | 0.81 | 0.84 | 0.79 | 0.85 |

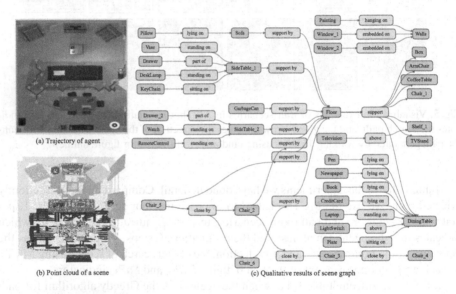

(a) Trajectory of agent

(b) Point cloud of a scene

(c) Qualitative results of scene graph

**Fig. 6.** (a) The trajectory generated by the agent walking 30 steps on the FloorPlan201 scene. The agent found 96% of the objects in the scene. (b) A 3D point cloud semantic map is generated. (c) Visual display of the scene graph.

## 5.1 Ablation Experiment

It takes time for the agent to explore forward, and the length of time it takes is closely related to the computational budget. Therefore, we conducted ablation experiments on the computational budget setting. We selected 50, 100, and 200 for comparison, and the results are shown in Table 2. It can be seen that the value of the computational budget has increased from 50 to 100, and the $SoP_{15}$ and $SoP_{30}$ indicators have increased by 0.02 and 0.03, respectively. However, from 100 to 200, the $SoP_{15}$ and $SoP_{30}$ indicators have only increased by 0.01, so we are not increasing the computational budget.

## 5.2   Representative Examples

In Fig. 5, we list representative examples for different scene categories. Obviously, the randomly selected paths all move near the starting point, and the search range cannot be expanded, we use the MCTS method. Starting from the starting point, the agent quickly moves where it can find the new objects. In the kitchen and living room scenes, the agent can follow the search path, such as the table and constantly change its orientation during the search process to find more objects. In the bedroom and bathroom scenes, the agent can approximately circle the room.

## 5.3   Scene Graph Generation

The agent constantly updates the point cloud and scene graph in the process of searching for objects. As shown in Fig. 6(a), our method can find a better route. On this route, the agent can observe most of the objects in the room. The generated point cloud and scene graph are shown in Fig. 6(b) and Fig. 6(c).

## 6   Conclusions

The agent needs to explore the room to discover all the objects and corresponding positions, to obtain complete scene information. We propose a scene graph generation method based on MCTS. When the agent explores the room, the agent uses MCTS to select the next step to be reached and find a path that can find the most objects. Experiments show that our method finds more objects within a certain number of steps compared to the agent's random exploration of the room. And then create a complete scene map. From a practical application point of view, it is not enough to solve the problem of building a map in a completely static environment; a dynamic environment should also be focused on. We will use MCTS to search for rooms in dynamic environment and improve the generated scene graphs' quality in future work.

## References

1. Yang, J., Lu, J., Lee, S., Batra, D., Parikh, D.: Graph R-CNN for scene graph generation. In Proceedings of the European Conference on Computer Vision (ECCV), pp. 670–685 (2018)
2. Tang, K., Niu, Y., Huang, J., Shi, J., Zhang, H.: Unbiased scene graph generation from biased training. In: Conference on Computer Vision and Pattern Recognition (2020)
3. Sünderhauf, N.: Place categorization and semantic mapping on a mobile robot. In: 2016 IEEE International Conference on Robotics and Automation (ICRA), pp. 5729–5736. IEEE (2016)
4. Johnson, J.: Image retrieval using scene graphs. In: Proceedings of the IEEE Conference on Computer Vision and Pattern Recognition, pp. 3668–3678 (2015)
5. Johnson, J., Gupta, A., Fei-Fei, L.: Image generation from scene graphs. In: Proceedings of the IEEE Conference on Computer Vision and Pattern Recognition, pp. 1219–1228 (2018)
6. Lee, S., Kim, J.-W., Oh, Y., Jeon, J.H.: Visual question answering over scene graph. In: 2019 First International Conference on Graph Computing (GC), pp. 45–50. IEEE (2019)

7. Wald, J., Dhamo, H., Navab, N., Tombari, F.: Learning 3d semantic scene graphs from 3d indoor reconstructions. In: Proceedings of the IEEE/CVF Conference on Computer Vision and Pattern Recognition, pp. 3961–3970 (2020)

8. Luo, J., He, W., Yang, C.: Combined perception, control, and learning for teleoperation: key technologies, applications, and challenges. Cogn. Comput. Syst. 2(2), 33–43 (2020)

9. Kattepur, A., Purushotaman, B.: Roboplanner: a pragmatic task planning framework for autonomous robots. Cogn. Comput. Syst. 2(1), 12–22 (2020)

10. Zhenyu, L., Li, M., Annamalai, A., Yang, C.: Recent advances in robot-assisted echography: combining perception, control and cognition. Cogn. Comput. Syst. 2(3), 85–92 (2020)

11. Kocsis, L., Szepesvári, C.: Bandit Based Monte-Carlo planning. In: Fürnkranz, J., Scheffer, T., Spiliopoulou, M. (eds.) ECML 2006. LNCS (LNAI), vol. 4212, pp. 282–293. Springer, Heidelberg (2006). https://doi.org/10.1007/11871842_29

12. Cameron B Browne, Edward Powley, Daniel Whitehouse, Simon M Lucas, Peter I Cowling, Philipp Rohlfshagen, Stephen Tavener, Diego Perez, Spyridon Samothrakis, and Simon Colton. A survey of monte carlo tree search methods. IEEE Transactions on Computational Intelligence and AI in games, 4(1):1–43, 2012

13. Krishna, R., et al.: Visual genome: connecting language and vision using crowdsourced dense image annotations. Int. J. Comput. Vis. 123(1), 32–73 (2017)

14. Zellers, R., Yatskar, M., Thomson, S., Choi, Y.: Neural motifs: scene graph parsing with global context. In: Proceedings of the IEEE Conference on Computer Vision and Pattern Recognition, pp. 5831–5840 (2018)

15. Yu, B., Chen, C., Zhou, F., Wan, F., Zhuang, W., Zhao, Y.: A bottom-up framework for construction of structured semantic 3d scene graph (2020)

16. Dhamo, H.: Semantic image manipulation using scene graphs. In: Proceedings of the IEEE/CVF Conference on Computer Vision and Pattern Recognition, pp. 5213–5222 (2020)

17. Tan, D.G.X.Z.F.S.S., Liu, H.: Towards embodied scene description. Science and Systems (RSS), In Robotics (2020)

18. Silver, D., et al.: Mastering the game of go with deep neural networks and tree search. Nature 529(7587), 484–489 (2016)

19. Song, H.: Joshua A Haustein, Weihao Yuan, Kaiyu Hang, Michael Yu Wang, Danica Kragic, and Johannes A Stork. A case study on planar nonprehensile sorting, Multi-object rearrangement with monte carlo tree search (2020)

20. Yoo, C., Lensgraf, S., Fitch, R., Clemon, L.M., Mettu, R.: Toward optimal FDM toolpath planning with Monte Carlo tree search. In: 2020 IEEE International Conference on Robotics and Automation (ICRA), pp. 4037–4043. IEEE (2020)

21. Sukkar, F., Best, G., Yoo, C., Fitch, R.: Multi-robot region-of-interest reconstruction with dec-mcts. In 2019 International Conference on Robotics and Automation (ICRA), pp. 9101–9107. IEEE (2019)

22. Eiffert, S., Kong, H., Pirmarzdashti, N., Sukkarieh, S.: Path planning in dynamic environments using generative RNNs and Monte Carlo tree search. In: 2020 IEEE International Conference on Robotics and Automation (ICRA), pp. 10263–10269. IEEE (2020)

23. Arora, A., Furlong, P.M., Fitch, R., Fong, T., Sukkarieh, S., Elphic, R.: Online multi-modal learning and adaptive informative trajectory planning for autonomous exploration. In: Hutter, M., Siegwart, R. (eds.) Field and Service Robotics. SPAR, vol. 5, pp. 239–254. Springer, Cham (2018). https://doi.org/10.1007/978-3-319-67361-5_16

24. Paxton, C., Raman, V., Hager, G.D., Kobilarov, M.: Combining neural networks and tree search for task and motion planning in challenging environments. In: 2017 IEEE/RSJ International Conference on Intelligent Robots and Systems (IROS), pp. 6059–6066. IEEE (2017)

25. Best, G., Cliff, O.M., Patten, T., Mettu, R.R., Fitch, R.: Decentralised Monte Carlo tree search for active perception. In: Algorithmic Foundations of Robotics XII. SPAR, vol. 13, pp. 864–879. Springer, Cham (2020). https://doi.org/10.1007/978-3-030-43089-4_55

26. Deng, X.G.N.Z.H.L.F.S.Y., Guo, D.: Mqa: Answering the question via robotic manipulation. Science and Systems (RSS), In Robotics (2021)
27. Li, X., Guo, D., Liu, H., Sun, F.: Robotic indoor scene captioning from streaming video. In: 2021 IEEE International Conference on Robotics and Automation (ICRA), pp. 6109–6115. IEEE (2021)
28. Qi, C.R., Su, H., Mo, K., uibas, L.J.: Pointnet: deep learning on point sets for 3d classification and segmentation. In: Proceedings of the IEEE Conference on Computer Vision and Pattern Recognition, pp. 652–660 (2017)
29. Kipf, T.M., Welling, M.: Semi-supervised classification with graph convolutional networks (2016). arXiv preprint arXiv:1609.02907
30. He, K., Gkioxari, G., Dollár, P., Girshick, R.: Mask R-CNN. In: Proceedings of the IEEE International Conference on Computer Vision, pp. 2961–2969 (2017)
31. Auer, P.: Finite-time analysis of the multiarmed bandit problem. Machine Learning, 47 (2002)
32. Kolve, E., et al.: Ai2-thor: an interactive 3d environment for visual ai (2017). https://ai2thor. allenai.org/ithor

# Predictive Maintenance Estimation of Aircraft Health with Survival Analysis

Jiaojiao Gu$^{(\boxtimes)}$, Ke Liu$^{(\boxtimes)}$, Jian Chen$^{(\boxtimes)}$, and Tao Sun$^{(\boxtimes)}$

Naval Aviation University, Yantai 264001, China

**Abstract.** Modern aircraft health estimation methods are too strict for predictive maintenance estimation and require a high degree of cleanliness of the data. It is preferable to develop thresholds for maintenance personnel to arrange repairs, especially for batches of equipment. The data collected in real scenes are usually incomplete, contain noise, and occupy a large proportion. Moreover, existing methods generally delete "NaN" data directly, which is actually a waste and unreasonable. Aiming at the problem, this study proposes using a survival analysis method for fault prediction. Incomplete data can also be used; they are usually removed in traditional machine learning methods, even in deep learning methods. This will greatly improve the efficiency of data usage. A maintenance evaluation model system was developed to conduct all experiments, which showed what. The results are close to those of the time-series analysis, which indicates that there is much room for improvement.

**Keywords:** Predictive maintenance · Survival analysis · Time-series data · Maintenance evaluation model system · Regression

## 1 Introduction

The main problem that needs to be solved for predictive maintenance based on big data is how to dig out valuable information such as the historical laws of device operation and the correlation between parameters from the massive historical data of device operation. This will enable the use of correlations between existing data to predict failures in a new situation. The application of big-data-related technologies is divided into two categories: data mining [1] and data analysis. Current mainstream data mining methods include linear and non-linear analysis, regression analysis, sequence analysis, and time-series analysis [2]. Excluding abnormal data and using mathematical methods to dig out the potential information in data are also at the core of equipment status analysis and fault diagnosis based on big data analysis technology.

It has been shown that during the actual process of maintenance support, especially for batches of equipment, it is better to propose a threshold or time-range suggestion for maintenance, but not a certain value, which is never certain owing to the complex internal structure of the equipment. There is no clear boundary between the certainty and uncertainty of the equipment. Overlap exists; in fact, we need the overlap threshold.

In big data analysis work, conventional time-series analysis methods have high requirements for data standardization, and the processing of "NaN" data, such as incomplete, ambiguous, noise, and outliers, is very strict. Further, the abnormal data are

F. Sun et al. (Eds.): ICCSIP 2021, CCIS 1515, pp. 416–426, 2022.
https://doi.org/10.1007/978-981-16-9247-5_32

usually deleted directly, which usually occupies a large proportion. Moreover, direct deletion is a waste of data. This kind of data can actually use unsupervised and other methods to extract certain useful information.

Given the above considerations, survival analysis [3] is used to develop failure prediction model systems and measure the lifespans of individuals in duration-type situations, such as predictive maintenance.

## 2 Background and Related Work

### 2.1 Predictive Maintenance

At present, aircraft personnel mainly adopt preventive maintenance methods to regularly inspect and maintain aircraft equipment. Regardless of whether the equipment fails, the equipment is maintained in accordance with the predetermined time and content. Preventive maintenance of equipment is low efficiency and high cost, which easily lead to under-maintenance or over-maintenance. If the maintenance interval is too long, it will be difficult to achieve the purpose of preventing failure; if the maintenance interval is too short, it may cause excessive maintenance, which not only wastes maintenance resources, but also introduces the risk of maintenance damage. Predictive maintenance aims to conduct condition-based maintenance based on the actual health status of equipment through reliable condition monitoring, which can greatly improve the safety of equipment system operation, reduce maintenance costs, and fully use the working life of equipment parts and maintenance materials so as to reduce maintenance costs and improve equipment maintenance efficiency and combat readiness.

Fault prediction methods based on single data produce insufficient accuracy and often have difficulty meeting the needs of predictive maintenance. There are now more equipment status parameters that can be monitored, analyzed, and processed. Big data technology can be used to mine useful information from a large amount of data and then obtain the operating status of equipment from multi-dimensional and multi-variable cross integration. Therefore, it is possible to more accurately judge the development trend of the equipment's operation and make predictions about possible failures.

There may be many failure signs corresponding to the same failure mode. For example, the failure prediction of electronic equipment can be realized by the change of key parameters, the dynamic power consumption of the equipment, the welding of solder joints, and the change in resistance. This method requires the current and historical data of electronic equipment, the observation sequence, the topological structure, and the prior and conditional probability.

The failure prediction of the aircraft is conducted using monitoring data collected by multiple sensors. Through the processing and analysis of a large amount of irregular data, the valuable laws behind all the data are unearthed, and then the equipment condition assessment is provided as a basis for decision-making. The purpose of data mining is to dig out the laws and patterns of equipment operation, establish a model of equipment health status, and use this as a basis to judge the equipment operation status for early warning of failures.

## 2.2  Data Cleaning

Analysis based on big data can be divided into three processes: data preparation, data mining, interpretation, and evaluation of results. Data preparation includes steps such as data integration, data selection, data cleaning, and data transformation, as shown in Fig. 1.

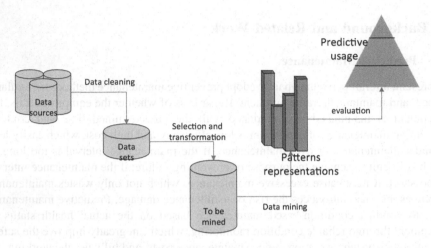

**Fig. 1.**  Processing flow of big data.

(1)  Data cleaning

Data cleaning refers to the process of cleaning a large amount of relatively unclear data with noise, depending on the situation. Generally, it is necessary to use knowledge in different fields to make preliminary judgments and then select the most appropriate cleaning method according to the specific situation.

(2)  Data integration

It is usually necessary to centralize a large amount of extremely different data to provide convenience for subsequent data processing. The key to data integration is to solve data differences caused by different conditions, such as types and platforms.

(3)  Data selection

Data selection involves extracting target data objects from the obtained data according to the goals of data mining.

(4)  Data transformation

The essence of data transformation is transforming the data type to complete the data mining process. For example, if you perform neural network calculations, the data should be converted from discrete to continuous, or the reverse conversion process should be performed. In addition, data transformation has other functions, such as reducing the dimensionality of the data, reducing the amount of data, and identifying the truly valuable data.

### 2.3 Data Mining and Analysis

After the data are prepared, data mining and knowledge representation are conducted to explain the mined stuff to obtain useful information. Generally, the information obtained can clearly describe the target result and can be directly input into the decision model to provide decision support; in addition, the data can be further mined (e.g., using PCA for data processing), and the information can be applied to new data. Under normal circumstances, data mining is a process of cyclical execution.

At present, trend state analysis methods are more mature methods for predicting equipment failure, which are trained with supervised learning. This kind of method includes traditional machine learning algorithms, such as SVC [4] regression, time-series analysis, random forest, and even modern neural network ways (e.g., MLP and LSTM) [5]. Although the trend state analysis method has achieved good application results, it cannot accurately describe the uncertain characteristics of different state transitions, which restricts its practical application in engineering. With the continuous emergence of advanced theories, many research institutions have made useful explorations of the use of new methods for fault prediction. For example, Vanderbilt University used the Taylor series expansion method of the feedforward signal to realize the failure prediction of avionics [6]. Further, Jingbo Gai1 and Yifan Hu from Harbin Engineering University used the method of combining singular value decomposition (SVD) and the fuzzy neural network (FNN) to extract and diagnose the fault features of diesel engine crankshaft bearings efficiently and accurately [7].

## 3 Research Method

Survival analysis is a branch of statistics that analyzes the expected duration of time until one event occurs, such as failure in mechanical systems. It can be used to predict remaining useful life. The algorithm is usually applied in epidemiology or studies for disease treatment (e.g., the proportion of a population that will survive past a certain time). For mechanical reliability, failure may not be well-defined if the failure is partial, a matter of degree, or not otherwise localized in time, which is exactly the situation encountered in predictive maintenance.

More broadly, survival analysis involves the modeling of time to event data, and failure is considered as an "event." The "duration" refers to the time of beginning the observation to the event or the end of the observation. Censoring occurs if no event is observed about that subject after the time of censoring. A censored subject may or may not have an event after the end of the observation time.

Right-censored definition refers to subjects that have not come to a breakdown (less than actual lifetimes). Traditional machine learning methods simply delete right-censored samples, which is not appropriate. In a typical predictive maintenance situation, a great portion of the data are incomplete. In airplane predictive maintenance, we cannot afford to wait for an airplane to break down to collect data, so the breakdown data must be collected in some other way, such as in comparison to other types of airplanes.

In Fig. 2, the red lines denote the lifespan of individuals where the event has been observed, and the blue lines denote the lifespan of the right-censored individuals (event that has not been observed). If the right-censored individuals are simply deleted, the true average lifespan will be severely misunderstood.

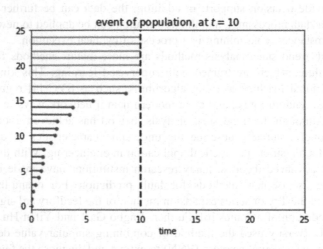

**Fig. 2.** Explanation of incomplete data. (Color figure online)

One of the advantages of survival analysis is to include airplanes that do not break down in the model. Survival analysis was originally developed to solve this type of problem, that is, to deal with estimation when data is right-censored. However, even in the case where all events have been observed (i.e., there is no censoring), survival analysis is still a useful tool to understand duration and rates.

The observations need not always start at zero either. An airplane can enter at any time; for example, when transferred from another airport, and it need not necessarily enter at time zero. In survival analysis, duration is relative: individuals may start at different times. Only the duration of the observation is needed, and not necessarily the start and end time.

In mathematics, the survival function defines the probability that the death event has not occurred yet at time t, or equivalently, the probability of surviving past time t as in Eq. (1).

$$S(t) = \Pr(T > t) \tag{1}$$

Hazard function defines the probability of a death event occurring at time t (given that the death event has not occurred yet) as in Eq. (2).

$$h(t) = \lim_{\delta t \to 0} \frac{\Pr(t \leq T \leq t + \delta t | T > t)}{\delta t} \tag{2}$$

The survival function and hazard function can be converted as in Eq. (3). H(t) is the cumulative hazard function, and the transformation is shown in Fig. 3.

The true survival function or hazard of a population is not observed. It must be estimated using the observed data, such as Kaplan–Meier [8, 8], which is explained in the next section.

$$h(t) = \frac{-S'(t)}{S(t)}$$

$$S(t) = \exp\left(-\int_0^t h(z)dz\right) = \exp(-H(t))$$

(3)

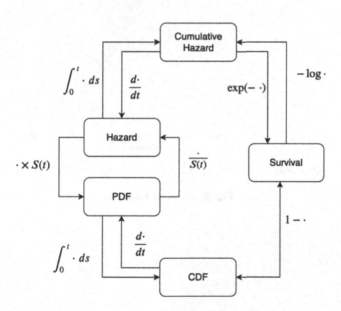

**Fig. 3.** Transformation used in survival analysis

## 4   Experiments

Unlike the turbofan engine degradation simulation data set, which is simulated by C-MAPSS [10], the datasets used here were collected from a real airplane. The structure was especially made in the format of NASA's format.

The initial step was using the Kaplan–Meier estimator to derive the survival function and then gaining insight in the functional time and probabilities of airplanes [11], as in Fig. 4. The plot is a crude tool to estimate the probability of survival past time $t$. The hazard rates are estimated using the Nelson–Aalen estimator [12, 12] to get the cumulative hazard function, as in Fig. 5. All experiments are done with Python package lifelines [14].

The cumulative hazard has a less obvious to understand than the survival functions, but the sum of estimates is much more stable than the point-wise estimates, and the rate of change of this curve is an estimate of the hazard function. The hazard did not start until time point 128, and got bigger (as seen by the increasing rate of change).

Time-varying models were used owing to the time-series nature of datasets, and we incorporated changes over time into the survival analysis by using a modification of the Cox's proportional hazard model, with the mathematical description shown in Eq. (4):

$$h(t|x) = b_0(t) \exp(\sum_{i=1}^{n} \beta_i(x_i(t) - \bar{x}_i)) \tag{4}$$

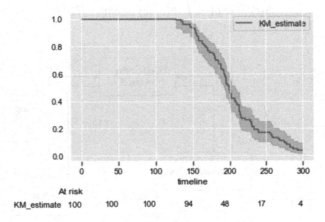

**Fig. 4.** Survival function

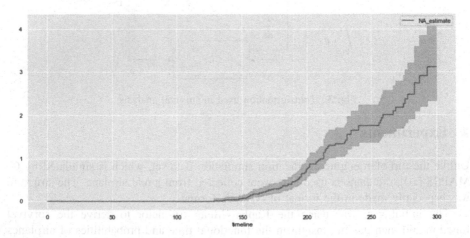

**Fig. 5.** Cumulative hazard function

The exp part in the mathematical description in (4) is a partial hazard, and $x_i(t)$ donates the time-varying part, which has covariates that can change over time. After training over 2000 periods, the get model log-likelihood factor was $-114.77$, which was calculated from CoxTimeVaryingFitter() in the lifelines package. This fit Cox's time-varying proportional hazard model, in (4). This indicates goodness of fit, as closer to 0 is considered better. $-114.77$ is a much lower value during the batch of running.

**Table 1.** Summary of Cox time-varying fitter

| | coef | exp(coef) | se(coef) | coef lower 95% | coef upper 95% | exp(coef) lower 95% | exp(coef) upper 95% | z | p | $-\log2(p)$ |
|---|---|---|---|---|---|---|---|---|---|---|
| Sensor 1 | 1.424213 | 4.154587 | 0.496882 | 0.450342 | 2.398084 | 1.568849 | 1.100207e+01 | 2.866300 | 0.004153 | 7.911630 |
| Sensor 2 | 0.021139 | 1.021364 | 0.032493 | -0.042547 | 0.084825 | 0.958345 | 1.088527e+00 | 0.650559 | 0.515331 | 0.956429 |
| Sensor 3 | 0.145099 | 1.156154 | 0.034326 | 0.077821 | 0.212377 | 1.080929 | 1.236614e+00 | 4.227072 | 0.000024 | 15.366263 |
| Sensor 4 | -0.89811 | 0.407335 | 0.352684 | -1.589366 | -0.206872 | 0.204055 | 8.131237e-01 | -2.54653 | 0.010880 | 6.522178 |
| Sensor 5 | -1.69807 | 0.183036 | 3.723479 | -8.995959 | 5.599812 | 0.000124 | 2.703757e+02 | -0.45604 | **0.648358** | 0.625138 |
| Sensor 6 | -0.00971 | 0.990337 | 0.026522 | -0.061693 | 0.042273 | 0.940171 | 1.043179e+00 | -0.36611 | **0.714277** | 0.485444 |
| Sensor 7 | 4.497159 | 89.761740 | 1.196104 | 2.152838 | 6.841480 | 8.609256 | 9.358729e+02 | 3.759839 | 0.000170 | 12.521985 |
| Sensor 8 | -1.64680 | 0.192665 | 0.414614 | -2.459433 | -0.834175 | 0.085483 | 4.342325e-01 | -3.97189 | 0.000071 | 13.775670 |
| Sensor 9 | 6.201192 | 493.336526 | 3.822620 | -1.291006 | 13.693389 | 0.274994 | 8.850411e+05 | 1.622236 | 0.104753 | 3.254939 |
| Sensor 10 | 0.026528 | 1.026883 | 0.029817 | -0.031912 | 0.084969 | 0.968592 | 1.088683e+00 | 0.889707 | 0.373623 | 1.420344 |
| Sensor 11 | 3.393975 | 29.784098 | 7.005694 | -10.336933 | 17.124882 | 0.000032 | 2.736792e+07 | 0.484459 | **0.628060** | 0.671026 |
| Sensor 12 | 0.244805 | 1.277372 | 0.148923 | -0.047078 | 0.536688 | 0.954013 | 1.710333e+00 | 1.643842 | 0.100209 | 3.318918 |
| Sensor 13 | -4.87282 | 0.007652 | 1.457906 | -7.730263 | -2.015377 | 0.000439 | 1.332702e-01 | -3.34234 | 0.000831 | 10.233304 |
| Sensor 14 | -3.72053 | 0.024221 | 2.152632 | -7.939618 | 0.498544 | 0.000356 | 1.646323e+00 | -1.72836 | 0.083923 | 3.574798 |

The model summary is shown in Table 1; it was also implemented in the lifelines package. The rows are sensors that recorded the equipment state from the datasets, which were scaled before the head. In Table 1, the p values for sensor 5, 6, and 11 are rather large [15]. The exp(coef) shows the scaling hazard risk, which indicates a large risk of breakdown, even for a small sensor value increment. Coefficients are shown as in Fig. 6, which displays the coefficients and confidence intervals of the features. Log partial hazard was then predicted with the lifeline package, which was plotted with remaining time as in Fig. 7. A higher log partial hazard means less time left before breaking down. The potential curve of log partial hazard over time could then be interpolated, which showed very clear potential over time.

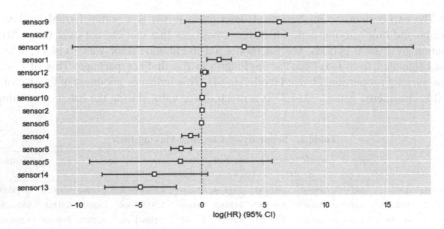

**Fig. 6.** Coefficient plot of the Cox time-varying variant fitter

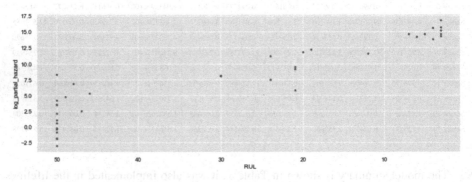

**Fig. 7.** Scatter of log partial hazard to remaining time

These two figures indicate information to perform predictive maintenance and we set a threshold for the log partial hazard, after which maintenance should be done.

With these models, an equipment health evaluation system was constructed to evaluate the equipment health level, as in Fig. 8. A health evaluation model was used to evaluate equipment health level as basic data for condition-based maintenance. Aiming at the failure mechanism caused by the environmental stress of the equipment in different mission profiles, we used methods based on data parameters, failure physics, and expert knowledge.

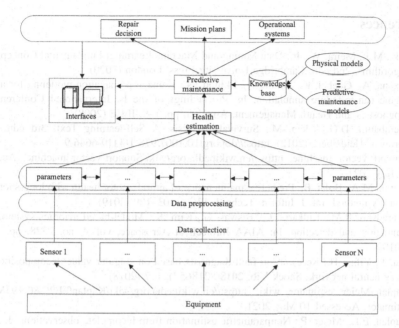

**Fig. 8.** A health evaluation model system

These could be used to establish the corresponding health evaluation model of each sub-system, with the help of various intelligent reasoning algorithms (i.e., neural network, data fusion, physical model) to assess the current health index. The Current status of equipment could be determined, which could provide a basis for timely maintenance and elimination of hidden dangers. The equipment verification system is generally divided into two parts, software and hardware. The software part includes monitoring databases, state assessment models, and fault prediction algorithms, and the hardware part includes computer platforms and maintenance support interfaces.

## 5 Discussion and Conclusion

Aiming at the problems mentions in the abstract, survival analysis was proposed for use in fault prediction and prediction of the remaining time range. This method can compute the hazard values of subjects at known observations, the baseline cumulative hazard rate, and baseline survival function. Its advantage is that incomplete data can also be used, which are usually removed in traditional machine learning methods. The method can greatly improve the efficiency of data usage. A health assessment and failure prediction evaluation system was developed to conduct all the experiments. First, we determined the correlation between equipment state parameters and failure modes, and then we optimized the monitoring parameters of the equipment health status through research on the correlation between state parameters and failure modes. The results indicate that the method can effectively improve the maintenance efficiency and integrity of equipment.

# References

1. Zaki, M.J., Meira, W., Jr.: Data Mining and Machine Learning: Fundamental Concepts and Algorithms, 2nd edn. Cambridge University Press, London (2020)
2. Saxena, A., Goebel, K., Simon, D., Eklund, N.: Damage propagation modeling for aircraft engine run-to-failure simulation. In: Proceedings of the Ist International Conference on Prognostics and Health Management, America, pp. 1–9. IEEE (2008)
3. Kleinbaum, D.G., Klein, M.: Survival Analysis: A Self-learning Text, 3rd edn. SBH. Springer, Heidelberg (2012). https://doi.org/10.1007/978-1-4419-6646-9
4. Support vector machine. https://en.wikipedia.org/wiki/Support-vector_machine. Accessed 21 July 2021
5. Kizrak, M.A., Bolat, B.: Predictive maintenance of aircraft motor health with long-short term memory method. Int. J. Inform. Technol. **12**(2), 103–109 (2019)
6. Bharadwaj, R.M., Kulkarni, C., Biswas, G., Kim, K.: Model-based avionics systems fault simulation and detection. In: AIAA Infotech at Aerospace, vol. 4, no. 3328, pp. 20–22 (2010)
7. Gai, J., Yifan, H.: Research on fault diagnosis based on singular value decomposition and fuzzy neural network. Shock Vib. **2018**(8218657), 1–7 (2018)
8. Kaplan–Meier estimator wiki. https://en.wikipedia.org/wiki/Kaplan%E2%80%93Meier_estimator. Accessed 10 May 2021
9. Kaplan, E.L., Meier, P.: Nonparametric estimation from incomplete observations. J. Amer. Stat. Assoc. **53**(282), 457–481 (1958)
10. PCoE Datasets. https://ti.arc.nasa.gov/tech/dash/groups/pcoe/prognostic-data-repository, https://en.wikipedia.org/wiki/Kaplan%E2%80%93Meier_estimator. Accessed 10 May 2021
11. Morris, T.P., Jarvis, C.I., Cragg, W., et al.: Proposals on Kaplan-Meier plots in medical research and a survey of stakeholder views: KMunicate. BMJ Open **9**(9), 1–7 (2019)
12. Nelson Aalen estimator wiki. https://en.wikipedia.org/wiki/Nelson%E2%80%93Aalen_estimator. Accessed 10 May 2021
13. Jones, A.M., Rice, N., D'Uva, T.B., Balia, S.: Duration data. Appl. Health Econ. **2**(3), 139–181 (2013)
14. Davidson-Pilon, C., et al.: https://github.com/CamDavidsonPilon/lifelines. Accessed 01 July 2021
15. Likelihood ratio. https://stats.idre.ucla.edu/other/mult-pkg/faq/general/faqhow-are-the-likelihood-ratio-wald-and-lagrange-multiplier-score-tests-different-andor-similar/. Accessed 01 July 2021

# Vehicle Trajectory Prediction Based on Graph Attention Network

Zhuolei Chaochen[1,4], Qichao Zhang[2,3(✉)], Ding Li[2,3], Haoran Li[2,3], and Zhonghua Pang[1]

[1] North China University of Technology, Beijing 100144,
People's Republic of China
[2] The State Key Laboratory of Management and Control for Complex Systems,
Institute of Automation, Chinese Academy of Sciences, Beijing 100190,
People's Republic of China
zhangqichao2014@ia.ac.cn
[3] College of Artificial Intelligence, University of Chinese Academy of Sciences,
Beijing 100049, People's Republic of China
[4] Hunan University, Changsha 410082, People's Republic of China

**Abstract.** Trajectory prediction is one of the main challenges to autonomous vehicles. Except for the predicted vehicle historical trajectory information, viable solutions for this task must also consider the static geometric context, such as lane centerlines, and the dynamic interaction information among traffic participants, such as the influence of surrounding vehicles or pedestrians on the predicted vehicle. Recently, mainstream methods are mostly based on recurrent neural networks, which have achieved state-of-the-art (SOTA) performance on distance-based prediction metrics. In order to consider the influence of static geometric context and dynamic interaction information better for the vehicle trajectory prediction, we propose a two-stage prediction framework and a combined VAE-GAT model. Stage I estimates the future destination point of the predicted vehicle using a destination point estimation module based on VAE. In stage II, it produces multiple trajectories using a multiple trajectories prediction module based on GAT which consists of an LSTM-based encoder-decoder and a graph attention network. Finally, one specific trajectory is selected from multiple trajectories conditioned on the estimated destination point. The experimental results and performance comparison based on the Argoverse motion forecasting dataset are given to prove the effectiveness of the proposed method.

**Keywords:** Graph attention network · Vehicle trajectory prediction · Multimodal prediction · Long short-term memory · Variational auto-encode

## 1 Introduction

Predicting the future trajectory of moving vehicles in a real-world environment is a fundamental problem for the autonomous driving system. To improve the safety and comfort of autonomous vehicles (AVs), it is essential to predict the future state accurately with the understanding of both moving objects (e.g., pedestrians and vehicles) and road

© Springer Nature Singapore Pte Ltd. 2022
F. Sun et al. (Eds.): ICCSIP 2021, CCIS 1515, pp. 427–438, 2022.
https://doi.org/10.1007/978-981-16-9247-5_33

428     Z. Chaochen et al.

context information (e.g., lanes). In this paper, the concerned agent for the prediction task is the vehicle, which is the most common moving object on the road.

There are three key challenges for vehicle trajectory prediction: the prediction uncertainty, the understanding of static geometric context, and the influence of dynamic interaction information.

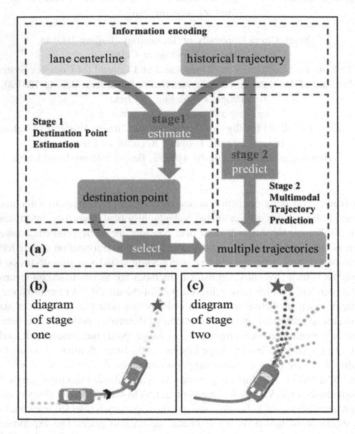

**Fig. 1.** (a): visualizations of our two-stage prediction framework. Stage I estimates the destination point (red patch). Stage II predicts multiple trajectories (blue patch) and selects one that is the closest to the destination point. (b): diagram of stage I. (c): diagram of stage II. The components' colors of these three subgraphs are corresponding to each other. Green solid lines and green patches represent historical trajectories. The green dotted line is the ground-truth future trajectory in (c). Yellow represents lane centerlines in (a) and (b). Blue represents multiple trajectories in (a) and (c). The red star represents the estimated destination point, and the red dotted line is the final predicted trajectory. (Color figure online)

(1) Prediction uncertainty: Due to not knowing the latent intentions of the predicted vehicle and other surrounding objects, a vehicle usually has a multi-modal distribution of futures: its trajectories could tend to turn, go straight, change lanes, etc. One approach to model the multimodality of trajectories is making multiple predictions, which is also used in this work.

(2) Static geometric context: To improve the prediction accuracy, the topological structure of the current traffic scene based on HD maps should be considered. These special rules are usually added as prior information in the prediction tasks [1].

(3) Dynamic social interaction: Similarly, social interactions between all objects have a great influence on the future trajectory. The dynamic social interaction information is very important to improve the prediction accuracy [2].

To address these challenges, a two-stage prediction framework and a combined VAE-GAT model are proposed as shown in Fig. 1a and Fig. 2 respectively. In stage I, we use the lane centerline which a vehicle drives along to represent the static geometric context. A variational autoencoder (VAE) is used to encode the static geometric context and vehicle's historical trajectory as the input features. Then it estimates a vehicle's destination point using the VAE-based destination point estimation module (shown in Fig. 1b). In stage II, a graph attention network (GAT)-based multiple trajectories prediction module is designed to predict multiple trajectories with the consideration of the social interaction information. Finally, we utilize the estimated destination point in stage I to choose one specific trajectory which is the closest to the destination point from all multiple trajectories (shown Fig. 1c). In conclusion, the trajectory prediction module can take full advantage of the static geometric context and dynamic interaction information by combining the stage I and II. The experimental results on the Argoverse [3] motion forecasting dataset demonstrate the effectiveness of the proposed method by comparing it with several baselines.

The contributions in this work are twofold. **First**, we propose a combined VAE-GAT model which consists of a VAE-based destination point estimation module and a GAT-based multiple trajectories prediction module. The former is given to encoding the static geometric context and the latter is designed to consider dynamic social interaction. **Second**, a two-stage prediction framework is proposed that estimates one destination point in stage I, predicts multiple trajectories, and selects one trajectory using the estimated destination point in stage II.

## 2   Related Work

The prediction tasks in traffic scenarios usually refer to human trajectory prediction and vehicle trajectory prediction tasks. The methods of both of them can be borrowed from each other due to the common key challenges for prediction tasks which are intention uncertainty, static geometric context, and dynamic social interaction. For human trajectory prediction, [4] uses a spatial-temporal attention model (ST-Attention) to learn the importance of historical trajectory information and a deep neural network to measure the different importance of the neighbors. PECNet [5] predicts trajectory endpoints using VAE to assist in multi-modal human trajectory prediction. Motivated by this, we employ VAE to estimate the destination point by combining the static geometric context.

With the development and application of graph neural networks (GNN) in recent years, GNN-based methods are recognized to be considered successful in their application to many areas such as semantic segmentation [6], visual navigation [7], and trajectory prediction which we study right here. GNN-based methods have received much attention in prediction tasks. Recently, many SOTA trajectory prediction models [8–10] introduce GNN in their architecture and have been achieved remarkable results on mainstream prediction benchmarks. VectorNet [8] leverages a local GNN to obtain actor-lane features and a global interaction GNN the higher-order interactions among all components with vector representations. Khandelwal et al. leverage two attention modules to describe the static interaction between road and actor, and the dynamic interaction among all actors respectively [9]. LaneGCN [10] exploits a fusion GNN consisting of four types of interactions to capture the complex interactions between objects and maps.

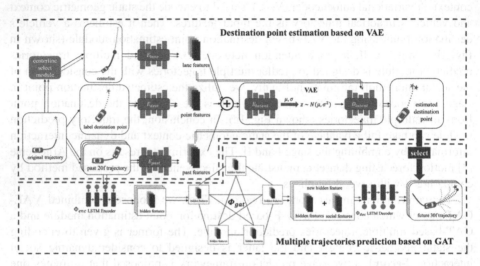

**Fig. 2.** The architecture of combined VAE-GAT. The destination point estimation module based on VAE uses historical trajectory $T_p^i$ and lane centerline $C^i$ along with ground truth endpoint $D$ to train a VAE for estimation. The multiple trajectories prediction module based on GAT uses $T_p^i$ to predict multiple $K$ trajectories $\hat{T}_f^{ik}$. Ground-truth destination points are denoted by yellow stars and estimated destination points are denoted by red stars. Green solid lines represent historical trajectories. Yellow represents lane centerlines and light blue represents multiple trajectories. Red connections denote the parts utilized only in training. Further details in IV. METHOD. (Color figure online)

In order to improve the prediction accuracy, many methods [11, 12] design a subtask to assist the prediction task. Multipath [11] leverages a fixed set of future state-sequence anchors that correspond to each mode of future trajectory in order to capture the intent uncertainty of the vehicle. Based on Multipath, a three-stage model TNT [12] is proposed. It generates trajectory sequences at stage II conditioned on predicted targets at stage I and estimates trajectory likelihoods for selection at stage three. Note that TNT uses the hierarchical graph network VectorNet as a context encoder. Our work is most related to TNT and Multipath. We propose a two-stage learning method. We predict the destination point (corresponding to the targets in TNT and anchors in

Multipath) of the predicted vehicle and multiple trajectories in stage II (corresponding to the target prediction and motion estimation in TNT respectively). Instead of the scoring and selection stage in TNT, we select one trajectory which is the closest to the destination point from multiple trajectories.

## 3 Formulation

Given a sequence $T_p^i = \{(x^i, y^i)\}_{t=0}^{t_p}$ of past observed states in the fixed time step $t_p$ for single vehicle $i$, the goal of vehicle trajectory prediction is to predict its future states $T_f^i = \{(x^i, y^i)\}_{t=t_p}^{t_p + t_f}$ up to the fixed time step $t_f$. We propose the two-stage framework to disassemble this goal as a step-by-step task.

### 3.1 Destination Point Estimation

The goal for stage I is to estimate the state $\{(\hat{x}^i, \hat{y}^i)\}_{t_p + t_f}$ in the last time step $t_f$ of the fixed time step for single vehicle $i$, given the past trajectory $T_p^i = \{(x^i, y^i)\}_{t=1}^{t_p}$. In addition, we also use the lane centerline sequences $C^i$ which vehicle $i$ drives along to take static geometric context into account. This last state, which we call destination point $\hat{D}^i$, will be the criterion of trajectory selection in the next stage.

### 3.2 Multimodal Trajectory Prediction

In stage II, we predict $K$ trajectories $\hat{T}_f^{ik} = \{(\hat{x}^{ik}, \hat{y}^{ik})\}_{t=t_p+1}^{t_p + t_f}$ $(k = 1, 2...K)$ multimodally using the past trajectory $T_p^i = \{(x^i, y^i)\}_{t=1}^{t_p}$ for vehicle $i$. Then we select one particular trajectory $\hat{T}_f^i = \min_k EucDist(\hat{T}_f^{ik}, \hat{D}^i)$ based on the destination point $\hat{D}^i$ we estimated in stage I.

## 4 Methods

Our proposed combined VAE-GAT architecture (Fig. 2) predicts one destination point and multiple trajectories of the predicted vehicle and gets the one trajectory with specific driving intent by selecting the closest trajectory to the estimated point from multiple trajectories. Because the destination point is only introduced to describe the driving intent of the predicted vehicle. Dynamic interaction among all traffic participants is not considered in stage I.

### 4.1 VAE Destination Point Estimation

The destination point estimation module based on VAE is for stage I in our two-stage prediction framework. It estimates the state of point $\hat{D}^i = \{(\hat{x}^i, \hat{y}^i)\}_{t_p + t_f}$ in the last time step of the fixed time step $t_f$ for vehicle $i$. As mentioned above, prediction for AVs are closely related to static offline map data. In order to take static geometric context into account, we use a concatenated lane centerline of each road segment that the vehicle drives along. We obtain the most relevant centerline from the underlying vector map using a heuristic-based polyline proposal module which is proposed in WIMP [5] based on Argoverse API. During the training phase, we respectively extract and encode the observed historical states $T_p^i = \{(x^i, y^i)\}_{t=1}^{t_p}$, ground-truth destination point $D$, and fixed-length lane centerline sequences $C^i$ for the predicted vehicle $i$ by an MLP-based encoder $E_{past}$, an MLP-based encoder $E_{dest}$, and an MLP-based encoder $E_{lane}$. These yield us $E_{past}(T_p^i)$, $E_{dest}(D^i)$ and $E_{lane}(C^i)$ which are respectively representations of the motion history, true intent, and geometric context. Then these representations are concatenated together and are considered as the input features of the latent encoder $E_{latent}$ of VAE, then it produces parameters $(\mu, \sigma)$ for the latent variable $z = N(\mu, \sigma)$. Next, it samples possible destination points from and concatenates them with $E_{past}(T_p^i)$. Finally, we decode the concatenated features using the latent decoder $D_{latent}$ to obtain destination point $\hat{D}$. Since the ground truth $D$ is not available in the real scene, during evaluation and test we don't use the encoder $E_{dest}$ and don't get $E_{dest}(D^i)$ naturally. We sample $z$ from a standard normal distribution $N(0, \sigma_T I)$ instead.

$$\hat{D}^i = \begin{cases} D_{latent}(E_{latent}([E_{lane}(C^i), E_{past}(T_p^i), E_{end}(D^i)])) & during\ train \\ D_{latent}(E_{latent}([E_{lane}(C^i), E_{past}(T_p^i)])) & otherwise \end{cases} \tag{1}$$

### 4.2    GAT Multiple Trajectories Prediction

The multiple trajectories prediction module based on GAT is for stage II in our two-stage prediction framework. In order to take **dynamic social interaction** into account, we encode historical trajectories of not only vehicle $i$ but its neighbors $j$ via a shared LSTM-based encoder $\Phi_{enc}$ in every time step t and we predict trajectories multiply to describe the uncertainty of the prediction.

$$h_t^i = \Phi_{enc}(T_t^i, h_{t-1}^i), \quad i = 1, 2, ..., N \tag{2}$$

$$h_t^j = \Phi_{enc}(T_t^j, h_{t-1}^j), j \in neighbor(i) \tag{3}$$

As $\Phi_{enc}$ runs independently, we employ a GAT module $\Phi_{gat}$ to incorporate other neighbors' interaction information within the scene as follows [13]:

$$\alpha_{ij}^r = \text{softmax}_j(a^r \odot [W^r h_t^n, W^r h_t^j]) \tag{4}$$

$$\bar{h}_t^i = \sigma(h_t^i + \frac{1}{R}\sum_{r=1}^{R}\sum_{j \in N\setminus i} \alpha_{ij}^r W^r h_t^j) \tag{5}$$

where $R$ denotes the number of attention heads, $W^r$ and $\alpha^r$ are learned parameters, $[,]$ is a concatenation operator, $\odot$ represents the inner product operation, $\sigma$ denotes a non-linear activation function. An LSTM-based decoder $\Phi_{dec}$ is used to generates multiple predictions, and then we obtain the output $o_t^i$ and state $s^{ik}$ generated by output $o_t^i$ via a bivariate Gaussian function $\Phi_{pred}$ for a future time-step $t$ as follows:

$$o_t^i, \bar{h}_t^i = \Phi_{dec}(\bar{h}_{t-1}^i) \tag{6}$$

$$\hat{s}^{ik} = (\hat{x}_{t+1}^i, \hat{y}_{t+1}^i)^k = \Phi_{pred}(o_t^i) \ (k = 1, 2, ..., K) \tag{7}$$

Finally, based on the estimated destination point, we select one specific trajectory from all multiple trajectories $\hat{T}_f^{ik} = \{\hat{s}^{ik}\}_{t=t_p+1}^{t_p+t_f}$ as follows, where EucDist(,) represents a euclidean distance operator:

$$\hat{T}_f^i = \min_k \text{EucDist}(\hat{T}_{t_f}^{ik}, \hat{D}^i) \ (k = 1, 2, ..., K) \tag{8}$$

### 4.3   End-To-End Loss

We use the loss functions respectively to training the end to end modules, the loss function in destination point estimation module based on VAE is as follows:

$$L_1 = D_{KL} + L_{point} = D_{KL} + \text{MSE}(D, \hat{D}) \tag{9}$$

where the KL divergence term is used for training the VAE, and the $L_{point}$ term describes the offset between estimated point and ground-truth. MSE(,) represents a mean square error operator.

The loss function of the multiple trajectories prediction module based on GAT is as follows, where $N$ denotes the total number of prediction tasks, $s_i^t$ denote the agent $i$'s $(x, y)$ coordinates at time step $t$, and $\hat{s}_i^{kt}$ represent the agent $i$'s predicted future state under the mode $k$ at time step $t$:

$$L_2 = \frac{1}{N} \min_{k \in \{1,...,K\}} |s_i^t - \hat{s}_i^{kt}| \tag{10}$$

## 5   Experiments

### 5.1   Dataset

We conduct our experiments using the Argoverse [2] dataset, a large-scale vehicle trajectory dataset containing more than 300,000 scenarios. Given a 2-s trajectory history of not only the agent but the nearby (social) neighbors as input to predict the future motion of the predicted vehicle over the next 3 s.

## 5.2    Implementation Details

**Normalization.** Before all the other calculations, every sequence (trajectories, lane centerlines, etc.) of each scenario in global Argoverse world coordinates within should be transformed to a local coordinates which is normalized on the basis of the predicted vehicle $i$. We use an affine transformation a to make sure that the predicted vehicle's heading (i.e. the angle between $s_i^{t=0}$ and $s_i^{t=20}$, where $s_i^t$ denotes the $(x, y)$ coordinates) is aligned with the positive X-axis and the first coordinates $s_i^{t=0}$ is at the origin of the local coordinates. i.e., $y_i^{t=20} = 0$ and $s_i^{t=0} = (0, 0)$.

**Experimental Settings.** We train the model on a 1050Ti GPU and 4-2080 TITAN GPUs. For training in stage I, we use the ADAM optimizer, and the learning rate is initialized to 0.0001 and increases by an order of magnitude in subsequent experiments (0.001 and 0.01). For stage II, we use the RMSPROP optimizer for the three components (LSTM-based encoder, LSTM-based decoder, and GAT) and the learning rate is set to 0.0001, 0.00001 and 0.00005. Validation metrics are computed after every training loop for both stage I and stage II. Each model requires 200 epochs approximately to train on average.

**Metrics.** For Evaluation, We use these widely adopted prediction metrics: the Average Displacement Error (ADE), the Final Displacement Error (FDE), and Miss Rate (MR) which are commonly used in current prediction tasks [4, 4, 4, 4, 4]. they are defined as follows [14, 14]:

$$\text{minADE} = \frac{1}{N} \min_{k \in \{1,\ldots,K\}} \sum_{i=1}^{N} \frac{1}{T} \sum_{t=1}^{T} ||s_i^t - \hat{s}_i^{kt}||_2 \tag{11}$$

$$\text{minFDE} = \frac{1}{N} \min_{k \in \{1,\ldots,K\}} \sum_{i=1}^{N} ||s_i^t - \hat{s}_i^{kt}||_2 \tag{12}$$

$$\text{MR} = \frac{M}{N} = \frac{\begin{cases} M+1, & \text{if } \text{FDE} > 2m \\ M, & \text{otherwise} \end{cases}}{N} \tag{13}$$

where N denotes the total number of prediction tasks, M denotes the number of "miss" circumstances and K is the number of modals.

## 5.3    Experiments Results

In order to train our model to the optimum efficiency, we set experiments under different settings of hyperparameters. (Shown in Table 1 and Table 2).

From Table 1, we can find the best hyperparameters setting for the VAE destination point estimation model: epochs are 500, the batch size is 256, and the learning rate is 0.0001. From Table 2, we can notice the best hyperparameters setting for GAT multiple trajectories prediction model: epochs are 200, the batch size is 128, and the learning rate is 0.0001.

**Table 1.** Experimental results under different settings of hyperparameters for VAE Destination Point Estimation model.

| Epoch | Batch size | Learning rate | Validation loss | minFDE |
|---|---|---|---|---|
| **500** | **256** | **1e−4** | **3.99** | **3.84** |
| 200 | 256 | 1e−4 | 4.34 | 4.17 |
| 200 | 256 | 1e−4 | 4.28 | 3.99 |
| 200 | 128 | 1e−3 | 4.34 | 4.19 |
| 500 | 128 | 1e−2 | 5.53 | 5.21 |
| 500 | 128 | 1e−3 | 4.44 | 4.26 |

**Table 2.** Experimental results under different settings of hyperparameters for GAT multiple trajectories prediction. (Void item is Because Data is too large to be valuable).

| Epoch | Batch size | Learning rate | Validation loss | minFDE (K = 6) | minADE (K = 6) | MR (K = 6) |
|---|---|---|---|---|---|---|
| 1000 | 128 | 1e−4 | 10.57 | 12.63 | 8.47 | |
| 200 | 128 | 1e−5 | 1.74 | 2.61 | 1.51 | 0.23 |
| **200** | **128** | **5e−5** | **1.55** | **2.37** | **1.32** | **0.19** |

We compare combined VAE-GAT to several baselines: LSTM+map(prior) and NN +map(prior) are baselines provided by Argoverse [3].

**Table 3.** Trajectory prediction performance evaluated on the Argoverse in minADE, minFDE and MR, with multi-modal number K = 6 (↓indicates lower is better).

| Model | minFDE (K = 6) | minADE (K = 6) | MR (K = 6) |
|---|---|---|---|
| **Ours** | **1.32**↓ | **2.37**↓ | **0.19**↓ |
| LSTM+map(prior)(Baseline) [3] | 2.08 | 4.19 | 0.67 |
| NN+map(prior)(Baseline) [3] | 2.28 | 5.32 | 0.75 |

**Table 4.** Ablation studies with different architecture components. Quantitative results reported for (K = 6) metrics on validation set (↓indicates lower is better).

| Model | Learning rate | minFDE (K = 6) | minADE (K = 6) | MR (K = 6) |
|---|---|---|---|---|
| LSTM+GAT | 1e−5 | 1.74↓ | 1.51↓ | 2.61↓ |
| LSTM | 1e−5 | 1.85 | 1.58 | 2.81 |
| LSTM+GAT | 5e−5 | 1.55↓ | 1.32↓ | 2.37↓ |
| LSTM | 5e−5 | 1.86 | 1.59 | 2.66 |

From Table 3, we can see our method is superior to the LSTM+map baseline by 50.5% on average and is superior to the NN+map baseline by 59.7% on average. This is because both static geometric contexts and dynamic social interaction are considered. Considering the limitations on computing resources, we simplify our model by reducing the number of layers and deleting the attention module which is supposed to describe the local geometric interaction in each time step. These modifications lead to some performance degradation.

In order to demonstrate how the GAT component of our architecture contributes to overall prediction performance, we perform an ablation study under two sets of hyperparameters and summarize the results in Table 4. All the hyperparameters except the learning rate are all the same (The batch size is 128, epochs are 200, etc.), so only the learning rates were given in Table 4. We can notice the maximum 14.8% decrease on average of metrics due to the GAT component, which proves its effectiveness (↓indicates lower is better).

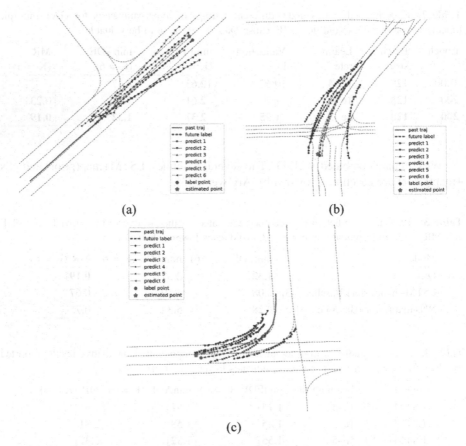

**Fig. 3.** Visualizations of three prediction scenarios which are straight (a), curve trajectories (b), and intersection turn (c). Green solid lines are past observed trajectories and green dotted lines are ground-truth future trajectories. Blue dotted lines are multiple trajectories and the red dotted lines are the final trajectories selected by the estimated points which are red stars. (Color figure online)

Finally, we visualize our results in several specific scenarios in 2D maps provided by Argoverse in Fig. 3. The results shown in Fig. 3 are trained under the hyperparameter which epochs are 200, the batch size is 128, and the learning rate is 5e−5. We can observe that all multiple trajectories (grey dotted lines) have a strong tendency to fit the ground-truth (green dotted lines) and the estimated destination point (red star) can correctly select the trajectory mode which fits ground-truth best (red dotted lines). We only compared results of quantitative metrics rather than visualizations, and that is expected to be improved in subsequent work.

# 6  Conclusion

In this work, we propose a two-stage prediction framework and the combined VAE-GAT architecture to handle the vehicle trajectory prediction tasks. We estimate the destination point which describes the driving intent in stage one and predict multiple trajectories which describe the uncertainty of prediction in stage II. We select one specific trajectory which is the closest to the estimated destination point in stage I from multiple trajectories, i.e., we predict one possible future trajectory under the specific driving intent. Finally, we conduct our experiments using the Argoverse and observe that our method had a lot of improvement over baselines (50.5% superior to LSTM +map and 59.7% superior to NN+map on average), which proves its effectiveness. The availability of the GAT component is proved by ablation studies. Our method uses offline map data as prior knowledge and large-scale datasets such as Argoverse for training. In practical application scenarios, real-time trajectory data and static map information are collected and retrieved for online dynamic prediction.

**Acknowledgement.** This work is partly supported by the Beijing Municipal Natural Science Foundation under Grants L191002, by National Natural Science Foundation of China (NSFC) under Grants No.61803371, and by Baidu Times Technology (Beijing) Co., Ltd.

# References

1. Lu, Y., Chen, Y., Zhao, D., Li, H.: Hybrid deep learning based moving object detection via motion prediction. In: Chinese Automation Congress (CAC), pp. 1442–1447 (2018)
2. Alahi, A., Goel, K., Ramanathan, V., Robicquet, A., Fei-Fei, L., Savarese, S.: Social LSTM: human trajectory prediction in crowded spaces. In: IEEE Conference on Computer Vision and Pattern Recognition (CVPR), pp. 961–971 (2016)
3. Fang, C., et al.: Argoverse: 3D tracking and forecasting with rich maps. In: IEEE/CVF Conference on Computer Vision and Pattern Recognition (CVPR), pp. 8740–8749 (2019)
4. Zhao, X., Chen, Y., Guo, J., Zhao, D.: A spatial-temporal attention model for human trajectory prediction. IEEE/CAA J. Automatica Sinica **7**, 965–974 (2020)
5. Mangalam, K., et al.: It is not the journey but the destination: endpoint conditioned trajectory prediction. In: Vedaldi, A., Bischof, H., Brox, T., Frahm, J.-M. (eds.) ECCV 2020. LNCS, vol. 12347, pp. 759–776. Springer, Cham (2020). https://doi.org/10.1007/978-3-030-58536-5_45

6. Lu, Y., Chen, Y., Zhao, D., Liu, B., Lai, Z., Chen, J.: CNN-G: convolutional neural network combined with graph for image segmentation with theoretical analysis. IEEE Trans. Cogn. Dev. Syst. **13**(3), 631–644 (2021)

7. Lu, Y., Chen, Y., Zhao, D., Li, D.: Graph neural network-based inference in a Markov network for visual navigation. Neurocomputing **421**, 140–150 (2021)

8. Jiyang, G., et al.: VectorNet: encoding HD maps and agent dynamics from vectorized representation. In: 2020 IEEE/CVF Conference on Computer Vision and Pattern Recognition (CVPR), pp. 11522–11530 (2020)

9. Siddhesh, K., William, Q., Jagjeet, S., Andrew, H., Deva, R.: What-if motion prediction for autonomous driving. arXiv preprint arXiv:2008.10587 (2020)

10. Liang, M., et al.: Learning lane graph representations for motion forecasting. In: Vedaldi, A., Bischof, H., Brox, T., Frahm, J.-M. (eds.) ECCV 2020. LNCS, vol. 12347, pp. 541–556. Springer, Cham (2020). https://doi.org/10.1007/978-3-030-58536-5_32

11. Chai, Y., Sapp, B., Bansal, M., Anguelov, D.: MultiPath: multiple probabilistic anchor trajectory hypotheses for behavior prediction. In: Proceedings of the Conference on Robot Learning, pp. 86–99 (2020)

12. Zhao, H., et al.: TNT: target-driveN trajectory prediction. arXiv preprint arXiv:2008.08294 (2020)

13. Veličković, P., Cucurull, G., Casanova, A., Romer, A., Liò, P., Bengio, Y.: Graph attention networks. arXiv preprint arXiv:1710.10903 (2017)

14. Interaction Prediction – Metrics. https://waymo.com/open/challenges/2021/interaction-prediction/

15. Argoverse Motion Forecasting Competition - CVPR 2021 competition. https://eval.ai/web/challenges/challenge-page/

# Time-of-Flight Camera Based Trailer Hitch Detection for Automatic Reverse Hanging System

Yaqi Liu[1,2], Chunxiang Wang[1,2(✉)], Wei Yuan[3], and Ming Yang[1,2]

[1] Department of Automation, Shanghai Jiao Tong University,
Shanghai 200240, China
wangcx@sjtu.edu.cn
[2] Key Laboratory of System Control and Information Processing,
Ministry of Education of China, Shanghai 200240, China
[3] University of Michigan - Shanghai Jiao Tong University Joint Institute,
Shanghai Jiao Tong University, Shanghai 200240, China

**Abstract.** With the development of autonomous vehicles, trailer-mounted self-driving cars are widely used for goods transportation. However, self-driving cars still use a manual way to hitch a trailer. To address this problem, this paper proposes a two-stage trailer hitch detection algorithm using a Time-of-Flight (ToF) camera to hitch the vehicle to a trailer automatically. The algorithm is divided into two parts: trailer detection and trailer hitch detection. An algorithm based on a 2D color image is used for trailer detection. To hitch a trailer successfully, the accurate pose of the trailer hitch is needed. This paper proposes an algorithm that combines coarse matching and fine matching in trailer hitch detection, which provides the 3D coordinate and the pose of the hitch. The method's performance is evaluated on real data. The experiments show the proposed method achieves high accuracy and high efficiency.

**Keywords:** Automatic reverse hanging system · Trailer hitch detection · Point clouds recognition

## 1 Introduction

Trailers are widely used to transport goods due to their convenience and easy expansion. Self-driving cars can realize the function of towing a trailer by adding a hitch at the rear. The application of trailer-mounted self-driving cars helps improve the efficiency of the transportation process and reduce labor costs. Although the trailer-mounted self-driving car can transport things on routes without drivers, it still uses a manual method to hitch a trailer. A worker needs to move the trailer into place manually, position the trailer hitch precisely underneath the vehicle's hitch and then connect them. An automated system can take the place of the workers and help the car automatically reverse to a stationary trailer.

© Springer Nature Singapore Pte Ltd. 2022
F. Sun et al. (Eds.): ICCSIP 2021, CCIS 1515, pp. 439–450, 2022.
https://doi.org/10.1007/978-981-16-9247-5_34

The key step of the automated hitch system is to detect the precise and specific position of the trailer hitch, so as to obtain the final target position of reversing. Detecting the trailer hitch accurately and reliably is important for automatically reversing to a trailer. This paper proposes a two-stage trailer hitch detection algorithm using a ToF camera to hitch the vehicle to a trailer. Our main contributions are: 1) Design a distance-driven two-stage trailer hitch detection system. 2) Develop a 2D detection method based on color images for detecting the trailer when the front self-driving car is far from the trailer. 3) Develop a 3D detection method based on point clouds and grid images for detecting the trailer hitch and estimating its pose when the front car and the trailer are close to each other.

## 2    Related Work

Atoum et al. [1] presented an automated monocular-camera-based computer vision system for autonomous self-backing-up a vehicle towards a trailer, by continuously estimating the 3D trailer coupler position and feeding it to the vehicle. They proposed a distance-driven multiplexer convolutional neural network (CNN) method, which selects the most suitable CNN using the estimated coupler-to-vehicle distance. Dahal et al. [2] designed a CNN that detects a trailer, its coupler, and the vehicle's tow ball by using the rear-view fisheye camera. Ramirez-Llanos et al. [3] proposed two semi-autonomous methods to reverse a vehicle to a trailer. The method uses visual servo to position the truck tow ball under the trailer coupler.

Our approach in this paper is different. First, we do not use the deep-learning based method, which means the algorithm can be implemented on an embedded system that does not have any graphical accelerator. Second, we use a ToF camera instead of a monocular camera, so the accurate distance can be measured and the algorithm based on point clouds is able to use under poor light scenarios. Third, the whole system is automatic which does not needs the user's assistance.

## 3    Method

### 3.1    Platform Overview

The goal of detection is to obtain the pose of the trailer hitch. Specifically, assuming that the position of the sensor installed behind the vehicle is the origin, three pose parameters between vehicle and trailer are needed, including lateral offset, longitudinal offset, and yaw angle (See Fig. 1). Compared with 2D images, the use of 3D point clouds to describe objects can more highlight the shape characteristics of the object. The detection result will not have a large difference due to the change of perspective so the sensor should have the function of collecting depth data. A ToF camera can produce a depth image, each pixel of which encodes the distance to the corresponding point in the scene [4]. These cameras can be used to estimate 3D structure directly, without the help of traditional computer-vision algorithms. The existing ToF camera can obtain a color image and a depth image at the same time, which is a suitable choice for realizing the system.

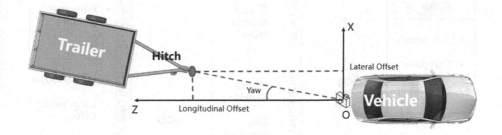

(a) Definition of the Pose Parameters

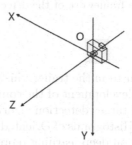

(b) Definition of the 3D Coordinate System

**Fig. 1.** Pose parameters and coordinates system

Since the ToF camera has a limited measurement range, and when the front vehicle is far from the trailer, the point clouds will be too sparse to detect the hitch, this paper proposes a two-stage detection method for the trailer and the trailer hitch (See Fig. 2). When the distance between the front vehicle and the trailer is far, the 2D color image is used for detection. Assuming the trailer is in the field of view of the camera, this work presents an image-based system to automatically detect the trailer and continuously provide location. An automatic control system may use the estimated position to control the vehicle's movement. After reaching the distance at which the trailer hitch can be detected, the 3D data is used to execute the detection algorithm based on point clouds to detect the hitch. Finally, the relative pose between the front vehicle and the trailer hitch is obtained.

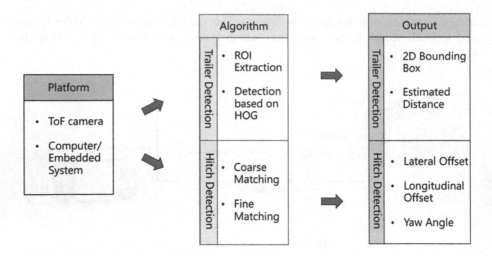

**Fig. 2.** The framework of the detection system

## 3.2  Trailer Detection

When the vehicle ahead is far from the trailer, this work detects the trailer based on a color image. With the development of the computer vision, there have been many excellent image-based target detection algorithms, such as the traditional methods represented by the Histograms of Oriented Gradients (HOG) [5] descriptors and the methods based on deep-learning represented by the RCNN [6] and the YOLO [7]. Data is key to learning an accurate convolutional neural network (CNN). Because of the lack of public large-scale datasets in this field, this work uses traditional methods that only require small-scale datasets. This paper proposes a two-stage method for trailer detection. First, color segmentation is used to extract the region of interest (ROI), and then the detection algorithm is executed in the ROI.

**ROI Extraction.** Extracting the region of interest can improve the operating efficiency of detection and avoid false detection effectively. Since the trailers are mostly not fully enclosed, which cannot cover the background behind them completely, and the background will have a great impact on the detection results. It is necessary to segment the trailer from the background. The color of the trailer is determined, but the color of the background is complex and changeable. Therefore, color segmentation can be used to segment the trailer from the complex background and then perform object detection. HSV is a color space based on the perceptual variables hue (H), saturation (S), and value (V) or brightness (L) [8]. Compared with the RGB color space, the HSV color space can express the hue of the color more intuitively. Therefore, the HSV color space is easier to focus on objects of a certain color and is often used for segmentation in computer vision.

We convert the images from the RGB color space into the HSV color space, delimit the maximum and minimum values of each channel, and then filter each channel separately to obtain an image mask. The mask is a binary image like a hard attention map. Every pixel value in a mask corresponds to whether the pixel in the raw image is the color we want. For each detected contour, the contour length and the area enclosed by the contour are calculated. The contours whose length and area are both greater than the threshold are kept. This paper regards the minimum enclosing rectangles of those retained contours as the regions of interest.

**Object Detection.** Object detection is to determine whether there is a trailer in each region of interest and give the specific location. Histograms of Oriented Gradients (HOG) descriptors are widely used in object detection. In the algorithm, the detector window is tiled with a grid of overlapping blocks in which Histograms of Oriented Gradients feature vectors are extracted and is scanned across the image at all positions. For each previously extracted ROI, an image pyramid with a set of layers of different sizes is constructed. Features are extracted for each layer in the image pyramid so that trailers of different sizes can be effectively detected.

The combined feature vectors of each detector window are fed to a machine learning model for object or non-object classification. Support Vector Machine (SVM) is a classic two-classification model. This work uses a soft margin linear SVM. We denote the train dataset as $T = (x_0, y_0), (x_1, y_1), \ldots, (x_N, y_N), x_i \in \mathbb{R}^n, y_i \in -1, +1, i = 1, 2, \ldots, N$. Construct the convex optimization problem as follows:

$$\min_{\alpha} \frac{1}{2} \sum_{i=1}^{N} \sum_{j=1}^{N} \alpha_i \alpha_j y_i y_j (x_i \cdot x_j) - \sum_{i=1}^{N} \alpha_i \tag{1}$$

with $\sum_{i=1}^{N} \alpha_i y_i = 0, 0 < \alpha_i < C, i = 1, 2, \ldots, N$. The $C$ parameter is a penalty term. Before training, the bounding boxes of trailers in images are marked. A two-stage training method can be used to improve the performance of the SVM. All positive and negative training examples are fed to train a preliminary SVM. Each negative training example is searched for false positives. Then, the method trains the SVM model again by using the initial negative examples and the false positive examples.

## 3.3   Trailer Hitch Detection

In order to hitch a trailer successfully, the pose (includes position and orientation) of the trailer hitch should be estimated. The detection results based on color images are often affected by changes in the viewing angle. Furthermore, it is difficult to obtain accurate 3D hitch coordinate with 2D images, so this work uses 3D point clouds to detect and estimate the pose of the hitch. The point clouds can be converted from a depth image by using a camera projection matrix. This paper proposes an algorithm that combines coarse matching and fine matching. The hitch cluster is extracted in the coarse matching stage, and the pose of the hitch is estimated in the fine matching stage.

**Coarse Matching.** A pass-through filter is used to filter out points outside the usable range of the ToF camera. The error measured distance by the ToF camera will cause sparse outliers, which will affect the object detection. To address this problem, a statistical outlier removal filter which uses point neighborhood statistics to filter outlier data is used. Since the hitch and the trailer are connected together, it is hard to use a segmentation algorithm based on point clouds to separate them clearly. Also, algorithms based on point clouds often involve problems such as massive calculations and inefficient. This work proposes a hitch detection method based on grid images, which transforms point clouds from 3D space into 2D space. The trailer hitch is located in the front of the trailer. We project the point clouds from a bird's eye of view because the hitch has strong morphological characteristics from this view.

The grid image is a 8-channel grayscale image. Each pixel in the grid image corresponds to a position in the real world. The point clouds are first sent to a pass filter to limit the value of $z$-axis and $x$-axis. Suppose the minimum value of the $x$-axis is $x_{min}$ and the maximum value is $x_{max}$ after filtering, so as the $z$-axis, and then do the transformation(see Algorithm 1).

---

**Algorithm 1:** Bird's Eye of View Grid Image Projection

---

**Data:** point clouds data $P$ which each point is denoted as $(x, y, z)$, step size for discretization $d$, height of the desired grid image $h$, width of the desired grid image $w$.

**Result:** a grid image $G_{w \times h}$ encodes height information of $y$-axis..

1  Initialize a grid image as zero matrixes with size $(w, h)$;
2  **foreach** *point p of P* **do**
3      $\quad p_u \leftarrow \lfloor \frac{z_{max} - z}{d} \rfloor$;
4      $\quad p_v \leftarrow \lfloor \frac{x - x_{min}}{d} \rfloor$;
5      $\quad p_{value} \leftarrow -y$;
6      $\quad$ **if** $p_{value} > G(p_u, p_v)$ **then**
7          $\quad\quad |\quad G(p_u, p_v) \leftarrow p_{value}$ ;
8      $\quad$ **end**
9  **end**
10  Normalize the grid image;
11  Convert the grid image to 8-bit grayscale;

---

The image is first dilated and then eroded to remove noise and join disparate elements [9]. Then the grid image is binarized and searched for contours. The contour feature can represent the shape feature of objects, and it is translation, rotation, and scale-invariant. This paper uses Hu moment invariants and contour scale feature as the feature vector to establish the similarity matching function between the template and the scene. Centralized moment $\mu_{pq}$ are geometric moments of the image $I_{xy}$, with the center of mass $(\bar{x}, \bar{y})$:

$$\mu_{pq} = \sum_{x=1}^{M} \sum_{y=1}^{N} (x - \bar{x})^p (y - \bar{y})^p I_{xy} \tag{2}$$

Nomarlized moments are defined as:

$$N_{pq} = \frac{\mu_{pq}}{\mu_{00}^{\gamma}}, \; with \; \gamma = \frac{p+q}{2} + 1, \forall p + q \geq 2 \tag{3}$$

Seven Hu Moments can be obtained from the centralized moments [10]. Our work use Hu Moments based on the second order moment, which can be used for scale, position, and rotation invariant recognition:

$$T_1 = N_{20} + N_{02} \tag{4}$$

$$T_2 = (N_{20} - N_{02})^2 + 4N_{11}^2 \tag{5}$$

Suppose the width of the minimum enclosing rectangle of the contour is $w$, and the height is $h$. The contour area is $s$. Scale features are defined as:

$$S_1 = \frac{w}{h} \tag{6}$$

$$S_2 = \frac{s}{w \times h} \tag{7}$$

A 1-by-4 feature vector $\vec{F}$ is defined as:

$$\vec{F} = [T_1 \; T_2 \; S_1 \; S_2]^T \tag{8}$$

During detection, suppose the feature vector of the contour in scene is $\vec{F_1}$ and the feature vector of the template is $\vec{F_2}$. The similarity function is defined as:

$$f\left(\vec{F_1}, \vec{F_2}\right) = -\sqrt{\sum_{i=1}^{4} \left(\vec{F_{1i}} - \vec{F_{2i}}\right)^2} \tag{9}$$

The larger the function value is, the more similar their shapes are. When the similarity function value is greater than the threshold, the contour is considered as the contour of the hitch. The positions of the four vertices of the minimum enclosing rectangle are re-transformed to the 3D coordinate of the real space. Then, we traverse the point clouds and keep the points located in the 3D bounding box as candidate point clouds cluster for hitch detection.

**Fine Matching.** Point cloud registration algorithm is widely used in object detection and robot localization [11]. To get the pose of the hitch, the point clouds of the hitch cluster need to be fine matched. This paper uses a fine matching algorithm based on Point Pair Feature (PPF) [12] and Iterative Closest Point (ICP) [13] to obtain the final accurate pose. PPF describes the relative position and orientation of two oriented points. There are two stages in the PPF method: model globally and match locally. The global model is represented as a hash table indexed by a set of PPF with similar feature vectors being grouped together. For local matching, a voting scheme is used for the downsample point clouds to get the final pose.

The Iterative Closest Point (ICP) method is used to do the further fine matching. The algorithm iteratively revises the transformation needed to minimize the distance from the scene to the reference model point clouds. The final translation matrix and rotation matrix are obtained. The lateral offset, longitudinal offset, and yaw angle can be calculated from the translation matrix and the rotation matrix.

## 4 Experiments

This work uses an Azure Kinect ToF camera installed at the rear of the vehicle ahead to collect the dataset. The dataset contains six bags consisting of 1506 frames. Each bag contains a video showing the process of a vehicle backing up towards a trailer. Each frame contains a color image, a depth image, and camera information. The bounding box of the trailer is labeled at every frame. The algorithm was implemented in C++ based on the Robot Operating System (ROS). The experiments were run on a 1.80 GHz Intel Core i7-8550U with 16 GB RAM.

Intersection Over Union (IOU) is used to check the accuracy of the algorithm. If the IOU between the predicted box and any ground truth box is greater than 0.5, the detect result will be considered as positive. The testing dataset contains 280 color images from one bag. The training dataset contains 500 color images randomly drawn from rest bags. This work used a soft margin linear SVM. The $C$ parameter in SVM trades off the correct classification of training examples against the maximization of the decision function's margin. Table 1 illustrates the high performance of our model under different $C$.

**Table 1.** Trailer detection results under different $C$

| C | Precision | Recall | Accuracy |
|---|---|---|---|
| 0.01 | 98.53% | 97.46% | 96.07% |
| 0.1 | 98.89% | 97.11% | 96.07% |
| 1 | 98.89% | 97.11% | 96.07% |
| 10 | 98.89% | 97.11% | 96.07% |

The $C$ parameter in SVM has little effect on the classification results. All models have good performance. Then, the IOU values of different models are compared to find the model with the highest average IOU value. A higher IOU value means that the 2D coordinate of the trailer is more accurate. We have counted the IOU values in different intervals, see Table 2. This work finally chooses a model with the $C$ of 1. Figure 3 shows some detection results. As visible in Fig. 3, trailers can be detected clearly and positioned accurately under challenging situations.

**Table 2.** IOU value count under different $C$

| C | (0.95,1.00) | (0.90,0.95] | (0.85,0.90] | (0.80,0.85] | Average |
|------|------|------|------|------|--------|
| 0.01 | 75  | 145 | 47 | 2 | 0.9302 |
| 0.1  | 106 | 153 | 10 | 0 | 0.9408 |
| 1    | 109 | 151 | 9  | 0 | 0.9424 |
| 10   | 96  | 149 | 24 | 0 | 0.9376 |

In order to verify that the ROI extraction algorithm helps enhance the algorithm efficiency, the runtime of the algorithm combined with the ROI extraction and HOG is compared with the algorithm only used HOG. The overall mean runtime of the algorithm combined with the ROI extraction and HOG is about 0.0995 s. The overall mean runtime of the algorithm only used HOG is approximately 9.7996 s. The results indicate that the ROI extraction algorithm is useful for improving efficiency.

In the trailer hitch detection, our algorithm can obtain an accurate pose of the trailer hitch by using point clouds successfully. Two examples of the detection results in the coarse matching can be seen in Fig. 4. The Hu Moments and the similarity function values of two examples are shown in Table 3. The similarity function values of the two contours are very close. The value is almost zero, which proves that the detected hitch contour is very similar to the model. The hitch cluster is extracted in the coarse matching stage, and the pose of the hitch is estimated in the fine matching stage.

**Table 3.** The Hu Moments and the similarity function values of two examples

| No | Hu Moments 1 | Hu Moments 2 | Similarity function value |
|----|------|------|---------|
| 1 | 0.4298 | 0.1457 | −0.0185 |
| 2 | 0.4213 | 0.1424 | −0.062 |

Figure 5 shows two examples in the fine matching, while the left column is the results of PPF and the right column is the results of ICP. The scene point

(a) Long-distance                    (b) Short-distance

(c) Reversing from the Side          (d) Poor Light

**Fig. 3.** Detection results under different situations

clouds and model point clouds are basically matched but there are still some errors. As shown in the right column, the point clouds of the scene and the model are matched well after ICP pose refinement. After trailer detection and hitch detection, we can detect the trailer and get the pose of the hitch. The hitch point clouds cluster is shown as red and an accurate 3D bounding box is shown in Fig. 6. The runtime of the trailer hitch detection algorithm is 0.214 s in which the coarse matching stage takes 0.038 s and the fine matching stage takes 0.178 s.

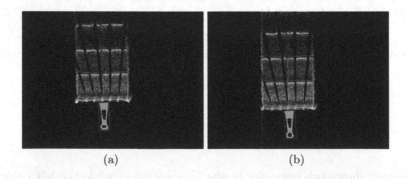

(a)                                  (b)

**Fig. 4.** Detection results in the grid image

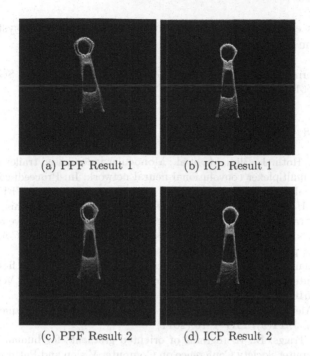

<table>
<tr><td>(a) PPF Result 1</td><td>(b) ICP Result 1</td></tr>
<tr><td>(c) PPF Result 2</td><td>(d) ICP Result 2</td></tr>
</table>

**Fig. 5.** Results in the fine matching stage

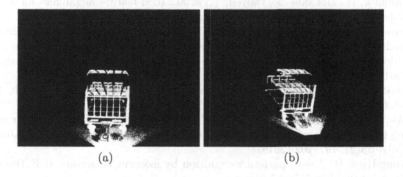

(a)                    (b)

**Fig. 6.** Trailer hitch detection

# 5   Conclusion

This paper focuses on the task of automatically revering to a trailer which is a
rising topic these years. We proposed an efficient two-stage algorithm to detect
the trailer and the trailer hitch by using a ToF camera. First, we use color
images to detect the trailer. The ROI extraction algorithm is used to enhance
the algorithm's efficiency. And then, the accurate pose of the trailer hitch can be
obtained by using depth images. The trailer hitch detection is divided into two
stage: coarse matching and fine matching. A dataset for automatically revering

to a trailer is collected. We demonstrated that our detection system achieves good results on the dataset.

**Acknowledgement.** This work was supported by National Natural Science Foundation of China (61873165/U1764264).

# References

1. Atoum, Y., Roth, J., Bliss, M., et al.: Monocular video-based trailer coupler detection using multiplexer convolutional neural network. In: Proceedings of the IEEE International Conference on Computer Vision, pp. 5477–5485. IEEE (2017)
2. Dahal, A., Hossen, J., Sumanth, C.: DeepTrailerAssist: deep learning based trailer detection, tracking and articulation angle estimation on automotive rear-view camera. In: Proceedings of the IEEE International Conference on Computer Vision Workshops, pp. 2339–2346. IEEE (2019)
3. Ramirez-Llanos, E., Yu, X., Berkemeier, M.: Trailer hitch assist: lightweight solutions for automatically reversing to a trailer. In: IEEE Intelligent Vehicles Symposium, pp. 510–517. IEEE (2020)
4. Foix, S., Alenya, G., Torras, C.: Lock-in time-of-flight (ToF) cameras: a survey. IEEE Sens. J. **11**(9), 1917–1926 (2011)
5. Dalal, N., Triggs, B.: Histograms of oriented gradients for human detection. In: IEEE Computer Society Conference on Computer Vision and Pattern Recognition, pp. 886–893. IEEE (2005)
6. Girshick, R., Donahue, J., Darrell, T., et al.: Rich feature hierarchies for accurate object detection and semantic segmentation. In: Proceedings of the IEEE Conference on Computer Vision and Pattern Recognition, pp. 580–587. IEEE (2014)
7. Redmon, J., Divvala, S., Girshick, R., et al.: You only look once: unified, real-time object detection. In: Proceedings of the IEEE Conference on Computer Vision and Pattern Recognition, pp. 779–788. IEEE (2016)
8. Smith, A.R.: Color gamut transform pairs. ACM Siggraph Comput. Graph. **12**(3), 12–19 (1978)
9. Wu, W., Yang, M., Wang, B., Wang, C.: Pallet detection based on contour matching for warehouse robots. Shanghai Jiaotong Daxue Xuebao/J. Shanghai Jiaotong Univ. **53**(2), 197–202 (2019)
10. Ming-Kuei, H.: Visual pattern recognition by moment invariants. IRE Trans. Inf. Theory **8**(2), 179–187 (1962)
11. Li, L., Yang, M., Wang, C., Wang, B.: Point set registration algorithm based on Gaussian mixture model-earth mover's distance. Huazhong Keji Daxue Xuebao (Ziran Kexue Ban) **45**(10), 65–69 (2017)
12. Besl, P.J., McKay, N.D.: Method for registration of 3-D shapes. In: Sensor Fusion IV: Control Paradigms and Data Structures, pp. 586–606. International Society for Optics and Photonics (1992)
13. Drost, B., Ulrich, M., Navab, N., et al.: Model globally, match locally: efficient and robust 3D object recognition. In: IEEE Computer Society Conference on Computer Vision and Pattern Recognition, pp. 998–1005. IEEE (2010)

# Precise Positioning and Defect Detection of Semiconductor Chip Based on Microvision

Xu Zhao[1,2(✉)], Yingjian Wang[3], Lianpeng Li[1,2], and Fuchao Liu[1,2]

[1] Beijing Information Science and Technology University,
Beijing 100192, China
zhaoxu@bistu.edu.cn
[2] Beijing Key Laboratory of High Dynamic Navigation Technology,
Beijing Information Science and Technology University, Beijing 100192, China
[3] Beijing University of Posts and Telecommunications, Beijing 100876, China

**Abstract.** This paper proposes a high-precision chip positioning and defect detection technology based on machine vision. Divided into low-high double precision detection process, the probe are roughly aligned with the initial test point at low magnification, the fine alignment and feature detection at high magnification. First, the chip image was pre-processed at a low magnification to obtain the MER, and the orientation of the initial test point was obtained by the template matching method, the rough position of the probe tip was obtained by Harris detection. At high magnifications, an improved positioning algorithm is used to obtain the sub-pixel coordinates of the center of the test point and the probe tip. Combined with the clustering method, the row and column spacing of the test point array is obtained. At the same time, the characteristics of test points are extracted in the test point detection process and compared with the standard database to detect defects.

**Keywords:** Machine vision · Chip detection · Positioning accuracy · Defect detection

## 1 Introduction

The flourishing of information technology has paid great attention to the microelectronics industry. In the aspect of integrated circuit, the performance of semiconductor chip will directly determine the quality of IC chip [1]. The vast majority of chips are precision components with extremely small dimensions Parts, and develop on the road of smaller size and higher integration. The difference in technology level leads to defects in the production stage of the chip. Efficient and accurate chip performance testing not only guarantees the reliability of IC chip packaging, but also improves yield and reduces economic losses [2]. This paper based on the micro-visual imaging technology, the precise location of the probe and the grain is realized through the detection process of low-high double-scale multiplier, the test point feature anomaly detection algorithm is used to achieve parameter acquisition and defect identification. And carry out chip screening to improve subsequent yield and reduce manufacturing costs. At present, there are mainly two types of mechanical and optical positioning

© Springer Nature Singapore Pte Ltd. 2022
F. Sun et al. (Eds.): ICCSIP 2021, CCIS 1515, pp. 451–462, 2022.
https://doi.org/10.1007/978-981-16-9247-5_35

methods. Among them, the mechanical positioning accuracy is low, and the chip is easily damaged by the mechanical positioning device. With the high-frequency repetitive work, the accuracy is gradually reduced, which cannot meet the accuracy requirements of the whole machine. The optical imaging and measurement components perform feature detection on the chip, and realize the positioning of the chip through artificial intelligence and image recognition algorithms. At this stage, machine vision technology has been applied to the detection of coarse defects on the surface of the chip, but machine vision needs to be improved in detection efficiency and accuracy. The detection of low and high double standard multiples proposed can realize the accurate identification and positioning of the chip, and further realize the abnormal detection of the chip test point.

## 2    System Composition and Process Block Diagram

The chip detection system consists of three parts: motion perception, microscopic imaging and performance analysis. The motion perception part realizes the 3d space and rotation motion of the tested chip, Microscopic imaging provides illumination and low-resolution imaging for wafers. The performance analysis part realizes wafer parameter analysis and processing through multi-source excitation. During the wafer inspection process, analyze the microscopic imaging characteristics of the wafer, drive the wafer test points to contact the probe, obtain the test point signals through source excitation, and analyze to achieve wafer parameter detection.

The chip detection system and microscopic imaging part are shown in Fig. 1:

**Fig. 1.** Chip detection system and microscopic imaging part

The imaging acquisition is fixed on the gantry structure frame, which is driven by a precise motor to collect the focused image of the chip with low/high multiplier. The wafer imaging is shown in Fig. 2:

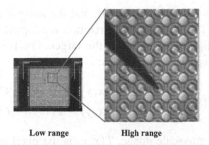

Low range          High range

**Fig. 2.** Focused image of the wafer at low\high magnification

The overall layout of the semiconductor chip is rectangular, and the test point are circles with a diameter of about several tens of microns.

The wafer precise positioning and inspection process in this paper mainly includes two stages. The first stage is mainly the probe-initial grain alignment under low magnification and wide viewing angle. The second stage is mainly the center of the crystal grains at high smagnification and narrow viewing angle-precise positioning of the probe, extraction of grain features and defect detection.

# 3 Probe-Initial Coarse Grain Alignment

Initial grain alignment drives the initial grain to move to the tip of the probe under low magnification and wide Angle imaging.

First, pre-processing and template matching methods are used to identify the edge information of the wafer and the marking position, then the corner position is detected to realize the probe tip positioning. Drive the initial grain point to move to the point coordinates to achieve the initial grain coarse alignment.

## 3.1 Image Preprocessing

The operation process of chip image preprocessing is shown in Fig. 3:

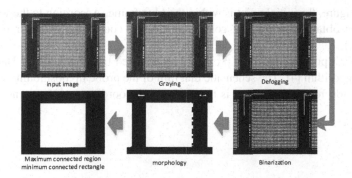

input image          Graying          Defogging

Maximum connected region
minimum connected rectangle          morphology          Binarization

**Fig. 3.** Chip image preprocessing process

First, the original image is grayed out [3], and the noise is suppressed by Gaussian filtering and defogging. Then, adaptive binarization is adopted to reduce the amount of data in the image, highlight the contour of the target. The basic principle of adaptive threshold segmentation can be expressed as:

$$I(x,y) = \begin{cases} 255 & |f(x,y) - T(x,y)| \geq C \\ 0 & |f(x,y) - T(x,y)| < C \end{cases} \tag{1}$$

Where: f is the original grayscale image, $T(x,y)$ is the pixel adaptive threshold of the weighted sum of a block neighborhood in $(x,y)$, C is a predetermined constant.

Morphological processing eliminates small and meaningless noise and fills some holes. The maximum connected region retains only the edge information of the chip, and extract the minimum external rectangle. The chip edge information and the maximum\small horizontal\vertical value were obtained by the above preprocessing: $x_{max}$, $x_{min}$, $y_{max}$, $y_{min}$.

## 3.2  Coarse Orientation of Initial Test Point

An identifier exists on the edge of a single wafer. In this paper, a high-speed template matching algorithm is used to compare the defogged wafer image with the template identifier. The schematic diagram of chip identifier is shown in Fig. 4:

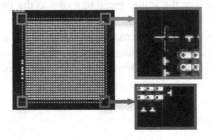

**Fig. 4.** Identifier diagram

In the figure, the initial point is within the blue frame. According to the wafer frame information obtained in 2.1, the coarse positioning coordinate of the initial point is $(x_{max}, y_{min})$.

The rough positioning of the probe is implemented by the traditional Harris corner detection algorithm [4]. The schematic diagram of the probe tip positioning is shown in Fig. 5, the top red point marked is the positioning coordinate of the corner point.

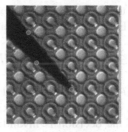

**Fig. 5.** Schematic diagram of probe tip positioning (Color figure online)

The coordinate information of the probe tip and the initial test point is fed back to the motion sensing part, and the driving chip realizes the rough alignment between the probe and the initial test point.

# 4  Fine Positioning of Chip Test Points

After realizing the coarse alignment of test points, adjust the multiplier and amplification factor. Further achieve precise alignment of the probe tip and the effective area of the crystal grain under high magnification and narrow viewing angle, to achieve test grain feature extraction and defect detection.

## 4.1  Rapid Detection and Location of Test Points

The chip image contains multiple and small grains. The positioning accuracy of grains directly affects the row spacing and the accuracy of parameter calculation. The multi-circle quick positioning algorithm is adopted [5], as shown in Fig. 6.

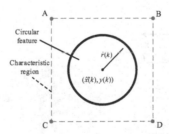

**Fig. 6.** Schematic diagram of fast center positioning

First, the Kalman filter is used to calculate the characteristics of the effective area of each grain, and the linear discrete system state equation is established to estimate the circle center coordinates and radius. Subsequently, the significantly different edge responses are eliminated, and a new circle observation vector is obtained using the least squares ellipse fitting method. Effective judgment basis for circle feature positioning:

$$[Av(k)]^T[Av(k)] \leq \gamma tr\{[H(k)p(k|k-1)H^T(k)+R(k)]A^2\} \tag{2}$$

Among them: $[Av(k)]^T[Av(k)] \leq \gamma tr[H(k)p(k|k-1)H^T(k)+R(k)]$ is the basis for determining filter convergence, A is the weight matrix, $\gamma$ is the reserve coefficient and $\gamma \geq 1$, $tr$ is the matrix trace. If the decision is invalid, the state filtering value of the particle filter at time $k$ is directly used as a measurement value.

The rapid detection and positioning process of a circle is shown in Fig. 7:

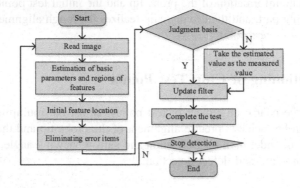

**Fig. 7.** Flow chart of rapid circle detection and positioning

## 4.2    Wafer Row and Column Calculation

The schematic diagram of initial grain detection is shown in Fig. 8:

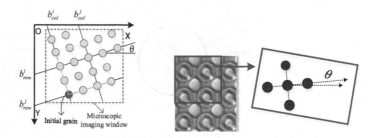

**Fig. 8.** Schematic diagram of initial grain inspection

### 1). Rotation Angle of adjacent grains

If rotation Angle $\theta$ exists, the rotation Angle of the grain is $\theta$, and the row line passing through the grain on the same row has the same row intercept. Therefore, we classify all the grains into the corresponding row set according to the row-line intercept of each grain, and perform the same operation on the grains on the same column. Grain array recognition includes two stages: calculating the direction of the test points and intercepting the clustered test points by row and column lines. Details as follows:

As shown in Fig. 10, for a single grain, the typical rotation angle corresponding to the adjacent grain $i$ is:

$$\Delta\theta_i = \pm\arctan(\frac{y^i_{adi} - y_{center}}{x^i_{adi} - x_{center}}) \pm 90°  \tag{3}$$

Among them: $(x_{center}, y_{center})$ and $(x^i_{adi}, y^i_{adi})$ are the coordinates of the center of the circle selected and its neighboring grains.

### 2). Line intercept clustering

The rotation Angle $\Delta\theta$ is calculated, then the row line of the grain can be expressed as:

$$y = \tan(\Delta\theta)x + b_{row}  \tag{4}$$

The grain alignment can be described as:

$$y = \tan(\Delta\theta + 90°)(x - b_{col})  \tag{5}$$

The centroid coordinates of a given test point are:

$$(x^i_{center}, y^i_{center}), (i = 1, 2, 3, ..., N)  \tag{6}$$

The intercept of the row line can be calculated through the center of mass:

$$b^i_{row} = y^i_{center} - \tan(\Delta\theta)x^i_{center}  \tag{7}$$

The intercept of the column line is:

$$b^i_{col} = x^i_{center} - \frac{y^i_{center}}{\tan(\Delta\theta + 90°)}  \tag{8}$$

Thus, $\{b^1_{row}, b^2_{row}, b^3_{row}, b^4_{row}\}$ and $\{b^1_{col}, b^2_{col}, b^3_{col}, b^4_{col}\}$ of the corresponding balls are obtained, and the crystal grains having roughly equal row and column intercepts are respectively classified into one class. And calculate the average size of grain spacing between adjacent rows and columns. The grain points in the schematic diagram of the initial grain inspection are regarded as an $4 \times 4$ order matrix, including 16 grain circle information and fitted row and column line intercept information.

### 4.3   Quick Positioning of Probe Tip

Harris fast corner detection algorithm based on gray difference and template is adopted. First, the gray corner difference and the 8-neighborhood circular template are used to screen the initial corner points [6]. The 8-neighborhood circular template is shown in Fig. 9:

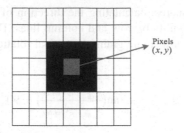

**Fig. 9.** 8 Neighborhood ring template

Calculate the gray difference absolute value in the four directions around the target pixel point $(x, y)$, The relationship between the judgment and the threshold T is preliminary screened, When the template is at a corner point, the number of similar pixels in the template is between the noise point and the edge point, that is, the number of similar pixels is in the closed interval, otherwise it is regarded as a non-corner point. The screening flowchart is shown in Fig. 10:

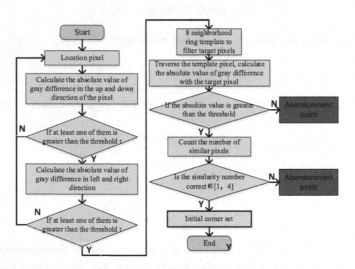

**Fig. 10.** Initial point screening flow chart

After preliminary screening, there are still some pseudo-corner points with a similar number of pixels of 4. The circular template with a radius of 3 is adopted for traversal, as shown in Fig. 11:

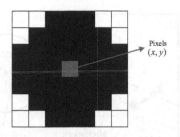

**Fig. 11.** Circular template

When the circular template traverses an initial corner point with four similar pixels, if the number of similar pixels is less than 18, it is retained. If the number of similar pixels is equal to 18, calculate the 6 Euclidean distances between 4 similar pixels to determine whether the target pixel is a corner point. If the number of Euclidean distances between 4 similar pixels is 1 is less than 3, that is, the distribution of 4 similar pixels is discontinuous, then it is retained. If the number is equal to 3 and the distribution of 4 similar pixels is continuous, it is eliminated.

After a large number of non-corner points are eliminated in the above two steps, the response function value of the initial corner point is calculated, and the expression is:

$$CRF(x, y) = \det(M) - k(tr(M))^2 \tag{9}$$

Where:$k$ is a constant term and the value range is $0.04 \sim 0.06$, $\det(M)$ and $tr(M)$ are the determinant and trace of the matrix C.

Non-maximum suppression is performed by the response function, and the maximum point obtained at the local position is the final corner point.

### 4.4    Precise Alignment of the Probe with the Effective Region of the Grain

Combined with the rapid positioning of the crystal circle radius and the center of Sect. 3.1, the row and column spacing values of Sect. 3.2, and the probe tip positioning of Sect. 3.3. Accurate alignment of the probe with the initial grain under high magnification is realized. According to the obtained row and column spacing information, the motion parameters of the driven grains are obtained. Due to the repeated positioning consistency accuracy error of the motion sensing part, after the grain is driven a certain number of times by the row and column spacing information, the probe may deviate from the center of the grain circle. In view of this problem, after the T grains are detected, the 3.1 pitch circle detection positioning is used to make auxiliary corrections, so that the probe tip is accurately positioned with the current grain circle center again to ensure that both the probe and the grains are in contact with the effective inspection area. The contact range of the grain detection process and the effective range of the probe tip is shown in Fig. 12:

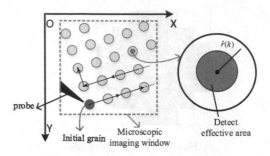

**Fig. 12.** Test point effective range

## 4.5 Grain Feature Extraction and Defect Detection

Grain may have characteristic defects such as defects, missing, oversized area, undersized, deformed and offset. Feature extraction of grains, including roundness, area, and centroid deviation of the grains. The grain area is the number of pixels contained in each detection point, and the roundness can be calculated as:

$$R = \frac{P^2}{4\pi A} \tag{10}$$

Among them: A is the grain area, P is the perimeter.

The circle center deviation is the distance between the actual grain circle center and the expected position, which is the intersection of the corresponding row match and column fit line obtained in Sect. 3.2. The actual center position of the circle is calculated by the fast circle detection algorithm.

Grain defect detection is mainly divided into two parts: off-line training part and online identification part [7]. Off-line training marks a large number of defect-free grains and performs feature extraction to establish a standard grain database. This database will serve as a reference for online defect inspection, where not only the grains are diagnosed, but also the location of the defective grains. Finally, the defective grains were extracted. The frame diagram is shown in Fig. 13:

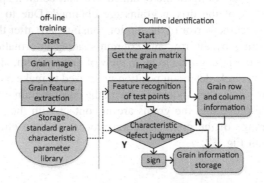

**Fig. 13.** Flowchart of defect detection algorithm

## 4.6    Grain Detection Process

The row-to-column distance of the test points of the chip, the coordinates of the center of the circle, the radius of the circle, and the coordinates of the tip of the chip are obtained through the above algorithm and the like. During the chip test, the single step of the motion system is the distance between the test points and columns. Taking the i-th test point as an example, when the motion perception is moved so that the center point coordinates of the test point coincide with the probe tip coordinates, and get the center coordinates of the (i + 1)-th test point. At this time, the Z axis is driven to move the chip upward, and then the test point is in contact with the needle tip to obtain various photoelectric parameters. At the same time, the characteristics of the test point and the defect detection are performed. Then lower the Z axis to make the needle point away from the test point, calculate the center coordinate of the (i + 1)-th test point based on the line spacing and the center coordinate of the i-th point, and calculate the center coordinate of the (i + 1)-th test point using the center positioning algorithm, and calculate the difference between the two. If the difference is within the valid range of the test point detection, the step distance is used as the line spacing value. If the difference is too large, so that the contact point of the needle tip exceeds the valid range of the test point, then adjust the movement distance parameter and locate the single point by positioning the test point center Step motion distance is corrected.

# 5    Conclusion

In order to improve the accuracy of semiconductor chip detection, a micro-chip-based high-precision detection technology is proposed. It is mainly divided into low-high double-precision detection technology, which are rough alignment of the probe and the initial test point at low magnification, fine alignment at high magnification, and feature detection. Firstly, the chip image was preprocessed at a low multiplier to obtain MER, the deflection Angle was calculated, and the orientation of the initial test point was obtained by template matching method. The rough position of the probe tip is obtained through Harris detection, and the motion system is driven to move the initial test point to the initial test point. In the case of high multiplication rate, the sub-pixel coordinates of the center of the circle were obtained by means of multi-circle quick positioning method, precise positioning of pinhead sub-pixel was achieved by improved Harris, and the row and column spacing of the test point array was obtained by clustering method, the coordinate information was fed back to the motion system, and the motor was driven to achieve precise alignment. At the same time, the extracted features of the test points were compared with the standard database to detect the defects. Experiments show that this method can greatly improve the detection efficiency and positioning accuracy, and meet the engineering requirements.

# References

1. Bai, L., Yang, X., Gao, H.: Corner point-based coarse-fine method for surface-mount component positioning. IEEE Trans. Ind. Inform. **99**, 1–1 (2017)
2. Tao-Tao, B.O.: Research and application on IC shallow detection based on machine vision and image processing. J. Hebei North Univ. (2015)
3. Liu, H., Su, Z., Wan, C., Yin, L.: Method for detecting wafer offset angle of probe station based on machine vision. Instrum. Tech. Sensor **431**(12), 91–94 (2018)
4. Harris, C.: A combined corner and edge detector. Proc. Alvey Vision Conf. **1988**(3), 147–151 (1988)
5. Wang, X., et al.: Multi-circle rapid positioning method in complex background using region estimation. J. Central South Univ. (Sci. Technol.) **7**, 2266–2272
6. Zhang, L., Huang, X., Lu, L., et al.: Harris corner detection fast algorithm based on gray difference and template. Chinese J. Sci. Instrum. **2**, 2018
7. Gao, H., Jin, W., Yang, X., et al.: A line-based-clustering approach for ball grid array component inspection in surface mount technology. IEEE Trans. Ind. Electron. **99**, 1–1 (2016)

# Gobang Game Algorithm Based on Reinforcement Learning

Xiali Li[iD], Wei Zhang, Junren Chen, Licheng Wu[(⊠)][iD],
and Cairangdanghzhou

School of Information and Engineering, Minzu University of China,
Beijing 100081, China
wulicheng@tsinghua.edu.cn

**Abstract.** The traditional Gobang game program generally evaluates the chess type, and the game power mostly depends on the developer's understanding of Gobang. Reinforcement learning combined with Monte Carlo tree search and upper confidence bound algorithm is introduced into the Gobang game in this work. Convolutional Neural Network is used to evaluate the current game board situation. Besides, the article also adjusts the neural network structure, introduces a small amount of calculation kill, artificial knowledge, and other programs to improve reinforcement learning. After 100,000 times of game training, the winning rate of the game program applied proposed methods has increased from 13% to 100% compared with the open-source Gobang game program Pela.

**Keywords:** Reinforcement learning · Convolutional neural network · Monte Carlo tree search · Upper confidence bound algorithm · Gobang

## 1 Introduction

The level of computer games such as Go and Chess has surpassed the strongest professional chess players [1]. Gobang is also one of the most popular chess games in the world. Players only need to connect five consecutive pieces horizontally, vertically, or diagonally to win. The black player in Gobang has tremendous advantages. Figure 1 is a standard opening "Hua Yue" of Gobang. Even if some restrictive rules are added, it is still be concluded that black players will win through the exhaustive algorithm.

Therefore, professional rules are more complicated to restrict the first player (namely the black player) to add the "banned hands," five-handed N-play, "three-handed exchange," etc. Most of the current Gobang game algorithms are Alpha-Beta pruning algorithm, which increases the number of layers while ensuring time efficiency. And human knowledge has an essential effect on the programs. This paper introduces reinforcement learning into the Gobang game and uses Monte Carlo tree search and upper confidence bound algorithm. Convolutional Neural Network is used to evaluate the current situation. Finally, the article also adjusts the neural network structure, introduces a small amount of calculation kill, artificial knowledge, and other programs to improve reinforcement learning according to the problems in the training process. After 100,000 times of game training, the winning rate of the game program applied proposed methods has increased from 13% to 100% compared with the open-source Gobang game program Pela.

F. Sun et al. (Eds.): ICCSIP 2021, CCIS 1515, pp. 463–475, 2022.
https://doi.org/10.1007/978-981-16-9247-5_36

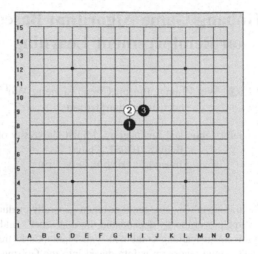

**Fig. 1.** Gobang "Hua Yue" opening

## 2 Related Works

DNN (deep neural networks) and MCTS (Monte Carlo tree search) can achieve superhuman performance even without supervision on human gameplay datasets. But for the majority of the research community, the training performance of the deep learning model is not obvious due to limited hardware resources. Before the advent of deep practical learning, classical search methods enjoyed initial success. The Methods used in Gomoku include the Alpha-Beta pruning algorithm, Temporal-Difference algorithm, Markov decision process, and Bayesian equilibrium algorithm. The Alpha-Beta pruning algorithm is a re-cursive tree search algorithm based on the Minimax algorithm combined with the pruning method, and the evaluation method uses static situation assessment, relies on a large amount of expert knowledge to support the opening library, and the complex design of the valuation function. The system based on the Temporal-Difference algorithm is fiercely over-reliant on human knowledge. The Markov decision process is based on the numerical iterative method and the policy strategy method, so the strength is limited by the iterative method. The Bayesian equilibrium algorithm is based on scoring different patterns of the chessboard and then accumulating the scores of all patterns, but it is impossible to systematically and comprehensively evaluate [2]. The evaluation methods based on Monte Carlo tree search (MCTS) can be used for high branching factor board games, including Go, chess, Gomoku, and even full-size games with good results. These algorithms build the dynamic evaluation into the tree search process, taking current board positions as the root of the game tree, including the selection of branches with good evaluation, expansion of the tree according to certain methodology, simulation of the endgame randomly, and backpropagation of the evaluation made by winning ratio of simulation. It can cease after any desired time or level while statistics are kept for each possible move from the current board state. Subsequently, the movie with the best overall results is returned, and average results are used as the evaluation value of current board positions. In order to optimize searching speed and evaluation accuracy, the MoGoGo program initially proposed the Rapid Action Value Estimation (RAVE) heuristic to quickly evaluate the values of the same move in different positions. Based on the strategy, Fuego introduced a new lock-free multithreading model that significantly improved the performance. Pachi used an algorithm based on an incrementally built probabilistic minimax tree and several domain-specific heuristics to improve the accuracy of the evaluation. Additionally, in order to balance the relationship between exploitation and exploration, a few studies introduced the upper confidence bounds applied toUpper Confidence Bound Apply to Tree (UCT) algorithm [3]. Deep reinforcement learning algorithms used in the Atari series of games, including Deep Q Network (DQN) algorithm, 51-atom-agent (C51) algorithm, and those suitable for continuous fields with low search depth and narrow decision treewidth, have achieved or exceeded the level of human experts. In the area of computer games, pattern recognition, reinforcement learning, deep learning, and deep reinforcement learning algorithms are used in Go, including Monte Carlo algorithm and upper confidence bound applied to tree (UCT) algorithm, temporal difference algorithm, the deep learning model combined with UCT search algorithm, and DQN algorithm, and they have also achieved quite good results in computer Go game, which shows that the idea of a deep reinforcement learning algorithm can adapt to the computer game environment. In addition, the application of deep reinforcement learning algorithms in Backgammon, Shogi, chess, Texas poker, Mahjong, and StarCraft II has achieved human excellence and even exceeded human achievements [4].

In [5], proposed and designed a gobang program based on a linear evaluation function. However, this evaluation function was not static but constantly learned during the course of games, and the learning method was called the TD learning algorithm. In [6], intelligent Gobang algorithms are analyzed to construct the valuation function, game tree, and $\alpha$-$\beta$ pruning algorithm is used to improve game-tree search efficiency, enhancing the level of computer intelligence. The paper [2] proposed an improved method to accelerate the MCTS search on the basis of the characteristics of Gobang. And this model can improve the chess power in a short training time with limited hardware resources. The paper [7] proposes an improved online sequential extreme learning machine (IOS-ELM), a new evaluation method, to evaluate chess board positions for the AZ-style algorithm. In the research of Tibetan Jiu chess, this paper [4] proposed a learning strategy that uses SARSA($\lambda$) and Q-learning algorithms combining domain knowledge for a feedback function for layout and battle stages. It can make the neural network learn more valuable chess strategies in a short time, which provides a reference for improving the learning efficiency of the deep reinforcement learning model. The paper [8] extracted the important chess shapes of JIU and proposed a chess-shaped pattern-matching algorithm based on matrices. The paper [9] shows that the UCT algorithm can implement the search work in Amazon's human-computer games and get satisfactory search efficiency. It not only overcame the problem that traditional Alpha-Beta's and Nega-Max algorithm's search hierarchy is shallow, and avoid the obstacle about Monte-Carlo evaluation methods need a huge amount of calculation. This paper [10] explores the possibility of improving DNN structures to increase the efficiency of deep reinforcement learning for application in Go programs and shows a feasible and effective scheme for speeding up the deep reinforcement learning algorithm by improving the DNN.

## 3  Gobang Game Algorithm

The Gobang game algorithm mainly involves the Monte Carlo tree search structure and convolutional neural network. The two parts are trained by the reinforcement learning method. In the algorithm model, the movie is mainly chosen according to the Monte Carlo tree search. For the nodes in the Monte Carlo tree search process, the situation assessment is completed by the convolutional neural network (CNN). The framework of the Monte Carlo search tree and neural network algorithm can be simply described in Fig. 2. Instead of a handcrafted evaluation function and move ordering heuristics, the framework utilizes a deep neural network $(p, v) = f_\theta(s)$ with parameters $\theta$. This neural network takes the board position s as an input and outputs a vector of move probabilities p with components $p_i$. For each action a, and a scalar value v estimating the expected outcome z from position s, it learns these move probabilities and value estimates from selfplay.

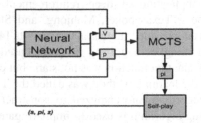

**Fig. 2.** The framework of the Gobang game algorithm

### 3.1  Monte Carlo Tree Search Combined with Reinforcement Learning

We use s to represent the current Gobang chessboard state, a to represent the tree branch corresponding to a certain move. Each node in the Monte Carlo tree contains the following information: $N(s, a)$ represents the number of visits of nodes, $W(s, a)$ represents the value of actions, $Q(s, a)$ represents the average value of actions, and $P(s, a)$ represents the prior probability of nodes.

The first step is selection by using the UCT algorithm to select branches. The specific formula used as shown in (1), (2):

$$U(s, a) = c_{puct}P(s, a)\frac{\sqrt{\sum_b N(s, b)}}{1 + N(s, a)} \tag{1}$$

$$a_t = \arg\max(Q(s_t, a) + U(s_t, a)) \tag{2}$$

Among them, $c_{puct}$ is the exploration constant. In addition, the Monte Carlo tree search will select the largest branch of $Q + U$ to search and conduct simulating sampling until the winner is determined or the node of the Monte Carlo tree without finality. If you reach the Monte Carlo tree node with no end, then you will enter the expansion stage of the Monte Carlo tree search. For the leaf node state $s$, the convolution neural network is used to predict the leaf node, and the possible strategy p and the corresponding value $v$ of the node are obtained. At this time, a new node $s_N$ is newly created in the Monte Carlo tree, and its branch information is initialized as shown in formula 3:

$$\{N(s_N, a) = 0, W(s_N, a) = 0, Q(s_N, a) = 0, P(s_N, a) = P_A\} \tag{3}$$

After the expansion, the leaf node $s$ will become an internal node. When the expansion and simulation are completed, it is necessary to trace back, and the parent node is updated as follows:

$$N(s_t, a_t) = N(s_t, a_t) + 1 \tag{4}$$

$$W(s_t, a_t) = W(s_t, a_t) + v \tag{5}$$

$$Q(a|s) = \frac{W(s_t, a_t)}{N(s_t, a_t)} \tag{6}$$

Monte Carlo tree search will be carried out 1600 times for getting a move. And each search will be followed by selection, expansion, simulation, and backtracking. After the completion of the Monte Carlo tree search, the algorithm can select the move based on the following formula (7) under the root node $s$ of the Monte Carlo tree search.

$$\pi(a|s) = \frac{N(s, a)^{1/\tau}}{\sum_b (s, b)^{1/\tau}} \tag{7}$$

Among them, $\tau$ is used to control the degree of exploration. The larger $\tau$ is, the larger the proportion of exploration is. The smaller $\tau$ is, the more inclined to choose the current best move. In the self-play stage, the algorithm should encourage exploration as much as possible in the early stage, so set the parameter $\tau = 1$ in the first 15 steps. With the development of the game progress, the parameter $\tau$ gradually is reduced to 0. In addition, when the man-machine game is played, the algorithm will set the parameter $\tau$ to 0 to ensure that the algorithm selects the best move each time.

## 3.2   Convolutional Neural Network

This section elaborates on the designed CNN, including input and output.

**Input.** After several experimental adjustments, the final input, which represents the state of the current game, is a tensor of 15 * 15 * 5, and each element takes a value of

0 or 1. Since the Gobang's chessboard is 15 * 15, the vector of 15 * 15 is chosen as the state of the chessboard. First of all, enter the chessboard information in black and white. If the current player is black, the value of the existing move is 1, and the value of its opponent is 0 (including the white move or the position where there is no move). In addition, in order to provide more information for the CNN, the input chess state includes not only the current chess board but also the game status corresponding to the first two steps of black and white. Therefore, there is a total of 4 levels of chessboard state in the game tree. Finally, a 15 * 15 vector is used to mark the side of the current player. In the case of the black player, all elements under this vector take the value 1. On the contrary, when the white moves at the current time, the value of all the elements will be 0. Therefore, the final input data of the CNN is the 15 * 15 * 5 tensor.

**Output.** The output of the CNN includes two parts, namely the strategy part and the value part. For the strategy part, the CNN will predict the winning rate of each feasible possible move, and the probability of the illegal move will be set to 0. Since Gobang includes 15 * 15 points, the probability output of the strategy is a 15 * 15 vector. For the value part, the output is a floating-point number with a value range of $[-1,1]$, which represents the evaluation value of the current position for the chess player.

**Network Structure.** After a lot of experiments, the final network structure is shown in Fig. 3. This is a deep residual network composed of a CNN:

The classic ResNet structure network is adopted and illustrated in Fig. 3. The loss function of the CNN is shown in formula 8:

$$L = (z - v)^2 - \pi^T log(p) + c\|\theta\|^2 \tag{8}$$

The formula consists of three parts. The first is the mean square error loss function $(z - v)^2$ which is used to measure the difference between the outcome predicted by the CNN and the actual outcome. The second is the cross-entropy loss function $\pi^T log(p)$, which is used to measure the difference between the strategy $p$ output by the CNN and the strategy $\pi$ output by the Monte Carlo tree search in the self-play data. The last part is the regularization term $c\|\theta\|^2$. Though training the convolutional neural network, its parameters $\theta$ are continuously optimized to guide the subsequent Monte Carlo tree search.

### 3.3    Self-play

Since this algorithm does not use the method of supervised learning, it does not need to use the game of professional Gobang players for learning. Correspondingly, a large amount of self-play is required to obtain data to train the subsequent convolutional neural network. This stage is also the process of learning through self-play between models, resulting in a large number of chess game samples.

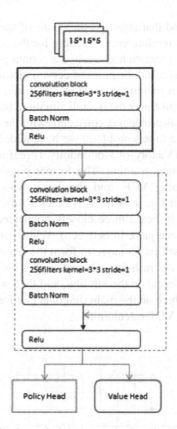

**Fig. 3.** Convolutional neural network structure

In the self-play stage, the selection of each step is completed by a Monte Carlo tree search. During the Monte Carlo tree search, if the chess state is not in the tree, the result of the convolutional neural network prediction is used to update the content obtained by the Monte Carlo tree search. In each round of iterations, for the game state $s$, 1600 times of Monte Carlo tree search are used to simulate and select moves. The final Monte Carlo tree search will give the best move strategy $\pi$. It should be noted that this strategy $\pi$ needs to be distinguished from the strategy output $p$ of the convolutional neural network. After each round of the match, you can get the final victory reward $z$, with a value of 1 or $-1$, representing victory and defeat, respectively. In this way, we will obtain a large number of training samples $(s, \pi, z)$ and these data will be used for training the subsequent convolutional neural network.

## 4   Human Knowledge

After about a month of iterations (the training process will be described in detail below), we found that the algorithm cannot really connect the five pieces together to win the game.

After analysis, we found that although the result of the game is a draw, the valuation of the winning rate of reinforcement learning for the current situation is as high as 97.43%. We found that the program had reached a certain point of victory in the replay chess game, but it had not reached the point of certain victory, and it was impossible to form five consecutive pieces to win the game successfully. We find that reinforcement learning has reasonable control over the overall situation, but the calculation of kill in a small range is not good. This problem is consistent with the nature of the convolutional neural network. In response to this problem, we have added a small amount of human knowledge such as VCT (Victory of Continuous Three) and VCF (Victory of Continuous Four) to reinforcement learning. The former wins the final game by continuously using VCT and doing VCF, and the latter wins the final game by VCF consecutively. As shown in Fig. 4, when it is black's turn, it can choose E9 move to form a vertical live-three (It means three closely connected chess pieces of the same color or three pieces with one piece in between). White can only choose to defend on the E column. Black then selects F8 move to form the live-three on the main diagonal, at the same time forming the rush-four (It means that only one point can form four pieces connected by five pieces) on the 8th line, and then white can only choose G8 to defend. At this time, the Three on the main diagonal can form the rush-four in order to win the game through the VCT calculation.

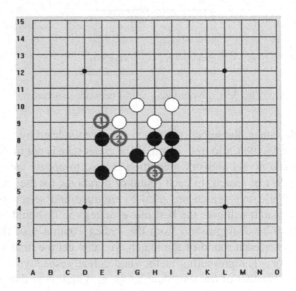

**Fig. 4.** VCT example

## 5    Experimental Results and Analysis

This section discusses the selection of language framework, convolutional neural network parameters, and the feature configuration in implementing the algorithm and gives the experimental results and analysis of the Gobang game algorithm based on reinforcement learning.

### 5.1    Development Tools and Development Environment

This chapter tests the hardware environment and software environment used by the Gobang game algorithm based on reinforcement learning as shown in Table 1 and Table 2:

**Table 1.**  Hardware situation

| Hardware | Detailed description |
|---|---|
| CPU | Intel 6th Generation Core i7–3220 @ 3.30 GHz octa-core |
| RAM | Kingston DDR4 1333 MHz 16 GB |
| Graphics card | NVIDIA GeForce GTX 1080Ti |
| hard disk | Seagate ST500DM002-1BD142 7200 rpm/min 1 TB |

**Table 2.**  Software situation

| Software | Detailed description |
|---|---|
| Operating System | Windows 10 Enterprise Edition 64-bit |
| Integrated Development Environment | Microsoft Visual Studio 2017 Enterprise Edition |
| Development language | C++, Python |
| Version Vontrol | Git |
| Deep Learning Framework | Tensorflow |

### 5.2    Training Improvement and Experimental Result Analysis

The training time is nearly three months, and the number of self-play games has reached more than 100,000 times. The training is divided into two stages. The first stage uses Python and TensorFlow to generate self-play data. In the second stage, C++ is used to refactor the code, some default configurations of neural network parameters are updated, and training continues, and finally, a better effect is achieved. In this process, we chose Pela as the benchmark of the Gobang game algorithm based on reinforcement learning. We played our program against Pela for several rounds, and the final winning rate was used to measure the improvement of chess ability.

Pela is an open-source Gobang AI with strong chess power. Its basic situation is shown in Table 3:

**Table 3.** Basic information of Pela

| Attributes | Specific information |
|---|---|
| Algorithm | Minimax Search Algorithm |
| Optimization | Alpha-Beta Pruning Algorithm |
| Author | Petr Lastovick |
| Development time | 2006 |
| Elo Ratings | 1511 |

**Analysis and Improvement of Experimental Results of the First Stage of Training.** In the first stage of training, the default parameters used are shown in Table 4:

**Table 4.** Default parameters used in the first stage

| Serial number | Parameter name | Parameter value | Parameter description |
|---|---|---|---|
| 1 | playout | 120 | Monte Carlo tree search simulation times |
| 2 | mse_factor | 1.0 | Mean square deviation factor |
| 3 | dir_noise | 0.03 | The amount of noise |
| 4 | use_rotate | false | Whether to use a rotating chessboard for training |
| 5 | block | 5 | Basic building blocks of Convolutional Neural Networks |
| 6 | filters | 48 | Filter |
| 7 | input | 15 * 15 * 17 | Input tensor |
| 8 | lr | 0.05 | Learning rate |

The training in the first stage has a total of 20 iterations, and every ten rounds are tested with Pela. In the first ten rounds of iterative games, a loophole in the training code was discovered, which would lead to a high winning percentage for the white player. We fixed the loophole. In the last ten rounds of iterative self-play, it was found that Python plus TensorFlow generated self-play data too slowly, so we started to use C ++ for code refactoring, stopped the first test, used C++ to generate self-play data, added the Piskvork protocol, and used software to assist in testing. The iterative game information and winning rate are shown in Fig. 5.

It can be seen from Fig. 5 that in the initial stage of training, the iterative winning rate is relatively high. As the number of iterations increases, the winning rate slowly converges to 50%. This is in line with expectations. At the beginning of the training, the model did not learn too much knowledge. As the number of self-play continues to increase, the model can learn less and less knowledge, so the winning percentage is declining. After ten rounds of self-play, the winning rate against Pela was 13%. After 20 rounds of self-play, the winning rate against Pela was 46%, indicating that Gobang's ability needs to be improved.

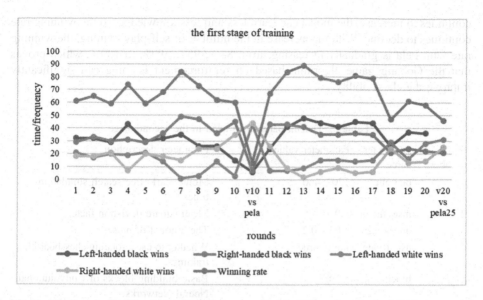

**Fig. 5.** The improvement process of the first stage training (20 iterations in total, and a game test with pela every ten rounds)

**Analysis of the Experimental Results of the Second Stage of Training.** In the first stage of training, the training speed of the Convolutional Neural Network is unusually slow. It takes a few days to complete one iteration (each iteration needs to have a winning rate of 60% against the previous iteration), so we proposed two solutions: we need to reduce the input tensor size and the number of feature layers. At the beginning of the implementation, the size of our input tensor is 15 * 15 * 17, with the information of the previous eight steps of the black and white players. After experiments, the tensor size input to the Convolutional Neural Network is finally reduced to 15 * 15 * 5. That is, the tensor only contains the previous two-step history information of the black and white players. In addition, we reduced the original 39-layer deep residual network to 19 layers. Some improvements have also been made in other areas. The specific parameters are shown in Table 5.

In the second stage, there are 40 iterations in total and a game test with pela every ten rounds. The specific iterative game and the winning rate are shown in Fig. 6.

In the 11th round of the game, it was observed that the winning rate of convolutional neural network in many games was very high, and there were many chances to win, but it failed to reach the point of winning, so the VCT and VCF expert knowledge calculation kill module was added. After the 20th round of the game, we adjust the learning rate to 0.005. After the 33rd round of the game, we adjust the learning rate to 0.002. It can be seen from Fig. 6 that in the first ten rounds of training, the winning rate is very high, the highest is 97%; in the 11–20 rounds of training, the winning rate is significantly reduced, the highest is 70%; in the 21–30 rounds of the game, the winning rate is decreased; in the 31–40 rounds of the game, the winning rate dropped significantly, less than 60%. This is in line with expectations. At the beginning of the training, the model did not learn too much knowledge. As the number of the self-play game continues to increase, the model can learn less and less knowledge, so the winning rate continues to decline. With the increase in the number of self-play training, the winning rate with Pela is gradually increasing, from 88%, 95%, 98%, to 100%, which proves that the Gobang game algorithm based on reinforcement learning can significantly improve the chess ability.

**Table 5.** Default parameters used in the second stage

| Serial number | Parameter name | Parameter value | Parameter description |
|---|---|---|---|
| 1 | playout | 120→400 | Monte Carlo tree search simulation times |
| 2 | mse_factor | 1.0 | Mean square deviation factor |
| 3 | dir_noise | 0.03→0.2 | The amount of noise |
| 4 | use_rotate | false→true | Whether to use a rotating chessboard for training |
| 5 | block | 5→6 | Basic building blocks of Convolutional Neural Networks |
| 6 | filters | 48→64→96 | Filter |
| 7 | input | 15 * 15 * 17→15 * 15 * 5 | Input tensor |
| 8 | lr | 0.05→0.002 | Learning rate |

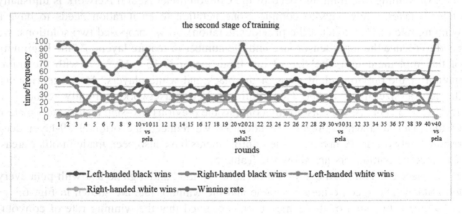

**Fig. 6.** The improvement process of the second stage training (40 iterations in total, and a game test with pela every ten rounds)

## 5.3  Consumption Comparison of Training Resources

After optimization (language version reconstruction, model adjustment, adding a small amount of artificial knowledge, etc.), the requirement of the final algorithm for training resources is greatly reduced. Compared with AlphaGo, the training resources required for the Gobang algorithm based on reinforcement learning have been greatly reduced. The specific training resource consumption is shown in Table 6.

**Table 6.** Comparison of resource consumption

| Algorithm | Resource consumption |
|---|---|
| AlphaGo Zero | 5000 TPU |
| ELF open Go | 2000 GPU |
| Leela Zero | Distributed architecture, about 100 GPU |
| The improved algorithm in this paper | One NVIDIA GeForce GTX 1080Ti |

# 6 Summary

This Gobang search algorithm based on reinforcement learning was given and implemented based on reinforcement learning and Monte Carlo tree search. The program applied the proposed algorithm is with a high winning rate compared with other programs while reducing the complexity for training. Certainly, this algorithm is only appropriative for Gobang, which is a kind of sufficient information game with visible states. When encountering problems with asymmetric information, such as mahjong, StarCraft, and other battle games, the algorithm needs to be modified and improved a lot.

**Acknowledgment.** This work is funded by the National Natural Science Foundation of China under Grant 61873291 and Grant 61773416.

# References

1. Silver, D., Hubert, T., Schrittwieser, J., et al.: A general reinforcement learning algorithm that masters chess, shogi, and go through self-play. Science **362**(6419), 1140–1144 (2018)
2. Li, X., He, S., Wu, L., et al.: A game model for Gomoku based on deep learning and monte carlo tree search. In: Proceedings of 2019 Chinese Intelligent Automation Conference (2019)
3. Browne, C.B., Powley, E., Whitehouse, D., et al.: A survey of monte carlo tree search methods. IEEE Trans. Comput. Intell. AI Games **4**(1), 1–43 (2012)
4. Li, X., Lv, Z., Wu, L., et al.: Hybrid online and offline reinforcement learning for Tibetan Jiu chess. Complexity **2020**, 1–11 (2020)
5. Cheng, Y., Lei, X.: Self-learning Gobang program based on TD algorithm. In: IEEE International Conference on Information Management and Engineering (2011)
6. Deng, H., Xun, Z., Qin, L.: Research and implementation of intelligent Gobang-playing. In: International Conference on Intelligent Information Technology Application (2010)
7. Li, X., He, S., Wei, Z., et al.: Improved online sequential extreme learning machine: a new intelligent evaluation method for AZ-style algorithms. IEEE Access **7**, 124891–124901 (2019)
8. Li, X., Wang, S., Lv, Z., et al.: Strategy research based on chess shapes for Tibetan JIU computer game. ICGA J. **2018**(40), 318–328 (2018)
9. Li, X., Liang, H., Wu, L.: UCT algorithm in Amazons human-computer games In: Control and Decision Conference. IEEE (2014)
10. Li, X., Lv, Z., Liu, B., et al.: Improved feature learning: a maximum-average-out deep neural network for the game go. Math. Probl. Eng. **1–6**, 2020 (2020)

# Research on Machine Learning Classification of Mild Traumatic Brain Injury Patients Using Resting-State Functional Connectivity

YuXiang Li[✉], Hui Shen, Hongwei Xie, and Dewen Hu

College of Intelligence Science and Technology, National University of Defense Technology, Changsha, Hunan, China

**Abstract.** In recent years, the incidence of mild traumatic brain injury (mTBI) has been increasing, especially in the military because of soldiers' special working environment. Current diagnostic systems relying too much on patients' self-description leads to improper diagnosis and treatment. Finding biomarkers of mTBI becomes significant for diagnostic accuracy improvement. We used machine learning methods to extract highly discriminative functional connectivity features and to discriminate mTBI patients from healthy controls. 31 mTBI patients and 31 healthy controls with matching age, gender and education level underwent resting-state functional magnetic resonance imaging. A promising classification accuracy of 75.81% was achieved using resting-state functional connectivity as features. Moreover, some functional connectivities between certain brain regions of the cerebellum and the sensorimotor were found to exhibit the highest discriminative power, which might provide a new idea for the discovery of stable biomarkers of mTBI.

**Keywords:** mTBI · Biomarkers · Machine learning · Resting-state functional connectivity

## 1 Introduction

As a public health epidemic in recent years, mild traumatic brain injury (mTBI) which refers to a kind of craniocerebral injury that causing the body to have a loss of consciousness or memory dysfunction in a short time but without obvious structural abnormalities, has a higher incidence in the military [1]. Due to their special working environment, soldiers are more vulnerable to mTBI and produce a series of complications such as post-traumatic stress disorder (PTSD) and depression. Traumatic brain injury is divided into mild, moderate and severe according to its severity. Among them, most patients with traumatic brain injury belong to mild condition (76% ~ 83%) [2]. First, neurological and neuroimaging examinations (CT/MRI) for mild brain trauma are basically normal [3]. Second, diagnosis of mTBI is often based on the patient's subjective feelings and self-description. Finally, mTBI patients lack objective biomarkers in neuroimaging and laboratory testing [4]. In summary, finding biomarkers of mTBI can help improve diagnostic accuracy [5, 6].

© Springer Nature Singapore Pte Ltd. 2022
F. Sun et al. (Eds.): ICCSIP 2021, CCIS 1515, pp. 476–483, 2022.
https://doi.org/10.1007/978-981-16-9247-5_37

Previous studies of classification analysis in mTBI focus mainly on EEG methods, whose spatial resolution is low. Because the electrodes measure the electrical activity on the surface of the brain, it is difficult to know whether the signal is generated in the cortex or a deeper area [7, 8]. However, as an important method to study the neuroanatomical basis of cognitive dysfunction and its treatment, fMRI has rarely been studied to examine changes in brain function of patients after mTBI.

FMRI-related experimental design is mainly divided into two kinds. The specific task of the event-related state triggers a large change in the BOLD signal, resulting in a relatively high false positive result. The resting state can better reduce practice, fatigue effects and head movements. Moreover, the experimental operation of the event-related state is relatively complicated, relying too much on the experimental design itself, and the resting state avoids these problems, and is currently widely used in the research of neural mechanisms of various diseases [9, 10].

In this paper, we focused on the classification problem of mTBI using resting-state fMRI data. Section 1 introduces the research background and significance of this

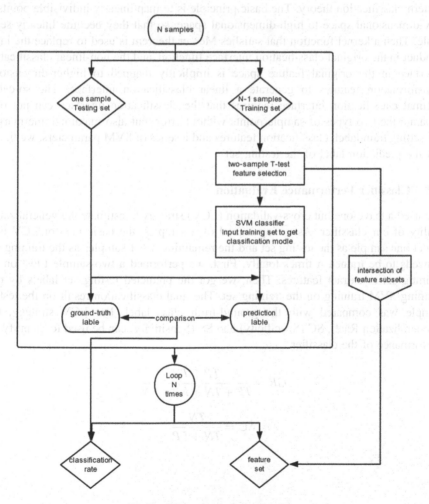

**Fig. 1.** Flow chart of the classifier.

article. Section 2 introduces the classifier used in this article and the evaluation method of the entire classification algorithm. Section 3 introduces the entire experiment process and final experimental results of this article. Firstly, we used two-sample t-test methods to select features, then the classifier was designed for classification based on support vector machines (SVM). Finally, the leave-one-out cross-validation strategy was used to evaluate the performance of the classifier designed by us (see Fig. 1 for detail). This study uses a SVM-based classifier to find potential biomarkers of mTBI, which has a profound impact on improving the accuracy of clinical diagnosis of mTBI.

## 2   Methods

### 2.1   Classifier Based on SVM

In order to distinguish patients from healthy controls, we used a supervised Support Vector Machine (SVM) classifier. The method of SVM is derived from the statistical pattern classification theory. The basic principle is to map linearly indivisible points in low-dimensional space to high-dimensional space, so that they become linearly separable. Then a kernel function that satisfies Mercer theorem is used to replace the inner product in the original classification interface function, and the non-linear classification interface in the original feature space is implicitly mapped to higher-dimensional transformation features to generate a linear classification interface. The so-called optimal classification interface requires that the classification interface can not only separate the two types of sample points without error, but also maximize the margin. By setting train label, classification features and a series of SVM parameters, we finally got the prediction label of the testing set.

### 2.2   Classifier Performance Evaluation

We used a leave-one out cross-validation (LCV) strategy to estimate the generalization ability of our classifier. Assuming a total of n samples, the basic idea of LCV is to select one sample as the testing set and the remaining n − 1 samples as the training set. It needs to be trained n times totally. First, we performed a two-sample t-test on the training set to extract features. Then, we got the predicted testing set labels by performing SVM training on the training set. The final classification result on the testing sample was compared with the ground-truth class label. For LCV strategy, GR (Generalization Rate), SC (Specificity) and SS (Sensitivity) can be used to quantify the performance of the classifier.

$$GR = \frac{TP + TN}{TP + TN + FP + FN} \tag{1}$$

$$SC = \frac{TN}{TN + FP} \tag{2}$$

$$SS = \frac{TP}{TP + FN} \tag{3}$$

Here, TP: the number of patients correctly predicted;
TN: the number of controls correctly predicted;
FP: the number of controls classified as patients;
FN: the number of patients classified as controls.

And the overall proportion of samples correctly predicted was evaluated by GR. The proportion of controls correctly predicted was evaluated by SC. The proportion of patients correctly predicted was evaluated by SS. In the end, we used receiver operating characteristic (ROC) curve to evaluate the classifier we designed. The ROC curve is a comprehensive index reflecting the continuous variables of sensitivity and specificity. The sensitivity is used as the ordinate and 1-specificity as the abscissa. On the ROC curve, the point closest to the upper left of the graph is the critical value with higher sensitivity and specificity.

## 3  Experiments

### 3.1  Data Acquisition

Subjects included 31 mTBI patients and 31 healthy controls. mTBI patients (within 3 days after injury) treated in the emergency department of the third Xiangya Hospital of Central South University from April 2014 to March 2016 were recruited. Healthy controls with matching age, gender and education level were recruited by advertisements (Table 1). In the resting-state experiments, participants were instructed to keep eyes closed and remain awake simply. The 3.0 T PHILIPS MRI was adopted for the use of imaging. It is equipped with 15-channel head coil to reduce the head movements. All subjects received axial-gradient spin echo sequence scan. The imaging parameters are as follows: TR = 2000 ms, TE = 39 ms, FOV = 240 mm × 240 mm, FA = 90°, matrix = 80 × 80, slice thickness = 3.0 mm.

Table 1.  Matching information of patient group and health controls.

| Variable | Health controls | Patient group | P value |
| --- | --- | --- | --- |
| Age (years) | 33.94 ± 9.85 | 30.26 ± 9.66 | 0.14 |
| Sex (M/F) | 18/13 | 16/15 | |
| Education (years) | 12.97 ± 3.44 | 13.68 ± 3.93 | 0.45 |

## 3.2   Data Preprocessing

The BOLD data were preprocessed using SPM12 (statistical parametric mapping) software package based on MATLAB R2017a. The first 5 volumes of each subject were discarded because of magnetic saturation effects. The remaining 235 volumes were slice-time corrected and realigned for head motion. Then the images were normalized to the standard EPI template in the Montreal Neurological Institute (MNI) space. Next, volumes were spatially smoothed with a Gaussian filter of 6 mm full-width half-maximum kernel and temporally filtered with a Chebyshev band-pass filter (0.01–0.08 Hz). We used 160 ROI template to extract the signals. Each ROI contains 27 voxels, including the center point of the ROI and the surrounding 26 voxels (radius = 6 mm) [11]. The average value of the signals of all voxels in each ROI is taken as the signal of the ROI. Each regional mean time series was further corrected for the effects of head movement by regression. We evaluated the functional connectivity between each pair of regions by using Pearson correlation coefficients. For each subject, we obtained a 160 × 160 functional connectivity matrix. Removing diagonal elements, we extracted the upper triangle elements of the matrix as classification features. The feature space for classification was spanned by the (160 × 159)/2=12720 dimensional feature vectors.

## 3.3   Feature Selection

Firstly, we needed to select a small number of highly discriminative features to construct the feature space for classification. From many feature selection methods, we chose the two-sample t-test method. Secondly, we chose two-sided two-sample t-test with p that can make the classification accuracy rate reach the maximum. The leave-one out cross-validation (LCV) strategy was used to estimate the performance of our classifier. During each iteration, a small number of features were selected for each subject. As a result, the common features of all participants were selected as the final classification features. Because the 160 ROI template we used is divided into 6 network modules, we also counted the proportion of extracted functional connectivities between and within each network to explore the pathology of mTBI.

## 3.4   Results

Choosing the right p was very important for two-sample t-test method. If p was too large, difference between mTBI patient group and healthy control group does not meet classification requirements. In contrast, the p was too small and too few features were selected to describe the difference. It can be seen from Fig. 2 that when p is 0.0060 to 0.0066, the classification accuracy rate reaches the maximum of 75.81%. Because the smaller the value of p, the more significant the difference, so p was set to 0.0060.

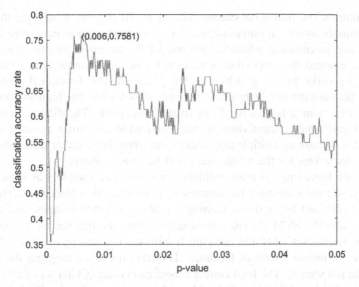

**Fig. 2.** Relationship between p-value and classification accuracy rate.

For 62 subjects, from 74 to 130 features of each subject were selected. Finally, 61 common features were selected as the final classification features. We extracted 61 functional connectivities between 74 ROIs in the end. The test statistics t in Eq. (1) tell us if t < 0, the functional connectivity of mTBI patients is weaker than that of healthy controls because we set mTBI patients as X. Conversely, if t > 0, the functional connectivity of mTBI patients is stronger (see Fig. 3-a). Consistent with previous research [8–10], the functional connectivity of mTBI patients are mostly weaker than

a                                        b

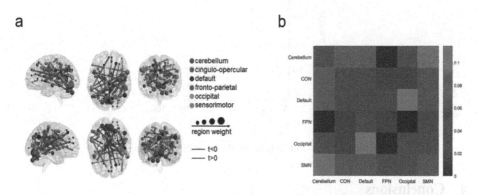

**Fig. 3. a)** The 61 functional connectivities between 74 ROIs extracted in the end. If the test statistics t < 0, the functional connectivity of mTBI patients is weaker than that of healthy controls. Conversely, if t > 0, the functional connectivity of mTBI patients is stronger. In this six brain mode, the top row from left to right are left side, top side and frontal side, while the bottom row from left to right are right side, bottom side and back side. **b)** The proportion of extracted functional connectivities between and within 6 networks.

healthy controls.The functional connectivity of mTBI patients is stronger than that of healthy controls mostly in cingulo-opercular. This phenomenon may exist due to the compensation mechanism, which is also one of the directions of our research in the future. We counted the proportion of extracted functional connectivities between and within 6 networks (see Fig. 3-b). As we expected, the functional connectivities extracted between the cerebellum and the sensorimotor has the highest proportion of 11.48% (7/61), which is also the focus of our next work. The difference in the proportion of functional connectivities between and within networks is small suggesting that mTBI is damage to multiple networks of the whole brain rather than local damage, so mTBI biomarkers for the whole brain will be more effective.

Using the leave-one-out cross-validation strategy, one sample was selected as the testing set, and the remaining 61 samples were used as the training set. The training model was obtained by inputting training set labels, selected features, and a series of parameters into the SVM classifier for training. Then the training model was used to predict the testing set label and compare it with the real testing set label. The above steps were performed a total of 62 times. The nth time of training got the prediction label of the nth sample. The final correct classification rate (CCR) was 75.81% (with 7 out of 31 patients and 8 out of 31 healthy subjects incorrectly classified) by using 61 features. GR, SS and SC of the classifier on LCV strategy are 75.81%, 77.42% and 74.19% respectively which suggested good classification performance and generalization of the algorithm. The ROC curve of the classifier we designed was shown in Fig. 4. The AUC (Area Under Curve) of the ROC curve is 76.7%. Significance level P < 0.001 (<0.05) suggested that our results are statistically significant.

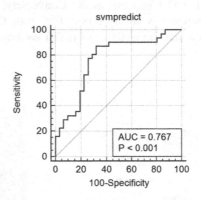

**Fig. 4.** The ROC curve of the classifier we designed.

## 4    Conclusions

In our study, we have successfully classified the mTBI patients from healthy subjects by selecting resting-state functional connectivity as classification features. The proposed classification method was able to capture the underlying difference of resting-state functional connectivity between patients and controls.

# References

1. Bhattrai, A., Irimia, A., Van Horn, J.D.: Neuroimaging of traumatic brain injury in military personnel: an overview. J. Clin. Neurosci. **70**, 1–10 (2019)
2. Mayer, A.R., Hanlon, F.M., Dodd, A.B., et al.: A functional magnetic resonance imaging study of cognitive control and neurosensory deficits in mild traumatic brain injury. Hum. Brain Mapp. **36**(11), 4394–4406 (2015)
3. Salat, D.H., Robinson, M.E., Miller, D.R., et al.: Neuroimaging of deployment-associated traumatic brain injury (TBI) with a focus on mild TBI (mTBI) since 2009. Brain Inj. **31**(9), 1204–1219 (2017)
4. Shetty, T., Nguyen, J., Cogsil, T., et al.: Clinical findings in a multicenter MRI study of mild TBI. Front. Neurol. **9**, 836 (2018)
5. Kawasaki, Y., Suzuki, M., Kherif, F., et al.: Multivariate voxel-based morphometry successfully differentiates schizophrenia patients from healthy controls. Neuroimage **34**(1), 235–242 (2007)
6. Fan, Y., Shen, D., Gur, R.C., et al.: COMPARE: classification of morphological patterns using adaptive regional elements. IEEE Trans. Med. Imaging **26**(1), 93–105 (2006)
7. Lewine, J.D., Plis, S., Ulloa, A., et al.: Quantitative EEG biomarkers for mild traumatic brain injury. J. Clin. Neurophysiol. **36**(4), 298–305 (2019)
8. Mcnerney, M.W., Hobday, T., Cole, B., et al.: Objective classification of mTBI using machine learning on a combination of frontopolar electroencephalography measurements and self-reported symptoms. Sports Med. Open **5**(1), 14 (2019)
9. Shen, H., Wang, L., Liu, Y., et al.: Discriminative analysis of resting-state functional connectivity patterns of schizophrenia using low dimensional embedding of fMRI. Neuroimage **49**(4), 3110–3121 (2010)
10. Zeng, L.L., Shen, H., Liu, L., et al.: Identifying major depression using whole-brain functional connectivity: a multivariate pattern analysis. Brain **135**(5), 1498–1507 (2012)
11. Dosenbach, N.U., Nardos, B., Cohen, A.L., et al.: Prediction of individual brain maturity using fMRI. Science **329**(5997), 1358–1361 (2010)

# Research on Physiological Parameters Measurement Based on Face Video

Baozhen Liu[✉], Kaiyu Mu, and Congmiao Shan

Astronaut Center of China, Beiqing Road. 26, Beijing 100094, China

**Abstract.** Based on imaging photoplethysmography (IPPG) technology, this paper proposes a physiological parameter measurement method based on facial video. This method achieves non-contact measurement of heart rate, respiratory rate, and blood oxygen saturation ($SpO_2$) through steps such as face tracking, template matching, signal filtering, independent component analysis (ICA), and Fourier transform. By experiments, the results are verified to be consistent with standard instruments. Compared with traditional contact measurement, this method has the advantages of non-contact, low cost, simple operation and convenience for long-term monitoring, and will be widely applied in the future medical and health field.

**Keywords:** Imaging photoplethysmography · Non-contact · Physiological parameter measurement · Face video

## 1 Introduction

In recent decades, the development of imaging technology and computer technology has expanded the analysis and application of video information. Facial video analysis with identity recognition as the core has been widely applied in public security management, criminal investigation, sentiment analysis, entertainment and etc. Identity recognition based on facial video conforms to human perception habits, which is accessible and easy-to-understand. Actually, facial video also contains rich physiological information, which can be used for physiological parameter measurement, and has attracted increasing attention.

Imaging photoplethysmography (IPPG) was first proposed by Schmitt et al. in 2000, and is a further development of traditional photoplethysmography (PPG) technology [1]. IPPG senses blood perfusion changes in superficial subcutaneous vessels through slight changes of skin color and extracts blood volume pulse waves (BVP) to calculate physiological parameters [2].

IPPG uses light as the information medium and is a non-contact physiological parameter measurement method, which can compensate for the limitations of contact measurement methods, such as the physiological monitoring of patients with open wounds, the search for survivors in disaster or battlefield environments, avoiding discomfort caused by wearing the sensor for a long time, and non-cooperative

F. Sun et al. (Eds.): ICCSIP 2021, CCIS 1515, pp. 484–494, 2022.
https://doi.org/10.1007/978-981-16-9247-5_38

physiological parameter monitoring. Non-contact physiological parameter measurement can also be achieved through ultrasound waves or electromagnetic waves. In contrast, IPPG has low hardware requirements, which can obtain physiological information such as heart rate, respiratory rate, and blood oxygen saturation (SpO$_2$) by a mobile phone or computer camera. This continuous, non-contact, low-cost measurement method makes daily health monitoring more convenient, and has important value for the promotion and popularization of mobile medical, telemedicine, and home medical care.

Based on IPPG, this paper realizes the extraction of heart rate, respiratory rate, and blood oxygen saturation from face video. The effectiveness and feasibility of the algorithm is demonstrated by comparison with standard instruments.

## 2 Biological Basis of IPPG

In each pulsation cycle of heart's diastole and contraction, the arteries will expand and contract correspondingly. This periodical pulsation is called pulse, and the fluctuation of blood volume is called blood volume pulse wave, or pulse wave for short. Therefore, physiological parameters such as heart rate, respiratory rate, and blood oxygen saturation can be obtained through the pulse wave [3].

Like PPG, IPPG uses Lambert-Beer law as its basic principle [4]. Lambert-Beer law describes the relationship between the absorption strength of a certain material for light with the certain wavelength, the light-absorbing material's concentration and the light-absorbing material's thickness. Its formula is:

$$I = I_0 \times e^{-\varepsilon(\lambda)CL} \tag{1}$$

where $I$ is the intensity of the outgoing light, $I_0$ is the intensity of the incident light, $\varepsilon(\lambda)$ is the absorption coefficient related to the light wavelength $\lambda$ and the light-absorbing substance, $C$ is the concentration of the light-absorbing substance, and $L$ is the light's path distance in the light-absorbing substance. Therefore, when light irradiates the skin, as the heart beats, the blood volume in the vessel changes periodically, and the intensity of reflected light shows similar changing rule with the pulse wave, which lays a theoretical foundation for detecting physiological parameters from facial video.

## 3  Measurement Method

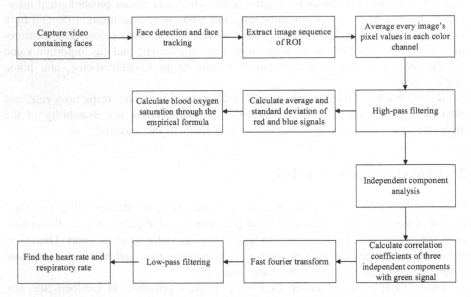

**Fig. 1.** The flow diagram of detecting physiological parameter from face video

The process of detecting physiological parameter from face video is illustrated in Fig. 1, which can be summarized into the following steps: obtaining the image sequence of region of interest (ROI) from the original video, extracting BVP from the image sequence, and calculating the physiological parameters according to BVP.

### 3.1  Video Processing

The purpose of video processing is to obtain the image sequence of ROI from the original video, and the position and perspective of ROI in each image should be consistent. Considering that the face video for physiological parameter measurement usually has the characteristics of stable external light, strong temporal correlation between adjacent frames and consistent movement of local areas of the face, this paper applies Kanede-Lucas-Tomasi (KLT) algorithm to realize the real-time tracking of human face [5].

The initial position of face in video is achieved by AdaBoost algorithm, which realizes face features expression and detection by joint effect of many weak classifiers [6]. First, Harr-like features are used to encode facial features as candidate weak classifiers; then, construct a strong classifier through multiple iterations and weighted voting; finally, cascade several trained strong classifiers as the final face detector. After retrieving the face position in the first frame, KLT algorithm is used for tracking based on feature points. In this paper, we use Harris corner point as the feature descriptor and match adjacent frames based on second-order derivative gradient local search, resulting in feature points positions in the next frame and the relative change of faces between adjacent frames [7]. According to position results, the face fragments are rotated to ensure the consistency of perspective. Figure 2 shows some examples of face detection and tracking, from which we can find that our method has high accuracy even in situations such as face swaying, viewpoint changing and partial occlusion.

**Fig. 2.** Some examples of face detection and tracking

The face fragment obtained by the above method contains many background pixels and is not all for BVP extraction. Therefore, the detected face is matched with a preset template, removing the background pixels and eyes areas, which are not covered by skins but instead of introducing noises by eye blinking. The remaining pixels are used as ROI (as shown in Fig. 3).

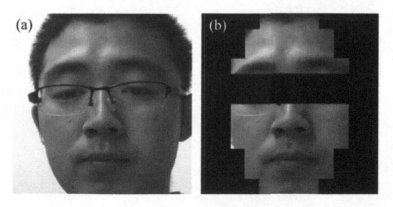

**Fig. 3.** Detected face and ROI

## 3.2   BVP Extraction

RGB channel separation is performed per frame and the average of ROI pixels is calculated in each color channel. The resulting three one-dimensional average pixel values as the function of time are looked as initial BVP signals, which are then interpolated to the sampling rate of 60 Hz by piecewise cubic Hermite.

Initial BVP signals are noisy and subject to considerable low-frequency variations, which mainly come from head movements and external illumination changes [8]. To eliminate the influence of low-frequency noises, a high-pass Butterworth filter is used on average pixel value signals. Figure 4 shows examples of average pixel signals in RGB color channels and corresponding filtered signals.

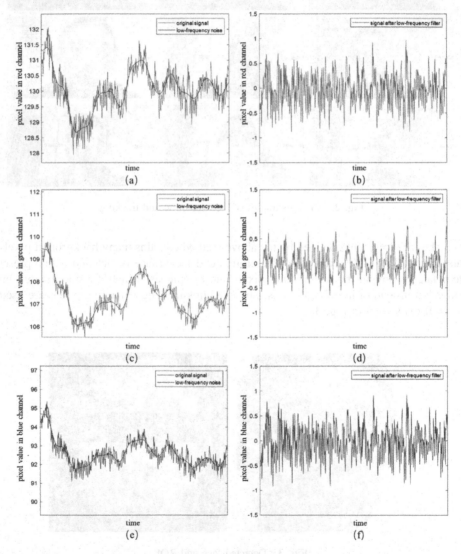

**Fig. 4.**   Average pixel signals in color channels and corresponding filtered signals.

A large number of literatures have shown that blind source separation (BSS) is necessary and effective when realizing physiological parameters measurement based on colorful videos [9–11]. BSS is a signal processing method developed in the 1980s, which refers to the process of extracting and separating the original signals that cannot be directly measured from several observed signals. Independent component analysis (ICA) is a classical BSS algorithm based on the non-Gaussianity and independence of source signals. For IPPG, heart pulsation has little correlation with noises including motion artifacts and illumination changes, so all source signals can be assumed as independent of each other. Meanwhile, both BVP and noises are non-Gaussian signals apparently. Consequently, it is highly appropriate that applies ICA in IPPG to implement noise reduction and signal optimization.

After ICA processing, three independent components can be obtained. According to relevant literatures, oxyhemoglobin and deoxyhemoglobin prefer to absorb green light among three different colors [12, 13]. Thus, the independent component most similar to the average pixel value signal of green channel is selected as the BVP in the next step. The similarity is measured by Pearson Correlation Coefficient (PCC), which is calculated by:

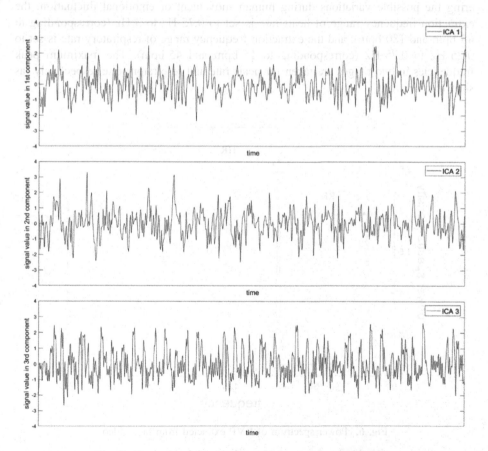

**Fig. 5.** Example of three independent components after ICA.

$$r = \frac{1}{n-1} \sum_{i=1}^{n} \left( \frac{X_i - \overline{X}}{s_X} \right) \left( \frac{Y_i - \overline{Y}}{s_Y} \right) \tag{2}$$

where $n$ is the number of sample points, $\overline{X}$ and $\overline{Y}$ respectively are averages of two signals, while $s_X$ and $s_Y$ are standard deviations.

Figure 5 shows the example of three independent components outputted by ICA, among which the second has the maximum PCC with original green channel signal and used for further physiological parameters calculation.

### 3.3    Calculation of Heart Rate and Respiratory Rate

Heart rate and respiratory rate are frequency characteristics, which are reflected in the BVP waveforms. Fast Fourier transform (FFT) is applied to the independent component obtained after ICA to get its power spectrum in frequency domain. Then a low-pass filter is employed to filter out irrelevant stray peaks.

Literatures have shown that heart rate of healthy Chinese people is between 50 to 95 beats/min (bpm), and respiratory rate of adults is between 12 to 20 bpm. Considering the possible variations during human movement or emotional fluctuation, the extraction frequency range of heart rate is set to 0.75 Hz to 3 Hz (corresponding to 45 bpm and 180 bpm), and the extraction frequency range of respiratory rate is set to 0.25 Hz to 0.75 Hz (corresponding to 15 bpm and 45 bpm). The maximum peak frequencies in two ranges are taken for heart rate and respiratory rate respectively (as shown in Fig. 6).

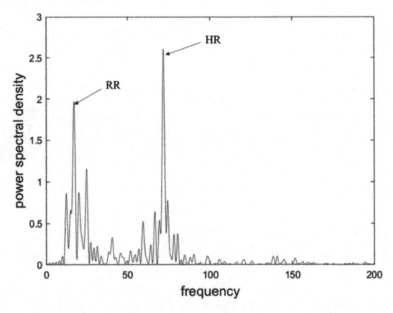

**Fig. 6.** Power spectrum of BVP extracted from face video.

### 3.4 Calculation of Blood Oxygen Saturation

Blood oxygen saturation is a non-frequency characteristic and cannot be obtained by the similar method with heart rate or respiratory rate. It refers to the concentration percentage of oxyhemoglobin of all hemoglobin and its formula can be written by [14]:

$$SpO_2 = \frac{C_{HbO_2}}{C_{HbO_2} + C_{Hb}} \times 100\% \tag{3}$$

where $C_{HbO_2}$ and $C_{Hb}$ are concentrations of oxyhemoglobin and deoxyhemoglobin respectively.

According to Lambert-Beer law and relevant derivations, blood oxygen saturation can be calculated from the relative pulsation amplitude of two kinds of light:

$$SpO_2 = A \times \frac{(I_{ac}/I_{dc})_{\lambda 1}}{(I_{ac}/I_{dc})_{\lambda 2}} + B = A \times R + B \tag{4}$$

where A and B are empirical coefficients, and $I_{ac}$ and $I_{dc}$ are amplitudes of alternating current component and direct current component of light respectively.

Since two kinds of hemoglobin have similar absorption coefficients for blue light and significantly different absorption coefficients for red light, blood oxygen saturation can be calculated using average pixel signals of red channel and blue channel in color video.

In this paper, we consider the average of red and blue channel signals as direct current component amplitude and the standard deviation as alternating current component amplitude. A and B are obtained by linear fitting between R values measured by IPPG and the synchronous measurements of contact pulse oximeter. In our implementation, subjects need hold their breath to obtain the variation of blood oxygen saturation.

## 4 Experiments

Experiments are carried out by a mobile phone and a contact pulse oximeter. The former is used as the video acquisition tool and the latter provides the true values of heart rate and blood oxygen saturation. The control value of respiratory rate is counted manually by subjects.

To prove the effectiveness of our algorithm, we conduct two experiments. The first is a resting state experiment, in which the subjects face the camera and breathe steadily, keeping as still as possible. The second is a head movement experiment, with the subjects facing the camera and moving their heads freely. Every experiment consists of 20 videos and each video lasts for 30 s. During the shooting of every video, the subject's heart rate and blood oxygen saturation are recorded every 5 s, and the mean is used as control values. The accuracy of results is evaluated by mean absolute error (MAE), standard deviation of error ($SD_e$) and root mean squared error (RMSE). The consistency between our method and the standard instrument is illustrated by Bland-Altman plot [15].

**Table 1.** Statistics of measurement of the resting state experiment

| Physiological parameter | MAE | SD$_e$ | RMSE |
|---|---|---|---|
| Heart rate | 1.4691 | 1.7237 | 1.6863 |
| Respiratory rate | 0.8619 | 0.9839 | 0.9648 |
| Blood oxygen saturation | 0.8651 | 0.9272 | 0.9830 |

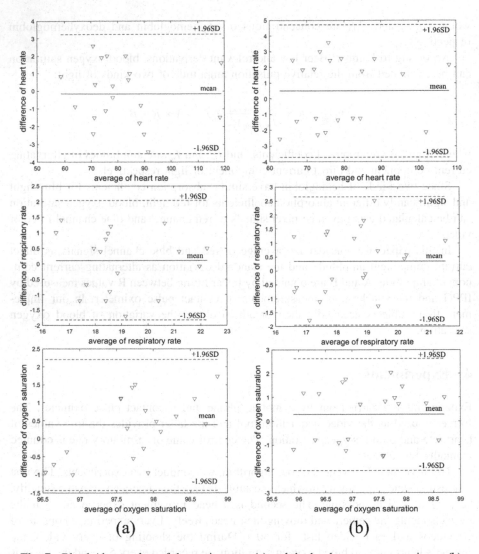

(a)                                    (b)

**Fig. 7.** Bland-Altman plots of the resting state (a) and the head movement experiment (b).

The experimental results of the resting state are shown in Table 1 and Fig. 7. Compared with the control values, the MAE of heart rate obtained from face video is 1.4691 bpm, and the RMSE is 1.6863 bpm; the MAE of respiratory rate is 0.8619 bpm, and the RMSE is 0.9648 bpm; the MAE of blood oxygen saturation is 0.8651%, and the RMSE is 0.9830%. In the Bland-Altman analysis, the average difference of heart rate between the two measurement methods is 0.1461 bpm, and the 95% confidence interval is [−3.5244, 3.2323] bpm; the average difference of respiratory rate is 0.1059 bpm, and the 95% confidence interval is [−1.8224, 2.0343] bpm; the average difference of blood oxygen saturation is 0.3868%, and the 95% confidence interval is [−1.4304%, 2.2040%].

As can be seen from the plots, for heart rate, respiratory rate, and blood oxygen saturation, all the measuring results are within the confidence interval, indicating that two measurement methods have good consistency when subjects are in resting state. Moreover, the MAE of heart rate is far lower than the error standard ($\leq 5$ bpm) in pharmaceutical industry standard of the People's Republic of China. These analyses prove that physiological parameters measurement based on face video has sufficient precision and accuracy for practical applications.

**Table 2.** Statistics of measurement of the head movement experiment

| Physiological parameter | MAE | SD$_e$ | RMSE |
|---|---|---|---|
| Heart rate | 2.0643 | 2.1486 | 2.1537 |
| Respiratory rate | 1.0383 | 1.1742 | 1.1966 |
| Blood oxygen saturation | 1.1391 | 1.1974 | 1.2002 |

The experimental results of head movement are shown in Table 2 and Fig. 7. Compared with the control values, the MAE of heart rate obtained from face video is 2.0643 bpm, and the RMSE is 2.1537 bpm; the MAE of respiratory rate is 1.0383 bpm, and the RMSE is 1.1966 bpm; the MAE of blood oxygen saturation is 1.1391%, and the RMSE is 1.2002%. In the Bland-Altman analysis, the average difference of heart rate is 0.5029 bpm, and the 95% confidence interval is [−3.7083, 4.7141] bpm; the average difference of respiratory rate is 0.3494 bpm, and the 95% confidence interval is [−1.9520, 2.6507] bpm; the average difference of blood oxygen saturation is 0.2801%, and the 95% confidence interval is [−2.0668%, 2.6269%]. We can find that the MAE, RMSE, and confidence interval of head movement get worse than resting state, but still maintains a higher accuracy and consistency with the control device.

## 5 Conclusion

This paper realizes the measurement of heart rate, respiratory rate and blood oxygen saturation from face video. We reduce influence of motion artifacts through KLT face tracking algorithm and improve the signal-to-noise ratio through face template matching and multiple filtering. Experiments results demonstrate the method's stability, accuracy and consistency with pulse oximeter. The measurement based on face video can make up for the limitations of traditional contact methods and will play a practical role in several fields such as daily health care, contactless sleep monitoring and hidden measurement of physiological parameters.

**Acknowledgement.** Project supported by the "Fei Tian" Foundation of Astronaut Center of China (Grant No. 2019SY54B0702).

# References

1. Wu, T., Blazek, V., Schmitt, H.J.: Photoplethysmography imaging: a new noninvasive and noncontact method for mapping of the dermal perfusion changes. Proc. SPIE **4**(163), 62–70 (2000)
2. Yankun, X.U., Ping, S., Hongliu, Y.U.: Progress on human physiological parameter detection based on imaging PPG. Beijing Biomed. Eng. **6**, 102–108 (2017)
3. Sanyal, S., Nundy, K.K.: Algorithms for monitoring heart rate and respiratory rate from the video of a user's face. IEEE J. Transl. Eng. Health Med. **6**, 2700111 (2018)
4. Kuo, J., Koppel, S., Charlton, J.L., et al.: Evaluation of a video-based measure of driver heart rate. J. Saf. Res. **54**, 55–59 (2015)
5. Mstafa, R.J., Elleithy, K.M.: A video steganography algorithm based on Kanade-Lucas-Tomasi tracking algorithm and error correcting codes. Multimedia Tools Appl. **75**(17), 10311–10333 (2015). https://doi.org/10.1007/s11042-015-3060-0
6. Viola, P.A., Jones, M.J.: Rapid object detection using a boosted cascade of simple features. In: Proceedings of the 2001 IEEE Computer Society Conference on Computer Vision and Pattern Recognition. IEEE, Kauai (2001)
7. Ranganatha, S., Gowramma, Y.P.: A novel fused algorithm for human face tracking in video sequences. In: 2016 International Conference on Computation System and Information Technology for Sustainable Solutions. IEEE, Bengaluru (2016)
8. Unakafov, A.M.: Pulse rate estimation using imaging photoplethysmography: generic framework and comparison of methods on a publicly available dataset. Biomed. Phys. Eng. Express **4**, 045001 (2018)
9. Poh, M.Z., Mcduff, D.J., Picard, R.W.: Advancements in noncontact, multiparameter physiological measurements using a webcam. IEEE Trans. Biomed. Eng. **58**(1), 7–11 (2010)
10. Sebastian, Z., Alexander, T., Daniel, W., et al.: Cardiovascular assessment by imaging photoplethysmography – a review. Biomed. Eng. **63**(5), 617–634 (2018)
11. Davis, S., Watkinson, P., Guazzi, A., et al.: Continuous non-contact vital sign monitoring in neonatal intensive care unit. Healthc. Technol. Lett. **1**(3), 87–91 (2014)
12. Fan, Q., Li, K.: Noncontact imaging plethysmography for accurate estimation of physiological parameters. J. Med. Biol. Eng. **37**(5), 675–685 (2017). https://doi.org/10.1007/s40846-017-0272-y
13. Bal, U.: Non-contact estimation of heart rate and oxygen saturation using ambient light. Biomed. Opt. Express **6**(1), 86–97 (2015)
14. Bagha, S., Shaw, L.: A real time analysis of PPG signal for measurement of $SpO_2$ and pulse rate. Magn. Reson. Chem. **48**(1), 61 (2011)
15. Myles, P.S., Cui, J.: Using the Bland-Altman method to measure agreement with repeated measures. Br. J. Anaesth. **3**, 309–311 (2007)

# Multi-modal Signal Based Childhood Rolandic Epilepsy Detection

Yixian Wu[1,2], Dinghan Hu[1,2], Tiejia Jiang[3], Feng Gao[3], and Jiuwen Cao[1,2(✉)]

[1] Machine Learning and I-health International Cooperation
Base of Zhejiang Province, Hangzhou Dianzi University, Hangzhou 310018, China
jwcao@hdu.edu.cn
[2] Artificial Intelligence Institute, Hangzhou Dianzi University,
Hangzhou 310018, Zhejiang, China
[3] Department of Neurology, The Children's Hospital,
Zhejiang University School of Medicine, National Clinical Research Center
for Child Health, Hangzhou, Zhejiang, China
{jiangyouze,epilepsy}@zju.edu.cn

**Abstract.** Electroencephalogram (EEG) is the common signal used in epilepsy analysis but suffered from the inconvenient issue in data acquisition, especially when applied to children with Rolandic epilepsy. In this paper, we present a study on multi-modal signal based epileptic seizure detection for children suffered from Rolandic epilepsy, where EEG combined with the synchronized surveillance video is included for analysis. The Mel frequency cepstrum coefficient (MFCC) and linear prediction cepstrum coefficient (LPCC) features are taken to characterize EEG. The spatiotemporal interest points (STIP) are extracted from video sequences to construct a bag of words model, which are based on the descriptors of histograms of oriented gradient (HOG) and the histograms of oriented optical flow (HOF) in the neighborhood. The histograms of word frequency (HWF) features are obtained for video representation. Direct feature fusion on the EEG based MFCC+LPCC and video based HWF is applied for classifier training. Data of 13 children with Rolandic epilepsy recorded from the Children's Hospital, Zhejiang University School of Medicine (CHZU) are applied in the experiment. The results show that the model trained on the multi-modal features of EEG and video can achieve the highest overall accuracy of 98.2%.

**Keywords:** Epilepsy · EEG · Seizure detection · Multi-modal features · Spatial-temporal interest points

## 1 Introduction

Epileptic patients make up about 1% of the world's population, and most of them are children. The incidence of Childhood epilepsy is 10–15 times that of

---

Y. Wu and T. Jiang—Contribute equally to the paper.

© Springer Nature Singapore Pte Ltd. 2022
F. Sun et al. (Eds.): ICCSIP 2021, CCIS 1515, pp. 495–510, 2022.
https://doi.org/10.1007/978-981-16-9247-5_39

adult [1,2]. The treatment of epilepsy has become one of the focus issues around the world. However, the randomness, repetition and unpredictability of epileptic seizures are challenging in epilepsy analysis. EEG, that can reflect the information of the patient's brain electrical activity, has been comprehensively studied for epilepsy analysis in clinical diagnosis [3–7]. Temko et al. [7] used multi-channel EEG signals to distinguish between seizure and non-seizure periods in neonatal patients, and controlled the final decision by selecting different confidence levels. James et al. [8] extracted EEG features based on wavelet transform, and obtained convincing seizure detection performance by random forest (RF). Parvez et al. [9] extracted the features of EEG based on empirical mode decomposition (EMD) and discrete cosine transform (DCT), and adopted the least-square support vector machine (SVM) for seizure detection. Abbasi et al. [10] used the long-short term memory (LSTM) to detect seizure, which was superior to SVM. Ansari et al. [11] used deep convolutional neural networks (CNN) and RF to automatically achieve feature optimization and epilepsy detection. Cao et al. [12] used the softmax layer of CNN to extract the probabilistic feature vectors, and improved the performance through using adaptive and differentiated feature weighted fusion (AWF) by stacked CNNs.

Among the various types of epilepsy, Rolandic epilepsy deserves more research attention because patients are at risk of sudden death. Rolandic epilepsy can be roughly divided into several categories: myoclonics seizures, clonic seizures, epileptic spasms, tonic seizures and generalized tonic-clonic seizures (GTCS). Similar movement patterns exist in each category and can be captured in video. Considering the inconvenience of EEG acquisition, researchers have also set their sights on the video-based epilepsy detection methods. Geertsema et al. [13] detected tonic-clonic seizures by calculating the power ratio of the effective component of the group velocity signal of the video optical flow sequence. In [14], Kouamou et al. proposed the average brightness signal of video sequence, which can detect clonic seizures by evaluating the periodicity of the average brightness signal. Lu et al. [15] used clothes of different colors on different parts of the body to assist limb segmentation, and quantified the characteristics of epilepsy through motion trajectories. Cuppens et al. [16] distributed the intensity to the pixels through the optical flow algorithm, and took the average of the highest motion vector percentage to achieve seizure detection by a thresholding method. Cuppens et al. extended their work by extracting temporal and spatial interest points (STIP) features from video sequences to detect seizures in patients with myoclonus [17]. Karayiannis et al. [18] used the optical flow method to extract the time motion intensity signal of the video to quantify baby's motion, and adopted neural network for seizure detection. Achilles et al. [19] applied CNN to build a real-time epileptic seizure detection system, where the AUC (Area Under the Curve) of 78.33% can be achieved. Yang et al. [20] designed a CNN+LSTM network for the generalized tonic-clonic seizure detection based on video sequence, and an average sensitivity of 88% and specificity of 92% were obtained. Besides merely using video, multi-modal signal based seizure detections, including the combination of EEG and Electrocardiograph (ECG) [21,22], accelerometer and

Electromyography (EMG) [23], EEG and video [24], were also studied in the past.

For children suffered from the Rolandic epilepsy, performing the long-term EEG recording is always challenging due to the inconvenience of EEG acquisition and the poor autonomous control of children. Using the synchronized video combining with EEG becomes popular and essential for epileptic seizure detection of children [25–27]. To this end, we present a study on using EEG and video sequence for childhood Rolandic epilepsy seizure detection in this paper. Figure 1 shows the overall flowchart of the proposed method. The Mel Frequency Cepstral Coefficients (MFCC) and Linear Predictive Cepstral Coefficients (LPCC) are extracted for EEG characterization. The histograms of word frequency (HWF) feature based on STIP is derived on the video representation. To address the imbalance issue existed between the interictal and seizure period, the SMOTE+TomekLinks approach is employed to generate the synthetic feature samples for model training.

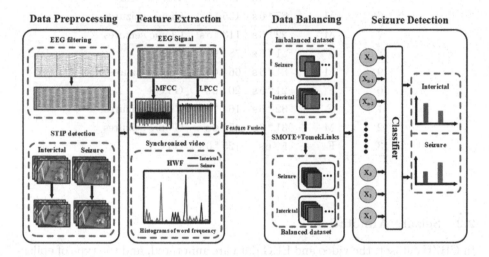

**Fig. 1.** The proposed multi-modal epileptic seizure detection algorithm

## 2  Dataset and Method

### 2.1  Dataset

The data used in this paper are collected by the Children's Hospital, Zhejiang University School of Medicine (CHZU), which consists of the 21-channel scalp EEG and the synchronized video data of 13 childhood patients suffered from the Rolandic epilepsy. Particularly, there include 3 types of epileptic seizures, clonic seizure, GTCS, and tonic seizure, respectively. Each subject has been recorded continuously for more than 24 h, and the total time of data exceeds 200 h. Among them, the sampling frequency of EEG is 1000 Hz, and the electrode position follows the international 10–20 standard system. The resolution of the video data is $480 \times 360$ pixels, and the frame rate is 20 frames per second. Table 1 shows the detailed specifications of the dataset. For instance, for subject 1, 6 clonic seizures with a total duration of 6 min were captured in the 2 d' recording, for experiment, the 6 min seizure data and 4 min interictal data were used, and meanwhile, the synchronized video sequences are also obtained for analysis.

**Table 1.** The specification of CHZU dataset.

| Subjects | Gender | Seizure | Interictal | Category |
|---|---|---|---|---|
| 1 | M | 60 * 6 s | 40 * 6 s | Clonic seizures |
| 2 | F | 11 * 6 s | 58 * 6 s | Clonic seizures |
| 3 | M | 60 * 6 s | 78 * 6 s | GTCS |
| 4 | M | 29 * 6 s | 19 * 6 s | Clonic seizures |
| 5 | F | 10 * 6 s | 54 * 6 s | Tonic seizures |
| 6 | M | 87 * 6 s | 155 * 6 s | Clonic seizures |
| 7 | M | 22 * 6 s | 113 * 6 s | Clonic seizures |
| 8 | F | 31 * 6 s | 78 * 6 s | GTCS |
| 9 | M | 81 * 6 s | 66 * 6 s | Tonic seizures |
| 10 | F | 21 * 6 s | 20 * 6 s | GTCS |
| 11 | F | 32 * 6 s | 164 * 6 s | Clonic seizures |
| 12 | M | 31 * 6 s | 47 * 6 s | Clonic seizures |
| 13 | F | 5 * 6 s | 123 * 6 s | GTCS |

## 2.2 Seizure Annotation

In CHZU dataset, the video and EEG data are annotated, and the type of epileptic seizure and the onset time of the seizure are determined by 2 neurologists. When EEG and video reflect the patient's seizure for the first time, it is marked as the beginning of the clinical seizure, and when the patient's behavior returns to normal, it is marked as the end of the clinical seizure. The specific types of seizures and the desirability of their detection are shown in Table 2. For the first category, this is an important factor of sudden unexpected death in epilepsy (SUDEP). So it is the most urgency detection in Rolandic epilepsy analysis. The second category is the type of seizures that need to be detected due to its serious harm. The third category is mild attack that is usually difficult to detect only by video sequences, and thus, EEGs are normally required to assist the detection. At the same time, the affections during the seizure onset are relatively minor.

**Table 2.** Seizure categories and the urgency need for detection.

| Category | Description | Detection need |
|---|---|---|
| 1 | Convulsive seizure (CS): Tonic-clonic seizures or generalized clonic seizures | Essential |
| 2 | Tonic seizures | Desirable |
| 3 | Non-motor seizures | Nonclinically vital |

## 2.3   Feature Extraction

For feature extraction, the EEG and video data are divided into sample segments of 6 s with the overlap rate of 50%. It can ensure that the EEG signal is cut without losing the characteristic information at both ends. The multichannel EEGs are filtered to remove 50 Hz power-line interference. In addition, the median filtering is also used to remove the noises in EEG.

**EEG Feature Extraction.** MFCC is a popular acoustic signal feature proposed by Mermelstein. It maps the signal frequency to a non-linear Mel filter bank and converts it to the cepstrum domain. MFCC can give higher weight to these frequencies in order to represent the signal more accurately. MFCC [28] is define as

$$MFCC_i = \sum_{m=1}^{M} s(m) \cos[i(m - \frac{\pi}{M})], i = 1, 2, ..., L,  \tag{1}$$

where $m$ represents the number of triangular filters, $s(m)$ represents the logarithmic energy output by each filter bank, and $L$ represents the order of the MFCC which is set to be 12 in this paper.

Linear predictive coefficient(LPC) is widely used in speech recognition and the main idea of LPC is to predict current or future samples based on previous signal. It has a small amount of calculation and is easy to implement. LPCC inherits the advantages of LPC. The LPC cepstrum is derived by

$$H = \frac{G}{A(z)} = \frac{G}{1 - \sum_{k=1}^{p} a_k z^{-k}}  \tag{2}$$

where $A(z)$ is a inverse filter and $a_k$ is the linear prediction coefficient ($k = 1, 2...$) [29]. Then, the LPCC can be calculated iteratively by the following formula

$$LPCC_n = \begin{cases} a_1, & n = 1, \\ a_n + \sum_{k=1}^{n-1}(1 - \frac{k}{n})a_k LPCC_{n-k}, & 1 < n \leq p, \\ \sum_{k=1}^{p}(1 - \frac{k}{n})a_k LPCC_n - k, & n > p. \end{cases}  \tag{3}$$

where $a_i$ is LPC. In this paper, the order of LPCC is set to be 16.

500 Y. Wu et al.

For the 6 s EEG segment, it is divided into short frames with the frame
length of 1024 samples and the frame overlap rate of 50%. For each frame, the
MFCC and LPCC features are extracted from all 21 channels, where $21 \times 120$
and $21 \times 160$ feature matrices of MFCC and LPCC are obtained, respectively.
These features are finally concatenated into a long feature vector with 5880
dimensions. Figure 2 shows the histogram comparisons of the 12th and 16th
features of MFCC ($MFCC_{12}$) and LPCC ($LPCC_{16}$) obtained from the EEGs
of seizure and interictal stages, respectively. As shown in the figure, $MFCC_{12}$
from the EEGs of seizure generally distributes around 11, while $MFCC_{12}$ from
the EEGs of interictal normally concentrates around 12. Similar difference can
be found from the distributions of $LPCC_{16}$, for the EEGs of seizure, $LPCC_{16}$
mainly distributes around $-2.1$ with a small variance, while for the EEGs of
interictal, $LPCC_{16}$ concentrates around $-1.8$ with a relatively large variance.

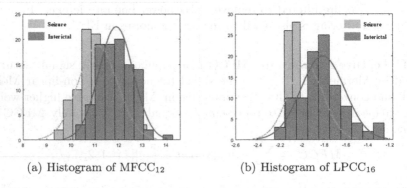

(a) Histogram of $MFCC_{12}$        (b) Histogram of $LPCC_{16}$

**Fig. 2.** Histograms of $MFCC_{12}$ and $LPCC_{16}$ on EEGs of seizure and interictal.

**Video Feature Extraction.** To synchronize with EEG sequence, the video
segment with 6 s is applied for feature extraction. As the frames per second
(FPS) is 20, there have a total of 120 frames for feature extraction for each
sample. To capture the motion information of Rolandic epilepsy, the statistical
features based on the spatiotemporal interest points (STIP) [30] from the video
sequence are derived, where we have extended the idea of Harris corner detection
algorithm from 2-D to 3-D here. STIP captured the points where the pixels of
the local area of the image have significant changed on the space and time
axis as spatiotemporal interest points, and will not detect points that make a
uniform linear motion on the time axis. Figure 3 shows the overall flowchart of
the proposed video sequence feature extraction algorithm on Rolandic epilepsy.
Particularly, the feature extraction is conducted in the following steps.

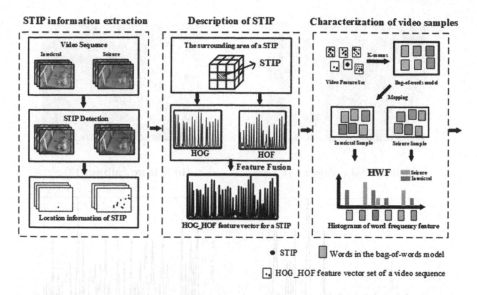

**Fig. 3.** The video sequence feature extraction on Rolandic epilepsy analysis.

1) STIP

To model a video sequence, we construct its linear scale-space representation by convolution of $f$ with a Gaussian kernel with independent spatial variance $\sigma_l^2$ and temporal variance $\tau_l^2$ as

$$L(\cdot; \sigma_l^2, \tau_l^2) = g(\cdot; \sigma_l^2, \tau_l^2) * f(\cdot), \tag{4}$$

where $f(\cdot)$ and $g(\cdot; \sigma_l^2, \tau_l^2)$ represent the video sequence and the Gaussian kernel respectively. The Gaussian kernel is $g(x, y, t : \sigma_l^2, \tau_l^2) = \frac{1}{\sqrt{(2\pi)^3 \sigma_l^4 \tau_l^2}} \times \exp(-(x^2 + y^2)/2\sigma_l^2 - t^2/2\tau_l^2)$. Then, the spatial-temporal second-moment matrix is calculated as

$$\mu = g(\cdot; \sigma_i^2, \tau_i^2) * \begin{pmatrix} L_x^2 & L_x L_y & L_x L_t \\ L_x L_y & L_y^2 & L_y L_t \\ L_x L_t & L_y L_t & L_t^2 \end{pmatrix} \tag{5}$$

where the integration scale $\sigma_i^2$ and $\tau_i^2$ are related to the local scale $\sigma_l^2$ and $\tau_l^2$. The definition of each first-order derivatives are $L_x(\cdot; \sigma_l^2, \tau_l^2) = \partial_x(g * f)$, $L_y(\cdot; \sigma_l^2, \tau_l^2) = \partial_y(g * f)$, and $L_t(\cdot; \sigma_l^2, \tau_l^2) = \partial_t(g * f)$. By calculating the three eigenvalues $\lambda_1$, $\lambda_2$, $\lambda_3$ of the matrix $\mu$, the Harris corner function in the space-time domain is defined as

$$\begin{aligned} H &= det(\mu) - k * tr^3(\mu) \\ &= \lambda_1 \lambda_2 \lambda_3 - k(\lambda_1 + \lambda_2 + \lambda_3)^3 \end{aligned} \tag{6}$$

where $det(.)$ represent the determinant of a matrix and $tr(.)$ represent the trace of a matrix. Then, we can get the spatio-temporal interest points by calculating

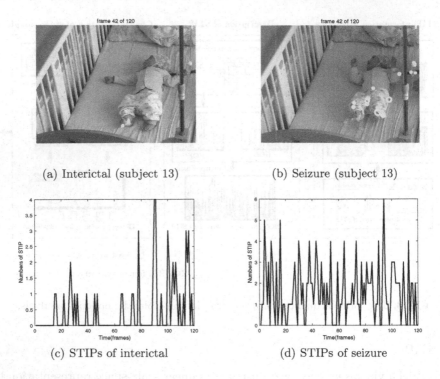

(a) Interictal (subject 13)          (b) Seizure (subject 13)

(c) STIPs of interictal              (d) STIPs of seizure

**Fig. 4.** STIPs detected within one video frame of interictal and seizure, respectively.

the positive maximum value of $H$. In this paper, $k$ is set to 0.001, $\sigma_l^2$ and $\tau_l^2$ are set to 4 and 2 respectively. $\sigma_i^2$ and $\tau_i^2$ are set to 8 and 4, respectively. Figure 4(a) and (b) show the results of STIP detection from the video frames in interictal and seizure states of the 13th subject, respectively. Figure 4(c) and (d) present the number of STIPs of different frames in the interictal and seizure. As observed, during the seizure, the number of STIP presents a regular and periodic change, that is different to the interictal state.

2) HOG and HOF Extraction

The histograms of oriented gradient (HOG) and the histograms of oriented optical flow(HOF) have been widely used in computer vision. Both features are obtained by calculating and counting the oriented histogram of the local area of the image. The difference is that HOG performs the weighted statistic on the gradient changes of the image, and HOF is derived on the orient of optical flow.

For HOG, the gradients of the horizontal and vertical coordinates of the image are firstly derived by

$$
\begin{aligned}
G_x(x,y) &= H(x+1,y) - H(x-1,y) \\
G_y(x,y) &= H(x,y+1) - H(x,y-1)
\end{aligned}
\tag{7}
$$

where $G_x(x, y)$, $G_y(x, y)$, $H(x, y)$ respectively represent the horizontal gradient, vertical gradient and pixel value at $(x, y)$. The gradient magnitude $G(x, y)$ and orient $\alpha(x, y)$ at the pixel are

$$G(x, y) = \sqrt{G_x(x, y)^2 + G_y(x, y)^2},$$
$$\alpha(x, y) = \cot(\frac{G_y(x, y)}{G_x(x, y)}). \tag{8}$$

By dividing the 360° into $n$ bins, the histogram with the weight of the gradient amplitude is calculated to get HOG.

For HOF, similarly, the optical flow field of each frame is calculated, and the optical flow vector of each pixel is obtained. The angle between the optical flow vector and the horizontal axis is obtained, which is then projected into the corresponding histogram bin according to the angle value and performed the weighting according to the magnitude of the optical flow. The detailed feature extraction of HOG and HOF is shown in Fig. 5.

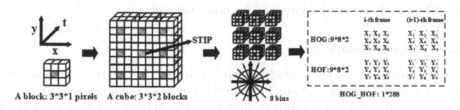

**Fig. 5.** HOG and HOF feature extraction on STIP locations.

3) HWF Extraction

The feature vectors of HOG and HOF of each spatiotemporal interest point from the video samples are obtained to construct a vocabulary set. The K-means algorithm based clustering is then performed on the vocabulary set to build a bag-of-words model for the video frame characterization. The number of clusters are set to be 50 in this paper, and the histograms of word frequency (HWF) with a vocabulary of 50 are extracted for video frame representation. The purpose is to reduce redundant information and extract discriminative feature to characterize the motion in the video sequence. Figure 6 draws the HWF vectors obtained from the video frames captured during seizure and interictal states, respectively, where Fig. 6(a) presents the HWF vector of single video frame and the Fig. 6(b) shows the average HWF vector of all video frames. Obviously, one can find there have significant differences in HWF between seizure and interictal samples. Further, the histograms of the 98-$th$, 129-$th$, and 13-$th$ features in HOG, HOF and HWF on video frames captured in the seizure and interictal states are also depicted in Fig. 7 for comparison. In Fig. 7(a), the $HOG_{98}$ of seizure

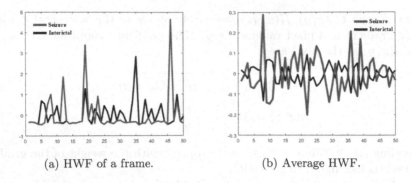

(a) HWF of a frame.                    (b) Average HWF.

**Fig. 6.** HWF comparisons.

generally distributes around 0.1, while that of interictal distributes around 0.3. In Fig. 7(b), the $HOF_{129}$ of seizure widely distributes between 0 to 0.7, while that of interictal concentrates around 0.1. Through the dimensionality reduction and feature clustering by the bag-of-words model, the difference between the feature distribution of seizure and interictal becomes more obvious.

## 2.4   Dataset Balancing

Dataset imbalance always exists in epileptic seizure detection due to the sudden and transient nature of seizures. To solve this problem, a minority sample generating method based on the synthetic minority oversampling technique (SMOTE) combining with the TomkLinks approach (SMOTE+TomekLinks) [31] is adopted in this paper. The SMOTE method generated new sample by the following rule

$$x_{new} = x + rand(0,1) * |x - x_n|, \tag{9}$$

where $x_{new}$ is the new sample, $x$ is a sample in the minority class, $x_n$ is randomly selected from the $k$ nearest neighbors. After that, the TomekLinks method, is applied to eliminates the overlaps between most of the samples. TomekLinks are defined as follow:

$$(x,y) \in a\ tomek\ link, \quad if \quad d(x,z) < d(x,y) \quad or$$
$$d(y,z) < d(x,y), \quad z \notin C_1, C_2, \quad x,y \in C_1, C_2, \tag{10}$$

where $d(\cdot)$ represents the distance between two samples, $C_1$ and $C_2$ are two different categories. Then we remove every matching tomek links. Table 3 lists the number of samples extracted from the CHZU database before/after using the SMOTE+TomekLinks approach. The ratio of seizure and interictal samples reached 1:1 when using the dataset balancing method. It is noted that for dataset balancing, the hybrid feature sample by direct concatenating the EEG features with the video features is used in the SMOTE+TomekLinks approach. With loss of generality, for the classifier training, the mixed data with the partial original feature samples and all generated samples by SMOTE+TomekLinks are used,

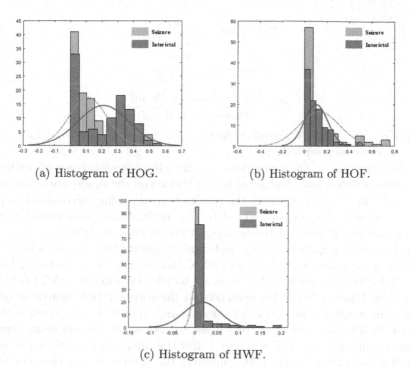

(a) Histogram of HOG.

(b) Histogram of HOF.

(c) Histogram of HWF.

**Fig. 7.** Histograms of the 98-*th*, 129-*th*, and 13-*th* features in HOG, HOF and HWF on video frames captured in the seizure and interictal states.

while for the performance testing, only the original feature samples are used. The 10-fold cross validation is applied in the performance evaluation, but in the testing stage, the generated samples are removed.

**Table 3.** Dataset balancing by SMOTE+TomekLinks.

| Epileptic state | Seizure | Interictal |
| --- | --- | --- |
| Original dataset | 923 | 2002 |
| Balanced dataset | 2002 | 2002 |

## 3   Results and Comparisons

For performance evaluation, the overall accuracy (Acc), precision (Pre), recall rate (Rec) and $F_1$ are calculated, defined respectively as

$$Accuracy = \frac{TP + TN}{TP + TN + FP + FN}, \tag{11}$$

$$Precision = \frac{TP}{TP + FP}, \tag{12}$$

$$Recall = \frac{TP}{TP + FN}, \tag{13}$$

$$F_1 = \frac{2 * Precision * Recall}{Precision + Recall}, \tag{14}$$

where $TP$, $TN$, $FP$, $FN$ represent the true positive, true negative, false positive and false negative, respectively.

In the experiment, the comparisons on the following aspects are presented: 1) the results between fused feature of EEG+Video and the single modal feature of EEG and Video, respectively, 2) the results between using the original and the balance datasets, respectively. The detection performance is evaluated using 4 popular machine learning methods: support vector machine (SVM), decision tree (DT), K-nearest neighbor (KNN), and random forest (RF). Decision tree (DT) is CART tree. In K-nearest neighbor (KNN), the number of nearest neighbors is set to 3. In RF, the number of trees is set to 100. Decision tree (DT) is CART tree and the Gini coefficient has been used as the criterion. In K-nearest neighbor (KNN), the number of nearest neighbors is searched on 3, 5, 7, 9, which is finally set to 3. In RF, the number of trees is set to 100, where the minimum number of observations per tree leaf is set to 1 and the number of variables randomly selected at each decision split is the square of the number of variables. For SVM, the 'Gaussian' kernel is used and the penalty coefficient is set to 1.

Tables 4 and 5 present the detection results obtained using the original and the balance datasets, respectively, where the results on the features of EEG+Video, EEG and Video are all given. From the table, we can observe that 1) the fused feature of EEG+Video based classifiers generally perform the best when comparing with the single modal feature based classifiers, 2) the EEG feature based classifiers perform better than the video feature based classifiers, 3) when merely using the video signal, the performance is acceptable after performing the dataset balancing, and for all classifiers, the overall accuracies are higher than 83%, 4) applying the dataset balancing generally enhances the performance for almost all classifiers and all kinds of features, where the enhancement is more obvious on the video signal, 5) overall, the best performance is obtained by the SVM algorithm on the fused EEG+Video feature after the dataset balancing, where the algorithm can achieve the accuracy of 98.23%, precision of 97.73%, recall rate of 98.75% and $F_1$ score of 98.23%, which are 1.1%, 1.59%, 4.05% and 2.82% over the ones before dataset balancing, respectively.

To have a better understanding, Fig. 8 shows the confusion matrices of overall classification accuracy on the seizure and interictal categories, respectively. The results on the original dataset and the balanced dataset obtained by SVM are given. It is obvious that the performance has been significantly improved after data balancing, especially for the video signal based epilepsy detection. For the seizure category, the classification accuracy with the original dataset by video is only 61.97%, while using the dataset balancing by SMOTE+TomekLinks, the accuracy on seizure category increases to 86.16%.

**Table 4.** Results (%) on the original dataset.

| Classifier | EEG | | | | Video | | | | EEG+Video | | | |
|---|---|---|---|---|---|---|---|---|---|---|---|---|
| | Acc | Pre | Rec | $F_1$ | Acc | Pre | Rec | $F_1$ | Acc | Pre | Rec | $F_1$ |
| SVM | 96.07 | 93.81 | 93.72 | 93.77 | 84.14 | 83.50 | 61.97 | 71.14 | **97.13** | 96.14 | **94.70** | **95.41** |
| DT | 92.24 | 88.67 | 86.46 | 87.55 | 81.89 | 74.84 | 64.14 | 69.08 | 95.18 | 94.63 | 89.82 | 92.16 |
| KNN | 96.03 | 95.59 | 91.66 | 93.58 | 83.69 | 80.30 | 64.03 | 71.25 | 96.62 | **98.13** | 91.00 | 94.43 |
| RF | 96.10 | 95.00 | 92.20 | 93.57 | 82.84 | 76.89 | 65.22 | 70.57 | 96.51 | 95.46 | 93.39 | 94.41 |

**Table 5.** Results (%) on the balanced dataset.

| Classifier | EEG | | | | Video | | | | EEG+Video | | | |
|---|---|---|---|---|---|---|---|---|---|---|---|---|
| | Acc | Pre | Rec | $F_1$ | Acc | Pre | Rec | $F_1$ | Acc | Pre | Rec | $F_1$ |
| SVM | 97.48 | 97.17 | 97.80 | 97.49 | 86.81 | 87.30 | 86.16 | 86.73 | **98.23** | **97.73** | **98.75** | **98.23** |
| DT | 93.33 | 94.79 | 91.71 | 93.22 | 83.59 | 85.38 | 81.07 | 83.17 | 95.83 | 95.58 | 96.10 | 95.84 |
| KNN | 95.45 | 96.00 | 94.86 | 95.43 | 85.66 | 86.61 | 84.37 | 85.48 | 97.58 | 97.04 | 98.15 | 97.59 |
| RF | 95.80 | 97.07 | 94.46 | 95.75 | 85.46 | 85.82 | 84.97 | 85.39 | 97.88 | 97.33 | 98.45 | 97.89 |

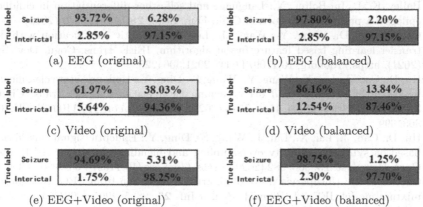

(a) EEG (original)  (b) EEG (balanced)

(c) Video (original)  (d) Video (balanced)

(e) EEG+Video (original)  (f) EEG+Video (balanced)

**Fig. 8.** Confusion matrices comparisons, where the results is obtained by SVM.

## 4  Conclusions

In this paper, the detection algorithm of childhood Rolandic epilepsy based on the multi-modal features of EEG and video was proposed. For signal characterization, MFCC and LPCC have been taken for EEG representation, and the STIPs based histograms of word frequency (HWF) have been derived for video sequence characterization. For the synchronized EEG signal and video sequence, these features were directly concatenated to achieve better detection performance. The dataset balancing approach by SMOTE+TomekLinks was applied to generate syntectic samples of the seizure category to address the imbalance issue between seizure and interictal states. The EEG and video data of 13 children with Rolandic epilepsy recorded from the Children's Hospital, Zhejiang University School of Medicine (CHZU) have been conducted for analysis. The results showed that the multi-modal signal based model can achieve better performance than that using single modal. Besides, the SMOTE+TomekLinks approach can effectively improve the classification accuracy of the minority category, which is practically significant in real applications.

**Acknowledgements.** This work was supported by the National Key Research and Development Program of China (2021YFE0100100), the National Natural Science Foundation of China (U1909209), the Open Research Projects of Zhejiang Lab (2021MC0AB04), the Key Research and Development Program of Zhejiang Province (2020C03038), and the Zhejiang Provincial Natural Science Foundation (LBY21H090002).

# References

1. Malarvili, M.B., Mesbah, M.: Newborn seizure detection based on heart rate variability. IEEE Trans. Biomed. Eng. **56**(11), 2594–2603 (2009)
2. Bailey, K.M., Im-Bolter, N.: Language and self-other differentiation in childhood epilepsy: a preliminary report. J. Child Fam. Stud. **28**(4), 971–979 (2019)
3. Cao, J., Hu, D., Wang, Y., Wang, J., Lei, B.: Epileptic classification with deep transfer learning based feature fusion algorithm. IEEE Trans. Cogn. Dev. Syst. (2021). https://doi.org/10.1109/TCDS.2021.3064228
4. Hu, D., Cao, J., Lai, X., Wang, Y., Wang, S., Ding, Y.: Epileptic state classification by fusing hand-crafted and deep learning EEG features. IEEE Trans. Circuits Syst. II Exp. Briefs **68**(4), 1542–1546 (2021). https://doi.org/10.1109/TCSII.2020.3031399
5. Hu, D., Cao, J., Lai, X., Liu, J., Wang, S., Ding, Y.: Epileptic signal classification based on synthetic minority oversampling and blending algorithm. IEEE Trans. Cogn. Dev. Syst. **13**, 368–382 (2020). https://doi.org/10.1109/TCDS.2020.3009020
6. Cao, J., et al.: Unsupervised eye blink artifact detection from EEG with gaussian mixture model. IEEE J. Biomed. Health Inf. **25**, 2895–2905 (2021). https://doi.org/10.1109/JBHI.2021.3057891
7. Temko, A., Thomas, E., Marnane, W., Lightbody, G., Boylan, G.: EEEG-based neonatal seizure detection with support vector machines. Clin. Neurophysiol. **122**(3), 464–473 (2011)
8. James, D., Xie, X., Eslambolchilar, P.: A discriminative approach to automatic seizure detection in multichannel EEG signals. In: 2014 22nd European Signal Processing Conference (EUSIPCO), pp. 2010–2014. IEEE (2014)
9. Parvez, M.Z., Paul, M., Antolovich, M.: Detection of pre-stage of epileptic seizure by exploiting temporal correlation of EMD decomposed EEG signals. J. Med. Bioeng. **4**(2), 1–7 (2015)
10. Abbasi, M.U., Rashad, A., Basalamah, A., Tariq, M.: Detection of epilepsy seizures in neo-natal EEG using LSTM architecture. IEEE Access **7**, 179074–179085 (2019)
11. Ansari, A.H., Cherian, P.J., Caicedo, A., Naulaers, G., De Vos, M., Van Huffel, S.: Neonatal seizure detection using deep convolutional neural networks. Int. J. Neural Syst. **29**(4), 1850011 (2019)
12. Cao, J., Zhu, J., Hu, W., Kummert, A.: Epileptic signal classification with deep EEG features by stacked CNNs. IEEE Trans. Cogn. Dev. Syst. **12**(4), 709–722 (2019)

13. Geertsema, E.E., et al.: Automated video-based detection of nocturnal convulsive seizures in a residential care setting. Epilepsia **59**, 53–60 (2018)
14. Ntonfo, G.M.K., Ferrari, G., Raheli, R., Pisani, F.: Low-complexity image processing for real-time detection of neonatal clonic seizures. IEEE Trans. Inf Technol. Biomed. **16**(3), 375–382 (2012)
15. Lu, H., Pan, Y., Mandal, B., Eng, H.-L., Guan, C., Chan, D.W.: Quantifying limb movements in epileptic seizures through color-based video analysis. IEEE Trans. Biomed. Eng. **60**(2), 461–469 (2012)
16. Cuppens, K., Lagae, L., Ceulemans, B., Van Huffel, S., Vanrumste, B.: Automatic video detection of body movement during sleep based on optical flow in pediatric patients with epilepsy. Med. Biol. Eng. Comput. **48**(9), 923–931 (2010)
17. Cuppens, K., et al.: Using spatio-temporal interest points (STIP) for myoclonic jerk detection in nocturnal video. In: 2012 Annual International Conference of the IEEE Engineering in Medicine and Biology Society, pp. 4454–4457. IEEE (2012)
18. Karayiannis, N.B., Tao, G., Frost, J.D., Jr., Wise, M.S., Hrachovy, R.A., Mizrahi, E.M.: Automated detection of videotaped neonatal seizures based on motion segmentation methods. Clin. Neurophysiol. **117**(7), 1585–1594 (2006)
19. Achilles, F., Tombari, F., Belagiannis, V., Loesch, A.M., Noachtar, S., Navab, N.: Convolutional neural networks for real-time epileptic seizure detection. Comput. Meth. Biomech. Biomed. Eng. Imaging Vis. **6**(3), 264–269 (2018)
20. Yang, Y., Sarkis, R., El Atrache, R., Loddenkemper, T., Meisel, C.: Video-based detection of generalized tonic-clonic seizures using deep learning. IEEE J. Biomed. Health Inform. **25**, 2997–3008 (2021)
21. Mporas, I., Tsirka, V., Zacharaki, E.I., Koutroumanidis, M., Megalooikonomou, V.: Online seizure detection from EEG and ECG signals for monitoring of epileptic patients. In: Likas, A., Blekas, K., Kalles, D. (eds.) SETN 2014. LNCS (LNAI), vol. 8445, pp. 442–447. Springer, Cham (2014). https://doi.org/10.1007/978-3-319-07064-3_37
22. Mporas, I., Tsirka, V., Zacharaki, E.I., Koutroumanidis, M., Richardson, M., Megalooikonomou, V.: Seizure detection using EEG and ECG signals for computer-based monitoring, analysis and management of epileptic patients. Exp. Syst. Appl. **42**(6), 3227–3233 (2015)
23. Milošević, M., et al.: Automated detection of tonic-clonic seizures using 3-d accelerometry and surface electromyography in pediatric patients. IEEE J. Biomed. Health Inform. **20**(5), 1333–1341 (2015)
24. Aghaei, H., Kiani, M.M., Aghajan, H.: Epileptic seizure detection based on video and EEG recordings. In: 2017 IEEE Biomedical Circuits and Systems Conference (BioCAS), pp. 1–4. IEEE (2017)
25. Alving, J., Beniczky, S.: Diagnostic usefulness and duration of the inpatient long-term video-EEG monitoring: findings in patients extensively investigated before the monitoring. Seizure **18**(7), 470–473 (2009)
26. Velis, D., Plouin, P., Gotman, J., da Silva, F.L., ILAE DMC Subcommittee on Neurophysiology: Recommendations regarding the requirements and applications for long-term recordings in epilepsy (2007)
27. Rubboli, G., et al.: A European survey on current practices in epilepsy monitoring units and implications for patients' safety. Epilepsy Behav. **44**, 179–184 (2015)
28. Handayani, D., Yaacob, H., Wahab, A., Alshaikli, I.F.T.: Statistical approach for a complex emotion recognition based on EEG features. In: 2015 4th International Conference on Advanced Computer Science Applications and Technologies (ACSAT), pp. 202–207 (2015). https://doi.org/10.1109/ACSAT.2015.54

29. Antoniol, G., Rollo, V.F., Venturi, G.: Linear predictive coding and cepstrum coefficients for mining time variant information from software repositories. In: Proceedings of the 2005 International Workshop on Mining Software Repositories, pp. 1–5 (2005)

30. Laptev, I.: On space-time interest points. Int. J. Comput. Vis. **64**(2–3), 107–123 (2005)

31. Fernández, A., Garcia, S., Herrera, F., Chawla, N.V.: Smote for learning from imbalanced data: progress and challenges, marking the 15-year anniversary. J. Artif. Intell. Res. **61**, 863–905 (2018)

# A Tensor-Based Frequency Features Combination Method for Brain–Computer Interfaces

Yu Pei[1,2] , Tingyu Sheng[3] , Zhiguo Luo[1,4] , Liang Xie[1,4(✉)] , Weiguo Li[2], Ye Yan[1,4] , and Erwei Yin[1,4]

[1] Tianjin Artificial Intelligence Innovation Center (TAIIC), Tianjin 300450, China
[2] School of Software, Beihang University, Beijing 100000, China
[3] Tianjin University, Tianjin 300000, China
[4] National Institute of Defense Technology Innovation, Academy of Military Sciences, Beijing 100081, China

**Abstract.** With the development of the brain-computer interface (BCI) community, motor imagery-based BCI system using electroencephalogram (EEG) has attracted increasing attention because of its portability and low cost. Concerning the multi-channel EEG, the frequency component is one of the most critical features. However, insufficient extraction of it hindered the development and application of MI-BCIs. To deeply mine the frequency information, we constructed a new feature set based on tensor-to-vector projection (TVP), fast fourier transform (FFT), common spatial pattern (CSP), and feature fusion. We designated it the tensor-based frequency feature combination (TFFC). With two datasets, we use different classifiers to compare TFFC with the state-of-the-art methods. The experimental results showed that our proposed TFFC could robustly improve the classification accuracy ($p < 0.01$), which approximately 5%. Also, a complementarity between weighted narrowband features (wNBFs) and broadband features (BBFs) was observed from the averaged fusion ratio. This article certificates the importance of frequency information in the MI-BCI system and may provide a new direction for designing a feature set of MI-EEG.

**Keywords:** Brain-computer interface (BCI) · Electroencephalogram (EEG) · Motor imagery (MI) · Common spatial pattern (CSP) · Tensor-to-vector projection (TVP) · Fast fourier transformation (FFT)

## 1 Introduction

The brain-computer interface (BCI) is a communication control system directly established between the brain and external devices (computers or other electronic devices), using signals generated during brain activity [23]. BCIs have shown potentials in applying various fields such as communication, control, and rehabilitation [1]. Electroencephalogram (EEG) is one of the most common signals used for building a BCI system

Tianjin Artificial Intelligence Innovation Center (TAIIC), Tianjin, 300450, China.

F. Sun et al. (Eds.): ICCSIP 2021, CCIS 1515, pp. 511–526, 2022.
https://doi.org/10.1007/978-981-16-9247-5_40

because of its cost-effectiveness, noninvasive implementation, and portability. Throughout numerous BCI studies, growing attention has been dedicated to analyzing EEG signals, especially by movement imagination, called motor imagery (MI) [12,18]. This interest is due to MI-BCI's ability to allow both healthy and disabled people to self-regulate brain signals without an external stimulus to control electronic devices. No external stimulus, which is a distinctive feature of the MI-BCI, brings its excellent application potentials.

The MI-BCI system's framework is based on the fact that the brain's activity in a specific area will be changed when the patients (or subjects) imagine moving any part of their bodies [17]. The spatial distribution and frequency-band's energy are two essential aspects of the EEG characteristics of MI [14]. Around the design of the spatial filter, a large amount of work has been produced to decode the MI-EEG signals [9, 10, 22]. Among these works, the most important one is the CSP algorithm, which is the root node of other algorithms, and a large amount of work is derived from it. CSP-rank is a filtering channel selection algorithm [2], which is used to remove redundant channels while improving BCI systems' performance. It sorts the importance of channels according to the coefficients of spatial filters, and the optimal channel sets correspond to the highest cross-validation accuracy. For the same channel selection problem, CCS-CSP used a correlation-based method to select the channels that contained more correlated information [8]. To include a spatial priority in the learning process, SRCSP added a regularization term that penalizes spatially non-smooth filters [13]. Because the L1-norm has lower sensitivity to the outlier, DRL1-CSP [9] defined a new L1-norm-based feature ranking function to select the more efficient features. Also, DRL1-CSP further used Dempster-Shafer Theory to fuse the L1-norm-based feature ranking and Fisher scores ranking to rearrange the importance of features to build a more robust feature selection mechanism.

We found a commonality after sorting out these works: Almost all of these methods use 8–30 Hz band-pass filters. Therefore, in this article, the features extracted by these methods are called broadband features (BBFs).

Moreover, the FBCSP architecture created another trend [3,4]. This architecture uses multiple narrowband bandpass filters rather than classic single bandpass filter and successfully extracts narrowband features related to MI. This architecture also has achieved good results on public datasets. Based on the FBCSP framework, many works has also been derived. Nevertheless, these methods are very dependent on feature selection. These methods calculate features in each narrow frequency band and select the $k$ frequency bands (features) with the most discriminative ability, which is an unfavorable operation.

To this end, we constructed a spatial-spectrum tensor based on FFT and used a tensor analysis method, named UMLDA [16], to extract more discriminative wNBFs hidden in narrow frequency bands. We fused these features with BBFs to obtain a more robust feature set named TTFC. Classifiers trained on this feature set have better classification performance. To our knowledge, we are the first team to use tensor analysis and feature fusion methods to study the fusion of broadband information and narrowband information in the field of BCI. The contribution of this article can be summarized as follows:

1. A spatial-spectrum tensor was constructed by FFT.
2. The wNBFs were extracted by the tensor analysis method named UMLDA.
3. The BBFs and wNBFs were fused to obtained a more robust feature set named TFFC.

The remainder of this article is organized as follows. Section 2 discusses the methods used in our study. In Sect. 3, we briefly introduce our dataset. The baseline methods and the experimental results are discussed in Sect. 4. Finally, Sect. 5 concludes this article.

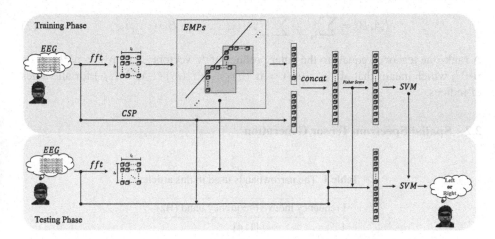

**Fig. 1.** Overall Architecture. The training phase is divided into two branches. In the first branch, the segmented MI-EEG trial is processed by band-pass filtering and FFT transform to construct the spatial-spectrum tensor. The UMLDA algorithm projects the spatial-spectrum tensor into a feature vector, which is the wNBFs. In the second branch, the CSP algorithm extracts a feature vector of length 6, the BBFs, from the segmented and band-pass filtered MI-EEG trial. The classifier is trained on the TFFC, which is a combination of wNBFs and BBFs. The downward arrow (↓) in the picture represents the parameters that need to be learned in the training set.

## 2 Method

This paper follows the notation conventions in multilinear algebra, pattern recognition, and adaptive learning literature. Vectors are denoted by lowercase boldface letters, e.g., $\mathbf{x}$; matrices by uppercase boldface, e.g., $\mathbf{X}$; and tensors by calligraphic letters, e.g., $\mathcal{X}$. Their elements are denoted with indices in parentheses. Indices are denoted by lowercase letters, spanning the range from 1 to the uppercase letter of the index, e.g., $p = 1, 2, ..., P$. In addressing part of a vector/matrix/tensor, ":" denotes the full range of the respective index and $n_1:n_2$ denotes indices ranging from $n_1$ to $n_2$. In this paper, only real-valued data are considered. The overall architecture of our method is shown in Fig. 1, and more details are as below:

## 2.1  Tensor Algebra

An $N$th-order tensor is denoted as $\mathcal{A} \in \mathbb{R}^{I_1 \times I_1 \times \cdots \times I_N}$ [6]. It is addressed by $N$ indices $i_n, n = 1, 2, ..., N$, and each $i_n$ addresses the $n$-mode of $\mathcal{A}$. The $n$-mode product of a tensor $\mathcal{A}$ by a matrix $\mathbf{U} \in \mathbb{R}^{J_n \times I_n}$, denoted by $\mathcal{A} \times_n \mathbf{U}$, is a tensor with entries

$$(\mathcal{A} \times_n \mathbf{U})(i_1, ..., i_{n-1}, j_n, i_{n+1}, ... i_N)$$
$$= \sum_{i_n} \mathcal{A}(i_1, ..., i_N) \cdot \mathbf{U}(j_n, i_n). \tag{1}$$

The scalar product of two tensors, $\mathcal{A}, \mathcal{B} \in \mathbb{R}^{I_1 \times I_1 \times \cdots \times I_N}$ is defined as

$$\langle \mathcal{A}, \mathcal{B} \rangle = \sum_{i_1} \cdots \sum_{i_N} \mathcal{A}(i_1, ..., i_N) \cdot \mathcal{B}(i_1, ..., i_N) \tag{2}$$

A rank-one tensor $\mathcal{A}$ equals to the outer product of $N$ vectors: $\mathcal{A} = \mathbf{u}^{(1)} \circ \mathbf{u}^{(2)} \circ \cdots \circ \mathbf{u}^{(N)}$, which means that $\mathcal{A}(i_1, ..., i_N) = \mathbf{u}^{(1)}(i_1) \cdot \mathbf{u}^{(2)}(i_2) \cdots \mathbf{u}^{(N)}(i_N)$ for all values of indices.

## 2.2  Spatial-Spectrum Tensor Generation

Table 1. The narrowbands used in this article

| Frequency index | Frequency band (Hz) |
| --- | --- |
| 1 | [1, 4] |
| 2 | [4, 8] |
| 3 | [8, 12] |
| 4 | [12, 16] |
| 5 | [16, 20] |
| 6 | [20, 24] |
| 7 | [24, 30] |
| 8 | [30, 35] |
| 9 | [35, 40] |

The original segmented EEG data is $M$-order tensor $\mathcal{X}_{eeg} \in \mathbb{R}^{I_T \times I_C}$, where the number of modes $M$ is 2, $I_C$ is the number of channels, and $I_T$ is the number of sample points. A transformation from spatial-temporal formulation to spatial-spectrum formulation is desperately needed to conduct a spatial-spectrum tensor analysis. We use Fast Fourier Transform (FFT) to complete the purpose (Table 1).

$$\mathcal{X}'_{eeg} = fft(\mathcal{X}_{eeg}) \tag{3}$$

$fft(\bullet)$ calculates the one-sided FFT along with the first mode with 1024 points. Note that the frequency components in $\mathcal{X}'$ are under $f_s$ according to Nyquist sampling theory, where $f_s = \frac{F_s}{2}$ and the $F_s$ is the sampling frequency. The motor imagery-related frequency components are not high. Since the frequency components related to motor imagery are mainly located between 8 Hz and 30 Hz, we need to extract the components of interest from $\mathcal{X}'$ and discarded the unrelated parts. Following the FBCSP algorithm's setting, we established nine narrow frequency bands to extract the interested components. The extraction process is defined below.

$$\mathcal{X}_F(i,j) = log((\frac{\sum_{k=a_i}^{b_i} \mathcal{X}'_{eeg}(k,j)}{b_i - a_i + 1})^2)$$

$$a_i = \frac{l_i \times 1023}{f_s} + 1, b_i = \frac{h_i \times 1023}{f_s} + 1 \qquad (4)$$

where $l_i$ and $h_i$ are the lower cut-off frequency and the upper cut-off frequency of the $i$-th frequency band. The $\mathcal{X}_F \in \mathbb{R}^{I_F \times I_C}$ is the spatial-spectrum tensor we wanted, where the $I_F$ is nine.

## 2.3   Common Spatial Pattern Extraction

The CSP algorithm is an effective spatial filtering method commonly used to extract features in MI-based BCI systems. The spatial filters are considered projection vectors and are calculated to maximize the variance of one class while minimizing the other class's variance. Consider two classes of EEG signals $\mathbf{X}_{i,1}, \mathbf{X}_{i,2} \in \mathbb{R}^{I_T \times I_C}$ from the experimental $i$th trial, where $I_C$ is the number of channels, and $I_T$ denotes the number of sampling points. The spatial covariance matrix of class c is computed as follows:

$$\sum_c = \frac{1}{n_c} \sum_{i=1}^{n_c} \mathbf{X}_{i,c}^T \mathbf{X}_{i,c} \qquad (5)$$

where $n_c$ represents the number of trials in class c. Then, the spatial filter that maximizes the variance of one class and minimizes the variance of the other can be calculated by

$$\mathbf{J}_c(w) = \frac{w^T \sum_c w}{w^T \sum_{\bar{c}} w} \quad s.t. \|w\|_2 = 1 \qquad (6)$$

where $w$ is the spatial filter. The optimization of the Rayleigh quotient can be converted to the generalized eigenvalue problem

$$\sum_c w = \lambda \sum_{\bar{c}} w \qquad (7)$$

where $\lambda$ and $w$ are the generalized eigenvalue and eigenvector. The spatial filters $\mathbf{W}_{csp}$ are formed by eigenvectors corresponding to $m$ maximum and minimum eigenvalues.

The projection signal $\mathbf{Z}$ of the signal trial is given by

$$\mathbf{Z} = \mathbf{W}_{csp}\mathbf{X} \qquad (8)$$

Then, the $p$th feature of the single trial can be obtained as follows:

$$f_p = log(\mathbf{Z}_p \mathbf{Z}_p^T) \qquad (9)$$

where $\mathbf{Z}_p$ is the $p$th row of $\mathbf{Z}$ ($p = 1, 2, ..., 2m$). And $\mathbf{f}_{csp}$ is the final feature vector, where $\mathbf{f}_{csp} = [f_1, f_2, \cdots, f_{2m}] \in \mathbb{R}^{2m}$.

## 2.4  Multilinear Spatial-Spectrum Feature Extraction

The tensor's projection has two types which are tensor-to-tensor projection (TTP) [15] and tensor-to-vector projection (TVP) [16]. We used the UMLDA algorithm, a TVP method, to project a tensor $\mathcal{X} \in \mathbb{R}^{I_1 \times I_1 \times \cdots \times I_N}$ to a vector $\mathbf{y} \in \mathbb{R}^P$ by a set of elementary multilinear projections (EMPs) learned from data, denoted as $\{\mathbf{u}_p^{(1)^T}, \mathbf{u}_p^{(2)^T}, \cdots, \mathbf{u}_p^{(N)^T}\}, p = 1, 2, \cdots, P$. $P$ is the number of components we wanted and the $p$th component of $\mathbf{y}$ is obtained from the $p$th EMP as $\mathbf{y}(p) = \mathcal{X} \times_1 \mathbf{u}_p^{(1)^T} \times_2 \mathbf{u}_p^{(2)^T} \cdots \times_N \mathbf{u}_p^{(N)^T}$. The UMLDA's objective is to determine a set of P EMPs $\{\mathbf{u}_p^{(n)^T}, n = 1, \cdots, N\}_{p=1}^P$ that maximize the scatter ratio while producing features with zero correlation. In this study, $N$ is 2 corresponding to space mode and spectrum mode, and P is set to 50. We apply the UMLDA algorithm on the space-spectrum tensor $\mathcal{X}_F$ as below:

$$\mathbf{f}_{ss}(p) = \mathcal{X}_F \times_1 \mathbf{u}_p^{(1)^T} \times_2 \mathbf{u}_p^{(2)^T}, p = 1, 2, \cdots, P. \tag{10}$$

where $\mathbf{f}_{ss} \in \mathbb{R}^P$ is the extracted wNBFs.

## 2.5  Features Fusion and Fisher Score Rank

We use vector concatenation to fuse features from CSP algorithm and UMLDA algorithm.

$$\mathbf{F} = concat(\mathbf{f}_{csp}, \mathbf{f}_{ss}) \tag{11}$$

where $\mathbf{F} \in \mathbb{R}^{2m+P}$ is the fused feature vector.

As more features can not improve the training accuracy, we need a feature selection mechanism to find out the most discriminative features. After feature extraction, we employed a Fisher score strategy for feature selection [5]. The Fisher score is defined as

$$S_F = \frac{|\mu_1 - \mu_2|^2}{\sigma_1 + \sigma_2} \tag{12}$$

where $\mu_i$ and $\sigma_i$ denote the mean and variance of class $i$ over an individual feature. We sort these features in descending order by the value of $S_F$, and then take the top k features to train the classifiers. The optimal $k$ is calculated by 10-fold cross-validation.

## 2.6  Classifier Tool

The support vector machine (SVM) is used in this work, which finds a hyperplane to segment the two classes. This hyperplane can be represented as $\mathbf{w}^T \mathbf{x} + b = 0$, where $\mathbf{w} \in \mathbb{R}^d$ denotes the weight vector and $b$ denotes the bias [11]. The principle of the segmentation is to maximize margins between two classes and, finally, transform the problem into a convex quadratic programming problem [7], in which

$$\min_{b, \mathbf{w}, \xi} \frac{1}{2} \|\mathbf{w}\|^2 + C \cdot \sum_{i=1}^n \xi_i \tag{13}$$

$$s.t. \quad y_i(\mathbf{w}^T \mathbf{x}^{(i)} + b) \geqslant 1 - \xi_i, \xi_i > 0, i = 1, 2, ..., n.$$

where $\mathbf{x}^{(i)}$ denotes the feature vector of the $i$th training sample, $\xi$ denotes the slack variable, $C$ denotes the penalty parameter of the error term, and $\mathbf{y}$ denotes the class label [19]. We used the radial basis function (RBF) kernel in this work.

## 3  Data Acquisition and Pre-processing

(See Table 2)

**Table 2.** Statistics of the two datasets

|  | Number of subjects | Days per subject | Number of channels | Sample rate (Hz) | Trials per subject |
|---|---|---|---|---|---|
| Dataset 1 | 7 | 3 | 59 | 1000 | 400 |
| Dataset 2 | 7 | 1 | 59 | 100 | 200 |

### 3.1  Participants in Dataset 1

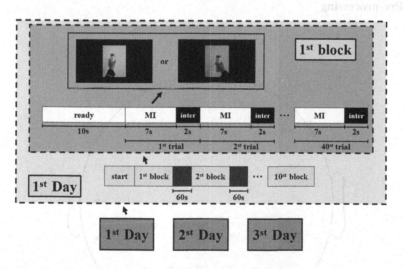

**Fig. 2.** Each subject needs to complete a motor imagery experiment three times on different days. Each experiment includes 10 blocks. Each subject has 10-s preparation time before the start of each block. There is a 60-s interval between blocks.

Seven subjects (aged 23–26: one female and six males) participated in the experiments with written consent. Among them, 6 subjects (S2–S7) were naive BCI users, and only one (S1) had a previous BCI experiment. The overall design of our experiment was shown in Fig. 2. Each subject needed to conduct three successive days of experiments. Each day of the experiment was divided into 10 blocks; each block included 40 trials, where 20 trials were for left-hand motor imagery, and 20 trials were for right-hand motor imagery. We obtained 400 (40 × 10) trials for one subject in one day. We used $Sx.y$ to represent the experiment of the $x$th subject in the $y$th day. At the beginning of the experiment, the subjects were seated comfortably in a chair with armrests 60 (±5) cm from a 20-in LCD monitor (refresh rate: 60 Hz and resolution: 1600 × 1200). During the experiment, participants were asked to relax and minimize their eye and muscle movements.

### 3.2    Participants in Dataset 2

Dataset 2 was from BCI-Competition-IV-1. Dataset 2 was recorded from seven subjects (A, B, C, D, E, F, G), including four real human subjects (named A, B, F, G), and three artificially generated "participants" (named C, D, E). Two motor imagery classes were selected for each subject from the three classes: left hand, right hand, and foot. Here we only used the calibration data because of the complete marker information. There were 200 trials for each subject. We randomly split these trials into ten blocks for 10-fold cross-validation. The details of the competition, including ethical approval and the raw data, can be downloaded from http://www.bbci.de/competition/iv/.

### 3.3    Pre-processing

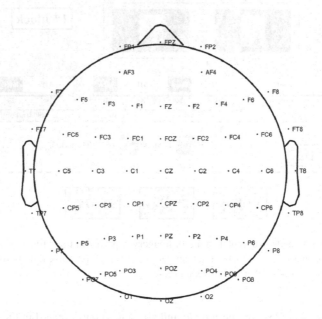

**Fig. 3.** Location of electrodes.

In each experiment, 59 EEG electrodes were used to record the EEG signals, with a sample rate of 1000 Hz for dataset 1 and 100 Hz for dataset 2. The EEG electrodes' location configuration is shown in Fig. 3. The EEG electrodes' impedances were maintained below $20\,k\Omega$ during the entire experiment and checked before the start of each phase. Each sample was segmented from [0, 4] s for dataset 1 and [0 2.5] s for dataset 2 by marks. To reduce the high computational burden from the sample rate of $1000\,Hz$ for dataset 1, we downsample it into $200\,Hz$. For the CSP algorithm, the recorded EEG signals were band-passed with a 10-order Butterworth filter between $8\,Hz$ and $30\,Hz$; For the UMLDA algorithm, the recorded EEG signals were band-passed filtered with a 10-order Butterworth filter between $0.1\,Hz$ and $40\,Hz$.

# 4    Results

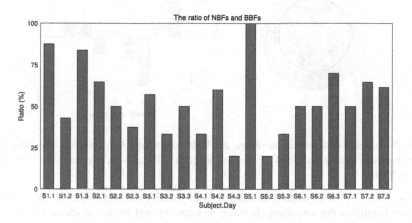

**Fig. 4.** The ratio of number of selected wNBFs and number of selected BBFs.

**Table 3.** Paired $t$-Test ($\alpha = 0.01$) for Table 4. **Boldface** Highlights significant differences.

| $\alpha = 0.01$ | | SVM | | | NN | | |
|---|---|---|---|---|---|---|---|
| | | CSP | UMLDA | FBCSP | CSP | UMLDA | FBCSP |
| TFFC | SVM | **0.0000** | **0.0000** | **0.0000** | **0.0000** | **0.0000** | **0.0000** |
| | NN | **0.0013** | **0.0002** | **0.0029** | **0.0000** | **0.0001** | **0.0000** |

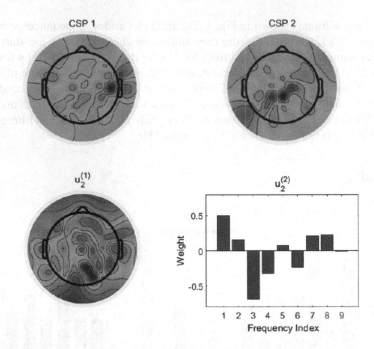

**Fig. 5.** The selected CSP projection vectors and EMP for subject A in dataset 2. The sub-pictures in the upper row are the selected CSP projection vectors. The sub-pictures in bottom row are the selected EMP.

**Table 4.** Mean (%) and standard deviation (%) of baselines methods and the TFFC method. **Boldface** highlights the maximum classification accuracy and minimum stantard deviation for individual classifiers.

| Subjects | SVM | | | | NN | | | |
|---|---|---|---|---|---|---|---|---|
| | CSP | UMLDA | FBCSP | **TFFC** | CSP | UMLDA | FBCSP | **TFFC** |
| A | 63.00 | 56.50 | 79.00 | **88.50** | 60.00 | 67.00 | 78.00 | **87.50** |
| B | 68.50 | 50.50 | 69.50 | **70.00** | 69.50 | 60.00 | 59.00 | 68.50 |
| C | 84.50 | 44.00 | 78.00 | **83.00** | 81.00 | 55.50 | 72.50 | 79.00 |
| D | 94.50 | 69.50 | 84.00 | **95.00** | 91.50 | 68.00 | 82.50 | **93.00** |
| E | 95.50 | 74.00 | 83.00 | **96.50** | 97.00 | 72.50 | 78.50 | 95.00 |
| F | 74.50 | 67.00 | 82.50 | **94.50** | 71.00 | 64.50 | 83.50 | **91.50** |
| G | 93.50 | 70.50 | 91.00 | **94.00** | 90.50 | 70.50 | 87.50 | **94.50** |
| S1.1 | 59.75 | 63.75 | 58.00 | **71.50** | 63.25 | 63.00 | 54.50 | **69.00** |
| S1.2 | 70.75 | 70.75 | 74.50 | **77.50** | 65.00 | 68.75 | 67.75 | **72.25** |
| S1.3 | 60.00 | 63.00 | 65.75 | **69.75** | 59.25 | 63.75 | 60.50 | **65.50** |
| S2.1 | 61.25 | 69.75 | 71.00 | **72.50** | 59.25 | 70.75 | 63.75 | **69.25** |
| S2.2 | 50.50 | 60.75 | **64.50** | 64.25 | 53.75 | 60.25 | 60.25 | **65.75** |

*(continued)*

**Table 4.** (*continued*)

| Subjects | SVM | | | | NN | | | |
|---|---|---|---|---|---|---|---|---|
| | CSP | UMLDA | FBCSP | TFFC | CSP | UMLDA | FBCSP | TFFC |
| S2.3 | 65.25 | 65.50 | 67.50 | **71.00** | **66.00** | 64.00 | 64.50 | 65.75 |
| S3.1 | 54.25 | 58.75 | **64.75** | 62.00 | 54.00 | 59.00 | 59.00 | **59.25** |
| S3.2 | 54.75 | 62.00 | **62.25** | 62.00 | 53.75 | **62.75** | 57.50 | 62.25 |
| S3.3 | 57.00 | 62.00 | 51.25 | **63.50** | 52.75 | 61.25 | 53.25 | **62.00** |
| S4.1 | 82.50 | 88.75 | 95.50 | **96.75** | 85.00 | 86.50 | **97.50** | 95.00 |
| S4.2 | 80.00 | 91.25 | **94.50** | 94.25 | 77.25 | 89.75 | **93.75** | **93.75** |
| S4.3 | 94.50 | 90.00 | 94.00 | **97.50** | 95.50 | 90.75 | 94.50 | **98.25** |
| S5.1 | **67.00** | 63.00 | 52.50 | 63.00 | **68.25** | 61.75 | 53.75 | 61.50 |
| S5.2 | **63.25** | 60.25 | 57.25 | 61.75 | 57.50 | 59.25 | **62.75** | 60.75 |
| S5.3 | **76.00** | 63.25 | 61.50 | 74.25 | 70.75 | 64.25 | 55.25 | **72.25** |
| S6.1 | 54.00 | **59.50** | 59.25 | 57.50 | 52.75 | 58.50 | 59.00 | **63.75** |
| S6.2 | 62.25 | 61.00 | **72.00** | 64.50 | 56.50 | 61.00 | 59.75 | **63.25** |
| S6.3 | **66.75** | 60.50 | 61.75 | 66.25 | **61.50** | 59.25 | 56.25 | 61.25 |
| S7.1 | 57.25 | 62.50 | 57.00 | **66.25** | 52.25 | **61.75** | 54.00 | 60.75 |
| S7.2 | 57.00 | 59.50 | 57.50 | **62.25** | 53.25 | 61.00 | 58.00 | **61.75** |
| S7.3 | 52.25 | 57.00 | 60.25 | **64.50** | 55.00 | 57.25 | 59.25 | **64.25** |
| Mean | 68.58 | 65.17 | 70.34 | **75.15** | 66.89 | 65.80 | 67.37 | **73.45** |
| Std | 13.99 | **10.66** | 13.25 | 13.66 | 14.17 | **9.21** | 13.82 | 13.71 |

---

**Algorithm 1.** Tensor-Based Frequency Features Combination (TFFC)

**Input:**
The training dataset $\{(\mathcal{X}_{eeg}^{(i)}, \mathbf{Y}^{(i)})\}_{i=1}^{n_{tr}}$;
The number of selected features, $k$;
The number of EMPs, $P$;

**Output:**
$\mathbf{F}'$, $\mathbf{W}_{csp}$ and $\{\mathbf{u}_p^{(n)^T}, n = 1, \cdots, N\}_{p=1}^{P}$.

1: Using (3) and (4) to obtain the $\mathcal{X}_F$.
2: Obtain $\{\mathbf{u}_p^{(n)^T}, n = 1, \cdots, N\}_{p=1}^{P}$. Using the same method as [16] to train EMPs on the training set.
3: Extracting the spatial-spectrum bilinear weighted features $\mathbf{f}_{ss}$, using (10).
4: Using (8) and (9) to obtain $\mathbf{W}_{csp}$ and $\mathbf{f}_{csp}$.
5: Concatenate $\mathbf{f}_{csp}$ and $\mathbf{f}_{ss}$ to form $\mathbf{F}$ by (11).
6: Sort $\mathbf{F}$ in descending order with the Fisher-Score calculated by (12).
7: Selecting the best $k$ features from $\mathbf{F}$ to construct the $\mathbf{F}'$.

---

## 4.1   Baselines and Comparison Criteria

In this work, the decoding accuracies of the different methods were evaluated in Matlab2020a. Computer hardware resources include 32 GB RAM, 2.21 GHz Intel Core I7 CPU. Since each experiment includes 10 blocks, each experiment was also divided into 10 folds according to the 10 blocks, 9 folds are used as the training set and 1 remaining fold is testing set. We did not use the random division method for cross-validation like the other articles, instead, we divide the block as the smallest unit, which can avoid randomness on the experimental results as much as possible. We used 10-fold cross-validation to evaluate the performance of each algorithm. Specifically, each time we select one fold as the testing set and all other folds as the training set and then perform the machine learning process. Repeat this process for ten times. The averaged decoding accuracy overall folds was used as the metric.

The following methods have been chosen for performance comparison.

1. Common Spatial Pattern (CSP) feature extraction. Because of the CSP algorithm's unshakable status in the field of MI-BCIs, we chose it as the baseline algorithm for this research. This feature extraction method has an unshakable position in the field of MI-EEG signal decoding. In the CSP algorithm process, each segmented EEG signal was first filtered by a pass-band filter with [8, 30] Hz and projected by a spatial projection matrix. The column number of the spatial projection matrix was set to 6 as [10].
2. Filter bank common spatial pattern algorithm (FBCSP), which is an extended version of the CSP. FBCSP is an extended version of the CSP. In the FBCSP algorithm, each segmented EEG signal passes through multiple narrowband filters, and the CSP algorithm extracts features in each frequency band. These features form a feature set, and $k$ optimal features are selected as the final feature set through a feature selection method. In this article, we used the mutual-information-based feature selection method and selected 4 pairs of CSP features [4]. The source code can be downloaded from https://github.com/stupiddogger/FBCSP.
3. Uncorrelated multilinear discriminant analysis (UMLDA), which is a framework for the recognition of multidimensional objects, known as tensor objects. We used this method to extract wNBFs and show the SVM classifier's decoding performance when only wNBFs are used.
4. Tensor-based Frequency Features Combination (TTFC) method, which is a feature extraction and fusion method that focuses on both narrowband and broadband features, simultaneously. For wNBFs, this method constructs a spatial-spectrum tensor and uses UMLDA, a tensor analysis method, to extract spatial-spectrum bilinear weighted features. For wNBFs, this method integrates the features extracted by CSP. The overall proposed algorithm was shown in Algorithm 1. We have opened part of the source code and sample data to promote the development of BCI field, which can be downloaded from https://github.com/iuype/TFFC.

To obtain a more objective comparison, the dataset's division is consistent among different algorithms.

### 4.2 Decoding Accuracies

The left part of Table 4 showed the accuracies in the individual day for the four methods when the SVM is used as the classifier. We observed that our TFFC method outperformed the other three approaches, where the average accuracies of TFFC, FBCSP, UMLDA and CSP were 75.15%, 70.34%, 65.17% and 68.58%. In addition, the proposed TFFC consistently outperformed other three methods for all subjects in dataset

2. It had better accuracy than FBCSP in 23 out of 28 subjects, than UMLDA in 25 out of 28 subjects and than CSP in 24 out of 28 subjects. The results indicated that the proposed TFFC method provided a 4.81% improvement with respect to FBCSP, a 9.98% improvement with respect to UMLDA and a 6.57% improvement with respect to CSP.

The right part of the Table 4 showed the accuracies in the individual day for the four methods when the KNN [24] is used as the classifier. We observed that our TFFC method outperformed the other three approaches, where the average accuracies of TFFC, FBCSP, UMLDA and CSP were 73.45%, 67.37%, 65.80% and 66.89%. It had better accuracy than FBCSP in 25 out of 28 subjects, than UMLDA in 24 out of 28 subjects and than CSP in 22 out of 28 subjects. The results indicated that the proposed TFFC method provided a 6.08% improvement with respect to FBCSP, a 7.65% improvement with respect to UMLDA and a 6.56% improvement with respect to CSP.

To verify the reliability of our experimental results, a paired $t$-test was used between the baseline algorithm and our proposed algorithm. Specifically, the matlab function *ttest* was used to test the Table 3. All improvements were statistically significant ($p < 0.01$). The paired $t$-test's results were shown in Table 3. The eight averaged accuracies were denoted as CSP-SVM, UMLDA-SVM, FBCSP-SVM, TFFC-SVM, CSP-NN, UMLDA-NN, FBCSP-NN, TFFC-NN, respectively.

### 4.3   Visualization of Feature Selection

Figure 6 and Fig. 7 showed the influence of the number of selected features on the proposed method's classification accuracy on the training set and the testing set. The dotted line represented the experimental results of each subject on each day. The solid line was the average accuracy of all experimental results. Note that we selected the peak value on each dotted line as the final metric for each experiment.

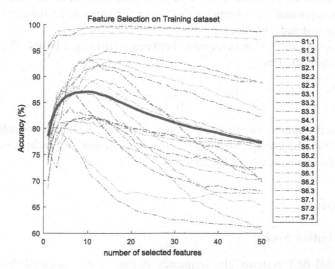

**Fig. 6.** Feature selection on training dataset. The dotted line represents the experimental results of each subject on each day. The solid line is the average of all experimental results.

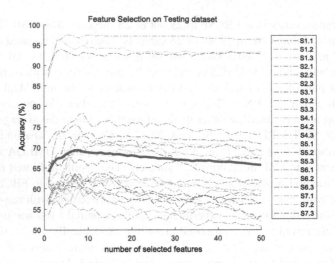

**Fig. 7.** Feature selection on testing dataset. The dotted line represents the experimental results of each subject on each day. The solid line is the average of all experimental results.

### 4.4 Visualization of Feature Fusion

After repeated experiments, the optimal feature selection parameters were determined for each subject. The optimal parameter of feature selection for subject A was 3, which contained two BBFs and one wNBF obtained by (8), (9) and (10). The selected two CSP projection vectors and EMP were visualized in Fig. 5. In Fig. 5, the pictures in the upper row were the selected CSP projection vectors, and the pictures in the bottom row were the selected EMP. We observed that the value of each element in the vector $\mathbf{u}_2^{(2)}$ is not equal, which supported our viewpoint that better features can be obtained by linearly weighting narrowband components.

Figure 4 shows the fusion percentage between wNBFs and BBFs. The fusion percentage was calculated by

$$Ratio = \frac{n_1}{n_1 + n_2} * 100\% \tag{14}$$

where $n_1$ was the number of selected wNBFs and $n_2$ was the number of selected BBFs. We observed that the average fusion percentage was around 50%, which indicated that both types of features were equally important.

## 5    Discussion

### 5.1    Contribution Area

Concerning MI-BCI systems, the frequency is one of the essential feature dimensions besides spatial distribution. Optimization techniques [3,20,21,25] for frequency bands can often bring definite classification performance improvements. However, the state-of-the-art methods have some shortcomings, which have been discussed in the introduction section. Focusing on these problems, we constructed a new feature set, named TFFC, based on CSP, FFT, and UMLDA. To verify the TFFC method, we conducted many experiments on dataset 1 and dataset 2. Experimental results and corresponding significance test were shown in Table 4 and Table 3.

## 5.2 Meaning of Extracted Features

After repeated experiments, the optimal feature selection parameters were determined for each subject. The optimal parameter of feature selection for subject A was 3, which contained two BBFs and one wNBF obtained by (8), (9) and (10). The selected two CSP projection vectors and EMP were visualized in Fig. 5. In Fig. 5, the pictures in the upper row were the selected CSP projection vectors, and the pictures in the bottom row were the selected EMP. The sensorimotor cortex is located in the parietal lobe of the brain and mainly controls the movement of human limbs [14]. We can see that the values around sensorimotor cortex were higher than other place, which indicated that CSP 2, the spatial filter, have captured the neural activity around the sensorimotor cortex. Also, we observed that the value of each element in the vector $u_2^{(2)}$ is not equal, which supported our viewpoint that better features can be obtained by linearly weighting narrowband components.

## 6  Conclusion

As we known, the CSP algorithm only extracted one single broadband feature and the FBCSP extracted feature in multiple narrow frequency bands, which was improved compared to CSP. However, each feature was either selected or discarded, which may lead to the neglect of discriminative fusion information between these features. To further explore the discriminative information related to motor imagery in the frequency band, we used FFT to construct a spatial-spectrum tensor and applied tensor analysis to mine the discriminative information. We successfully extracted discriminative features related to short frequency bands and used feature cascade to fuse them with standard CSP features. The final feature set was named TFFC. The TFFC method can significantly improved the classifiers' classification performance for MI-EEG signals. Our experiment constructed a more robust feature set, verified the complementarity of broadband features and narrowband features, and successfully introduced tensor analysis to classify motor imagery EEG signals, which proved this method's feasibility. This article certificated the importance of frequency information in the MI-BCI system and may provide a new direction for designing a feature set of MI-EEG.

## References

1. Abdulkader, S.N., Atia, A., Mostafa, M.S.M.: Brain computer interfacing: applications and challenges. Egypt. Inf. J. **16**(2), 213–230 (2015)
2. Alotaiby, T., Abd El-Samie, F.E., Alshebeili, S.A., Ahmad, I.: A review of channel selection algorithms for EEG signal processing. EURASIP J. Adv. Sig. Process. **2015**(1), 1–21 (2015)
3. Ang, K.K., Chin, Z.Y., Wang, C., Guan, C., Zhang, H.: Filter bank common spatial pattern algorithm on BCI competition IV Datasets 2a and 2b. Front. Neurosci. **6**, 39 (2012)

4. Ang, K.K., Chin, Z.Y., Zhang, H., Guan, C.: Filter bank common spatial pattern (FBCSP) in brain-computer interface. In: 2008 IEEE International Joint Conference on Neural Networks, pp. 2390–2397. IEEE World Congress on Computational Intelligence. IEEE (2008)
5. Bishop, C.M.: Pattern Recognition and Machine Learning. Springer, New York (2006)
6. Cichocki, A., Zdunek, R., Phan, A.H., Amari, S.: Nonnegative Matrix and Tensor Factorizations: Applications to Exploratory Multi-way Data Analysis and Blind Source Separation. Wiley (2009)
7. Cortes, C., Vapnik, V.: Support-vector networks. Mach. Learn. **20**(3), 273–297 (1995)
8. Jin, J., Miao, Y., Daly, I., Zuo, C., Hu, D., Cichocki, A.: Correlation-based channel selection and regularized feature optimization for MI-based BCI. Neural Netw. **118**, 262–270 (2019)
9. Jin, J., Xiao, R., Daly, I., Miao, Y., Wang, X., Cichocki, A.: Internal feature selection method of CSP based on L1-norm and Dempster-Shafer theory. IEEE Trans. Neural Netw. Learn. Syst. **32**, 4814–4825 (2021)
10. Koles, Z.J., Lazar, M.S., Zhou, S.Z.: Spatial patterns underlying population differences in the background EEG. Brain Topogr. **2**(4), 275–284 (1990)
11. Lal, T.N., et al.: Support vector channel selection in BCI. IEEE Trans. Biomed. Eng. **51**(6), 1003–1010 (2004)
12. Lee, M.H., Fazli, S., Mehnert, J., Lee, S.W.: Subject-dependent classification for robust idle state detection using multi-modal neuroimaging and data-fusion techniques in BCI. Pattern Recogn. **48**(8), 2725–2737 (2015)
13. Lotte, F., Guan, C.: Spatially regularized common spatial patterns for EEG classification. In: 2010 20th International Conference on Pattern Recognition, pp. 3712–3715. IEEE (2010)
14. Lotze, M., Halsband, U.: Motor imagery. J. Physiol. (Paris) **99**(4–6), 386–395 (2006)
15. Lu, H., Plataniotis, K.N., Venetsanopoulos, A.N.: Multilinear principal component analysis of tensor objects for recognition. In: 18th International Conference on Pattern Recognition, ICPR 2006, vol. 2, pp. 776–779. IEEE (2006)
16. Lu, H., Plataniotis, K.N., Venetsanopoulos, A.N.: Uncorrelated multilinear discriminant analysis with regularization and aggregation for tensor object recognition. IEEE Trans. Neural Netw. **20**(1), 103–123 (2008)
17. McFarland, D.J., Miner, L.A., Vaughan, T.M., Wolpaw, J.R.: Mu and beta rhythm topographies during motor imagery and actual movements. Brain Topogr. **12**(3), 177–186 (2000)
18. Nicolas-Alonso, L.F., Gomez-Gil, J.: Brain computer interfaces, a review. Sensors **12**(2), 1211–1279 (2012)
19. Suykens, J.A., Vandewalle, J.: Least squares support vector machine classifiers. Neural Process. Lett. **9**(3), 293–300 (1999)
20. Thomas, K.P., Guan, C., Tong, L.C., Prasad, V.A.: An adaptive filter bank for motor imagery based brain computer interface. In: 2008 30th Annual International Conference of the IEEE Engineering in Medicine and Biology Society, pp. 1104–1107. IEEE (2008)
21. Thomas, K.P., Guan, C., Tong, L.C., Vinod, A.P.: Discriminative filterbank selection and EEG information fusion for brain computer interface. In: 2009 IEEE International Symposium on Circuits and Systems, pp. 1469–1472. IEEE (2009)
22. Wang, Q., et al.: A motor-imagery channel-selection method based on SVM-CCA-CS. Meas. Sci. Technol. **32**(3), 035701 (2020)
23. Wolpaw, J.R., et al.: Brain-computer interface technology: a review of the first international meeting. IEEE Trans. Rehabil. Eng. **8**(2), 164–173 (2000)
24. Zhang, M.L., Zhou, Z.H.: ML-KNN: a lazy learning approach to multi-label learning. Pattern Recogn. **40**(7), 2038–2048 (2007)
25. Zhang, Y., Wang, Y., Jin, J., Wang, X.: Sparse Bayesian learning for obtaining sparsity of EEG frequency bands based feature vectors in motor imagery classification. Int. J. Neural Syst. **27**(02), 1650032 (2017)

# Trajectory Planning of 7-DOF Humanoid Redundant Manipulator Based on Time Optimization

Hui Li, Quan Zhou, Zeyuan Sun, Yifan Ma, Minghui Shen, Jinhong Chen, and Zhihong Jiang[✉]

Beijing Advanced Innovation Center for Intelligence Robots and System, School of Mechatronical Engineering, Beijing Institute of Technology, Beijing 100081, China
jiangzhihong@bit.edu.cn

**Abstract.** Because of redundant degrees of freedom and elbow offset, inverse kinematics (IK) of 7-DOF redundant manipulator is difficult to solve, which brings challenges to trajectory planning. In order to meet the planning requirements in different scenarios, an analytical IK algorithm and a time optimal trajectory planning algorithm are proposed. Specifically, the included angle (arm angle) between the plane of the shoulder, elbow and wrist of the manipulator and the reference plane is parameterized to represent all possible IK solutions within the specified arm angle range. Based on S velocity curve planning, joint angle is interpolated in joint space, and arm angle, end position and attitude are interpolated uniformly in Cartesian space to determine the unique IK solution. Simulation experiments verify the feasibility of the algorithm, and show good motion performance based on the actual manipulator platform.

**Keywords:** 7-DOF manipulator · Inverse kinematics · S velocity curve · Time optimal

## 1 Introduction

Joint manipulator varies from 2-DOF to redundant degrees of freedom [1]. Redundant degrees of freedom give the manipulator good obstacle avoidance ability and high operational flexibility [2,3], but at the same time, IK solution often becomes more difficult. IK solutions are mainly divided into numerical methods and analytical methods. The numerical method is mainly divided into Jacobian method [4] and meta-heuristic method [5]. But the numerical method always has two obvious shortcomings: low real-time performance and difficulty in

Supported by the National Key Research and Development Program of China (2018YFB1305300), the National Natural Science Foundation of China (61733001, 61873039, U1713215, U1913211, U2013602) and the China Postdoctoral Science Foundation under Grant (2020TQ0039, 2021M690017).

F. Sun et al. (Eds.): ICCSIP 2021, CCIS 1515, pp. 527–544, 2022.
https://doi.org/10.1007/978-981-16-9247-5_41

solving multiple IK solutions. In trajectory planning, it is necessary to consider searching multiple IK solutions to determine the best solution [6], and sometimes there is a real-time requirement, so the analytical method is more suitable for our research.

Hollerbach [7] defined the included angle between the arm plane and the reference plane of the manipulator as the arm angle, and confirmed that the configuration with spherical-revolute-spherical (SRS) [8] structure is the best configuration. Kreutz [9] introduced arm angle into redundancy resolution, Dahm [10] defined the circle formed by elbow rotating around the axis of shoulder and wrist as redundant circle, calculated elbow position through redundant circle radius and redundant angle, and solved inverse kinematics problem by analytical method. Shimizu [11], based on Kreutz's work, proposed an IK algorithm with limited joints. On the basis of Shimizu's work, Singh [12] studied the inverse kinematics problem with elbow offset. Furthermore, Sinha studied the joint deviation of shoulder, elbow and wrist in [6]. However, none of the above studies have targeted the trajectory planning, and the optimal IK solution cannot be determined.

Trajectory planning is divided into basic trajectory planning and optimal trajectory planning [13]. Basic trajectory planning includes joint space planning, Cartesian space linear planning, circular arc planning and so on. The impact of joint instantaneous acceleration will lead to vibration, mechanical wear and other problems, and reduce the motion accuracy [14]. Fang [15] introduced the quintic polynomial into iiwa manipulator to ensure the continuity of acceleration, but did not consider the basic trajectory planning. It is worth noting that the existence of redundant degrees of freedom may make the traditional planning algorithm invalid, and as far as we know, almost no literature discloses the trajectory planning algorithm of 7-DOF manipulator in joint space and Cartesian space.

Based on Sinha's work, this paper puts forward a targeted redundant degree of freedom processing algorithm: introducing virtual elbow joint points to simplify IK solution process; limit the rotation range of arm angle to solve the specified range of IK; propose an evaluation function based on joint angular velocity to determine the optimal solution of IK; propose a planning algorithm based on S-speed curve to obtain the optimal time planning. In Cartesian space, there is no algorithm to effectively realize the unified interpolation of attitude and position [1], the corresponding solution is also proposed in this paper.

This article is organized as follows. In Sect. 2, we derived IK algorithm, and then introduced the basic trajectory planning algorithm based on S velocity curve in Sect. 3. The kinematics analysis of planning results is carried out based on Matlab in Sect. 4. Section 5 shows the application of actual manipulator platform. And finally, the conclusion is given in Sect. 6.

# 2    Proposed Inverse Kinematics Algorithm

## 2.1    Manipulator Model

Based on the work of Hollerbach [8], we design the manipulator as SRS structure (see Fig. 1), and its DH parameters are given in Table 1. Compared with DH parameters in [8], the elbow of our manipulator is not on the shoulder-wrist axis, that is, there are offsets between joint 3, 4 and joint 4, 5. The design of elbow joint offset can make the manipulator obtain longer wingspan. The origin of shoulder three-joint coordinate system coincides, elbow joint is offset by 0.03 m, and the origin of wrist three-joint coordinate system coincides.

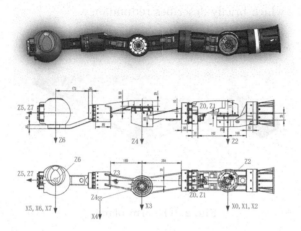

**Fig. 1.** The robot arm model and coordinate system

**Table 1.** DH (modified) parameters for the 7-DOF manipulator

| i | $a_{i-1}(m)$ | $\alpha_{i-1}(rad)$ | $d_i(m)$ | $\theta_i$ | Limits (rad) | |
|---|---|---|---|---|---|---|
| | | | | | Upper | Lower |
| 1 | 0 | 0 | 0 | $\theta_1$ | −2.967 | 2.967 |
| 2 | 0 | $\pi/2$ | 0 | $\theta_2$ | −2.094 | 2.094 |
| 3 | 0 | $-\pi/2$ | 0.4495 | $\theta_3$ | −2.967 | 2.967 |
| 4 | 0.03 | $\pi/2$ | 0 | $\theta_4$ | −2.792 | 2.094 |
| 5 | −0.03 | $-\pi/2$ | −0.4495 | $\theta_5$ | −2.967 | 2.967 |
| 6 | 0 | $\pi/2$ | 0 | $\theta_6$ | −2.181 | 2.181 |
| 7 | 0 | $-\pi/2$ | 0 | $\theta_7$ | −2.967 | 2.967 |

## 2.2   Redundancy Resolution

Hollerbach [8] defines the rotation of elbow joint around the axis connecting shoulder and wrist as self-motion, and defines the angle between the plane where shoulder, elbow and wrist lie and the reference plane as arm angle. In this method, the arm angle is the redundancy angle. As shown in Fig. 2, we define the origin of shoulder three-joint coordinate system as point $B$, elbow coordinate system as point $E$, and wrist three-joint coordinate system as point $W$. What is different from [8] is that we introduce an unbiased elbow joint virtual origin point $E'$ in the arm angle plane, which is the vertical point of point $E$ on the big arm axis and the origin of the third joint coordinate system. The reference plane is defined as the vertical plane where the straight line $BW$ lies, that is, the reference plane of our selection is not fixed, and the arm angle is set as $\beta$ (see Fig. 3), which briefly describes redundancy.

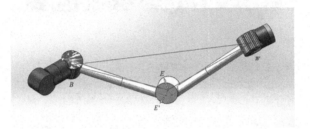

**Fig. 2.** The arm plane

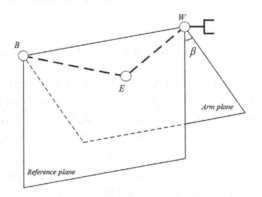

**Fig. 3.** The definition of $\beta$

## 2.3   Redundancy Resolution

Shimizu [12] has proposed the inverse kinematics solution of typical SRS type 7-DOF manipulator with unbiased elbow. For the case of elbow offset, Singh [13] puts forward the inner elbow posture and outer elbow posture of manipulator according to the relative position of elbow, proves that the outer elbow posture can cover a larger space by cosine theorem, and describes all possible postures by generating circles and upper and lower joint circles. The main difference of our work is to describe all the possible postures concisely by introducing virtual elbow joint points.

For each IK problem to be solved, the reference plane is obtained according to the expected terminal position, as shown in Fig. 4.

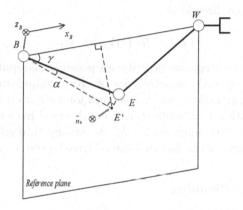

**Fig. 4.** Representation of the origin of the elbow coordinate system below the reference plane

We use cosine theorem for $\Delta BEW$ to calculate the fourth joint rotation angle $\theta_4$ in the outer elbow posture. A temporary coordinate system $\{B\}$ is established at point $B$, which is based on the base coordinate system $\{O\}$. It takes the direction of vector $\boldsymbol{BW}$ as the $x$ axis and the direction perpendicular to the paper plane inward as the $z$ axis. It is easy to get the transformation relationship $_B^O R$ between the two coordinate systems and the representation of point $E'$ under the coordinate system $\{B\}$

$$^{B}\boldsymbol{E'} = (l_{BE'} \cos(\alpha + \gamma), l_{BE'} \sin(\alpha + \gamma), 0) \tag{1}$$

where $l_{BE'}$ is the fixed distance from point $B$ to point $E'$, $\alpha$ is the fixed angle of elbow joint offset, and $\gamma$ is the variable angle related to the terminal position, which can be calculated according to the cosine theorem.

Then, we rotate point $E'$ by $\beta$ radians around the axis where $\boldsymbol{BW}$ is located, and get all possible positions, and then express them in the base coordinate system $\{O\}$:

$$^{O}E' = {}^{O}_{B}R \cdot R\left(BW, \beta\right) \cdot {}^{B}E' \tag{2}$$

where $R\left(BW, \beta\right)$ is the relative rotation matrix obtained after rotating $\beta$ degrees around the axis where $BW$ is located.

We specify the direction vector $n_4$ of the rotation axis of the fourth joint, which is perpendicular to the paper plane inward and can be obtained by cross multiplying the vector $BW$ and the vertical downward vector $n_v$

$$n_4 = BW \times n_v \tag{3}$$

Specially, when vector $BW$ goes straight down, the above formula cannot be calculated, we make the vector $n_4$ the specified value.

Then we rotate vector $n_4$ by $\beta$ radians around the axis of the vector $BW$ to get all the possible directions

$$n_4' = R\left(BW, \beta\right) \cdot n_4 \tag{4}$$

Through the above steps, we describe all possible manipulator postures with $\beta$. According to the special characteristics of SRS manipulator, we can calculate the first joint rotation angle $\theta_1$ and the second joint rotation angle $\theta_2$ from point $^{O}E'$, the third rotation joint angle $\theta_3$ can be obtained from $\theta_1$, $\theta_2$ and $n_4'$, and then solve the last three joint angles $\theta_5$, $\theta_6$ and $\theta_7$ through $^{4}_{7}T$, which is the posture change matrix of the fourth joint relative to the terminal.

## 2.4    Redundancy Planning

We need to filter out IK solutions beyond the joint limit, and then search for the optimal solutions according to the evaluation function

$$F = \sum_{i=7}^{7} k_i \left|\theta_i + \theta_{i''} - 2\theta_{i'}\right| \tag{5}$$

where $\theta_i$ represents the rotation angle of the $i$th joint at the current moment, $\theta_{i'}$ represents the rotation angle of the $i$th joint at the last moment, $\theta_{i''}$ represents the rotation angle of the $i$th joint before the last moment, and $\left|\theta_i + \theta_{i''} - 2\theta_{i'}\right|$ $(i = 1, 2, \cdots 7)$ represents the relative variation of angular velocity of the $i$th joint. When $\theta_i = \theta_{i''}$, the optimization evaluation function degenerates into the sum of joint angle changes with weights, which can satisfy the real-time and non-real-time IK solutions respectively. $k_i$ represents the weight factor of the velocity variation of each joint, which is given by

$$k_i = \sum_{i=1}^{7} \dot{\theta}_{iMax} / \dot{\theta}_{iMax} \tag{6}$$

where $\dot{\theta}_{iMax}$ is the maximum angular velocity of the $i$th joint. The smaller the value of $F$, the better the solution, that is, the optimal solution is the group

with the smallest weighted velocity variation or angular variation. We describe
the IK algorithm as:

$$res = IK(\boldsymbol{\theta}_{init}, \boldsymbol{P}_{final}, \beta_{down}, \beta_{up}) \qquad (7)$$

where $\boldsymbol{\theta}_{init}$ are the current joint angles, $\boldsymbol{P}_{final}$ is the desired posture, and
$[\beta_{down}, \beta_{up}](-\pi \leq \beta_{down} \leq \beta_{up} \leq \pi)$ is the search range of $\beta$.

## 3  Trajectory Planning

Our research focuses on point-to-point (PTP) trajectory planning with initial
and final velocity of zero. Under a given motion mode (such as joint space motion,
Cartesian space linear motion, etc.), the discrete position of each joint angle is
given according to the working cycle of the driving motor, so that the joint acceleration is continuous. In theory, it can replace the traditional quadratic interpolation method and only perform one interpolation. Spatial trajectory planning is
relatively simple and has a large working range, but the terminal postures during the trip is uncontrollable, Cartesian space trajectory planning is controllable,
but it is suitable for small-scale precise operation occasions.

### 3.1  S Speed Curve Planning

S-speed curve has acceleration, uniform speed and deceleration stages. As shown
in Fig. 5, the whole process can describe as follows:

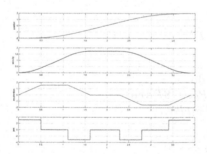

**Fig. 5.** S velocity curve

1) Uniform jerk stage: with constant jerk $j$, the acceleration is increased from 0
   to the set value $a$.
2) Uniform acceleration stage: accelerate with constant acceleration $a$.
3) Uniform jerk stage: with constant jerk $-j$, the acceleration is reduced from
   $a$ to 0.
4) Uniform speed stage: moving at the maximum constant speed $v$.
5) Uniform jerk stage: with constant jerk $-j$, the acceleration is reduced from 0
   to the set value $-a$.

534     H. Li et al.

6) Uniform acceleration stage: decelerate with constant acceleration $-a$.
7) Uniform jerk stage: with constant jerk $j$, the acceleration is increased from $-a$ to 0.

Obviously, the S-speed curve is based on the maximum specified jerk, acceleration and speed, which ensures the continuity of acceleration and has the ability of time optimal control.

## 3.2   Joint Space Trajectory Planning

Trajectory planning in joint space is mainly based on cubic and higher-order polynomials [1], but these methods do not make full use of acceleration and jerk, and it is difficult to realize time optimal control, while S-velocity curve planning can. We describe the algorithm as:

$$res = MoveJ(\boldsymbol{\theta}_{init}, \boldsymbol{P}_{final}) \tag{8}$$

where $res$ is a series of planned joint angles. The planning process is shown in Algorithm 1.

---
**Algorithm 1.** Joint Space Trajectory Planning

---
**Input:** current joint angles $\boldsymbol{\theta}_{init}$, desired pose $\boldsymbol{P}_{final}$;
**Output:** a series of planned joint angles $res$;
1: $\boldsymbol{\theta}_{final} = IK(\boldsymbol{\theta}_{init}, \boldsymbol{P}_{final}, -\pi, \pi)$;
2: **for** i=1:7 **do**
3:     $SPara = SParaCul(\boldsymbol{\theta}_{init}[i], \boldsymbol{\theta}_{final}[i])$;
4:     $T[i] = SPara[k]$;
5: **end for**
6: $T_{max} = max(\boldsymbol{T})$;
7: $num = floor(T_{max}/T_c)$;
8: **for** $i = 1:7$ **do**
9:     $t = 0$;
10:     **for** $j = 1:num$ **do**
11:         $res[i][j] = SPos(t, \boldsymbol{SPara})$;
12:         $t = t + T_c * T[i]/T_{max}$;
13:     **end for**
14: **end for**
15: $res[num+1] = \boldsymbol{\theta}_{final}$;
16: **return** $res$;

---

Firstly, we use the IK method to get desired joint angles $\boldsymbol{\theta}_{final}$, then plan the S velocity curve for the initial and final value of each joint angle so that we can get a series of motion parameters, in which the $k$th parameter is the planning time $T$, find the longest motion time $T_{max}$ among seven joints. Then, the number of planning points is determined by $T_{max}$ and driving motor cycle $T_c$. Finally, a series of joint planning points res can be obtained by sampling according to the function of joint angle with respect to time obtained by S velocity curve planning.

## 3.3  Linear Trajectory Planning in Cartesian Space

Cartesian space planning usually requires controllable terminal position and orientation, that is, terminal position and orientation must be planned at the same time. For redundant manipulators, unlike general six-degree-of-freedom manipulators, redundancy angle brings new challenges to planning. Therefore, it is necessary to plan three key parameters: terminal position, orientation and arm angle at the same time. We describe the algorithm as:

$$res = MoveL(\boldsymbol{\theta}_{init}, \boldsymbol{P}_{final}) \tag{9}$$

The planning process is shown in Algorithm 2.

---

**Algorithm 2.** Linear Trajectory Planning in Cartesian Space

**Input:** current joint angles $\boldsymbol{\theta}_{init}$, desired pose $\boldsymbol{P}_{final}$;
**Output:** a series of planned joint angles $\boldsymbol{res}$;
  1: Calculate $dist$, $\boldsymbol{A}_{rr}$, $\theta_{rr}$, $\beta_{init}$, $\beta_{final}$ and $\boldsymbol{\theta}_{final}$ by $\boldsymbol{\theta}_{init}$ and $\boldsymbol{P}_{final}$;
  2: $\boldsymbol{SPara1} = SParaCul(0, dist)$;
  3: $\boldsymbol{SPara2} = SParaCul(0, \theta_{rr})$;
  4: $\boldsymbol{SPara3} = SParaCul(\beta_{init}, \beta_{final})$;
  5: $\boldsymbol{T}[1] = SPara1[k]$;
  6: $\boldsymbol{T}[2] = SPara2[k]$;
  7: $\boldsymbol{T}[3] = SPara3[k]$;
  8: $T_{max} = Max(\boldsymbol{T})$;
  9: $num = floor(T_{max}/T_c)$;
 10: $\boldsymbol{SPara\_t} = SParaCul(0, 1)$;
 11: Calculate $a_p$, $\boldsymbol{\theta}_{pr}$ and $\beta_p$ by $\boldsymbol{T}$, $T_{max}$ and $\boldsymbol{SPara}$;
 12: **for** $i = 1 : num$ **do**
 13:    Calculate the process position by $a_p$;
 14:    Calculate the process orientation by $\boldsymbol{\theta}_{pr}$ and $\boldsymbol{A}_{rr}$;
 15:    Combine the process position and orientation to get the process pose $\boldsymbol{P}_p$;
 16:    $\boldsymbol{res}[i] = IK(\boldsymbol{\theta}_{init}, \boldsymbol{P}_p, \beta_p[i], \beta_p[i])$;
 17:    $SafeCheck(\boldsymbol{res}[i])$;
 18: **end for**
 19: $\boldsymbol{res}[num+1] = \boldsymbol{\theta}_{final}$;
 20: **return** $\boldsymbol{res}$;

---

Firstly, we plan the S speed curve for the linear motion distance of the terminal, and obtain the motion time $\boldsymbol{T}[1]$. Then, the relative rotation axis $\boldsymbol{A}_{rr}$ and relative rotation angle $\theta_{rr}$ are calculated from the rotation matrix of the terminal relative to the initial posture. We plan the S speed curve for $\theta_{rr}$ to obtain the motion time $\boldsymbol{T}[2]$. Then, we get the initial arm angles $\beta_{init}$ and final arm angles $\beta_{final}$ through the initial and final posture, and then plan the S speed curve for them to obtain the motion time $\boldsymbol{T}[3]$. Then we find out the longest time $T_{max}$ in $T$, and determine the planning points based on $T_{max}$ and $T_c$. It is worth noting that the terminal track is transformed into a straight-line reference equation. We plan the straight line parameter t to realize the smooth interpolation of the position. The relative rotation matrix is obtained by $A_{rr}$ and $\theta_{rr}$, then the process orientation is obtained by combining the initial orientation, and then the unique optimal IK solution under the specified arm angle is obtained by combining the process arm angle $\beta_p$. Because of the inherent problems in Cartesian space planning, such as high joint rate near the singular point, it is necessary to check the safety of the planning points, and stop planning if the speed exceeds the limit. Under normal circumstances, a series of joint planning points res can be obtained.

### 3.4  Circular Trajectory Planning in Cartesian Space

As same as linear trajectory planning, we also plan these three key parameters for circular arc trajectory planning. We describe the algorithm as:

$$res = MoveC(\theta_{init}, p_2, p_3) \tag{10}$$

where $p_2$ is the middle point on the circular trajectory, while the $p_3$ is the final point. The planning process is shown in Algorithm 3.

---

**Algorithm 3.** Circular Trajectory Planning in Cartesian Space

---

**Input:** current joint angles $\theta_{init}$, middle point $p_2$, final point $p_3$;
**Output:** a series of planned joint angles $res$;
  1: Calculate $r$, $A_r$, $\theta_r$, $T_{32}$ of the three-point circle;
  2: Calculate $P_{final}$ by $\theta_{init}, A_r$ and $\theta_r$;
  3: Calculate $\beta_{init}$ and $\beta_{final}$ by $\theta_{init}$ and $P_{final}$;
  4: $SPara1 = SParaCul(0, \theta_r)$;
  5: $SPara2 = SParaCul(\beta_{init}, \beta_{final})$;
  6: $T[1] = SPara1[k]$;
  7: $T[2] = SPara2[k]$;
  8: $T_{max} = Max(T)$;
  9: $num = floor(T_{max}/T_c)$;
 10: Calculate $\theta_p$ and $\beta_p$ by $T$, $T_{max}$ and $SPara$;
 11: **for** $i = 1 : num$ **do**
 12:     Calculate the process position by $r$, $A_r$, $\theta_p$, and $T_{32}$;
 13:     Calculate the process orientation by $\theta_p$ and $A_r$;
 14:     Combine the process position and orientation to get the process pose $P_p$;
 15:     $res[i] = IK(\theta_{init}, P_p, [\beta_p[i], \beta_p[i]])$;
 16:     $SafeCheck(res[i])$;
 17: **end for**
 18: $res[num + 1] = \theta_{final}$;
 19: **return** $res$;

---

Firstly, according to the three-point circular arc composed of the initial point, the middle point and the final point at the terminal, we calculate the geometric parameters of the arc, such as rotation radius $r$, rotation axis $A_r$, rotation angle

$\theta_r$, and the transfer matrix $T_{32}$ from the three-dimensional space to the two-dimensional plane. Then we get $T[1]$, the time needed for position and attitude motion. And then, we get the initial posture $P_{final}$ and final arm angle $\theta_{final}$ from the current joint angles $\theta_{init}$, $A_r$ and $\theta_r$. We plan the S speed curve for the arm angle to obtain the time $T[2]$ required for the arm motion. After getting the planning points, we calculate the process position with $r$, $A_r$ and process rotation angle $\theta_p$ obtained by sampling. The process orientation is obtained by $\theta_p$ and $A_r$, and then the unique optimal IK solution under the specified arm angle is obtained.

Of course, we can also specify the desired attitude in Algorithm 2 or keep the attitude unchanged during planning to meet different working conditions.

## 4  Simulation and Analysis

### 4.1  Accuracy of IK Solution

We specify initial joint angles as $[\theta_1, \theta_2, \cdots, \theta_7]$, and obtain the terminal posture through forward kinematics, and take it as the expected position to do the IK solution. Under the situation of not taking care of obstacles, the range of $\beta$ is $[-\pi, \pi]$. See Table 2 for IK solution and Matlab running time corresponding to different scanning intervals $\Delta\beta$.

**Table 2.** IK results under different $\Delta\beta$

| $\Delta\beta\,(rad)$ | $\theta_1$ | $\theta_2$ | $\theta_3$ | $\theta_4$ | $\theta_5$ | $\theta_6$ | $\theta_7$ | $t(s)$ |
|---|---|---|---|---|---|---|---|---|
| – | −2 | 0.5 | 1.5 | −1 | 1 | 2 | −1 | – |
| 0.01 | −1.999 | 0.499 | 1.502 | −1.000 | 0.998 | 2.001 | −1.001 | 0.063 |
| 0.05 | −1.999 | 0.489 | 1.518 | −1.000 | 0.978 | 2.009 | −1.007 | 0.025 |
| 0.1 | −1.999 | 0.489 | 1.518 | −1.000 | 0.978 | 2.009 | −1.007 | 0.019 |
| 0.5 | −2.008 | 0.537 | 1.439 | −1.000 | 1.076 | 1.968 | −0.979 | 0.015 |

It can be seen that the smaller $\Delta\beta$, the greater the probability of scanning the initial arm angle, and the closer the IK solution is to the given value, but the calculate complexity is also increasing. Therefore, we use trichotomy to scan the arm angle, gradually reduce the scanning range of the optimal arm angle and reduce the scanning interval, so as to improve the search efficiency and accuracy, and generate a series of joint angles based on Monte Carlo method to repeat the above experiments, further verifying the correctness of IK method.

### 4.2  Joint Space Trajectory Planning

We specify initial joint angles as $\theta_{init} = [-1.5, 1, 1, -2, 0, 1, 1]$, then take a group of joint $angle = [-2, -1, 2, -1, 1, 2, -1]$ to obtain the desired position $P_{final}$

through forward kinematics, finally obtain the desired joint angles $P_{final} = [0, -1.95, -0.5, 0.99, -1, 1.97, 1.5]$ through IK method.

As shown in Fig. 6, the curves of joint angle *position*, angular velocity *velocity*, angular acceleration *acceleration* and angular jerk *jerk* related to time $t$ are shown. According to the acceleration curve, the second joint reaches the maximum speed first, indicating that the longest time in this planning appears in the second joint, and other joints take the time required by the second joint to sample the joint position, finally realizing the optimal time planning.

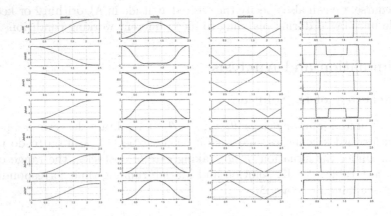

**Fig. 6.** Kinematic parameter of *MoveJ*

## 4.3   Linear Trajectory Planning in Cartesian Space

Firstly, the trajectory and orientation of linear motion are specified, as shown in Fig. 7.

In order to verify the influence of planning arm angle on the stability of trajectory planning of redundant manipulator, we put forward the following three planning strategies and carried out corresponding experiments

1) test1: Three key parameters, namely terminal position, orientation and arm angle, are planned.
2) test2: Only two key parameters, namely terminal position and orientation, are planned, and $\beta$ at next moment is dynamically solved within the specific range that depends on the maximum speed of the third joint and the driving motor cycle. Greedy method is used for optimization, and IK evaluation function is the smallest weighted speed change;
3) test3: on the basis of test2, the IK evaluation function is the smallest weighted angle change.

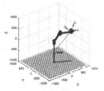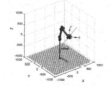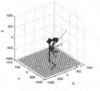

**Fig. 7.** Movement of $MoveL$

See Table 3 with the average running time of the last three experiments, and see Fig. 8 with the kinematic parameters obtained by planning, this time we added the analysis of the arm angle $\beta$.

**Table 3.** Average running time of $MoveL$

| Test | 1 | 2 | 3 |
|------|------|------|------|
| $t(s)$ | 0.117 | 0.563 | 0.557 |

It can be seen from Table 3 and Fig. 8 that different planning strategies lead to different results of joint angles, running time and acceleration curve smoothness. The first strategy not only has the advantages of smooth speed and acceleration, but also has the best real-time and stability. While the effect of the second strategy is close to that of the first strategy, but the joint angle changes a lot, and the time consumption is nearly five times that of the first strategy. And the angle and angular velocity curves of the third strategy are similar to those of the first strategy, though the acceleration curve performed badly, it can be improved by fine interpolation of position again.

In addition, we find that the arm angle of the second strategy remains unchanged during the movement, so we can improve the real-time performance based on the IK method with specified $\beta$. The movement parameters of the fourth joint angle in three experiments are completely consistent, because the fourth joint angle is a function only about the terminal position.

### 4.4 Circular Arc Trajectory Planning in Cartesian Space

Also based on the three planning strategies in the linear trajectory planning, we carried out the experiments test4, test5 and test6 in turn. The trajectory and posture of the specified arc motion are shown in Fig. 9, the average running time of the above three experiments is shown in Table 4, and the kinematic parameters obtained by planning are shown in Fig. 10.

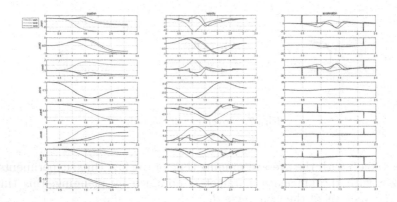

**Fig. 8.** Kinematic parameter of *MoveL*

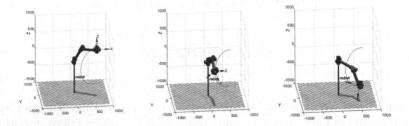

**Fig. 9.** Movement of *MoveL*

We get a similar conclusion with linear trajectory planning, but the latter two strategies have more impact on the acceleration than the linear trajectory planning, so we adjust the arm angle scanning interval $\Delta\beta$ of the second strategy, carried out two groups of experiments test7 ($\Delta\beta = 0.001$ rad) and test8 ($\Delta\beta = 0.0001$ rad), and compared with the results of test5, as shown in Fig. 11.

We can find that the smaller $\Delta\beta$ is, the smoother the motion parameter curve solved by greedy method is, but the acceleration still has an impact. It can be seen from the velocity curve that when $t = 1.35$ s, the acceleration of $\beta$ suddenly changes, so does the joint acceleration. It can be judged that we can get a smooth joint acceleration curve if we carry out S velocity curve planning or polynomial interpolation on $\beta$. However, IK solution based on greedy method is very time consuming. To solve this problem, we can appropriately increase the sampling period for coarse interpolation, and then carry out fine interpolation

**Table 4.** Average running time of *MoveC*

| Test | 4 | 5 | 6 |
|------|-------|-------|-------|
| $t(s)$ | 0.118 | 0.462 | 0.457 |

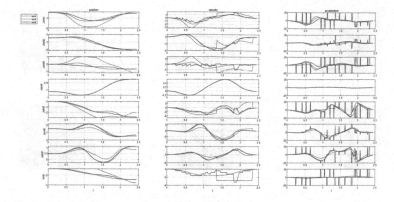

**Fig. 10.** Kinematic parameter of *MoveC*

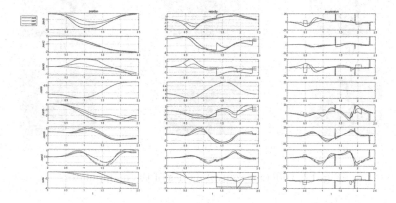

**Fig. 11.** Planning results for different $\Delta\beta$

by polynomial interpolation methods to improve the real-time performance of the second planning strategy.

## 5  Implementation of Manipulator Platform

We complete the construction of hardware platform. In Ubuntu, we added real-time kernel patch Xenomai and installed EtherCAT master station IgH to build real-time Linux operating system. The actual control algorithm runs in C++.

Figure 12 shows the motion. According to the simulation analysis in the Sect. 4, we designed 4 motion stages. In stage 1, the manipulator performs self-motion to show redundancy performance (Fig. 12(a)–(c)). In stage 2, the manipulator moves in a wide range in the joint space (Fig. 12(d)–(f)); In stage 3, the manipulator moves linearly in a small range in Cartesian space (Fig. 12(g)–(i)); In stage 4, the manipulator moves in a small arc in Cartesian space (Fig. 12(j)–(l)). During the motion, the manipulator moves smoothly and meets the requirements of control accuracy, stability and real-time.

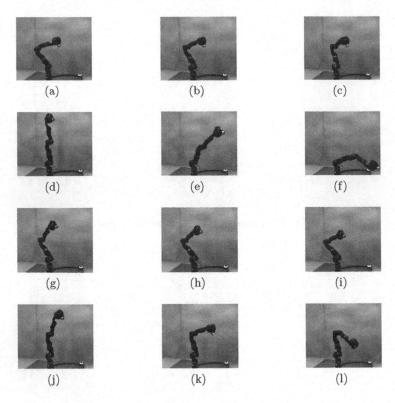

**Fig. 12.** Different control modes of the manipulator

# 6   Conclusion

Taking the 7-DOF redundant manipulator as the research object, we established the D-H model based on Matlab. Based on redundant arm angle and offset elbow angle, we proposed IK method suitable for trajectory planning, and then applied S velocity curve to joint angle, terminal posture and arm angle. Kinematic parameter analysis based on Matlab simulation proved that the fourth joint angle is only related to terminal position. The rest joints are functions of terminal position, orientation and arm angle. The S velocity curve planning of these three key parameters in Cartesian space can significantly reduce the acceleration impact. We verified the feasibility of the algorithm in Matlab. In practical application, we translate the algorithm into C++, and send the planning points of each step to the driving motor in real time, instead of waiting for the whole planning to end, so that we can achieve millisecond real-time performance. Trajectory planning in joint space is highly stable. Based on discrete sampling of desired trajectory, trajectory planning in Cartesian space has high accuracy. However, trajectory planning in Cartesian space has great limitations, one of which is that the expected orientation in the process can easily exceed the maximum rotation range of joints. The strategy based on dynamic solution of arm angle can avoid the joint limit as much as possible, avoid the problem that IK solution cannot be solved under the specified arm angle, and improve the planning success rate.

In the future, we will focus on the planning of arm angle. We hope to improve the trajectory planning algorithm in the presence of obstacles, put obstacles in the rotation space of the arm angle, and limit the rotation range of the arm angle by introducing visual information, so as to avoid obstacles. In addition, the evaluation function of IK can be replaced by an evaluation function that can characterize singular points, such as operability, so as to avoid the singular configuration in the planning process and improve the stability of the terminal motion in Cartesian space.

# References

1. Li, L.I., et al.: Research of trajectory planning for articulated industrial robot: a review. Comput. Eng. Appl. **54**, 36–50 (2018)
2. Luo, R.C., Lin, T.W., Tsai, Y.H.: Analytical inverse kinematic solution for modularized 7-DoF redundant manipulators with offsets at shoulder and wrist. In: 2014 IEEE/RSJ International Conference on Intelligent Robots and Systems. IEEE (2014)
3. Stevenson, R., Shirinzadeh, B., Alici, G.: Singularity avoidance and aspect maintenance in redundant manipulators. In: International Conference on Control. IEEE (2002)
4. Buss, S.R.: Introduction to inverse kinematics with Jacobian transpose, pseudoinverse and damped least squares methods. IEEE Trans. Robot. Autom. **17**(1), 16 (2004)
5. Dereli, S., Köker, R.: A meta-heuristic proposal for inverse kinematics solution of 7-DOF serial robotic manipulator: quantum behaved particle swarm algorithm. Artif. Intell. Rev. **53**(2), 949–964 (2019). https://doi.org/10.1007/s10462-019-09683-x
6. Sinha, A., Chakraborty, N.: Geometric search-based inverse kinematics of 7-DoF redundant manipulator with multiple joint offsets. In: 2019 International Conference on Robotics and Automation (ICRA) (2019)
7. Nakamura, Y., Hanafusa, H.: Inverse kinematic solutions with singularity robustness for robot manipulator control. J. Dyn. Syst. Meas. Contr. **108**(3), 163–171 (1986)
8. Hollerbach, J.M.: Optimum kinematic design for a seven degree of freedom manipulator. In: International Symposium of Robotics Research (1985)
9. Boudreau, R., Podhorodeski, R.P.: Singularity analysis of a kinematically simple class of 7-jointed revolute manipulators. Trans. Can. Soc. Mech. Eng. **34**(1), 105–117 (2010)
10. Kreutz-Delgado, K., Long, M., Seraji, H.: Kinematic analysis of 7 DOF anthropomorphic arms. In: IEEE International Conference on Robotics and Automation. IEEE (1990)
11. Dahm, P., Joublin, F.: Closed form solution for the inverse kinematics of a redundant robot arm (1997)
12. Shimizu, M., et al.: Analytical inverse kinematic computation for 7-DOF redundant manipulators with joint limits and its application to redundancy resolution. IEEE Trans. Rob. **24**(5), 1131–1142 (2008)

13. Singh, G.K., Claassens, J.: An analytical solution for the inverse kinematics of a redundant 7DoF manipulator with link offsets. In: IEEE/RSJ International Conference on Intelligent Robots and Systems, pp. 2976–2982. IEEE Xplore (2010)

14. Rubio, F., et al.: A comparison of algorithms for path planning of industrial robots. In: Ceccarelli, M. (eds.) Proceedings of EUCOMES 2008. Springer, Dordrecht (2009). https://doi.org/10.1007/978-1-4020-8915-2_30

15. Gasparetto, A., et al.: Experimental validation and comparative analysis of optimal time-jerk algorithms for trajectory planning. Robot. Comput. Integr. Manuf. **28**(2), 164–181 (2012)

16. Fang, S., et al.: Trajectory planning for seven-DoF robotic arm based on quintic polynormial. In: 2019 11th International Conference on Intelligent Human-Machine Systems and Cybernetics (IHMSC). IEEE (2019)

# Author Index

Printed in the United States
by Baker & Taylor Publisher Services

Printed in the United States
by Baker & Taylor Publisher Services